The Great Religions

The Great Religions

Quinter Marcellus Lyon
Professor of Philosophy
University of Mississippi

The ODYSSEY PRESS, *Inc.* *New York*

Third Printing

To

My best helper—my wife

Preface

Some years ago I conceived the desire to write the story of man's religions, and to incorporate a philosophy of religion which should be loyal to the fundamental values in our Hebrew-Christian tradition while at the same time remaining in harmony with what is sound and true in all human experience. Despite a heavy teaching schedule I managed to dictate to a student-secretary an outline which has grown over the years. Finally, instead of further revising my story I completely discarded the old manuscript and began again at the beginning, examining fresh sources in the meantime.

The composition of a philosophy of religion has met with difficulties and rewards. It has called for much patience and effort. A philosophy of religion is not something which can easily be spun out of sheer imagination. It must grow out of a broad knowledge of man's religious experience. It must overcome many deep prejudices—my own and those of others, prejudices in favor of one's own religion and prejudices against all religions. No literature is more vast or varied than religious literature, and a knowledge of it requires a lifetime's devotion.

My story has assumed the following form. I have discussed in Chapter I some tentative criteria by which to compare and judge the religions of mankind. In succeeding chapters I have presented, with a casual informality, the religions of man from prehistoric times to the present, from Oriental mysticism to Semitic monotheism. I have sought to make clear by example the basic techniques of obtaining historical facts, and have applied them to all religious traditions. I have tried to apply the criteria of maturity to all religions as they have been passed in review. Finally in the concluding chapter I have presented a sketch of a philosophy of religion which should be justifiable and adequate for the experience of an enlightened man today. So far as I know, no other textbook attempts to unify the three fields of history of religion, comparative religions, and the philosophy of religion.

Readers are expected to regard the author's criteria as exploratory and experimental, in no sense final. Additional criteria may be used or substituted for some here suggested.

The chapter on Hindu Schools of Philosophy (XV) may be omitted from an elementary course in the great religions. Other chapters may be used in a different order. Those on Jainism and Buddhism (XI-XIII) may be read after completing a study of Hinduism (XIV-XV), while those on Islam (XXXVIII-XXXIX) might come before the religion of Israel (XXVII-XXX) for certain reasons. The present order is considered historically desirable.

Several persons have given me the benefit of their advice and criticism, including my colleagues, Dr. Charles P. Bigger III, Dr. Doris Raymond, and—in the area of creative writing—Dr. John Pilkington, Jr. My son, Dr. David B. Lyon, became one of my frankest critics, albeit constructive. My daughter, Mrs. Gilbert L. Keck, has asked persistent questions and has made specific contributions to this text as an illustrator and artist. Publication of my manuscript was inspired largely by the interest of my students in it over a period of years. Without the sympathetic criticism of my wife throughout these years I could have accomplished little. She also undertook most willingly the arduous task of reading the complete page-proofs for me. My secretary, Mrs. John Pilkington, Jr., besides being efficient, has been inquisitive and critical as she has worked through the manuscript.

To other colleagues I am indebted: to Professor William H. Willis for counsel on linguistics, to Professor David Moore Robinson for advice on archaeological problems, to Professor Dwight Van de Vate for his stimulating thought on some of my problems, and to numerous members of the Department of English. My friend and former adviser at Ohio State University, Professor Albert E. Avey, has helped me more than he realizes. Dr. T. Z. Koo, professor emeritus of Oriental Studies at the State University of Iowa, has advised me on some problems in Neo-Confucianism. I wish there were space to mention all who aided and inspired me.

To the University of Mississippi library staff for its cooperation in providing me a secluded study, book orders, and inter-library loans, I am grateful. To the University administration I am also grateful for encouragement of the life of scholarship.

My purpose in mentioning the persons to whom I am indebted is not to implicate them in responsibility for my story's shortcomings. The fact is that despite excellent and objective suggestions, I often persisted in doing things my own way.

Q. M. L.

To the University of Mississippi library staff for its cooperation in providing me a secluded study, book orders, and interlibrary loans I am grateful. To the University administration I am [illegible] grateful for encouragement of the [illegible] scholarship.

My purpose in mentioning the persons to whom I [illegible] is not to implicate them in responsibility for my [illegible]. The fact is that despite excellent and objective [illegible] often persisted in doing things my own way.

Acknowledgments

For PERMISSION to quote copyrighted material, grateful acknowledgment is hereby made to the publishers or other copyright owners of the following books: George Allen and Unwin, James H. Moulton, *Early Zoroastrianism,* Sarvepalli Radhakrishnan, *Indian Philosophy* (2 vols.), and Arthur Waley, *Analects of Confucius;* American Historical Association (copyright) and Appleton-Century-Crofts, John K. Shryock, *Origin and Development of the State Cult of Confucius;* University of California Press, Cyril Bailey, *Phases in the Religion of Ancient Rome;* University of Chicago Press, H. G. Creel (copyright), *Chinese Thought from Confucius to Mao Tse-tung;* The John Day Company, H. G. Creel (copyright), *Confucius, the Man and the Myth;* E. P. Dutton and Co., Ernest Richard Hughes, *Chinese Philosophy in Classical Times;* Harper and Brothers, Swami Nikhilananda, *The Upanishads* (2 vols.); Johns Hopkins Press, William Foxwell Albright, *From the Stone Age to Christianity;* Indiana University Press, Philip Wheelwright, *The Burning Fountain;* Liberal Arts Press, Isaac Mendelsohn, *Religions of the Ancient Near East;* The Macmillan Company, Lewis Browne, *The World's Great Scriptures,* Fung Yu-lan, *Short History of Chinese Philosophy,* John B. Noss, *Man's Religions,* James Bisset Pratt (Mrs. Pratt, copyright), *Pilgrimage of Buddhism,* Sarvepalli Radhakrishnan, *Indian Philosophy* (2 vols.), Arthur Waley, *Three Ways of Thought in Ancient China;* John Murray, Lionel Giles, *Musings of a Chinese Mystic* and *The Sayings of Lao Tzu;* Kelly and Walsh, Lionel Giles (copyright), *Chuang Tzu, Mystic Moralist, and Social Reformer;* Thomas Nelson and Sons, and the National Council of Churches of Christ in the U.S.A. (copyright), *Holy Bible, Revised Standard Version;* New American Library, R. B. Blakney (copyright), *The Way of Life: Lao Tzu;* Oxford University Press, Robert E. Hume, *The Thirteen Principal Upanishads;* Philosophical Library, Vergilius Ferm, ed., *Forgotten Religions;* Princeton University Press, John Clark Archer, *The Sikhs in Relation to Hindus, Moslems, Christians and Ahmadiyyas,* Jack Finegan, *Archeology of World Religions,* and *Light from the Ancient Past,* Fung Yu-lan, *History of Chinese Philosophy* (2 vols.), Edward Jabra Jurji, ed., *Great Religions of the Modern World,* James B. Pritchard, ed., *Ancient Near*

Eastern Texts Relating to the Old Testament; Routledge and Kegan Paul, M. Anesaki, *History of Japanese Religion,* Rafael Karsten, *Origins of Religion;* Charles Scribner's Sons, James Henry Breasted, *The Dawn of Conscience,* James Hastings, *Encyclopedia of Religion and Ethics;* Vedanta Society of Southern California, Swami Prabhavananda and Christopher Isherwood, *Bhagavad-Gita.*

Contents

The Great Religions

PART ONE

Introduction

I. TOWARD A MATURE PHILOSOPHY OF RELIGION

RELIGION IS of first importance in human life. It is of the very essence of religion to possess such importance. Ever since man has been man, his concern over certain values has had the quality of religious experience. Religion existed in human experience long before it was recognized as such or organized as an institution. The logic of the human situation compels us to believe that man will always possess a deep feeling concerning the importance of certain vital experiences and relationships, and this deep feeling will always be the essence of his religion.

We are concerned with the realization of three goals. First, we want to develop a concept of religion in its broadest sense, so as to include under the appropriate genus and differentiae all human experiences which may properly be classed as religious. Second, we must develop a standard by which to judge religions as relatively more or less mature. And finally, we should describe the religions of mankind from the most primitive to the most mature, and try to apply to them our criterion of relative maturity as objectively as possible.

What Is Religion?

Many have tried to define religion, with varying success. Most of the definitions apply only to some phase of religion. It is not the case that just one definition of religion is true and all the others false.[1*]

All partial definitions of religion may be classified as of three types. The first is intellectualistic, defining religion in terms of belief. The second is affectivistic, defining it in terms of the emotions. The third is voluntaristic, regarding the will as the core of religion.

A typical intellectualistic definition of religion is that of Martineau. Religion, he says, is "the belief in an ever living God, that is, in a Divine Mind and Will ruling the Universe and holding moral relations with mankind." Schleiermacher's definition illustrates the second type: "The essence of religion consists in the feeling of absolute dependence" upon a being higher than ourselves. Kant exemplifies the third type: "Religion is [considered subjectively] the recognition of all duties as divine commands."[2]

These are all partial definitions. The truth is that religion must have some intellectual basis as well as an emotional qualification. Most important of all, however, is the role of will in religion. Perhaps as good a definition as any would be the following: Religion is commitment of the person or group to a way of life based on certain beliefs and attitudes, and conceived as most likely to guarantee the conservation and increase of life's dearest values. Perry characterizes religion briefly in a similar manner when he says that in a "generic and universal sense, religion is man's deepest solicitude, his concern for the fate of that which he accounts most valuable."[3]

The test of a definition is whether it describes all cases commonly regarded as instances of the thing to be defined, and whether it covers only such instances. The test of my definition may be made as we survey primitive and mature religions. It is not proposed as the one and only valid definition of religion, but only as a working definition to guide our study. It is broad enough to include magic as a type of religion—the most primitive type—and the religion

* Superior figures refer to Chapter Notes, pp. 665-688, inclusive.

of Jesus, for whom the kingdom of God was primarily a moral-spiritual experience. It may be maintained that humanism and communism are covered by my definition.

Mature Religion

Mature religion is, of course, one species of religion. It is to be distinguished from immature religion by carefully chosen criteria, which must be set forth before going further. The unfortunate thing is that one must seem dogmatic and arbitrary by introducing at this point any criteria of religious maturity, since we have not yet examined man's religions. Despite such risk, however, I venture to suggest the following criteria, with the understanding that they are purely tentative, designed to stimulate thought and encourage independent judgment.

1. Mature religion differs from immature or primitive religion by excluding the element of magic. In the next chapter it will be explained that man's religions generally have gone through the stage of magic. There are many survivals of magic even in the best of man's religions today. We may well wonder why religion clings to certain magical practices while science generally disavows them. Some religions are freer from magic than others, and the religious experience of many individuals and groups in the great religions are, in principle at least, entirely free from magic.

2. Mature religion also excludes the element of literal mythology. There is a sense in which myth is compatible with the most mature religion, as Plato used myth in his dialogues to convey meanings which lay beyond the bounds of logical exposition. In this sense it may even be maintained that the most primitive myths had more vitality at first than later, since they were originally regarded as pure symbolism whereas later they came to be taken literally.[4] Whatever one may think about the origin and proper uses of mythology, certainly the traditional insistence upon regarding the myths as literally true is a mark of religious immaturity. Here myth and magic become confused, for if one's salvation depends upon belief or credal statement conforming to literal myth, then salvation is made into a magical formula, the use of which gains certain very im-

portant ends, such as victory over death and demons. If you believe the myth you will be saved. If you do not believe it, you will be sent howling into hell. This seems naive and immature.

3. On the positive side, mature religion calls for commitment to truth wherever you find it, when that truth is relevant to religious experience. This involves the so-called conflict between science and religion. Actually there can be no conflict between science and mature religion, for the latter is based on a fundamental commitment to truth, and science by definition is knowledge of facts and relations which constitute the truth in a given area. Traditional religious cosmology is often found to be in conflict with science, but that is an accidental relationship, not at all fundamental. Mature religion outgrows its primitive cosmology. The idea that God's dwelling place is up above the earth, that the earth is the center of the universe, and that hell is underneath the earth's surface, is part of a cosmology which is not essential to the fundamental elements of Christianity. Essential are such teachings as that the kingdom of God is spiritual, and that membership in it is conditioned by acceptance of the Christian way of life.

Commitment to the truth entails not only the acceptance of well established theories of physical science, such as that the sun is the center of our universe, but also loyalty to the principles of historical criticism. Now it is easy for us to apply such principles to other religions than our own, and to non-religious affairs in our own traditions. The Christian will not hesitate to conclude that, since most of the Confucian Classics were not mentioned by Confucius or by Mencius or later Confucians, and since the Classics generally reflect later cultural conditions, therefore they were not written by Confucius. The Christian must be equally willing to apply the principles of historical criticism to his own sacred literature.

Similarly in all human relations we must be committed to the truth, if our religion is to be mature. When sociological problems arise in the interpretation of our religious traditions, if sociology has any definite conclusions to offer, we must be ready to apply them to the problems at hand. We must exercise due caution lest we apply a scientific theory before it is well established. But when it is well authenticated, nothing is to be gained by dogmatic denial of the facts of life for the sake of some mistaken tradition. It is better to reinterpret the tradition and come out with a more mature religion.

4. Mature religion also requires a commitment to the principles of psychological health and the facts of human nature. We must recognize the fact that our ancestors were somewhat superstitious about psychological facts. Today we are familiar with such terms as frustration, fundamental drives, schizophrenia, and psychosomatic diseases. Most religious traditions show immaturity in this area and need to be reinterpreted. The greatest prophets in all the religions need reinterpreting in certain respects, without any damage to their essential message. Mature religion does not hesitate to make such reinterpretations.

Truth scales on which Maat, Egyptian truth goddess, balanced the departed soul against a feather to determine its freedom from guilt.

5. Mature religion is ethical religion. It ministers not only to the strengthening of the group and of the individual within the group but also encourages the sensitivity of the individual to ethical relations with other individuals. The emphasis in mature religion is not on God's power or on miracle, but on God's moral demands upon the person. This is a principle which will find ample application in the Hebrew-Christian tradition, as in other religious traditions of mankind. It is an important characteristic of religious maturity.

6. Religious ritual is often thought of as that human experience which is distinctly religious, while ethical and social dimensions are classified on another level. This raises the question of judging religious maturity in terms of its rites and symbols.

The development of a meaningful set of symbols regarded as essentially nothing more than symbols is one criterion of mature religion. When symbols are first used they may indicate more maturity than later when they have acquired idolatrous significance as ends in themselves. Further experience and enlightenment may reinterpret idols as mere symbols, thus restoring an earlier quality of maturity.

It seems as though a beautiful religion—one filled with aesthetically pleasing and ethically inspiring ritual regarded as purely symbolic—should not be condemned as necessarily formalistic. Many sincere people have been unable to choose between Quakerism and Episcopalianism because of their inability to deal properly with the subject of religious symbolism versus idolatry. It is not the symbols or their lack that make a religion mature or immature, but the success of either a symbolic or plain type of religion in inspiring a life of love, service, and purity.

Sacrifice occupies a unique place in religious symbolism. Originally the sacrifice was a symbolic meal set out for the sustenance of a departed member of the family. As an ancestor took on the proportions of deity the sacrifice was regarded with more awe, and the demands of deity aroused reactions of magic and literalness. It took millennia to reorientate the sacrifice to its symbolic use as an aid to communion with deity, or to substitute more suitable forms of worship.

Prayer is another element of religious ritual needing evaluation. It lends itself to magical uses, but may also be employed as a symbolic approach to communion with deity. Like other elements of religious ritual, it cannot be evaluated by itself but only in relation to the total religious experience. If the ritual generally is regarded aesthetically and evaluated in terms of its success in (a) adjusting man to universal forces and (b) inspiring him to moral and spiritual achievement, then a high level of religious maturity has been achieved.

7. Mature religion is universal or inclusive. The earlier stages of some of the great religions have been exclusive, nationalistic, or racistic. The God of the early Israelites was conceived to be intensely Hebrew. He was for the Israelites and against all others. Shinto has remained exclusively Japanese until very recently. Mature religion must possess qualities which can apply to man as man. It must lose those qualities which divide sect against sect and nation against nation.

8. Lest we forget it amid the emphases of modernity, we have saved until last the further criterion of mystic sensitivity. Very primitive religion may show the quality of mystic sensitivity and thus be mature in this one respect while immature in others. On the contrary a modern religion may show freedom from magic and literal myth, it may be committed to truth, psychological health, and

ethical principles. But if it lacks a certain mystic sensitivity it is not completely mature. In fact, this final lack may disqualify it from being a religion at all, in the estimation of some critics.

In my opinion this last criterion does not rule out humanism or communism as religions, but it does raise a question about their real maturity. Perhaps some types of humanism may still qualify even as to maturity. This is to say that in order to have a mature religious experience one must possess the awareness of a Presence in the world of human experience—a Presence that is perhaps personal, perhaps transpersonal, symbolizing the universal or spiritual forces which may be tapped for help in times of individual or group need. The need may be emergency, or it may be routine, everyday humdrum which is made tolerable by one's mystic sensitivity. Prayer is essentially communion with this imaginative (not imaginary) Presence whose reality is vivified by a poetic nature. If freed from the characteristics of magic and literal mythology, such an awareness is likely to unite the other characteristics of a mature religion into a vital and successful experience in the modern world.

Religious Value

A distinction has been made between religion as such, and religious value as derivative from religion. Here we must be careful, for there is no religious value apart from all other positive values, just as there is no such experience as religion apart from the human effort to conserve and enhance life's values. Religious value is a synthesis of all other values, and is expressed in the form of a concern for their conservation and increase.

The concept of religious value as a synthesis of all human values was suggested by Plato when he said that the archetype of all archetypes is the Good, and that the Good comprehends the two other main types of value, the True and the Beautiful. Now if this trinity of values includes all other values, then there is no separate category for religious value. Religious quality is breathed into these or any other conceivable values by the essential religious attitude, which is one of zealous regard for their human or cosmic significance, for their universal recognition, and for their conservation.

Man's perennial concern for the conservation of values is necessarily attached to whatever cosmology he happens to have. We could not expect prehistoric man, primitive man, or ancient classical man—not even Jesus—to believe in the Copernican or Einsteinian cosmology. No more should we expect primitive man to understand that love to God and one's neighbor is the principle by which all values may be transformed into religious values.

There is no absolute norm of mature religion. The most enlightened prophet may have lived in times when the limitations of his culture prevented him from reaching a certain type of maturity. Even today there are people whose educational advantages have been small but whose insights into the meaning of religious value are far advanced. Of such people we may say that their religion is more mature than their science. The tendency today, unfortunately, is such that we must say of large segments of mankind, especially in the western world, that they are more mature scientifically than religiously. I say unfortunately, because man is in danger of destroying himself for this very reason.

The prevalence of immature religion in much of the world today, and still more in the distant past, does not prove that religion is by nature immature and can never grow into maturity. We may concede that religion arose out of magic. But so did science. Magic was the first stage of the technology for catching game, growing crops, healing diseases, and winning battles. We do not condemn mature science on that account. Nor should we condemn mature religion because it was once magical—and still is for many people. Instead of condemning religion because of its immaturity, we should promote the mature product as a means of integrating and perpetuating the worthwhile values of the human spirit.

Factors Contributing to Scientific Maturity

It will be instructive to ask why it is that science has reached maturity before religion, in the experience of most people. The answer to this is threefold.

1. Science reached maturity in the popular mind before religion because it is easier to overcome prejudices of science than of religion. Even when prejudice prevented the acceptance of new scientific

ideas, it was more likely religious than scientific prejudice which was at fault. So it was with the Copernican theory of the universe, and the Darwinian theory of biological evolution. Yet despite this complication people did gradually come to accept Copernicus and apparently are doing the same thing for a modified Darwinism. The young science of anthropology has made remarkable headway in a brief span of years, partly because Darwinism had already paved the way and partly because the evidence for prehistoric man is literally overwhelming. Many times Darwinism is accepted only provisionally, with the understanding that biological evolution does not apply to man but only to the lower animals. And the existence of prehistoric races is rationalized by saying that these races were pre-Adamic, and were somehow destroyed before God created Adam. So religious prejudice triumphs even when scientific prejudice is reduced. Even scientists sometimes have naive religious concepts and are denominationally prejudiced. Sectarian prejudices within each religion still run deep, and between the great religions of mankind there is still too little understanding or sympathy. The hopeful sign seems to be that more and more people are overcoming religious prejudice today. There is a growing insistence on religious toleration in America and in parts of Europe. And East and West are making concerted efforts to understand each other. These are indications of a growing religious maturity.

2. Science is more mature popularly than religion because the mature product of science has been systematically cultivated by our educators for generations, while religion, conceived to be divisive, has been kept out of our schools. It is a fitting testimony to the power of the classroom, with its day-to-day endeavors to enlighten and explain, that it has popularized the knowledge of science and society. If our schools were allowed to do the same thing for religion, we might make some very essential progress toward maturity in that important area of human experience. Of course we do not advocate that the schools should teach any one religion; rather they should teach the generally accepted facts about all religions. Adult education could then supplement the efforts of the public schools and colleges, and the churches could take up where these agencies leave off. In this way religious illiteracy would be reduced and mutual understanding promoted among people of differing religious

traditions. Considering the gravity of world conditions, it seems that we should forget our petty differences and cooperate toward the goal of human understanding and goodwill, which is the fundamental object of commitment in any enlightened religion. This can best be accomplished through the use of the classroom.

3. The rapid progress of modern science is largely due to the fact that Bacon and Descartes and their successors developed a sound scientific methodology, whereas religion still lacks an accepted methodology. Francis Bacon laid stress on the methods of scientific induction. Perhaps he overemphasized induction, but that overemphasis was needed in those days, in order to combat the scholastic tendency to assume the premise and to argue deductively thereafter. Descartes accepted the basic principles of induction but insisted also that deduction must be used. His contribution of analytic geometry symbolized the important part which mathematics was then playing and was to play increasingly in the phenomenal development of modern science. Like Bacon, Descartes urged individuals to look with suspicion upon all who would set themselves up as authorities, and to learn to be independent in making one's own careful judgments. This method was in fact not really different from the method of Socrates, except for the modern emphasis upon mathematics and experimentation. But now it was set forth systematically at a time when scientific experiment was in the air. Descartes described the methods which were actually being used so successfully by Copernicus, Galileo, Tycho Brahe, and Kepler. Newton and Leibnitz further systematized scientific method and contributed significantly to its mathematics. In fact an important reason why modern physical science has commanded universal assent has been the absolute certainty of the mathematical reasoning at its basis. The measurement of the universe by increasingly accurate devices has yielded data which cannot be denied. John Stuart Mill formulated some important canons of induction, and many others since have contributed to the logic of science.

Methodology and Religious Maturity

Unfortunately this is not the situation with regard to religious methodology. And my diagnosis of the malady in religious discussion is that theologians—both learned and lay—are arguing about their conclusions, whereas they should be arguing about their methods. Agreement on conclusions is not likely to be reached until agreement is first reached on the fundamental principles which shall constitute a methodology for the discovery of truth in religion. If we can ever come to agreement on methodology, then and only then can we expect to reach a high general level of religious maturity. By following this methodology in the study of religion we should eventually arrive at common conclusions regarding the nature of religion, its truth values, and its moral and spiritual essence.

The Problem of Religious Knowledge

The basic issue of methodology in religion is the problem of knowledge. This is a complex issue which requires a complex solution. Yet there are a few simple principles to guide us toward a satisfactory conclusion.

Man is not omniscient. Therefore man must be satisfied with something less than absolute knowledge in any field of human experience. This is especially true of religion, in which the conflict of "absolute authorities" is so dramatic that it creates skepticism and irreligion in the minds of many thoughtful people.

Reason has a place in religion, as in any other area of human experience. Certainly one of the concerns of religion is truth, and truth is a function of reason. Any one who considers himself a religious devotee must include truth as one of the objects of his devotion. In committing himself to God, he necessarily commits himself to the truth. Therefore wherever he discovers truth, in science or other human experience, he must seek to make particular truths cohere with his cosmic view of truth and religion.

Rationalism, however, has its limitations. Aesthetic experience lies largely outside the limits of reason. This is perhaps less true of religion than of art, yet to some extent it is true of both. Religion's special concern with values of course includes reason or truth as one of its concerns. Goodness, beauty, and love are other values sought by religion, and these are only in part governed by reason —though it should be said that they are at least harmonious with reason.

In our search for religious knowledge, one of the primary guides should be the principle of inclusiveness. The student must not be satisfied with his knowledge of one religious tradition—and that perhaps only partially understood. He must seek to know sympathetically all the religions of mankind, and to understand why each has claimed for itself the same ultimate authority which all the others claim. If the student knows only one religion he is a most unsatisfactory judge of any religion. How can he know that the claims of other religions are unsound or fraudulent if he knows nothing about them? Without prejudice he must read their literature and become familiar with their traditions if he wants to be an impartial judge; only then will he be able to understand the part which religion plays in the life of man. He must become familiar not only with the world's living religions but also with its ancient but now dead religions, and with the religions of primitive peoples. With this knowledge as a background he will be better prepared to interpret the data which the anthropologists have accumulated regarding the religion of prehistoric man. He may then be prepared to describe the origin and nature of religion.

Of special importance are the experiences of the great prophets and mystics of all traditions. No one is in a position to draw final conclusions for a religious philosophy without first seeking a sympathetic understanding of the experiences of these great men. They all afford data of human experience which are relevant to the problem of religious knowledge. It seems immature to assert that mystics in some religions have received divine revelation while denying it in others.

The experience of the religious mystics raises the question as to whether or not there is an intuitive path to religious truth, quite apart from the rational-empirical path which we have been describing. But certain qualifications immediately become evident. If there is such an intuitive path, certainly its results cannot conflict with the results of the empirical approach. It may be surmised, furthermore, that the inspirations or "intuitions" of the mystics are in reality not essentially different from the creative insights of the scientists in their moments of triumph. A scientific genius is aware of a multitude of facts which need organization. Suddenly the integrating idea comes to him and in his inspiration he finds the way to unify a large field which until that moment lacked unity. So also, perhaps, the religious genius had been aware of a multitude of moral, social, and religious experiences which needed organization. His genius lay in his ability to grasp the trend of human experience in its relation to life's greatest values, and his "intuition" may indeed be as valid in the religious realm as the scientist's insight in the other area. The two may not be far apart in their fundamental experience.

All of this merely proves that the path to truth is much the same, in principle, in every field. And the laws of thought must be accepted by scientist and religionist alike. Both scientist and religionist need a vast amount of experience as a background from which to draw valid conclusions in their own special fields.

Three Approaches to a Religious Philosophy

We should not leave this discussion of religious methodology without taking note of certain specific methods or techniques for implementing the general principles already described. These techniques have been perfected over the last century and a half. Tsanoff[5] enumerates the three methods most used by recent scholars for the study of religion, each complementary to the others: (1) the historical, (2) the comparative, and (3) the psychological. In the historical method we gather together, with the aid of the expert historian, all the information we can about any given religion. We learn about its rise, its crises, its developments. In terms of its cultural growth and broad human experience we can better understand any religion, including our own. The comparative method seeks to find parallels and contrasts between different religions, their histories, and their great experiences, as a means to understanding each one better. Sometimes the parallels may be explained in terms of the influence of one religion on another. But at other times parallel developments take place in religions which have not been in contact. For example, "The belief that thunderstorms, eclipses, and volcanic eruptions are caused by powerful evil spirits, often conceived directly as disembodied human souls, is probably universal among savage peoples all over the world."[6] Karsten cites the parallel between the Kafirs of South Africa and the Jibaro Indians of South America. Not only is their ideology the same, but their ritual also is alike. On the approach of a storm they rush out and brandish their weapons and shout at the clouds, thinking that by frightening the spirits in the storm they can divert it. "Here we have a remarkable uniformity of beliefs between peoples in different parts of the world who cannot be assumed to have influenced each other. It would be easy to add similar instances from other quarters of the globe."[7] The explanation of such parallels must be in terms of a common human nature which responds similarly to similar experiences. This illustrates the use of the psychological method.

All three of these methods or techniques must, of course, be used harmoniously with the fundamental principles on which the pursuit of all truth is based. Furthermore, each field of human learning has its special techniques which have proved to be fruitful in the pursuit of knowledge in that particular area. So archaeology, anthropology, and history use special techniques for acquiring knowledge. These will be illustrated as we apply them to the general area of religion.

Our particular concern in the chapters which follow will be with the history of religion and its philosophical interpretation. In dealing with the history of religion it will be necessary also to deal with the history of culture, since religious values are not something apart but can be understood only in relation to cultural values and cultural achievements. I shall deal first with prehistoric religion and with anthropology as it yields data on which to base a philosophy of the origin of religion and of man. Primitive religion as we have been able to observe it in contemporary cultures will also be noted. Then I shall describe and evaluate the great historic religions of mankind, reserving for final treatment the monotheistic religions of the Near East. Nothing is so broadening as familiarity with the experiences of the people of other cultures. Nothing is so challenging as a frank presentation of the strengths and weaknesses of our own traditions.

PART TWO

Truth and Myth in Ancient Religions

II. PREHISTORIC AND PRIMITIVE RELIGION

WHAT IS MAN? How did he come into being? When did his experience of religion begin? The young science of anthropology can give us some help in answering these questions.

Man is to be defined under the genus animal. However, the most important part of the definition of man is not the genus, but the differentiae. Certain biological characteristics were very important conditions of the human synthesis. Among these are the rotating forearm and opposable thumb; the pronounced double curvature of the spine; the large convoluted brain, particularly the frontal lobes encased by a high forehead; and the power of speech. The large convoluted brain is a prerequisite to human intelligence. The high frontal cortex is a prerequisite to abstract thinking. The thumb and rotating forearm are conditions of human artistry and technology. And the power of speech, itself a synthesis, makes possible his whole system of culture, passed on from generation to generation. But the thing that makes man human is not the physical conditions themselves, but their emergent qualities or "synthesis." And the most important characteristic of the human synthesis is man's fundamental concern for the conservation of his values. Man's experience of values is not by addition, but by organic synthesis. That is, all his values are organically interrelated and mutually interdependent. And man's fundamental concern for the conservation of his values is what made him both human and religious at the same time. It is this awareness that unites primeval man with primitive man today, and with progressive man.

The Creation of Man

When the human synthesis took place, that is, when man became man, he became aware of values such as goodness, beauty, truth, love, and deity in some form. It was precisely this awareness of goodness, beauty, truth, love, and deity that made him man. What happened at this important crisis in cosmic growth was that there occurred a synthesis of inward experience which we properly characterize as human. There is no special reason to doubt that that synthesis took place suddenly, as in a biological sport. Other evolutionary changes took place in that way, and so it is reasonable to believe that man came into existence as a biological sport, whose new powers of synthesis gave him true human qualities for the first time in terrestrial life. His biological ancestors were merely animals. But when he became value-conscious as man, his (spiritual) father was God. Such a sport may properly be described as a divine creation. It was something new in the world. From then on the question of man's origin was irrelevant. Heaven was his destination, and that alone was important. Heaven, of course, was to have many interpretations in the course of man's spiritual experience.

In discussing the problem of human origins Professor Weiss argues[1] that the first human embryo to be born from an animal body was different from its biological parent in that from the beginning it resisted the body's animal concerns and, instead, quickened its body by a concern with the moral self. On the other hand the late Professor Ralph Linton, eminent Yale anthropologist, in conversation with me said that Weiss' view was too abrupt. In his opinion man did not become man quite that suddenly. He suggested "cerebral hypertrophy" as the genetic process by which the simian species gave birth to man. It seems to me that this could have happened in one generation. But regardless of this issue, the principle still remains. Whenever a simian sport achieved the human synthesis and became aware of values, he became the first man. That was what made him man. That was the divine creation of man in the image of spirit.

Man still knows little about the details of his origin. Did he come from one original human stock, or were there several independent human origins? When one human mutation occurred, did others also occur in various parts of the world? It is quite possible that they did. For the creative nature of evolution implies that there is a certain purposiveness immanent within the process itself, so that it might be expected that when conditions were ripe the human synthesis would take place independently in various parts of the world. A mere thousand, ten thousand, or hundred thousand years difference in time of independent origin would be insignificant in comparison with geological time.

The main scientific objection to the theory of multiple origins of the human race is the biological fact of fertility whenever mating occurs between the members of any two races of men. But this evidence is inconclusive. And the fact that we find fossil remains of manlike creatures in far distant parts of the earth as far back as half-a-million years ago lends some support to the theory of multiple origins.

The important consideration, however, is not whether all races came from one common stock, but rather that they are now one in nature, and that their nature is essentially not biological but spiritual. That is, man characteristically enjoys values and shares a culture. His inherent concern for the conservation of values is his religion, however superstitiously conceived.

The theory of this chapter is that religion began at least as early as Neandertal man. It may have begun earlier than that, perhaps with Heidelberg man, who may in fact have been only an early or variant form of Neandertal man. Or it may have begun with the Peking "Sinanthropus," or with the Java "Pithecanthropus." That is, it may be that these humanoids already had a crude form of language and were concerned with the experience and conservation of values. Their brains were large enough theoretically to achieve the human synthesis. But we have absolutely no evidence either of language or of culture in the case of these protoanthropic organisms. Hence there is no basis for argument. But in the case of Neandertal man there is abundant evidence of culture and religion.

Neandertal Man's Religion

Of Neandertal man there are dozens of specimens, in various parts of Europe and even outside Europe. Some of his skeletons are complete while others are fragmentary. His accompanying tools and artifacts are abundant. He represents a definite type, different both from later and from earlier humanoid types. And for the first time, in his case, we find convincing evidence of a religious attitude. Some of the specific evidence will now be cited in order to make the student more vividly aware of the reality and nature of prehistoric religion.

*Table I—Cultural Chronology**

Paleolithic	
Chellean and Acheulian	before 50,000 B.C.
Mousterian (Neandertal, Pleistocene)	50,000–25,000 B.C.
Aurignacian (Cro-Magnon, Upper Paleolithic)	25,000–18,000 B.C.
Solutrean	18,000–16,000 B.C.
Magdalenian	16,000– 8000 B.C.
Mesolithic (Postglacial)	7000– 3000 B.C.
Neolithic	6000– 2000 B.C.
Chalcolithic	4000
Bronze	– 1000 B.C.
Iron	1400

* Approximate dates, differing with locale. Gleaned from tables and discussions in A. L. Kroeber, *Anthropology,* Rev. Ed. 1948, chaps. 16 and 17. Harcourt, Brace and Company.

The most significant of the evidences of Neandertal man's religion are his burial practices. When an animal dies the other animals leave his body wherever it perished. But when Neandertal man died, his fellows showed their social characteristics by burying his body with ceremony. This normally included folding the body, and surrounding it with useful or precious objects.

Anthropologists are not entirely agreed as to the exact interpretation of Paleolithic burial practices. Some believe that the reason why Paleolithic man folded his dead was because that was the typical sleeping position for primitive man. But this explanation leaves many questions unanswered. Did he, for example, believe that the dead was merely sleeping and would some day awake? Or was his sleep permanent? The theory is too naive; it fails to account for certain things. For instance, sometimes the dead were not folded. And oftentimes they were bound and weighted. We need a theory broad enough to account for all these things.

Other anthropologists believe that primitive man folded his dead in order to simulate the position of the foetus: just as man came from the foetus, so he must return to it. But this theory imputes to Paleolithic man a higher degree of sophistication than seems plausible. It errs in the opposite direction from the first theory.

The third theory is that fossil man folded his dead in order to conserve burial space. After all, it is more of an effort to dig a large hole than to dig a small one. And when we consider the fact that fossil man often buried his dead in the very caves and shelters where he lived, naturally he would want to conserve space. But against this theory is the fact that oftentimes the dead were folded even when they were buried in spacious natural ditches.

Three conclusions seem justified by the evidence. First, Paleolithic man believed in the continued existence of the dead. This is inferred from his having painted the body or bones of the dead with red ochre, the color of life-blood. Perhaps the red paint was conceived to have magical power, guaranteeing the continued existence of the deceased. Or it may merely have symbolized his belief that the dead were somehow still alive. In either case, his exact concept of the future life has been lost to us. We have no way of knowing whether he thought that the body was dead and the soul alive, or that the body was not really dead but only asleep, likely to wake up at almost any time. He must have believed in one or the other of these concepts, for why else would he surround the dead with tools, weapons, and food?

Second, Paleolithic man feared what the dead might do to the living. This is inferred from the fact that he trussed up the dead as if to prevent them from moving, and that he fixed them in place with heavy stones.

Third, Paleolithic man revered the dead. It is more than obvious by this time that his conduct was far removed from mere animal behavior. The care with which he put away his dead is a definitely human characteristic. Besides all the ceremonials which we have mentioned was the further significant fact that valuable personal possessions were buried with the dead, such as precious stones, charms, and amulets, as well as weapons, tools, and food. Thus if the dead were feared, it is also true that they were revered. Ancestor worship among primitive peoples today, as among the Chinese and other civilized folk, is based partly on the fear of what the ancestral ghost might do to the living if the body were not properly buried and his memory duly respected.

Paleolithic man's burial customs were evidently bound up with an endeavor to conserve values, based upon some kind of belief in a power higher than themselves. The exact nature of their concept of deity is of secondary importance. Of first importance is the fact that they based their efforts toward the conservation of values upon a belief in some power higher than themselves. It is also significant that the Neandertal belief in the soul's survival indicates a recognition of the value of the individual.

As one concrete example proving that Neandertal man was religious, we cite the fossils discovered in the cave of La-Chapell-Aux-Saints, in the Department of Correze, France. This skeleton was buried in an approximately rectangular ditch dug in the marl of the cave's floor. The skull was against a corner of the ditch, fixed securely in place by stones and pieces of bone.[2] One arm was stretched out, but the other was probably folded, bringing the hand near to the head. The legs were folded also, so as to bring the knees breast-high.[3] From the grave were taken some excellent flints and flint flakes of varying colors, together with fragments of red sandstone. But of special interest were the objects surrounding the grave. Near the feet was a black flint scraper, near the head some other flints and stones, and near the right hand an ox foot and reindeer cerebral column, both arranged correctly as in living anatomy, indicating that these fresh meat morsels had been placed near the dead man's hand for food in his continued life.[4]

Other evidence of early Paleolithic funerary ritual is found in connection with skeletons discovered at Le Moustier, La Ferrassie (Dordogne), and elsewhere. Both during early Paleolithic times and later Paleolithic times the dead were often deposited in the caves where men lived. Some strongly felt superstition must have motivated the cultivation of such a disagreeable relationship with the dead. Prehistoric man must have had a conviction that his burial customs were divinely ordered, and that both the living and the dead would prosper if the customs were followed.

Cro-Magnon Man's Religion

The Mousterian culture, characterizing the life of Neandertal man at its high period, is abundant in its remains, but not nearly so rich as the Aurignacian, Solutrean, and Magdalenian cultures of Cro-Magnon man. These people of the upper Paleolithic era practiced variants of the burial customs of earlier men, and drew significant pictures on the walls of their caves and carved statues of animals and human beings. The female statuettes may have been small idols, representing the power of fertility in primitive mythological religion. Their grotesque exaggeration of the female characteristics suggests such an interpretation. Many of the cave drawings were apparently of magical significance, representing the wounding of prehistoric animals upon whom the Cro-Magnon men depended for their food. The drawings were made deep within their caves, by the light of fatty-oil lamps, and were probably the objects of ceremonials before the hunt, designed to impart to the hunters a supernatural power over their prey. Other drawings refer to some type of ritual, such as the composite painting on the wall of a cave at Cogul, Province of Lérida, Spain.[5] The artistic qualities of these drawings are in themselves sufficient to identify Cro-Magnon man as human and therefore as religious. A sense of aesthetic values is itself a mark of reverence toward intrinsic values, and hence an indication of the capacity for religion, to say the least.

Much of Paleolithic art may have been produced for purely aesthetic reasons, but certainly some of it was created for reasons of magic, in order to conserve socially recognized values. When magic is practiced for this purpose, it becomes religion in its early stages.

It is also certain that some of the art of Cro-Magnon man pictures the magician practicing his profession. Such is the case of the man with a long beard and a horse's tail, found on a schist plaque near Lourdes.[6] So also with the "dancing sorcerer" engraved and painted on the wall of the cave of Trois-Freres at Ariege.[7] These drawings are clear proof that Cro-Magnon man, from twelve to twenty-five thousand years ago, was practicing magic. Certainly a part of his magic was for the purpose of enhancing and conserving values, and was related to his belief in a power higher than himself.

Primitive Religion Today

So far in discussing the contribution of anthropology to a philosophy of religion we have dealt almost entirely with that part of anthropology which is concerned with prehistoric man. But a very large part of anthropology is concerned with the study of primitive societies today. Many of these societies had not come under the influence of western Christendom or other advanced civilizations before being observed by the anthropologist.

There is a strong probability that these isolated, primitive groups of people still believe and behave essentially as did their ancestors ten thousand or even twenty thousand years ago. In the eighteenth century there was a popular belief, encouraged by Rousseau, that the savage was the freest and therefore the happiest of individuals. But anthropologists' careful and widespread observations have proved the opposite. For primitive society is so bound by custom and tradition that the individual has no real freedom. This is evidence for our theory that primitive peoples today believe and behave as they have done for thousands of years. It is only after the idea of change gets a foothold in a civilization that change is tolerated; finally it spirals in its pace until we get in the habit of expecting change and of deliberately planning it.

In an essay on "The Dawn of Religions,"[8] Dr. Phyllis Ackerman has given evidence for believing that contemporary primitive peoples have many ideas which are similar to those of prehistoric men. She shows apparent parallels of belief between prehistoric and contemporary primitive peoples which witness to a background of what many anthropologists have called animatism. She suggests that dynamism or vitalism would be a better term than animatism. We shall adopt the term dynamism. The discussion of dynamism at this point does not mean that we are committed to the theory that dynamism is more primitive than animism.

Dynamism is held to be the primitive belief that there is a marvelous power diffused throughout nature, but also concentrated especially in certain types of natural phenomena. The Melanesian word for this power was "mana," as Bishop Codrington has reported it; but its equivalent exists in many primitive societies today, expressed in different words. "To the Polynesian 'mana' was like an electric fluid that could charge persons and things and be diverted from one to another. Any conspicuous success was due to 'mana,' failure to its absence or loss. . . . In short, good luck, efficiency, outstanding wisdom, were the outer signs of 'mana' as the operative cause."[9]

It is not necessary to assume that one society influenced another in its belief in dynamism. The common belief may be explained in terms of common human nature responding psychologically to similar human experiences.

Ackerman offers a number of examples from prehistoric and contemporary anthropology which suggest that primitive people revere a life-force. One is the bovine figures on the walls of the cave of the Trois Freres at Tuc d' Audoubert. These "indicate almost beyond question bovine rites. . . . Other remains in the same cave-complex indicate phallic rites. . . . The pregnant women represented by late palaeolithic figurines are about to create life, thus demonstrating their possession of a high degree of vital power."[10] From other prehistoric remains and from Chinese, Egyptian, Indian, and other cultures Miss Ackerman shows the evidences of a human tendency to revere blood and breath, food and water, procreative organs, revivified life in the springtime, and evergreen trees—all as symbolizing the life-force.

Lowie uses the term "impersonal supernaturalism" to describe what we have called dynamism.[11] Such supernaturalism is evident in the practice of imitative and contagious magic—terms used by Lowie but first suggested by Sir James G. Frazer in his voluminous report, *The Golden Bough*. That animism is also present in imitative and contagious magic will presently be seen.

Magic and Religion

Lowie classifies totemism as an example of imitative magic and, as such, of impersonal supernaturalism. It is true that the tribe, in its totemic emblem, imitates its imagined ancestor and regards the totem as possessed of a magical power. Usually that power is regarded as dangerous, bringing harm to anyone who kills a totemic species, for example. But on closer inspection its impersonal character must be questioned. For the origin of totemism is now known to be the primitive belief that ancestral spirits entered into the totemic species, making it sacred forever. This is the real reason why the totem was regarded as the ancestor of the tribe. As such it served a purpose by promoting the unity of the group.

Totemism may be observed in the making, among certain South American Indian tribes. "The Arawaks in Guiana, for instance, imagine not only that they are descended from certain animals and plants, but also from inanimate objects like rocks and stones, into which the souls of their dead kinsmen are believed to transmigrate. These natural objects tend consequently to become totems. . . ."[12]

Totemism is religious in the broad sense of the word, in that through magical means a group sought to conserve its values. Like the Republican elephant and the Democratic donkey, the totem was a symbol which aroused deep feelings in a group. As Lowie says, "though the actual [formal?] worship of the totem is rare, Australians usually go through elaborate rites at sacred spots supposedly hallowed by their totemic ancestors, the object being to increase the animal or plant species. Totemism thus ranges from the simple heraldic use of convenient symbols to a complex system of religious and magical observances."[13]

The dynamistic character of imitative magic is more clearly seen when a Hopi Indian tries to attract rain by drawing pictures of clouds and dropping rain, or by throwing water into the air. His expectation is that nature will imitate his example. He believes that he may cause a storm by imitating thunder or rain according to a prescribed ceremony. When an Australian aborigine wants rain he takes water into his mouth and squirts it in various directions, expecting that nature will follow his example.

Another illustration of imitative magic is the effigy. One might make an effigy of his enemy and then abuse it in order to bring disaster on the enemy. In this case, however, the primitive belief is that any likeness of a person is certain to attract that person's soul into it. This is why a primitive will not allow anyone to take his picture, for the likeness is believed to give another a certain power over the subject. The effigy therefore illustrates a confusion of animistic and dynamistic magic.

Again, the fertility rites of the ancient Celts constitute another example of imitative magic. For these rites men and women went into the fields openly at the time of their festival to Beltane, in order to set an example for the sun god and the rain god to follow for the sake of making the soil fertile.

Contagious magic, on the other hand, is at work when a potent object is brought in contact with one who needs that magical potency. An example is rubbing fish-hawk eyes over a sleeping baby's eyelids to give him the fish-hawk's keen sight. Or by carrying a tiger's tooth, a savage thought he would catch the tiger's courage. By eating his courageous and strong enemy's flesh the cannibal thought he would strengthen himself and gain courage. The elements of animistic magic can readily be seen in these examples.

Fetishism, another example of contagious magic, is one of the most common practices of primitive people, especially of the natives of west Africa. Fetishes were generally artifacts, or collections of natural objects modified in some way. They were either carried about on the person or lodged in the village or home. Every house possessed its fetishes. Religious ritual was observed in their presence, such as the offering of food and drink. The fetishes were supposed to insure success in the undertaking to which they were related in primitive imagination. An amulet is a kind of fetish, made to be worn on the person, often as an ornament, but always for the purpose of preventing or healing a disease or bringing good luck. The fact that fetishes in many cases are regarded as the abode of a spirit shows, again, that contagious magic is not solely based upon dynamism but also contains a large element of animism.

Taboo is still another example of contagious magic. It is attached to objects which are sacred, that is, which are inhabited by impersonal mana or by some personal supernatural being. When an object is taboo it is not to be touched. To do so would be to offend the supernatural being or to get badly injured by contact with the supernatural force. Pork is taboo to Jews, while the sacred cow is taboo to the Hindus. To the ancient Babylonians the sabbath (seventh) day was an unlucky day. It had a bad character because of the magical number seven. The Hebrews, however, learned to observe the taboo resting upon this day because, they said, it was a day beloved by their god.

Lowie mentions divination and spells as still other manifestations of impersonal supernaturalism.[14] He cites divination techniques among the Siberians, Mongols, Eskimos, West Africans, South Africans, Indians, and Hawaiians. They were also common among the Babylonians, Greeks, and Romans.

One divination technique was to throw dice in order to discover the divine will. This was done in ancient India and in primitive South Africa. Another method was to cut open an animal and read the future from the position of the entrails. Another was to watch the flight of birds. The magician was of course the final authority on the interpretation of these and other omens of the divine intent.

Magic as practiced by primitive tribes today may be said to contain three elements. First, there is the formula of words or numbers. This formula must be repeated exactly or the potency is lost. A single misspoken word or number, or the wrong intonation, may break the spell. Sometimes absolute silence is required. The barking of a dog or the hooting of an owl might spoil everything. Second, there is the ritual. If the moon is seen over the right instead of the left shoulder, the magical event will not occur. Every motion must be exactly correct. Finally, there is the force which is conceived to be either personal or impersonal, but subject to the magician's wiles.

Animism

We have mentioned that anthropologists are divided over whether dynamism or animism came first. Recent work seems to favor the latter view, making animism the mother of dynamism. If this is true, then animism is founded upon a prior concept of the human soul.

The conception of the human spirit or soul is believed to have had its origin, in part, in man's dream life. Dreams apparently carried the soul far away from a man's body, but when he awoke his body was exactly where he had gone to sleep. He could not doubt that somehow he had been on the journey about which he had been dreaming. Even today primitive peoples regard their dreams as having just as much reality as their waking experiences. So their souls are conceived to be different from their bodies. Yet the soul is like the body, for besides seeing it in his dreams a man would catch glimpses of it in the clear surface of the lake or stream, or in the shiny side of his stone axe, or even in his shadow. He also saw his friends or enemies in his dreams, as well as other evidences of their souls. At times in his dreams he saw images of departed friends; this convinced him that they were not really dead but were living and trying to communicate with him. Sometimes they would tell him about the future.

The second main source of the idea of the soul was man's experience of death. When a man died his fellows were deeply affected and caused to wonder. What was it that made the difference between life and death? The body was just as real after death as before. But something was missing. That something must be the soul, they reasoned. And they identified the soul variously with the breath, or with the blood, or with the nails or the hair whose remarkable growth was a sure sign of vitality. In fact primitive peoples seem to have believed in multiple souls for each man, such as a body-soul and a spirit-soul, each behaving according to its functional relationship. During historic times the Egyptians assigned several souls to each individual, as we shall see in the next chapter.

Belief in the soul's survival may have been the basic primeval experience which in turn led to ancestor worship, animism, dynamism, polytheism, and finally monotheism. Let us state the case for this theory, so ably supported by Karsten.

Our earliest knowledge of prehistoric man finds him believing in the survival of the human soul, as in the case of Neandertal man described above. Cro-Magnon man's art, coming much later in time, indicates a widespread belief in magic, which certainly contains elements of dynamism. The presumption is that dynamism grew out of a more primitive belief in a world of souls.

That ancestor-worship and animism arose out of man's belief in the soul's survival is supported by what we know about primitive man today. Karsten cites many specific cases where tribes imagine that the souls of their ancestors have entered into animals, plants, and inanimate objects such as rivers, hills, stones, clouds, and stars. The living propitiate the ancestral spirits by various means and try to prevent them from bringing harm. That is why they make offerings to the dead and supply their souls with food, tools, and possessions.

Even totemism is based on the concept that ancestral spirits enter into some plant or animal or inanimate object of nature or into an artifact.

Gods and local deities usually turn out to be ancestral spirits of earlier times. "The water-spirits of the Indians, for instance, frequently belong to this species. If an Indian loses his life in a rapid river or a cataract, his soul is changed into a demon who haunts that spot. According to the belief of the Jibaro Indians, the spirits of their forefathers inhabit the small waterfalls in the cordilleras where they are used to taking their ritual baths. The water, therefore, in these falls has magical power which fills the Indian bathing there. The natives think that the enormously deep and ice-cold lagoons in the Andes are haunted by the souls of malevolent sorcerers who send disease. It is natural that these spirits, especially the spirits of people drowned in the lake or river, should be regarded as malevolent and dangerous beings."[15]

The Kafirs of South Africa and the Chaco and Jibaro Indians of South America, among others, are cited as believing that the souls of departed warriors, or hostile or evil spirits, inhabit the thunder clouds and can be frightened by appropriate human action. A Kafir village, led by its medicine men, will rush to a nearby hilltop and yell at the storm in order to repel it.[16] The Jibaros behave in much the same manner, whereas the Chaco Indians, huddled in a hut, shout loudly at each clap of thunder "in order to frighten away the molesting supernatural visitors."[17]

In the animistic stage of culture all nature was thought to be alive with souls. Some were benevolent and some malevolent. The ancestral origin of some of the spirits and demons came to be forgotten, while others were remembered for a longer period of time.

The spirits of some parts of nature were considered beneficent by one tribe and malevolent by another. Volcanoes and storms were usually thought to harbor malevolent souls or demons. Rivers bringing fertility and trees bringing shade were usually considered beneficent. But a river could also destroy, and even the life-giving sun could scorch the earth.

For many years anthropology was influenced by Marett's belief that dynamism preceded animism. Some scholars still prefer Marett's view, while to others dynamism seems a more advanced concept than animism.

Birth of the Gods

Polytheism seems also to have stemmed from animism. It was inevitable that some souls would become more important than others and come to be thought of as the greater deities. The more important the object in the life of a people, the greater its divine soul was considered to be. The sun was one of the most important objects of nature, and its soul became a high god. Part of nature was thought of as male and part as female. The star, Venus, was commonly regarded as female. The Nile River contributed a great god, Osiris, greatly adored by the Egyptians. A mountain in Midian contributed a Semitic god whose spiritualization has fathered at least three great religions. Among the Greeks, the Romans, the Indo-Aryans, the Teutons, and many other tribal groups, imagination in the course of time organized polytheism into a system and attributed a social life to the gods. And so the pantheons of the various peoples were born. Being manlike, it was thought that the gods could be prevailed upon to aid men, even against their wills.

One school of thought, represented by Gusinde, Lang, and Schmidt, maintains that the earliest men were monotheists, and that polytheism, animism, and magic were degenerations from that primitive simplicity. Father Schmidt, author of *Der Ursprung der Gottesidee* (1912-36), cites the dynamistic belief in "mana" as evidence of a primeval monotheism. Since dynamism has been shown to be a derivative of animism, however, this argument is disproved. Anyhow, the "mana" idea is far removed from the spiritually more advanced concept of monotheism, which historically is known to be an outgrowth of polytheism. Schmidt's efforts to show that primitive peoples believe in a "supreme being" while they also believe in an animistic and polytheistic universe have been at best only partially successful.

Magic and Modern Man

Frazer thought that religion did not come into being until men gave up the magical practices of trying to force nature to do man's bidding, and instead prayed to the gods or spirits to give aid. When magic gave way to prayer, that was religion, said Frazer. We have chosen to define religion more broadly so as to include the practice of magic. The magical stage of religion is, of course, the primitive stage, from which mankind still has need to be freed. It would be well if everyone knew more about anthropology, in order that they might recognize the survivals of magic even in advanced religions.

In an effort to clarify the relation between dynamism, animism, magic, and religion, the late Professor Linton in a manuscript on magic and religion argues that there are three aspects of the development of magic. First, there is the impersonal supernaturalism which has been so often described, in which the magician presumes to be in control of the impersonal magical forces of the universe. Second, there is the aspect, once assumed to have appeared later in time, in which the supernatural powers are conceived to be not impersonal but personal. The witchcraft of our own tradition would illustrate this stage, since it was thought that the witch derived her power from a demon. But there is also an overlapping middle phase, says Linton, in which magic presumes both impersonal forces and personal beings. This occurs for example when supernatural beings are presumed to control supernatural forces, and when human beings presume to control supernatural beings. Linton cites an historic case at Santa Fe, New Mexico, in which the statue of the Virgin was ceremoniously paraded on the occasion of prayer for rain. If after a fixed time the rain did not come, the Virgin was publicly spanked. In another case, in Mexico, the deity was invoked to bring rain. When the rain did not come the priests released their parishioners from certain minor obligations in an effort to force the deity to send rain. When that did not work they released them from more serious obligations, finally threatening to release them from the ban on incest and murder. In these two instances of magic there seem to be elements of both impersonal and personal supernaturalism. In both cases, also, the religious element is present. Through magic the people sought to conserve values which to them were of great importance.

These citations show to what extent the phases of a culture may be blended into one complex experience. They remind us that in our present state of culture there are elements of scientific enlightenment paralleling animistic and dynamistic concepts—sometimes in the same individuals. How many people call in scientifically orientated physicians while they still believe in the dynamistic power dwelling in charms, four-leafed clover, the bones of saints, or ancient customs. There are people today who are afraid to start something on Friday the thirteenth, or to sit down at a table where the number of guests adds up to thirteen. Hotels have no thirteenth floors because of such people. Bad luck is said to follow the breaking of a mirror. Crops will not grow if planted while the moon is waning. Tea-leaves and daisy-petals and the flipping of a coin are taken to reveal the future. If you are in trouble, open the Bible and the pages will fall open by divine guidance to just the right place; you will find the needed aid. Prayer is sometimes thought of as magic: it cannot fail to bring miraculous results if used in precisely the right way; the hand of God will be forced, even against his own will.

Many of the characteristics of primitive religion and magic will be found in the anicent historic religions of the Mediterranean and Mesopotamian areas. (See pages 44, 70-71, 79-80, 104-106.)

Evaluation of Primitive Religion

Naturally there is little in the way of maturity in prehistoric and primitive religion. It is precisely from the animism, dynamism, and magic of primitive man that we wish to free modern religion.

By the time one comes in contact with primitive culture, even its mythology has taken on the characteristics of literalness. Primitive man's religious ritual is deadly serious, at times involving even human sacrifice. The symbolism is there, but he does not regard it as symbolism. Rather his ritual is a part of his cosmos which he tries to control not by prayerful communion but by simple magic. Custom rules his moral life. He has no freedom. He has little concept of truth, beauty, or goodness in the abstract; these values are merely implicit in his intuitive experience. His mystic sensitivity is probably his greatest claim to maturity, but even here he confuses deity with nature, and stresses power and miracle over moral value. But, then, this all reflects his cosmology, just as should be expected. More blameworthy is modern man whose scientific cosmology is one thing while his religious cosmology is another.

III. RELIGION IN ANCIENT EGYPT

RELIGION AND CULTURE in Egypt did not suddenly begin after Noah's descendants spread over the earth. In order to demonstrate how Egypt's culture did emerge out of a long past, it will be necessary to try the reader's patience by many—but I hope not too many—details. These details will illuminate the facts of Egypt's religions.

Prehistoric Egypt

The Nile Valley has been traversed by man from early periods of the Old Stone Age. At least 200,000 years ago Chellean flints were left on its banks by Paleolithic man, and Acheulian flints picked up by modern archaeologists were deposited there 150,000 years ago. These facts show that hunters of the Old Stone Age made at least occasional excursions into the thin strip of penetrable territory that was then the Nile Valley.[1]

Four phases of paleolithic culture are distinguished by Hayes,[2] the first two prior to 12,000 B.C., the other two from 12,000 to 5000 B.C. At that time began the Neolithic culture, during which men of the New Stone Age built permanent dwellings first of wood, then of brick, and then of stone. The Neolithic "Tasian" Culture was primarily pastoral, evolving into a sedentary, agricultural society of organized villages.[3] The organization was inspired by nature, for only groups in cooperation could drain swamps, build dykes and reservoirs, and irrigate their fertile land. They came to live in clusters of little villages or nomes, which in the course of time were united to form the earliest political associations of Old Egypt, namely, the Two Kingdoms, the Upper and the Lower. The latter occupied the Egyptian Delta. The former extended from there to the First

Cataract of the Nile. These kingdoms brought to a close the Stone Age and introduced the use of copper and painted pottery. The Chalcolithic (Copper-Stone) Age began in Egypt well before 4000 B.C. and extends to about 3200 B.C., when the First Dynasty of the Historic Period begins.[4]

The Neolithic and Chalcolithic Egyptian cultures may be thought of as forming roughly a chronological order, although sometimes they overlap or suggest continuous cultural development and influence. For example, the Tasian (late Neolithic) and Badarian (early Chalcolithic) cultures show some notable differences, and yet may be regarded as essentially earlier and later phases of the same culture. Tasian pottery was comparatively primitive, while Badarian pottery was delicate, polished, painted, and finely decorated. Then the Amratians developed a rich culture between 4000 and 3600 B.C., but left no indications of being war-like. They were succeeded by the more warlike Gerzeans, whose vases conveyed drawings of their boats, and whose emblems are associated with the later hieroglyphic sign suggesting a hill god, very similar to the Yahweh of the Old Testament.[5] They perfected the methods of making beautiful painted pottery. They built brick houses and played games such as ninepins. They confused religion and magic, as their ancestors had done and as their descendants continued to do.

The Tasians are the first people known to bury their dead at a distance from their dwellings. They created cemeteries on the desert's edge, and there placed the dead in a grave, the body folded and lying on its side as if in sleep. With the dead were buried both useful and precious objects for the success and happiness of the soul. Thus in the fifth millennium B.C. the proto-Egyptians were practicing the rudiments of the religion for which later Egyptians became famous. By the middle of the fourth millennium the Gerzeans were burying their dead with the head toward the north, facing the rising sun, thus supplying evidence that at this early date a solar religion was being practiced.[6] In all probability it was Horus whom these prehistoric peoples worshiped, for he it was whom the Egyptians were worshiping when they entered the horizons of history. It would be interesting to know whether Horus had already lost his right eye at this early date. But conjecture must end somewhere; it may as well be here.

First Dynasty of Egyptian History

History properly begins with Narmer-Menes, whose dynasty (the first) and the one succeeding it are traditionally credited with having united Upper and Lower Egypt and gained control over Syria and Palestine. A conservative date for Menes (Meny) lies between 3100 and 2900 B.C. Petrie dated him as early as 4777 B.C. Hayes dates the entire first dynasty between 3200 and 2980, and the second dynasty between 2980 and 2780 B.C. Hayes insists that he is being conservative in adopting these dates.[7]

The early adoption of Egypt's astral calendar of 365 days affords a clue to the remarkable development of culture in that ancient land. Whenever this calendar was first adopted, its New Year's Day was undoubtedly that long-awaited day in the springtime when the star Sirius could be observed to set at dawn. Each day thereafter it would set a little earlier in the darkness before dawn until finally it became invisible in the daylight. The next year when the early riser saw it setting at dawn he knew that spring was once more at hand—and the imminent overflowing of the Nile.

For a reason which is easy to understand, the fixed calendar of 365 days was introduced. That reason was in order to enable the priests and laymen to know definitely, year after year, on what days to celebrate the great religious feasts. The presumption is that in the year when the fixed calendar was initiated, the New Year's Day coincided with that glorious day of spring when the star Sirius could be observed setting at sunrise. But because the true year is 365¼ days long, every four years thereafter Sirius set at sunrise one day later. After 1460 years the New Year's Day of the fixed calendar would again coincide with the Sirian New Year's Day. This event is known to have happened in 139 A.D., and in 1321 B.C., and also in 2781 B.C. Going back another 1460 years would take us to 4241 B.C. Winlock regards this as far too early in Egyptian history to conceive it possible that the fixed calendar had been invented. But that it was invented in 2781 B.C. is quite probable, since it was used in the religious texts of the pyramids of the Fifth and Sixth Dynasties, between 2550 and 2200 B.C. Winlock makes an excellent case for the theory that from the very beginning of its history Egypt followed a "vague calendar" based upon empirical observation of the rise and fall of the Nile River, on which Egyptian life and culture depended, and of the connection between the appearance of Sirius and the coming of the life-giving waters.[8]

It is therefore evident that Egyptian culture was far advanced by the beginning of the third millennium B.C. Not only did Egypt enter this millennium with the invention of writing, but it also developed mathematics and astronomy to a sufficiently high degree to account for the invention of the astral calendar. Then, too, mathematics and practical engineering were far enough advanced to enable Djoser, founder of the Third Dynasty (2780-2761 B.C.), to build the first pyramid. This was the so-called Step-Pyramid at Saqqara. The Age of the Pyramids followed.

Age of the Pyramids

The Old Kingdom, known as the Age of the Pyramids, comprised the Third to the Sixth Dynasties, 2780-2280 B.C. Probably the greatest of all pyramids was that built at Giza by Khufu, founder of the Fourth Dynasty. "Upon a square base covering some thirteen acres, he heaped up 2,300,000 blocks of yellowish limestone, each weighing on the average two and one-half tons, until the whole pyramid towered originally 481 feet into the sky. According to Herodotus, laborers toiled on the monument in groups of 100,000 men, each group for three months at a time. Ten years were required to make the road whereon the stones were dragged and twenty years more for the pyramid itself. . . . The stonework was done with a precision involving seams of one ten-thousandth of an inch, and the entire exterior was covered with an exquisitely fitted casing of fine white limestone."[9]

When we learn that the pyramids were royal tombs, intended to house the divine royal body until the resurrection day, we realize how much attention the early Egyptians were paying to some religious aspects of life. But religion was not merely an outward form even in those ancient times, as may be seen in the proverbs composed throughout the period of the Old Kingdom. Ptahhotep, a grand vizier of the Fifth Dynasty, counseled his son, "Be not arrogant

*Table II—Egyptian Chronology**

Paleolithic	before 8000 B.C.
Mesolithic	8000–6000 B.C.
Neolithic	6000–4000 B.C.
Chalcolithic and Predynastic (Tasian, Badarian, etc.)	4000–3200 B.C.
Early Dynastic	
I (King Meny)	3200–2980 B.C.
II	2980–2780 B.C.
Old Kingdom (Age of the Pyramids)	
III (Memphis) (Kings Djoser, etc.)	2780–2680 B.C.
IV (Kings Snefru, Khufu, etc.)	2680–2560 B.C.
V (Vizier Ptahhotep)	2560–2420 B.C.
VI (Pyramid Texts)	2420–2280 B.C.
First Interregnum	
VII (Seventy kings)	2280 B.C.
VIII (Fifteen kings)	2280–2242 B.C.
IX (Herakleopolis)	2242–2133 B.C.
X (Coffin Texts)	2133–2050 B.C.
Middle Kingdom	
XI (Thebes)	2134–1991 B.C.
XII (It-towy)	1991–1778 B.C.
Second Interregnum	
XIII (Fifty-four kings)	1778–1625 B.C.
XIV (Xois) (Seventy-six kings)	1778–1594 B.C.
XV (Hyksos)	1675–1567 B.C.
XVI (Thebes)	1660–1600 B.C.
XVII (Last of Hyksos)	1600–1567 B.C.
New Kingdom	
XVIII (Ahmose I, Amenhotep I-IV [Ikhnaton], Thutmose I-IV, Hatshepsut, etc.)	1567–1320 B.C.
XIX (Ramses I-II, etc.)	1320–1200 B.C.
XX	1200–1085 B.C.
Late Dynastic	
XXI (Tanite) (Amenemope)	1085– 950 B.C.
XXII (Libyan)	950– 730 B.C.
XXIII (Bubastite)	817– 730 B.C.
XXIV (Saite)	730– 715 B.C.
XXV (Ethiopian)	715– 656 B.C.
XXVI (Saite)	663– 525 B.C.
XXVII (Persian)	525– 404 B.C.
XXVIII (Saite)	404– 398 B.C.
XXIX (Mendesian)	398– 378 B.C.
XXX (Sebennytic)	378– 341 B.C.
Second Persian Period	341– 332 B.C.
Greek (Ptolemaic) Period	332– 30 B.C.
Roman Period	30 B.C.– 364 A.D.

* Dates primarily from Hayes, *The Scepter of Egypt,* especially p. xx.

because of thy knowledge, and be not puffed up for that thou art a learned man. Take counsel with the ignorant as with the learned. . . . Goodly discourse is more hidden than the precious green-stone, and yet it is found with slave-girls over the millstones. . . . Covetousness is an incurable malady, [but] a man shall thrive if he be truly righteous."[10]

Egypt's pyramids became a symbol of immortality.

The period from 2280 to perhaps 2052 B.C. is sometimes called the First Interregnum, or First Intermediate Period, because the glory of the Old Kingdom had departed. Weak rule, disintegration, and division are reflected in the literature of the period. Such is seen in "The Admonitions of Ipuwer":

> Behold, he that possessed wealth now spendeth the night athirst;
> He that begged of him his dregs is now a possessor of wine-vats.
> Behold, they that possessed clothes are now in rags;
> He that wove not for himself now possesseth fine linen.[11]

The Seventh to the Tenth Dynasties came during the First Interregnum. The Eleventh Dynasty ran concurrently with the Tenth Dynasty, and brought order out of chaos.

The Middle Kingdom began with the Eleventh Dynasty in 2134 B.C., and came to an end when the Twelfth Dynasty ceased in 1778 B.C.

Then followed the Second Interregnum or Second Intermediate Period. The thirteenth and Fourteenth Dynasties ran concurrently, beginning in 1778 B.C. The Thirteenth came to an end in 1625 B.C., while the Fourteenth continued until 1594. Meanwhile the Fifteenth or Hyksos Dynasty had arisen in 1675 to challenge the divided native dynasties, and gained the real mastery over Egypt while the native dynasties were contented with their role as puppets or fought among themselves. The Sixteenth Dynasty (1660-1600 B.C.) and the Seventeenth Dynasty (1600-1567 B.C.) completed the Second Intermediate Period.

Hyksos Kings

But who were the Hyksos kings? Scholars are again favoring the older tradition that the Hyksos kings of Egypt were probably Semites of Asiatic origin who invaded Egypt in a time of its weakness and gained control over it. The theory has come back into favor that the Israelites found asylum in Egypt during the reigns of these kings who, themselves Asiatics and Semites, would be likely to be friendly to Hebrews of similar origin.[12] During this Interregnum Egypt lost control over Syria and Palestine. Then finally arose some native patriots who drove out the Hyksos kings, with the result that Egypt's golden age was ushered in. This was the period of the New Kingdom, comprising Dynasties Eighteen to Twenty, 1567-1085 B.C.

Most noted dynasty in all the history of Egypt was the Eighteenth. It produced one of the great women of history, the capable and wilful Hatshepsut. When she no longer ruled indirectly through her husbands she ruled independently as a self-proclaimed "king." A great temple and other architectural achievements survive to her credit. Ahmose and Thutmose I, II, and III belonged to this famous dynasty, as well as Amenhotep II, III, and IV. The last changed his name to Ikhnaton for religious reasons, as we shall presently explain.

Then in the Nineteenth Dynasty came Ramses II, and Merenptah. Ramses III was the most noted king of the Twentieth Dynasty.

While it is not definitely proved, yet the most likely theory is that Ramses II was the Pharaoh of the oppression, enslaving the Israelites in his Lower-Egypt building program about 1300 B.C., the year after his accession. A stela of Merenptah names the Israelites as "widowed" masters of Palestine by about 1229 B.C. That leaves a fair amount of time for an exodus and at least a partial conquest of Palestine in the intervening seventy years.[13]

Decline of Egypt

The famous Tell El-Amarna letters, written to Amenhotep III and Ikhnaton in the fourteenth century B.C., describe Palestine and Jerusalem as under attack by the "Habiru," and appeal to the

Pharaoh for help. The Habiru may have been a nomadic branch of the family of Hebrews, cousins of the Israelites. Or they may possibly have been the Israelites themselves and their allies.

Egypt was in a state of general decline during the centuries when Israel and Judah were at the height of their culture in Palestine. The Twenty-first Dynasty, beginning about 1085 B.C., saw the rise of the priesthood to such power that Upper Egypt was practically an independent kingdom ruled by priests, while Lower Egypt was ruled by the Pharaoh, after a fashion, from Tanis in the Delta. It was during these days that Amenemope composed his verses of "wisdom." Some of his verses parallel the Proverbs of the Hebrews. Egyptian influence seems evident in Proverbs 22:17, 18, 24 among other passages. Compare these with Amenemope:

> Incline thine ears to hear my sayings,
> And apply thine heart to their comprehension.
> For it is a profitable thing to put them in thy heart,
> But woe to him who transgresses them.
>
> Fraternize not with the hot-tempered man,
> And press not upon him for conversation.[14]

The Late Dynastic Period saw the rise and fall of Dynasties Twenty-one to Thirty. Sometimes two dynasties ruled concurrently. Most often they were short-lived. The decline of Egypt was brought to a rout when about 525 B.C. the Persian King Cambyses II invaded the land and subjected it to Persian rule. Dynasties Twenty-seven to Thirty were on the whole under Persian subjection. Then in 332 B.C. came Greek rule and, after 323, rule by the Ptolemies. Cleopatra was the last of the Ptolemies. Following the matrilinear customs of Egypt she married first her elder brother and then her younger brother, to legitimize their rule. Then when Julius Caesar invaded Egypt she married him, thus legitimizing his rule as a Ptolemy. Later Anthony married her, thus becoming a Ptolemy in Egypt, even though in Rome he had another wife. But when Anthony was killed and Octavius showed his intention to marry Cleopatra, "she very wisely preferred death."[15]

When Rome thereupon annexed Egypt in 30 B.C. as an imperial province, a glorious history was ended. Its history may not seem glorious when we think of many of its customs and its magical, idolatrous, and polytheistic religious ideas. But these judgments would be unfair in the light of its positive achievements, its art, especially architecture, and its moral ideals. Breasted makes a strong case for the theory that in Egypt we see the very earliest "dawn of conscience."[16]

It is quite certain that Israel learned much from Egypt. The emergent moral ideals of Egypt quite apparently affected the Hebrew prophets and through them the whole world. Providence and moral law are seen in Egyptian writings. Hebrew writers virtually translated Egyptian wisdom literature, and the psalms and prophets are deeply rooted in Egyptian philosophy, in much the same way as Babylonian mythology and law were the roots from which Old Testament stories and laws were derived.[17]

Book of the Dead

We are indebted to the Pyramid Texts for much of our knowledge of early Egyptian history and religion. These are inscriptions found on five pyramids at Saqqara, dating between 2560 and 2280 B.C. It is quite certain that these texts quoted earlier texts which have not been recovered as yet, and which in some cases date back to before 3000 B.C.[18] When these texts grew by being inscribed on coffins, and modified in the process, they developed into what is called the Coffin Texts. The next step was to gather many of these together on papyri to form the earliest edition of the so-called *Book of the Dead*. This book was never definitive, but in its several forms contains collectively about two hundred independent chapters. Its collection began during the Eighteenth Dynasty, after 1567 B.C.

Some Characteristics of Egyptian Religion

It is useless to look for order that does not exist in Egyptian religion. The fact is that Egypt had not one religion but many. In an easy going manner, people of different times and various localities in Egypt chose certain of the traditional gods as of special importance, and in practice neglected others. The priests at given times and places emphasized certain gods rather than others. They were superseded by other priests who thought differently, and occasionally by a king who ordered changes in religious customs. The different classes of people, too, tended to have their favorite gods and to observe their preferred ritual. Religion which appealed to the aristocrats was not likely to be the choice of the oppressed classes.

There are legends which suggest that Egypt's prehistoric religion contained elements of crude savagery. Ra, as supreme ruler, is said to have ordered Sakhmet, the lion goddess, to destroy mankind. Sakhmet failed in her appointed task only because she became intoxicated with blood. At certain religious festivals people representing the enemies of the gods were beaten almost to death, while other participants beat themselves bloody. War prisoners were actually killed and animals were consumed by the altar fires. In historic times such crude behavior gave way to symbolic rites using wax figures and magical ceremonies. The gods, in turn, came to stand for moral and social values and the guarantors of eternal justice.

There is some disagreement as to whether Egypt's prehistoric religion was totemic.[19] "It is clear that nothing quite like the types of totemism known from Australia, Africa, or America had ever existed in Egypt. Nearly all the local gods, each of whom was revered in a town or district (from which arose the later system of forty-two nomes) were represented in animal form, as we know from later idols, hieroglyphs, and allusions in Egyptian religious literature. . . . But there does not appear to be a trace in early texts of specifically totemic phenomena such as . . . exogamy. . . ."[20] On the other hand writers like Mercer, Murray, and Noss refer approvingly to prehistoric totemism in Egypt. The disagreement seems to be a matter of definition. The fact is that each of the village groups in prehistoric Egypt probably regarded a certain animal or other symbol as its common ancestor and, as such, sacred. Evidence for this lies in the fact that the customary representation of the gods was in the form of a man's body with the head of an animal or other totemic symbol. Ra, for example, was pictured as a falcon-headed man wearing a sun and a serpent, while Anubis, god of the tomb at Cynopolis, appeared as a jackal-headed man.[21] The bull was sacred at Memphis, Thebes worshiped a ram (Amen), and the swallow was personified and deified in Isis, while Set took the form of a greyhound. Thoth was pictured as an ibis or an ibis-headed man. Examples are manifold, witnessing to the primitive Egyptian belief in a power strong enough to hold a community together and deserving worship for its own sake.

How large a part was played by animals in Egyptian religion from earliest times is illustrated by bull worship. A divine bull by different names was worshiped at four different places: Memphis, Heliopolis, Hermonthis, and Canopus. The worship of the Apis-bull at Memphis is the best known. Herodotus wrote:

> This Apis . . . is the calf of a cow incapable of conceiving another offspring. This calf, which is called Apis, has the following marks: it is black, and has a square spot of white on the forehead; and on the back the figure of an eagle; and in the tail double hairs; and on the tongue a beetle. [At the birth of an Apis] the Egyptians immediately put on their richest apparel and kept festive holiday.[22]

Apis was identified with the Nile, hence was so closely associated with Osiris as to be considered his visible soul. This made him divine, justifying his worship. He "suffered the same fate as the human incarnation of the divine Spirit. He was not allowed to die of old age, but was ceremonially [drowned] and a new bull installed in his place."[23] It seems likely that there was a communion feast on his flesh, and royal honors paid to inedible parts of the carcass.

Those anthropologists who follow Marett find a trace of dynamism in the origin of some of the Egyptian deities. It seems simpler to say that the Egyptian deities, like others, show a mixture of dynamistic

Hieroglyphic pictograph for life, a key carried by the gods. The tau cross may be discerned here in its most ancient form. The life force is revered in all primitive religions, usually with sex-symbols.*

and animistic characteristics. Apparently the impersonal power of fertility flowed from the personal Osiris. In Egypt in historic times the power of fertility was identified with the River Nile, which so obviously gave life to the valley by its annual overflow and thus sustained human life and culture. Since Osiris was the divine soul of the Nile, he was also the god of fertility, the sustainer of Egyptian

* See Wheelwright, *The Burning Fountain*, pp. 138-140.

life and culture. Osiris was possibly, therefore, of animistic origin. A similar case may be made for the other gods who together formed the Egyptian pantheon.

Dynamism is revealed in the magical formulas or rites whereby the Pharaohs were expected to be brought back to life.[24] These ceremonies provide for revivifying the corpse through the life-giving water of the Nile, with which the god Osiris was identified, and by reciting religious texts. Magical formulas were suggested to the dead monarch whereby he might fool the ferryman on the river of death and sneak into heaven without the permission of the gods. By repeating these formulas the Pharaoh was presumed to be making contact with an impersonal, supernatural force which assured him success in a most critical undertaking. The formulas were quotations from the Pyramid Texts, Coffin Texts, and *Book of the Dead.*

It is of course evident that Egyptian religion was prevailingly polytheistic. Its polytheism probably arose there—as Marett claims it has everywhere—out of animism. The souls of the most potent parts of nature came to be feared and in due time worshiped. So the sky (nut) was conceived of as the god Nut; the earth (geb) became the god Geb; and the sun (ra) became the god Ra.

Like polytheism elsewhere, that in Egypt was completely anthropomorphic. Their gods were like the men who created them. They were thought to be limited in knowledge, subject to sorrows, injuries, and even death, emotionally responsive to insults and praise, and sufficiently impotent to be controlled by magic. They fought with each other, killed and even ate other gods, and might be seen by men under certain conditions, in which case they would usually be found to have manlike bodies.

As mythology developed, certain gods and goddesses played a more prominent part than others. It would be tedious to make a complete list of these. But because of the importance of sun-worship and the later triumph of Osiris, we should mention first, Ra, the sun god of Heliopolis. Ra was usually pictured as a man with the head of a falcon and associated with the sun's disc. At Thebes Amen was conceived to be the creator-god, associated with a ram. At Memphis, Ptah was thought to be the divine cosmic architect, usually pictured as a manlike idol with legs together. Set was a primitive god of the atmosphere, having a man's body and an animal head. He was originally independent of the Osiris myth but in the course of time came to be thought of as the brother and slayer of Osiris. Then there was the goddess Isis, who shared with Osiris the function of fecundity; she was the sister-wife of Osiris in the developed mythology. Horus, one of the earlier independent sun gods, became even more prominent through participation in the Osiris drama. In his struggle with Set he took on the characteristics of a war god. Other than Isis, perhaps the most important goddess was Maat, who personified truth. The list has hardly begun, but must end here.

Two Rival Cults

As numerous types of religious faith and experience issued out of this multitude of gods, two principal rival systems emerged in Egyptian history. One was the sun cult, centering in Ra, the sun god of Heliopolis. The theologians of this triumphant city regarded Ra as the creator-god. He was conceived to be kingly himself and the father of the Egyptian Pharaohs. When they died the Pharaohs were thought to have gone to be with their heavenly father, Ra, in the sun's abode. In this way, as we see, the religion of Ra was aristocratic, appealing to royalty and its retinue. It was made into a state religion in order to bolster patriotism and kingly pride and was more concerned with cosmology and government than with the spiritual needs of the people. It emphasized the present world and the life-giving powers of the sun, referring to the next world only to assure the king's survival, surrounded by all his courtiers and earthly comforts in the celestial land of the sunlight. The boats found near the tombs of the Pharaohs were supposed to carry the souls of the Pharaoh and his friends across the sky in daily company with the divine sun.

The second principal religious cult was that revolving about Osiris. It is possible that Osiris was originally a human being who was later raised to deity. There is other evidence of ancestor worship in ancient Egypt, and this theory of the origin of Osiris would fit in with that. And yet a religion is what it comes to be, not merely what it was originally. The great significance of Osiris lay in the development of the popular mystery cult of Isis and Osiris.

The myths told about Osiris are varying and not always coherent. One mythical tale has it that the wicked Set, his brother, killed him and boxed him in a casket which he set afloat on the River Nile. The widow, Isis, mourned and searched for him and, finding him at last, concealed his body. Another story relates how Set stole the body, cut it to pieces, and scattered the pieces throughout Egypt. The forlorn and pertinacious widow wandered about the land until she had found and buried every single piece. The agricultural significance of this myth is seen in the interesting detail that wherever a piece of his body was buried, there sprang up living vegetation. Horus was represented in these myths as having been born of Isis from the seed of Osiris, which Isis had taken up into herself after first finding the body of her slain beloved. Gratefully Horus set out to avenge his father's death, and the struggle with Set ensued. During the struggle Horus lost an eye, which was later restored. When he offered it as a sacrifice he was rewarded by the resurrection of his father who, however, did not thereafter roam heaven and earth but descended into the lower regions. There he became the ruler of the realm of the dead and, as such, the personal judge of all those who entered that abode. The story about the eye of Horus accounts for the symbolism of the eye of Egypt, which later entered into western symbolism. It is the eye of God, which sees all and knows all, and is offered as a sacrifice for another's salvation from death.

The eye of Horus has influenced western symbolism, as the all-seeing eye of God who, seeing all, knows all.

As time went on the Osiris myth was appropriated by the common people, while the cult of the sun correspondingly declined. Even before 1850 B.C. the symbolism of the Osiris story was acted out on festival occasions as an ancient Passion Play. Like all of the mystery myths of the ancient Near East, the one about Osiris symbolized the annual death of vegetation and its rebirth in the spring. The earlier emphasis in the Osiris myth was upon the dependence of nature, man, and culture on the mysterious cycle of death and rebirth, as personified by the Nile. But the later Osirian mystery cult, in which not only kings but also commoners put their trust, stressed the salvation of the soul in the future life. This other-worldly function of Osiris finally became his chief role, along with that of being judge of the dead.

The royal pyramid-tombs of Egypt are monuments to man's irrepressible notion of immortality. In anticipation of the hoped-for resurrection, the body of the pharaoh was carefully embalmed in order that it might still be in good condition when the soul returned to animate it. Meanwhile the shadowy soul was supplied with food, drink, furniture, jewels, and all the comforts of his earthly palace while waiting for the return to his body. Ordinary mortals who could not afford the luxury of scientific embalming had to depend on a soaking with salt water to mummify the body till that great day when the soul should return to the resurrected body. The common man's longing for immortality is attested by the growth of the Osiris cult as it eclipsed or absorbed the sun-cult.

Doctrine of Man

Egyptian psychology was confusingly complex. The Egyptians thought of the soul, "Ba," in the form of a bird with a human head. After death the "Ba" hovered about, making its temporary home in the statue of the deceased which customarily was placed in the tomb. In addition to the "Ba" they pictured the "Ka" as a ghost-like image of the individual. They hypostasized a man's name, "Ren," and his intelligence, "Khu," as well as his heart, "Ab," and other aspects. But the "Ka" was the most important of all; it was that which needed food and drink and other useful or precious objects in the continued life after death. The Egyptian cult of the dead centered around the "Ka."

Frankfort[25] has shown rather conclusively that the Egyptians from earliest times regarded the "Ka" as a "vital force," similar in character to the primitive Roman "genius"—an impersonal twin-like accompaniment of the individual but surviving death to lead him like a guardian angel into immortal blessedness. Primitive Egyptian art sometimes represents the royal "Ka" in concrete imagery, while the "Ka" of commoners is never so represented. However, an abundance of texts prove that even the royal "Ka" was regarded as his divine vital force linking him to his father-god.

The "Ba," often represented as a birdlike image, is the Egyptian concept of a spirit or "ghost" which hovers about the old haunts and seeks to rejoin the body. It is conceived sometimes as flying to heaven, but as seeking generally to be near the dead body and to enjoy the food and possessions which it enjoyed in life.

It seems that no curious philosopher or theologian arose in ancient Egypt who felt the challenge to reconcile the contradictory views that (1) the soul hovered in the tomb until the proper time came for it to reenter the resurrected body; (2) the soul went to the underworld where Osiris, after judging its qualifications in morals or magic, welcomed it to eternal bliss; (3) the souls of kings and their courtiers went upward to the cheerful realm of the sun's abode.

This is a good place to mention the very ancient Egyptian doctrine of the divinity of the Pharaoh. Frankfort has given evidence that even before Menes united the upper and the lower Egypt into "The Two Kingdoms," the Egyptian kings were regarded as divine.

> This was the fundamental concept of Egyptian kingship, that Pharaoh was of divine essence, a god incarnate; and this view can be traced back as far as texts and symbols take us. It is wrong to speak of a deification of Pharaoh. His divinity was not proclaimed at a certain moment, in a manner comparable to the *consecratio* of the dead emperor by the Roman senate. His coronation was not an apotheosis but an epiphany.[26]

The Monotheistic Idea

Egyptian religion is not merely a story of animism, polytheism, magic, and Pharaoh worship. One of the most dramatic stories in the history of all religion is that of the rise in Egypt of monotheism during the reign of Ikhnaton, or Amenhotep (Amenophis) IV, who succeeded his father Amenhotep III in 1377 B.C. The story has become somewhat complicated by the fact, more recently discovered, that Amenhotep IV was not solely responsible for the initiation of the monotheistic doctrine, and that the doctrine was not purely monotheistic. It is most likely that the idea was promoted by his mother, a woman of foreign birth, probably from Syria. Amenhotep IV came to the throne when he was no older than eleven, and he may have been as young as eight at his accession. He reigned for only seventeen years. It is not impossible that such a youthful king should have dreamed up a kind of monotheism all by himself. But since we find reference to the idea of Aton-worship during the reign of his father, it becomes still more plausible to believe that Ikhnaton was influenced by others. It is now known that in the Near East, with which Egypt was then in close contact, the doctrine of theological universalism was being expressed. This was the doctrine that various gods in different places and with different names are not really different gods at all.[27] It was only a step further to monotheism.

But no matter who influenced him, Ikhnaton was powerfully overcome by the idea of one god, whom he identified with the sun's disc. He was repelled by the more primitive animistic idea of worshiping the deified souls of the objects of nature. He was fascinated by the notion that the sun itself, by its daily journey across the earth, gave warmth and light to man, beast, and herb. So Aton was the Lord of all, insisted Amenhotep IV, who even changed his name to Ikhnaton in honor of the great god. Not only that, but Ikhnaton also moved his capital from Thebes to a new spot which he named Akhetaton, and there built a great temple. He also ordered the old inscriptions at Thebes, Karnak, and elsewhere, referring to Amen-Ra and other gods, to be changed to Aton. This was accomplished. A new set of priests was installed at the new temple at Akhetaton to promote the new religion.

Ikhnaton stressed the need for truth and reality, and initiated a reform in art in the direction of realism. He also laid emphasis upon family love and happiness, and fought against the old magical superstitions.

It is now quite certain that Ikhnaton was not truly monotheistic. For example, he adhered to the Egyptian tradition of believing in his own kingly divinity, as the son of Aton, even though he must have been conscious of his own personal deformity and weakness. He also seems to have believed that some entity, housed in the new temple, united him with his father Aton. Apparently he also worshiped Ra and Horus, perhaps as other names for the sun-god; and he regarded the Mnevis bull as a divine incarnation.

Murray greatly discounts the significance of Ikhnaton (which she and some others spell Akhnaten). She reveals hymns to the sun which rival his well-known poem. She describes him as a king who lacked legitimate claim to the throne (i.e., he could not claim the customary matrilinear descent); as one who may have been forced to leave Thebes for his new capital for some unworthy reason; as a worshiper of "Re, Horus, and the Mnevis bull; and as one who neglected his declining empire for a sentimental religion which exalted the physical sun."[28]

It is generally held, however, that Ikhnaton's religious ideas were in advance of his day. He used his position as god and king to force a temporary religious reformation. But upon his death the merchants, priests, and people conspired to restore the old order. The restoration occurred with some vengeance when even his new capital was demolished, to be replaced later by Tell-el-Amarna. The probable truth is that his religion was so far ahead both of the magic-dominated priests and of the ignorant masses that they could not appreciate the fine features which it possessed. They longed only for Osiris by whose power they might overcome sickness and death. The hot sun's disc in torrid Egypt held little enchantment for them.

The most immortal deed which Ikhnaton ever performed was the writing of the celebrated "Hymn to the Sun." There is no special reason to doubt the tradition that he was its author. And its beauty is such that it holds inspiration even for our day. We quote some of its beautiful lines, which compare favorably with Psalm 104:

UNIVERSAL SPLENDOUR AND POWER OF ATON

Thou dawnest beautifully in the horizon of the sky,
O living Aton who wast the Beginning of life!
When thou didst rise in the eastern horizon,
Thou didst fill every land with thy beauty.
Thou art beautiful, great, glittering, high over every land,
Thy rays, they encompass the lands, even to the end of them;
Thou bindest them for thy beloved son [the Pharaoh].
Though thou art far away, thy rays are upon earth;
Though thou art in the faces of men, thy footsteps are unseen.

NIGHT AND MAN

When thou settest in the western horizon of the sky,
The earth is in darkness like death.

They sleep in their chambers,
Their heads are wrapped up,
Their nostrils are stopped,
And none seeth the other,
While all their things are stolen,
Which are under their heads,
And they know it not.*

NIGHT AND ANIMALS

Every lion cometh forth from his den,
All serpents, they sting.
Darkness broods,
The world is in silence,
He that made them resteth in his horizon.*

DAY AND MAN

Bright is the earth when thou risest in the horizon;
When thou shinest as Aton by day
Thou drivest away the darkness.
When thou sendest forth thy rays,
The Two Lands (Egypt) are in daily festivity.
Men waken and stand upon their feet
When thou hast raised them up.
Their limbs bathed, they take their clothing,
Their arms uplifted in adoration to thy dawning.
Then in all the world they do their work.*

DAY AND THE WATERS

The barques sail up-stream and down-stream alike.
Every highway is open because thou dawnest.
The fish in the river leap up before thee.
Thy rays are in the midst of the great green sea.*

. . . .

REVELATION TO THE KING

. . . .

There is no other that knoweth thee
Save thy son Ikhnaton.
Thou hast made him wise
In thy designs and in thy might.

* CF. Psalm 104:20-26.

UNIVERSAL MAINTENANCE

The world subsists in thy hand,
Even as thou hast made them.
When thou hast risen they live,
When thou settest they die;
For thou art length of life of thyself,
Men live through thee.[29]

The beauty of this poem shines like the sun through the clouds of Egyptian superstition. It is one of the truly great contributions of ancient Egypt.

Social Values in Egyptian Religion

Another excellence of ancient Egypt was its recognition of the values of family life. A thousand years before Ikhnaton, as the pyramid inscriptions reveal, family life in Egypt was cultivated from prehistoric times. One of the pyramid inscriptions tells how a certain son traveled into the savage Sudan to recover the body of his murdered father and give it proper burial.[30] The story was cited as proof that the son had observed the duties of filial piety and should therefore be judged sympathetically by the gods. There are many other evidences of a pervasive feeling of family loyalty in the Age of the Pyramids and earlier.

Furthermore the dead man's tomb usually contained inscribed evidence that the deceased had been just and kind to others besides his family. So the steward Meni showed evidence, for example, that he had been most fair and just in paying the workmen who were building his tomb.[31] Harkhuf of Elephantine has written on the walls of his tomb: "I was . . . beloved of his father, praised of his mother, whom all his brothers loved. I gave bread to the hungry, clothing to the naked, I ferried him whom had no boat. . . . Never did I judge two brothers in such a way that a son was deprived of his paternal possession."[32]

Both in the earlier and later parts of the *Book of the Dead,* the loftiest social values of Egyptian society are reflected in the promise of reward and threat of punishment. One of the noblest passages in all religious literature is that passage in the *Book of the Dead* in which the soul is represented as having earned the right to say to the gods in the next world,

I have not done iniquity. . . . I have not robbed with violence. . . . I have not done violence to any man. . . . I have not committed theft. . . . I have not made light the bushel. . . . I have not acted deceitfully. . . . I have not purloined the things which belong unto God. . . . I have not uttered falsehood. . . . I have not defiled the wife of a man. . . . I have not committed any sin against purity. . . . I have not struck fear into any man. . . . I have not been a man of anger. . . . I have not made myself deaf to the words of right and truth. . . . I have not stirred up strife. . . . I have not judged hastily. . . . I have not multiplied my speech overmuch. . . . I have not fouled water.[33]

One feels that there is a certain amount of self-righteousness in this bit of ritual. And always there was added to the reflection of high moral aspiration their accompanying superstition that the very use of these formulas of righteousness might suffice to gain magic entry into heaven. Yet the more noteworthy is the fact that the Egyptians so long ago felt the moral compulsions indicated in this remarkable chapter of the *Book of the Dead*.

The role of truth and justice in ancient Egypt was dramatized by the goddess Maat. This goddess first arose as the symbol of personal and family righteousness. But in the course of time she came to personify the orderliness, justice, and stability which Egyptians believed to characterize all their affairs. Breasted has pointed out[34] how the Egyptians of the Age of the Pyramids looked back on a thousand years of Egyptian history and were convinced that order and justice alone could explain the success of Egyptian cultural experience. Maat came to stand not only for the truth and justice according to whose standards the individual was judged in the next life, but also for the lawfulness of human society. As Maat in the next world placed a feather in the scales to weigh against the soul of the deceased, in order to determine if there was any sinfulness to weight it down, so in this world the human judge wore an image of Maat which at the conclusion of the trial he turned symbolically in the direction of the winner. The Pharaohs thought of themselves as personifying and enforcing Maat and as obligated to suppress those things which she opposed, namely, lawlessness, injustice, and untruthfulness. As Breasted points out, conscience had dawned in ancient Egypt. Indeed, the evidence is strong that it had dawned much earlier; in Egyptian culture it merely took a specific direction and exerted historic influences which we today can trace down into our times.

Egyptian religion inevitably became highly institutionalized and its priests acquired great influence. Its feasts and its solemn occasions recurred with seasonal regularity. On such occasions the priests of the various cults were generally clothed in white, closely shaven, and clean. There were also priestesses who served as musicians, among other things. Temple architecture developed into a pattern, with the holy "cella" at the center. Only the priests went into the holy sanctuary to attend the gods, to bathe them, and to offer sacrifices. On special occasions they would take the gods out to the people for a solemn or joyful procession, as the ritual demanded. Undoubtedly many hearts were lifted up as they witnessed the pageantry and thought of the dependence of man upon the will of the gods, in this life and the next. The pious would make fresh resolves to live worthily of the favor of the gods, hoping that by all means available they would be saved now and for eternity. Of course there were always those who lived for today, willing for tomorrow to take care of itself. And on the whole it is probable that ignorance, fear, and superstition prevented most people from obtaining a coherent religious experience. But Egyptian society cultivated religion as a means of expressing its concern for the conservation of those values which it held most dear. As we have seen, those values were moral, aesthetic, social, and to an unusual extent other-worldly. But Egypt's faith in immortality was in itself a recognition of the intrinsic worth of the individual, who should make himself worthy to live forever.

Emerging Maturity in Egyptian Religion

Certain values of maturity can easily be seen in Egypt's religions. The interest in immortality indicates an implicit faith in the value of the individual. There certainly was an ethical sensitivity in their culture. The Egyptian deification of truthfulness (Maat) implies a certain commitment to the truth, without providing techniques for discovering the full nature of truth. Egyptian science was largely confined to mathematics, astronomy, and engineering. Cosmology was of course inadequate in science as in religion. And magic tainted the ethical insights of the *Book of the Dead,* while literalness corroded the earlier freshness of many myths, preventing Egyptian religion from gaining any large measure of maturity. There was much beauty in the religious symbolism of Egypt, as in the pyramids and the mystery myths symbolizing immortality. Here too magic and formalism detracted. The implicit qualities of religious maturity had to wait for some other experience which Egypt failed to produce; therefore Egyptian religion remained in a state of relative immaturity throughout most of Egypt's long cultural epochs.)

IV. RELIGION IN THE ANCIENT NEAR EAST

FROM THE POINT OF VIEW of the Judeo-Christian tradition we should be more interested in the religion of the Near East than in that of Egypt. Not that there is any doubt that Egypt influenced Israel both during the centuries of its sojourn in Egypt and later in Palestine. For in those later years there must have been repeated contacts with Egypt which kept Israel aware of its great achievements. But the Hebrew relation with Near Eastern culture was more direct and pervasive. The influence was permanent and unavoidable. For Abraham was himself a Mesopotamian and a Semite, like his neighbors in Mesopotamia. The Hebrews carried Mesopotamian culture into Palestine and on down into Egypt. On returning to Palestine the Israelites came into daily contact with their Semitic cousins of Canaan, Phoenicia, and Syria, absorbing many of their customs and ideas.

Near Eastern Prehistory

Egyptologists and Near Eastern archaeologists rival one another in their efforts to push history and prehistory back farther and farther. Up to date there are no definitive results of this rivalry. It may be that ascertainable settlements in the Near East are earlier than those of Egypt. But apparently history began in both areas at about the same time.

The cultural remains of prehistoric man in the Near East are abundant and ever increasing. Excavations there began about 150 years ago, and have multiplied in the last few decades. Tepe Gawra, Ur, Erech (Uruk), Ras Shamra (Ugarit), Ghassul, Jericho, and many other sites have now been uncovered.

Neolithic villages have been discovered in the Near East dating back to between 6000 and 5000 B.C.[1] In fact, the Near East appears to be the home of Homo sapiens, for the twelve bodies embedded in limestone in two caves near Mount Carmel, probably 100,000 years old, have the general characteristics of Paleolithic Neandertal man but, with one exception, also show some significant anatomical likenesses to modern man.[2] Nowhere except in the Near East does this occur. We also have evidence of continuous development of Neolithic Palestinian man, except for the period from *c.* 20,000 to *c.* 10,000 B.C.

*Table III.—Mesopotamian Cultural Periods**

Paleolithic	25,000–7000 B.C.
Mesolithic and Neolithic	7000–4500 B.C.
Chalcolithic	4500–2800 B.C.
Halafian	4500–4000 B.C.
Obeidian	4000–
Uruk	–3000 B.C.
Bronze	
Early Dynastic	3000–2500 B.C.
Classical Sumerian	2800–2360 B.C.
Sumero–Akkadian	2360–1960 B.C.
Western Semitic and Old Babylonian	1960–1550 B.C.
Assyro-Babylonian	1100–539 B.C.[3]

* See Kroeber, *Anthropology,* 2nd ed., p. 706. Harcourt Brace and Co., 1948.

Following the Neolithic came the Chalcolithic ("Copper-stone") Age, which began about 4500 B.C. Its earliest culture is called Halafian, after Tell Halaf where its remains were first discovered in northwestern Mesopotamia. Other remains of this primitive culture were found at Carchemish and at Tepe Gawra. Skilfully glazed pottery of great beauty characterizes this culture. A culture comparable in date and artistry was found in excavations at Ghassul near Jericho.

Of special significance for us is the fact that the people of the Halafian period in the fifth millennium B.C. had developed institutional religious practices. Certain massive buildings with circular ground-plan have been identified as shrines, partly because of the concentration of fertility figurines around them. At Ghassul frescoes have survived well enough to prove that they represented a god and goddess having some cultic significance.

Lower Mesopotamia, or Sumeria-Babylonia, was an uninhabited marshland during the period of the Halafian culture. The earliest culture in lower Mesopotamia is called Obeidian, from Tell el-Obeid near ancient Ur. Deep excavations at Ur also reveal the Obeidian culture as its earliest. In the north, too, at Tepe Gawra, levels XIX to XIII are Obeidian. Level XIX, the earliest of the Obeidian levels at Tepe Gawra, reveals the oulines of what Finegan describes as "by far the oldest religious structure known to man."[4] Albright is convinced of the existence of shrines in the earlier Halafian period,[5] yet all this seems to have taken place in the fifth millennium B.C.

Level XIII at Tepe Gawra has been dated by Finegan at about 4000 B.C.[6] At this level elaborate temple structures were discovered. There were three large buildings in the main courtyard. As one entered the court, the building on the right was the white Eastern Shrine, on the left, the red brick Northern Shrine, and straight ahead, the Northern Temple. So imposing was this group of buildings that one can be sure that only a populous community could have erected them. Both religious and social progress are indicated.[7]

No written records have come down to us from 4000 B.C., so we have no way of ascertaining the names of the gods whom the Obeidians worshiped. One of them probably was the moon god, another the sun god, another a fertility goddess. That the stages of animism and dynamism had passed into the era of polytheism is quite evident, for when we first learn the names and functions of their gods, they turn out to be the deified souls of the powers and objects of nature.

The cosmopolitanism of the Obeidians is shown by their trading habits. Lapis lazuli and amazonite beads among the remains of the Obeidian culture are positive evidence that at this early period Mesopotamia had trade relations with central Asia and India, from which these stones came. Other evidence accrues to confirm this theory.

The next, the Warkan or Uruk Period, before 3000 B.C., showed northern influences, probably from Transcaucasia and Anatolia. The potter's wheel was used in this period, and new methods and styles of painting were introduced. The ziggurat, too, is first found in the Uruk culture. This was a temple in the symbolic form of a small mountain with the sacred shrine at its pinnacle. The ziggurat became the most characteristic form of sacred architecture in the subsequent history of Babylonia. The oldest ziggurat known (at Uruk) stood about thirty feet high and was much wider at the base than at the top. The "tower of Babel," noteworthy in Biblical lore, was a ziggurat. Not so famous but remarkably well preserved was the ziggurat at Ur, apparently built on an earlier and smaller ziggurat. It was restored by Nabonidus, father of Belshazzar, in the sixth century B.C. This ziggurat was originally about seventy feet high, with a rectangular base 200 by 150 feet. Its pinnacle shrine was approached by three large outside stairways. The shrine was constructed entirely of blue enameled bricks. "The ziggurat stood on a high raised terrace surrounded by a double wall. Partly on this terrace and partly at its feet lay the large temple for the moon-god Nanna with a wide outer court surrounded by numerous store-chambers and offices. Not far from it was a temple dedicated to both Nanna and his wife Ningal; then came a building which may have been used as a 'court house;' then the temple sacred to Ningal known as Giparku, which itself contained two separate temples as well as a host of private and storage rooms. All in all the Ekishnugal must have contained the outstanding group of buildings in ancient Ur."[8]

But far more important than the ziggurat were the Uruk contributions of the cylinder seal and writing. The cylinder seal was made of stone, with artistic figures cut into it so that as it was rolled over a moist clay surface it left an impression in relief. These cylinder seals came to be of great importance and were exported to places as far away as Egypt and India. The seals provide artistic illustrations of many elements of ancient culture, religious and social. The early artistic seals of Uruk were used to identify private ownership, while others developing in the same culture displayed pictographic writing which in the course of time evolved into the Babylonian cuneiform. The cuneiform script in turn became a medium for the writing of many different languages, in contrast with the limited use of Egyptian hieroglyphics. Even before 3200 B.C. it is known that temple records were kept on clay tablets, revealing an elaborate economic and political organization in Mesopotamia. Thus with the invention of writing, history began in

Mesopotamia in the Predynastic Period, during the fourth millennium B.C.

Although there are "almost no religious texts" from the fourth millenium B.C., yet we may learn from "votive building documents and administrative lists" something about their religious ideas and practices. From such evidence we infer that "in the major temple of each city there were offered daily sacrifices consisting of animal and vegetable foods, libations of water, wine, and beer, as well as the burning of incense. In addition there were, of course, the new moon feasts and other monthly celebrations. Finally there was the prolonged New Year celebration with its human and divine processions culminating in the hieros-gamos ceremony."[9]

The Sumerian Culture

The next main historic period of Babylonia is called the classical Sumerian period, and lasted from about 3000 or 2800 to about 2360 B.C. This period Finegan calls the "Early Dynastic Period," whose records confuse fact and legend. For example, some of its earlier dynasties are credited with thousands of years, while others in odd small figures are more evidently correct. The Sumerian King List in its present form was put into writing no later than about 2000 B.C., but undoubtedly is based on much earlier records.

The Sumerian language appears to be unique in linguistic history. It is definitely non-Semitic and no one has proved its relation to any other historical language. But it was the first language to be written, and for a thousand years was the only written language of Mesopotamia (about 3500-2500 B.C.).[10] For another 2500 years it was the universal learned language of the Near East, like the Latin of medieval Europe.

While the Sumerian culture was extremely influential over a period of several millennia, in politics it was a different story. For in this field the Semites gained the upper hand. By Semites we mean a large family of peoples. "The Akkadian, Assyrian, and Babylonian dialects constitute the older East Semitic branch of this family, while Hebrew, Aramaic, Phoenician, Syriac, Arabic, and Ethiopic are included in the West Semitic."[11] There is much evidence of an infiltration of Mesopotamia by Semites over a long period of time. The infiltration may have taken place violently from time to time, but for the most part was probably peaceful. Finally with the appearance of Sargon the Akkadian about 2360 B.C. the Semitic political domination became complete. However, as when the Hellenes conquered the Mycenaeans, and the Romans conquered the Greeks, when the Akkadians conquered the Sumerians, the conqueror retained and further developed the culture of the conquered. For this reason the period from Sargon I to the fall of the Third Dynasty of Ur, c. 2360-1960 B.C., is called the Sumero-Akkadian Age.

Sargon was a man of humble birth but of great achievement. A favorite story of the near East was told about him, and later about Moses. One of his inscriptions explains that he did not know his father and that his mother hid him in an ark among the bulrushes where he was found by an irrigator. "Akki the irrigator hauled me out. . . . Akki the irrigator took me to be his son and brought me up."[12] Out of gratitude Sargon founded the city of Agade, giving the name Akkad to the surrounding country and the name Akkadians to his Semitic people. Sargon's empire extended from Elam in the east to the Mediterranean in the west.

It is difficult to distinguish between the Sumerian gods and those of the Akkadians. The Akkadians accepted the gods of Sumer and added some of their own or changed the Sumerian name to that of a Semitic god having the same function. One of the most important gods was Enlil (or Ellil), the air-god and creator of sun, moon, and stars. He was widely revered by both Sumerians and Akkadians, but was especially the patron of Nippur where his temple was. Enki—known later as Ea—was the water-god in an irrigation culture. His importance therefore is easily seen. He, too, was widely revered but was the special patron deity of Eridu. Through his gift of water he brought the arts and crafts to man. Nanna—known to the Akkadians as Sin—was the moon-god, as universal as the moon in his appeal; but Ur regarded him as its patron deity and built his grandest temple.

Among the peculiarly Sumerian gods was Nammu, goddess of the primeval sea. Nammu was thought of as having been self-produced, a myth symbolizing the supposedly self-producing and creative character of primeval water. An (Anu), heaven-god, was her son, and Ki, earth-goddess, was her daughter. Utu, the sun-god, was the son of Nanna, the moon-god. And so the gods were believed to have had a natural origin after the manner of human families, and to have their special duties as men also have.

Two important Akkadian gods were Shamash, the sun-god, and Ishtar, goddess of love and beauty—and of the star which is better known to us as Venus. Shamash, like the sun, was universal, but was regarded as the special patron of Larsa in the south and Sippar in Akkad. He was thought of as dispensing both light and justice to all mankind, and was the subject of many beautiful poems or psalms. The following passages from a later composition illustrate how uplifting a spiritualized concept of the sun-god could become:

TO THE GOD OF RIGHTEOUSNESS

At thy rising the gods of the land assemble;
Thy terrible radiance overwhelms the land.
From all lands together resound as many tongues:
Thou dost know their designs; thou dost behold their footsteps,
Unto thee do all men look up together.
Thou causest the evil-doer . . . to tremble;
Out of the depths thou bringest those who perverted justice.
O Shamash, by the just judgment which thou dost speak
Thy name is glorious,
Thou standest beside the traveller whose way is toilsome;
To the voyager who fears the flood thou givest (courage).
On paths that were never explored thou (guidest) the hunter;
O Shamash . . .
Whoso devises wickedness, his horn thou destroyest.
Whoso meditates oppression, his dwelling is overturned.
The wicked judge thou causest to see bonds;
Whoso takes a bribe, and does not judge righteously,
on him thou inflictest punishment.
Whoso takes no bribe, but makes intercession for the weak,
Well-pleasing is this to Shamash, he increaseth his life. . . .

Whoso gives money for excessive interest, what does he increase?
He overreaches himself for gain, empties his own purse,
Whoso gives money for just interest . . .
Well-pleasing is this to Shamash: he increaseth his own life. . . .

Thou hearest, O Shamash, prayer, supplication, and homage,
Submission, kneeling, whispered prayer, and prostration.
From his deepest breast the needy crieth unto thee,
The feeble, the weak, the afflicted, the poor—

With a lament, a petition, he ever appeals to thee,
He whose family is far away, whose city is a great way off.
The shepherd, with the fruits of the field, appeals to thee . . .
The travelling merchant, the trader who carries the bag,
Appeals to thee; the fisher of the deep,
The hunter, the slaughterer, the keeper of cattle,
The fowler . . . appeals to thee.
The house-breaker, the thief—though an enemy of Shamash—
The vagrant upon the way of the desert, appeals to thee.
The wandering dead one, the fleeting shadow. . . .[13]

Nature Myths of Sumer

The goddess Ishtar may teach us much about ancient Mesopotamian religion. Her name is Semitic, but the myths about her undoubtedly came from the Sumerians or even earlier.[14] Ishtar personally symbolizes the large part which sexual love and beauty play in the life of man. The Akkadians frankly recognized that fact and gave it universal status. There was something very earthly and hedonistic about the influence of Ishtar or her Sumerian counterpart, Siduri or Inanna, as when she is represented as having advised Gilgamesh,

Fill thou, O Gilgamesh, thy belly.
Be merry day and night.
Every day prepare joyfulness.
Day and night dance and make music.

Let a wife rejoice in thy bosom,
For this is the mission of man.[15]

The reason for this carefree advice was that man must die, and therefore he might just as well get all the happiness he can while the getting is good.

The story is told of how Ishtar, the shady lady of Sumer-Akkad,[16] sometimes called the Queen of Heaven—stormed the gates of death in order to secure the restoration to life of her principal lover, Tammuz. But Deadland seems to have had several gates, and as she passed each gate she had to leave an article of her clothing—perhaps as security that she would return from places where she did not belong. When she reached the heart of Deadland she hadn't one piece of clothing left. She was very unhappy, suffering from many diseases and great humiliation. Meanwhile through her absence from the land of the living all nature wilted and died too. So finally she was released, picking up her clothing as she passed the seven gates back to the land of the living, where life again burst forth to greet her return.[17]

The descent of Ishtar into the underworld to secure the release (resurrection) of Tammuz, her beloved, is wholly in accord with Ishtar's this-worldliness. For the myths about the death and resurrection of a god originally symbolized the annual cycle of the death of vegetation and its rebirth in the springtime. Only in the course of time did these myths evolve into the mystery cults teaching the immortality of the soul. This evolution occurred in Egypt before it did elsewhere. One of the most remarkable contrasts between Egyptian religion and that of Mesopotamia is, indeed, the Mesopotamian contentment with the doctrine of the mortality of man. Even the kings in Mesopotamia were regarded as merely human and therefore mortal, in contrast with the Egyptian concept of the divinity and immortality of its kings. Apparently all that the Sumerians and Akkadians wanted from their gods was long life, prosperity and happiness. The kings, on their part, asked merely that the gods grant prosperity to their kingdoms, power to their arms, inviolability to their borders, and death to their enemies. These cultural characteristics must be accorded a large degree of sophistication, since the admitted polytheism of their prehistoric culture was based on the still more primitive animism and ancestor worship—forms of belief in immortality.

A fragment from Nippur contains a broken Sumerian account of a previous flood which brought grief to men and gods. One human hero, King Ziusudra, played the part of Noah in this story except that in the end he achieved divinity and immortality.

Floods and Death

The ancient Sumerian story of the flood was modified when it was incorporated into the later Epic of Gilgamesh. In this Ziusudra becomes Utnapishtim, and Gilgamesh, legendary king of Uruk, makes a voyage to Never-Never-Land where the immortal Utnapishtim dwells, in order to gain immortality for himself.

Ishtar (Siduri) pessimistically advises Gilgamesh, just as Shamash had done earlier:

> O Gilgamesh, whither wilt thou go?
> The life thou seekest thou shalt not find.
> When the gods created mankind,
> Death they prepared for man,
> But life they retained in their hands.[18]

But Gilgamesh longed for immortality, and he went through hell and high water—literally, in the story—to gain it. When he reached Never-Never-Land Utnapishtim told him how he had been favored by the gods when a great flood came upon the earth. By building an ark according to divine instructions he rode out the storm and became divinely immortal. But such a boon is not to be expected by others, said he, as he repeated the advice of Shamash and Siduri on how to be happy though mortal. Yet as a parting token he told Gilgamesh about an herb growing at the bottom of the sea which would renew one's youth. Gilgamesh heroically secured this plant, but later on his joyful way home he stopped to bathe and left the herb on the banks with his clothes. A serpent came along and ate the precious plant, forthwith shedding its skin and renewing its youth. So after all Gilgamesh had to submit to death, as all mankind must.

There was indeed, in Mesopotamian tradition, a concept of some kind of survival after death. But the type of survival was far from desirable. It gave rise to no longing for "that blessed isle of peace and joy." It was death, unwanted and unglorified, from which there was no escape. Hence the Mesopotamian stress was upon the present life.

From predynastic times the Epic of Gilgamesh and Utnapishtim's story of the flood were probably recited in one form or another, for the instruction and enjoyment of all. That a great flood did actually cover Ur in the middle of the Obeidian Period is proved by the eight-foot clay deposit in that ancient city separating one level of its early culture from the next. This fact, however, is hardly sufficient justification for believing as the epic states, that it was magically sent by the gods (the punishment for sin seems to be an afterthought), or that Utnapishtim was especially favored by the gods.

The story of the flood in the Epic of Gilgamesh is obviously more primitive in its conception of the gods than the Biblical narrative. Whether it was in the direct line of descent or only in a collateral line is of no importance; certainly the problem cannot now be solved. That the poem does not exhibit the dignified conception of God found in the Biblical narrative is evident from the following lines:

> The gods were terrified at the deluge,
> Withdrew and ascended to the heaven of Anu.
> The gods, crouched like dogs, lay by the outer walls.
> Ishtar cried like a woman in travail.
>
> The gods, the Anunnaki, wept with her.
> The gods sat dejected in weeping.[19]

Utnapishtim weathered the flood in the ark which Ea had instructed him to build. With wild beasts, cattle, and kin safely inside he floated for seven days, at the end of which the ark was grounded. Opening a window, he released a dove, but the dove returned without finding a place to alight. The same thing happened later when he sent out a swallow. But when finally he sent forth a raven it did not return. Telling the story to Gilgamesh, Utnapishtim said:

> I poured out a libation on the top of the mountain. . . .
> The gods smelled the savor,
> The gods smelled the sweet savor,
> The gods crowded like flies about the sacrificer.[20]

Another parallel between the Epic of Gilgamesh and the Biblical tradition lies in the story of the serpent. In the former the serpent robs Gilgamesh of the herb of immortality just before his disappointed return from the land of the sunset to his native place. Shortly thereafter the serpent demonstrated the renewal of its youth by shedding its skin. We will recall that in the Biblical narrative the serpent beguiled Eve to eat of the tree which robbed her and her descendants of immortality.

On the fall of Sargon's Akkadian dynasty the Gutians dominated Mesopotamia for a century, at the end of which there occurred a remarkable Sumerian renaissance, followed by the famous Third Dynasty of Ur. The founder of the latter dynasty, Ur-Nammu, called himself "King of Sumer and Akkad." His dynasty came to an end when the Elamites and Amorites invaded the land and the rival cities fought one another. In this situation an Amorite succeeded in gaining mastery over Babylon and establishing a new West-Semitic dynasty. Of the sixth generation of this dynasty was Hammurabi, whose military genius enabled him to bring to an end the inter-city conflict and to establish Babylonian rule first over southern Mesopotamia and later over the north as well. One northern city which he had to conquer twice was Mari, where more than 20,000 tablets have been recovered from the royal palace during the past decades.

Hammurabi and Old Babylon

The Amorites and western Semites dominated Mesopotamia from c. 1960-1550 B.C., constituting our fourth main period which we have called the Western Semitic and Old Babylonian. Of this period the years from c. 1830-1550 B.C. are known as the Old Babylonian period. Hammurabi's dates are c. 1728-1676 B.C.

The Mari tablets have supplied us with a vast store of information about Old Babylonia. Many of our citations so far date from the records of this period. Yet in most cases they did not originate in this period, but were merely recorded there in the particular form in which we find them. Both the flood legend and the creation myth were undoubtedly common folk-knowledge during the Sumerian and the Sumero-Akkadian periods.

With the rise of Old Babylon new gods came into prominence. One of these was Marduk, patron deity of Babylon, whose political ascendency explains the rise of Marduk at the same time. It is easy to understand why the victorious Babylonians wished the Mesopotamians to accept the myth of the supremacy of Marduk, the Babylonian god.

For ulterior purposes, therefore, the Old Babylonians retold the Epic of Creation, using the names of Marduk and Tiamat. The earlier Sumerian epic had conceived of heaven and earth as originally one, but as having been separated in order to provide a fitting place in which mortal man might dwell. The revised myth represents Marduk as the god of universal order or cosmos, while Tiamat was the goddess of chaos. So Marduk entered into combat with Tiamat, and his victory allegorized the creation of the cosmos.

> Then joined issue Tiamat and Marduk, wisest of gods.
> They strove in single combat, locked in battle.
> The lord spread out his net to enfold her,
> The Evil Wind, which followed behind, he let loose in her face.
> When Tiamat opened her mouth to consume him,
> He drove in the Evil Wind that she closed not her lips.
> As the fierce winds charged her belly,
> Her body was distended and her mouth was wide open.
> He released the arrow, it tore her belly,
> It cut through her insides, splitting the heart.
> Having thus subdued her, he extinguished her life.
> He cast down her carcass to stand upon it.

The fleeing bodyguard was caught and imprisoned, after which Marduk came back to Tiamat's dead body.

> Then the lord paused to view her dead body,
> That he might divide the monster and do artful works.
> He split her like a shellfish into two parts:
> Half of her he set up and ceiled it as sky. . . .[21]

Marduk then put the earth in place, and made the abodes of the gods: Anu in the sky, Enlil in the air, Ea in the subterranean waters, and so forth. And from the blood and bone of Tiamat he created man to serve the gods.[22]

It is easy to see that the earlier Sumerian myth was simpler than the Babylonian. The Sumerian myth really contained the substance of the Hebrew-Christian story of the creation of the world by the divine word. All that the god needed to do, it seemed, was to utter the word and magically the world came into being. Old Babylon complicated this by resorting to allegory; Judeo-Christianity simplified it by eliminating the pantheon.

Hammurabi's greatest fame lies not in his inspiration of a novel mythology, but in his much more significant codification of law. The letters which Hammurabi wrote reveal him as a great administrator who paid due attention to details. Hammurabi collected and harmonized the laws which had come down to him from Sumerian times. The resulting code lasted for a thousand years. We are fortunate to have recovered a copy from the ruins of Susa; the copy is on a stela now in the Louvre. At the top of the six-foot stela is a bas-relief of Hammurabi receiving from Shamash, sun-god and divine patron of law and justice, the symbols of royal power.

The code of Hammurabi is remarkably complete and shows some most interesting parallels with both the Mosaic Code and the Deuteronomic Code. Finegan finds the following Biblical passages paralleled by the Hammurabic Code: Exodus 21:16; 22:2; 21:23-25; Leviticus 20:10; Deuteronomy 19:18f.; 24:1; 22:22; 19:21.[23] That there were cultural exchanges between Palestine and Mesopotamia cannot be doubted.

There are almost 300 paragraphs in the code of Hammurabi. They provided that false accusation of a capital offense was punishable by death (par. 3), as were also certain types of theft, kidnaping, burglary, certain types of adultery, and builder's criminal negligence (pars. 6, 14, 21, 129, 229). They provided for the law of retaliation (pars. 200-209). If the physician bungled at an operation or caused a death thereby, his hand was to be cut off (pars. 215-225). Marriage and divorce were regulated (pars. 128, 142).[24]

As the Old Babylonian Empire declined in power, the Assyrian Empire gradually arose to take its place. Tiglath-pileser I (c. 1114-1076 B.C.) extended Assyrian power westward to the Mediterranean. Some of his famous successors were Ashur-nasir-pal II (883-859), Shalmaneser III (858-824), and Tiglath-pileser III (744-727). The latter extended Assyrian rule southward over Babylonia. Shortly afterward a usurper who called himself Sargon II (721-705) established a new dynasty. His first famous act was to complete the destruction of Samaria, capital of northern Israel. Sennacherib (704-681) was the next Assyrian king, followed by his favorite son, Esarhaddon (680-669), who restored Babylon after his father had destroyed it. Then came the great Ashurbanipal (669-633), who is famous for the library which he collected, the discovery of which has provided a bulwark of our knowledge of antiquity. Ashurbanipal's scribes copied and translated many of the priceless treasures of ancient Mesopotamia.

In 612 B.C. Nineveh, the Assyrian capital since Sennacherib chose it after 704, fell to Nabopolassar of Babylon and Cyaxares the Mede. This date marks the beginning of the New Babylonian Empire, 612-539. Nabopolassar's son, Nebuchadrezzar II, defeated the Egyptian army at Carchemish in 605 and extended the rule of the new Babylonian Empire over all of western Asia. It was he who brought about the fall and destruction of Jerusalem in 598 and 587. Nebuchadrezzar died in 562 after which Babylonian rule was weak and divisive until its end in 539.

The Persian Empire (539-331 B.C.) succeeded the New Babylonian Empire, and was in turn brought to an end by Alexander the Great. The Persian Empire introduced Zoroastrianism to Mesopotamia, whereas Alexander offered Greek culture.

Canaanitic Gods

Before leaving the topic of Near Eastern religions we should mention Baal, El, Elohim, and El Shaddai in particular. Baal or Bel was the name of the storm-god of northern Mesopotamia, the land of rain-agriculture. He was invoked because of his special powers over the moisture-bringing storms. So he was connected with the fertility of the soil. In Canaan, too, he was a fertility god. In a fourteenth century B.C. Ugaritic text Baal is described as "slain by monsters and carried to the land of death. . . . After Baal's death all life on earth languishes, so his sister, 'the virgin' Anath, finds Mot [Death], kills him in a terrible battle, after which she performs an interesting dynamistic ritual with his body:

> She seized Mot, son of El;
> With the sword she cut him up, with the sieve she winnowed him,
> In the fire she burned him, in the mill she ground him.
> In the field she sowed him,
> In order that the birds might eat their portion, in order that they might destroy the seed. . . .

. . . The purpose of this ritual was not to revive Mot but to revive Baal by sympathetic action."[25] The worship of Baal ("Lord") was really a survival of magic in the attempt to tap the sources of fertility for man's uses.

The story of Baal allegorizes the annual cycle of rain, flowing rivers, drought, and the return again of rain and its ensuing cycle. Baal brings the rain and the storms when he is brought back to life. The streams and rivers are filled with water. But when the rains cease the streams and rivers subside and cease, and drought returns when Baal is tricked by Mot in the nether world. So the seasons recur.[26]

A late Ugartic myth makes Baal the divine giver of metals, symbolizing the cultural change from a stone culture to the culture of gold, silver, bronze, and iron. Baal outwits his superior, El, by securing his permission to build himself a house, in view of his intended marriage. When he builds it, it turns out that the bricks which he promised to use were made of gold and silver, thus insuring his triumph over the other gods.[27]

In Canaanitic-Hebrew traditions El was the supreme god. The polytheistic Canaanites gave El a consort, the goddess Asherat. The derivation of monotheism from this background was on the right track for the spiritualization of the concept of one god. El Shaddai, "god of the mountains," was a "high god" associated with the mountains near Harran, and may originally have been a local deity. Elohim, literally "the gods," may have been used by the Hebrews as a term of majesty. But most of the Semites did not think in such terms. Their religion, more akin to the northern Mesopotamian, was polytheistic, dynamistic, and animistic. As in Mesopotamia, they sought primarily long life, prosperity, and happiness through the favor of the gods or by means of magic-bearing ritual.

Priests performed a number of valuable functions in ancient Mesopotamia. They set an example of business-like organization and conduct of temple affairs, keeping records of temple transactions and responsibilities from before 3200 B.C. They taught school in the temple compounds. And they practiced the science—or art—of divination. The latter function was carried on by interpreting dreams, reading sheep's liver, and observing the stars. The purpose of such observation was to foretell the future through these omens of the divine will. By astrological divination the ancient Babylonians were pioneering in the science of astronomy. Modern astronomy is indebted to them in somewhat the same sense as modern enlightened religion is indebted to them.

Evaluation of Near Eastern Religion

Because of the magical element, Near Eastern religion must of course be judged as immature. Mythology, so far as can be ascertained, came early to be regarded as literally true, though we find an imaginative freshness in its most primitive tales suggesting that they were not always so regarded. Such is true, for example, in the myth of Gilgamesh and the herb of immortality.

Commitment to scientific truth is a criterion which is inapplicable to Near Eastern religion, since science was not yet born. Nor was there any understanding of human nature or psychological health.

Ethical and social norms in the Near East showed glimpses of maturity mixed with crudeness, as in the code of Hammurabi. The hymn to Shamash reveals a kind of devotion to goodness from motives of fear.

Crude was the concept of sacrifice in the flood legend. Mesopotamian ritual was on the whole regarded magically, and its symbolism was largely idolatrous.

Mystic sensitivity in the Near East was on a level with the religious experience of most primitive cultures. There was an awareness of divinity in the animistic-dynamistic-polytheistic ideas of the fertile crescent, but the concept of deity was too crude to warrant a judgment of religious maturity.

V. THE DEVELOPMENT OF GREEK RELIGION

HISTORICAL GREEKS appear on the scene only after the Egyptians and Sumerians had already gone through a highly sophisticated cultural cycle. History does not begin in Greece until 776 B.C., the date of the first Olympiad. The Prehistoric Minoan and Mycenaean cultures are known mostly through their physical remains because their inscriptions and the tablets continually coming to light are as yet only partially understood by us. Work on decipherment of the scripts has already made great progress, however, since it was discovered that some of the tablets were written in a primitive Greek.[1] Present scholarship is doing much to clarify the relations between those cultures and that of historic Greece. The Greek alphabet, Semitic in origin, is extant in inscriptions as early as the seventh century B.C. and was probably introduced into Greece in the eighth century, at the time of the great colonizations, or earlier in the form of the primitive Greek Minoan-Mycenaean script. The *Iliad* and the *Odyssey,* probably completed in their present form during the eighth century, though they were not written down until the time of Pisistratus, are the products of an earlier age and represent the "folk-memory" of early Greek history. Some of the *Iliad* is older than the *Odyssey* and may have been composed in the ninth century. Both poems were known to Hesiod when he wrote his poetry early in the eighth century B.C.

But who were the Greeks?[2] What was their origin? What stage of religious development is represented by the poetry of Homer and of Hesiod? What influences can be identified with that religious development? These are some of the questions which must be answered before we can understand and appreciate the Greek religion.

Prehistory in Greece, starting with the archaeological evidence of stone age culture, concerns at least two, and possibly three, racial strains: the non-Indo-European tribes, which may have been indigenous; the inhabitants of Crete; and the Indo-European ancestors of the Greeks. The latter group did not begin to appear in the peninsula until about 2000 B.C. In other words, the ancestors of the classical Greeks did not appear in their future homeland until the Bronze Age culture was well on the way. The earliest mainland cultures, chalcolithic and neolithic, were related to cultures of Asia Minor and were rather stagnant. The culture of Crete, emerging from the neolithic to the Bronze Age about 3500 B.C., developed almost in isolation for the better part of a millenium; then in contact with Egypt and the Syrian coast, it made rapid progress while retaining its own identity.[3]

By the time that the Greeks appeared in Greece, the mainland culture had been modified somewhat by the Minoan, and Minoan areas of influence or domination appeared in southern Greece. The influence appears architecturally, ceramically, in artistic motifs, and in religion. We do not know the relations between Minoans and Mycenaeans. Evans was inclined to favor the view that the Minoans had some political control over the Mycenaeans, while Wace and others doubt it.[4] The superior culture of the islanders certainly caused changes on the mainland; it would seem that the mainlanders finally retaliated and, in an expedition of which the Theseus-and-the-Minotaur story is the only record, destroyed the great Palace at Cnossos.[5] This left the way clear for Greeks to become Greeks.

Before the migration of peoples in the twelfth century it is likely that the Achaeans and Aeolians, branches of the Greek parent-stock, wandered in small bands into Greece, and that finally in the twelfth century a great band of "Dorians" completed the migration. This last group were acquainted with iron prior to their arrival and thus brought about the end of the Bronze Age about 1100 B.C. The several tribes settled in various parts of the Greek peninsula and the coast of Asia Minor, conscious of their kinship and speaking a mutually intelligible language, whatever its dialectic peculiarities. They still called themselves by their tribal names; Hellas and Hellenes were not used before the time of Hesiod. The name "Greek" is itself a Latin word, based by historical accident upon an obscure Hellenic tribe called *Graios*.

Concerning the identity of the ancient Greeks, we can know one thing for certain, namely, that they were a mixed race. Their language is certainly Indo-European, and some of their ancestors were certainly Indo-European. But the important thing is that they came to think of themselves as being culturally one people, and thereby they were able to create what we know as the Greek or Hellenic civilization. At the dawn of their history we find the Greeks strongly conscious of cultural unity.

For legendary tales about prehistoric Greece, we are indebted to Homer, Hesiod, Herodotus, Plato, and many lesser Greeks. The former distrust of these legends is being replaced by credence in them, since archaeology is helping to find their thread of historical truth. From the time of Heinrich Schliemann (c. 1870) to the present excavations by the Americans at the site of Troy,[6] legend has been proved more often than it has been disproved. Even Aeschylus' account, at the beginning of the *Eumenides*,[7] of the history of the Delphic oracle has been proved credible.

Of course we should not know whether Homer's tales were legendary or purely imaginative except for the light of archaeology. The great pioneers in Greek archaeology were Schliemann and Sir Arthur Evans. Schliemann did the first work in excavating the sites of ancient Troy, Tiryns, and Mycenae, beginning in 1850. He was followed by the more expert Dorpfeld and others. Evans pioneered about 1900 in excavating the great palace at Cnossus in Crete. There he uncovered the treasures of the Minoan civilization, named after the Minos, or King, of Cnossus. From these relics and from many more found in Crete, Greece, and Asia Minor we are able now to reconstruct the elements of the religion which preceded Homer and which had a large influence in the development of the Greek religion. The story will be more complete when the Minoan script is more fully mastered.

Pre-Homeric Religion

In pre-Homeric religion four kinds of places were sacred: caves, mountain tops, groves, and shrines constructed in connection with dwelling houses.

The cave cult is well illustrated by the cave of Amnisus near Herakleion, in Crete. In this cave two isolated cylindrical stalagmites are surrounded by a stone wall. No idols were found in the cave, but the many vases are evidence that liquid offerings were made to the stalagmites which were in some manner identified with the divine spirit. Homer in the Odyssey, Book XIX, has Odysseus refer to the "port of Amnisus by the cave of Eileithyea," so it is evident that local legend regarded the cave as sacred. From early prehistoric to Christian times the people of Crete worshiped the goddess Eileithyia in the Amnisus cave. In many other places of Crete the cave cult was practiced, and a few caves on the Greek mainland have been identified as cultic.[8]

Mountain-top sanctuaries are found both in Crete and in Greece. They are parallel in many respects to the cave sanctuaries. For example, no icons have been found in them, and pillars built of baetylic stones correspond to the stalagmites of the caves. That the pillars were sacred objects is proved by representations on a cylinder seal from Mycenae, on two glass plaques from the lower town of Mycenae, and on signet rings from Crete and Mycenae. On these relics we see a man between two columns worshiping with upraised hands, or pouring libations over the columns, or otherwise indicating religious ceremonial.

A peak sanctuary has been excavated on Mt. Juktas near Cnossus, and another at Petsofa. "In both cases well-built walls support a terrace and surround an enclosure within which were found deep layers of ashes mixed with charcoal and filled with votive offerings, mainly figurines of men, women, and animals."[9]

Sacred trees are found to have been worshiped in the peak sanctuaries. But trees and groves also came to be regarded as sacred apart from other sanctuaries, at least as long ago as Middle Minoan times. In their art we find trees or boughs placed between "horns of consecration," which indicate that libations were poured upon such sacred objects. The tree cult was especially popular among country people.

The fourth type of sacred place was the shrine, erected in homes and royal palaces. "Temples, in the common sense of the term, i.e., special buildings standing by themselves and serving as the abodes of the god or as the places for communal worship, were as a rule unknown to the prehistoric Greeks. The only exception to the rule is the shrine of Gournia which was not incorporated in the palace or in a house, and apparently served the entire village."[10]

The royal and domestic shrines were usually relatively small single rooms. The royal shrines were, of course, the larger and are often referred to as "pillared rooms" because of the single pillar standing in their center. The pillared rooms were crypts over which columnar shrines were built.

Another type of shrine was the sunken area, a rectangular depression in the pavement used for purification rites and the worship of chthonic deities.[11] The underlying assumption probably was that in subterranean shrines one would be most likely to come in contact with underworld deities, powers, or ghosts of the dead, and there would be the best place to placate them.

*The Greek cross as a symbol of deity far antedates (1600 B.C. at Cnossus) its later Christian use in the same form.**

Ritual aids or symbols used in pre-Homeric religion included pillars, crosses, double axes, horns of consecration, vases for libations, and figurines for symbolic sacrifice. Scholars are not agreed as to the origin and meaning of the double axes and the horns of consecration. The latter may have come to have sacred meaning as a result of the custom of hanging up the head of the sacrificed bull. As to the double axe, whatever its origin and meaning, all are agreed that to the Minoan it "was as important a religious sign as is the cross to the Christian and the crescent to the Moslem. . . . [It] was considered as the aniconic image and the embodiment of the Minoan Divinity."[12]

It seems that the earliest religion of Minoan-Mycenaean times was non-anthropomorphic. But later the objects of worship took on human form, appearing as a mother-goddess and young male attendant and snake goddess in a fertility cult. In some representations the snake goddess—Eileithyia—is associated with the harmless household snake. At other times she is handling venomous snakes.

* Evans, *The Palace of Minos,* I, pp. 511-517.

Other goddesses are seen with doves or animals. These facts have led Professor Nilsson to infer that the Minoans were polytheists, believing in a number of goddesses and subordinate gods. But Evans and Mylonas argue that there was only one goddess with several functions, a concept approximating monotheism.

The snake and the bull were the two animals in prehistoric Greek religion most often associated with divinity. The snake earned its sacred reputation from its habit of going underground for a part of its existence. The presumption was that the snake was in touch with the nether regions and so might well be a link between men and ghosts or other-world forces. There is reason to connect the snake with the concept of fertility also, which concept played a large part in the religious life of early man. The realm of the dead, below the earth's surface, was the realm where the powers of life were temporarily held in restraint—during the winter months. Then in the spring they came forth again.

In Minoan times, as in ancient Egypt with which the Minoans were in concourse, the bull was the most sacred animal of all, probably "because of his enormous strength, his size, his rage, in fine, as anthropolgists call it, his *mana*. . . . The tremendous *mana* of the wild bull indeed occupies almost half the stage of pre-Olympian ritual." Primitive Cretan religion "is permeated by the bull of Minos. The heads and horns are in almost every sacred room and on every altar."[13] But it was not the bull itself that was divine; only the *mana* was divine. "There was no god there, only the raw material out of which gods are made. You devoured the holy animal to get its *mana,* its swiftness, its strength, its great endurance, just as the savage now will eat his enemy's brain or heart or hands to get some particular quality residing there."[14]

Murray is here suggesting that the prehistoric religion of Greece and Crete was less anthropomorphic than the later mythological religion, and that it was originally dynamistic. Certainly the primary purpose of the early Minoans and Mycenaeans was to get in touch with the life-force. The values which they sought through these means were always more life, health, happiness, prosperity, victory in war, and peace of mind. In these respects they were like most people before and since.

Emergence of Homeric Religion

One of the best examples of the emergence of Homeric religion out of Minoan-Mycenaean religion is the character of Hermes. In Homer Hermes is Zeus' very gracious messenger with winged feet. In order to carry out the command of Zeus

> . . . the Shining One with might
> Took wing, and mounting the Pierian height
> Out of the sky on ocean darted down
> And swift across the billows urged his flight
> As a sea-eagle that his finny prey
> Chases, his thickest plumage wet with spray,
> Through the dread gulfs of sea unharvested,
> Over the thronging waves he sped his way.[15]

Odysseus is overcome by the beauty of Hermes:

> . . . in that place
> Gold-wanded Hermes met me face to face
> In likeness of a youth when the first down
> Fledges his lip in earliest manhood's grace.[16]

Despite the graceful mobility of the Homeric picture of Hermes, there seems to be no doubt whatsoever that this messenger of the gods evolved out of the simple pillar ("herm") of pre-Homeric times. The pillar, of course, is universally regarded as a phallic symbol of the power of fertility. On searching further into the matter we find that, even in Homer, Hermes is described on one occasion as a guide for the souls of the dead, descending for this purpose into the nether regions.[17] We know, too, that pillars were set up both as boundary markers and as memorials to the dead, and that even in historic times in Greece people often used a pillar as a means of seeking an oracle. In known cases the pillar had already partially evolved into the humanized god, Hermes, for it was surmounted by a bearded head. The oracle-seeker was always one who had a problem. For advice he would first go to the elders. But when they could not help he would seek the advice of the still older generation lying beneath the ground. Would not a tombstone be the proper place to commune with the departed soul? He would whisper his question to the departed one and turn away listening. Thereafter the first words which he heard from any human mouth would be the oracle's words, the clue to his answer.

Furthermore the dead, having descended beneath the earth, were thought of as having some power over the seeds which also were buried beneath the soil. So the "herm" symbolized not only the dead but also the power of fertility coming from that lower world with which the "herm" brought the individual in close touch.

Pausanias, wandering about Greece in the second century A.D., saw and described so many of these "herms" and the customs associated with them that we can be quite confident that the Hermes of Homer was also the "herm" or pillar of the pre-Homeric religion, evolving into a truly manifold character. Pausanias goes on to mention that a large number of *unwrought* stones were worshiped as divine, and that "in the olden time all the Greeks worshiped unwrought stones instead of images."[18] It seems like a Cinderella story, then, to find that Hermes eventually became a god who dwelt on Mt. Olympus.

But the stories of the other gods are no less fascinating than that of Hermes. Poseidon was one such god. King of the sea, according to Homer, we might expect him to be purely elemental. But such is not the case. Instead of merely personifying the sea we find him undergoing complex metamorphoses.

For one thing, Poseidon is described in poetry and art as carrying a trident. This forms a clue to a part of his complex character. For the trident turns out to be nothing but the spear with which the Greek fisherman caught his fish. So Poseidon represented a function which was very important to a people who depended on fish, as the sea-girt Greeks did.

But Poseidon also rode a horse, furiously surmounting the waves. A Homeric hymn describes him both as the "Tamer of horses and the succour of ships." Horse sacrifices were offered to Poseidon in ancient times, the horses being drowned in the sea, or on other occasions in fresh water, showing that the element of the sea was not the most prominent source of his character.

One step farther brings us to his immediate origin. It is most significant that Poseidon was associated with the bull. In art he is represented as riding the bull. In poetry he *is* the bull. And since the bull was especially sacred to the Minoans, it is believed that Poseidon came from Crete to Greece. In Harrison we read the startling statement. "The god Poseidon is primarily and in essence none other than the Cretan Minotaur."[19] This of course simplifies the situation too much, as she goes on to say. But from Minoan art of the fifteenth century B.C. comes evidence corroborating Herodotus' statement that Poseidon brought the horse from Libya to Greece. But he did so by way of Crete where he was changed from a horse-god to a bull-god. The Greek myth of Theseus slaying the Minotaur was invented later, according to some scholars, to explain how the Mycenaeans threw off the yoke of Minos but returned with much of his culture. Theseus is said, in this myth, to have been the son of Poseidon. Thus Poseidon was naturalized by being made a citizen of Mt. Olympus. But his immigrant accent always clung to him. "At times he exists in order to be defeated; defeated in Athens by Athena, in Naxos by Dionysus, in Aegina by Zeus, in Argos by Hera, in Acrocorinth by Helios though he continues to hold the Isthmus. In Trozen he shares a temple on more or less equal terms with Athena. Even in Troy he is defeated and cast out from the walls his own hands had built."[20]

The Greek way of naturalizing Poseidon was to give him a trident, thus making him perform a function related to Greek survival. Of course he could not continue to be a mere fisherman, so he had to be made ruler of the seas. At times he rode a horse, at times he rode a bull. At other times he *was* the horse or the bull. Though he became a brother to Zeus, he was likely to be at odds with his family, thus suggesting that he belonged only by adoption.

Turning now to another Homeric development out of Minoan materials, there was the figure of the unnamed Mountain-Mother. All the art of Crete is consistent in portraying motherhood as superior to fatherhood. The Minoan society therefore may be thought of as matrilinear, while the Indo-European Greek society was patriarchal. Zeus was supreme in Olympus, but the Mountain-Mother was supreme in Crete. The Minoan Mountain-Mother was the source of all gifts to mankind, of life, love, law, and hope. So the Mountain-Mother survives in Homer variously in the goddesses who inherit her nature. "To Hera she lent her 'sacred marriage,' to Demeter her mysteries, to Athena her snakes, to Aphrodite her doves, to Artemis all her functions as 'Lady of the Wild Things.' And most of all the functions of the dominant goddess with the subordinate figure of the male attendant, half-son, half-lover."[21]

Hera, the Homeric wife of Zeus, turns out to be an earth-mother from Arcadia. Her name means "year," and at Stymphalus she was worshiped as child, as mother, and as widow, symbolizing the spring, the summer of fruitfulness, and the autumn of death. The jealousy and quarreling which Homer describes between Hera and Zeus may reflect the marriage of invading Greek and native Pelasgian. Perhaps Dione was the original northern wife of Zeus.[22] At any rate, the Arcadian myth helps us to understand how at one time Hera can be thought of as a virgin while at another time she is pictured as the loyal wife of Zeus.

Athena, however, is the idealized maiden ("parthenos"—"maid of Athens"). Dear to her were animals and plants and her native city of Athens, for which she fought her successful fight with the immigrant Poseidon. The owl of wisdom was one of her symbols; the snake another. Still another was the olive branch. The snake, her counterpart, was the guardian of the household. The olive tree was the fate of Athens, for on it her prosperity was largely based. Above all, of course, Athena stood for Athens itself.

Aphrodite, goddess of love and beauty, continues the functions of the Earth-Mother. The dove is her sacred bird, and Eros (love) is her son. The Greek Eros should be thought of not as a pudgy Roman cupid, but as the spirit of life. Eros is more prominent in Greek thought than Mother-Aphrodite, it seems.

It was the fateful privilege of Paris, son of Priam King of Troy, to choose between Hera, Athena, and Aphrodite. In choosing Aphrodite he unwittingly precipitated the Trojan war. But the primary meaning of his choice was the evaluation of the three typical divine gifts to man. And Paris chose love rather than royalty or wisdom. In any event, however, all three goddesses were native creations, although some functions and symbols were either imported or used to supplant those of the Mountain-Mother.

And now we come to the two gods who, with Athena, compose the most truly native Greek triad: Apollo and Zeus.

Zeus came to Greece with the northern invaders. Like the other Indo-Europeans, they thought of him as god of the sky. The sky might be bright with sun, moon, or stars, or it might be dark with clouds, rain, and thunder, but there was Zeus in any case. Reflecting the heroic times in which his myths were created, Zeus was king of the gods. And symbolizing the successes of the invaders, Zeus was varyingly married to different wives, mistreating all of them and being faithful to none. But of all the divinities, he comes closest to being identified with the element which he symbolized, namely, the sky. With all his power, however, he does not create but only design. He himself is born of Chronos, time, who is the father of all. And with all his racial purity, he absorbed into his own self many of the functions of foreign or Pelasgian origin. Zeus Aphiktor (suppliant) was of Minoan origin, Zeus Meilichios (of placation), probably of Pelasgian origin, and as such was the spirit of placation, not Zeus at all.

Apollo held a prominent place on Mt. Olympus next to Zeus. He carries the bow and takes quick vengeance on enemies. Thus he brings disease and death, but also healing. He is the god of medicinal herbs, especially the peony—he is sometimes called the god Paeon. He was also a god of trees, especially the apple and the poplar, as well as the oak of Zeus, and the laurel. The laurel wreath was the sign of his responsiveness at the oracle, although Homer knew nothing of his oracular functions. He came to be the god of the lyre and of song, and by slaying the Python whom he displaced at Delphi he became the oracular divinity there. Finally he became the sun god. In art he is often pictured with Artemis, the huntress and goddess of the moon.

Ares, of Thracian origin, was a sun-god and god of war. Son of Zeus, he was "treated as a mere bully and coward and general pest." He commits adultery with Aphrodite, whose husband is the lame Hephaestus, god of the forge and of fire.

Dionysus was an illegitimate son of Semele by Zeus. Hades, god of the underworld was, like Zeus, the son of Chronos and Rhea, and Demeter, earth-goddess, had the same parents.

These and many other gods of composite origin and function composed the Greek pantheon. Most of them were made to dwell on Mt. Olympus—wherever that was—and conceived to be associated with one another in families, with some semblance of political order. Their aristocratic individualism reflected the heroic era of the prehistoric Greeks and Mycenaeans. Their personal characters were far removed from the primitive animism-dynamism out of which they had evolved. It is, of course, impossible to know how literally Homer regarded his characters. Perhaps his descriptions of their personalities were meant to be taken no more literally than St. Gaudens' statue of Grief.

The myths of Homer and Hesiod became the core of the official religion of the Greek city states. As such we must call it a nature religion, for its gods certainly stood for nature's elements and forces. And it was a religion of this world, viewing darkly the prospects of the world to come. When Homer pictures Odysseus visiting the nether world and trying to comfort the dead Achilles the latter is made to answer, "Nay, speak not comfortably to me of death, oh great Odysseus. Rather would I live on ground as the hireling of another, with a landless man who had no great livelihood, than bear sway among all the dead that be departed."[23]

The esthetic detachment of the Olympic cult, as the Homeric religion is often called, did not make for fanaticism. Family groups participated in it in a simple manner, without the aid of priests or scriptures. What was really in the heart of the common man is difficult to say. One must wonder whether he ever did get beyond the Mycenaean Herm, for example, to the Homeric Hermes. More "religious" in the modern sense were the mystery cults, to which we now turn.

Greek Mystery Religions

In contrast with the Olympic religion, the mystery cults were non-naturalistic, other-worldly, and intimately personal in their experience. And while everybody automatically belonged to the state religion, only the initiated belonged to the mystery cults. The simple family rites of the Olympic cult were replaced in the mystery cults by elaborate, mystic symbolism, rites of purification, passion plays, and liturgies in which the individual was swept into a state of ecstasy.

The mystery cults were imported into Greece toward the end of the prehistoric period. Thrace was the immediate source of two of these cults, the Dionysian and the Orphic. The origin of the other principal cult, the Eleusinian, is unknown. We have already traced the development of Egyptian and Near Eastern mystery religions, and we know that during the Bronze Age Greece was in cultural intercourse with Egypt, Crete, and Asia Minor. But regardless of their origin, the theme was the same in all the mystery cults; only the names of the gods and the details of the myths differed.

The Greek mysteries enjoyed two periods of great popularity. The earlier period was in the sixth century B.C. The later one was during the Hellenistic Age, becoming especially strong just preceding and during the early years of Christianity.

Because of the secret character of the cults there remains much that we do not know about them to this day. Yet we do know a great deal which we have gleaned from works of art and from literature, particularly the *Bacchae* of Euripides which reveals much concerning the Dionysian cult. We have learned about the Eleusinian cult through the excavations at Eleusis, a town about fourteen miles from Athens. Here was discovered an ancient temple which existed in the fifteenth century B.C., supporting the late Mycenaean existence of the Eleusinian cult, the oldest of the three so far as Greece is concerned.[24]

According to the Theban myth Semele, a mortal woman, so strongly desired to live with Zeus that she willingly endured the consuming flames of that radiant deity. As a result she died, but Zeus took the unborn Dionysus and hid him in his thigh until his birth. His worshipers believed that Dionysus later died and was brought back to life, thus symbolizing the death and life cycle of vegetation and—what is more—of the human soul.

Dionysus was indeed a primitive deity in Thrace. There he was originally like Hermes, a mere post of a tree surmounted by a human head. Grapes, ivy, honeycombs, and figs were represented as growing from him, revealing him as the god of all growing things. In the course of time he became known as the god of the vine, and the drinking of wine became an important part of his worship.

The name "Semele" clearly indicates her Thracian origin. There she was the Earth-Mother, and as such her worship was a prominent part of the Dionysian worship. "The worship of Dionysus is always dual, of mother and son." "The satyrs project Dionysus, but the Maenads project the figure of the Mother."[25]

The Dionysian festival was preceded by fasting. It may be remarked that one would need to be hungry in order to eat what the Dionysus worshipers were supposed to eat. Also the fasting would help to put the worshipers in a receptive emotional attitude. The devotees dressed themselves like the god and met during the night, carrying decorated spears and torches. Then they wandered through the country until they had found a suitable "mountain-top" on which to fulfil their rites. Wild dancing and drinking of wine would follow until the devotees reached a high pitch of excitement, that is, until they had become "mad," which to them meant the loss of their own self-possession and the attainment of possession by the god himself. The divine mania enabled persons to perform miracles, it was believed. But the central fact was that the worshipers thought that they had attained oneness with the god.

The culmination of the rites came when in great frenzy "the initiates attacked and dismembered with their own hands an animal —a goat, a fawn, or preferably a bull—separated the flesh from the bones and in a frenzy ate particles of raw flesh reeking with blood." "The animal was considered the embodiment of the god, and in eating its live raw flesh, the initiates believed that they were taking in them the god of life."[26]

Undoubtedly there was much orgiastic abandon and crudeness in this cult. Yet the religious character of the yearning for unity with the god is revealed in ancient verse. The Bacchants of Euripides sing:

> Appear, appear, whatso thy shape or name,
> O Mountain Bull, Snake of the Hundred Heads,
>   Lion of the Burning Flame
> O God, Beast, Mystery come![27]

>   And all the mountain felt,
> And worshipped with them; and the wild things knelt
> And ramped and gloried, and the wilderness
> Was filled with moving voices and dim stress.[28]

Thus we witness the evolution of a mystic concept out of primitive magic, the transformation of the search for the *mana* of the bull into an aspiration for unity with God and his world, together with a yearning for immortality in him.

The Orphic mystery cult also revolved around Dionysus, but in a somewhat more reserved manner. Orpheus was a legendary human figure reputed to have been the leader of the cult to which he gave his name. The cult regarded itself as the reformed branch of Dionysus worship. They even told a different myth about Dionysus, who in this story is called Dionysus Zagreus, the son of Zeus and of Persephone, Zeus' daughter. Zagreus is eaten by the wicked Titans, all except his heart which Athena rescues and delivers to Zeus. To Semele then Zeus gives the heart of Zagreus, dissolved in a potion, and she brings him back to life as Dionysus. With his thunderbolt Zeus cremates the Titans and then makes man from their ashes. Thus man was part evil—the original sin being inherited from the Titans—and part divine, from the god whom the Titans had eaten. This is the myth underlying Orphic dualism. Man therefore needed redemption and might find it by suppressing his evil (Titanic) body and reinforcing his divine soul by the proper rites. Transmigration of the soul gives it repeated opportunity to be saved and thus escape from the recurrence of physical life.

Salvation might be secured through a knowledge of the scriptures, through participation in the rites of initiation, and through reunion with the god. From Euripides again we learn that in the Orphic cult, too, a part of the ritual consists of eating the raw flesh of the sacred animal. Thereafter the Orphic abstained from eating meat, and practiced those strict virtues which characterised Orphism as a way of life.[29]

Orphism formed into brotherhoods after the manner of later religions. One of its centers of strength was Athens. Many scholars believe that Orphism influenced the development of Christianity in certain ways. For example, medieval dualism and asceticism may have been encouraged by Orphism.

The Eleusinian mystery cult had its center at Athens and nearby Eleusis. Semele does not figure in this myth at all. Instead it is Demeter who is Earth-Mother or rather, in this case, Corn-Mother. And instead of a son she has a daughter Persephone, the Corn-Maid. Of this pair Miss Harrison says, "They are but the younger and the older forms, each of the other."

Simply told, the myth has Hades, King of the Dead, snatch Persephone and take her to his abode as wife. Mother Demeter mourned and sought her everywhere, finally coming to Eleusis. There at length she cast off her disguise and called on the people to build her a temple. This they did, but the goddess still was forlorn, and so long as she continued thus no seed grew from the earth. Finally Zeus yielded to her pleas and sent Hermes down to rescue Persephone, who meanwhile had eaten the pomegranate seeds upon the crafty urging of Hades. This precluded her complete rescue to the land of the living, but as a compromise she was ordained to spend the winter with her husband and the spring and summer with her mother.

The mythical reference to seasonal growth and decay is of course obvious. But what makes this a mystery religion is its ulterior reference to human death and the soul's immortality. Eleusinianism emphasized ethical values and the need for living in the light of eternity.

The other mysteries might be dramatized any time and anywhere, but the Eleusinian mysteries were always dramatized in September at Athens and Eleusis. First the sacred objects were brought to Athens. Next day proclamations and purifications began, and a few days later the initiates started on their long procession—a kind of passion play—to Eleusis. The fourteen-mile "via sacra" was traversed with appropriate songs and ceremonies from morning until midnight. "With burning torches Proserpina (Persephone) is sought, and when she is found, the rite is closed with general thanksgiving and a waving of torches," writes Lactantius.[30] The evidence is very incomplete, but seems to support the conclusion that a sacramental meal was a part of the ceremonial. Mylonas thinks it highly possible that "acts such as the elevation of the sacred host and others were borrowed by the Christians from the Eleusinian rites."[31]

The Eleusinian cult lived for two thousand years to ennoble an increasingly large number of human beings. The theory that its passion play was debased by a "holy marriage" may be rejected on archaeological evidence. Some of the world's greatest men believed in the Eleusinian mysteries, and perhaps a part of their greatness was due to their having so believed.

In Hellenistic times, especially when Rome ruled, the mysteries spread far and wide. Besides the revival of the three cults described above, others were imported, like the worship of the Great Mother,

Cybele, and her dying and risen lover Attis, from Phrygia, and the revived cult of Isis and Osiris from Egypt. Most impressive of all late mystery religions was Mithraism. In this cult Mithra, the Indo-European sun-god, is conceived to exercise the power of light and goodness. He was always warring against evil and darkness, and was pictured as the helper of the pious and the judge of all after death. Eternal life might be gained through Mithra, the savior-god, in like manner as in the other mystery cults. But great emphasis was placed upon purity of life. In this respect Mithraism became one of the strongest rivals of Christianity. One reason why Christianity won the struggle was because Jesus was an historical and most attractive personality while Mithra was purely mythical. Another reason was that Christianity appropriated Mithra's sacred days, such as Sunday and December 25, and so made the transition from Mithraism to Christianity easier for many.

Most writers conclude their discussion of the mystery religions by saying that they were a preparation for Christianity, and that "in the fulness of time God brought forth his Son." The mysteries had made religion a matter of personal conviction, had developed the consciousness of sin and the need for redemption, had conceived of gods as universal and of the brotherhood of mankind. They encouraged the quest for immortality, and propagandized their faith. In a syncretistic age they even moved toward monotheism.[32]

Greek Philosophy and Religion

Gilbert Murray divides Greek religion into five phases, as follows: Pre-Homeric, Olympian, Stoic and Epicurean, Later Hellenistic, and Pagan revival by Julian and Sallustus.[33] I have discussed his stages one, two, and four. We have not space for a discussion of stage five but should like to refer briefly to the part played by Greek philosophy in the religious experience of the Greeks.

The humanizing of Greek religion, after the manner of Homer, was bound to present problems to the thoughtful. When an impersonal force like *mana* brought about unfortunate results one can only wonder. But when one conceives as personal the power that strikes people dead for touching a holy object, such as an ark toppling behind the oxen, more serious problems arise. Why should a good god kill a man whose very pardonable offense was to try to keep the holy ark from falling? In Israel and in Greece men were troubled by problems such as these. In Greece men were troubled by the indecencies of the gods themselves, and by the obvious injustices which they permitted on the earth. One such man was the poet Aeschylus. Another was Sophocles. Both tried to justify the ways of the gods, and incidentally to suggest that in reality the gods were all one—a stage of monotheism. Moreover, independent of any capricious divine wills were the powers of fate, *moira,* and of nemesis—a universal force which punished any one who sought to become more powerful than the gods. (Some claim to see in fate and nemesis a survival of dynamism.) At any rate, the two poets try to show that the universe exhibits a just moral order, and that the rule of the gods or of God must be according to that law. Sophocles causes Antigone to say, concerning the unjust ruling which her uncle, King Creon, had made:

> Nowise from Zeus, methought, this edict came,
> Nor Justice, that abides among the Gods
> In Hades, who ordained these laws for men.
> Nor did I deem thine edicts of such force
> That they, a mortal's bidding, should o'erride
> Unwritten laws, eternal in the heavens.
> Not of today or yesterday are these,
> But live everlasting, and from whence
> They sprang none knoweth. I would not, for the breach
> Of these, through fear of any human pride,
> To heaven atone. I know that I must die;
> How else? Without thine edict that were so.
> And if before my time, why, this were gain.
> Compassed about with ills, who lives, as I,
> Death, to such life as his, must needs be gain.
> So is it to me to undergo this doom
> No grief at all: but had I left my brother,
> My mother's child, unburied where he lay,
> Then I had grieved; but now this grieves me not.[34]

The poet Euripides, a younger contemporary of Aeschylus and Sophocles, apparently began his poetic career possessed of the same high faith as they had. But wide open eyes convinced him sadly that justice did not rule in human affairs. Even his beloved Athens acted notoriously in destroying their peaceful neighbors on Melos.

As they did so he wrote *The Trojan Women,* projecting into the conflict with Troy his own outraged feelings about the Athenian rape of Melos. He seemed to be saying that if there was no supreme divine law there ought to be—but probably there really was not! In his *Bacchae* Euripides comes to some such conclusion, in a poetic sort of way. But later in the *Medea* Euripides suggests a moral order based upon human moderation or self-government. It is the absence of this human restraint which Euripides laments—and Plato takes up where he leaves off.

The three tragic poets belong to the fifth century B.C., during which time the poet Pindar tried also to reform Homer. But early in the sixth century Thales had already thrown a thunderbolt at Zeus by asking people to seek the explanation of natural events by analyzing the relations between the events, not by analyzing the mind of Zeus to see what his intentions were. A few years later Heraclitus complained that "Hesiod is most men's teacher. Men are sure he knew very many things, a man who did not know day or night." Homer, he said, "should be turned out of the lists and whipped." Heraclitus did not deny God, but seemed to identify him with the world process. "God is day and night, winter and summer, war and peace, surfeit and hunger; but takes various shapes, just as fire, when it is mingled with spices, is named according to the savour of each." For Heraclitus "the wisest man is an ape compared to God, just as the most beautiful ape is ugly compared to man."[35]

A more direct attack on the Homeric religion, however, was made by Xenophanes during the sixth and early fifth centuries B.C. This philosophical, mystical bard was dissatisfied with Homer's immoral heaven, with his equally immoral universe in which the gods often punished men for no other reason than that they had offended the feelings of the gods; and he was dissatisfied with Hesiod's effort to make the Homeric religion appear to suggest that the universe is moral and that the rule of the Homeric gods is really for the good of man. Said he, "Both Homer and Hesiod have attributed to the gods all things that are shameful and a reproach among mankind: theft, adultery, and mutual deception." Again, "But mortals believe the gods to be created by birth, and to have their own [mortals'] raiment, voice, and body." "But if oxen (and horses) and lions had hands or could draw with hands and create works of art like those made by men, horses would draw pictures of gods like horses, and oxen of gods like oxen." "Aethiopians have gods with snub noses and black hair, Thracians have gods with grey eyes and red hair." "There is one god, among gods and men the greatest, not at all like mortals in body or in mind." "He sees as a whole, thinks as a whole, and hears as a whole." "But without toil he sets everything in motion, by the thought of his mind."[36]

The tendency to monotheism was strong among the early Greek philosophers. In other words, as they endeavored to substitute science for superstition, so also they tried to substitute mature for immature religion. Plato went so far, in his effort to cultivate mature religious concepts, as to urge that Homer be expurgated for educational purposes. On the positive side it would take us too long a journey to really do justice to Plato's contribution to religion. But briefly stated, Plato had a mystical reverence for the Ideas, and especially for the ideal of truth, beauty, and goodness. The Idea of the Good was, to him, the supreme concept, ruling the realm of absolute reality as the sun rules the day. For Aristotle, too, God was one, the Unmoved Mover, whose perfect embodiment of the ideal constituted the motivation of all things to seek the realization of their own ideals in a universe of forms. God is the form of forms, pure actuality, who apparently, for Aristotle, has consciousness and yet transcends consciousness.

The Cynics and Stoics, as well as the Epicureans after their fashion, developed a practical religious way of life. The two points of view, while opposite in important respects, were nevertheless one in insisting that salvation was primarily for the present life, within the realm of nature, and that such salvation was to be found within one's own spirit. For Epicurus salvation consisted in the achievement of peace of mind, which could best be attained by philosophically undermining fear of death and of the gods. Positively salvation consisted in contentment with simple joys, above all the joys of friendship and philosophy. Salvation could best be attained without the help of the gods, who were too wise to be concerned about human affairs anyhow, said Epicurus. As for death, "When we are, death is not; when death is, we are not." So why be afraid? In a broad sense, this was truly a religious philosophy.

As a way of life Cynicism and Stoicism also sought peace of mind, or "imperturbability"; but the technique and presuppositions were different from Epicureanism. After all, Epicureanism was egocentric in its reference, whereas Stoicism was oriented to the universe of human relations and the primacy of moral responsibility. Human nature, for the Stoic, was not merely a refined animal nature; it was indwelt and infused by a spark of the divine. Therefore one should live worthily of his divine kinship, as a child of God and as a brother to all men. Duty was the first consideration, and the good will was all that counted. The Stoics cultivated the ascetic ideal, choosing the hard life in preference to the life of ease. In this manner one could best nurture the soul and make it independent of its physical relationships. On the death of the body the soul would then return to the divine fire of which it was but a spark—although some Stoics believed that the individual soul would survive until the great conflagration in which the universe as a whole would return to God, to start once more on a new world cycle. The Stoics believed in divine providence and justice, and equated the divine fire with reason, which we can recognize within ourselves as the essence which unites us all with God and our fellowmen. As with Heraclitus, so also with the Stoics, the Logos—the abiding law or rationality of all things—was that which changeth not. This was obscure in Heraclitus but becomes explicit in the Stoics. In modified form it influenced Philo, a contemporary of Jesus, and John, author of the Fourth Gospel.

The religious quality of Stoicism is seen in the hymn of Cleanthes, written in the mid-third century B.C., and in the almost Christian attitude of Epictetus toward the end of the first century A.D. Cleanthes wrote, "Most glorious of immortals, O thou of many names, all-powerful ever, hail!" He thus gave expression to the growing monotheistic conviction of the Greeks that the many gods were really not many but one and all-powerful. He describes God as the guide of "universal Reason—the moving principle of all the world." The world is just, he says: "Thou canst make the crooked straight, bring order from disorder, . . . For out of all goes forth a single everlasting Reason. This all the wicked seek to shun, unhappy men, who, ever longing to obtain a good, see not nor hear God's universal law: which, wisely heeded, would assure them noble life."[37] His was a strong faith.

Epictetus was sure that "There is a god and . . . he provides for all things; also . . . it is not possible to conceal from him our acts, or even our intentions and thoughts." Epictetus was definitely pantheistic: he regarded man as a fragment of God. Yet he also speaks of God as our maker, and of our duty to live worthily of our creator. Whatever he has given us is good, and when he takes it away, it is also good. More than most Stoics, Epictetus was otherworldly. "Ask you whether a man shall engage in the administration of the state . . . ? Ask me too if he shall govern; and again I will answer, Fool, what greater government shall he hold than that he holds already?" [government of moral affairs.][38] He wanted only to be "wholly attentive to God and to his orders and commands."[39] This seems close in spirit to one of the themes of early Christianity. Indeed some think he was definitely influenced by Christian thought, although there is no proof of that. It matters not, for by now it is quite clear that Greek religious philosophy had moved in the same direction as the monotheism and piety of the Judeo-Christian philosophy.

Maturity of Greek Religion

No doubt the evaluation of Greek religion has by now become basically clear. Yet our judgment dare not be too simple. For the maturing process is relative at best.

Was Homeric or Minoan religion free from magical concepts? Were the Greek myths originally poetic and symbolic? These questions are ultimately unanswerable except on the basis of uncertain theory. But we are sure that many Greeks in classic times had come to interpret the myths prosaically and literally, and Socrates seems to have been executed because he was not a literalist. So we must distinguish between the relative immaturity of the common man's religion and the relative maturity of the religion of Socrates, Plato, Aristotle, Heraclitus, Xenophanes, the Stoics, and many others.

The growing dissatisfaction of thoughtful Greeks with their religious traditions was in large part due to their growing moral sense. Therefore their reformed type of religious conviction was deeply ethical, although not entirely free from superstition. From Thales to Aristotle and on to Archimedes there was a kind of commitment, in principle, to the truth wherever it might be found. Devotion to the divine Logos, to truth and wisdom, was a philosophical ideal which played a fateful part in the religious experience of our Greek cultural heroes. Greek cosmology became the prototype of our own modern cosmology. The principle of loyalty to the concept of nature and human nature was recognized by prophetic souls in classic Greece, where Socrates and Plato stressed the supreme importance of the "tendance of the soul."

When we think of the artistic greatness of classic Greece we are led to seek beauty in Greek religion. Certainly there was beauty in the poetic expression of Greek myths, in the artistic symbolization of her deities, and in the developed symbolism of Greek mystery cults. Prayer and sacrifice seem to have known many mature expressions in Greek history—a topic too involved to be adequately treated here.

The criterion of mystic sensitivity has a variety of applications in Greek religion. We have seen it expressed in primitive myth, and perhaps more crudely but fervently in the earliest Greek mystery cults. It was also evident in a refined but profound sense in the experience of Socrates, who was ever faithful to the divine voice deep within his spirit. God was intimately present to him, and his mystic sensitivity was reflected in the fine perceptivity of the spirit of Plato and later in the Stoics.

The universality of Greek religion was a development of the philosophers. Plato's universality of concepts, necessarily applied to all thinking beings, and the Stoic insistence on the fatherhood of God, the divine universal fire, affected the thoughts of men in all nations.

Much of the maturity of modern Christianity may be recognized as a gift of the Greeks. This will be brought out in the discussion of the Hebrew-Christian tradition.

VI. UNIQUE QUALITIES OF ROMAN RELIGION

As a brief historical background for an examination of Roman religion, it is necessary to glance at the various elements, cultural and ethnic, which gave the Roman state its characteristics. Anthropologists are uncertain as to the origin of the oldest remains in Italy, along the Ligurian coast, for they bear resemblances to deposits in Europe and in North Africa.[1] The neolithic period brought the so-called Mediterranean race, whose south Italian members were in contact with the eastern Aegean. It is not until the developed Bronze Age, when the *terramare* folk came into north Italy, that a distinct cultural pattern emerges. Even here progress was slower than in Greece, for example.[2] These people, probably of Indo-European cultural background, spread down to the area of Rome, and their descendants in the early Iron Ages (known in the north as Villanovans) probably are buried in the cemeteries found on the Esquiline and in the Roman Forum.[3] They and their relatives lived in nine groups of communities in northern and central Italy. The religious practices of these people, little known as they are except by inference, underlie the Roman religion.

The Etruscans, the other major source of Roman culture, remain an enigma. Tradition says they came from the east, Lydia to be exact, with whose language their own seems to have some affinities. On the other hand, there seems to be no break in the cultural tradition in central Italy, as evidenced by grave finds. They appeared in the area recognizably at least as early as 800 B.C.[4] The whole Etruscan question is awaiting solution. None the less, their remains are indicative of the influence of their religion[5] upon the Romans, whether the facts of history resemble Roman tradition or not.

According to unreliable tradition of late origin Rome was founded by a mythical person, Romulus, in 753 B.C. While the hills that go to make up Rome were inhabited prior to this—settlement on the Palatine commencing perhaps before 900 B.C.—yet the Rome of the Four Regions could not have been organized before late in the seventh century. At that time or shortly afterward the Etruscan kings, the Tarquins, wrested the monarchy from the earlier Latins. Tradition becomes partially reliable about this time. But history properly does not begin until the fall of the monarchy and the organization of the republic, which probably occurred about 450 B.C. rather than in 509 B.C., the traditional date.[6]

In the first century B.C., when Augustus was trying to restore the old Roman religion and to end the religious Babel, Varro and others reported the ancient Roman calendar of public festivals. The calendar included names of gods and goddesses whose original functions had been forgotten, as Greek and oriental gods had come in to replace them or to join with them in new functions. Varro and his contemporaries did not know any more about them than we do—perhaps less, considering new sources of our information, particularly our knowledge of philology and of comparative religions. Also significant was the absence from the calendar of certain names of deities who had been thought of as originally Roman. Some, like Juno, were absent because of the variable character of the date for her festival. But others were missing simply because they were not Roman gods at all; they were introduced later from foreign sources.

Native Roman Deities

Who, then, were some of the original deities of early Rome? What were their functions—when they can be ascertained? And what do they reveal concerning the nature of primitive Roman religion? We must keep in mind, of course, that primitive Roman religion was still two millennia more recent than the primitive religions of Egypt and Mesopotamia, but roughly comparable in time with Homeric Greece.

By analyzing the divine names for clues to their functions, and noting the time of year when their festivals occur, we can be quite sure of some of the early religious beliefs of the Romans. Sometimes tradition supports our conclusion, but at other times tradition has been prejudiced by Greek or other influences. The simplest explanation is likely to be the best, for it soon becomes evident that the Romans were concerned with practical things, like agriculture, fertility, peace, and war. And their gods at the dawn of history turn out to be powers or functions of nature. In the earliest historical periods we may catch glimpses of Roman gods as they pass from one cultural stage to another. Under Etruscan and Greek influences they definitely assumed anthropomorphic shapes like the Homeric gods.

Writers on Roman religion are accustomed to pointing out that it went through the stages of primitive magic and dynamism, then animism, and finally polytheism. This, of course, reflects the anthropological views of Marett. In the case of Roman religion there may seem to be more support for Marett's theory than in most other anthropological studies. Yet even in this instance we do not have enough information to be conclusive. All that we can say for certain is that Roman history begins at a time when the neighborhood of Rome apparently accepted magic, which, as we have seen, may be impersonal, personal, or a mixture of the two. They also believed in powers or functions (*numina*) of nature, which in some instances seem to be purely impersonal or abstract and in others seem to be personal. This could indicate that the *numina* were in a stage of transition. But was the transition from impersonal functions to personal spirits or vice versa? Or did the primeval Romans conceive of the numinal powers or functions as really emanating from ancestral spirits—or from souls akin to ancestral spirits?

Since the *numina* represent the heart of the Roman contribution to religion, we should note that there are two general types of *numina*. First, there are the local *numina*, like the local spirits of ordinary animism. Second, there are the functional *numina*. Of these, some are agricultural and others are pastoral, while still others have to do with the organization of human society.

A mysterious combination are these ancient Roman *numina*. It was usually assumed that they had sex, although the worshiper was not always sure what its sex was. "Be thou god or goddess, to whom this wood is sacred," the Roman farmer recited as he made a clearing in the wood, "as it is right to make expiation by the offering of a pig because of the clearing of this sacred wood, for this cause, that all may be rightly done. . . . I make pious prayer that thou wouldest be kind and gracious to me, my home, my household, and my children. . . ."[7]

In the above illustration the implication is clear that the ancestors of the Romans considered trees as being indwelt by souls, perhaps by ancestral spirits, and thought that to cut them down was to run the risk of offending those spirits. Apparently Roman animism was already so ancient when history began that the worshipers no longer knew the tradition regarding the origin of local *numina*. The same is no doubt true concerning functional *numina*.

That the *numina* were animistic is clearly indicated. Bailey refers to numinism as "the higher animism."[8] That it is animism of some sort is certain. "The word *numen* appears to denote 'a being with will power,' and it is as such that the 'spirits' are approached by their worshippers."[9]

Probably the soundest conclusion is that magic and taboo represent a predominantly dynamistic phase of Roman religion, while numinism represents a predominantly animistic phase of the same. Neither is exclusively one or the other.

The best way to see these things is to make a brief survey of the divine Roman *numina* and of Roman magic and taboo. Thus we shall get a concrete picture of Roman religious practice and development.

As far back as we have information, then, the earliest Roman gods were *numina*. "The word *numen* is everywhere employed, where a divine action, an activity or function is meant." "A god, when he expresses himself in a special direction or action and when that expression, for the immediate present, forms the focus of interest, can be designated simply as numen."[10] Illustration will help to make this clear.

Agricultural Gods

Saturn was one of the gods of early Rome. "His name is found in the byform Saeturnus and is certainly connected with the root of *serere*, to sow; a legend attributed to him the invention of the processes of agriculture. Unfortunately we know nothing of him in this character, as his cult very early became overlaid with Greek influence. He was identified with Chronos and figures as the mythical king of Italy in the golden age; his festival in the city of Rome lost its agricultural character and became, as we all know, the occasion of friendly visits and gifts and of considerable license for the slaves—the prototype of the Christian Christmas."[11]

As Saturn was originally the divine act, function, or spirit of sowing, so Ceres was the spirit of the corn crop. Bailey is confident that her name is derived from the root of *creare,* to create. "She is then the spirit of the birth and growth of the corn. Later the conception of Ceres was corrupted by her assimilation to Demeter and the consequent attachment of underworld notions."[12]

By similar reasoning it is possible to identify Consus with the function of storing the crops: Consus is the spirit of the granary. Ops, associated with Consus, was the wealth represented by the stored crops in a day when money as such did not exist. Flora was the spirit of flowers, but was later associated with the games which became a public institution in 238 B.C., in which flowers were the sign of gayety. Pomona was the ripening of fruit, conceived as a function, act, power, or process.

Vesta was the spirit of the hearth, keeping the fires going in order to cook the food or bring warmth and cheer. The Lar familiaris was the spirit or function of protection of the household in its comings and goings, including the family and its servants, from generation to generation. The Lares may originally have been the spirits of the farm-fields, but came to be worshiped in the household along with Vesta and the Penates. It has long been held, but cannot be proved, that the Lares have something to do with a cult of the dead.[13]

Pales was the guardian-spirit or protecting power of the flocks of the pasture. Sometimes spoken of as masculine, at other times feminine, perhaps Pales was originally a pair of spirits whose functional rather than local nature was recognized. The name of Pales almost certainly survives in the Palatine Hill of Rome, where the divinity Pales was given a home and a flamen, or priest.[14] (Latin "flare" means "to blow." The priests originally were, apparently, people whose duty it was to kindle and blow up the sacred fires.) But though Pales was given a local habitation, yet he or she was worshiped wherever there were flocks to be guarded.

Faunus and Fauna were the male and female *numina* of idyllic rustic character embodied in the woodlands surrounding the fields and pastures. Literally, Faunus was "the kindly one" (from *favere,* to favor, not from *fari,* to speak.)

Fons illustrates a unique characteristic of Roman religion. He or she seems to signify the individual spirit of a spring of water, wherever it is found. All springs (*fontes,* fountains) were sacred. All were indwelt by Fons, sometimes possessing a special name but usually not. At the Fontinalia festival on October 13 "it was still the individual springs and wells which were garlanded, and it seems clear that Fons never achieved any strong personality: the old animistic notion of the spirit in each spring survives throughout."[15] Fons, then, seems to illustrate the "local" type of *numen,* although it is hard to exclude the functional as well.

Social Gods

Janus in some ways was the most important deity of primitive Rome. Prayers always began by first invoking him. Janus means literally "going," symbolized by the open door whenever Rome went to war.[16] There is some scholarly controversy over the early function of Janus, but in some manner it is connected with the door (hence our word Janitor). Perhaps Janus was the spirit of defense which activated the free men of Rome or Latium when war threatened and they opened the door and went forth to defend their homes. That spirit always stands at the door, ready to go forth.

But we really have not mentioned as yet the most prominent of all Roman deities. At the head of the list probably should stand Jupiter (Juppiter), whose Indo-European derivation links the Latins with the Greeks, Iranians, and Indians. Jupiter and Zeus Pater were descended from a common Indo-European word-form, as the sound indicates. As Indo-European, Jupiter was a sky-god, and is recognized as such in Roman tradition. Yet the earliest function associated with him in the agricultural calendar was as protector of the vine. Jupiter, with Mars and Quirinus, formed the supreme triad of the earliest Roman religion. "We may think of them as even then gods rather than spirits, but not of course conceived as yet in human form."[17]

Mars and Quirinus both were war gods. Mars was widely worshiped in Italy in early times. But besides being the martial spirit, he was besought as protector of the farmers' possessions and activity. Quirinus, perhaps of Sabine origin, was always a god of war, and never had agricultural functions so far as we know. The importance of the war gods from earliest times indicates that war was an habitual accompaniment of Italian life, rather than an exception. Mars and Quirinus are sometimes spoken of as "doublets," that is, gods from adjacent locales whose functions were in some respects identical, but whom neither group was willing to abandon. So they both survived in the native Roman triad, Jupiter, Mars, and Quirinus. The "doublets" were virtually synthesized in Jupiter.

Of less importance was Neptune in early times when he was spirit of the water. When Greek influence came in he was, of course, made the equivalent of the more important Poseidon. When this happened, Neptune was conceived not functionally nor even locally but anthropomorphically.

Still to be mentioned are the Genius and Juno. Every man had his Genius and every woman her Juno. We might call the Genius the "spirit of manhood," and the Juno the "spirit of womanhood," thus seeing these *numina* in their functional or activist natures. The Genius is the virile power that makes a man a man. The Genius was not conceived of as a man's soul, although this may have been its original nature. Historically the Genius was closer to being conceived of as a man's guardian angel. In the development of Roman religion it became somewhat more animistic, but originally, like the other *numina,* it represented a functional concept in human experience. The situation with regard to the original concept of Juno was parallel until she was personalized by the Etruscans and eventually was thought to be the wife of Jupiter, just as the Greek Hera was thought to be the wife of Zeus Pater.

It was customary in primitive Rome for each man to pay reverence to his own Genius on his birthday, and for the whole household to worship the Genius of the paterfamilias on the latter's birthday. This suggests ancestor worship, although the Genius which was held in such regard always belonged to a living person, the head of the household. The Genius of the Emperor led to Emperor worship, on the theory that the people of the empire were members of his household, since even slaves were included in the family of the paterfamilias.

The Di Manes—"kindly gods"—in primitive Roman religion most likely were thought of as the "collective powers of the underworld, the chthonic deities."[18] As such they were probably not spirits of the dead, who apparently were not worshiped in Roman religion. Even the spirits of the dead were conceived as in some manner collective, not as individual, but were functionally associated with the Di Manes. Ancestor worship is believed by some to have arisen late in Roman religion.

There were still other *numina* among early Roman deities, like the Penates, protectors of the store-cupboard. Some of the *numina* remain only as names, their functions having been entirely forgotten and unrecovered. These included, for example, Furrina, Falacer, and Palatua. The names of others indicate a minute subdivision of function. Thus Neptune, the spirit of waters, was aided by Volturnus, spirit of the rolling waters, and by Portunis, spirit of the landing place. The Lares, spirits of the fields, were aided by Terminus, spirit of boundaries.

Terminus is of special interest as evidence of the survival of early magic. As a god Terminus is of late origin. The termini were at first merely magical or sacred stones which marked the boundary between fields. The Terminalia was a feast celebrated on February 22, at which the owners of adjoining fields met and decorated the boundary stones, made sacrifice and feast, and thus symbolized the renewing of the original boundary compacts. In the course of time it is believed that these magical stones came to be thought of as containing spirits, "termini;" such *numina* appear to be both local and functional. Finally as "deus" Terminus was worshiped, although he never did acquire the image of man as did Hermes, his Greek counterpart.

Formalization of Roman Religion

According to tradition Numa, the supposed successor to Romulus as king of Rome, made the Roman religion the official state religion by drawing up a list of the deities and assigning to each its festival or festivals. He decreed how each one should be worshiped, and where. The king assumed the function of head of the Roman religion as well as its civic ruler. When the monarchy was overthrown and the republic established in 509 B.C., the religious and civic functions of the state were placed under different officials. Presiding over the religious functions were, first, the Pontificial College of three persons, chief of whom was the Pontifex Maximus. The college was self-perpetuating and had authority to appoint priests and servants of the many gods of Rome. Second, there was the Rex Sacrorum, who "was always reckoned as the first of the priesthoods and he had the first seat on ceremonial occasions. . . . He, like the Pontifex Maximus, had the right of entry to the *sacrarium* of the Regia, the king's palace, and was entrusted with the secrets of the *ius divinum*. It is indeed probable that in the early republican period he played a large part, but later on his functions were mostly usurped by the Pontifex Maximus. . . ."[19] Finally there were the individual Flamines, especially the priests of Jupiter, Mars, and Quirinus. The Flamines were surrounded by primitive taboos characteristic of the presence of the sacred and the magical.

As time went on there was a tendency for the ritual to become more and more elaborate, punctilious, and stereotyped, and thus to get further and further away from the magical simplicity with which it had begun. Sometimes, however, the ritual revealed not only the increasing formality of the later Romans but also some unique survivals of primitive magic. Sacrifices of vegetable or animal offerings were everyday occurrences. The common motive of the sacrificer was to strengthen the deity, to appease him, or to gain his favor. But the sacrifice of the pregnant cow was most extraordinary. In historic times this offering was made to Tellus, conceived originally as the function or spirit of fertility inhabiting the soil. In this offering the foetus was extracted from the victim and burned, and the ashes were used to insure the fertility of the crops. Here is an excellent illustration of the survival of the sympathetic magic of primitive Latium.[20] The blood of the October horse was used in a similar manner.[21] In historic times its magical significance was forgotten, and the October horse came to be regarded as a thank-offering for victory in war.

Magic and Taboo

Stones were particularly reminiscent of primitive Roman magic. The *termini* have already been cited. Stones were used especially as sacred or magical bases for a holy oath. Such was the nature of the most sacred stone in the very ancient temple of Jupiter Feretrius. This temple never housed a statue, but only the sacred stone.

Another magical stone famous in Roman religion was the *lapis manalis,* used as a rain charm. Water was poured over it and allowed to drip down in imitation of the rain which it was supposed to induce: a clear instance of imitative magic.

Besides magic stones we may note the survival of magic spells in Roman practice. Some of these are embedded in the literature of Ovid, Virgil, Horace, and others. There were love charms, health charms, and charms to avoid pestilence. In the state religion it was customary for the consul, in time of pestilence, to drive a nail into the inner shrine of the capitoline temple, in order to end a pestilence.[22] In the feast of the Lupercalia nearly naked youths ran around the city, making what must have been regarded originally as a magic circle to keep out evil. With thongs of fresh goat hide they struck bystanders, particularly the women, in order to make them fertile. "The thongs, cut from the skin of the sacred victim, convey his mystic power to those whom they touch, and the whipping is the driving away of evil spirits, which might hurt the community and especially the spirits which cause sterility and hinder childbirth."[23]

There are also numerous survivals of taboo in Roman religion. Taboo is classed as an example of contagious magic. The Flamen Dialis, or special priest of Jupiter at Rome, was surrounded with taboos. For example, he might not ride a horse—this may have indicated merely the conservatism of the priests. But neither might he see an army in formation—since his god was not a war god and had nothing to do with war magic. He might not take an oath, since an oath usually called down bad luck on one who failed to keep it, and the very thought of bad luck was repugnant to so sacred a person as the Flamen Dialis. "He must wear no ring, unless it is cut through, and have no sort of knot in any part of his clothing. . . . Knots are very bad magic, as a rule. . . . Once cut, his hair trimmings and nail parings must be buried under a lucky, that is, a fruitful tree. There, they would not only be safe from hostile magic, but exposed to good magic, a most desirable precaution. There were a number of things unlucky for one reason or another which he might not touch or even name. Naming is a kind of touching, for the name is part of the thing, to the primitive thinker."[24] Beans were also forbidden to him, because they were contaminated by being associated with mortuary ritual. The "Flamen Dialis must not touch a dead body or enter the place where a corpse had been burnt, nor must he touch or mention a goat or a dog, animals with chthonic associations. . . ."[25]

There were taboos for everyone, to degrees only less than those resting upon the Flamen Dialis. The soldier was under a taboo of blood-guiltiness and might not enter Rome except by following the laurel-decorated chariot of a general; this purified him and permitted him safely to enter Rome. There were days of the calendar which were taboo, or unlucky, and everyone refrained from getting married, or starting an important undertaking, on such days.

The examples of taboo and magic in early Roman religion are endless. Those cited will easily show that the early Romans were endeavoring to gain success and happiness through the proper ordering of the forces of the universe, while at the same time they sought to be in right relation to the *numina* or spirits of the world.

Etruscan and Greek Influences

The process of personalizing the Roman *numina* was encouraged by the Greek influence, as well as by the Etruscans. Varro stated that there were no images of the gods during the first 170 years of

Rome, that is, until the Etruscans built the temple to Jupiter, Juno, and Minerva on the Capitoline hill. Whether the Greeks took up where the Etruscans left off personalizing the gods, as some writers say, or whether the Etruscans were in reality merely following the leadership of the Greeks, as Altheim insists, is not important.

It will be noted that Minerva's name was absent from the early Roman calendar of festivals. Her case illustrates how the Roman pantheon grew. As the craftsmen became more numerous in monarchical Rome they needed a protector. So Minerva was brought from Falerii, on the upper Tiber, to serve this need. Later Diana, spirit of the grove at Aricia, was also brought to Rome and given a grove on the Aventine hill. The latter event may have symbolized the transfer of Latin leadership from Aricia to Rome. Fortuna, especially important to women, and Venus, guardian of gardens and fruit trees, were also early introduced to Rome. But the characters of all of these deities were destined to grow and change beyond recognition. Under Greek influence Minerva became the Athena of Rome. Diana became the moon goddess, like Artemis of Greece. Fortuna evolved from an Italian deity of fertility and childbirth, into the Grecianized personification of Chance. And rustic Venus, from Ardea, became the equivalent of the Greek Aphrodite, goddess of fecundity and of beauty.

Apollo found his way to Rome from the Greek city of Cumae during the monarchical period. Later a temple was built for him in 431 B.C. He came not as a sun god, but only as the god of healing. Even his name was not Latinized when his services were appropriated by Rome. Augustus later made him patron of the arts and of literature. Early Rome knew him only as a kind of Greek physician.

But Apollo was not allowed to exercise his oracular powers in Rome. These were associated with the Sibyls in Greek Italy. The Sibyls had arisen in Greece in connection with the Orphic mysteries. One Sibyl had gained a stronghold in Italy at Cumae, to which the early Romans journeyed in search of their oracles. The Romans, being acustomed to seeking omens through divination, might well be expected to take up with the Sibyl in order to discover the divine will by a different method.[26]

The introduction of the Sibylline Books at Rome was of momentous importance. Tradition assigns this event to the time of the late monarchy. Foreign (that is Greek) priests were imported to interpret the Sibylline Books. When the superstitious Romans, including officials, appealed to the Sibylline oracles in time of danger or disaster, their Greek priests were likely to recommend the acquisition of a new Greek god or the Grecianizing of old Roman deities. The latter happened to Ceres, Liber, and Libera, for example, about 493 B.C. when they took on the respective characteristics of Demeter, Dionysus, and Kore. It was then, too, that Mercury appeared as the equivalent of the Greek Hermes as patron deity of commerce.[27] Through Sibylline influence arose the custom of offering sacrificial meals to images of the deities. In early Roman religion a token meal was merely thrown into the hearth fire but the new Greek influence brought the gods personally to dinner. So here, too, anthropomorphism increased in Rome.

More tragic was it when, through Sibylline intervention, human sacrifice was required. Unknown to Latins since the fifth century, this is recorded as having occurred in 226, 216, and 114 B.C.[28] Unfortunate, too, was the Sibylline introduction of the worship of the Great Mother from Phrygia, complete with Phrygian priests and orgiastic rites, between 204 and 191 B.C.[29] The occasion, as usual, was a great crisis, in this case the war with Hannibal. Five years later the Senate, alarmed at the oriental corruption of Roman traditions, passed a decree prohibiting the celebration of the Bacchanalian rites. The prohibition was only temporarily successful.

With the Roman annexation of Greece in 146 B.C. the Greek influence became complete. Efforts were made to stop it, but they were futile. The result was a hodge-podge of religions which might be described for the most part as Greco-Roman, but which included elements which were neither Greek nor Roman.

Emperor Worship and the Mysteries

It has been held that the demoralization of the family and the society of Rome was the result of the degeneration of the old Roman religion. In fact the first Caesars so believed, for Julius and Augustus both made statesmanlike efforts to put religion on a sounder basis of Roman tradition. Probably their motive was to make Roman religion a better servant of the empire. Julius Caesar was more than ready to accept divine acclaim which came to him from the provinces, where the idea of the god-king was already a native tradition. In Rome he accepted Senate honors, including the assignment of a *flamen* to his service. After his death the Senate legislated his divinity and provided for a temple of Divus Julius, which Augustus dedicated in 29 B.C.

Augustus was more reluctant to accept divinity than Julius Caesar had been. He built imperial temples to certain old and new deities in order to cultivate an appropriate synthesis of religious traditions. "He could not altogether prevent the worship of his person in the provinces, but insisted that it should not be allowed except in conjunction with that of the Dea Roma. In Rome, in full accord with his general policy and his attitude toward the revival of religion, he was at pains to link up the new cult with the old Republican traditions. In his new house on the Palatine the cult of his Genius was of course a natural form of domestic worship: he permitted this to be extended in the city and to be combined with that of the Lares Praestites."[30] Augustus was in turn deified upon his death in 14 A.D. By the end of the first century it had become a matter of custom to deify the deceased emperor.

Augustus was in effect taking all Rome into his family by permitting Romans to regard his Genius as divine. Romans, understanding the traditional religion to this extent, did not regard the living emperor himself as divine. But the provinces, particularly some oriental provinces and Egypt, were accustomed to the idea of the divinity of the living monarch. To his subjects the emperor indeed took the part of a god by bringing to them fateful retribution or prosperity, and they tended to regard him as divine in this manner. Augustus was revered especially for having brought peace to the empire. And if Augustus was not morally perfect, neither were the gods, according to the myths which told of them.

When Christianity arose to threaten the old religion certain policies were adopted which could be interpreted as efforts to forestall the victory of Christianity. The cult of the emperor certainly was stressed as a means of securing a feeling of unity within the empire. Once Severus Alexander (193-211 A.D.) tried to secure unity through eclecticism and mutual toleration. In his private chapel he included images of Christ, Abraham, and Orpheus. His predecessor had tried to save the empire by exalting the worship of a Syrian sun god. Aurelian a little later adopted a more chaste version of sun worship than the emperor Elagabalus had introduced. And after him Mithras, still another sun god, was raised by Diocletian above all other gods of the empire.

The mystery religions needed no help from the state. They were already popular in the empire. So popular did the Eleusinian cult become that, despite the long journey, many Romans traveled all the way to Athens and Eleusis to be initiated. But more popular than Eleusinianism was Mithraism. This cult offered consolation and magical help for this life and immortality in the life to come for all male human beings who had partaken of the mysteries of Mithras, the god who died and came forth from the rock in perpetual youth. Also popular was the Phrygian cult of the Great Mother, Cybele, whose son Attis died from excessive emasculation but was resurrected. Devotees sometimes actually emasculated themselves during the rites and believed that they had thereby sufficiently identified themselves with Attis to insure their resurrection with him. There is little doubt that the original meaning of the cult, as also of Mithraism, was the practice of sympathetic magic designed to bring about the rebirth of vegetation in the spring. But such an interpretation would certainly not have made the cult popular in late Roman times. For the sake of eternal life people were willing to mutilate themselves and to endure the drenching by the blood of the bull in the taurobolium ceremony.

It is true that Stoicism offered an escape from the confusion of Roman syncretism by stressing the unity of God and the necessity of living the good life. The Stoics also insisted that salvation was primarily in this world, not in the world to come, and that it consisted in the attainment of equanimity through the performance of duty and the realization of independence of one's environment. There was a fundamental piety in the Stoic philosophy which might have saved Roman society if the people had laid hold upon it. But the reason why the Roman people did not take up with Stoicism was because they were not heroes, as Stoic philosophy required them to be. They were ordinary human beings, most of them, ignorant and superstitious, reluctant and even afraid to die without some deep assurance of salvation. The mystery religions—the cults of Mithras, Attis, Serapis, and others—held out this assurance primarily through magic and emotionalism. Certainly they did not stress moral behavior as an essential on the pathway to salvation. This Christianity did, offering at the same time an emotional release and the hope of immortality. Christianity therefore may well be regarded as the religion which was best prepared to satisfy the innumerable unintegrated religious desires of the people of the Roman Empire two thousand years ago.

It may be true, as some insist, that many chose Christianity rather than the mystery religions because salvation was free in Christianity, whereas one had to purchase the bull in certain of the cults. It is difficult to detect the motive for choosing one thing rather than another. But surely one reason why Christianity triumphed over Mithra and Attis was because it offered more of the ethical values to people whose cultural outlook was expanding, and because its fundamental mysticism, which it held in common with the other cults, was more refined and offered infinitely more room for spiritual and social growth in a world which needed that kind of salvation.

Evaluation of Roman Religion

In terms of our basic criteria, then, we must judge Roman religion as generally immature because it was permeated by magical assumptions on the whole. There is no way of knowing how literally Roman mythology was interpreted, but it seems a safe bet that most people regarded it as literally true, in some vague manner.

As to the commitment to truth in science, cosmology, history, and human relations, these were undeveloped fields in Roman culture and as such could scarcely command any kind of loyalty or commitment. The Stoics produced an advanced concept of nature and human nature, entitling them to the highest claim to maturity in the Hellenistic-Roman era. But the Stoic definition of human nature called for too great inhibition of the human emotions.

The Roman and Stoic sensitivity to ethical demands and to the demands of universal law justify Rome's most rightful claim to maturity. Roman law stands high in cultural achievement and reflects to some degree on its religion, particularly on its adopted religion of Stoicism.

The ritual of Roman religion, while reflecting a certain simple beauty and strength, was also permeated by magical concepts, as we have seen. And the mystic sensitivity of the Roman devotee was not especially different from that of other primitive civilizations where myth and magic mingle. The claims of late Roman statesmen and of the historian Edward Gibbon that native Roman religion was unusually mature cannot stand careful scrutiny. Yet such as it was, Roman religion was practiced for the purpose of conserving those values which the Romans held dear.

PART THREE

The Pageant of India's Religions

VII. PRIMEVAL INDIA

OUR STUDY SO FAR has covered some of the so-called "forgotten religions"—religions which are no longer practiced as such, although their influence is noteworthy in the development of modern culture. Now our interest turns to religions which are still living as cultural organisms. Some of these living religions began long before Greece and Rome existed. As we trace their histories we shall find that from crude and superstitious beginnings have evolved some of the world's most mature faiths. We shall also observe superstitions multiplying in some instances. Tragic are those cases where prophets and reformers have, in effect, founded new and mature religions, only to have them transformed into their opposite by unperceiving followers.

Among the world's living religions, four have originated in India. They are Hinduism, Jainism, Buddhism, and Sikhism. These four religions are about as closely related as Catholicism and Protestantism. In order to understand the Protestant sects we must understand the mother church from which they branched off. So also in order to understand Jainism, Buddhism, and Sikhism we must understand Hinduism, their ancient mother. In order to understand Hinduism we should briefly look at its cultural and historical background.

Cultural Importance

If a study of Indian culture needs to be justified at this point, it may be suggested that (1) India contains about one fifth of the human race. (2) Its culture is more ancient and continuous than that of perhaps any other part of the earth. (3) It contributed some very important social inventions, such as the use of zero and the place-value number system. (4) It gave birth to some of the world's greatest prophets, such as Gautama Buddha and Mahatma Gandhi. (5) It produced some of the most remarkable texts of all religious literature. (6) Its historical schools of thought include points of view quite harmonious with Christian thought, as well as others not so harmonious. (7) As the world grows smaller there is correspondingly greater need for us to understand one another. (8) India may indeed hold the key to international reconciliation and world peace amidst our international-intercultural tensions. As Americans or Europeans interested in world unity we cannot afford to remain ignorant of so great a tradition as that of India.

Geographically India is divided into four main types of areas, each of which affected cultural development. The northern semicircle is mountainous, with the highest mountains in the world reaching up into the regions of eternal snow and sloping downward into the densely forested hills. South of the mountains lies the second area, the heart and center of India, reaching from the pleasant valleys of the Indus River and its tributaries on the west to the delta of the Ganges on the east. The climate of the Punjab in the northwest is very desirable, whereas Calcutta, in the Ganges delta, lies at sea level below the Tropic of Cancer. Between these two limits lies the Ganges river system and the important province of Magadha, famous in Indian history and rich in resources. Besides the Indus and the Ganges river systems south of the Himalayas, there is also the Brahmaputra river flowing from the northern slopes of the Himalayas, skirting the eastern terminus of the mountains and joining the Ganges at its delta. The third geographical area is the Deccan plateau forming the center of the peninsula. The fourth is the coastal area fringing the peninsula.

The races of India are many. All the typical human races are represented there. But the main racial ingredients of Hinduism are two: Aryan and Dravidian. Scholars are not entirely agreed on the story, but it seems most likely that during the third or second millennium B.C. the Aryans invaded the most attractive part of India, the Punjab in the northwest, and drove many of the dark-skinned Dravidians southward. In the course of time despite racial prejudice intermarriage took place, leaving the Aryans dark-skinned too. Seeing what was taking place, the Aryans became frightened and set up rigid caste barriers against the Dravidians. As a result, although his skin is dark, the Hindu has retained the essential ethnic characteristics of the Aryan peoples. He is probably as purely Aryan today as most Europeans or Americans are.

For that matter, even the Dravidian racial classification is far from having been established. It is believed that the Dravidians were the masters of India before the coming of the Aryans. Yet they were probably not the aborigines of India. Modern Dravidians of southern India exhibit such diverse racial and cultural characteristics that they are of no help in determining their origin. The Dravidian languages, however, are as distinct a type as the Aryan group of languages. If linguistic unity proves that all Aryan language groups are racially pure, then it should prove the same thing for Dravidians. This would indicate that the original Dravidians were neither negroid nor Aryan but unique, which may indeed be true.

Modern archaeology has pushed back the horizons of our knowledge of Indian religion and culture. New historical studies, too, combined with philology, have added greatly to our information, although there is still much that we do not know about the development of Hinduism from earliest times.

It woud be a mistake to identify Hinduism with the primeval Aryan religion, which the ancestors of the Hindus shared with the ancestors of their Persian and European cousins before they began their migrations. Rather, Hinduism is the religion which evolved after the Indo-Aryans moved down into the Punjab, mingled with their enemies, the Dravidians, and absorbed many of the native religious elements. As time went on Hinduism became more and more Dravidian. But it is now possible, with the help of archaeology and philology, to distinguish between Aryan and native or Dravidian elements in Hinduism as it developed. In fact archaeology reveals some of the details of the Indus culture and religion before the Aryans invaded the Punjab and composed the Vedas. Certain features of this native religion and culture are definitely recognizable in later Hinduism.

Like the rest of the world, India has relics of an Old Stone Age, a New Stone Age, a Copper-Stone Age, a Bronze Age, and finally the Iron Age. A brief account of its Bronze Age in the Indus Valley will be a fitting preface to a discussion of Hinduism itself.

Indus Bronze-Age Culture

In 1922, almost by accident, the whole civilization of the Indus valley of 5,000 years ago was laid before us through the discovery in Sind of the mound of Mohenjo-daro—"the place of the dead." The city of Harappa four hundred and fifty miles to the north in the Punjab had already yielded similar treasures, but much of their value was ruined by the long-time operation of a brick quarry on the site, and by more recent industrial developments there. The two sites together, however, witnessed to the breadth of the Indus civilization which is now dated between 3300 and 2500 B.C.[1]

Of special interest is the fact that the Indus civilization was in contact with contemporary civilization in ancient Sumer. Sir Aurel Stein has identified the stations of a caravan route by which products were exchanged between the two civilizations. At Ur was discovered "the little figure of a squatting monkey precisely similar to figures unearthed at Mohenjo-daro, while around 2500 B.C. at Tell Asmar other Indian animals—the elephant, rhinoceros, and gharial or fish-eating crocodile—appear on a seal of undoubted Indian workmanship."[2] Certainly the Indus civilization learned the art of seal-making from the Sumerians, and possibly also of writing. A pottery jar recently uncovered at Mohenjo-daro dating between 2800 and 2500 B.C. contains a Sumero-Babylonian cuneiform inscription. Most of the seals have short inscriptions on them, but efforts to decipher them have not met with success.[3]

That the Indus civilization belonged to the copper-bronze age is evident from the fact that there is an abundance of these metals in its artifacts but none of iron.[4] Some catastrophe overtook it before it had gotten beyond the use of bronze.

The modernity of Mohenjo-daro may be assumed because it was a well planned city. Three of its seven levels were excavated prior to 1948, with still more cities showing below the water level. The evidence is that the city was laid out with broad straight streets running north-south and east-west, and with commodious middle-class houses standing at equal distances from the streets, which were thirty-three feet wide.[5] The houses were built of burnt bricks, and most of them contained bathrooms with sloping floors and wall drainage as in modern India. "The drainage system of Mohenjo-daro was better than anything known in Europe before the 19th century. Every street and lane and passage had its own covered conduit of finely chiselled brick, laid with extraordinary precision. The drains had manholes and other cleaning facilities at regular intervals."[6] It is a paradox that much of modern India does not have city engineering which equals that of ancient Mohenjo-daro.

Modern, too, were many of the artifacts of Mohenjo-daro. The oldest piece of cotton cloth known to man was found there, preserved by the corrosion covering a silver jewel-jar which had been hidden under the floor of one of the houses.[7] A large number of pottery spindles have been found, together with ivory and stone dice, clay whistles, toy animals and carts, bronze razors, a bronze figurine of a dancing girl, and innumerable articles of personal adornment such as rings, bracelets, and necklaces of precisely-cut precious stones.

That many of the seals were intended to be worn as amulets is proved by the perforated knob on the back. Many of these magical seals show profiles of typical Indian animals or of mythological creatures such as the unicorn or a double-headed or triple-headed animal. Usually in front of the animal is an object which by the comparative method should be interpreted as an altar. On one seal appears to be a three-headed horned god sitting cross-legged on a stool, which in many cultures is a sign of deity. The posture is a typical Indian attitude of meditation. Animals are grouped around the deity as if in adoration. Another seal portrays a tree spirit with a man worshiping before it.[8] The worship of Shiva may be foreshadowed in the former seal,[9] while the tree worship prevalent among some primitive tribes today is seen in the latter seal. Still another indication of religion in the Indus civilization is the discovery of large numbers of clay images of the Mother Goddess, foreshadowing later Shaktism in Hindu India.

We have no historical knowledge of the relation between the Indus civilization and that of modern India. If there are survivals, as in Shiva worship, tree worship, and fertility worship, there is complete ignorance as to the path of survival. Sen is convinced that the Indus civilization came to an abrupt end between 2700 and 2500 B.C. She speculates[10] as to whether some natural catastrophe such as floods or plagues, or some human catastrophe such as invasion was the cause. The absence of weapons among the ruins might mean that the Indus people were not prepared for self-defense. And the fact that the civilization came to an end over a rather wide territory within a brief time would indicate human agency rather than a natural catastrophe.

There is just a possibility that the Dravidians themselves may have been the progenitors of the Indus civilization. It is known that the Dravidians were the masters of India prior to the coming of the Aryans, and that they were experts in city-building and in agriculture, commerce, and industry. Much of our knowledge comes from the Aryans' own first literature, the Vedas, in which the invaders brag about the proud race which they conquered, although they usually describe them as slaves—"dasas" or "dasyus"—and as "black-skinned" and "noseless."

Whether or not the Dravidians were the progenitors of the Indus civilization, at least they fell heir to much of its culture. And when the Aryans invaded India their prime enemy was the Dravidians. The Aryans came with their families and their fighting equipment, which included horses and chariots, swords, battle-axes, javelins, slings, and bows and arrows. Their warfare was too efficient and powerful for the enemy. As a result the Aryans pushed the Dravidians southward into the Deccan plateau and the coastal regions, and later followed them peacefully, mutually to impart and absorb culture. The Hindu tendency toward an abstract, monistic type of religion was therefore modified by the Dravidian tendency to think of deity as a Mother Goddess, or as a fertile Shiva, or even as a lingam (phallus) or other symbol of sex and vitality. The Dravidians ultimately became a part of Hinduism when, with castely caution, the Aryans admitted them as shudras, that is, members of the fourth or lowest caste, the servant caste. They did not become members of the twice-born castes, went through no initiation ceremonies and received no sacred thread to be worn as a symbol. Yet they were granted a position higher than the outcastes or untouchables of India.

Meanwhile the Stone Age aborigines of southern India had passed into the ages of bronze and iron, but not without leaving behind them numerous megalithic relics which are worthy of mention. These were huge stone shelters or burial places, comparable with Stonehenge in England. One of the most famous of these sites is the burial ground in the Tinnevelly district near Madras. It has yielded treasures which reveal a highly developed civilization. The huge stones indicate a strong effort to insure the safety of the soul after death. Their emphasis on personal survival after death is out of harmony with the philosophy which was later developed in the Upanishads, as we soon shall see.

The Indo-Aryans

Concerning the culture and history of the early Indo-Aryans, our principal source of information is the Rig Veda, called "the oldest book in the world." Its archaic Sanskrit identifies it certainly as

The swastika, found in all parts of the world became stylized in this form in India. Here one may discern an early form of the cross. *See page 179.*

the oldest of all Indo-European literature. Originally nomadic, the Indo-Aryans became more and more agricultural on settling in the valleys of the Indus river system. They introduced into India cows, sheep, goats, dogs, and horses. The last, with chariots, gave them great military superiority over the inhabitants of the Punjab. They ate meat and drank milk and "soma"—an intoxicating liquor combining milk with the juice of an unidentified plant. They formed tribes, each having a king or "rajah"—same as Latin "rex, regis." The principle of the division of labor gave rise to the warrior class who helped the king protect the people, the priestly class who served rulers and people, and the farmer-herdsmen who outnumbered all the rest.

Social organization among the Indo-Aryans, as among the European Aryans, was patriarchal. Head of the family and owner of its property was the father or "pitar"—same as Latin and Greek "pater," German "vater," English "father." More dignified and free than later Indian womanhood was the mother or "matar"—same as Latin "mater," Greek "meter," German "Mutter," English "mother." The primeval unity of the Indo-European Aryans is seen not only in its philology but also in its social institutions and attitudes. Such unity is also seen in the gods which they had in common. The best known illustration of the latter is Dyaus Pitar, the sky god, known to the Greeks as Zeus Pater and to the Romans as Deus Pater or Jupiter.

A certain democratic freedom is perceivable in Vedic references to early Indo-Aryan life. The home was pictured as a scene of affection and moral growth. The community was thought of as an association deserving one's loyalty and devotion, and in which honesty is encouraged in barter and contract. Each village was governed by a council or, as it grew in size, by an assembly. Of course the conquered "dasyu" had not so much liberty as his masters, yet even he was left alone for the most part after the division of labor was settled. Only later did the caste system arise to subjugate all shudras. Only later, too, did such customs arise as "sati," which required a widow to be burned on the funeral pyre with her husband. The primeval Aryan never dreamed of subjugating women or setting up a caste system.

Creative in many aspects of culture, the Indo-Aryans were especially creative religiously. Their first product in this area was the poetry of the Vedas.

VIII. VEDIC RELIGION

THE WORD "veda" (rhymes with "made a") is from the same root as our word "wit" and the German word "wissen," to know. In Hinduism the Vedas are believed to contain the divine wisdom necessary for man's salvation. Nothing is quite so sacred in Hindu tradition as the four Vedas, especially the Rig Veda.

The term "Veda" is used in two different senses. The most common usage denotes the collections of sacred hymns which are regarded by Hindus as the source of all religious inspiration. Later literature, inspired by them, includes the Brāhmanas, the Upanishads, and other writings. But according to the other usage the Vedas *include* the Brāhmanas and the Upanishads, as well as the Mantras or hymns themselves. This is the sense in which Radhakrishnan uses the term in his classic discussion of Indian philosophy.[1] According to his analysis, what is usually referred to as the Vedas should really be called the Sanhita, meaning the collection of hymns or mantras. We shall try so far as possible to observe the technical usage of the term in this book.

There are four principal Vedas: Rig Veda, Sama Veda, Yajur Veda, and Atharva Veda. Of these the Rig Veda is the most ancient and most important. It is composed of more than a thousand hymns addressed to seventy-six different deities. It is divided into ten books. Its hymns are phrased in the most archaic Sanskrit and were recited at prehistoric Indo-Aryan sacrifices. The Sama Veda is primarily an arrangement of Rig Vedic hymns, with some others, for use in the Soma sacrifice. The prayers and formulas of the Yajur Veda served ritualistic purposes also, and largely repeat the Rig Veda. The Atharva Veda is later and independent in its composition. It "contains mostly spells, incantations, and medical recipes, and is really a very ancient book on magic."[2] Because of the primitiveness of its magical ideas many writers argue that the Atharva Veda really represents earlier Hindu experiences than the other Vedas, although the collection is admittedly later.

The Vedic hymns are believed by the pious Hindus to have been literally inspired. More than that, they are believed to have been in existence eternally. This does not necessarily mean that they existed in written form from eternity, but that they are eternal as truth is eternal. In fact it is well known that for many centuries there was systematic objection to the writing of the Vedas, on the theory that to do so would subject them to critical contact with the unworthy and the profane. The Vedas were handed down by word of mouth from teacher ("guru") to pupil. The student learned not only the sacred words themselves, but even their intonation. Everything about them was believed to be too sacred to be changed. When the pupil had learned his lessons perfectly and had demonstrated his ability to repeat the sacred words, with the proper intonations and the correct explanations, then he was ready to be commissioned as a rishi himself.

It is not a matter of too great doubt, therefore, to believe that the Vedic hymns did exist, in virtually their present form, for some centuries before they were reduced to writing. How many centuries this went on is a matter for conjecture. On this point Radhakrishnan writes, "Some Indian scholars assign the Vedic hymns to 3000 B.C., others to 6000 B.C. The late Mr. Tilak dates the hymns about 4500 B.C., the Brahmanas 2500 B.C., the early Upanishads 1600 B.C. Jacobi puts the hymns at 4500 B.C. We assign them to the fifteenth century B.C. and trust that our date will not be challenged as being too early."[3] His supporting reasoning for this date seems sound. Buddhism arose in the sixth century out of a background of Vedantism. That is, it presupposed the Hymns, the Brahmanas, and the Upanishads. But it must have taken at least a thousand years for this literature to grow and become established. So the fifteenth century can scarcely be considered too early a date for the Vedic hymns to have come into oral existence. Sen conjectures that the Vedic literature may have been composed over a period of two thousand years.[4] The Rig Veda in its present form was probably reduced to writing by about the eighth century B.C. As a book, therefore, this would make it about as old as the Book of Amos in the Old Testament, though not as old as the Egyptian *Book of the Dead* or the Sumerian epic.

That the Vedic hymns are not dead literature in a modern age is evident when we realize with what reverence they are still regarded. No Christian fundamentalist is more insistent on the sacredness of each holy word than the orthodox Hindu is with regard to the authority of the Vedic scriptures. An orthodox Hindu to this day governs his life's activities according to the Vedas, at least as interpreted by some school of thought. He may dispense with the images which are such a common element of popular Hinduism, realizing that images are a later accretion, not belonging to Vedic religion at all. But daily prayers are still taken from the Vedic poems, and Hindu social relations are strictly regulated by reference to what the Vedas say.

A Religion of Nature

The religion of the Rig Veda is properly characterized as a nature religion. The earliest Indo-Aryans built no temples and carved no images until some one thought of the magical device of carrying an image of Indra into battle. The primitive Vedic poets wrote hymns to the souls of the natural objects which they loved. They communed with the living presences in nature. They called the objects of nature "devas," literally "shining ones." We use this root in our words deity and divine. Strangely enough, we also use it in our word devil, following the influence of Zoroastrianism, which we shall explain later. But for the Vedic seer the "sun, the moon, and the sky are devas because they give light to all creation. Father and Mother and spiritual guides are also devas. Even a guest is a deva. We have to take into account only that notion of deva which answers at least roughly to the modern conception of God. It then means bright."[5] Even the ancestors of the Hindus are classed with the divine in two of the hymns (X.15 and X.54).

For the most part, however, the Vedic hymns are found to be invoking the objects of nature as gods who may help man to be successful and good. One of the earliest of such shining ones was Dyaus Pitar, whose very name is based on the root of deva: "div," to shine.[6] Dyaus refers to the whole sky which includes the sun, moon, stars, clouds, and the dawn. In this inclusive sense therefore Dyaus suggests the unity of god, and may have been one of the factors which led to the Hindu doctrine of monism. Furthermore Dyaus Pitar was the father of men—literally—and Prithivi Matar was their mother and likewise brightly divine. In the Rig Veda heaven and earth together were conceived to be the parents of both men and gods. The heavenly bodies no less than the fire, the wind, and the rain were their children.

It is to be observed that the Vedic gods had overlapping functions. It may be somewhat puzzling to hear first that Dyaus was the divine sky, and then to be told that Varuna was god of the wide expanse of sky and ocean. That Varuna was an ancient Aryan god is seen when we compare his name and function with that of the Greek Uranus and the Persian Ahura Mazda. Somehow Varuna came to have a strongly moral quality, as the ancient Hindus besought him to forgive and to lead in the spirit of sympathy.

> Our sin that sinless Varuna discovered, the Wondrous-
> Wise hath long ago forgiven. R.V. vii.28.4.
>
> According to his wisdom Varuna knoweth all: may he,
> the Holy, hallow times for sacrifice. R.V. x.11.1.
>
> O Varuna, a hundred balms are thine, a thousand; deep
> and wide-reaching also be thy favors.
> Far from us, far away drive thou Destruction. Put
> from us e'en the sin we have committed. R.V. i.24.9[7]

Breathing a spirit perhaps somewhat less of fear but equally of moral and spiritual devotion is the following, poetically rendered. Its first lines also reflect more of the primitive Aryan's wonder at nature's magical perfection.

> None, verily, hath ever let or hindered this the
> most wise god's mighty deed of magic,
> Whereby with all their flood, the lucid rivers
> fill not one sea wherein they pour their waters.
>
> If we have sinned against the man who loves us, have
> ever wronged a brother, friend, or comrade,
> The neighbor ever with us, or a stranger, O Varuna,
> remove from us the trespass.

If we, as gamesters cheat at play, have cheated, done
wrong unwittingly or sinned of purpose,
Cast all these sins away like loosened fetters, and,
Varuna, let us be thine own beloved.[8]

The origin of the concept of Varuna as a moral overseer relates to his function as custodian of the law. This law, or "rita," means literally "the course of things," and refers originally to the orderliness of nature. Rita originally meant the "established route of the world, of the sun, moon, and stars, morning and evening, day and night."[9] From this function Varuna progressed to become the keeper of the moral law, the preserver of the ways of justice.

But other gods besides Varuna were invoked to keep men good. Mitra (Persian Mithra, whom we have already met in a mystery religion) is closely associated with Varuna: often the two are invoked together. Mitra is identified with the sun or the sunlight. Like Varuna, he too upholds the law and forgives sin. In the course of time Mitra becomes identified with the morning light and Varuna with the brilliance of the sky at night.

Other sun-gods (or names of the sun-god) are Surya, Pusan, Vivashvat, Savitri (or Savitar), and Vishnu. About ten hymns are addressed to Surya, who rises daily to survey man's condition, to protect the traveler and the needy, and to watch man's deeds of good and ill.[10] He comes to be the world's creator and governor.[11]

In the Rig Veda Vishnu occupies a relatively subordinate position. But there is enough there to substantiate the fond imaginings of later Vaishnavism. He is represented as "the god of three strides. He covers the earth, heaven, and the highest worlds visible to mortals. . . . In the Rig Veda . . . Vishnu is described as . . . having the world for his body. . . ."[12]

Indra and Agni

More popular than any of the above gods, however, was Indra, god of the rain and the storms. Two hundred and fifty hymns of the Rig Veda sing his praises. He is represented as ruler of the heavens and king of the gods. No wonder, for he wielded the thunder and the lightning. Since the invading Aryans found that they were utterly dependent upon the fortunes of rain, they virtually made the rain-god their national god. In time Indra displaced Varuna in the imagination and affection of the Hindus. Rig Veda ii.12 relates these stirring thoughts about Indra:

> He who, just born, chief God of lofty spirit by power
> and might became the God's protector,
> Before whose breath through greatness of his valour the
> two worlds trembled, He, O men, is Indra.
>
> He who fixed fast and firm the earth that staggered,
> and set at rest the agitated mountains,
> Who measured out the air's wide middle region and
> gave the heaven support, He, O men, is Indra. . . .
>
> Of whom, the Terrible, they ask, Where is He? or
> verily they say of him, He is not.
> He sweeps away, like birds, the foe's possessions.
> Have faith in him, for He, O men, is Indra.[13]

Thus Indra became the god of battles, the divine spirit, who sees all and whose very thought inspires men to become their best. Besides wresting the divine leadership away from Varuna he is even represented as overcoming Krishna, of whom we shall hear more shortly.

Very seldom mentioned is the god Rudra. He too hurls the thunder and sends the lightning. But he could not compete with Indra. Later he became identified with Shiva, changing his whole personality in the transition.

Close to Indra in popularity was Agni, god of fire (Latin "ignis," as in ignition). Two hundred or more hymns are addressed to him. These images of fire's various sources are found in the hymns: the burning sun, the lightning, flint on flint, and fire sticks.

> Agni, accept this flaming brand, this waiting
> with my prayer on thee.
> Between both races, Agni, Sage, well skilled thou
> passest to and fro
> As envoy friendly to mankind. R.V. ii.6.

As the fire of earth and the fire of heaven Agni comes to occupy an important place, drawing men and gods together. His most sacred appearance was in the fire of the Vedic sacrifice. The place which he held in the hearts of the faithful may be gleaned from the following:

> Worthy is Agni to be praised . . .
> He shall bring forward the Gods.
> Through Agni man obtaineth wealth . . .
> Agni, the perfect sacrifice which thou encompassest about
> Verily goeth to the Gods . . .
> To thee, dispeller of the night, O Agni, day by day with
> prayer
> Bringing thee reverence, we come
> Ruler of sacrifices, guard of Law eternal, radiant One,
> Increasing in thine own abode.
> Be to us easy of approach, even as a father to his son.[14]

A strange deity is the Soma, already mentioned as an intoxicating liquor. He is the same as Haoma of the Persian Avesta, and like Dionysus of the Greeks. The ancient Aryans had no scruples about intoxicants. On the contrary, to the primitive man the state of intoxication seemed like being possessed by the deity. His exhilaration and extraordinary powers were a proof that he was moved by divine inspiration. Therefore the Soma was deified by the Indo-Aryans. Soma is incompletely personalized. Plant and juice are so real to the poet's imagination that he does not easily deify them. The hymns to Soma were intended to be recited while the juice was being pressed from the plant. . . . "In viii. 48.3 the worshiper exclaims: 'We have drunk the Soma, we have become immortal, we have entered into light, we have known the gods.' "[15]

The very natural and human character of the Vedic religion is easily perceived in the hymns to Soma. The following beautiful hymn illustrates further this fact.

> Where there is eternal light, in the world, where the sun is
> placed, in that immortal, imperishable world, place me,
> O Soma.
> Where the son of Vivasvat reigns as King, where the secret
> place of heaven is, where these mighty waters are,
> make me immortal.
> Where life is free, in the third heaven of heavens, where
> the worlds are radiant, there make me immortal.
> Where wishes and desires are, where the bowl of the bright
> Soma is, where there is food and rejoicing, there make
> me immortal.

Where there is happiness and delight, where joy and pleasure
reside, where the desires of our desire are attained,
there make me immortal.[16]

Another Vedic deity was Yama. According to the myth he was the first human being to die and reach the other world. By virtue of that fact he became the king of the dead.

Still other noteworthy Vedic deities were, Prajapati, lord of all creatures; Hiranyagarbha, the golden god of all that exists; Brihaspati, supreme lord; and Vishvakarman. The latter is pictured as an all-seeing god, with eyes, faces, arms, and feet on all sides, whose movements produce all things and whose being is beyond mortal comprehension.

Vedic Monotheism

It may seem that with some seventy deities mentioned in the Rig Veda there is nothing but polytheism there. But the logic of the several hymns led to monotheism. For from time to time first one and then another of the deities was described as all-powerful, as lord of all, creator, guide, law-giver, moral guide, and friend of man. But not all gods could be thus supreme at the same time. Therefore poets became philosophers and foresaw the development of later monotheism. At times it was seen in Varuna. "Varuna is the heaven, Varuna the earth, Varuna the air, Varuna is the universe and all besides." At other times Agni was held to be all the gods. In the later Vedic religion it was Prajapati or Vishvakarman or one of the other deities. But some form of monotheism is forcast from early times.

So monistic is the Hymn of Creation that we must surmise it to be one of the latest compositions included in the Rig Veda:

Then was not non-existent nor existent: there was no
realm of air, no sky beyond it.
What covered in, and where? and what gave shelter?
Was water there, unfathomed depth of water?
Death was not then, nor was there aught immortal:
no sign was there, the day's and night's divider.
That One Thing, breathless, breathed by its own nature:
apart from it was nothing whatsoever.

Darkness was there: at first concealed in darkness this
All was indiscriminated chaos.
All that existed then was void and formless: by the
great power of Warmth was born that Unit.[17]

The typical Vedic god is half way between the precisely conceived personality of the Greek gods and the monistic concept of the Hindu Upanishads. In the Vedic hymns we find that the gods are sometimes personalities ruling nature's phases, while at other times they are the essence of nature's powers. This is in contrast with the Homeric society of gods, as also with the gods in the Puranas and other late Indian tales. In the Vedic hymns the gods merge into one another, with no clear distinction. In the later tales their personalities are unique, like their epic deeds.

The early concept of Agni pictures the god, as fire, housed in the sticks of wood until he leaps forth in brilliant flame, devouring the suppliant's sacrifice.

His flames that wax not old, beams fair to look upon
of him whose face is lovely, shine with beauteous sheen.
The rays of Agni, him whose active force is light, through
the nights glimmer sleepless, ageless, like the floods.
R.V. i.143.3.

Treating Vata, the wind, in the same manner, the suppliant reverently would say:

Travelling on the paths of air's mid-region . . . where
did he spring from?
Germ of the world, the Deities' vital spirit, this God
moves ever as his will inclines him.
His voice is heard, his shape is ever viewless. Let us
adore this Wind with our oblation.
R.V. x.168.3-4.[18]

When we turn from the Rig Veda to the Atharva Veda we seem to find ourselves in a new world. In it one feels that the hymns of the Rig Veda have been jumbled, its deities mistaken for each other or combined in a pantheon with many new gods. Hell is now met with as a place of torture. And Brahmaloka is first mentioned as the Heaven of pleasure for the blest. Charms and evil incantations are multiplied. It is true that in the Rig Veda are found incantations, spells, charms, witchcraft, and hymns to inanimate things and demons; yet these seem out of place there. In the Atharva Veda they are its sum and substance. This has been explained by the failure of the Indo-Aryan to absorb a conquered people without compromising with its religion and culture. The Rig Veda reveals a background of conflict between Aryan and Dravidian. The Atharva Veda, on the other hand, suggests a later period of peace and harmony between Aryan and native. "The spirit of accommodation naturally elevated the religion of the primitive tribes but degraded the Vedic religion by introducing into it sorcery and witchcraft."[19]

There is, of course, much that is life-affirming in the Atharva Veda. In it we read a love charm, an appeal to a magical plant to heal a broken bone, a charm to destroy hostile priests, a charm against witchcraft, a charm to grow hair, another to bless a child's first teeth, one against fear, another against sterility, and one to bless barley. But even in its life-affirming character the Atharva Veda is magical in its philosophy. In contrast with the Rig Veda, therefore, it obviously reflects the lower culture of native India as the Aryans compromised with it and absorbed it. Whitney writes:

> In the Rig Veda the gods are approached with reverential awe, indeed, but with love and confidence also. . . . the divinities of the Atharva are regarded rather with a kind of cringing fear. . . . it knows a whole host of imps and hobgoblins. . . . The most prominent feature of the Atharva is the multitude of incantations which it contains.[20]

A few of the Atharva hymns are speculative and mystical. Most of them, however, are priestly, popular, magical, and superstitious, in contrast with the sophistication of the Upanishads.

Although the gods of the Rig Veda were both male and female, the male gods were more prominent. In the Atharva Veda the opposite is the case. This helps to explain why in the Tantric philosophies sex becomes so important. The worship of the cow is one case of female divinity.

> The Atharva Veda, the result of so much compromise, seemed to have had a good deal of trouble in obtaining recognition as a Veda. It was regarded with contempt, since its central feature was sorcery. It contributed to the growth of a pessimistic outlook in India. Men cannot believe in a devil and the tempter and yet retain joy in life. To see demons close at hand is to shudder at life.[21]

In retrospect, therefore, we shall think of the Rig Veda as the main Veda and as the noblest contribution of the Aryan Hindus to religious experience. We must recognize in it a kindred spirit to the poetry of Homer, representing as it does the parallel religious growth of another group of Aryans. And just as the Homeric mythology was transformed by great dramatists and philosophers who contributed in turn to the development of Christian thought, so the Aryan Vedic mythology was transformed by the Brahmins and other philosophers who contributed to the development of Upanishadic mysticism, which we shall now take up.

Evaluation

Formal evaluation of Vedic religion will be deferred until the end of Chapter X.

IX. POETS, PRIESTS, AND PHILOSOPHERS

THERE IS SOMETHING about poetry that resists analysis. Many of the beautiful things spoken by the poets would be meaningless if interpreted literally. Yet understood imaginatively they may prove to be the truest of all true sayings. Perhaps the poet himself would be puzzled and skeptical if confronted by a literal prosaic statement of what he has already said poetically. I am sure that this would have been true of the Vedic poets who wrote with reverent feeling about the divine qualities of nature. The parts and processes of nature were so closely akin to themselves that they spoke of them as though they were personal or nearly personal.

The earliest Indo-Aryans must have been happy to be able to use the fresh-spoken words of their poets as they offered sacrifices to the powers of nature. Without thinking too seriously or too literally about the ultimate truth of those poems, they entered into the spirit of them. No compulsion other than their own inner feelings motivated their worship. No slavish following of tradition, no literalistic interpretation of scriptures whose origin was long forgotten, compelled their reverence. They loved nature, and loved the poems which gave expression to that love. Not that there were no superstitions. But their superstitions were born of the ignorance of the childhood of the race, and may have harmed them no more than the superstitions of our own young children.

But all too soon in Indian experience that situation was to change. Just as the life of the maturing individual becomes complicated, so the simple life of the Indo-Aryans became complicated by the division of labor and the rise of the caste system. The evidence that caste did not exist in early Aryan times is reflected by the fact that there is only one mention in the Rig Veda of the four groups who later composed the four main castes of India. These groups were the Brahmins, or priests; the Kshatriyas, or warriors and rulers; the Vaishyas, or general Aryan population of farmers and merchants; and the Shudras, or non-Aryan servant class. Then as life grew complex and the division of labor was reinforced by the desire to keep the Dravidians in their place, these four groups became four castes. Rulers and warriors became a professional caste, priests another, and the common Aryans a third, with the Dravidian Shudras at the bottom.

At first there was no thought of distinguishing between the three upper or "twice-born" castes in social value. But in the course of time the priests, or Brahmins, secured for themselves the position of supreme authority, leaving the rulers and warriors to occupy a close second place, with the common Aryans below them both. Thus, two thousand years before their time, what was to be the fondest dream of a Gregory VII or Boniface VIII—the church lording it over the state—was realized in an Indian setting.

It has been held that caste was merely a logical development of a social situation in India. This is partly true, for two reasons. First, there was the social need for a division of labor, as noted above. And second, something had to be done about the Dravidians. They were, like the Canaanites, too numerous to exterminate or to push into the forests. Somehow, therefore, they had to be incorporated into Hindu society. As a matter of fact, some did flee into the forest rather than submit to servitude to the Aryans. When they filtered back into the later encrusted Indian society they became the outcastes, still lower than the Shudras. But the bolder Dravidians either held their ground in northwest India where they were partially absorbed by the Aryans and partially made servants, or they retreated into the Deccan which the Aryans later penetrated more peacefully, accepting the natives again as Shudras.

One large difference between the Shudras and the other castes was that the former were regarded as "once-born," while the latter were said to have been "twice-born." The second birth, or birth of the spirit, was believed to occur when the members of the three upper castes were initiated into the mysteries of the higher Aryan wisdom. At that time they received the sacred thread which they wore forever afterward as a symbol of their spiritual birth.

It hardly behooves western society, which tolerated slavery for many centuries and still tolerates brutal warfare, to be too critical of Hindu society for its caste system. Nevertheless it is a fact that the caste system, arising during the period of the Brahmanas, was encouraged by the Brahmanic appeal to the racial pride of the Aryans. Thus a religious sanction was given to a rising social institution, causing it to become rigid. One must wonder what might have happened if prophets in India had taken a stand such as the prophets of Israel took when the priests were corrupting religion.

Rise of Sacerdotalism

Sacerdotalism is perceivable even in the Yajur Veda, for there the life has passed out of the spontaneous hymns, which are arranged for ritualistic purposes. As Radhakrishnan puts it, "The religion of the Yajur Veda is a mechanical sacerdotalism. A crowd of priests conducts a vast and complicated system of external ceremonies to which symbolical significance is attached and to the smallest minutiae of which the greatest weight is given. The truly religious spirit could not survive in the stifling atmosphere of ritual and sacrifice. The religious feeling of the adoration of the ideal and the consciousness of guilt is lacking. Every prayer is coupled with a particular rite and aims at securing some material advantage."[1]

This situation is still more evident when we turn to the Brahmanas. By this time the authority of the Vedas had been fully established as divine revelation. Seers were no longer needed nor expected; priests interpreted the sacred texts and performed the traditional rites. So religion became authoritative, uncreative, imitative, scholastic, and prosaic. The religion of the Brahmanas was Pharisaic, legalistic, formalistic, magical in its assumptions, and uninspiring. The nearest thing to the Brahmanas in the Hebrew-Christian tradition is the book of Leviticus, written by post-exilic priests and detailing the minutiae of the ritual requirements in worship and sacrifice.

The power of the Brahmins was strengthened by the fact that the religious ritual had become so complicated that only professional priests could successfully conduct it. Even the priests had to have textbooks. The Brahmanas became those textbooks, which every Brahmin learned by heart, as he also learned the Vedas. And since the priest gained a monopoly over religious ceremonies such as prayers and sacrifices, he made proud use of his monopoly. The Brahmins as an hereditary caste used their authority as priests to gain for themselves the pinnacle of castely authority. Then they insisted that prayers and sacrifices were necessary to the smooth operation of human affairs and even of nature itself. In one passage it was asserted that the individual's salvation depended on paying fees to the priest. In another the claim was made that the sun would not rise without the performance of the appropriate sacrifice. So the Brahmins set forth the claim that they controlled Brahman, the creative principle of the universe. This was turning religion back into magic. By magic the Brahmins would make themselves supreme among men, immortal, and superior even among the gods. Says the Shatapatha Brahmana, "Verily there are two kinds of gods; for, indeed, the gods themselves are gods, and the Brahmins who have studied and teach the sacred lore are the human gods."[2]

One wonders why, in view of all this, there was no popular rebellion by the rank and file of Hindus against the authority of the Brahmins. Radhakrishnan replies to this by saying that the priests really did not tyrannize over the people, but only insisted on the fulfilment of social obligations.[3] Perhaps the real reason why the people submitted is that there was no alternative to the traditional Aryan way, as interpreted by a growing priestly caste. They had to take it or leave it, and they were afraid to leave it.

It should not be thought, however, that the Brahmanas are worthless. Hidden among the dry reeds are gems of spiritual insight, as when the Shatapatha Brahmana insists that all sacrifice is a means to spiritual freedom.[4] Godliness, man's prime duty, is said to consist in trying to be good, truthful, and faithful to the divine ideals. Adultery is declared to be sinful, especially displeasing to Varuna. And confession is held to reduce one's guilt.

Individual immortality was still the accepted theological doctrine in the age of the Brahmanas. The ideas of karma and of the transmigration of souls appeared in the Brahmanas, but their emergence there merely indicates that the influence of the aborigines was beginning to be felt in Hindu thought. For these ideas did not come from the Vedic hymns, and they were not prominent in the Brahmanas.

Among the cosmological ideas which appear in the Brahmanas is the story of the flood. This parallels the story found among so many peoples over the whole earth, such as the Babylonians, the Hebrews, the Egyptians, and American Indian tribes. The Shatapatha Brahmana tells of Manu's miraculous escape from the flood. It is related that a fish warned Manu of the approaching flood and instructed him to build a ship. He did so and embarked when the floods came. The fish then came and guided the ship to a mountain top where it was fastened to a tree. After the flood Manu piloted the ship down the mountain as the flood subsided. Producing a woman through the magic of sacrifice, he and she together became the progenitors of a new human race.[5]

Rise of Speculative Religion

Transitional between the Brahmanas and the Upanishads are the Aranyakas, or forest-treatises. Dasgupta refers to them as "a further development of the Brahmanas." Nikhilananda also describes the Upanishads as "mostly the concluding portions of the Aranyakas," which illustrates how closely associated are the sacred writings of the Hindus in their development.[6] Dasgupta goes on to say, "These works were probably composed for old men who had retired into the forest and were thus unable to perform elaborate sacrifices requiring a multitude of accessories and articles which could not be procured in forests." The reference here is to the ancient division of the individual Hindu's life into four stages. The first stage is that of the celibate student, under the guidance of a guru, or teacher. The second stage is that of the householder, with husband and wife following the religious ritual of ancient tradition. In the third stage, when the hair was greying and the face wrinkling, the householder and his wife both became forest-dwellers. In the fourth stage one renounced the world and became a sannyasin, a monk devoted to the contemplation of Brahman.[7] In the last two stages recognition was given to meditation as a suitable substitute for sacrifice. In fact, certain types of meditation gradually came to be recognized as having more merit than sacrifice.

In the first chapter of the Brihadaranyaka Upanishad, paralleling a passage from the Shatapatha Brahmana, the forest-dweller is instructed how to substitute meditation for the very elaborate horse-sacrifice. "Om! Verily, the dawn is the head of the sacrificial horse; the sun, his eye; the wind, his breath; universal fire, his open mouth. . . ."[8] Considering the fact that the horse sacrifice took a whole year, many priests, and 609 animals to complete it, the forest-dweller was the gainer in time, trouble, expense, and above all, spirituality. Actually, the horse sacrifice was required only of a king who had conquered other kings.[9] It was one way of bankrupting the royal treasury. So when the lowly forest dweller was encouraged to gain the benefits of the horse sacrifice by simple, solitary meditation, certainly that was a gain in democracy as well as spirituality.

In point of time, therefore, the speculative period of Indian philosophy followed the era of the Brahmanas. The speculative period is usually referred to as the age of the Upanishads.

Who were the authors of the Upanishads? This is a difficult question. Authorship is sometimes referred to some deity, such as Indra, or to an ancient hero. Very little is really known about specific authorship. But there is a controversy over whether the Upanishads were written by Brahmins or by Kshatriyas. Dasgupta reviews the controversy and concludes that they were primarily the work of Brahmins, but he admits that there was considerable influence from Kshatriyas and even from women.[10] Radhakrishnan, without reviewing the controversy, comes to the conclusion that there was a considerable amount of influence from the warrior caste in the composition of the Upanishads. Most significant is the story cited from the Chandogya Upanishad which teaches that "Brahminhood does not depend on birth, but on character." It is worth quoting:

> Once upon a time Satyakama Jabala addressed his mother Jabala: "Madam! I desire to live the life of a student of sacred knowledge. Of what family, pray, am I?"
>
> Then she said to him: "I do not know this, my dear—of what family you are. In my youth, when I went about a great deal serving as a maid, I got you. So I do not know of what family you are. However, I am Jabala by name; you are Satyakama by name. So you may speak of yourself as Satyakama Jabala."
>
> Then he went to Haridrumata Gautama, and said: "I will live the life of a student of sacred knowledge. I will become a pupil of yours, sir."

To him he then said: "Of what family, pray, are you, my dear?"

Then he said, "I do not know this sir, of what family I am. I asked my mother. She answered me: 'In my youth, when I went about a great deal serving as a maid, I got you. So I do not know this, of what family you are. However, I am Jabala by name; you are Satyakama by name.' So I am Satyakama Jabala, sir."

To him he then said: "A non-Brahmin would not be able to explain thus. Bring the fuel, my dear. I will receive you as a pupil. You have not deviated from the truth."[11]

If this story was written by a Brahmin, it was certainly a different type of Brahmin from the ones met with in the Brahmanas, which of course is entirely conceivable. But it is evident, from this story and other references like it, and from the spontaneity and freedom of the Upanishads in contrast with the legalism and ritualism of the Brahmanas, that non-Brahmins at least influenced the writing of the Upanishads. Radhakrishnan further points out that in one Upanishad a Kshatriya, Sanatkumāra, teaches the Brahmin Nārada about Brahman. Elsewhere in the Upanishads others besides Brahmins discussed philosophy and religion. Kings called religious gatherings and taught gurus important matters. Many were interested in philosophical discussion. "The Brahmin editors of the Upanishads had so sincere a regard for truth that they were ready to admit that Kshatriyas took an important part in these investigations. Women, though they were much sheltered so far as the struggle for life was concerned, had equal rights with men in the spiritual struggle for salvation."[12]

No definite dates can be assigned to the period of the Upanishads, or to the other literary periods before or after. The important point is that the age of the Vedic hymns was followed by that of the Brahmanas which in turn was followed by the period of the Upanishads. But these eras overlapped. Not all the hymns were composed before the first Brahmanas were written. Nor were all the Brahmanas completed before any of the Upanishads were created. In fact some of the earliest Upanishads may have antedated the latest of the Vedic hymns. Dasgupta assigns the earliest Upanishads to the seventh century B.C. Radhakrishnan, on the other hand, says, "The accepted dates for the early Upanishads are 1000 B.C. to 300 B.C."[13]

General Character of the Upanishads

In distinction from the Vedic hymns, the Upanishads are concerned solely with the knowledge of truth and reality, while the hymns are the free expression of the poetic imagination reflecting the religious ideas and experiences of early Indo-Aryans. The conclusions to which the Upanishads come are far removed from the poetic concepts of the early hymns. Yet in the Hindu tradition the Upanishads are regarded not as contradicting the hymns but as constituting their fulfilment. For that reason they often refer to the Upanishads as the Vedanta, meaning "the end of the Vedas."

Not only is there considerable distance between the meaning of the hymns and the philosophy of the Upanishads, but also there is divergence between the doctrines of the various Upanishads. An orthodox Hindu, of course, would not admit either of these statements to be true. Whatever he does accept as true and right in faith and practice, he tries to think of as well founded in both the Vedas and the Upanishads. But it is a common experience for any devotee to read his own beliefs, however gained, back into his scriptures. We Christians have a saying that even the devil can quote scripture, and that almost anything can be proved by citing scriptural texts. It is, of course, much easier for Christians to find inconsistencies and contradictions in Hindu scriptures than in our own; the opposite of course is just as true for the Hindu.

Our purpose is not to expose the inconsistencies or contradictions of the Upanishads, but rather to reveal their value. It is easy to discover superficial incongruities. But if we look more deeply we shall find that the Upanishads have a message for the occident which might be of great value in an age of scientific materialism. We shall find that the Upanishads deal with speculative philosophy, but not in the same spirit as Plato and Aristotle. In the Upanishads it seems that speculation is built upon some of the persistent and fundamental intuitions of mankind. Of course Plato and Aristotle found room for intuition, but most prominent in their works, as in those of many western philosophers, is rational logic. What western philosophers have tried to rationalize are such concepts as the good, the true, the beautiful, the nature of the state, the nature of man, duty, and the problem of evil. The dominant motive throughout western philosophy has been humanistic. With the Upanishadic authors the motive was religious. They were searching for the truth about God, and about man and the universe in relation to God. More or less incidentally they also discussed human psychology and the principles of logic and a great variety of other things.

There are many Upanishads. Radhakrishnan puts the total number at one hundred and eight, while Dasgupta lists one hundred and twelve but later says that there are one hundred and eight. There are only a few really ancient ones. R. E. Hume conveys to western readers "the thirteen principal Upanishads." Nikhilananda is in process of translating eleven Upanishads in four volumes,[14] including notes from the commentaries of Shankara. Radhakrishnan reduces the number of really great, that is, original prose Upanishads to eight.[15] They are the Chandogya, the Brihadaranyaka, the Taittiriya, the Aitareya, the Kaushitaki, the Kena, the Isha, and the Mandukya. Parts of some of these represent later additions. Nikhilananda includes all these except the Kaushitaki, and adds the Shvetashvatara, the Prashna, the Katha, and the Mundaka. Of these the Katha and the Mundaka are the most popular. Hume includes the Maitri Upanishad in addition to all of those mentioned above. In his recent translation Radhakrishnan includes all of the above, and adds the Subāla, Jābāla, Paingala, Kawalya, and Vajrasūcikā Upanishads—eighteen in all.[16]

Speculative Prophets

If Indian freedom showed a decline in the Brahmanas, it experienced a renaissance in the Upanishads. Compared with the traditionalist Brahmanas the Upanishads were creatively non-conformist and boldly speculative. At the same time they were sincerely religious. Like the prophets of Israel, the writers of the Upanishads were intuitively certain that they possessed new wisdom fresh from God which superseded earlier revelation and contradicted the ritualism of the priests. Unlike the prophets of Israel, however, they were speculative in their approach to the knowledge of God and the way of life.

In a real sense, therefore, the authors of the Upanishads had arrived at the position of freedom of thought and independence of tradition. This was a most important development in human affairs, comparable with the philosophy of Descartes more than two thousand years later. These Hindu philosophers antedated Plato and Aristotle and, in some cases, even Thales and Xenophanes.

The Upanishads carried out the suggestion of the Aranyakas that meditation was better than sacrifice. They regarded life itself as the truest sacrifice, which should be consecrated through meditation. In one Upanishad we read: "Verily, a person is a sacrifice. His [first] twenty-four years are the morning libation. . . . When one hungers and thirsts and abstains from pleasures these constitute the initiatory rites. And when one eats and drinks and enjoys pleasures, then he joins in the Upasada ceremonies. And when one laughs and eats and indulges in sexual intercourse, then he joins in the chant and recitation. And austerity, almsgiving, uprightness, non-violence, truthfulness, these are the gifts for the priests. . . . Death is the final bath [after the ceremony]."[17]

While the Upanishads did not deny the sacredness of the Vedic hymns, yet they were indifferent to their authority. Instead, they proposed a new kind of knowledge that was superior to the revelation of the mantras. The Chandogya Upanishad quotes Narada as saying, "I know the Rig Veda, Sir, the Yajur Veda, the Sama Veda . . . with all this I know the Mantras only [and] the sacred books; I do not know the Self."[18] In the Mundaka Upanishad we read, "Two kinds of knowledge must be known . . . the higher and the lower. The lower knowledge is the Rig, the Yajur, the Sama, the Atharva Veda, Ceremonial, Grammar . . . but the higher knowledge is that by which the indestructible Brahman is apprehended."[19]

We turn now, therefore, to the "higher knowledge" which the Upanishads presume to give.

X. MAIN TEACHINGS OF THE UPANISHADS

WHILE THERE ARE many different points of view in the Upanishads, justifying the various schools of thought which later interpreted them, yet we may say that there is a general trend in the development of Upanishadic teachings. It is this general trend that we propose now to summarize, with the understanding that it must necessarily be incomplete. The various schools of interpretation will be summarized in a later chapter.

(1) The *Doctrine of Brahman* is the very heart and strength of the Upanishads. In the Vedic hymns Brahman meant the "power of prayer," or a "magical spell" such as might be identified with the primitive notion of prayer. In the Brāhmanas the word Brahman denoted the hymns and chants used in the ritual, conceived as a magical power. Then there emerged the speculative notion that the "holy power" or "power of prayer" whereby the priests changed the course of events must be the central principle of the universe, the creative power itself, which the priests had been fortunate enough to make contact with.

The word Brahman is said to come from the root "brih," meaning to swell or grow. Radhakrishnan, reviewing the various meanings assigned to the word, concludes, "To us, it is clear, Brahman means reality, which grows, breathes, or swells."[1] This is the basic notion which the authors of the Upanishads took up and developed.

First of all, the word Brahman is neuter gender. The appropriate pronoun to use in referring to Brahman is it, not he, although some Upanishads use he. The word Brahma is also found in the neuter gender, meaning the same as Brahman; its final *a* is short and the accent, as with Brahman, is on the first syllable. Then there is the very different word Brahmā, with the final *a* long. In this case the accent is on the last syllable, and the gender is masculine. Masculine

Brahmā is conceived as a personal god, the first in the trinity of Brahmā, Vishnu, and Shiva. As such he is the creator of the universe and enters into personal relationship with man. In the Maitrāyanī Upanishad Valakhilyas (Valikhilyas) insists that there is only one god. "But which one? Agni, Vayu, Aditya, Kala, . . . Brahma, Rudra, Vishnu?" The answer is, "These are but the chief manifestations of the highest, the immortal, the incorporeal Brahman. . . . Brahman, indeed, is all this, and a man may meditate on, worship or discard also those which are its manifestations."[2]

In this book we shall not use Brahma as a neuter word equivalent to Brahman, because of its confusion with Brahmā (masculine, with accent on the last syllable).

The other two related words are Brāhmin, meaning a member of the priestly caste, and Brāhmana (accent on the first syllable, since the first *a* is long) meaning a treatise on the conduct of the Vedic ritual.

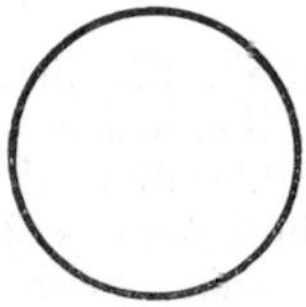

*The circle was regarded by the Greeks as the perfect figure, symmetrical, without beginning or end. It became a universal symbol of deity, the ground of all reality. In Egypt it symbolized the self-sufficiency and unity of God, the preserver. Originally it may have represented the serpent.**

Generally speaking, the Upanishads take up the monistic suggestions found in a few of the Vedic hymns and develop them at great length. The hymns merely dropped the hint that all the gods were really one, whereas the Upanishads make this their central theme. Besides, the Upanishads were not satisfied to accept mere monotheism, which is as far as the latest hymns ever got; the Upanishads went on to a complete monism in which even Brahmā was not ultimately real, because the ultimate reality is not differentiated as to personality or sex. Not Brahmā but Brahman is the object of contemplation and faith in the Upanishads, as suggested in the above passage quoted from the Maitrāyanī Upanishad. Brahman alone really exists. It is all that is real.

It is very likely that the authors of the Upanishads came to these conclusions freely, without attempting to square their doctrines with the Vedic hymns. Yet if I were a Hindu I might argue that the

* See Wheelwright, *The Burning Fountain*, pp. 134, 152.

Upanishads rightly interpreted the essential teaching of the Vedas in this respect. For in the hymns the various deities really represent nature itself in its functions and parts. So when the hymns suggested that all the gods were really Brahmā, did they not mean that nature is really one whole, and that Brahmā is all of nature? And since nature is really not masculine or personal, therefore Brahmā is really Brahman. Toward those whose experience had not prepared them to think abstractly of god as the Absolute Brahman, the Upanishads were tolerant, since meditation on the manifestations of the Absolute might lead one on to the discovery of Brahman Itself. Even the authors of the Upanishads found difficulty in dispensing with the personal pronoun as they referred to Brahman.

The use of the personal pronoun in the following quotation from the Maitrayani Upanishad does not necessarily mean that the author believed Brahman really to be personal. The passage does demonstrate how great was the composer's inspiration as he objectified Brahman in the world of nature:

> Verily, in the beginning this world was Brahma(n), the limitless One—limitless to the east, limitless to the north, . . . limitless in every direction. . . . Incomprehensible is that supreme Soul, unlimited, unborn, not to be reasoned about, unthinkable—He whose soul is space! In the dissolution of the world He alone remains awake. From that space He, assuredly, awakes this world, which is a mass of thought. It is thought by Him, and in Him it disappears. His is that shining form which gives heat in yonder sun and which is the brilliant light in a smokeless fire, as also the fire in the stomach which cooks the food. For thus it has been said: "He who is in the fire, and he who is here in the heart, and he who is yonder in the sun—he is one."[3]

In the Chāndogya Upanishad Brahman is said to be the whole of impersonal reality, the source and goal of all things:

> Verily, this whole world is Brahma(n). Tranquil, let one worship It as that from which he came forth, as that in which he will be dissolved, as that in which he breathes.[4]

Inseparable from Brahman is (2) the *Doctrine of Atman.* Spelled with a small *a,* the atman is the individual self of any human being. Spelled with a capital, Atman is the same as Brahman. Atman is the Brahman regarded subjectively yet impersonally. Just as my identity is the same whether regarded spiritually from within my own personality, or physically by an external observer, so the Atman and the Brahman are identical. "Brahman is the Atman and the Atman is the Brahman. The one supreme power through which all things have been brought into being is one with the inmost self in each man's heart."[5]

In Sanskrit as in most languages the word for self or soul was originally a word meaning breath. This is the meaning of atman in Rig Veda x. 16. 3. But by the time of the Upanishads the self had been rationalized and analyzed to form the basis for the doctrine of Brahman-Atman. In a conversation between Indra, the pupil, and Prajapati, the teacher, in the Chandogya Upanishad[6] a definition of the self is developed. The lowest meaning is the physical or organismic self. Second is the self of sense experience. Third, we may say, is the transcendental self, comparable with Kant's "transcendental unity of apperception." Highest is the absolute self, comparable with Bradley's Absolute Experience. This could be implied in Prajapati's teaching as he points out, "This body is mortal and always held by death. It is the abode of that self which is immortal and without body. . . . There is the person of the eye; the eye itself is the instrument of seeing. He who knows, let me smell this, he is the Self; the nose is the instrument of smelling. . . . He who knows, let me think this, he is the Self; the mind is his divine eye. . . ."[7] Just as the bodily self and the empirical self are shown to be inadequate concepts of the real self, so also the transcendental self is seen to be too abstract and insufficient to represent what we really are. At least Radhakrishnan concludes from his analysis of Prajāpati's discourse that the only adequate concept is the Absolute Self. It is "an active universal consciousness, existing, to adopt Hegel's phraseology, both in itself and for itself. . . . It is both subject and object. [Atman and Brahman?] The objects we know in experience are based on it. The true infinite self . . . is none of the limited things, but yet the basis of all of them. It is the universal self, which is immanent as well as transcendent. The whole universe lives and breathes in it. 'The moon and the sun are its eyes, the four quarters of the sky its ears, the wind its breath.' . . . Our small selves are included in it and transcended by it."[8]

It is really rather startling to an occidental that the Hindu writers should so boldly identify their little selves with the Ātman or Brahman. But that is exactly what they claimed in so many words. "This great, unborn Self (Atman), undecaying, undying, immortal, fearless, is indeed Brahman. Fearless is Brahman, and he who knows this becomes verily the fearless Brahman."[9] In the Chāndogya Upanishad Uddālaka exclaims to his son Shvetaketu, at the climax of each analytical discourse, "That which is that subtile essence, in it all that exists has its self. It is the True. It is the Self (Atman), and thou, O Shvetaketu, art it." He was analyzing, for example, the essence of a tree (its sap), nyagrodha fruit (the contents of a seed), and salt water (pervasive salt).[10]

Another doctrine integrally related to those of Brahman and Atman is (3) the *Doctrine of Pure Consciousness,* in which is epitomized the essence of Indian idealism. Perhaps the best way to convey this doctrine to the reader is to quote verbatim the shortest of all the ancient Upanishads, the Māndukya. This text distinguishes four stages of consciousness: the waking, the dreaming, deep sleep, and "turiya" meaning "the fourth" . . . which includes the other three. This last might be defined as "pure intuitional consciousness which is unaware of the difference between subject and object, and which is necessary to tie together the universe of experience." "Turiya" is a state of "ānanda" or perfect bliss, because it links the individual self with the Absolute Atman.

The Māndukya Upanishad consists of twelve verses. It begins with "Harih Aum!" which is roughly equivalent to our expression, "Gracious Lord!" AUM—sometimes spelled OM, as it is pronounced —is a word having no meaning apart from its primary symbolism, which will be clear on reading the Upanishad:

I

HARIH AUM! AUM, the word, is all this [i.e. the whole universe]. A clear explanation of it is as follows: All that is past, present, and future is, indeed, AUM. And whatever else there is, beyond the three-fold division of time—that also is truly AUM.

II

All this is, indeed, Brahman. This Atman is Brahman. This same Atman has four quarters.

III

The first quarter is called Vaisvānara, [pronounced Vaishvānara] whose sphere of activity is the waking state, who is conscious of external objects, who has seven limbs and nineteen mouths, and who is the experiencer of gross objects.

IV

The second quarter is Taijasa, whose sphere of activity is the dream state, who is conscious of internal objects, who is endowed with seven limbs and nineteen mouths, and who is the experiencer of subtle objects.

V

That is the state of deep sleep wherein one asleep neither desires any object nor sees any dream. The third quarter is Prājna, [prononuced Prajnya] whose sphere is deep sleep, in whom all experiences become unified, who is, verily, a mass of consciousness, who is full of bliss and experiences bliss, and who is the door leading to the knowledge [of dreaming and waking].

VI

He is the Lord of all. He is the knower of all. He is the inner controller. He is the source of all; for from him all beings originate and in him they finally disappear.

VII

Turiya is not that which is conscious of the inner (subjective) world, nor that which is conscious of the outer (objective) world, nor that which is conscious of both, nor that which is a mass of consciousness. It is not simple consciousness nor is It unconciousness. It is unperceived, unrelated, incomprehensible, uninferable, unthinkable, and indescribable. The essence of the Consciousness manifesting as the self [in the three states], It is the cessation of all phenomena; It is all peace, all bliss, and non-dual. This is what is known as the fourth (Turiya). This is Atman, and this has to be realized.

VIII

The same Atman [explained before as being endowed with four quarters] is now described from the standpoint of the syllable AUM. AUM, too, divided into parts, is viewed from the standpoint of letters. The quarters [of Atman] are the same as the letters of AUM, and the letters are the same as the quarters. The letters are A, U, and M.

IX

Vaisvānara Atman, whose sphere of activity is the waking state, is A, the first letter [of AUM], on account of his all-pervasiveness or on account of his being the first. He who knows this obtains all desires and becomes first [among the great].

X

Taijasa Atman, whose sphere of activity is the dream state, is U, the second letter [of AUM], on account of his superiority or intermediateness. He who knows this attains a superior knowledge, receives equal treatment from all, and finds in his family no one ignorant of Brahman.

XI

Prājna Atman, whose sphere is deep sleep, is M, the third letter [of AUM], because both are the measure and also because in them all become one. He who knows this is able to measure all and also comprehends all within himself.

XII

The fourth (Turiya) is without parts and without relationship; It is the cessation of phenomena; It is all good and non-dual. This AUM is verily Atman. He who knows this merges his self in Atman—yea, he who knows this.[11]

It may be difficult to understand what is meant by the fourth part in the analysis of AUM. Apparently there is no fourth part, since obviously there are only three letters. But the author refers to the enveloping silence which precedes and follows the pronunciation of AUM, and which is just as much a part of the word as any one letter—in fact, more truly a part in that it unites the three letters into one whole. The silence is undifferentiated, like Brahman-Atman itself, and like it, also includes differentiations in that it envelops AUM within itself. It is to be noted that each letter of this sacred word, representing waking, dreaming, and deep sleep, respectively, stands for a different aspect of the Atman. But the subtlest essence of Atman is the Turiya, which itself is completely undifferentiated.

The doctrine of "pure consciousness" is a difficult concept for one unfamiliar with the Indian traditions. It may help to point out that to the Indian the universe is not a meaningless, mechanistic system of matter; rather it is enveloped in the "pure consciousness" that constitutes the nature of Brahman-Atman. Such "pure consciousness" is certainly not the same as ordinary human consciousness, waking or sleeping, since our conscious experience is limited, exclusive, and personal. Our consciousness is aware of the distinction between subject and object, or between self and not-self. But Brahman-

Atman, as "pure consciousness," is an intuitive, all-inclusive awareness which does not distinguish between self and not-self, since there really is nothing that is not-self. Yet within that consciousness there is variety of all kinds. And that variety needs something to unify it. That something, say the Upanishads, is like the silence coming before and after AUM, the silence of a universe of meaning whose reality gives life and meaning to all particulars in the universe.

The fact is that the letters of any word are meaningless apart from their unity. The system of unifying relationships that constitutes a word's meaning is the most important part of any word. That unity is grasped not consciously but intuitively.

If this explanation does not prove the existence or clarify the character of "pure consciousness," that is because reason is limited. The only way to understand reality is through intuition, say the Hindu sages. This leads us to the fourth Upanishadic doctrine.

(4) The *Doctrine of Mysticism* may be found in the Māndukya as in all the other Upanishads. Mysticism is present in all religions in varying degrees; in Hinduism it exists in the highest degree. The common features of all mysticism are that (1) the Real is conceived as being indescribable and incomprehensible by logical means; (2) the mystic nevertheless tries to understand and to communicate his experience of the Real to others; (3) such communication is usually attempted by negatives; that is, by explaining what God is not, they hope that they can help others to intuit what God is; (4) union with the Real is possible, it occurs in the experience of saintly persons, and it bestows upon the subject a state of ecstasy or perfect bliss, inasmuch as the experiencer is unaware of any separation from the object of his contemplation. He who contemplates Brahman may be rewarded with the experience of unity with it, together with the perfect bliss that comes from the feeling that nothing is lacking—absolutely nothing. The mystic does not demand the reward as a right earned by what he does, but only hopes for it as a gift freely bestowed upon one who has put himself in a condition to receive it. "This Atman cannot be attained by the study of the Vedas, or by intelligence, or by much hearing of sacred books. It is attained by him alone whom It chooses. To such a one Atman reveals Its own form."[12]

Verses VII and XII illustrate mysticism in the Māndukya Upanishad. The author, presumably himself a mystic who has experienced the ecstatic union, asserts that the experience of the Atman cannot be communicated, yet all the while he is trying to communicate it. He does use some affirmative terms, such as "all peace, all bliss," and "all good." But he also uses negatives, such as "non-dual," and "cessation of phenomena." In verse VII Turiya is said to be "not that . . . nor that . . . nor that . . ." repeating the negative six times. Then he goes on to say "It is *un*perceived, *un*related, etc.," for six more negatives. The conclusion of the Upanishad stresses the union of the soul with God: "He who knows this merges his self in Atman."

A favorite method by which the mystic tries to communicate his knowledge of the Absolute is by means of paradoxes. "Atman, smaller than the small, greater than the great, is hidden in the hearts of all living creatures," states the Katha Upanishad.[13] "It moves and moves not; It is far and likewise near. It is inside all this and It is outside all this."[14]

The goal of all mystics is, of course, to experience unity with God and, in that experience, to be filled with unspeakable bliss. Brahman is said to be Sat-Chit-Ananda, or Existence, Consciousness, and Bliss. So when the mystic is one with Reality and Truth, he is also one with Bliss. In the Taittiriya Upanishad the son asks his father to explain to him the nature of the real from which all things are derived. The father tries to lead the son to discover his own answer. Dramatically, as in a Platonic dialogue, the son proposes first matter, then life, then perception or sensation, then intellect. Each of these in turn is seen to be less comprehensive than the next, and even intellect is incomplete and imperfect. So finally he arrives at the all-inclusive "Ananda," or the Bliss of immediate, intuitive union of subject and object. This is the absolutely real, the Atman or Turiya. It is the Nirvāna of Buddhism.

In this connection it should be noted that it is not quite correct to speak of the doctrine of Brahman as "Hindu idealism." This is because, as we have seen, mind is not regarded as the ultimate reality. Rather, the real according to the Upanishads is the intuitive experience in which distinctions of difference are not consciously made. The more correct term is "Hindu mysticism," as we have indicated. Yet the term "idealism" has expansive meaning and, in contrast with materialism, is frequently used to describe the Upanishadic philosophy.

(5) The *Doctrine of Pantheism* is a corollary of what has already been said. Pantheism is the view that God is the sole reality, and that all the multiplicity of the universe can be reduced to God. The later Vedantic *Doctrine of Māyā* is based on this view, although it is not identical with it. Māyā is the view that the world is an illusion since Brahman alone is real. But this does not necessarily follow from the doctrine of pantheism, as pointed out by Radhakrishnan.[15] Pantheism is compatible with the view that the multiplicity of the universe derives its being from God, or Brahman. As such it is not an illusion. Its being is relative, not absolute. This seems to be the view which the Upanishads support.

In the Mundaka Upanishad we read: "As from a blazing fire, sparks essentially akin to it fly forth by the thousand, so also, my good friend, do various beings come forth from the imperishable Brahman and unto Him again return."[16] Again it states, "That immortal Brahman alone is before, that Brahman is behind, that Brahman is to the right and left. Brahman alone pervades everything above and below; this universe is that Supreme Brahman alone."[17] Again, "He who knows the Supreme Brahman becomes Brahman."[18]

It is easy to see how the doctrine of māyā was derived from passages such as the second one above. But even that one may be interpreted as basically pantheistic rather than as teaching māyā. The sparks referred to in the first passage may be regarded as not unreal, but as depending for their reality upon the fire, symbolic of Brahman. So the whole universe, in the second passage, depends upon or manifests Brahman. In the third quoted passage the individual is represented as passing from a state of separation from Brahman to one of identification with him. The passing, however, is truly one of illusion, for no one can exist apart from Brahman. That is the lesson of the Chāndogya Upanishad, as in the following passage:

"Fetch me from thence a fruit of the Nyagrodha tree." "Here is one, Sir." "Break it." "It is broken, Sir." "What do you see there?" "Not anything, Sir."

The father said: "My son, that subtle essence which you do not perceive there, of that very essence this great Nyagrodha tree exists. Believe it, my son, That which is the subtle essence, in it all that exists has itself. It is the True. It is the self, and thou, O Svetaketu, art it."[19]

But if Brahman is the subtle essence of the whole world, he is also the essence of the gods, according to the Upanishads. And if the world is not an illusion neither are the manifold gods an illusion. "This that people say, 'Worship this god! Worship that god!'—one god after another—this is his creation indeed! And he himself is all the gods. . . . Whoever worships one or another of these—he knows not; for he is incomplete with one or another of these. One should worship with the thought that he is just one's self [atman], for therein all these become one. . . .

"Verily, in the beginning this world was Brahma[n].

"It knew only itself: 'I am Brahma[n]!' Therefore it became the All. Whoever of the gods became awakened to this, he indeed became it. . . .

"So whoever worships another divinity [than his Self], thinking, 'He is one and I another,' he knows not. . . ."[20]

That the universe of matter, the persons of the gods, and the self of man are dependent beings, while Brahman alone is absolutely real—this seems to be what the Upanishads mean by the doctrine of pantheism.

The basic assumption of the doctrine of Brahman-Atman, as of Pantheism, is that the real is the timeless and the changeless. The subtle essence that is ultimately real, as Brahman-Atman, is thus conceived of as not subject to change, for change is a sign that the thing that is changing is less than perfect. Or if it is perfect in one state, then when it changes to another state it becomes something less than the perfection which it was before.

But the unanswered question of the Upanishads is, if the subtle essence that is Brahman is so perfect, how can it manifest itself in something less than perfect—for surely the world which is its manifestation is less perfect than the Brahman. Also Brahman is spoken of as the unconditioned and the unrelated. If this is the case, how can the world be the manifestation of Brahman without being related to it? These are questions which later commentators sought to answer, as we shall explain in another chapter.

The doctrine of pantheism implies, of course, the immanence of God. God is not far away; he is even here within my heart. "In him we live and move and have our being." "God is love, and he who abides in love abides in God, and God abides in him." Love in the heart is God in the heart.[21] Christianity truly shares with Hinduism the view that God is immanent, and that his most fitting abode is in the heart of man. We may also agree with Hinduism that God is the only Absolute Being, and that the existence of the world is a dependent one. This is the point of view found in the Upanishads and in the writings of modern interpreters of Hinduism such as Radhakrishnan, whose education in Madras Christian College helped him to acquire a sympathetic understanding of Christian philosophy side by side with his deep and abiding loyalty to the best in the Hindu tradition.[22] The Christian philosopher should sincerely endeavor to gain an equally sympathetic understanding of Hinduism, and to avoid views which would caricature its pantheistic and other doctrines.

Concerning (6) the *Doctrine of the Transmigration of Souls,* our next topic, the situation is different. For there is not much in common between Hinduism and Christianity on this view, except that both religions teach that the soul survives death. This doctrine is also called *reincarnation.* Sansara is the Sanskrit word to denote the phenomenal world of unceasing births and deaths in which transmigration prevails.

Some scholars believe that the idea of transmigration came into Hindu thought from the Dravidians or earlier inhabitants of India. We have already seen that primitive peoples in many parts of the world even today believe that a man's soul passes at death into animal or plant bodies or other forms. Possibly the Aryans themselves once believed this. But at the time the Vedas were composed the Hindu Aryans had mostly passed beyond this belief. Then in the period of the Upanishads it may have come back into Hinduism through absorption from the lower culture.

The doctrine of rebirth first appears in the Brāhmanas, and is developed in the Upanishads. The earliest Brahmanic doctrine is that the good are born again in a better world to die no more, while those who have not attained Brahmanic wisdom and who fail in their duties are born in a different world only to die again and again.[23] Even in some of the earliest Upanishadic passages the soul's rebirth is conceived as taking place not on earth but in heaven or hell. Fear of hell in the Chāndogya Upanishad reminds one of the Persian Zoroastrian doctrine of retribution: "May I never go to the white, toothless, devouring abode."[24]

However we do find passages in the early Upanishads teaching that the soul is reborn in this world, and that its fortunes in the next rebirth depend on how one lives in this life. "Those whose conduct has been good will quickly attain some good birth, the birth of a Brāhmin, a Kshatriya, or a Vaishya. But those whose conduct is evil will quickly attain an evil birth, the birth of a dog, or a hog, or a candāla."[25] This is the simplest statement of the Upanishadic doctrine of transmigration. But we frequently find various strands of thought woven together in the Upanishads. For example in the Chāndogya Upanishad those souls which have done good deeds are recompensed by rising through smoke and darkness to the moon. After the influence of the good deeds has been exhausted the soul then "descends again through ether, wind, smoke, mist, cloud, rain, herbage, food, and seed, and through the assimilation of food by man he enters the womb of the mother and is born again."[26] In this passage the moon becomes a kind of heaven where time continues to operate. The length of one's sojourn on the moon depends on the number of good deeds one has done. After that one returns to earth and lives a new life to determine the soul's further transformations.

How far apart are East and West in one respect may be seen in Radhakrishnan's sincere rationalization of the doctrine of reincarnation. "The theory of rebirth is quite as logical," he writes, "as any other hypothesis that is in the field, and it is certainly more satisfactory than the theories of absolute annihilation or eternal retribution. It accounts for the apparent moral disorder and chaos of suffering. . . ."[27] The occidental must ask what is the moral significance of rebirth if the reborn has no recollection of his previous existences. If there is no continuity of unified experience, there would seem to be no moral value in the doctrine of reincarnation.

(7) The *Doctrine of Karma* is inseparable from that of transmigration. Karma is the law of character. Every deed that a man does influences his character. In the course of his lifetime his charac-

ter is formed from the totality of his deeds, good and bad. According to the degree of goodness or badness, karma impersonally decrees that the soul shall at death be reborn into another body, human or subhuman, and suffer or be rewarded according to a strict accounting of its deeds in the former life. The law of karma is inexorable. No person or god administers it. It is the impersonal law of the universe and cannot be evaded by any man.

Karma is an idea that is peculiar to India. The idea of moral law is universal among men, like the Rita of the Vedic period, but the idea of karma developed only in India, after the period of the hymns. In the earlier period it was believed that man could escape from the consequences of his sins by sacrificing to the gods and calling on them for mercy. But in the Upanishads we read that sacrifice is of no avail. It is true that the Upanishads do provide a way of escape from the effects of karma through the performance of disinterested deeds of social service. "While *thus* you live there is no way by which karma clings to you," says the Isha Upanishad.[28] So the law of karma, in its best expression, provides for a way of escape. "Those who depart from hence without having discovered the Self and those true desires, for them there is no freedom in all the worlds. But those who depart from hence, after having discovered the Self and those true desires, for them there is freedom in all the worlds."[29] The philosophical Hindu probably longs for rebirth in a world that is free from old age, disease, and death.

We may accept the above view as the most sympathetic interpretation of the Indian philosophy. It is certainly harmonious with Indian mysticism. Yet the average Hindu is unaware of this aspect of Upanishadic teachings, thinking of karma only as the inexorable moral law of cause and effect which necessarily condemns him to a hopeless round of rebirths. The cycle of reincarnations is sometimes referred to as the wheel, because it is virtually endless. Most men never seem able to do enough good or free deeds to insure their rebirth in pleasant circumstances. It is no wonder, therefore, that the common desire of religious Hindus has been to be released from the wheel, to be reabsorbed into Brahman.

(8) The *Doctrine of Caste* is embedded in the Upanishads, as it was in the Brāhmanas. This has already been referred to in the discussion of transmigration and karma, as well as in the preceding

chapter describing the rise of the Brāhmins. In the Upanishads the rigidity of caste is modified somewhat by the observation that true Braminhood depends on character more than on heredity. The practical subordination of castely privilege to genuine leadership is seen in those cases where Kshatriyas are found teaching Brāhmins about religion.

Nevertheless the prevalent assumption of the Upanishads is that caste is the divine rule in human life. Whatever one's station in life, apparently gained through heredity, it is right because of the deeds of the soul in previous lives. This gives a divine sanction to the social and economic status quo, imprinting on the Upanishads the mark of conservatism. There was not enough of that counteracting insight in the Upanishads to make them an instrument of social progress and reform as was the case with the prophets of Israel. Perhaps we should judge the Upanishads by what they failed to do, as well as by what they actually accomplished.

If the lowly Shudra thought about it at all, he would surely get small comfort from the doctrine that his lot in life was just, since his unremembered past lives had produced exactly the kind of karma which caused him to be reborn in his poor circumstances. If he was intellectually privileged so as to know about the doctrine of moksha, and if he believed the doctrine, then he would certainly be strongly inclined to regard this world pessimistically, as a vale of sorrows which it were better to leave. The related doctrines of caste, karma, and transmigration are much more likely to inspire a privileged Brahmin or Kshatriya than a Shudra. A Brahmin could live this life and feel that release from the wheel should perhaps be postponed while he enjoys his special privileges. The Shudra would be more likely to feel depressed by it all.

Some Hindus sincerely defend caste by explaining that it eliminates competition which is disadvantageous to the weak and that it promotes social harmony. Fear of being born into a lower caste is also a factor in motivation.

(9) The *Doctrine of Moksha,* or release from individual existence in this world, ties in with all that has been said so far. According to the ancient Upanishads such release was looked upon as a thing greatly to be desired. Release from individual, dependent existence meant reunion with the Absolute Brahman, in which is joy un-

speakable. This is the fulfilment of the philosophy of mysticism, wherever it is found, in Hinduism, in Christianity, or in Islam.

It has been argued that the desire for reabsorption in God is a mark of other-worldliness. It is asserted to be essentially the attitude of world-denial, or pessimism concerning the worth-whileness of individual human life. The mystic will be likely to deny these assertions. He will insist that the mystic vision transfigures ordinary life and gives to its true values an eternal significance. He will point out that while the life of the individual is necessarily incomplete, it finds fulfilment in the life divine (to use Aurobindo's expression). Certainly some of the world's mystics have found individual life meaningful and have taken more than average delight in it, as is true of St. Francis for example. And there is no denying the fact that there is a certain amount of other-worldliness in Christianity, if we want to point it out. We tend to emphasize its other aspects. So does the Hindu mystic. Radhakrishnan accepts the mysticism of his religion, yet he was sufficiently this-worldly to accept the post of Ambassador to the Soviet Union and later of Vice-President of India. This seems the culmination of a life of great variety and practicality on the part of a noble Hindu guru, and is cited as another proof that mystics can be, perhaps usually are, more practical than most men. "The Upanishads do not teach that life is a nightmare and the world a barren nothing," writes Radhakrishnan. "Rather it is pulsing and throbbing with the rhythm of the world harmony. The world is God's revelation of Himself. His joy assumes all these forms."[30] Perhaps this is an exaggeration of the part played in the Hindu scriptures by the ideal of joyfulness in the religious life. But that the idea is there should not be overlooked, and modern life in India and elsewhere may need such emphasis. It is certainly understandable that a great Hindu idealist should claim that the Hindu ethic is the ethics of self-realization. For that is the ethics of western idealism.

Finally, (10) the *Doctrine of Yoga* may be found even in the most ancient Upanishads. This is the doctrine that one can obtain Moksha, or release from individuality, even in present experiences by following certain practices. These practices may be described as essentially means to self-control. One of these means is identified as breath-control. Says the Brihadaranyaka, "Therefore let a man perform one observance only; let him breathe up and let him breathe down, that the evil death may not reach him. And when he performs it, let him try to finish it. Then he obtains through it union and oneness with that deity."[31] The Maitri Upanishad suggests six methods of gaining Moksha: "restraint of the breath, restraint of the senses, meditation, fixed attention, investigation, absorption, these are called the sixfold yoga."[32] If perchance these passages were insertions of a later age, still there are references to the life of tranquil meditation which prove that the method of the Yoga was derived from an early age. Such is the implication of the Chandogya Upanishad: "This whole world is Brahman, from which he comes forth, without which he will be dissolved and in which he breathes. Tranquil, one should meditate on it."[33]

The development of yogism awaited a later age. It will be discussed in another chapter.

Development of Hindu Maturity

If we accept the interpretation of Hinduism by its respected scholars, then we may conclude that the mythology of the early Rig Veda is both more primitive and more mature than the Homeric mythology. It captured the imaginations of the Indo-Aryans at an earlier stage than Homer in the case of a related culture. Vedic myth proves thus to be less anthropomorphic than Homeric myth.

Yet the presence of magic in the Vedas is even more marked than in Homer. And the transformation of a simple religion of nature into an anthropomorphic type of religion can be seen as it actually took place in the Vedas. Vedic magic became detailed in the Atharva Veda, as in portions of the Rig Veda itself. Vedic myth, being less anthropomorphic generally than Homeric myth, did not lend itself so easily as the latter to literalistic interpretation. The late development of Hinduism was unrestrained by this insight, but for centuries at least the Vedas formed a poetic background for a healthy religious development.

Then as the priestly class became a priestly caste, the brahmins searched the Vedas for proof texts which were to repress Indian society for many generations. As an antidote to the sacerdotal literalism of the Brahmanas there arose the Aranyakas and the Upanishads, produced in large part by enlightened Brahmins themselves. The magic of the Brahmanas gave way to the spirit of free inquiry and unrestrained mysticism of the Upanishads. This was an achievement of essential universalism in ancient times.

In Upanishadic religion we find much evidence of a free commitment of the individual to the truth, so far as that was attainable. In a prescientific age there were no such issues as a Copernican theory or biological evolution. The more remarkable was the sweep of Hindu intellectual intuition as it broke with priestly polytheism and magic, asserting instead the unity of God, the relativity of nature and human experience, and the underlying obligation of the individual to perform the works worthy of the God dwelling within our own spirits (atman). The pessimism which is found in the Upanishads may be admitted as evidence of their authors' realism in a difficult climate and a confused society. Psychological health may have been promoted in this manner, to a certain extent.

The primary criticism of Upanishadic ethics seems to be the endorsement of the caste system by the Upanishads. This criticism is only relative, however, and must be diminished as enlightenment in the social sciences and technology takes place in modern India.

Probably no religion achieved more beauty of religious symbolism and greater freedom from idolatry than the creators of the Upanishads. Regardless of what the outward forms were, they were always interpreted as merely symbolic. Reality was an inward, mystical experience which took the worshiper to the very heart of Brahman-Atman.

Need we say more about the further criterion of mystic sensitivity? Such has never been more brilliantly exhibited in any religious tradition than in the Hindu Upanishads. Among the great Hindu Upanishadic mystics were some who conceived Brahman as personal, and others who thought of him as transpersonal, even as some of Christendom's greatest theologians differ among themselves today.

The story of Hinduism in later ages was to take some odd turns. That is why we have paused to make an evaluation at this point in its development. Further evaluation will be undertaken at the end of our discussion of modern Hinduism.

XI. THE JAINIST PROTEST

It might seem that we are interrupting our study of Hinduism at this point in order to take up something different and unrelated. But such is not the case. For both Jainism and Buddhism—the subject of the next chapter—are vitally related to the development of Hinduism. Jainism as a movement had been stirring in eastern India perhaps for some centuries while the Upanishads were forming. Like Buddhism, it shows a large amount of influence from earlier Hinduism and in turn influenced the development of later Hinduism. It is difficult to tell the difference between modern Hinduism and modern Jainism. According to Radhakrishnan both Jainism and Buddhism are Hindu in background and spirit.

Technically, however, Jainism is a separate religion of India having much in common with Hinduism but also having much that is different. Just as Protestantism shares with Roman Catholic Christianity the great mass of its basic beliefs, yet differs from it in significant ways, so Jainism is like Hinduism in most respects while differing from it in others. Jainism may be understood historically as a protest against the philosophical monism of Hinduism, as well as a condemnation of the system of cruel—and costly—animal sacrifice.

Jainism has its own sacred writings on which we must rely for our knowledge of Jainist traditions, just as we must rely upon the Hebrew scriptures for most of the data of Hebrew tradition. Jainists reject the sacred literature of Hinduism, and principally for that reason were regarded as heretical.

The most reliable group of Jainist canonical scriptures is called the Siddhanta, with divisions.[1] Some of these divisions go to make up what is popularly known as the Jaina Sutras. The canon of Jainist scriptures was perhaps a thousand years in forming, although some of the writings go back at least to the fourth century B.C.[2] One Jainist sect rejects even this canon, having composed its own scriptures. Well into the Christian era a Jainist theologian, Umasvati, reduced the Jainist beliefs to brief, systematic statements generally accepted by all sects. On the basis of such evidences the following stories and doctrines are now repeated.

The Founder

Mahavira, the reputed founder of Jainism, was a contemporary of many of the world's great creative prophets. According to the tradition he was born in 599 B.C. and died in 527 B.C. Some modern scholars regard these dates as too early by perhaps half-a-century, although there is much to favor the traditional dates. If the dates are correct he was a contemporary of the Buddha in India, of the legendary Lao Tzu and Confucius in China, of Zoroaster in Persia, and Jeremiah, Ezekiel, and the Second Isaiah in Judaism.

Mahavira is sometimes called Nataputta, and sometimes Vardhamana. Nataputta was a family name, while the name given him at birth was Vardhamana, meaning "the Increasing One." After he had achieved the great spiritual victory of his life he was called Mahavira, the "Great Hero," or the Jain, or Jina, "the Victorious One." Mahavira, therefore, was an earned name comparable with "the Buddha," or "the Christ."

Strictly speaking, Mahavira was not the founder of Jainism but only its last and greatest prophet and organizer. Jain tradition has it that there have been twenty-four prophets or Tirthankaras, "guides across the sea of transmigration." The last of these was Mahavira. The one before him was known as Parshva. It is said that he lived in the ninth century B.C., that he was more than thirteen feet tall, and that he lived to be a hundred years old. His predecessor is said to have been fifteen feet tall, and to have lived to be a thousand years old, about 84,000 years before Parshva. The farther back we go, the more fantastic the Tirthankara story becomes. The likely conclusion is that Parshva and Mahavira were historical but legendary figures, while all the earlier Tirthankaras were purely mythological.

Mahavira was a member of the Kshatriya or ruler-warrior caste. He was a prince who was surrounded by every luxury that one could desire. It is rather disillusioning to learn that the territory over which his father was king was really only a kind of suburb of the small capital city of Vesali in the province of Lichavi, north of Magadha. But the royal family could still have been wealthy, as small-town mayors often are. And by marriage he was related to the kings of both Videha and Magadha.[3] Also it is significant that he was not the oldest son and so probably would not have inherited the royal suburb. This may help to explain why he chose to go into the service of the church rather than remain surrounded by luxury, although it could never explain why he went to the extremes of asceticism and reform as he did. His success may partially be explained by the fact that in eastern India, where he lived his strange life, the Kshatriya caste was inclined to be somewhat envious of the Brahminical claims to spiritual primacy. Many of his followers were of the second rather than the first caste.

From the Jaina Sutras[4] we learn that as a baby Mahavira was served by five nurses who greatly pampered him, and that as a growing youth he reveled in "the allowed, noble five-fold joys and pleasures" of the senses. He married a princess and became a father, but grew discontented with his manner of life. Meanwhile he continued to live at home in the royal palace, although he was already attracted by the manner of life displayed by the Parshva monks who lived in a park outside the town. This attraction came to him quite naturally, since his home influence also favored the Parshva way of life. We are told that his father and mother "were worshipers of Parshva and followers of the [ascetics],"[5] and that when they decided that it was time for them to die they insisted on the same manner of death as Parshva had chosen: "On a bed of kusa-grass they rejected all food, and their bodies dried up by the last mortification of the flesh."[6] This occurred when Mahavira was thirty years of age.

When his father and mother were dead Mahavira felt free to join the monks. His royal brother gave a delayed consent, after which he systematically gave away his treasures to the poor—apparently unaware of any obligation to his wife and daughter. "After fasting two and a half days without drinking water [he] put on a divine robe, and quite alone, nobody else being present, he tore out his hair [in five handfuls] and leaving the house entered the state of houselessness."[7] In order to join the monastic order of Parshva he was required to pledge: "I shall for twelve years neglect my body and abandon the care of it; I shall with equanimity bear, undergo, and suffer all calamities arising from divine powers, men, or animals."[8]

Renunciation

For some time after that he probably lived with the Parshva monks outside the town. But having become an ascetic he decided to carry asceticism to its logical conclusion. At that time his only possession was a flamingo robe. This he threw away and went completely naked all the rest of his life. Naturally we of the West raise our eyebrows at such conduct and wonder what diagnosis a modern psychiatrist would have made concerning his insanity. But the people of India did not look upon him as an exhibitionist nor put him in jail. They concluded that he was a genuinely holy man and revered him as such. For he had carried the Indian ideal of self-denial to its logical conclusion, refusing to own a house, jewelry, food, or even clothes. For his food he begged and gratefully accepted whatever was given.

For the next twelve years Mahavira sought, through asceticism, to cleanse his soul of material attachments and to attain complete salvation. He also took every precaution not to injure any kind of life whatsoever. Both of these ideas came to him by way of the Parshva order, but he gave them new life. It is said that during the rainy season he stayed in one place lest he step into muddy water teeming with life and injure some creature. He realized that many organisms were so small as to escape ordinary notice, and when he walked he was always most attentive to where he stepped. He is believed to have carried with him a soft broom with which to sweep away the insects, in order not to harm them. When he needed to rest he would make sure that the ground—or borrowed bed—was free from any kind of life. He used a cloth for straining his drinking water and as a covering for his mouth when speaking, lest he accidentally swallow some form of life. In begging he would not accept raw food, since to eat it would be to destroy vegetable life. Nor would he allow anyone to cook food especially for him, for cooking also destroys life. He would accept only left-overs that had been prepared for others, and thus not be directly responsible for the destruction of any life whatsoever.

All of this meticulous care for life contributed to his asceticism. But in order to perfect his soul he went to even greater extremes in disregarding the desires of his body. Even in the winter he would wander about, unshielded from the elements, refusing clothing, shelter, or fire. When the winter was cold he would sit meditating in the shade; in the hot summer he would squat in the full glare of the sun. "The Venerable One, exerting himself, did not seek sleep for the sake of pleasure; he waked up himself, and slept only a little, free from desires." "Purgatives and emetics, anointing of the body and bathing, shampooing, and cleansing of the teeth do not behoove him."[9]

The holy man refused on principle, except in the rainy season, to stay in any one place lest he become attached to it. This matter of personal detachment he carried to an extreme equal to his policy of non-injury. When people spoke to him he did not reply. Even when asked questions he did not answer. This earned him ill-will even when people were otherwise inclined to be friendly to the strange monk. Sometimes people would strike him to see if he would pay any attention, but as always he showed that his mind was centered on salvation. Dogs and other animals would attack him, but he would rather be torn to pieces than harm an animal. Human beings tormented him, throwing him in the air and letting him fall. "Abandoning the care of his body, the Venerable One humbled himself." Once some villagers lit a fire between his feet as he sat motionless: surely he would move to avoid being burned. But nothing conquered his will to impassivity.

Finally after twelve years he attained "moksha," that is, release from the wheel of transmigration. He entered Nirvana even while still living this life, and thus was assured that never again would he have to be born into the world of matter and sense experiences. It came about in this way:

"Outside of the town Jrimbhikagrama, on the northern bank of the river Rijupalika, in the field of the householder Samaga, in a northeastern direction from an old temple, not far from a sal tree, in a squatting position with joined heels exposing himself to the heat of the sun, with the knees high and the head low, in deep meditation, he reached Nirvana, the complete and full, the unobstructed, unimpeded, infinite and supreme, best knowledge and intuition, called Kevala ['total']. When the Venerable One had become an Arhat and Jina, he was a Kevalin, omniscient and comprehending all objects, he knew all conditions of the world, of gods, men, and demons; whence they come, where they go, whether they are born as men or animals . . . their open and secret deeds, their conversation and gossip, and the thoughts of their minds; he saw and knew all conditions in the whole world of all living beings."[10]

Thus he earned the title of Jina, or Jain, "the conqueror." For he had conquered his body with its needs and desires, and the soul with its pride, anger, and ambition.

After this mystic experience, beyond which nothing was to be desired, Mahavira devoted the rest of his life to evangelism. After nearly thirty years of such activity he died at the age of seventy-two—"in a fit of apopleptic rage," says Hopkins,[11] which seems utterly discordant with all else that has been said of him. At any rate, the record insists that during his preaching ministry he won an amazing following of 14,000 monks, 36,000 nuns, 159,000 laymen, and 318,000 laywomen.[12]

Development of Jainism

Among those won to his following were the whole Order of Parshva, which he had joined after his great renunciation and from whom he had departed within about a year. To the four rules of Parshva (non-injury, truthfulness, honesty, and poverty) Mahavira had added a fifth, namely, chastity. Furthermore it seems he interpreted the rule of poverty as forbidding the ownership of clothing. At least, these were the two points of difference reported by the Jain scriptures, in which the followers of Parshva accepted the reformation of Mahavira.

Subsequently some difference of opinion arose over whether the wearing of clothes was absolutely forbidden or only optional, depending on certain circumstances. This question was compromised for awhile. But when a large group, during a twelve-year famine, migrated to the south they formed the Digambara sect which insisted that a Jain should wear no clothes. Literally, the word Digambara means "sky-clad." The northern Jainists, however, the Shvetambaras or "white-clad," yielded to the demands of the weather and of polite society and relaxed the rule. Two other differences between the Shvetambaras and the Digambaras are that the former admit women to their order and concede that they may even enter Nirvana, while the latter regard women as the source of temptation and sin; also the Digambaras reject the Shvetambaras' sacred scripture, having written their own.

Jainism increased until its adherents numbered 1,250,000 to 1,500,000.[13] At the present period their number remains stationary.

The Jain contribution to art and logic has been significant through the centuries. Their painting, primarily illustrative of their manuscripts, has shown a boldness of line and color. Unique sculpture is found in their temples and sacred caves. The favorite sculpture is colossal statues of the twenty-four tirthankaras, each a copy of the other except for its symbolism. Another subject of sculpture was the Jaina saints. Medieval Jain temples appear in incredible location and artistry on remote mountain-tops of Rajputana and the Gujarat. In general literature and especially logic they have made remarkable contributions.

The following summary of Jainist teachings is presented to show the similarities and differences between Jainism, Hinduism, and Buddhism.

Some Jaina Doctrines

(1) *Animism* is fundamental in Jainist theory, in that it forms the logical foundation for the doctrine of non-injury. Animism is already familiar as teaching that souls inhabit the bodies not only of men but also of animals, plants, and even inorganic objects. The Jainas people heaven and hell also with "jivas" or souls inhabiting the bodies of gods and demons respectively. They believe that all souls are uncreated and indestructible, and that except for the

contamination of matter they would be perfectly good, wise, and powerful.

The crudeness of the Jainist animism is evidence of its being more ancient than Mahavira, and earlier than the relatively enlightened thought of the Upanishads which were being composed in and before the days of Mahavira. The Jain animism is very clean-cut: there is an absolute difference between soul and body. Everything else in the universe is made of atoms, but souls are purely spiritual, teaches Jainism. Its atomism sounds almost like that of the Greek philosophers, Democritus and Epicurus, except for the Jain failure to include souls among those things having atomic structure.

(2) *Pluralism.* The combined Jaina theory of uncreated, indestructible souls and universal atoms, forms an interesting contrast with Hindu monism. Radhakrishnan calls the Jaina theory "pluralistic realism," in contrast with the Upanishadic monistic idealism.[14] To the Jainas each soul and each atom is an uncreated, indestructible real, constituting a pluralistic universe, a universe made up of many, many substances.

(3) *Non-injury* is perhaps the most spectacular doctrine of Jainism, and rests solidly upon its fundamental animism. If the souls of gods, men, and lower forms of life are all essentially alike, then all life should be regarded as sacred. Dr. Albert Schweitzer accepts a modified form of the doctrine of non-injury, preferring to call it "reverence for life," and refraining from making his principle an absolute as the Jainists have done. We have already seen to what absurd extremes Mahavira carried his doctrine, essentially setting up the lower forms of life as having more value than human life itself. This, as we have seen, flows from the animistic assumption that there really is no difference between human life and all other forms of life. But practically it subordinates human life to the other forms of life.

Jainism was more emphatic than the Upanishadic thinkers in opposing animal sacrifice. The Upanishads merely argued that such sacrifice was unnecessary in the case of those who understood the oneness of all things with Brahman. But to Mahavira animal sacrifice was a heinous crime against the souls which dwelt in the bodies of the sacrificial animals. In this respect the doctrine of non-injury had positive value.

Today in Jainist India, however, the doctrine of non-injury is carried to the extremity of maintaining elaborate animal hospitals, not just for pets and domesticated animals as we do in the West, but for the most fantastic care of useless and even harmful animals. Hopkins cites an instance where "five thousand rats were supported in such a temple-hospital in Kutch. (The town was taxed to provide the food for the rats.)"[15]

(4) *Atheism* may be said paradoxically to characterize the Jainist faith, in one sense. No doubt this aspect of Jainism has been overemphasized. The substance of the accusation is that Mahavira denied the existence of Brahman. This world is a pluralistic universe, he said in effect, not a monistic, pantheistic universe. The world is made up of a vast number of uncreated and indestructible souls and atoms in a hierarchy of being. No Brahman or other deity was needed to create it, according to Jaina doctrine. Naturally the orthodox Hindus were horrified at this heresy. The charge of atheism must have originated with them.

But Jainism is not quite so atheistic as might appear. For Mahavira did believe in the existence of gods and demons, as already indicated. Certainly, however, the gods whom Mahavira admitted were not the kind whom we should deem worthy of adoration and prayer. They were too human for that. The whole universe, for Mahavira, was a sort of democracy of jivas or spirits in various stages of the wheel of transmigration. The gods were souls which had earned enough merit to be privileged for a time. But eventually their bliss would end and they would very likely be reborn as men or as animals. Demonic souls in the underworld might in their next rebirth be as well off as the gods. Justice would seem to be more divine than the gods themselves. And of course there were the Jinas, those like Mahavira who succeeded in freeing themselves from the lower world of matter, to rise to the heaven of spirit. Theoretically even they could not help a struggling, sinful mortal man because they had reached a place of complete detachment from all worldly things and so were above being prayed to. Yet the Jainist did practically make gods of the Jinas, adoring and imitating them even if they could not make practical connections with them.

At least in theory, therefore, Jainism is essentially humanistic. Prayer was condemned when its appeal was to any external power.

"Man! Thou art thine own friend; why wishest thou for a friend beyond thyself?"[16] The aspiration to become perfect was open to all. Any one who practiced the severe ascetic steps prescribed by Jainism could become divine like the Jina himself. "God is only the highest, noblest, and fullest manifestation of the powers which lie latent in the soul of man. All perfect men are divine, and there is no rank among them, since all are equal."[17]

It should be pointed out, however, that popular Jainism today is polytheistic, idolatrous, and supernaturalistic, just like popular Hinduism. In many cases its religious ritual is even conducted by a Hindu Brahmin.

(5) *Transmigration and karma* are closely related doctrines of Jainism, as of Hinduism, but with some unique features. In both religions transmigration takes place according to the law of karma. But in Jainism transmigration normally encompasses a wider scope than in Hinduism, for the soul of man may become god, demon, beast, plant, inanimate thing, or a pure spirit liberated from transmigration.

Karma, too, in Jainism, is unique in that it is a subtle form of matter which the soul attracts to itself by its bad desires and deeds. The soul leaves the body at death but carries its unperceivable karma atoms with it in the form of layers of encrustation. Much karma makes the soul sink to lower forms of existence. Little karma permits it lightly to rise. No karma may allow it to become an arhat in Nirvana. Karma, like all other matter, is conceived to be inherently evil. Of karma there are eight kinds, with 148 subdivisions, determining such matters as caste or species in the next rebirth.[18] No one can escape the effects of his karma. But to everyone is given the inherent power to follow the laws of the Jainist Order, and thereby scale off the karma crusts and head for Nirvana. This is an important element of freedom in Jainist theory.

(6) *Nirvana and moksha* also are related doctrines of Jainism. As in Hinduism and Buddhism, so in Jainism the goal is to become freed from the wheel of transmigration. But Nirvana is a unique concept in Jainism. Instead of the annihilation of conscious individuality, as in Hinduism and Buddhism, the Jainist seeks to rise to the highest heaven, free from all matter, and there live the life of an eternal, conscious individual. We read that "Perfected souls

. . . reside on the top of the world; they leave their bodies here, and go there, on reaching perfection. Twelve yojanas above the Sarvartha is the place called Ishatpragbhara. . . . This place, by nature pure, consisting of white gold, resembles in form an open umbrella. . . . There at the top of the world reside the blessed perfected souls, rid of all transmigration, and arrived at the excellent state of perfection. . . ."[19] It sounds as if heaven were made of atoms, albeit precious ones, just like the rest of the universe. But the arhats who go there are pure spirit: "The liberated is not long nor small . . . neither heavy nor light . . . he is without body, without resurrection, without contact [of matter], he is not feminine, nor masculine, nor neuter; he perceives, he knows, but there is no analogy . . . ."[20]

The arhats in Nirvana are far better off than the gods. For the gods still have karma which dooms them to further rounds of transmigration. The arhats, by freeing themselves of all worldly attachment and passion of all kinds, have shed all karma and live eternal lives of conscious individuality, unperturbed by anything in the universe.

(7) *Renunciation* is the heart of Jain morality. In this respect there is no difference between Jainism and Hinduism, for the way of asceticism is recognized in Hindu tradition as one of the ways to salvation. The five great vows of the Jain monk are really but modifications of the vows taken by Hindu ascetics before Jainism and Buddhism arose.

Each of the five vows of the Jain monk begins with the declaration, "I renounce." He first renounces all killing, whether directly or indirectly, by himself or by proxy. Then he renounces untruthfulness arising from anger, greed, fear, or mirth. He next renounces all dishonesty, with emphasis on strict observance of the spirit as well as the letter. The fourth vow renounces sex pleasure in deed, word, or thought. In the fifth he renounces all attachments to the world of the senses.[21]

Jain Values

On the whole the five Jain vows are most thorough and comprehensive and reveal the negative attitude toward life. As Radhakrishnan puts it, "Both Buddhism and Jainism admit the ideal of negation of life and personality. To both life is a calamity to be avoided at all costs. They require us to free ourselves from all the ties that bind us to nature and bring us sorrow. They glorify poverty and purity, peace and patient suffering."[22] He quotes as a caricature of Jainism Hopkins' statement that "A religion in which the chief points insisted upon are that one should deny God, worship man, and nourish vermin, has indeed no right to exist."[23] There is enough truth in the criticism, however, to make it worth our analysis. We have seen that Jainism is, in one sense, atheistic, and that it deifies any Jain who, conquering karma, rises to Nirvana. Unfortunately it is also true that, out of regard for all forms of life, the Jainist monk will nourish rats and vermin regardless of their effect on human values. While there are good things in Jainism, there are obviously some aspects of it which cannot be condoned.

Even suicide is justified in Jaina doctrine. This is not found, to my knowledge, in any other religion except Shinto. Jainism approves of suicide when one has tried and failed to lead the ascetic life. The assumption seems to be that bad karma is being stored up and had better be cut off as quickly as possible. The other justification of suicide is when one has spent twelve successful years as an ascetic and has thus become assured of entering Nirvana; the sooner the better.[24] This extreme point of view merely carries otherworldliness to its logical conclusion. If one is sure that there is another world, and that it is better than this one, why not die at once and go to it?

Jainism is a religion in which all sense pleasure is condemned. All that is spectacular, such as the theater or boxing, is said to influence the soul for evil. "What is discontent, and what is pleasure? One should live subject to neither. Giving up all gaiety, circumspect, restrained, one should lead a religious life. . . . First troubles, then pleasures; first pleasures, then troubles. These are the cause of quarrels."[25]

Women are regarded as a chief source of sinful pleasure, unless they too renounce all and seek salvation. "The world is greatly troubled by women. People say that women are vessels of pleasure. But this leads them to pain, to delusion, to death, to hell, to birth as hell-beings or brute-beasts."[26]

Jainism opposes the fundamental principles of caste, but condones the system after a fashion. The doctrine is that one becomes a Brahmin or other caste-member by his actions rather than merely through birth. "By one's actions one becomes a Brahmin, or a Kshatriya, or a Vaishya, or a Shudra. . . . Him who is exempt from all karmas we call a Brahmin."[27]

The trouble with Jainism was that it made life too deadly serious. Aside from the eccentricities of this ancient religion, its whole attitude toward life was upside down. Why should we accept unchallenged the Jaina assumption that all pleasure is bad, that life must be renounced in order to find salvation in a better life? It is easy to fall a prey to this idea, since it crops out in many religions.

Of course, the lay Jainas did not carry things so far as the monks and nuns. Most of the rules of Jainism were modified somewhat for the benefit of the laity. They were permitted to live the family life but were restricted in many normal habits of everyday experience. Most far-reaching for the laity was the required vow never knowingly to kill a sentient creature. This rule kept Jainists out of farming, fishing, and the army, and by a process of elimination sent most of the northern Jainists into business and the professions. There they have prospered and gained the respect of their fellows of other faiths through their devotion to a restrained and moderate manner of living.

As a parting thought, designed to emphasize something positive, we mention the three jewels of Jainism which are "faith in Jina, knowledge of his doctrine, and perfect conduct." Any Jain may earn merit by giving food, water, clothing, and shelter to those in need, always remembering of course the monks. Patience, humility, simplicity, contentment, kindness, self-control, and sincerity are among the virtues insisted upon by Jainism. If the Jainists are badly mistaken in some of their ideas, at least they are trying, in a deadly serious manner, to be good.

Evaluation

Popular Jainism is one of the most magical of magical religions today. In a sense even original Jainism was magical, in that Mahavira attributed a supernatural structure to the universe which brought disaster upon him who disregarded that structure. Such disregard might take the form of stepping carelessly on living creatures, or disobeying human laws of ethical relationship.

Jainist myth seems to have been taken most literally. Its animism was prosaic and literal, as were its doctrines of heaven, hell, and karma.

Even in a prescientific age it is hard to excuse Jainism for its extreme emphasis upon the negative in human conduct, and for its unnatural attitude toward women and sex. Jainism is one of the most ethically minded of all religions, but its ethics is too negative and too severe.

In denying the reality of Brahman, Jainism shows a lack of mystic sensitivity. Yet the attainment of Nirvana by Mahavira was itself a mystic experience. Nirvana probably remains in Jainist lore as a literal dogma, having little inspiration to mystic experience in the present. And Jainist ritual tends too much toward idolatry and the deification of its very human founder.

It is hard to see any progress of Jainism over its parent, Hinduism.

XII. ORIGINAL BUDDHISM

PROBABLY MORE WESTERNERS have been converted to Buddhism than to any other oriental religion. Certainly there is little in Jainism to appeal to a westerner, and much to repel him. The reverse is true of Buddhism. There is in it much to appeal to a westerner and relatively little to repel him. When a great scholar like the late J. B. Pratt uses two of his sabbatical leaves to make pilgrimages to Buddhist lands in order to get the full flavor of Buddhism and relay it to western minds,[1] we may be sure that a study of Buddhism is worth while. The Christian would do well to note the parallels in doctrine and history between Buddhism and Christianity.

Buddhism arose in the same century as Jainism—probably a generation later—in the same northeastern part of India. It may best be understood as, like Jainism, an effort at reform within Hinduism. To a certain extent it is also a reaction against the extremes of both Jainist and Hindu asceticism.

There are many similarities and also noteworthy contrasts between these two closely related religions. Like Jainism, Buddhism was personally founded. In both religions there sprang up orders of monks and nuns, as well as lay congregations. The stories of Mahavira and Buddha contain parallels—as well as contrasts. The same is true regarding their teachings.

Buddhist Scriptures

The sacred scriptures of Buddhism are referred to as the Tripitaka,[2] or "three baskets" (of the law). The first Pitaka (or basket) is the Vinaya, containing the rules of the monastic order. The second is the Sutta Pitaka, setting forth the teachings of Buddha. The third is the Abhidhamma Pitaka, dealing with metaphysical and psychological aspects of Buddhism and reflecting the later development of Buddhist speculation in the schools of thought. There is much repetition in the Vinaya texts, probably because the Buddha revised his sermons only slightly each time he initiated a new group of monks.

Most valuable to us is the Sutta Pitaka with its five divisions or Nikayas. This contains the famous "Sermon at Benares" and also the Dhammapada, a summary of Buddhist ethics. Parts of the Sutta Pitaka are undoubtedly of late composition, such as the folk tales gathered together in the Jataka for moralizing purposes. But generally speaking we may be sure that we are getting to the factual bases of the Buddha legends in the Sutta Pitaka more so than in the rest of the Buddhist canon. The Tripitaka was written down certainly by the first century B.C., and possibly in the third century B.C.[3] Before that it was transmitted orally.

The Questions of King Milinda is admitted into the canon by the Buddhists of Ceylon and Thailand. But the whole attitude of Buddha, as represented in this late text, is negative and dogmatic. Unfortunately this is the picture that has been impressed on western thought. We must re-examine our sources, therefore, and discover what the original Buddha was like, what he said and did, and what was his primary attitude toward man's nature, duties, and destiny.

The name Buddha is, of course, not a proper name but a title, like Christ. It means "the knower," or "the enlightened one," or "the one fully awake." The family name of the Buddha was Gautama, in Sanskrit. The name is often spelled Gotama, as in the Pali texts, reflecting the Prakrit of Buddha's time and locale—a variety of Sanskrit. Buddha's given name was Siddhartha—or Siddhatha in the Pali. Siddhartha means "he who has accomplished his aim." He was also called Shakyamuni, meaning "sage of the Shakyas," in much the same spirit as we refer to the "man of Galilee." The Shakyas were the tribe or clan to which his family belonged. The name Shakyamuni is most often used in the Far East. In the Pali texts he is also called the Tathagata, or "the perfectly enlightened one." Sometimes he is called simply "the Blessed One."

Life of Buddha

Gautama Siddartha was born about 563 B.C. and died eighty years later, which would be 483 B.C. The place of his birth was Kapilavastu, almost as far north as the border of mountainous Nepal. Like Mahavira, he was a Kshatriya. His father was king—or president, since he ws elected[4]—of the Shakya clan. He was educated as a prince and in due time married Yashodhara, his cousin, who bore him a son, Rahula, who later became his disciple. His sensitive nature was impressed by four sights from which, according to legendary accretions, his father tried to shield him, knowing that by viewing them he would be moved to renounce the world and become a Buddha. The four omens which he did eventually see, despite all precautions, were a decrepit old man, a very sick man, a corpse, and a calm ascetic. These sights made him realize that his own life was artificial, and that human life was at its foundation one of suffering and death. The ascetic was an object lesson to him on how to gain true peace in this tumultuous life.

Then came the great renunciation. He resolved to become an ascetic and go in search of salvation. In other words, Gautama was so disillusioned about life that he wanted to find release from the wheel of transmigration and avoid having to be reborn in human flesh. His motive was probably selfish, according to Hopkins,[5] although later traditions represented him as renouncing the world in order to save mankind. The temptation by Mara, the Indian Satan, was also a later tradition. Immediately after his enlightenment Mara suggested to Buddha that he enter Nirvana at once, but Buddha refused, preferring to live long and thus bring salvation to many.

The story of the renunciation is embellished by the details of how he took a last fond look at his sleeping wife and child and then departed. His charioteer drove him into the wilderness and, at the Buddha's command, returned alone with the horse and chariot and all of the Buddha's possessions. One of his last acts before the charioteer left him was to take a sword and cut off his beautiful black hair and beard and don the orange-yellow robe of a mendicant.

Discounting such embellishments, we still get the picture of a young Kshatriya, with a life before him that might have been filled with worldly success and political power, turning deliberately from it in favor of a life of self-denial. At first he sought the guidance of some Brahmin ascetics and followed the path of Yoga, which was well recognized by the Hinduism of his day as one path to salvation. This took him into the practice of meditation and speculation concerning the nature of reality and the nothingness of the universe. But such meditation brought him no peace, and he made up his mind to try the sort of asceticism advocated by the Jainists.

Once he was joined by five Brahmin ascetics who apparently were not displeased to accept a Kshatriya as one of their company. This would not be likely to happen in a later day, or even in Buddha's day outside of the neighborhood of Magadha. But there developed considerable rivalry among the six ascetics to see which of them could be most austere. Gautama outdid them all. He practiced the most extreme form of breath-restraint until it seemed that his head would split. He ate the most utterly disgusting foods, wrapped himself in the most irritating garments, stood or squatted in one position for long periods of time, reclined on a bed of thorns, sought the company of rotting flesh and bones, and allowed vermin and filth to accumulate on his flesh. He refused to eat more than one grain of hemp or rice a day. In the Majjhima Nikaya of the Sutta Pitaka we read Gautama's words: "When I was living on a single fruit a day, my body grew emaciated in the extreme; (my limbs became) like the knotted joints of withered creepers; like a buffalo's hoof were my shrunken buttocks; like the twists in a rope were my spinal vertebrae; like the rafters of a tumble-down roof were my gaunt ribs; like the starry gleams on water deep down in the depths of a well, so shone my gleaming eyes deep down in the depths of their sockets; and as the rind of a cut gourd shrinks and shrivels in the heat, so shrank and shrivelled the scalp of my head. . . . If I sought to feel my belly, it was my backbone which I found in my grasp."[6]

Meanwhile Gautama was becoming disillusioned with the method of extreme asceticism as a path to salvation. Austerity would never make him superhuman nor give him peace. Could there be another way?[7]

The five Brahmin ascetics, seeing his austerity beyond their endurance, were now anxious to become his disciples and share the enlightenment which should result from such heroism. But then, as Gautama went to the brook for a drink of water, he fainted. When he came to, he lay in the shallow water until he was refreshed and then suddenly decided that he was following the wrong path. He picked up his begging bowl and returned to civilization, abandoning the life of austerity. His five friends were disappointed at such lack of will power, as it seemed to them, and they went down to Benares where they were to meet the Buddha later.

Meanwhile without abandoning his quest he probably became more relaxed as he thought back over his unsuccessful experiences of the past six years. This critical meditation really brought him to the verge of a tremendous new insight that was to motivate much of Asia in the centuries to come.

Buddha's Enlightenment

Sitting under the sacred fig-tree, called the Bodhi-tree, or the Bo-tree—the Tree of Knowledge—in Bodhi Gaya of Magadha, one night everything became clear to him. This was his so-called enlightenment or great awakening which entitled him ever afterward to be called the Buddha. To him was revealed, as to the Vedic seers of old, the fundamental principles of salvation. These are known as the "Four Noble Truths of Buddhism."

It was all very simple—very simple, indeed. There was no need to torture oneself as he had done and as Mahavira and his followers did. All that was necessary to salvation was to realize that desire, or thirst—it is difficult to render the word into English—is the cause of all human suffering. Unenlightened humanity is full of desire. They are continually turning from one thing to another, literally hounded to hell by their insatiable desires. So the Buddha—the Enlightened One—said that in order to be saved we must recognize the nature of desire and then proceed to cut it off from our inward experiences. This would be the difficult thing to do, to be sure. But not all the austerity in the world would take the place of this simple insight. And for the person who understood this fundamental principle of salvation and acted on it, salvation was assured. Nirvana could be reached at any time. Meanwhile there was nothing to be gained in either of the extremes of life—either a life of luxury which left one unsatisfied in the end, or a life of severe austerity, which likewise failed to give peace by itself. Those who understood this truth but were still unable to live by it might well resort to the life of moderation, following the eight-fold noble path which constitutes the fourth of the noble truths of Buddhism. They could not do better than this.

According to the story, when these "noble truths" came to Gautama as he sat beneath the Bodhi-tree, he experienced the state of great ecstasy which is so characteristic of the mystic experience. In that moment he realized that he himself was utterly free from all desire. Now at last he was free from ignorance and darkness and was

*This ancient Buddhist swastika may symbolize a wheel in motion, or the sun emitting rays in four directions.**

filled with the brilliant light of the only important truth in the universe. Being an Indian and believing in transmigration and karma, he was absolutely convinced that rebirth was for him no more. He was in that moment of ecstasy experiencing the eternity of Nirvana, into which he was sure to enter on the death of his body.

The ecstasy having passed, then he was confronted with the inevitable temptation. Like Jesus at the time of his baptism, he had had a great experience. Now what should he do about it? His salvation was now assured, and that had been his goal for the past six years. Should he let it go at that? Mystics are all alike in that, having had the experience of salvation, they are on fire to share it with others. After thinking it over the Buddha, too, concluded that, having experienced salvation, now he must preach it to others.

His Mission

The story is that the Buddha's first thought was of the five friends who had shared his austerity but had turned away from him when

* See Wheelwright, *The Burning Fountain,* pp. 125-127.

he abandoned his austerity. He sought them out in the deer park near Benares. At first the ascetics, seeing him approach, resolved to ignore the renegade. But the Buddha's manner was so calm and benign that they could not carry out their resolution. They showed him every courtesy, meanwhile entering into a discussion with him concerning the way of salvation. Culminating the discussion was the famous "sermon at Benares" on "Setting in Motion the Wheel of the Law."[8] Here are some quotations from Rhys Davids' translation.[9]

There are two extremes, O Bhikkhus, which the man who has given up the world ought not to follow—the habitual practice, on the one hand, of those things whose attraction depends upon the passions, and especially of sensuality—a low and pagan way (of seeking satisfaction) unworthy, unprofitable, and fit only for the worldly-minded—and the habitual practice, on the other hand, of asceticism (or self-mortification), which is painful, unworthy, and unprofitable.

There is a middle path, O Bhikkhus, avoiding these two extremes, discovered by the Tathagata—a path which opens the eyes, and bestows understanding, which leads to peace of mind, to the higher wisdom, to full enlightenment, to Nirvana.

What is that middle path, O Bhikkhus, avoiding these two extremes, discovered by the Tathagata—that path which opens the eyes, and bestows understanding, which leads to peace of mind, to the higher wisdom, to full enlightenment, to Nirvana? Verily! it is this noble eightfold path; that is to say:

Right views;
Right aspirations;
Right speech;
Right conduct;
Right livelihood;
Right effort;
Right mindfulness; and
Right contemplation. . . .

Now this, O Bhikkhus, is the noble truth concerning suffering. Birth is attended with pain, decay is painful, disease is painful, death is painful. Union with the unpleasant is painful, painful is separation from the pleasant; and any craving that is unsatisfied, that too is painful. In brief, the five aggregates which spring from attachment (the conditions of individuality and their cause) are painful. This, then, O Bhikkhus, is the noble truth concerning suffering.

Now this, O Bhikkhus, is the noble truth concerning the origin of suffering. Verily, it is that thirst (or craving) causing the renewal of existence, accompanied by sensual delight, seeking delight, seeking satisfaction now here, now there—that is to say, the craving for the gratification of the passions, or the craving for (a future) life, or the craving for success (in this present life). This then, O Bhikkhus, is the noble truth concerning the origin of suffering.

Now this, O Bhikkhus, is the noble truth concerning the destruction of suffering. Verily, it is the destruction, in which no passion remains, of this very thirst; the laying aside of, the getting rid of, the being free from, the harboring no longer of this thirst. This then, O Bhikkhus, is the noble truth concerning the destruction of suffering.

Let us not think for one moment that the materialistic hedonists were absent from Buddha's India. There was a definite school of thought known as the Carvakas, who taught that the only real things in the universe were made of matter, that there were no gods in the universe or out of it, and that the only good was pleasure—as much pleasure as one could get while life lasted. These people, "hardened sensualists," represented one extreme while the austere ascetics of Jainism and Hinduism, "self-tormenters," represented the other. Neither was any better than the other. Nor was the householder accomplishing any merit for himself by means of traditional sacrifices and ritual. The way of salvation lay in the Four Noble Truths, including the Eightfold Noble Path of moderation.

Formation of the Sangha

At the conclusion of the Sermon at Benares the five Brahmin ascetics acknowledged conversion by the Buddha. Soon they were joined by large numbers of "the rich youth" of Benares. Thus the Buddhist Order, the Sangha, was born. It is said that a thousand Brahmins soon joined the Sangha in a body, under the leadership of three ascetic Brahmins.[10] Even members of the lower castes joined the order, although its greatest popularity seems to have been with the Kshatriyas.[11] The citizens of Magadha even complained that Gautama was robbing them of their youth. The Buddha's father sent him an invitation to come back home. He did so and received his father, mother, wife and son, as well as other relatives, into the order.

It was with some reluctance, apparently, that Buddha decided to admit women into an order of nuns. The story, which may reflect a later attitude rather than Buddha's, relates that the latter remarked that his religion would last for a thousand years if women were not admitted to it, but that if they were, it would only last for five hundred years. This legend may have arisen when the nuns were giving Buddhism some trouble.

Another feature of the Sangha was its division of laymen. The laymen were required to take only the first five of the ten vows which the monks took.

On joining the Sangha each new member made the following confession:

> I take my refuge in the Buddha;
> I take my refuge in the Dharma (the true law);
> I take my refuge in the Sangha (the order).

To become a monk one had to bind himself by the Ten Precepts:

1. Do not destroy life.
2. Do not take what is not given.
3. Be not unchaste.
4. Do not lie or deceive.
5. Do not drink intoxicants.
6. Do not eat immoderately or after noon.
7. Do not dance, sing, or observe theatrical or other spectacles.
8. Do not use garlands, perfumes, unguents and ornaments.
9. Do not use high or broad beds.
10. Do not accept money.

The first four of these precepts seem quite universal. Nearly everyone believes that it is wrong to kill, to steal, to be unchaste, and to lie. The matter of intoxicants is included in the list of common moral principles for Buddhist laymen. The last five may strike us as not conforming with the rule of moderation which Buddha accepted as a fundamental principle, even for monks. But we must think of this in the setting of Hindu and Jain asceticism. Relatively speaking, therefore, the last five precepts are indeed moderate. The sixth precept calls not for fasting but only for moderation in eating. Seven and eight call attention to the principle that true happiness comes from within. Number nine forbids luxury, and the last one reminds the monk that he is living the life of faith, having consecrated himself to the service of humanity through the Sangha. The Buddhist Bhikkhu was required to beg for his food. Two other requirements were that the head and face should be shaved and the monk should wear a yellow robe.

Buddhism became one of the most missionary of all religions, ranking with Christianity and Islam in this respect. The Buddha is said to have sent out his first disciples with this stirring commission: "Go ye now . . . and wander, for the gain of the many, for the welfare of the many, out of compassion for the world, for the good, for the gain, and for the welfare of gods and men."[12]

At first the Buddha himself ordained his disciples. But as time passed and his missionaries traveled great distances he commissioned them to ordain. Only during the rainy season did the missionary activity let up. At those periods each year the disciples would gather together for mutual edification and self-discipline.

The success of Buddhism was really phenomenal. It is said that Buddha personally converted Bimbisara, King of Magadha, at his capital in Rajagriha. There he also converted two young Brahmins, Maudgalyayana and Shariputra, who came to be famous leaders of Buddhism. His personal attendant was his cousin Ananda, who figures prominently in the early history of Buddhism. The Judas of Buddhism was another cousin, Devadatta who killed King Bimbisara, tried to kill Buddha, and organized a more extreme Buddhist sect. Pasenadi, King of Kosala, was another disciple. Parks, monasteries and nunneries were given to the order by wealthy patrons. The Buddha's success was tremendous even during his lifetime.

Legend has added much of the supernatural and the fantastic to the simple story of Buddha. It is said that he walked on the water, floated in the air, subdued a frightful serpent, disappeared into heaven to convert his mother who had died seven days after his birth, associated there with the gods, returned to earth by way of a jeweled staircase, and divided himself into multiple persons.[13]

But underneath all the legends there is the solid essence, well attested historically, of the noble Buddha who sincerely and earnestly sought peace of mind first by renouncing his princely life and going to the extremes of asceticism, only to find that he had failed to find peace there. Then he learned, apparently without effort, as the mystic insight flashed in upon his being, that neither in pleasure nor in self-torture is peace to be found, but in the inward cutting off of desire. This spiritual act called for suitable outward behavior. But the principle remained clear throughout.

After forty-five years of ministry, death came to the Buddha in a sal tree grove at Kusinara, an obscure town in the land of the Mallas about forty miles from where he had been born. Despite Buddha's efforts to teach his disciples how to escape sorrow by freeing themselves from emotional attachments to family, friends and earthly possessions, they became quite perturbed by his approaching death. Ananda slipped out to the cloister-building and stood "leaning against the lintel of the door . . . weeping." Ananda was called back to be with the Blessed One, who said, "Enough, Ananda, do not let yourself be troubled; do not weep. Have I not already, on former occasions, told you that it is in the very nature of all things most near and dear to us that we must divide ourselves from them . . . ? Whereas anything whatever born . . . contains within itself the inherent necessity of dissolution—how, then, can this be possible that such a being should not be dissolved? For a long time, Ananda, have you been very near to me by acts of love, kind and good, that never varies, and is beyond all measure. (This Buddha repeats three times.) You have done well. Be earnest in effort, and you, too, shall soon be free. . . ." The townspeople, when informed of the Buddha's approaching death, cried, "Too soon will the Blessed One die! Too soon will the Happy One pass away! Full soon will the Light of the world pass away! . . ." The Buddha's last words to his disciples were, "Behold now, brethren, I exhort you, saying, 'Decay is inherent in all component things! Work out your salvation with diligence.' "[14]

Main Teachings of Buddhism

So far as it is possible to reconstruct the teachings of Buddha, on the basis of our discussion so far, it would seem that they contained some traditional elements inherited from Hinduism, some novel elements contributed by the Buddha himself, and most important of all, the personality of the founder.

1. Among the traditional Hindu elements are the doctrines of *transmigration, karma,* and *moksha.* The Buddha did not invent these ideas at all. He did reinterpret them somewhat, in relation to other ideas of his own. But substantially he taught exactly as the Hindus of the Upanishads, and as Mahavira, with regard to transmi-

gration and its cause, karma, as well as the need for moksha or release from the cycle of death and rebirth. It seems unnecessary to discuss these three doctrines further, except to say that his concept of karma was more Hindu than Jainist. Jainist karma was based on Jainist atomism, in part. Buddhist karma was wholly spiritual.

2. Like the Hindus and the Jainists, Buddha believed in *gods* and in *heaven* and *hell*. Like the Jain, he believed that the gods were still in the cycle of deaths and births and would suffer reincarnation just as men would. Those arhats who had succeeded in gaining Nirvana were better off than any of the gods.

3. Against Buddha as against Mahavira the charge of *atheism* has been leveled, and for much the same reasons in both cases. The mortal gods whom Buddha recognized are hardly worthy of the name, although they are temporarily better off than men. And the Brahman of the Upanishads he refused to acknowledge as the sole reality of the universe, although he may have given Dharma, the eternal law, Brahman's place there.[15] Nor did he conceive that a creator was a necessary hypothesis for the explanation of the origin of the universe.

Yet there is really a vast difference between the theoretical atheism of Mahavira and Buddha. For whereas Mahavira denied the existence of Brahman and its identity with the Atman, Buddha merely held that Brahman was an inadequate concept of God. Radhakrishnan reports a dialogue[16] with the wandering monk Vaccha and his own disciple Ananda, in which the Buddha refused either to say that the Atman exists or that it does not exist. Later he explained to Ananda that he felt that both assertions would be false, since existence is not the proper category to apply to the Atman. It appears that Buddha was merely opposed to speculative theology. Religion to him was a very practical affair, and its success might very easily be impeded by theology. Too often theology is made a substitute for real religion. These matters of theological speculation, said the Buddha, "profit not, have not to do with the fundamentals of religion, tend not to absence of passion, quiescence, supreme wisdom, and Nirvana."[17] To Buddha "absence of passion, quiescence, supreme wisdom, and Nirvana" were the sum and substance of religion. The rest did not matter. Buddha did not mean to deny the existence of Brahman, or to insist on its existence for that matter, for the category of existence might well be misleading. He merely wanted to emphasize the point that religion was something other than credo.

4. Sometimes Buddha's view of the universe, as described above, is referred to as his *phenomenalism*. To summarize briefly, this is the view that there is no fundamental substance at the heart of the universe from which originates all that comes to be and to which all returns. According to such a view there is no being, but only becoming. "Buddha simply accepts the facts of experience. Things change."[18] Radhakrishnan feels that the tendency of Buddha's thinking is toward idealism, although he admits that Buddha suspends judgment when it comes right down to the issue. Buddha agrees with the Upanishads that the phenomenal world is a component world, a world made up of parts, and therefore not itself ultimately real but always changing its composition. But while the Upanishads go beyond the phenomenal world to its source in Brahman, Buddha refused to go behind the world of change. *Peace of heart* is the goal of life, said he, and to argue the problems of metaphysics is to run the risk of a fatal distraction from the real issues of life.

5. Closely related to the Buddha's so-called atheism and phenomenalism is his doctrine of the nature of *personality*. Like everything else in this phenomenal world, human personality is made up of component parts or aggregates called khandas. Five such khandas are distinguished: the body, feeling, sense-perception, mental processes and tendencies, and cognition. Other elements of personality are the five senses and the will to live. Buddha seems to have rejected the theory that karma causes rebirth. Rather, said he, rebirth is caused by the craving for life, or, as Schopenhauer put it, the will to live. Karma merely determines the kind of rebirth. So if one can extinguish the craving for life, one can end the cycle of rebirths.

As one element of personality, the body is obviously impermanent. "We can't take it with us." Even more impermanent is the mind, said Buddha. It changes from moment to moment. But the craving for life somehow keeps the four mental components of personality tied together so that when the old body dies the four mental khandas pass on to a new body, accompanied by their accumulated karma.

Pratt argues that inasmuch as Buddha rejects the view that the self is any one or all of its components, therefore he must have believed that the self is an indefinable something ultimately independent of its phenomenal self and its component parts. "The self is enduring, not subject to change, and as such, when by itself, not painful . . . . The moral earnestness of the Buddha and his insistence on responsibility would seem to demand some kind of real, identical, and abiding self."[19] It is apparent that Buddha rejected the crude animism of Jainism. But his refusal to put into words a substitute theory does not mean that he believed that there was no such enduring reality as might be connoted by the term personality. Radhakrishnan substantially agrees with Pratt's interpretation on this point.[20] Hopkins holds to the older view that for Buddha the person is nothing more than the bundle of khandas which, when dissolved by an act of enlightened will, cease to exist as a person.[21] Nirvana in Buddhism would mean, therefore, the extinction not only of desire but also of personality. But how could one, in Nirvana, enjoy the peace which passeth understanding if the person no longer exists? I must interpret Buddhism as Radhakrishnan and Pratt do in this respect.

6. The discussion so far leaves us in a good position to state simply the Buddha's view of *Nirvana.* To the Buddha Nirvana was the state of blessedness, happiness, joy unspeakable, that comes to the arhat who has extinguished the craving for life in all of its aspects. Since such blessedness is logically impossible without a person to enjoy it, I must reject the view that Buddhist Nirvana is the extinction both of desire and of the person. It is, of course, the extinction of the phenomenal person. It probably even means the extinction of the individuality of the person, or at least of the consciousness of limiting individuality. Words fail us. Neither existence nor nonexistence applies to Nirvana, says the Buddha. He tries to answer his disciples' questions about what has happened to Vakkali, an Arhat who had just died. Said he, "He has no consciousness anywhere and is utterly well."[22] Dealing with the same problem on another occasion he concluded by saying, "*Reborn* does not apply to him nor *not-reborn,* nor any combination of such terms."[23] His bliss is beyond the description of familiar terms or concepts. His being is more wonderful than the particularities of consciousness and sensation.

We are, of course, not sure that these were the actual words of the Buddha or whether they were put into his mouth by later Buddhists. But they seem to carry out the logic of his position in any case. And they certainly imply the persistence of the subject who, in the state of Nirvana, neither in time nor space, enjoys the peace unspeakable which comes from the extinction of desire.

7. Buddha's religion was fundamentally ethical. We may properly describe it as an expression of *ethical idealism*. Whatever else we may say about Buddha's views of the universe, we must admit that his universe was just. The most fundamental law of the universe was not gravitation or atomism but the law of karma, and this law insured that the wicked should be punished and the good rewarded. Further than that, he regarded man as free, so that when he became enlightened as to the sorrowful nature of life and its psychological causation, he could free himself from the law of karma and rise to Nirvana.

8. Essentially the Buddha's philosophy was *humanistic*. States Radhakrishnan, "He raised his voice in indignant protest against superstition and unreason. . . . He denied the divinity of the gods and undermined the authority of the Vedas."[24] The Buddha emphatically refused to believe something simply because it was traditional, or because it was in writing, or because a teacher said so, or even because he wanted to believe it.[25] This is like the freedom of the Greek philosophers and the thinkers of the Renaissance.

9. The Buddha left some teachings concerning the proper regard or reverence which the disciples should have for *the person of the Buddha*. Certainly one of the most important legacies of Buddhism was the very attractive personality of the Buddha. And while Gautama did not regard himself as a god nor expect his followers to worship him, yet he did apparently have an extraordinary opinion of himself—as Jesus did. It seems that he said certain things which led eventually to his exaltation to divinity. He is reported to have said, "He who seeth the Dharma, seeth me; he who seeth me, seeth the Dharma."[26] The Buddha became divinely precious in the memories of his disciples, as Jesus did in his. And his disciples accepted his teachings by faith, because they believed in him. They believed that he *knew*.

10. Reverence for the Buddha's relics, and *pilgrimages* to his

sacred places, may have been sanctioned by the Buddha. At least it is so represented in the earliest writings.[27] When the Buddha died his body was burned and the bones and ashes distributed to the faithful, who erected first a cairn and later a stupa over each deposit. Early Buddhism approved of the custom of paying reverence to the relics of the Buddha for the purpose of becoming calm in heart. Approved also was the custom of making pilgrimages to the four sacred places: (1) Kapilavastu, where he was born; (2) Bodhi-Gaya, where beneath the Bodhi-tree he received his enlightenment; (3) the deer park near Benares, where in his first sermon he started the

*The Buddhist "Wheel of the Law" may also represent the sun's disk, emitting its rays (the spokes) of light and truth.**

"turning of the wheel of the Dharma;" and (4) Kusinara, where he entered Nirvana upon the death of his body. Herein we have all the makings of the later Buddha worship. The tree, the wheel, and the stupa early became the sacred symbols of Buddha. His personal image did not enter into Buddhist worship until the first or second century A.D., through Greek influence.

Essence of Buddhism

The original genius of Buddhism lies in its ethical insight. Had Buddhism persisted in the land of its birth, it is quite likely that caste would have disappeared. Said Buddha, "Not by birth does one become an outcaste, not by birth does one become a Brahmin; by deeds one becomes an outcaste, by deeds one becomes a Brahmin."[28] Although its first appeal was primarily to Kshatriyas and then to Brahmins, yet it accepted all who came, regardless of caste. Thus it has done ever since. Its emphasis has always been on the moral worth of each individual. Its insistence on denying the craving for life was for the purpose of achieving a certain inward calmness of spirit.

* See Wheelwright, *The Burning Fountain,* p. 138.

The Noble Eightfold Path is a practical combination of faith and works. "Right views" refers to the need for a reasonable faith in the true way, as revealed through the knowledge of the Enlightened One. Right views include knowledge as well as faith, and are the necessary foundation for good character and a good life. The good life requires not ignorance but knowledge.

"Right aspiration" involves a conscious choice of worthy goals. The good life cannot be constructed without understanding the goals toward which one aspires. Let love and kindness motivate one's conduct, and the aspirations will be sure to be right.

"Right speech" calls for the elimination of lying, slander, and profane talk. It requires studied self-expression in order that our fellows may truly understand us and be influenced by our benevolence.

"Right behavior" is the substance of the moral life, outwardly observed. Perfectly good motives must not stop short of the fullest expression. Buddhism insists on purity of motive, but also requires the full outward expression of such motives in ethical conduct.

"Right livelihood" refers to the choice of such vocation by the laity as would not require or encourage killing, lying, stealing, for example. For the monks of course it refers to the proper monastic way of life.

"Right effort" calls for the active participation of the whole self in the moral life. One must always be alert to one's opportunities as also to the stumbling blocks in the way of success. No great task is accomplished unless one tries and tries hard.

"Right mindfulness" means that one should direct one's attention to those matters which are wholesome, which support those goals which one has consciously chosen. To let the attention wander to distracting events and purposes is to suffer defeat at the outset.

"Right concentration" is a further and more specific development of right mindfulness. A good way to overcome vices and temptations is to concentrate in meditation upon the ideal. This eighth path was probably borrowed from Hindu Yoga, with modifications. But the Buddha rejected the hypnotic aspects of Yogism and insisted that the individual concentrate his fullest consciousness on the objects which he has so carefully chosen for his moral aspiration. Such concentration should go far toward moral excellence and loving service to humanity, which is, after all, the main purpose of the Buddhist calm and the earnest goal of the founder of this remarkable religion.

Said Radhakrishnan, "In spite of the reforms which he wished to introduce, Buddha lived and died in the belief that he was restoring the principles of the venerable Aryan faith. . . . putting spiritual brotherhood in place of hereditary priesthood, personal merit in place of distinctions of birth, logical reason in place of Vedic revelation, moral life in place of ceremonial piety. . . . What made Buddha and his followers unpardonable heretics in the eyes of the Brahmin priests is the social revolution which they preached."[29]

XIII. THE GROWTH OF BUDDHISM

Paradoxically the religion of Buddhist lands today is not what we have described as Buddhism. The reason for this is not hard to find. Even as Gautama said, this is a world of becoming. Everything is in flux, including the religion which he bequeathed to the world as a strong tower in the midst of turmoil.

Even during the lifetime of Gautama certain changes were taking place. He himself started out by seeking his own salvation but, in the seventh year, turned compassionately to the task of teaching his fellows the way of salvation. As he won new converts they showed their individuality, in turn, by proposing variants of Gautama's teachings. When Devadatta could not convert Gautama to stricter ideas he tried to kill him. His accomplice, Ajatashatru, actually succeeded in killing Buddha's protector, King Bimbisara. On another occasion it became necessary to expel certain monks who had proved themselves unworthy of the Sangha. But others took sides with the unworthy ones. The Buddha reminded them that their example would influence the world. The factious brethren became insolent to the Buddha and told him that they understood their responsibility perfectly well. Buddha shrugged his shoulders and remarked, "Truly, these fools are infatuate." So he "leaves them, and goes into solitude, rejoicing to be free from souls so quarrelsome and contentious."[1]

If schisms could not be prevented during the lifetime of the founder, they were even more likely to occur later. And as Buddhism spread and took in more and more people, the cultural background of those people was certain to influence the development of Buddhist belief and practice.

Buddhist tradition, recorded in the Cullavagga and the Mahavamsa, reports that during the rainy season following the death of the

Buddha five hundred leading Arhats met at Rajagriha in the First Council of Buddhism. The council is supposed to have explored the extent of their agreement or disagreement on Buddhist doctrine and discipline. While there is no historical proof that such a council did meet, yet it seems only logical that it should have. Pratt accepts it with caution.

According to tradition the Second General Council of Buddhism met a hundred years later at Vesali to discuss the rules of the Sangha. Many monks thought the rules too strict, but the conservative party proved to be in the majority. So a schism resulted, and then there were two Sanghas instead of one. This is supposed to have happened about 383 B.C.

Influence of Ashoka

The next hundred years of Buddhism are too obscure to report. But then about 273 B.C. Ashoka (usually spelled Asoka, but the "s" is pronounced like "sh") came to the throne of Magadha and changed the whole history of Buddhism.

Ashoka inherited an expanding empire from his grandfather, Chandragupta Maurya, and his father, Bindusara. In turn Ashoka recklessly expended lives, according to his own confession, in further expansion until his empire included the kingdom of Kalinga in southeast India and everything north and northwest thereof to the Himalaya Mountains and the Hindu Kush.

After his conquest of Kalinga Ashoka became a Buddhist layman, and in 259 B.C. took the monastic vows. Upon his conversion he experienced, as he says in one of his Rock Edicts (XIII), "remorse for having conquered the Kalingas, because the conquest of a country previously unconquered involves the slaughter, death, and carrying away captive of the people. . . . (Now) His Sacred Majesty desires that all animate beings should have security, self-control, peace of mind, and joyousness."[2] These desires reflect his new Buddhist ideals.

Ashoka became inspired with missionary zeal and in the course of his reign of forty years sent missionaries throughout India and also to Ceylon, Syria, Egypt and Greece. On rocks and pillars he inscribed pithy statements of Buddhist doctrine, written in Prakrit, the language of the people. He went on a pilgrimage to many of the holy places of Buddhism. "By digging wells, planting trees, providing remedies (hospitals also may be intended) for both men and animals, and looking out for the comfort of travelers,"[3] he showed the sincerity of his religious convictions. He made justice more merciful, required his viceroys to travel and inquire into the needs of the people and instruct them in the law. He encouraged tolerance, genuine piety, humility, and love. Through his missionary zeal "he succeeded in transforming the local doctrine of a local Indian sect into one of the great religions of the world."[4]

The evangelization of Ceylon was accomplished by Mahinda, who was either Ashoka's son or younger brother. According to a legend Mahinda and his missionary party floated through the air when passing from the mainland to the island of Ceylon. The story goes on to say, more credibly, that Mahinda's sister later went to Ceylon to establish an order of nuns. There is abundant archaeological and historical evidence that the island of Ceylon was thoroughly won for Buddha. It still holds to that religion.

According to tradition Ashoka convened Buddhism's Third General Council in 241 B.C. Pratt and Radhakrishnan accept the historicity of this council and regard it as an effort to purify the Buddhist Sangha and verify the sacred scriptures which were in existence at that time. It is said that there were eighteen or more Buddhist sects in existence then. A general council was certainly needed, therefore.

About 185 B.C. Ashoka's dynasty gave way to the Shunga dynasty, ruling over a considerably smaller empire. Its Hindu King Pushyamitra is reported to have initiated a persecution of Buddhism. Nevertheless Buddhism was still vigorous during his reign and that of his dynasty, lasting until about 80 B.C. Many stupas have been discovered which date back to Shunga times, as also to Ashoka's times.

In the Punjab at this time appeared the Greek King Menander, who was called Milinda by the Indians. His reign was c.161-c.145 B.C., and he became a new champion of the Buddhist religion. Partly legendary and partly historical are the Questions of King Milinda, which has been incorporated into the canon of some of the Southern Buddhists. "Milinda" was a philosophical king who never met his philosophical equal until he learned of Nagasena. This venerable Buddhist monk was able to answer all the king's questions to his complete satisfaction. Finegan quotes one such conversation, as follows:

> The king said: "Nagasena, is there any one who after death is not reindividualized?"
> "Some are so, and some not."
> "Who are they?"
> "A sinful being is reindividualized, a sinless one is not."
> "Will you be reindividualized?"
> "If when I die, I die with craving for existence in my heart, yes; but if not, no."
> "Very good, Nagasena!"[5]

It is said that Milinda was converted by Nagasena, and that with his encouragement Buddhism became strong in northwestern India as it diminished in Magadha under Hindu kings.

The Greek dynasty in northwestern India was replaced by the Kushans (c.50-c.320 A.D.), Mongoloid nomads. Its King Kanishka in the second century A.D. chose Buddhism as his faith, yet was no narrow partisan. Well-disposed toward the other religions of northwest India, he was especially helpful toward Buddhism. Like Ashoka, he convened a Buddhist council, called the Fourth General Council in Buddhist tradition. The growing sectarianism alone was sufficient justification for such a council, which dealt with this problem in a fairly successful manner. The scholars at this council wrote extensive commentaries on the Tripitaka, and King Kanishka "had the discourses inscribed on copper sheets and enclosed in a stone receptacle, and over this he erected a stupa."[6]

Besides the eighteen or more fragmentary sects, the two main divisions of later Buddhism had already come into existence by the time of Kanishka, namely, the Hinayana and the Mahayana. Hinayana means literally "Lesser Vehicle," while Mahayana means "Greater Vehicle." The Mahayanists were responsible for inventing the names but the Hinayanists had to accept them, for they stuck. The implication was that the revised version of Buddhism offered by the Mahayana sects was a more adequate means, or vehicle, for conveying the essence of Buddhism than the more conservative version offered by the Hinayana sects.

Mahayana and Hinayana

The development of Mahayana Buddhism was forecast by the religious art of the period of Kanishka. In his northwest India Hellenism and Buddhism met, and the result for Buddhism was a more personalized religion. Before this time artists had represented the Buddha by such symbols as the Bodhi-tree, the wheel of the law, the empty seat or throne, or the footprints of the Buddha. Beginning at about this time we observe images of the human-divine Buddha, not with his head shaved but with short curling hair and Indra top-knot. About him frequently appear other Buddhas, Bodhisattvas and gods. Similar Buddha-images, seated or standing, are found in other parts of India dating back to the second and first centuries A.D. and showing that even at that early time Buddhism had produced the elements of the Mahayana faith. Indeed, the Buddha-images were to characterize both Mahayana and Hinayana Buddhism from this time on.

Generally speaking Hinayana Buddhism spread to southern lands such as Ceylon, Burma and Thailand, while Mahayana Buddhism spread to the northern lands, China, Korea and Japan. However, the story is not quite that simple, for Hinayana influence was strong in early Chinese Buddhism. At times the Mahayana was in the ascendancy in the southern lands, as in Ceylon and Burma. And there are definitely Mahayana features even in Hinayana Buddhism today. In India itself the Mahayana and Hinayana sects existed side by side, with sometimes one in the ascendancy and sometimes the other. Sometimes monks of both groups would live together in the same monastery, keeping to their own separate ideas regarding the interpretation of Buddhism.

Hinayana Buddhism has been called conservative because it is more in accordance with original Buddhism than the Mahayana. That is, the Hinayanists believe that the Buddha was originally quite human, and that he attained superhuman powers only through his enlightenment. They believe that the Buddha entered Nirvana upon death, and therefore that he no longer enjoys personal existence nor influences the affairs of men or nature. Such peace does he have that he is wholly unaware of the world of becoming.

The Hinayanists accept only the ancient Pali texts, described as the Tripitaka. However, we have already seen that the Tripitaka texts are not all equally ancient, and that even the most ancient ones contain accretions not in accord with the ideas of the historical Buddha—although this point is often hard to maintain. For example, the Pali texts in one place say that Gautama was not the only Buddha, but that there were six others who preceded him in earlier ages. In another place they say that twenty-four Buddhas preceded Gautama. In the same text we also read that Gautama is a divine being, perfect in his goodness and wisdom from eternity; that he accumulated merit through innumerable incarnations and lived in the Tushita heaven, which he deliberately forsook when he resolved to come to earth, enter the womb of Maya his virgin-mother, be born as a man and bring enlightenment and salvation to many. His teachings and example showed men how to live. Then he entered Nirvana and became finally unaware of the world of change. But the next Buddha—Maitreya—who is now a Bodhisattva, will come to earth in the fullness of time, will again attain enlightenment and teach men how to live before he, too, enters Nirvana. That this is legendary we have no doubt. But what substratum of Buddha's actual words were transformed into such legends, that is what we do not know.

Though Hinayana Buddhism is more conservative than the Mahayana, it has wandered far from the teachings of the man Gautama, as an examination of Ceylonese or Burmese Buddhism will prove. For example, there are the sacred relics. It is doubtful that Buddha ever said anything to show his approval of relic-reverence at all. If he did, it certainly was for no other purpose than to aid the disciples in achieving inward calm. But Ceylonese and Burmese relic-worship far exceeds such humanistic purposes.

For example, there was the worship of the Bodhi-tree. The Emperor Ashoka himself, in Magadha in the third century B.C., worshiped the Bodhi-tree and abdicated his throne in order to make it king. King Tissa, first Buddhist ruler of Ceylon, gratefully accepted a branch of the Bodhi-tree which he planted and made king in his stead.[7] Then in the fifth century A.D. Ceylon imported the left canine tooth of the Buddha from southern India. Annually the tooth was taken on a solemn processional between rows of images of the Bodhisattva of Gautama, while religious offerings were made to it with incense and burning lamps. So reports the fifth-century Chinese Buddhist pilgrim, Fa-Hien.[8] Although the tooth was destroyed by the Portuguese in 1560 and given twice within a few months' time to the King of Burma, yet the Ceylonese still revere the "original" tooth. These goings-on do not sound like the religion of Gautama the Buddha.

Hinayana Worship

In Ceylon Buddhism seems to be primarily a religion for monks. Monasteries and temples are found mostly in secluded places which are hard to reach, insuring privacy for monastic meditations. Buddhist laymen normally go to church only on "preaching days," which usually come twice a month. In contrast, Burma's monasteries are close to the centers of population and are frequented by laymen who singly or in groups enter to meditate and become calm in heart, and go out to be more like the Buddha.

*Symbol of the Buddhist tomb, or stupa, suggesting the triumph of life over death. Note the tau cross surmounting the tomb.**

In both Ceylon and Burma there are thousands of inferior deities, with just a few major deities borrowed from Hinduism (or, in Burma, from native animism) playing a prominent part. Indra (or Sakara), Brahmā, Vishnu, Shiva, and the Bodhi-tree are all important. Prayers are said to them—or to their images—in much the same way as a Roman Catholic prays to the saints. The Buddha is still the top god but is less approachable than these others, since he is in Nirvana, theoretically out of touch with the world of turmoil.

A typical monastery in Ceylon consists of the central shrine—the dagoba (stupa) presumably sheltering some sacred relic—and simple dormitories. The white dagoba is in the form of a hemisphere of solid masonry topped by a white "tee." The monastic dormitories are likely to be separated from the central shrine and to include a low tower.

* See Wheelwright, *The Burning Fountain,* pp. 137-138.

More impressive are the pagodas of Burma, guarded by carved beasts reminiscent of its recent animism. Shrine and dormitory are likely to be united in one piece of architecture in Burma. Actually the pagoda is a one-story affair, but a series of turned-up gables give the impression of several stories. The single large room "serves as meeting-place, dining room, temple, and usually as dormitory also. . . . The eastern end of the great hall is reserved for the Buddha and his altar, surrounded with offerings. . . . Both interior and exterior of the monastic building are decorated in high color, with much red and mosaic. . . . There is also much carving—especially of friendly nats (gods)—and perhaps frescoes, especially of the curiosities of hell."[9] Some of the large pagodas, such as those at Rangoon, Prome and Pegu, are most striking. One at Rangoon is higher than Saint Paul's Cathedral in London. There are many, many pagodas in Burma, largely because building a pagoda is a chief way of earning merit.

The primary purpose of monastic life seems to be to secure one's own salvation. "There are learned monks in both lands, but the great majority are decidedly ignorant."[10] The Burmese monks educate the young boys from the villages. They enjoy the respect of the people, the great majority of whom are Buddhists. Certainly some of the monks and at least a few of the laity understand the humanistic intent of Buddhism, and in that respect are faithful to the spirit of original Buddhism. And, as Pratt says, practically the whole population knows the moral side of Buddhism. "All the Burmese know the Five Precepts, the girls as well as the boys, the old folks as well as the young."[11]

Nationalism in southern Asia has led to a resurgence of Buddhism as a political force. "Naturally when these people think about their national heritage they must think about Buddhism, for no other force has contributed half so much as Buddhism has. To be a loyal Ceylonese, Burmese, or Siamese is to be a good Buddhist. In fact, Buddhist monks, especially in the large centers, are taking more and more interest in politics and in the affairs of the modern world. So much is this the case that older and more conservative monks are expressing concern lest 'true Buddhism' will not survive."[12]

Mahayana Mission

One of the chief differences between Hinayana and Mahayana Buddhism is that in the former the monastic life has always been regarded as ideal, while in the latter monasticism was rather regarded as a means to the propagation and ministry of Buddhism to the laity. Paralleling this contrast, the characteristic attitude of Hinayana Buddhism was other-worldly and pessimistic, while the Mahayana was other-worldly but optimistic. The latter also greatly exaggerated the supernatural aspects of Buddhism and added numerous mythological tales.

For example, the doctrine of the Bodhisattva was elaborated in the Mahayana. This is a term which occurs in some early texts and is used in both kinds of Buddhism. In its earliest use the term Bodhisattva described Gautama in the period before he became the Buddha, as the one who was destined to become enlightened. The Jataka Tales, of late origin but canonical even with the Hinayana, explain by means of mythology how the predestined Buddha had progressed through many incarnations, finally entering the Tushita heaven. From there he came to earth to redeem mankind.

Mahayana thinkers set up this redeemer ideal as higher than the ideal of the arhat who, "wandering alone like a rhinoceros," was concerned only with his own salvation. They conceived that there were many Buddhas throughout the ages who had done as Gautama had, and that there would be many more. Those who were yet to be Buddhas were even now going through the stages of perfection as Gautama had done in his previous existences. And a great many had already attained to perfection but were postponing their Buddhahood in order to use their superfluous merit for the salvation of mankind. That is what makes them Bodhisattvas. Some of the monastic disciples of Buddhism in the Mahayana sects took vows to become Bodhisattvas rather than Buddhas, that is, "to preach the Dharma . . . , comfort the afflicted, and accumulate merit through many incarnations for the use of others, and not enter into Nirvana till all are rescued."[13] The typical Bodhisattva, however, is not the human monk just starting on the enormous cycle of incarnations leading heavenward, but one of a great number who have already gone through the cycle and have now postponed their own Nirvana until they have saved all men. To them the Mahayana Buddhist prays for the needed merit or forgiveness and aid on the road of earthly existence.

Mahayana Deities

Somehow the Mahayanists learned the names of some of the most important of the really innumerable Bodhisattvas. Of first importance was Avalokiteshvara, "He who looks down in pity." The name is of Indian origin, where he gained his first popularity. But his greatest development took place in China, Korea, and Japan. There his sex changed and he became in China Kuan-Yin, Goddess of Mercy —a kind of Virgin Mary to the Chinese Buddhists. In Korea Koan-Eum, in Japan Kwannon, was her counterpart. The goddess of mercy was often pictured holding a babe tenderly in her arms. She helped women to bear children, and guided the faithful at death to the Western Heaven, the Pure Land of Amitabha.

Manjusri holds second place among the Bodhisattvas. He symbolizes or personifies wisdom, knowledge and meditation. He represents the intellectual side of Buddhism, carrying the sword of logic and the book of the Dharma. He knew the Dharma long before the first of the twenty-five Buddhas. The intellectual aspect of Buddhism makes him important, although not so important as the more emotional Avalokiteshvara ("the Lord Avalokita"). Chinese Buddhism knows him as Wen-Shu, Japanese as Monju.

Another prominent Bodhisattva was Kshitigarbha—Ti-Tsang in China, and Jizo in Japan. This strange being was credited by the Chinese with being able to divide himself into six persons—one for each of the levels of universal life. In the Orient his popularity seems due to his reputation for descending into hell, upon request, and delivering one's relatives from torment, taking them to heaven.

The Buddhas who have already gone to Nirvana are known as Manushi Buddhas. They are, of course, respected, admired, and even loved, especially Gautama. But the Bodhisattvas are supernatural beings on the way to Buddhahood who are not unapproachable in Nirvana. So they fill a place which the Manushi Buddhas could not.

There is a third type of being, the Dhyani Buddhas. Of these by far the most important is Amitabha. His name means "Measureless Light." As Amitayus, he is also "Measureless Life." The Chinese know him as O-mi-to, the Koreans and Japanese as Amida. He was once a Bodhisattva but passed beyond it to Buddhahood without, however, actually entering Nirvana. Many more of the Dhyani Buddhas have become such without going through the human experience of arhatship and enlightenment.

The special appeal of Amitabha lies in the fact that he is now presiding over the Western Paradise, "the Pure Land," while he postpones his own Nirvana. As lord of the Pure Land he hears the prayers of the faithful, forgives their sins and assures them of admission to that glorious country. This is salvation by faith, as a late Sanskrit work describes it: "Beings are not born in that Buddha country as a reward and result of good works performed in this present life. No, all men and women who hear and bear in mind for one, two, three, four, five, six, or seven nights the name of Amitayus, when they come to die, Amitayus will stand before them in the hour of death, they will depart this life with quiet minds, and after death they will be born in Paradise."[14] This could be salvation by faith, or it could be magic, depending on the cultural background of the faithful. But whichever it is, it is a far cry from the original ideal of Gautama who sought the extinction of desire and individuality in the peaceful calm of non-sensuous Nirvana.

We should perhaps also mention Vairocana, originally an oriental sun god who was adopted by Mahayana as an Eternal Buddha. He is of first importance in Javanese Buddhism and is popular in some sects of China and Japan. His origin and character dramatize the extremely mythological nature of Mahayana Buddhism.

But shall we say that Mahayana Buddhism is therefore inferior to Hinayana, or to the still more philosophical Buddhism of Gautama? That it answers better to the needs of human beings as they now are is admitted. Even so, it is of course more superstitious and far more mythological. In terms of human values as they are lived, perhaps Mahayana Buddhism, with its emphasis on the laity rather than on the monastic order, is more humanistic.

A further word should be said about Maitreya, the Messianic Buddha still to come. He is to be classified among the Bodhisattvas, since he has not yet attained Buddhahood. There is more of a social message in the doctrine of Maitreya than in any other aspects of Buddhism. For when Maitreya comes he promises to usher in an earthly kingdom of prosperity, good health, wisdom and virtue. Miraculous features will accompany his coming, but when he comes he will reward Kassapa, Gautama's faithful disciple, for his meditation deep within the earth. Then he will proclaim that not miracles but virtue, wisdom and mercy are of supreme importance. This coming of God's kingdom on earth through the instrumentality of Maitreya has in it many possibilities for a reinterpretation of Buddhism, which in its Mahayana form is out-going and evangelistic rather than inward and individualistic.

Buddhism in Northern Lands

A confused form of Buddhism is found in Tibet, where it shows strong mixtures of primitive animism, Tantrism, Shivaism, Shamanism, and sorcery. It may more properly be called Lamaism. Worship of the Shiva-devil (half male and half female) for warding off evil spirits, is as important as the worship of Buddha. Magic and sorcery are practiced by the shamans or priests, who are tremendously powerful. Even the Buddhist texts are more likely to be used magically than morally or doctrinally in Tibet.

There the Dalai Lama is a combination of pope and emperor, uniting church and state. When the Lama dies, his place is taken by an infant born at that moment. The priests of Lamaism feel competent to discern into which new-born body the soul of the departed Lama has entered, somewhat as the Calvinistic old lady undertook to name those about her whom God had predestined to be saved or damned.

Most Buddhist monks of Tibet marry. Even the Buddhas are represented as being married, each to his Shakti, or embodiment of female life-energy. Shaktism—or Tantrism—seems to have been original in Tibetan culture, and to have mixed quite naturally with the Buddhism which was imported.[15]

Although geographical contact between China and India is very difficult, it is possible that the Chinese heard about Buddha during Ashoka's reign in the third century B.C. But the official Buddhist mission to China did not take place until 65 A.D., according to tradition. At that time the Han Emperor Ming Ti is said to have had a dream of a golden image of Buddha entering his room with its head glowing brightly as the sun. Thereupon he sent twelve emissaries to India to secure more knowledge of the Buddha. The emissaries returned with two monks, their holy scriptures and Buddha images. The Emperor built them a monastery where they proceeded to translate their scriptures into Chinese. From these legends we may at least conclude that Buddhism gained a foothold in China during the first century A.D.

Apparently the first Buddhism to come to China was of the Hinayana type. The Confucian Chinese were inclined to be primarily interested in this world and its social values. A strong tradition reports that the Chinese forbade their own boys from entering any Buddhist monastic order. This is not surprising, since there is a logical antagonism between the Confucian family ideal and the Hinayana monkish ideal.

From the third to the sixth centuries China experienced a time of troubles. Nomadic tribes invaded China bringing division, misery, and in general a pessimistic outlook on life. Among the nomads were Mahayana Buddhists. Other Mahayana missionaries came to China too. The times were such that Mahayana Buddhism made a strong appeal. It proved also to be more adaptable to the Chinese temperament and tradition than had the Hinayana. Among other things, Mahayana added the Confucian virtue of filial piety to its list, and urged sons to make use of Mahayana masses for the dead, in order that the departed souls might be happy. Mahayana Buddhism also provided for the superstitious Chinese a more pleasant picture of the future life than they had been accustomed to in Chinese mythology. The Chinese equivalents of Avalokiteshvara and Amitabha became very popular. Northern China responded first, while southern China yielded more slowly to the new Buddhist effort.

Mahayana Buddhism entered Korea about the fourth century. This country's animistic culture was so inferior to any type of Buddhism that it yielded easily to the Buddhist mission. Before the sixth century was over Korea was exporting Buddhism to Japan.

According to the legend, a Korean monarch sent to the Japanese Emperior Kimmei, in 552 A.D., a golden image of Buddha, some

Buddhist scriptures, and a message concerning Buddhism, its magical and spiritual values. The message explained that this great religion had come all the way from India, that the Chinese had accepted it, and that it had done much good in Korea. After some discussion with his advisers, somewhat fearful that the native gods would be offended, the Emperor decided to let the Prime Minister erect the image in the territory of his people, the Soga clan. A pestilence followed and they threw the image into a canal. This story was virtually repeated during the reign of the next Emperor, with a sequel: when the Buddha images were thrown into the canal, the pestilence continued. Japanese logic then suggested that the reason for the pestilence probably was not the anger of native gods but the anger of the Buddhas at such a cool reception. Finally in 588 A.D. the regent, Shotoku Taishi, who had been converted to Buddhism, took steps to encourage Buddhism as well as to bring about governmental reform. Social reforms also were initiated, in which other Buddhists cooperated. This did much to advance Buddhism in Japan. Buddhism became popular when it took over the native gods by making them Buddhas and Bodhisattvas. This did not mean that the people abandoned either Shinto or Confucianism; on the contrary, they frequently found it advantageous to believe in all three at the same time. This was the pattern which Buddhism had followed successfully in China, and now it worked also in Japan.

Buddhism has undergone periods of bitter persecution in both China and Japan, and has survived them all. In 740 A.D. it is recorded that there were sixty-four monasteries and twenty-seven nunneries in the Tang capital of China alone. A century later, in 845 A.D., persecution destroyed 4,600 large Buddhist monasteries and 40,000 other Buddhist buildings, and 260,500 monks and nuns were required to abandon the order and become laymen. The persecution was inspired by the enemies of Buddhism, however, and the people remained loyal, compelling a return to tolerance. During the following centuries in China Buddhism prospered, even influencing the philosophy of the Confucian schools. In Japan a revival of Shinto in the seventeenth century led to some troubles for Buddhism, which proved to be temporary however. At the present time Buddhism is of course prospering more in Japan than in China where, under the Communist regime, no religion is officially tolerated.

Meanwhile Buddhism made consistent progress in India, the land of its birth, up to about the sixth or seventh century A.D. The invasions of the White Huns in the sixth century were hard on Buddhist monasteries in the north. Still more significant was the Hindu adoption of Buddhism, as when the Vishnu worshipers made Buddha the ninth incarnation of Vishnu. This confused the people who saw no reason to abandon Hinduism when it included Buddhism. Recent Hindu philosophy sees a fundamental kinship between Hinduism and Buddhism, and in effect claims to encompass the latter. The severest external blow against Indian Buddhism came with the Muslim invasion of the twelfth century. The Muslims, of course, would tolerate no polytheism and no image worship, so Buddhism was doomed wherever Islam went. Magadha was taken in 1193 A.D., and—until its recent revival—Buddhism virtually ceased to exist as an organized religion in the land of its birth.

Some Buddhist Sects

Our story would be incomplete without at least referring to some of the most important Buddhist sects or schools of thought of China and Japan, in order to suggest the sort of problem which confronts modern Buddhism. I shall not attempt to give the history of any sect named except as it may help to enlighten concerning its present character.

Three sects having much in common are the *Pure Land* sect (or school) of China, and the *Jodo* and *Shinshu* sects of Japan. Amitabha Buddha is central in these sects, the Eternal Buddha who is always ready to help some one in need, and in the hour of death to lead him to the Pure Land of Bliss in the Western Regions. Good works are unnecessary, though desirable. The Jodo and the Shinshu sects provide names or formulas, the repetition of which shall provide the means of salvation. One who has not the time or ability to engage in Buddhist meditation can easily see the advantages of this teaching. One novelty of the Shinshu sect is the marriage of the monks. Man is a citizen of eternity, said Shinran its founder, but he is also a citizen of this world. This made household religion as important as temple religion.

Two other sects are the so-called *True Word* sects, the *Chen Yen* in China and the *Shingon* in Japan. These are sometimes called the Mystery Sects. Chen Yen states that reality is a mystery too deep for words, and can best be represented by symbols. Its doctrine is that Vairocana, the Eternal Buddha who is identified with the sun, is the dynamic source of all being. In this way man is truly an emanation from the Infinite Buddha and therefore has the true Buddha nature within. By realizing this he can return to his source, becoming the Buddha once more. This doctrine is as pantheistic as the most pantheistic of the Upanishads. But popularly Chen Yen is associated with mystery and magic. The correct use of the right formula will bring a dead relative back from hell and take him magically to heaven. In Japan even emperors joined the Shingon sect, substituting the Sun Buddha for the Japanese sun goddess Amaterasu. The same mystic pantheism characterized Shingon in Japan as Chen Yen in China.

More rationalistic were the T'ien-T'ai sects of China and the Tendai of Japan. These schools originally took a broad-minded view of religious truth, insisting that there are many ways of arriving at salvation: "silent meditation and mystical communion with the eternal; ascetic discipline and meritorious work; and simple faith in the mercy of the all-compassionate Buddha."[16] The many-sidedness of these sects resulted in the founding of still newer sects standing for more specific things.

The Chinese Ch'an and the Japanese Zen sects stress meditation, looking inwardly into one's heart to find the true Buddha nature. Good works, scholarly research, asceticism and ritual are either futile or harmful if they do not lead to intuitive insight which enables the subject to come in contact with Buddha-reality. The emphasis of these sects upon intuition has led to the development of a distinctive, dreamy art-style, in both China and Japan. The Japanese discrimination in flower-arrangement is said to have been derived from Zen Buddhism. Zen monks have been habituated to making paradoxical and completely irrelevant statements, their purpose being to prod men into the meditative mood in order to come up with original insights. The theory is that reason cannot possibly give us truth or reality, which can only be learned by turning the attention inward. Japanese military men became fond of Zen Buddhism, apparently because it taught rigid self-discipline and a readiness to sacrifice oneself for king or country.

Finally Nichiren Buddhism arose in Japan as a protest against Buddhist sectarianism. Nichiren, the founder, insisted that the *Lotus Gospel* was the only true Buddhist Scripture, and he denounced the popular belief in Amida (Amitabha). He taught that the Buddhist should not be thinking about going to the Western Paradise, but about living good loyal lives here and now, especially for the glory of Japan. The Nichiren sect is influential in Japan even yet, but its influence is primarily patriotic and its present followers are mostly fanatics. They think of Nichiren as a great Bodhisattva.

Evidences of modernism and the ideal of social service may be noted especially in Zen and Nichiren Buddhism, as also in Japanese Buddhism in general.[17]

Buddhist Philosophers

It might seem, from this review, that the philosophy of Mahayana Buddhism is unimportant, or even that the word "philosophy" is a misnomer when applied to Mahayana. But the opposite is the case so far as history reveals.

Four philosophers are especially important in the history of Mahayana Buddhism. They are Ashvaghosha, Nagarjuna, Asanga and Vasubandhu. The first two were converted to Buddhism from Hinduism. The father of the latter two was himself a Brahmin. So we may anticipate that their philosophies were influenced by Hinduism.

Nagarjuna founded the Madhyamika school of thought. Some have described this system as nihilism, since it teaches that nothing exists from one moment to the next. This doctrine he took from the Hinayana philosophers who had said that being and consciousness are composed of dharmas or drops of reality which last only for a moment and are succeeded by other dharmas carrying the essence of the past into the future. Nagarjuna launched his philosophy by denying the reality of the momentary dharmas, and susbstituting for them the Void. Although there is much difference of opinion over what he meant, the tendency today is to interpret him as a kind of idealist. If this is correct, he was somewhat like Plato who, in his allegory of the cave, taught that the material world of the senses is non-being, while the world of Ideas is the only true being. Both Plato and Nagarjuna probably believed that the world of matter had a relative kind of being. F. H. Bradley taught a similar doctrine in very recent times.

The Madhyamika school influenced the Yogacara philosophy, initiated by Asanga and Vasubandhu. These philosophers seem to accept the Madhyamika doctrine of the Void, but insist as probably Nagarjuna believed, that if there is a Void there is also something which *is* void. Just as an illusion implies that someone is experiencing even the illusion, so a void implies that there is something which contains the void. These philosophers constructed a world which is dependent on consciousness of some sort. We might call it the subconscious, or mere intuitive awareness.

The striking feature of the Mahayana philosophy is seen when this ultimate reality—consciousness or awareness, call it what you will—is said to be nothing other than the Buddha nature itself. Ashvaghosha's little book, *The Awakening of Faith in the Mahayana,** carries out this idea with power. The very essence of all being, he insists, is absolute knowledge, unitary being. When one really understands the nature of the infinite Buddhas who have appeared during past world epochs, says Ashvaghosha, one realizes that the Buddhas are all one. The Buddha appears differently to each of us, depending on our degree of enlightenment. But even the historical Buddha was only an appearance. The real Buddha is an eternal being, of whom all manifestations are mere appearances. The Eternal Buddha was incarnate in Shakyamuni, as in all the other Buddhas. Knowledge of the eternal Buddha and love for all sentient beings is what leads to salvation, to Nirvana. "As ignorance is thus annihilated, the mind is no more disturbed so as to be subject to individuation. As the mind is no more disturbed, the particularization of the surrounding world is annihilated. When in this wise the principle and condition of defilement, and their products, with the mental disturbances that flow from them are all annihilated, it is said that we attain Nirvana."[18]

Nirvana, in *The Awakening,* as for Mahayana generally, turns

* It is not all certain that Ashvaghosha wrote it, but such is the tradition.

out to be not extinction, although this word is used. The *Lotus Gospel* describes an ancient Buddha as "completely extinct" in Nirvana, but when a certain stupa is opened, there he is "as if absorbed in abstract meditation."[19] Shakyamuni comes to him and they converse and share a throne. So Nirvana means here the extinction of illusion and self-centeredness. Essentially, for the Mahayana, Nirvana means the attainment of Buddhahood, or the full realization that the world of individuality is a world of appearance, and that reality is the Buddha-nature from which we come and to which we return. So in Mahayana Buddhism, at least for the philosophical, we have gone full circle and come back at last to the position of the Hindu Upanishads.

In Mahayana idealism, however, there is one important qualification which distinguishes it from certain Upanishads. That is that the Buddha-reality at the heart of the universe is personal, not an "It" like Brahman. That personal essence, for Mahayana, is best seen in the great love wherewith Shakyamuni loved his fellow creatures and all forms of sentient life. If the love of an ultimately single personal God is the essence of reality for the Mahayana Buddhism, perhaps we should be comparing it not just with the Upanishads, but with Christianity.

Maturity of Buddhism

It seems clear that in Buddhism we have found a religion with much maturity. Of course we find magic in its history and present practice, as in the special regard for Buddha's relics, like the worship of his tooth. And there is some idolatry, as when ignorant and superstitious people revere an oversize image of the Buddha. But ignorance is at fault in such cases, not original Buddhism or philosophical Buddhism. A sacred tooth can hardly be interpreted as anything but a magical fetish. But the quest of a quiet heart through the contemplation of a Buddhist stupa, or the search for aesthetic peace by means of contemplating a truly expressive image of Buddha, may be granted a high status of religious maturity.

There is undoubtedly much literalism in Buddhist interpretation of its myths. The question is, however, what are the potentialities of Buddhism for a mature religious experience? And the answer to this is that the potentialities are great. The myths of the Bodhisattvas, for example, can be used by enlightened Buddhists to stimulate the imagination to cooperate with the will in a life of compassion for God's children and God's creatures. Even the myth of the Buddha's virgin birth and high resolve to leave heaven behind him, like the myth of Maitreya, may be used poetically for a like purpose.

Buddhist pessimism may be defended to some extent, although mental health does not easily result from the effort to rid the self of desire. It may well be the case that an individual has too much ambition in comparison with his ability. Some Buddhist insight may be quite helpful in such instances. But in any case, and on the whole, the Buddhist stress on moderation is good. Gautama condemned equally the life of purposeless pleasure and the ascetic life as simply ineffective means of finding satisfaction. If one can reach the philosophical height of a kind of detachment from the innumerable petty goals that absorb most human hearts, and then through a kind of eightfold noble path evaluate one's daily quests with moderation and contentment, he may be truly happy.

Considering the basic Buddhist ideal of universal human compassion and selfless service, one must accord to Buddhism a high degree of maturity as judged by its ethical principles and social outlook.

Buddhist art and ritual, when rightly interpreted and correctly orientated, can point beyond idolatry to maturity. Its symbols have an intrinsic power, inspiring one to reverence for law, to peace of mind, and to human service.

The misinterpretation of Buddhist atheism has been a great historical injustice. Buddha sought the divine presence for six years, if tradition is true. Finding it, he was so happy that he wanted to share it with all. But the divine presence could not be expressed in neat formulas, so he tried to lead his disciples to personal discovery. Many of his followers made that discovery. Not the least of these was Ashvaghosha—or whoever wrote *The Awakening*.

Buddhism may be interpreted as an expression of the essential universalism of Hinduism, carrying its insights abroad as Hinduism failed to do.

We might be surprised to learn how many obscure but pious

Buddhists there are in the world today, who have carried modern enlightenment into the rich forms of Buddhist traditions, who think of the Buddha primarily as a prophet, but who have been inspired by him to think of God as love. Such are at least the mature potentialities of Buddhism among the religions of mankind.

XIV. THE GROWTH OF HINDUISM

Besides the early Upanishads or Vedanta, already discussed, later Upanishads sprang into existence through religious inspiration, and literature of an entirely different type was written. These works include legal writings such as the Code of Manu, and the great Epics like the Mahabharata, the Ramayana, and the Puranas. Included in the Mahabharata is the immortal Bhagavad Gita which forms the most treasured part of all Hindu literature today, in very much the same way as the Psalms and the Sermon on the Mount constitute the most treasured part of Christian scriptures today.

In addition to the Upanishads, the Codes, and the Epics, there came into existence quite early the various Sutras, in an effort to sum up as briefly as possible the teachings of the Upanishads. Out of the Sutras grew the six schools of Indian philosophy and their later commentators. One of these schools was called Vedanta, and the writings of this school are often referred to as Vedantic literature. This phase of Hindu philosophy will be dealt with in the next chapter. The present chapter will be confined to the scriptural sources.

The Code of Manu

It seems that the Code of Manu has been emphasized out of proportion to its importance by western scholars. It is true that Indian scholars continue to recognize it in expounding Hindu literature, as Radhakrishnan has done. But they probably do so because of the same accident that brought it to the attention of western scholars. When Warren Hastings became the first British Governor General of India he chose the Manava Dharma Shastra ("Code of Manu") from forty-seven Indian legal works submitted to him. He was anxious to govern by means of native law, and this seemed to him to epitomize the Hindu legal complex. Hence its singular importance.

The Code of Manu is not a book of law in the modern sense. At best it is a mixed collection, with one part sometimes contradicting another part. It is in Sanskrit verse-form, based on "an earlier prose treatise of religious, ethical, ceremonial, civil and criminal rules and precepts for right living and right conduct, as taught by a particular school of northwestern Brahmins called Manavas. Manu is only the mythical author whose name was written into the work to give it an age-old sanctity."[1]

The Code of Manu is dated at about 200 B.C. by Archer.[2] Other scholars differ as much as 1600 years on its date. In its versified form it probably belongs to the Gupta period beginning in the fourth century A.D.[3] "It glorifies custom and convention at a time when they were being undermined."[4] It approves of Vedic sacrifices, the rules of caste, child marriages as a guard against unchastity, the prohibition against the remarriage of widows, the subjection of women to fathers, husbands or sons, the supremacy of the Brahmin caste, the degradation of Shudras and outcastes. Caste duty is exalted as caste opportunity. "The tapas of a Brahmin is concentrated study, of the Kshatriya protection of the weak, of the Vaishya trade and agriculture, of the Shudra service to others."[5]

In defense of the Code it is maintained that Hindu society has been held together by its rigid principles. This is a hard statement to prove or disprove, since we cannot go back and try it again without the Code. And there are progressive ideas in the Code too. For instance, it indicates four ways of determining right and wrong: revelation, knowledge, custom, and conscience.[6] On the whole, however, the Code of Manu stresses the law of karma, the retribution taking place in reincarnation, and the supreme need for observing caste duty.

Ramayana and Mahabharata

The Ramayana and the Mahabharata have been likened to the Iliad and the Odyssey. The Mahabharata is an epic poem "seven times as long as the Iliad and the Odyssey together," "the longest poem in the world."[7] The Ramayana is less than half as long. In their present form both were in existence before the end of the second century A.D., but were being assembled by 400 B.C. Rama was probably a very human king who was transformed into a god sometime in the dim past. And the fratricidal war of the Bharatas probably actually took place about the tenth century B.C. or earlier. The essential stories of these two epics have been repeated and dramatized in India for thousands of years. "The Ramayana is still acted as a play all over India every autumn."[8]

The Ramayana is the story of Prince Rama and his loyal wife Sita who singly and together overcame many odds and proved themselves to be perfect in all the virtues. Rama was heir to the throne of his father, King Dasharatha of Kosala. He had recently married Sita and was about to be installed as crown prince when complications developed. For the King had three wives, and his second queen staged a bedroom scene which beguiled the old king into changing his mind in favor of her son, Bharat, and banishing Rama to the Dandaka Forest for fourteen years.

Since King Dasharatha had promised to grant her two requests, there was nothing else for him to do. So Rama was banished and Bharat, who was visiting an uncle and knew nothing of what was going on, was called home to be made crown prince. Bharat, however, proved too virtuous to accept the boon, preferring instead to go in search of Rama and his wife Sita who had loyally followed him into exile. Rama was found but refused to come home against his father's will. With a still younger brother, Lakshman, the royal couple spent years in the Dandaka Forest. At length, however, Sita was kidnaped by Ravana, King of Lanka (Ceylon). Birds, flowers, monkeys, and a magic circle all played their parts in the tragedy and the rescue. Hanuman, a miracle-working monkey-leader, son of the wind-god, found Sita, comforted her, and returned to lead a glorious expedition to rescue her. By this time the fourteen years of exile were about up, and the royal couple, with Lakshman the loyal, returned to Kosala where Bharat was still acting as regent for his older brother, whose golden sandals he had placed on the throne.

But people talked about Sita because she had spent some time in the palace of her kidnaper, King Ravana. So according to one ending she proved her innocence by submitting to an ordeal by fire. Another, perhaps later, ending has Rama reluctantly exile her as a matter of duty. But in the end she goes to heaven on the lap of a goddess.

In the Ramayana gods and demons were almost more common than men. Rama, from the earliest stages of the epic, was himself regarded as an avatar, the seventh incarnation of Vishnu. The latter had come into the world this time to destroy the evil demon Ravana. But the lasting value of the Ramayana lies in its insights into human character and motivation, and in the loyalty, devotion, and honor of its leading characters.

The Mahabharata is a more miscellaneous type of literature than the Ramayana. It contains a whole tradition of Indian myth, legend and philosophy. One of the pieces of its mosaic is the Bhagavad Gita. The work as a whole is called the Mahabharata because its main story is the epic of the war between two branches of the "Great Bharata" clans, the Kurus or Kauravas, and the Pandavas. The heroes of the story are the sons of Pandu, the five Pandava brothers, Yudhishthira, Bhima, Arjuna, Nakula and Sahadeva. After their father's death they are all reared by their blind uncle, Dhritarashtra, in the companionship of their much more numerous and jealous cousins—the Kurus. The great age of the Mahabharata is seen in that a Brahmin is made the military instructor of the five boys.

But intrigue secures the exile of the boys and Kunti, their mother. While in exile they attend a betrothing field day in disguise at the Panchala court. Arjuna wins the princess for his bride when he excels with bow and arrow. On taking the princess home Arjuna proudly announces that he has won a great prize. Without waiting to see what the prize was, mother Kunti innocently counsels him that whatever prize he has won he must share equally with his brothers. So the princess marries all five brothers, thus showing again how old the story was. Without doubt it was used originally to justify polyandry in an age when polyandry was still practiced somewhere in India, as it still is in Tibet.

For a time, with the support of the King of Panchala, the Pandavas are able to rule over half of their kingdom, pacifying the

Kurus by giving them the other half. But then the jealous Duryodhana, the Kuru king, devises a gambling venture and wins from Yudhishthira, the Pandava king, not only the kingdom and his wealth but also his brothers and their wife. Again they are exiled, with promise of restoration after thirteen years. But at the end of that time the Kurus are again faithless, so a civil war shapes up, with Indian kings and principalities taking one side or the other.

Fateful is the entry of Krishna, king of the Yadavas, into the struggle. For although earlier in the Mahabharata he was very human and really most immoral, seducing countless milkmaids through the soft music of his flute, yet in the Bhagavad Gita he turns out to be none other than an avatar, the eighth incarnation of Vishnu. Both sides asked his aid, but he proposed that his army should fight on one side while he acted as charioteer for the other. The Kurus chose the army, while Arjuna chose Krishna. The battle raged for eighteen days, during which the Kurus were destroyed with the exception of one brother, and on the Pandava side only the five brothers and Krishna were left. Yudhishthira thereupon took over the Pandava kingdom and offered the famous year-long horse sacrifice to show that he was now a king of kings—though the kings over whom he ruled were mostly dead by then.

But bad times set in. Krishna himself was accidentally killed. And the five brothers crowned Arjuna's grandson and renounced the world. They set out for heaven at the top of the Himalayas, with their wife and a dog which turns out to be a god. On the way up the mountains they display the utmost selflessness and are finally rewarded by being received within the Gates of Bliss.

The ethics of the Mahabharata is based on the assumption that pleasure is good and pain is bad, but that the contented life is one in which the individual is superior to the fortunes of either. Caste is accepted as the working basis for society, but morality transcends caste. "Thou shalt not do to others what is disagreeable to thyself," is the golden rule of the Mahabharata. "Truth, self-control, asceticism, generosity, non-violence, constancy in virtue—these are the means of success, not caste nor family." "Virtue is better than immortality and life. Kingdom, sons, glory, wealth—all this does not equal one-sixteenth part of the value of truth."[9]

The Bhagavad Gita

The Bhagavad Gita is regarded by most scholars as an insertion in the Mahabharata. Actually, the whole of the Mahabharata is a collection of stories and speculations woven together in the course of time. The Gita is hardly an exception in this regard. Radhakrishnan regards it as an integral part of the larger epic, and makes a good case for his view, mentioning for example the internal references to the Gita in the main body of the Mahabharata. He dates the Gita in the fifth century B.C.[10]

The Bhagavad Gita, or "Song of the Divine One," is "the most popular religious poem of Sanskrit literature."[11] Said Shankara, the most respected scholar in the history of Hinduism, "This famous Gitashastra is an epitome of the essentials of the whole Vedic teaching. A knowledge of its teaching leads to the realization of all human aspirations." Said Gandhi, "I find a solace in the Bhagavadgita that I miss even in the Sermon on the Mount. When disappointment stares me in the face and all alone I see not one ray of light, I go back to the Bhagavadgita. I find a verse here and a verse there and I immediately begin to smile in the midst of overwhelming tragedies—and my life has been full of external tragedies—and if they have left no visible, no indelible scar on me, I owe it all to the teachings of the Bhagavadgita."[12] Every unprejudiced seeker after religious truth will want to explore the classic riches of the Gita.

Envision the plain of Kuru, with the armies drawn up ready for the battle. In that dramatic situation Arjuna's heart beats with misgivings over the question of whether he should proceed with the killing of kinsmen—or be killed. He raises the question with King Krishna who has consented to be his charioteer. Krishna comes back with the view, essentially, that this life is the least real part of existence anyhow, and that the soul is immortal, going from one incarnation to another. Morally, therefore, every one should behave in accordance with the duties of his station in life. Krishna does not deny that salvation can be won by the way of asceticism. But he insists that it can also be won—even more assuredly—by doing the tasks which come before one in the ordinary course of events, so long as these tasks are done in the spirit of devotion to god. The new emphasis which we find in Krishna's teachings is upon bhakti, or devotion. The way of bhakti is open to all, whereas the way of ascetic contemplation is at best open to relatively few. And the way of devotion is best. This is the theme which comes to the front repeatedly in the Gita. Early Buddhist literature refers to the bhakti school of religious thought.

Through the incarnation of Vishnu in King Krishna, the highly philosophical religion of the Upanishads is made over into the very personal religion of the Gita. So the humdrum duties of daily life are transfigured into highly meaningful personal relations with a god whom one can know as intimately as a personal friend. Instead of confining the religious experience to sophisticated Brahmins or Rajas, the lower castes and women, even sinners, thus share in the essential religious privileges of Hinduism. It is no wonder, therefore, that so many have found spiritual delight in the Bhagavad Gita.

The counsel of detachment is prominent in the Gita, very much as it is in Buddhism. It is not so important what one does; the important thing is that we do not allow our spirits to become attached to material or worldly things. We must do whatever worthy deeds we do in an unselfish spirit, without expectation of reward. So we shall be free and ready to be released from the round of transmigration, joining God forever and ever.

The Gita does not deny that God is the impersonal Brahman, hard to appreciate and difficult to comprehend. Without denying Brahman, however, the Gita goes on to identify God with man, as revealed in Krishna, the friend of all. God is not far removed from man but is best known through human nature, which Vishnu assumes again and again throughout the ages. Krishna has passed through many incarnations, but he remembers them all. In that respect his reincarnation was different from that of Arjuna who, too, has often lived but does not remember his former lives.

We see, then, that the essential doctrines of the Gita are similar to those which characterize the Upanishadic religion. These are transmigration, karma, moksha, Nirvana, Brahman (as Vishnu-Krishna), and the several ways of salvation. But the most effective way of salvation through devotion to a personal God makes the Gita religion superior to all that went before. It seems significant that the Gita came into human experience at a time not too long before the beginning of the Christian era. And the parallels are so obvious that we can understand why the Gita is often spoken of as the New Testament of Hinduism.

The following passage illustrates the personal quality of the Gita religion, together with its dark view of life and its tendency to escapism:

> Quickly I come
> To those who offer me
> Every action,
> Worship me only,
> Their dearest delight,
> With devotion undaunted.
>
> Because they love me
> These are my bondsmen
> And I shall save them
> From mortal sorrow
> And all the waves
> Of life's deathly ocean.
>
> Be absorbed in me,
> Lodge your mind in me:
> Thus you shall dwell in me,
> Do not doubt it,
> Here and hereafter.[13]

Note that in this passage absorption in a personal God replaces absorption in an impersonal Brahman.

That the Gita, however, does not abolish the Upanishadic doctrine of pantheism is seen in the following passages which further illustrate the emotional and moral appeal of the Gita:

> A man should not hate any living creature. Let him be friendly and compassionate to all. He must free himself from the delusion of the "I" and "mine." He must accept pleasure and pain with equal tranquility. He must be forgiving, ever-contented, self-controlled, united constantly with me in his meditation. His resolve must be unshakable. He must be dedicated to me in intellect and mind. Such a devotee is dear to me.[14]

> He who dwells
> United with Brahman,
> Calm in mind,
> Not grieving, not craving,
> Regarding all men

With equal acceptance:
He loves me most dearly.

To love is to know me,
My innermost nature,
The truth that I am:
Through this knowledge he enters
At once into my being.[15]

The intimate and wide appeal of the Gita is further seen in the following passage of exquisite beauty:

Whatever man gives me
In true devotion:
Fruit or water,
A leaf, a flower:
I will accept it.
That gift is love,
His heart's dedication.

Whatever your action,
Food or worship:
Whatever the gift
That you give to another:
Whatever you vow
To the work of the spirit:
O son of Kunti,
Lay these also
As offerings before me.[16]

One mark of superiority in the Bhagavad Gita is its doctrine that the force of karma can be overcome through faithful devotion to the will of God:

Thus you will free yourself from both the good and the evil effects of your actions. Offer up everything to me. If your heart is united with me, you will be set free from karma even in this life, and come to me at the last.[17]

The doctrine of God's grace may even be found in the Gita:

My face is equal
To all creation,
Loving no one
Nor hating any.
Nevertheless,
My devotees dwell

Within me always:
I also show forth
And am seen within them.

Though a man be soiled
With the sins of a lifetime,
Let him but love me,
Rightly resolved,
In utter devotion:
I see no sinner,
That man is holy.

Holiness soon
Shall refashion his nature
To peace eternal;
O son of Kunti,
Of this be certain:
The man that loves me,
He shall not perish.[18]

In its attitude toward caste and God's love for all alike, the Gita approximates Mahayana Buddhism and Christianity:

Even those who belong to the lower castes—women, Vaishyas, and Sudras too—can reach the highest spiritual realization, if they will take refuge in me. Need I tell you, then, that this is also true of the holy Brahmins and pious philosopher-kings?[19]

If we look for complete logical coherence in the Gita we shall be disappointed. Its author was a seer rather than a philosopher, in the final analysis. His assertions, while dealing with speculative matters, did so in a forthright, dogmatic way. Recognizing the authority of experience, he did not try to make all his visions cohere. So we find him approving of qualified polytheism, monotheism, and Brahmanistic pantheism at different places.

On the whole, however, the Gita's emphasis is on personal, ethical religion in which the motivating power comes from a mystic experience of the presence and the care of God.

Puranas and Late Upanishads

The Puranas, or eighteen ancient tales, conclude the texts of the Hindu sacred scriptures. In these latest sacred writings new rules are found, new precepts and new ideals, and new gods to be worshiped. Side by side with the enlightened, though relatively pessimistic, philosophy of the Upanishads, these stories present a persistent form of animism. They encourage the fear of evil spirits and of eclipses. They teach a faith in the power of the stars over human life. They formulate deadly curses and charms and explain the magic of the evil eye.

More rewarding are the late Upanishads which were produced during the period of the epics. Indicative of the temper of the age, many of them parallel the Bhagavad Gita in insisting that god is personal and that devotion, or bhakti, is the path of salvation. Either Vishnu or Shiva is the supreme lord of the universe according to the Mahanarayana, the Ramatapanniya, the Shvetashvatara, the Kaivalya and the Atharvashiras Upanishads. To cite one example, the Shvetashvatara Upanishad differs from the Bhagavad Gita primarily in making Shiva rather than Vishnu lord of all, and also in the more speculative and less dogmatic approach. Like the Gita, the Shvetashvatara Upanishad presents a kind of personalistic pantheism which many describe as theism. Thus we read, "Thou art woman, thou art man, thou art the youth and even the maid, thou art the old man trembling on his staff, thy face is the universe."[20] Devotion and meditation are recognized as ways to salvation. By God's grace are men made free.

Hindu Sects

A remarkable phenomenon occurred in south India during the seventh, eighth and ninth centuries A.D. Evangelistic singers composed and sang devotional hymns as they walked about the land. They taught the path of devotion. Some made Vishnu the supreme lord, while others made Shiva the lord. This movement gave rise to the Vaishnavas, or Vishnuite Hindus, and to the Shivaites or Shaivites, that is, followers of Shiva. People from all castes became alvars, or singing saints, in this movement. And people from all castes were welcomed into these popular sects of Hinduism. Temples were built and an escape was provided from the social system and the Brahmin intellectualism which had dominated Indian religion for so long. This revival of Hinduism was the climax of the bhakti movement which had begun early in the Christian era and had undermined Buddhism by offering its equivalent within the Hindu tradition. It is said that by the Tamil saints, the singing evangelists, "Buddhism was sung out of the country."

Shaktism is still another path to religious experience for the common people of India. It is sometimes called Tantrism, because its literature is called Tantra. The goddess Shakti is found in the Rig Veda as the personification of power, "The supporter of the earth living in heaven."[21] Her essential characteristics for modern Shaktism, however, were probably inherited from the mother-goddess of the Dravidians or Indian aborigines. Shaktism is carried to an extreme by some who are overcome by their worship of sexuality. Others with a rich philosophical background see in Shaktism a recognition of the part played by creative energy in the world-system. Shakti came to play a part in both Vaishnavism and Shivaism. For the Mahabharata describes her as the sister of Krishna, Vishnu's avatar, and the Shivaites made her the wife of Shiva. In its best form Shaktism cultivates reverence and respect for women.

Hinduism developed its own favorite trinity of Brahmā, Vishnu and Shiva. In this trinity Brahmā is regarded as creator, Vishnu as preserver, and Shiva as destroyer. Creation would be useless unless preserved. And without a passing away there cannot logically be a creation. The three functions operate in a unity of rhythm and value. As destroyer Shiva was once greatly feared, but in the course of time his nature changed to one of compassion and kindness. Since he had in his hands the power of destruction, every time he listened to human prayer and withheld that power he built up, as it were, his reputation for mercy and kindness. So he became a great favorite with the common people, probably next to Vishnu. Brahmā as creator seemed to be farther removed from the popular everyday needs. Today in India there are hardly a half-dozen temples dedicated to Brahmā, while very many are dedicated to Vishnu and to Shiva.

Images of all the gods are worshiped, some having a more definite personality than others. Probably the personality of Vishnu is the most definitely formed in Hindu tradition. He usually appears with four arms and holds a mace, a lotus, a conch, and a disc.[22] Shiva, too, is multi-armed and is often seen performing his symbolic cosmic dance. But more often than not, Shiva is represented not by a statue but by a lingam or phallus, the male organ symbolizing the supposedly vital power at the heart of all being.[23] There are many temples in India which represent architecturally the form of the lingam, such as the Lingaraja at Bhuvaneshvara and the Kandarya Mahadeva at Khajuraho.[24] Sometimes Shiva and Brahmā are represented with four or five faces.[25] Of the three members of the Hindu trinity, Shiva, while more popular than Brahmā, nevertheless lost his personality through absorption in the personality of one of his wives. We have mentioned Shakti, who constituted a kind of mother-goddess of mercy for some and a sex-god for others. Kali and Durga were more likely to symbolize the sex theme and to lead to extravagant indulgence in sex emotions and ritual. Kali once required human sacrifices and still "consumes" goats sacrificed to her in the temple at Kalighat near Calcutta.[26] According to Baronte human sacrifice still takes place in India, despite organized effort to prevent it.[27]

Baronte sees little good and much evil in Indian culture, while Woodroffe (alias Avalon) views even Shaktism sympathetically.[28] Woodroffe is aware of abuses of Shaktism, but other religions witness abuses also. The ideas of the God-Mother, of the universe as the manifestation of energy-force, of universal insight into the nature of deity, of the distinction between the changing relative world and the unchanging eternal world—these are ideas derivable from Shakti philosophy.

The universality and spirituality of Shaktism may be glimpsed in four brief quotations from a Hymn of Mahakalarudra to Mahakali: "I torture not my body with penances" (to do so would be to torment God). "I lame not my feet in pilgrimage to holy places" (since my body is God's temple). "I spend not my time in reading the Vedas" (from which I get the religious experience of others while neglecting my own). "But I strive to attain Thy two Sacred Feet" (thus to do God's will as if my own).[29]

Some of India's greatest prophets have been devoted to Shakti or her equivalent, interpreting her as a symbol of the creative energy which, at some significant stage, must characterize the deity. Among other devotees of Shakti was the great Vedantic commentator and saint, Shankara. Of him we shall speak in the next chapter.

Still other devotees were "the notable Bengali saint Ramakrishna and his faithful disciple Rabindranath Tagore."[30]

Recent Hinduism

Ramakrishna, writing in the nineteenth century, stressed the theme of religious unity. He insisted that there is really only one God who is known in his various characters by different names. There are many paths leading to the one and only God. Jesus himself appeared to Ramakrishna one day during his ecstatic meditation. He came closer and closer, actually entering into him and becoming a part of him. Muhammad, Buddha, and others also came to him in a similar manner. Ramakrishna actually set up shrines representing the worship of several great religions, and felt no incongruity in bowing before each of them.[31] That God is available to all who seek is a Christian teaching vigorously seconded by the great Hindu philosopher. Ramakrishna recognized the importance of matching words by deeds. He called for less talk and more action. He did not believe in depending on providence when by our own efforts we could secure a desirable goal. He accepted the Golden Rule, restating it in simple, direct terms.

The tradition of Upanishadic mysticism is evident in Ramakrishna's writings, as when he speaks of Maya and the impermanence of the individual. This point of view makes him characteristically Hindu while at the same time he expressed a genuine appreciation of the values of other religions than his own.

The Ramakrishna Mission was organized by a disciple of Ramakrishna, Swami Vivekananda, late in the nineteenth century. This was a monastic order devoted to social service and Hindu missions abroad. By it Hinduism is represented as the superior religion of mankind because it is the most tolerant and all-inclusive.

The rise in India of religious leaders like Ramakrishna, the mystic poet Rabindranath Tagore and, more recently, Mahatma Gandhi, shows that even a religion of limited geographical appeal may produce great prophets and evolve ultimately into a universal type of religion. We occidentals are inclined to be impatient regarding the application of the principles of democracy to the Hindu caste system, while we ignore the abuses of democracy in our own culture. It is noteworthy, however, that recent legislation in India has removed the stigma of untouchability, while retaining the essentials of the caste system.

Caste and Illiteracy

On the debit side of Hinduism are, unfortunately, many factors. Caste is one of those factors. In our story so far we have taken slight account of the caste system. The truth is that it is difficult to get reliable statistics on caste in India today. Archer quotes figures for 1945 indicating that there were then 17,000,000 Brahmins, twice as many Kshatriyas, 30,000,000 Vaishyas, and 120,000,000 or more Shudras. Besides this there were about 60,000,000 outcastes or "untouchables"—people without any caste.[32] These all add up to about 261,000,000 Hindus and outcastes. Taken in 1945, this census applies to both India and Pakistan which at that time were still one under Britain. But the 1954 estimate (U.N.) is that out of 377,000,000 inhabitants of India, 320,000,000 are Hindus, while 10,000,000 of Pakistan's 75,000,000 inhabitants are Hindus.[33] These figures are confused but will give some notion of the relative size of the four main castes and outcastes.

However, the four main castes do not tell the whole story of the Hindu caste system. For these castes have been divided and subdivided many, many times through the exigencies of the situation. There are special castes for farmers who grow a certain crop, preventing them in effect from raising anything else. There are castes for different specialized artisans, requiring that a blacksmith's son become a blacksmith and marry a blacksmith's daughter. There are castes invented to include special tribes blanketed into Hinduism, and sectarian castes to accomodate new religious groups, such as a Vishnuite sect which arose partly in protest against caste. There are clean castes and unclean castes, the latter composed mostly of certain types of former outcastes who have been organized into very low Hindu castes. Members of the latter are required by Hindu tradition to keep their distance from people of higher castes who would otherwise have to undergo elaborate rites of purification.[34]

Recent legislation is designed to improve this situation, but conflicts with established customs.

Illiteracy is shocking in India also, being estimated recently at 82 per cent for the whole population, but at 97 per cent for women.[35] Of the Brahmins 60 per cent are said to be literate, of Kshatriyas only 25 per cent. The Vaishyas are said to be "fairly literate," but the lower castes and outcastes almost wholly illiterate.[36] There is one institution of higher learning in India for approximately every half-million of its population.

Education and Reform

Free India today realizes its educational deficiencies and is initiating reforms. Christianity—statistically the third religion of India—has tried to do something about it. By 1930 the Christian church alone was operating, in India, "55 colleges, 346 high schools, 571 middle schools, 11,414 primary schools, 108 training schools, and 203 schools of specialized character, or, all told, about a sixteenth of all educational institutions in the country."[37] In 1951 there were in India 500,000 primary schools—such as they were—and 200,000 secondary schools. There were twenty-eight universities and some 600 colleges and specialized schools. The government plans by 1965 to make education universal, compulsory and free for all children from six to fourteen years of age—even for the children of the outcastes, whom Gandhi always called the Harijans, that is, God's people. Pakistan has farther to go than India in making up for educational deficiencies. Given time, it will probably do so.

Free India has also taken steps to abolish the legal disabilities of the outcastes or untouchables. All may now vote, regardless of caste. And increasing travel and other social opportunities are throwing together the people of all castes. India's ancient and outmoded social and religious system surely cannot last long in a modern age. India tried for a time to resist industrialization, under the leadership of Gandhi. This was an ostrich philosophy and has been abandoned. As industry grows and old occupations cease to exist, caste will decline. With the growth of wealth, education and opportunity, caste will certainly be ignored. The efforts of prophets amounted to very little in relation to the total complex of the Indian social situation. The forces of modern life will soon dispose of problems which seemed insuperable only a short while ago.

What will happen to India's best religious and philosophical traditions? As its superstitious and oppressed people become enlightened they tend toward atheism. It is not surprising that they should go from one extreme to the other. Premier Nehru has no sympathy for the religious superstitions which India has inherited, and there are many like him in India today. But the national pride in India's great achievements will undoubtedly bring many to an enlightened religious point of view, such as has been established in the Brahmo Samaj, now more than a century old.

The Brahmo Samaj was established in Calcutta in 1828 by Ram Mohan Rai. An intelligent Brahmin, he perceived the common spiritual heritage of Hinduism, Buddhism, Zoroastrianism, Christianity and Islam and organized a following which has lasted until this day. It has broken up into sects, unfortunately. But they have, either actively or inactively, undermined the caste system and opposed polytheism, idolatry, transmigration, pantheism, animal sacrifices, polygamy, child marriage, the suttee (burning of the widow along with the corpse of her husband), and other abuses of Hinduism. Many of the ideals of the Brahmo Samaj have already been realized, due at least in part to its influence.

A visitor to India today is likely to be most impressed by the amazing freedom allowed to cows and monkeys to roam wherever they will. This is partly due to the Indian regard for all life, but especially because cows and monkeys are regarded as sacred. Cows are especially sacred in India, and even the late Mahatma Gandhi considered their veneration a central and wholesome feature of Hinduism. The Indian Mutiny of 1857 was caused by the erroneous belief that the British were using cow and pork grease on their guns. The position of the cow in India today as it moves toward modernism is a paradox which it is difficult to comprehend. Even the excrement of the cow is worshiped and given many uses. "Cow-dung is today used . . . . as a fuel; as a disinfectant element dissolved in the water used to wash floors, thresholds, and walls; as an ingredient in clay-mortar and mud-plaster; and as a medicine. In some rural regions, when a man is dying and wishes to assure himself a safe passage from this life into the next, he grasps the tail of a cow backed up to his bed-side, or should the room be inaccessible to the animal, he holds a rope fastened to a cow's tail outside the room."[38]

The lot of woman in India is not happy. They are the most illiterate of all. As mere girls they are required to marry according to the wishes of their parents, and may not remarry upon the death of their husbands. It may be pointed out, however, that the lower castes have not been inclined to observe the restrictions regarding remarriage. And the Indian government has been trying to liberate women and raise the age of consent.

From one point of view the animism, ritualism, idolatry, polytheism, pantheism, pessimism, legalism, and evangelical reform existing in the various types and movements of Hinduism have served to make that religion very adaptable. All comers could be satisfied. The intellectual Hindu could smile tolerantly at his superstitious fellows. He could be satisfied with his rationalized pantheism, while the rank and file demanded personal manifestations of Brahman in the form of Brahmā, Shiva, Vishnu, Shakti, or some avatar such as Rama, Krishna, or Buddha. Meanwhile the ignorant would remain ignorant, the poor would remain poor, and happiness would be remote from millions of superstitious, unwholesome homes.

But it is easier to criticize than to appreciate another culture than our own. And every culture has its dark side. Every culture likewise produces its own noble prophets. So our purpose will have been realized in these chapters on India if we have gained a fair appreciation of the true worth of the Upanishads, the epics, and the sincere quest of many after the true and the good. Buddhism for a time constituted a progressive social, moral and intellectual element in Indian life. And great saints, scholars and patriots in the past two centuries have added to the halo of glory which India justly deserves. No greater man of God has appeared in any civilization than India's Mahatma Gandhi, whose vows of chastity and strict diet, sometimes of death-bringing fasting, did more to free India and arouse its own people to an appreciation of its noblest heritage than any other single factor.[39]

No account of India's religions would be complete without taking careful note of its schools of philosophy and their great commentators. Westerners who aim to be broad-minded will not neglect these really great contributions to human culture.

XV. THE HINDU SCHOOLS OF PHILOSOPHY

A NUMBER OF SCHOOLS have developed out of the effort to interpret the Upanishads, or to solve the problems which are dealt with in the Upanishads. It is customary to list six schools, in logical rather than chronological order. They are: Nyāya and Vaisheshika, Sankhya and Yoga, Mīmānsā and Vedānta. In turn three additional schools have emerged from the Vedanta school, namely, the Advaita or Non-Dualism of Shankara, the Qualified Non-Dualism of Rāmānuja, and the Dualistic System of Madhva. This outline still does not cover all the philosophies of India, but it will reveal its best known and most significant philosophies, which in India happen always to be religious philosophies. It may come as a surprise to learn that ideas which emerged only recently in European philosophies appeared many centuries ago in Indian philosophy. Occidentals who strive to be broad-minded should study Indian philosophy. All that we hope to do in this chapter is to characterize briefly the various schools, and to suggest what has been accomplished by each.

The Sutras constitute a condensed body of literature in which the teachings of the several schools were summarized. They in turn required exposition, which was undertaken in due time by the commentators like Shankara and Ramanuja.

(1) NYAYA was a school primarily devoted to logic and logical analysis as a means of arriving at the truth. The traditional founder of the school was a man by the name of Gautama—which was probably as common among the Indians as Smith is in America. Gautama was the Aristotle of India. He listened to—and participated in—the scholastic debates of his day and came to the conclusion that agreement could better be reached if we would first take time out to study the principles of reasoning. He is credited with the Nyaya Sutra. Certainly some of this was composed in the third century B.C.[1]

Typical of the Nyaya logic is its statement of the four conditions of knowledge: (1) subject of knower, (2) object, (3) state of cognition, and (4) means of knowledge.[2]

Knowledge, according to Nyaya, reveals an existent external world. Such a world does not depend on knowledge, but knowledge is merely a sharpened instrument designed to bring to us awareness of reality and also of value, which attaches to matters of fact. So we classify Nyaya as realistic, with emphasis upon logical realism.

Knowledge may be acquired by four means, according to Nyaya: (1) intuition (which includes sense-perception), (2) inference, (3) comparison, and (4) verbal testimony.[3]

In the experience of intuition and perception the given includes sensible qualities and relations. "The mind of man is not an empty room into which sensations walk. Every perception is the result of an active reaction to a stimulus."[4]

Inference is made by means of a syllogism having five parts: (1) the proposition, (2) its supporting reason, (3) an explanatory example showing the principle involved, (4) its application in the given case, and (5) the statement of the conclusion.[5] This is of course not Aristotle's analysis of the syllogism, but it has its own merits. Nyaya also recognized inference or generalization through induction.[6] Discovery of the cause-effect relationship depends on a positive and a negative: the effect must always be there when the cause is present, absent when it is absent.[7] There are different types of causes, even as Aristotle pointed out (material, formal, efficient).[8]

Resemblance, or analogy, illuminates the relation between cause and effect or a thing and its attributes.[9] The test of analogical reasoning lies in successful performance—an anticipation of Pragmatism.[10]

Nyaya's acceptance of verbal authority leads it to an analysis of words as conveyors of ideas. Words are conceived to convey not only individual items but also universals and sub-universals.[11] Words are capable of conveying true knowledge thus.

Nyaya deals at length with the problem of fallacies of reasoning, and of the nature of truth. Its theory of truth, being realistic, should be classified as depending on correspondence. There must always be an appeal to facts in order to prove a thing.[12] The Pragmatic test is also mentioned.[13] But truth is not made; it is discovered.[14] "Error is the apprehension of an object as other than what it is."[15]

Nyaya realism involves the same difficulties as Locke experienced when he sharply differentiated between self and not-self. But Nyaya was no doubt trying "to save us from Buddhist subjectivism."[16] This was good as far as it went. It resulted in the atomic universe of the Vaisheshika school, which we would do well now to take up as complementary to the Nyaya school. In a word, however, Nyaya's metaphysics turns out to be pluralistic, not merely dualistic. Its ethics inclines strongly toward asceticism and accepts karma as a universal moral force. And in its earliest form it apparently had no need of god, since a real external world was eternal. Later Nyaya, however, was theistic.

(2) VAISHESHIKA, like Nyaya, was motivated by its antagonism toward Buddhist subjectivism and phenomenalism. The name is based on the Sanskrit word vishesha, meaning particularity, or the characteristics which distinguish one particular from everything else. The Vaisheshika metaphysics was atomistic, like that of Democritus but with a difference. For, unlike Democritus, it also taught the reality of souls and other substances which were not composed of atoms. Kanāda also taught that atoms are not all alike, as Democritus taught, but have differing qualities.

The Vaisheshika school arose probably at about the time of Mahavira and Buddha, in the sixth century B.C. Its reputed founder was Kanāda (accent on the second syllable), who according to tradition wrote the Vaisheshika Sutra. Kanada appears to have been his assumed name; his real name was Kashyapa.[17]

Just as the Nyaya practically accepts the Vaisheshika metaphysics, so the Vaisheshika practically accepts the Nyaya logic, making the two schools complementary.

Among the logical categories of Vaisheshika is that of substance, which this school views as something in addition to the sum of its qualities. This doctrine distinguishes Vaisheshika from idealism.

Fundamental in Vaisheshika are the nine substances: earth, water, fire or light, air, soul, mind (manas), ether (akasha), time, and space. The last three are all-pervading in nature, time and space being empty receptacles. Ordinarily imperceptible are soul, mind, ether, time, space, air, and the constituent atoms. Ether conveys sound.

The atomism of the Vaisheshika is rather confusing and really unrewarding. Its value today is not like that of the Greeks. For according to Vaisheshika certain atoms are the source of odor, others of flavor, others of form, and others of touch. The same atoms may combine certain of these qualities. Some substances are composed of atoms and some are not. Apparently the atomic substances are earth, water, fire, and air.[18] Like time and space, ether is a continuum not composed of discrete atoms.

Soul and mind pose problems. For Kanāda the body was instrumental and presupposed the soul. Mind, too, is an instrument of a different type, used by soul to perceive and organize the sense world and forms.

The soul is called atman when applied to its many finite instances. Like the atman is the Ishvara, or supreme soul.

Original Vaisheshika, like Nyaya, needed no god since the substances were regarded as uncreated and eternal. But the Dharma, the Eternal Law, occupied a place equal to divinity from the beginning. And later Vaisheshika felt the need for Ishvara, or the supreme guiding spirit of the universe.

We have the feeling that the Vaisheshika does not cohere as a philosophy. While it is not exactly materialism, neither is it idealism. "The shadow of materialism darkens the background, and souls are regarded as substances of the same nature as atoms, unintelligent in themselves."[19] The Vaisheshika is like a catalogue. Much more coherent is the dualism called the Sankhya System.

(3) It is remarkable how many systems of religious philosophy, dating from the same general period, originated in a kind of anti-Brahman atheism. We must now add the SANKHYA system to those of Nyaya, Vaisheshika, Jainism and Buddhism. For the Sankhya "substitutes evolution for creation" and makes the world a product of the activity of spirits (purushas) and the potentialities of nature, which they called prakriti. Yet Sankhya does not really argue that there is no god. Like Kant, it merely shows that his existence cannot be proved.

The reputed founder of Sankhya was Kapila, who probably lived in the seventh century B.C., the century before Buddha. Tradition is probably wrong, however, in attributing the Sankhya Sutra to him. Ishvarakrishna probably wrote the important Sankhya Kārikā about the third century B.C.[20]

The Sankhya analyzes cause and effect as two aspects of one thing. This view receives application in the doctrine that prakriti, or unmanifested, potential nature, is the uncaused cause of nature. Spirit or purpose is a part of the process whereby the world comes into existence, or evolves. Nature is the objective, while spirit is the knowing subject, called purusha. Prakriti and purusha are unrelated in essence. "Prakriti is non-consciousness, while purusha is consciousness. Prakriti is active and ever-revolving, while purusha is inactive."[21] This results in a clear-cut dualism.

But purusha is not the self, the individual. It is spirit universalized. Like it in essence, but individual in nature, is the jiva, the self, the changing ego. Just as prakriti causes individual objects of empirical nature, so purusha is the substance from which individual, active and changing souls have their being. In the individual are combined spirit and matter (or prakriti, the potentiality of nature). Without purusha the world of nature would be meaningless; it would have no plan or purpose and no motivation. "The purusha of the Sankhya is not unlike the God of Aristotle."[22]

Sankhya admits three sources of knowledge: perception, inference, and scripture. The emphasis, however, is on the first two of these. The Vedas are more or less ignored after being acknowledged. Yogic meditation is classed under perception, on the theory that the Yogin can actually see things past or future.

The Sankhya ethical outlook is based on the prevalence of suffering. The goal is freedom or release from suffering. Death is not that release. Freedom can only be attained when the individual soul succeeds in gaining the detachment of the universal spirit or purusha. "All ethical activity is for the fuller realization of the purusha in us."[23] It involves release from ignorance, egoism, desire, hatred and fear.

Sankhya teaches that there are fourteen grades of being through which the soul may pass in its rebirths. The soul can never be destroyed; but neither has it been created. Its eternity extends in both directions. Kant's criticism should apply to Sankhya: if the soul has always existed, it should already have passed through all the grades of the soul, leaving nothing for it to experience.

Sankhya has multiplied entities, contrary to the (much later) advice of William of Occam. Its unsolved problem would seem to be how to get these entities together when really they are so different. This is the problem of all dualisms, as the Cartesians realized.

(4) The YOGA system of Patañjali is the fourth of the six schools listed. "Yoga, according to Patanjali, is a methodical effort to attain perfection, through the control of the different elements of human nature, physical and psychical."[24] Yoga in one form or another appears in all Vedic literature, even in the Rig Veda. Patanjali is credited with the authorship of the Yoga Sutra, which may have been composed in the second century B.C. It makes use of the Sankhya system to an extent, showing that it is later.

There is little difference between the metaphysics of Sankhya and that of Yoga. The latter is somewhat more simplified. Yoga sees life as posing a dilemma and offering the individual an opportunity to rid himself of the influence of matter. The yogin tries to restore universal consciousness, getting rid of particularity, passion, and striving. He seeks physical health not as an end in itself but as a means of controlling human passions. He uses eight means of overcoming hindrances to inward calm: abstention, observance, posture, regulation of breathing, withdrawal of the senses, fixed attention, contemplation, and concentration. The first two media call for non-violence, truthfulness, honesty, continence, and non-avarice.[25] Posture, according to Patanjali, "must be firm, pleasant and easy." Yoga discipline of the body is not intended as self-torture or asceticism. It is often intended to make the body an unconscious, perfected means to spiritual goals. Breath control is another means of becoming calm and selfless. Sense-control is reflected in Whittier "Let sense be dumb, let flesh retire." Contemplation takes the attention away from the changing to the unchanging world. And concentration is useful for the accomplishment of any goal.

In Yoga, philosophy is not an end in itself, but a means. Will is higher than intellect. And the will to freedom from control by the world is the proper exercise of that will.

The yogin claims to be able to develop "supernormal powers" through his discipline, such as indifference to heat and cold, or the strength of a giant, or ability to see or hear a great distance or to communicate by direct means, without speaking.

Patanjali made use of the idea of a personal God as an object of meditation. Speculation did not interest him, however. He believed that one might get far in his meditation by thinking on the mystic syllable AUM. But his goal was not union with God, but separation from matter.

Many critics believe that Yoga is based on the understandable experience of self-hypnotism. This is not to deny its values.

(5) PURVA MIMANSA, the next Hindu school of thought, is literally the "earlier examination"—of the Vedas. The "later examination" from which it is distinguished is usually called the (6) VEDANTA, the last of the six schools. Traditional founder of the Purva Mīmānsā was Jaimini, author of the Mimansa Sutra. Since Jaimini was familiar with the Nyaya and the Yoga Sutras he must have lived no earlier than the fourth century B.C. His writings were commented on in the first century B.C. and earlier. Kumārila was a later great commentator.

On examining the foundations of knowledge, Jaimini admits perception, inference, and testimony, to which later disciples add comparison, implication, and non-apprehension. These scholars reject the yogic claims to mystic perception in time and space. Only the Vedas can give that kind of foreknowledge or past knowledge. This school regards the Vedas as eternal, not as the words of God spoken in time. They were, of course, written down in time, but prior to that they existed like mathematical propositions. All true knowledge is self-existent and self-justifying, including Vedic knowledge. But the logical aspect of the Purva Mimansa is its least rewarding or significant contribution to modern students of Hindu philosophy.

Based on Vedic testimony, the existence of the self is accepted by the Purva Mimansa. The self is not to be identified with the body, or with the senses or the understanding. It is present in perception and understanding, but cannot be the object of perception or of consciousness. It is what perceives and what is conscious.

The Mimansa theory is realistic in that it holds that perception or consciousness is of objects themselves, and not of their images in sense or imagination. One ancient scholar stated, "If it be the conclusion of those who know Brahman that all that is known is false, and that what is not known is true, I beg to part from them with a bow."[26] He accepts the universe as real independently of its being perceived, and at the same time as knowable.

But the Mimansa ethics is other-worldly. Sacrifice in a moderate degree is justified for the two upper castes, according to Mimansa ethics. The goal of life is happiness, not in this world but in the next. The law, the Dharma, leads to such happiness. The law is revealed in the Vedas, but is supplemented by utilitarian reasoning. Man is free to obey the law, since we obviously regard him as responsible for his acts. Karma is a strong influence in our behavior but may be overcome by starting justly at the very beginning of a series of moral acts. Release—moksha—may be gained by breaking the circle of karma. Knowledge is helpful to this end, said Kumarila.

Original Mimansa was inclined toward atheism, as were most of the other schools. That is, it denied that God's existence could be proved, and substituted the Vedic Dharma for him. But the later Mimansa thinkers admitted the gods. "The lacuna in the Purva Mimansa was so unsatisfactory that the later writers slowly smuggled in God."[27] Kumārila prayed to Shiva: "Reverence to him whose body is made of pure knowledge, whose divine eyes are the three Vedas, who is the cause of the attainment of bliss, and who wears the crescent moon."[28] But we must remember that Jaimini, founder of Purva Mimansa, was interested primarily in the duties and rewards of man as revealed in the Vedas—meaning by that term also the Brahmanas and the early Upanishads.

(6) The VEDANTA school, on the other hand, was primarily interested in the metaphysics and theology of the Vedas. This school was founded by Bādarāyana, who is reputed to have been the author of its fundamental literature, the Vedanta Sutra, called also the Shariraka Sutra and the Brahma Sutra. "In five hundred and fifty-five sutras (aphorisms, or short, pithy statements), which consist mostly of two or three words each, the whole of (his) system is developed. The sutras are unintelligible by themselves. . . ."[29] They challenged a host of commentators, among whom were Shankara and Ramanuja. Each commentator could justify his own favorite doctrine by referring to the same aphorisms. The Vedanta Sutra was composed between 500 B.C. and 200 B.C., according to most scholars. Whether Bādarāyana or Vyāsa composed it, or whether the two were the same individual, is not known for certain.

Like the Purva Mimansa, the Vedanta school was orthodox. That is, it regarded the Vedic literature as authoritative and sought primarily to interpret and summarize it. Badarayana regarded the

Veda as eternal, the revelation of absolute truth. Together with revelation (shruti) he admitted inference as the prime media of knowledge. Included in the revelatory literature were the Mahabharata (with its Bhagavad Gita) and the Code of Manu.

Based on such authority Badarayana reasoned that Brahman is the only reality, the one infinite substance. He (or It) created the world and entered into its parts, giving rise to an evolutionary process. Being a modification of Brahman, the universe cannot well be looked upon as illusion (maya). Brahman creates the universe as the fire creates heat, not externally but immanently. Brahman is not only the light of the universe and its cosmic air; he is also the subtle essence in the heart of man. Man's reincarnations are determined by his karma. Which means that God suffers the effects of karma in the experiences of all men, who are the manifestation of Brahman. The Brahma Sutra does not try to solve this paradox but merely states it as a revelation of scripture.

Another paradox of Vedanta lies in its assertion that Brahman is changeless and eternal, but that the world which he creates and into which he enters is changing and impermanent. Vedanta does not try to solve this paradox, preferring rather to believe both views since both are contained in the Upanishads. But its emphasis is certainly on the changeless character of the one eternal Brahman.

It becomes clear at once, therefore, that Vedanta is an idealistic system of Hindu philosophy, in contrast with the realism, for example, of the Purva Mimansa, the Nyaya and the Vaisheshika. Vedanta is not pluralistic in its metaphysics, nor dualistic like Sankhya and Yoga, but monistic in an absolute sense. This view is further developed along two lines by Vedanta's two greatest commentators, Shankara and Ramanuja, whom we shall now discuss.

Non-Dualism

Shankara was the Hegel of Hindu philosophy, but lived at least a thousand years before Hegel. He may also be likened to John Keats, having accomplished his monumental work in a few short years before he died at the age of thirty-two, according to the tradition. That he died early in the ninth century, or even earlier, is the concensus of most scholars. He was also the St. Thomas of Hinduism, interpreting and systematizing its scriptures and traditions.

(7) ADVAITA VEDANTA is the name given to the philosophy of Shankara. That he belonged to the Vedanta tradition is indicated by the second word. The first word means "non-dual." Monistic might seem a better word than non-dual, but Shankara preferred the negative, since the positive word, monism, might seem too definite a doctrine to assert concerning the Brahman.

Shankara adopted the life of a sannyasin at a very early age, that is, the life of a homeless wanderer. He founded monasteries, composed hymns, tried with considerable success to reform popular Hinduism, and wrote immortal commentaries on eleven or more of the ancient Upanishads as well as upon the Brahma Sutra. He was associated for a time with Govinda and Guadapada, of the non-dualist Vedanta. Guadapada is said to have taught Govinda, who taught Shankara. Guadapada was familiar with Buddhist teachings, which he incorporated into his system so far as they did not conflict with it. Shankara in turn was greatly influenced by Buddhism and transmitted much of its philosophy as an integral part of Hinduism. For this he was criticized by other Hindu philosophers. Yet his authority was not Buddhism but the Upanishads and the Vedanta Sutra.

Shankara's doctrine of the self—the Atman—was in accord with the Upanishadic teachings. The self is the fundamental reality, prior to consciousness, to truth or its opposite, to real and illusory, to the good and the evil. Even sleep implies the self which, unconscious, does not cease therefore to exist. The self is the intelligence which ties experience together and unites the cosmos. "The Atman is throughout nothing but intelligence; intelligence is its exclusive nature, as the salt taste is of the lump of salt," states the Brahma Sutra.[30] It is what is present in the individual and pervasive in the universal, which unites individual selves into a total reality. That reality is not dual (non-dual). It is not thought *and* extension, or mind and matter. Whatever it may be, it is not divided and so opposed to itself.

Knowledge, for Shankara, is far more than subjective imagination. He could not accept the subjective idealism which Buddhist thought developed. The objects of experience were not merely phenomenal, but real existences based upon the fundamental reality of Brahman-Atman. What we know of reality is directly perceived. Not that it is wholly independent of being perceived. But it is not subject to our fancies. Its reality is independent of the perceiving subject, yet it is internal to the perceptions of that subject. Hence truth is to be verified not by comparing images with external reality; but by the test of coherence between the elements of our total experience. Empirical knowledge apart from the implications of unified, total human experience, can bring no certainty. Intuition, intellect and revelation combine to give one knowledge and insight into reality.

Radhakrishnan compares Shankara in certain respects with Kant, Bergson, and Bradley. Against Kant's early philosophy, Shankara would not admit that there are plural reals.[31] Against Bergson, he would not admit that intellect breaks up the flow of life into dead analyzed components.[32] "Among Western thinkers Bradley comes nearest to Shankara, though there are fundamental differences between the two."[33] Both Bradley and Shankara are monistic idealists, whose reality is one and changeless but whose phenomenal world contains change, related in some ultimate way with the changeless Absolute or Brahman. Maya, for Shankara, is merely the doctrine that the world of change is a dependent world, the ultimate reality being Brahman-Atman.

The being of Brahman is, of course, a different kind of being from that which is ascribed to the objects of this world. Of Brahman it cannot be said either that he exists or that he does not exist, in the sense in which this world exists.

Brahman may be thought of as Nirguna Brahman or Saguna Brahman, said Shankara, trying to reconcile the greatest paradox in the Upanishads. It was said at times that Brahman was so Absolute as to be wholly unrelated to the world, for any relation would be a limitation, a mark of finiteness. At other times the Upanishads taught that the world is the manifestation of Brahman, perhaps through Ishvara the personal creator. So Shankara adopted the two concepts of Nirguna Brahman and Saguna Brahman.[34] Maya (the sense world) appears to limit Saguna Brahman but does not in fact, since Maya is not an independent real. Nirguna Brahman is sometimes described as Sat (Being), Chit (Consciousness), and Ananda (Perfect Bliss). But these are terms to relate Brahman not to an external independent reality but rather to the internal essence of himself.

Shankara, like Kant, examined the traditional proofs for the existence of God and found them all lacking because they all referred to existence in the external world, which is not at all the sort of being which we must conceive for God.

When Saguna Brahman comes into relation with the cosmos it is as Ishvara, the personal creator, that he is manifested. Such manifestation is less than the true and full nature of absolute being, but yet it is not to be thought of as having no truth. "Ishvara is thus the mediating principle between Brahman and the world, sharing the natures of both. He is one with Brahman, and yet related to the object world."[35]

The world is maya in the sense that it is not ultimately real. Its reality, to the extent that it exists, lies in its dependence on Brahman. Such dependence affects the world, but it does not affect Brahman whose being is such that the world naturally arises out of him.

Likewise pantheism may be ascribed to Advaitism and at the same time denied to it. For God is the world only in the derived sense but not in the absolute sense. Herein language fails us—or fails Shankara. And the reason why words fail is because of ultimate ignorance. We cannot know in the absolute sense, hence we cannot describe the distinction which lies in Hindu pantheism. Yet it is there, and we have no right to say that Shankara was a pantheist or to deny it. Certainly we must admit that the world, for Shankara, had a large degree of being, similar to the cosmic being which Plato taught, to say nothing of Bradley. There must be some reality to the world of experience and of imperfect human knowledge, because without this admission salvation from the world of human experience would be impossible. Our salvation consists largely in ridding ourselves of ignorance concerning the nature of the world. It consists of wisdom which recognizes the oneness of ultimate reality and our identity therewith. But wisdom would not be wisdom if it asserted that the world is maya, in the sense of having no reality at all. In each soul, as in the world, are the two aspects of the real and the dependent. "Each man is in essence the supreme reality, unchanging and unmodified and partless, and yet we speak of the rise and growth of the soul."[36] So the soul changes while it recognizes the changeless as its ultimate being and its goal. It must rise above the limited and arrive at deliverance through realizing its identity in essence with the Absolute.

Shankara was like Buddha in rejecting the rigidity of caste. All were welcome to his monasteries regardless of stations in life. He looked to anyone who might teach him, regardless of caste. "He who realizes the goal is the true Brahmin."[37] Other-worldliness characterized Shankara's ethics. Meekness, calmness, holiness, were the qualities of soul which he stressed. And of course he was sure that the better life was the universal one in which the individual became free from all particularity and identified himself with the Brahman-Atman. This was moksha. This was Nirvana.

Some criticise Shankara's ethics by saying that it negates all need for ethics, since if Brahman is all of reality, then nothing can be bad. But we have already seen that for Shankara the world of human experience is not unreal. It is merely a dependent world. In its relativity there is indeed much of both good and bad, and as we must live for a while in this relative or dependent world, we must abide by the best ethical insights which we can secure. In the Absolute perhaps there is neither good nor bad, but no one lives in the Absolute until he has reached Nirvana or its equivalent. Even then, in so far as his human life is relative and dependent it is also good or bad in a very real human sense—just as really as gravitation, which we do not ignore just because it is relative.

In a sense, for Shankara as for Bradley, self-realization is the principle of human ethics. That is, we become good or better as we universalize ourselves, making ourselves more and more real as we realize more and more of the relations with man and nature which lead us in the direction of the Absolute. So the good man is one whose life embodies the fullest realization of his human potentialities in relation to family, community, and all of nature. For Shankara the hindrances to moral life are selfishness, lust, bondage to the sense-life. Release from these is release from karma.

Brahman-Atman had a definitely religious quality for Shankara. While he did not recognize the personality of God as his truest aspect, yet he did think of him as personal in a lesser sense than the Absolute. He tried to find a common insight which he might share with the partisans of all six schools of Hindu philosophy, and with the various sects such as the Vishnuites, the Shivaites, and Shaktism. His philosophy was on the whole not skeptical nor irreligious. It was reformist and inspiring.

I have tried to interpret Shankara sympathetically, in order that we might see him at his best as we tend to see our own philosophers and church fathers at their best. There is no doubt that Shankara was one of the giants in the tradition of Hindu philosophy and religion. His background naturally was the complex of Hindu doctrines and Hindu experience, such as we related in discussing the Upanishads. We may all be happier for knowing something about Shankara and his predecessors in the Hindu schools of thought.

Theism in India

(8) But now we come to another great Hindu philosopher who seems to many Westerners more modern and more akin to Christianity than Shankara. That is Rāmānuja, who was born in 1027 A.D. It was his aim to harmonize the Upanishads, the Bhagavad Gita, the Brahma Sutra, and the Vishnu faith. Rāmānuja's Bhashya emphasized the theistic Upanishads in his effort to accomplish this aim.

Rāmānuja built upon the logical foundations of his predecessors, accepting perception, inference and scripture as the bases of knowledge. Like Shankara, he rejected Yogic claims to supernormal perception. Scripture may yield superhuman knowledge, he thought. He regarded the Vedas as eternal, hence was considered orthodox.

Individual selfhood was stressed by Rāmānuja. The self, he held, must be distinguished sharply from objects of perception and from being as a whole. Nor is the self identical with consciousness. The self may be conscious, but it is never consciousness.

But there is a unity among the elements of the cosmos, Rāmānuja held. That unity is God, whose infinity conserves the values of finite being. God is in personal relation to his world. Brahman is not an impersonal, unrelated Absolute, like the Nirguna Brahman of Shankara. He is the Saguna Brahman, and as such is to be conceived as a person. Being, consciousness and bliss (sat-chit-ananda) cannot characterize an impersonal, unrelated Brahman. These qualities of the divine character imply personality, said he. His personality is not limited or finite like ours, but infinite, omniscient, and eternal. Brahman has no sense organs. His knowledge is that of direct intuition. Finite souls and matter are moments of God. His omnipotence and his love brought the world into being. His omnipotence implies that karma is not a force which transcends the nature of God, but rather it is a means whereby God's love and justice are made real.

To Rāmānuja Ishvara is Brahman creating. Brahman is another name also for Vishnu. Brahmā and Shiva likewise are the same. In reality there is only one God, and the character of that God was best seen in the person of Vishnu, thought Rāmānuja. God is in close touch with human experience, encouraging and sustaining us in all good endeavor.

As moments of God, souls are individual, unique, and free. They have their existence as persons within the infinite personality of God, but are not mere phases of God acting. Souls are subject to karma, death and rebirth, as God is not. But God recognizes the intrinsic worth of each soul and he fashions nature in such a way as to insure opportunity for each person to work out his salvation from karma. Nature is not maya—illusion. Nature is not the imagination of ignorance, but is real, though dependent on God. It is a means to the realization of the good of souls.

Rāmānuja, as a representative of the Vishnu tradition, had a deep sense of sinfulness and of God's grace in saving from sin. Salvation was not to be earned by knowledge, meditation, or good works, but through devotion (bhakti) and God's grace. Karma cannot save us, through accumulation of good works. Nor can it master us, through our sinful deeds, if we call on God sincerely. On the other hand, bhakti or devotion is not mere sentimental emotionalism. It involves both intellect and will. "Bhakti is loving God with all our mind and with all our heart."[38] Rāmānuja's convictions apparently would be sympathetic towards the views of the Northern Bhagavatas, who hold that God's grace operates through the cooperation of man, as the monkey, being rescued from danger, holds fast to its rescuer. In contrast with this "monkey theory" of grace is the "cat theory" of the southern Bhagavatas, who liken God's grace to the cat saving the kitten by carrying it with its mouth, without the exertion of any effort by the kitten.

In principle Rāmānuja opposed caste. God's love and man's

worship make all men equal. Even outcastes were admitted to his temple at Melkote. Yet apparently he did not demand the actual abolition of caste, since it appeared to have a practical use.

Heaven, or the state in which one exists after moksha (release), Rāmānuja described as the condition in which the soul attains to the nature of God without being actually identical with him. The soul in heaven has an intuition of God and so is omniscient, a small god himself. The soul's release comes when it has no desire but to contemplate God. Desiring nothing, the soul has no attachment which will drag it down to rebirth. So the soul lives forever with God, in a heaven with "streams of living waters, trees laden with delicious fruits, gentle breezes and golden sunshine. . . . They sing and feast, listen to music of the heavenly choirs, and enjoy at times philosophic converse. . . ."[39] The incongruity of a natural heaven for bodiless souls is scarcely any more serious in Ramanuja's religious philosophy than it is in Islam, or in Christianity where we insist that such language is symbolic at best.

(9) Theistic like Rāmānuja was Madhva, who was born in 1199 A.D. He, too, belongs to the Vishnu tradition. He composed commentaries on the Upanishads, the Brahma Sutra, the Bhagavad Gita, and other sacred literature. But instead of maintaining some kind of monism as Shankara and Ramanuja did, he came out in favor of a dualistic philosophy similar in some ways to that of Descartes and the Sankhya system.

In Madhva's opinion there are two kinds of reality, independent and dependent. God, conceived as the supreme person, is the only independent reality. Dependent reality, in turn, is of two kinds: conscious souls and unconscious entities such as matter and time. His metaphysics becomes rather involved at about this point, and is not particularly rewarding.

Brahman is the supreme, independent, personal reality. He is said to create and destroy the world many times, and to rule the world absolutely. Yet Madhva also says that the world and souls are eternal though dependent on God. Brahman is the same as Vishnu, and the latter's consort, Lakshmi, has a kind of dependent relation to him.

Madhva makes much of the moral life as a life of freedom, and urges meditation as a means to receiving God's grace.

So we find that Hinduism has produced some remarkable philosophies which cohere with the Indian cultural background. We could not expect its philosophies to be exactly like our western systems. The amazing thing is that there are as many parallels as there are between certain philosophies of the two different civilizations, and that the Indian systems and original writings are, generally speaking, older than their comparable western systems. It is time now for a free exchange of enlightened insights between these two great cultures, the Indian and the European.

Hindu Maturity

Much has been written and said about the ignorance and superstition of India. The human fact is that ignorance and superstition go hand in hand, and that a religion with the greatest potential for maturity may produce the greatest superstition instead. Such seems to be the case with Hinduism which we have already judged mature on the basis of its achievements in the Upanishads.

When we examine modern Hinduism and note the growth of its myths, its epics, its bhakti literature and its schools of philosophy we find that, first, Hinduism has produced some of the great myths which can inspire if not taken too literally, and second, it has actually shown a tremendous vitality in its popular bhakti movement. As a matter of simple fact, Hinduism has continued to be magical for the great majority of its devotees, and its myths have hardened into literal norms. Despite these limitations Hinduism has shown a certain vitality for popular religious inspiration comparable with Christianity in its pre-enlightened centuries. Its philosophy, in turn, deserves much more attention than it has received from western scholars.

India failed to solve its social, economic and educational problems for centuries. Was this the fault of Hinduism, or was it the fault of a foreign exploiter who was not interested in India for its own sake? It is hard to be objective in dealing with such questions.

In applying the criteria of commitment to the truth and to principles of psychological health, or the criterion of ethics and social relationships, we may note that at least some of the great prophets and philosophers of India have tried to be loyal to the truth as objectively as possible. India's statesmen and leaders have sought to find the right path for political, social, and economic adjustment, as will generally be admitted in the case of men like Gandhi. And the people have been anxious to follow.

In judging the mystic sensitivity of later Hinduism, we think of the singing evangelists, saints, prophets, and reformers, as well as those who gladly followed them. India is sometimes described as the most religious nation in the world. That is because it has displayed unusual mystic sensitivity. If we were to judge only on the basis of this criterion, Hinduism would rank very high in maturity.

As to the cult itself, here we find complications. Even men like Ramakrishna and Gandhi were sentimental about the symbolism of their religious traditions. Ramakrishna was devoted to Shakti, while Gandhi ranked the cow highly in Hindu religious symbolism. The outside observer looks with suspicion on a religion which encourages cows and monkeys to take over the freedom of city streets and homes. Yet the ritual use of Vedic poems and the Gita in personal, daily devotions reveals a symbolism of beauty and freedom. The modern Hindu awareness of the values to be found in other great religions is also a sign of maturity.

Thus the case for Hinduism is confused. At best we may say that the potential is high, and that the potential has already been realized in many ways over the centuries. At worst we may conclude that up to date there is much magic, superstition, ignorance, and maladjustment in Hindu experience. Will universal education, political freedom, and economic progress combine to prove Hinduism one of the world's greatest religions?

XVI. SIKHISM AND MODERN INDIA

No study of Indian religion would be complete without taking note of Sikhism and the total religious situation of India today. With a membership of perhaps six million at the present time, Sikhism stands fourth among the religions of India. The first, of course, is Hinduism, and the second is Islam. Christianity ranks third, with perhaps ten million adherents today.[1] There is a strong tradition that Christianity was brought to India in the first century A.D. by the Apostle Thomas. Even if this is legendary, there is no doubt that Syrian Christianity existed in southern India from very early times, certainly no later than the third century. The Syrian Church in India is as nearly native as any other religion, depending on no foreign support. Islam is no more indigenous to India than Syrian Christianity is. So really that puts Sikhism second among the religions which were born in India. Native Buddhism has been almost completely absorbed by Hinduism, although its current revival may restore it to its native soil as a vital cultural factor. And Jainism, to the extent that it is different from Hinduism, is yet much smaller in numbers than Sikhism. There are now approximately one million Jains.

Sikhism may be thought of as a nationality as well as a religion. Religion has done much to make the Sikhs a cultural unit. And for a time they constituted a political unit as well. The Sikh population is concentrated geographically in the Punjab between the Sutlej and Ravi Rivers and the Himalayas. Unfortunately for their political aspirations—and otherwise—when Pakistan was separated from India half of the Sikh population was allotted to Pakistan and half to India. This seems a poor reward for the part they have played in Indian culture and British affairs. No doubt there are reasons why it had to be this way.

But we seem to have begun our story at the end. Let us go back to the beginning.

To begin at the beginning necessitates our going back before Nanak, the founder of Sikhism, to Kabir and Ramananda, his forerunners, and to the duoreligious predicament of India in those days, as now. For the Muslim conquest posed a serious religious problem which India has not settled even yet, a problem which both Kabir and Nanak tried to solve. Since this problem did not arise until close to the beginning of the modern period of history, Sikhism has become the newest and youngest of the world's great religions.

The Muslim conquest of India began when they invaded northwest India and annexed the Punjab in 1022 A.D. By the end of the next century northern India was in the hands of the Muslims, Delhi being occupied in 1191. By 1316 the Gujerat and the Deccan were subjected to Islam. Dynasty followed dynasty until the Mughal (Mogul) Empire was established in 1526. This empire expanded under its early strong kings, but declined under weak ones and came to an end in 1857 when the British took over.

Islam in India followed the usual policy of twofold taxation. Believers paid a moderate tax and unbelievers were required to pay a penalty tax. As usual, this policy led many natives to profess Islam for economic advantage. Some Indians were sincerely convinced of the truth of Islam, or were attracted to it by such doctrines as the equality of all believers. The general tendency among thoughtful Hindus, however, was to be tolerant of Islamic monotheism, since that point of view was so very much like the monotheism or monism of the Vedanta. It is significant that Ramanuja, whose Vedantism was theistic like the Muslim theology, lived shortly after the Muslims conquered northwest India.

But if Indians were tolerant of Islam, the reverse was not true. Muslims were most intolerant of Hinduism, especially of its idolatry and its polytheism. Monotheistic Hindus had their ways of rationalizing the popular polytheism and idolatry and of excusing its ignorance. But Islam was militantly missionary.

A story is told of the Muslim King Sikander of Delhi and Agra, whose intolerance was manifested in the destruction of many Hindu temples and idols. About 1500 A.D. he heard of a Bengali Brahmin who was teaching that Islam and Hinduism were both true, and that they were simply two paths to the same god. Sikander sent for the Brahmin and called together his theologians. Responding to the problem of what to do about the Brahmin, the theologians proposed that since he had admitted Islam to be true he should be required to accept it or be executed. The Brahmin refused to deny Hinduism by becoming a Muslim, so the King had him put to death.[2]

Whether or not this story is true—and it may well be true—it illustrates the problem of the relation between Islam and Hinduism in modern India. It was this problem that gave rise to Sikhism. The proposal of the Sikhs was, like that of the Brahmin and of the typical Hindu, that both religions were true. As so often happens when one religious group tries to reconcile two others, the result was a third, a new religion which was neither Hindu nor Muslim but a little bit of each.

Early Sikh Prophets

The first major figure who tried to reconcile Hinduism and Islam was Ramananda, who lived about 1400 A.D. He was a Vishnuite and a disciple of the great philosopher, Ramanuja. Later in life he founded a religious order which worshiped Rama and Sita, and admitted to his group members of all castes. It is said that he had among his disciples "a Muslim, a Jat, a shudra, a woman and an outcaste."[3] During his travels he came in contact with Muslims, as at Benares. One of his hymns was included in the Adi Granth, the original Bible of Sikhism. We quote.

> Whither shall I go, Sir? I am happy at home.
> My heart will not go with me; it hath become a cripple.
> One day I did have an inclination to go;
> I ground sandal, took distilled aloe wood and many perfumes,
> And was proceeding to worship God in a temple,
> When my spiritual guide showed me God in my heart.
> Wherever I go I *find only* water or stones.*
> But Thou, O God, art equally contained in everything.
> The Vedas and the Puranas all have I seen and searched.

* I.e., rivers on which pilgrimages are most easily made, and stone idols.

Go thou thither, if *God* be not here.
O true guru, I am a sacrifice unto thee
Who hast cut away all my perplexities and doubts.
Ramanand's Lord is the all-pervading God;
The guru's word cutteth away millions of sins.[4]

Ramananda had several disciples whose hymns were included in the Adi Granth. One of them was Kabir, whose traditional dates are 1440-1518 A.D.

Kabir was undoubtedly the most important forerunner of Nanak. His memory is revered not only by Sikhs but also by Muslims, and by some 650,000 Kabirpanthis (people who follow the "Kabir path") who consider him God's greatest prophet. According to the best evidence, Kabir was born of the union of a Muslim father and a Hindu mother, both of whom were weavers. He was born near Benares, which continued to be a center of Hindu influence despite Muslim political control. His father's faith seems to have been of the mystic Sufi type, which is closest of all forms of Islam to Hindu pantheism. In his own deeply religious experience Kabir became convinced that idolatry was sinful, that pilgrimages were useless, that religious ritual was misleading and pernicious, and that neither the Vedas nor the Koran should be regarded as authoritative. He taught that God is the True Name—not any one name in particular—and this teaching had great influence on Sikhism. He was a mystic, like the Muslim Sufis and the Hindu Vedantists, believing in the possibility and desirability of the soul's ultimate reunion with God. He believed in the Hindu doctrines of reincarnation and karma, but held that love to God can free one from the force of karma and bless the soul with mystic peace. He also felt that the individual needs a living leader or teacher to help him work out his salvation. All of these principles found a place in Sikhism a few years later.

The gist of Kabir's teachings may be found in the following selection.

God is one; there is no second. The One is everywhere.
Search in thy heart; there is His abode.
O men and women, seek the sanctuary of the One.
He pervadeth thy body and the universe as well. . . .

Sacrifice, the rosary, pilgrimage, fasting and alms are cloaks
of falsehood.

Why perform so many ceremonies! Of what avail to Hindus
to bathe, and to Moslems to pray at the mosque?

Some pride themselves on the practice of yoga.
Put away suspension of the breath and all the attitudinal in
devotion. . . .

Worship God, thou fool!
Renounce family, caste and lineage, lest thou think the Maker
thus distinguished men. . . .

Birth is in accordance with penalties for deeds;
Through wanderings and error man keeps coming to his house
[i.e., the body].
If attention be fixed on God, the dread of and the fact of
rebirth are at an end. . . .

I have met God who dwells within the heart. . . .

Renounce honors, renounce boasting.
They who crave for liquor and incline to drunkenness nowhere find content. . . .

When thy stewardship is ended, thou must render an account. . . .

Repeat the name of Ram, thou madman!
The ocean of existence is difficult to cross;
The name of God savest him who has tasted of its savour. . . .

I take no thought of sin or virtue; neither go I to a heaven
or a hell;
I shall not die as the rest of the world of men.
The soul that is joined with Him is indestructible. . . .[5]

The Story of Nanak

If Kabir was the John the Baptist of Sikhism, Nanak was its Christ. In many ways Nanak does indeed parallel Christ in Sikhism. His probable dates are 1470-1540 A.D. He was of humble Hindu parentage. His father is said to have belonged to the lower Kshatriya caste and to have engaged in trade and agriculture. His mother was probably of still more humble origin. The place of his birth was Talwandi, later called Rayapur, on the banks of the Ravi River near Lahore. Legendary accounts assert that divine beings and representative men welcomed his birth, predicting that through him the world should be saved. As a youth he attended an elementary school, but may have learned more out of school than in, through his association with Muslims, Hindu yogis, Parsis, Jews, and possibly Christians.[6]

At the age of nine he was initiated into the ranks of the Hindu "twice-born" by being invested with the sacred thread, the janeu. Legend has him question the ceremony by speaking these wise words, like the boy Jesus in the temple:

> Make mercy thy cotton, contentment the twisted thread and continence the knot,
> And thus make a janeu for thy soul. . . .
> A man dies, the thread is broken and his spirit departs without it. . . .
> By praise and adoration of The Name comes honor and the true janeu
> Which does not break, but lingers for man's entrance into the court of God.[7]

At nineteen Nanak was married and accepted a position as revenue-collector with a brother-in-law. He had several children but was unhappy as a family man. So, probably in his early thirties, he entered the "homeless state" as any Hindu might do, and began his life of wandering. There followed a period of spiritual preparation for his life's mission, which is believed to have begun at about the age of fifty. The tradition is that he received his commission to preach during a three-day retreat in the wilderness with his musician friend, Mardana. At the end of three days his worried friends searched for him and found him in an alarming condition. Thereupon he is represented as quoting his famous slogan, "There is no Hindu, nor is there a Moslem."[8]

The rest of his life he spent on journeys with Mardana. He would sing his verses and Mardana, a Muslim servant, accompanied him on the rebeck, a stringed instrument. According to the tradition their journeyings took them as far south as Ceylon, as far east as Benares, northwest into Afghanistan, and westward into Arabia to the sacred Muslim shrine at Mecca. The latter pilgrimage is held in serious doubt, for critical reasons. Yet the stories are good and may well be repeated.

For example, in the mosque at Mecca he lay down with his feet toward the qiblah (the direction of prayer), which was very disrespectful from the Muslim point of view. A Muslim rebuked him, but he replied by asking in what direction God is not, in order that he might turn his feet in that direction. He quoted the Koran's record of Muhammad's assertion that God is everywhere. He asserted that humility and genuine prayer carried with them more religious value than either the Koran or the Vedas.

But whether or not Nanak and Mardana ever visited Mecca, they came often in contact with Muslims. Tradition has it that Nanak humbled Babur, founder of the Mughal dynasty in northern India, who came to pay homage to Nanak. But Muslims were not generally converted to Nanak's faith. Muslims and Hindus alike were impressed by his message. But his lasting followers were won over a period of many generations in the Punjab area already referred to. In that area were many primitive animists, many Hindus, and some Muslims.

One of the most interesting legends of Nanak's life tells how Nanak got the best of some "thags"—from whom the word "thug" has come into our language. The thags were devoted to Shakti, Kali, or Durga, the female energy of Shiva. In her name they would set up a rest house with altars to Allah and Hindu deities, invite travelers to come and stay for the night, and while they slept would murder them for their possessions, quickly disposing of the body. Nanak and Mardana were thus entertained one night when, at bedtime, they sang their devout hymns to Sat Nam, resulting in the conversion of their host. The thag confessed his sins and promised to restore whatever he had stolen, and to establish a truly benevolent rest house for travelers. If this actually happened, in essence, it may have resulted in the first "gurdwara," or Sikh shrine with a connecting kitchen to feed travelers. Gurdwaras have become a Sikh institution.

Once Nanak joined some bathers in the sacred Ganges, and found them throwing water toward the east. Nanak started throwing water toward the west. The bathers were honoring their ancestors, and they demanded to know why Nanak was throwing water in the opposite direction. He explained that he was throwing water toward a garden which he had left far to the west, in hopes that it would bear fruit. When the bathers laughed at him he observed quietly that he thought his water would do his garden as much good as theirs would do to their ancestors.

Nanak realized that he had started a religious movement. When he knew that his death was approaching he selected Angad, one of his most worthy disciples, to be his successor. He deliberately passed over his own two sons, one of whom, Chand, was anxious to be his successor. But Chand's message was too ascetic to suit Nanak. So he established the policy whereby each guru (leader, teacher) should choose his own successor.

When Nanak's death was drawing near people who had felt his influence came to honor him. Some of his Muslim followers asked permission to bury him, while his Hindu followers desired to cremate him. Nanak bade both groups to place flowers beside him, saying that they whose flowers were unwilted next morning might have the honor of disposing of his body. Then he covered himself and the flowers with a sheet. Next day when they removed the sheet his body had disappeared and all the flowers were blooming. Consequently the Sikh burial custom includes either burial or cremation, although cremation is generally favored.

Essential Character of Sikhism

The religion of Nanak was not especially intellectual. It was more like the bhakti movement of Hinduism, yet had its intellectual side. A reading of the Japji (or Japuji)—Nanak's book of thirty-eight hymns included in the Adi Granth—reveals a genuine piety, a practical religious viewpoint, with a distinct emphasis on monotheism. Such emphasis is seen in the lines of the introduction to his Japji.

Unity, Active Om, True Name!
Actor, Pervader, Fearless, devoid of Enmity,
Whom Time and the Ages do not cumber,
Self-existent, perceptible Guru—
Praise!
Pre-eminent Truth, primordial Truth,
Truth that is, saith Nanak, and will abide forever.[9]

Meditation is emphasized as a path to wisdom, and obedience to the religious leader—the guru—is strongly urged by Nanak's hymns.

> Salvation's doors are opened by obedience,
> And one may save his family by obedience,
> Obedience to the Guru gets salvation;
> Who obeys, saith Nanak, is ne'er a lifelong beggar.
> The Name is such to him devoid of passion,
> Who knows him in his heart by due reflection.[10]

Asceticism does not meet with Nanak's approval. Instead he proposes the way of simple piety as the path to peace of mind.

> Nanak very humbly undertakes expression,
> Saying self-denial is of slight avail;
> To please thee is man's best aspiration,
> O thou who art eternal, dwelling ever in repose.[11]

Man is sinful and needs God's gracious forgiveness, taught Nanak.

> A worm is but a worm, and sin rests on the sinner,
> But he who forgives, saith Nanak, adds virtue unto virtue—
> No man exists who needs not added virtue.[12]

God's nature is known through the intuition of the heart. God is mystical, like the concept of the Sufi Muslim and the Hindu Vedantist.

> His state is indescribable who keeps the Name in mind,
> He repents it afterwards who undertakes description,
> No use of pen or paper is availing,—
> Let them think it in the pose of meditation.
>
> The Name is such to him devoid of passion,
> He knows him in his heart on due reflection.[13]
>
> Countless names and countless places,
> Regions too numerous to name,
> Countless praises humbly uttered,
> Names and praises couched in written signs.
> Knowledge, songs and recitation,
> Writing, speaking—all the while by signs.
> In symbol also is the tale of final union.[14]

God's providence rules and overrules the affairs of men and nature.

> Destiny is not disclosed in writing,
> As he alone commands so it befalls.[15]

Pilgrimages, ritual and good works are useless unless accompanied by devotion.

> Pilgrimage and penance and free-will giving
> Gain for one no single grain of merit,
> Unless one harken and his heart be loving,
> Cleansed within by a meditative bath.[16]

The Hindu doctrine of karma is mentioned in hymn 26, and the doctrine of maya is referred to in hymns 27 and 30, showing that Nanak's consciousness reflected the Hindu world. He also speaks of Rama, Sita, Shiva, Krishna, Vishnu, Brahmā and other Hindu gods as if devotion to and meditation upon any one of them were religiously effective—ways of conceiving Sat Nam, the True Name. But it is most evident, in his hymns, that Nanak had no systematic theology, no well thought philosophy of religion. His religion was practical, emphasizing the virtues of humility and self-restraint. His experience and his intuitions constituted the basis for the development of Sikhism.

It is quite clear from a cursory reading of his hymns that Nanak did not think of himself as superhuman. Legends later arose which illustrated the deified concept of Nanak which his disciples cherished. His followers in the course of time came to distinguish two Nanaks: one the historic, the other the "formless Nanak" who in death became the image of God. But Nanak himself taught very humbly, and would have been horrified at the thought of being divine.

> He [God] only knows of his own greatness,
> And gives to us, saith Nanak, of his mercy.[17]

The Bible of Sikhism is the Adi Granth or the Granth Sahib—sometimes called simply the Granth—composed of the hymns of Nanak, Kabir and others, plus certain supplementary writings. The first compilation of the Granth was made by Arjun, the fifth Guru of Sikhism, about sixty-five years after Nanak's death. The third and final edition was made by the tenth and last Guru, Gobind Singh, less than a century later. The final edition contained some verses of Gobind Singh and his father, the ninth Guru. Besides the hymns for morning worship and those for evening worship, there are many general psalms and also some verses in praise of the Gurus.

Less sacred but still highly revered is the Granth of the Tenth Guru, containing writings and translations of Gobind Singh and others. It included a biography of Gobind Singh, psalms to the goddess Durga, and stories of avatars of Hinduism, that is, incarnations of deities. This latter portion of the Granth of the Tenth Guru illustrates the qualified character of the Sikh monotheism, which teaches that God is one though he appears in various forms. It is easy to see, therefore, why Sikhism appealed to Hindus more than to Muslims.

Another group of writings treasured by the Sikhs is the Janamsakhis, or Birth Stories. These are legendary for the most part, and deal largely with Nanak's life.

But no writings quite equal the Adi Granth in the estimation of Sikhs. Their temples are rich in treasure but bare of images or idols. But in place of idols is a richly embellished copy of the Granth, occupying the most holy place of a temple. This is the case, for example, with the Darbar Sahib, or Golden Temple, built at Amritsar by Guru Arjun and rebuilt after its destruction by the Muslims. In many of the Sikh temples attendants reverently wave chauris over the sacred copy of the Adi Granth. Such is the case at the Shrine of Guru Arjun at Lahore, and at the temple of Tarn Taran where the Granth is wrapped in silk.

The traveler in search of the world's wonders would certainly go to Amritsar, the center of Sikhism. There the Golden Temple stands on an island in the Pool of Amritsar. The pavement around the five-acre pool is of marble, as are also the lower temple walls. The temple doors are usually silver, but eight golden doors for special occasions are kept in the Treasury on the edge of the Pool. A causeway leads to the temple. The Akal Takht, another temple by the Pool of Amritsar, houses Sikh treasures.

The Ten Gurus

There have been ten Gurus in the history of Sikhism. The first, of course, was none other than Nanak, founder of Sikhism. The second was Angad, personally chosen by Nanak, as his successor.

Angad (1540-1552), a leader of the Hindu Durga cult, had been converted by Nanak. He seemed to understand Nanak's purposes and to possess the qualities of leadership. As the second Guru he enlarged the services of the public kitchen which was shared by all regardless of race, caste or sex. He also had something to do with the adoption of a special alphabet as the medium of the vernacular in the Sikh region.

The third Guru was Amar Das (1552-1574), chosen by Angad because of his spiritual qualifications. He devoted his prophetic powers to social and religious reforms, the most significant of which was the condemnation of sati, or the burning of widows with their deceased husbands. He wrote poems which were critical of Hindu scriptures, polytheism, idolatry, and the Brahman priesthood. His other poems praised the life of virtue and piety.

But the family principle of succession was bound to come out sooner or later. This occurred when Amar Das designated his son-in-law, Ram Das (1574-1581), as his successor. Perhaps his only notable achievement was the establishment of a large public kitchen on the site later occupied by the Darbar Sahib, the Golden Temple.

Arjun (1581-1606), the fifth Guru and one of the greatest, was the son of Ram Das, designated by him as his successor. He made Amritsar the permanent home of Sikhism. But his greatest fame lies in his official compilation of the Adi Granth. In it he included some of his own really excellent hymns. His most difficult task was to decide what to exclude from the Sikh scriptures. Guru Arjun also expanded the Sikh institution of the public kitchen and provided for its adequate maintenance by imposing the tithe—a tax of ten per cent of one's gross income for the support of temples, kitchens, and the office of the Guru.

Under Arjun the Sikh community began to take on certain political aspects. The Mughal Emperors were the political overlords of the Sikh territory, and somehow the Sikhs became involved in the plot of the Emperor's grandson, Khusraw, to succeed to the throne instead of his father, Salim Jahangir. But the plot failed and Arjun was tortured and executed, thus becoming the first Sikh martyr. The odd historical fact is that Emperor Akbar, father of Salim Jahangir, had lost his faith in Islam as the exclusive religion and was searching for some means to reconcile Islam and Hinduism, along with the other religions with which he was well acquainted, including Christianity. The contemporary Muslim historians mention the other religions but fail to include Sikhism. It seems a pity that Sikh and Mughal at that time could not join forces and bring about a spiritual reform of religious India.

But the fact is that Sikhism took a turn toward militant politics through Arjun's experience and martyrdom. Nanak is credited with having said, "Take up arms that will harm no one; let your coat of mail be understanding; convert your enemies into friends; fight with valor, but with no weapon but the word of God." It was a different message that Arjun sent to his son and successor, Har Gobind:

> Bid him not mourn me, nor indulge in unmanly lamentation, but sing God's praises.
> Let him sit fully armed upon the (throne) and maintain an army to the best of his ability.
> Let him . . . observe the precedents to which now is added bearing arms!
> Do not cremate my body; let it float away on the bosom of the Ravi.
> I bear all my torture to set a good example to the teachers of True Name, that they may not lose patience, nor rail at God in their affliction. The true test of faith comes in the very hour of misery.[18]

So Sikhism became a religion of heroism, and came to characterize a small nation pressed by the larger interests of empire.

Har Gobind (1606-1645), the sixth Guru, was only ten upon his accession to office. He was the symbolic head of a religious order which had come to such maturity as not to require a strong man at its head. But he also felt that he was the head of a political and military community which was opposed to both Muslim and Hindu communities. No longer was Sikhism a noble effort to unite those of the two paths to God—Muslims and Hindus. It was now thought of as a distinct and superior religion, with nationalistic significance.

Har Rai (1645-1661), the seventh Guru, was the grandson of Har Gobind, succeeding his grandfather by the law of primogeniture. Har Rai intervened again in Mughal politics, on the losing side as before. His son, Ram Rai, became a hostage at the Muslim court and tried there to encourage religious tolerance. As a result he was passed over in the succession.

Har Kishan, grandson of Har Rai, became the eighth Guru (1661-1664) but was even less distinguished than his predecessor.

The ninth Guru, Teg Bahadur (1664-1675), was the son of Har Gobind, the sixth Guru. Fearful of the Mughal power, Teg Bahadur moved his headquarters a hundred miles eastward to Anandpur. But he could not escape the Muslim potentate. Probably for political rather than religious reasons, as claimed by the Sikhs, he was executed by the Muslim power, becoming still another martyr in Sikh tradition.

Gobind Rai, son and successor to Teg Bahadur, assumed the name of Gobind Singh ("lion") as the tenth and last Guru (1675-1708). Gobind Singh organized the Khalsa which effectively united church and state for the Sikhs. The Khalsa received fanatical support from all those who felt a common cause against the Muslim overlord. Initiation into the Khalsa was by means of a combined baptismal and communion service, during which sugar-water was stirred with a two-edged sword, and was both drunk by the communicants and sprinkled over them. A committee was organized to form policies and direct the affairs of the Khalsa. Certain habits were adopted for membership, including long hair wound into a top-knot, a comb, a steel bracelet worn on the left arm, a pair of shorts, and a two-edged dagger. Into the Khalsa were admitted people of all four castes as well as outcastes and outlaws.

The Khalsa was put into action by first attacking some weak allies of the Mughals in the hills. When Aurangzib, the Mughal Emperor learned of the nature of these developments he moved against Gobind Singh with overwhelming force. Chased into the desert, the decimated Khalsa forces carried on guerrilla activities. Also during this period of retreat Gobind further revised the Granth and composed additional literature.

Aurangzib died in 1707 and Gobind Singh and his loyal supporters were again free to come out into the open. The accounts are confused thereafter, but whether by Muslim violence or otherwise, Gobind Singh died in 1708, leaving no successor. From then on the Khalsa, with its governing committee, became successor to the Guru. There are disaffected elements among the Sikhs to this day, but all are relatively free to follow their convictions as Sikhs. Under the Muslims, who came to respect their fierce independence, and later under the British, the Sikh nationality persisted in a loose sort of confederation. At one time Ranjit Singh (1780-1839) became the raja of an active political state extending from the Sutlej River into Afghanistan. The British have from the beginning been impressed with the military capacities of the Sikhs, and have enlisted them in their service all over the East. Then on the division of India and Pakistan, a part of the land of the Sikhs was placed under Pakistan and a part under India, as already noted.

All of the sects of Sikhism today are united in their common regard for Nanak, its founder, and for the Adi Granth, the original Bible of Sikhism. In the years since politics and war enticed men of local patriotism, Sikhism has tended to restore its earlier emphasis upon the reconciliation of religions, devotion to the True Name, monotheism, and discipleship. A Sikh is, as the word indicates, a "disciple." This realization motivates many educated Sikhs, whose number is ever increasing, to learn more and more about the one God whom all peoples seek, and to live in peace with all of God's children. Their schools and colleges are encouraging a knowledge of science, history and the humanities in a world that is fast becoming one. It would be strange indeed if this minor religion, after wandering from its original path, should yet effect a reconciliation between the two major religions of India, namely, Hinduism and Islam. Highly respected by both groups as they are, and politically divided between them, they might well do so.

Religious Maturity of Sikhism

In applying the first criterion—the absence of magic—we must, of course, distinguish between popular Sikhism and enlightened Sikhism. As with other religions, there is a vast difference between the two categories. Magic and superstition are strong among the ignorant Sikhs, many of whom had animistic ancestors who were thrown in with the Sikhs for nationalistic reasons. Educated Sikhs are remarkably free from magic.

Educated Sikhs are also quite free from literalistic mythology. There was, as noted, a tendency to inject Hindu mythology loosely into the traditions of Sikhism. When this can be done without becoming enslaved to literal myth, the result is often happy.

Modern enlightened Sikhs seem well aware of the need for commitment to truth in science, cosmology, history, and human relations, showing Sikhism to be an unusually mature religion inherently.

There was an atmosphere of intellectual freedom and religious tolerance in the early traditions of Sikhism. So the fourth criterion seems also to characterize this religion as mature. Asceticism did not attract the Sikh prophets, nor did they encourage withdrawal from the world. God's world is a good world, where men may mingle in brotherhood and joy. The Gurus usually reared families and partook in politics and cultural pursuits. Faithfulness in social relationship was stressed, showing Sikhism to measure highly according to the fifth criterion.

Original Sikhism stressed the purely symbolic nature of all ritual, and marks the early religion as more mature than the later where the Granth Sahib came virtually to be an idol. Also there was the intermediate stage when the First Guru was worshiped as a god. Modern Sikhism, however, recognizes the humanity of Nanak and the merely instrumental nature of the Sikh Bible, which an educated Sikh enjoys for its real value. Magic is cast out. The ritual of the sacred kitchen became a means of expressing a social need and its fulfilment, thus stressing cultic maturity.

As to the criterion of mystic sensitivity, the Sikhs stand high. More mystical than monotheistic, the Sikhs have always been sensitive to the presence of spiritual power, available to the spirit of man at all times. This was conceived of not magically but as an avenue of kinship between man and the divine heart of the universe.

One of the world's smallest religions, Sikhism ranks essentially high in maturity. Its original genius lay in its insight that different religions really form a divine brotherhood of man. "There is no Hindu, nor is there a Muslim."

PART FOUR

Oriental Religions of Man and Nature

XVII. EARLY CHINESE RELIGION

TWO OF THE GREAT RELIGIONS of China were native to that land. A third made a strong bid for the Chinese faith. The two religions are known as Confucianism and Taoism. The third is Buddhism. Native to Japan was Shinto—or Shintoism. There, too, Buddhism made a strong appeal, and Confucianism became quite popular also. As in India, so in the Orient, Christianity also has been influential, especially during the past hundred years. Other religions appeared also. But in these next chapters our special interest will be those religions which are native to the Far East: Confucianism, with its emphasis upon man; Taoism, originally emphasizing nature in its mystical aspect; and Shinto, with its stress upon the state.

Before we enter upon a review of the essential nature of Confucianism and Taoism, however, we should make a brief survey of primitive Chinese culture as it was when these two religions were born. No religion is ever born out of nothing. And we can better understand the major religions if we first note the general state of culture when they were born.

In the first place, the Chinese civilization has a geographical background of an immense land-mass and large river systems. As in other parts of the world, early civilization grew around China's rivers, especially its northernmost great river, the Hwang Ho, or Yellow River. This river now empties into the Yellow Sea, but until quite recently it emptied much farther north into the Gulf of Chihli. The second river of China is the Yangtze, with its outlet close to Shanghai. The third is the Si, flowing into the South China Sea near Hong Kong.

Most of the stories about the origin of Chinese culture cluster about the Yellow River. It was not far from the mouth of the earlier Yellow River, in 1927, that Sinanthropus pekinensis was found. This fossil is said to have lived around 400,000 years ago. It is entirely possible that the present Chinese are descended from the relatives of Sinanthropus.[1]

Not far from the great bend of the Yellow River, in 1921 near Yang Shao Ts'un, were found the remains of a Neolithic settlement. From this and other sites, mostly in the same river valley, were gathered pieces of pottery, some of them fragmentary, proving that man tilled the soil, spun cloth, wove baskets and tended their domesticated animals there around 2000 B.C. or earlier.

Myth and Culture

There is a large mass of mythological traditions concerning the origins of Chinese culture. One such myth concerns the first man, P'an Ku, who formed earth and sky out of the primeval chaos that resembled the white and yolk of an egg. He was the Chinese Paul Bunyan who "transfigured himself nine times a day. The sky became ten feet higher each day, the earth ten feet thicker, and P'an Ku ten feet taller." He lived for eighteen thousand years, the world growing with him. His breath was the wind, his voice the thunder, his glance the lightning. "When he died his remains fell apart and formed the Five Sacred Mountains of China. . . . His eyes were transformed into sun and moon, his fat melted into streams and seas, and his hairs took root and covered the earth with plants."[2] There are other myths of celestial or human kings each of whom ruled for many thousands of years. Still other myths tell how Yu Ch'ao taught men to build houses; Sui Jen taught how to make fire; Fu Hsi taught how to fish with nets, domesticate animals, construct musical instruments and write Chinese characters; Shen Nung taught agriculture and medicine; and Huang Ti, the Yellow Emperor, invented civilized war, the keeping of records, and building with bricks. He is said to have constructed an observatory, corrected the calendar and built a temple, while his wife introduced the culture of the silkworm.[3]

The general consensus of scholars, quite apart from the myths, is that much of the Chinese culture originated by contact with the ancient West—the Near East—through travel, trade, or migration, or by some combination of these factors.

But the primitive religion of China possessed a combination of characteristics which distinguished it from others. It was animistic, of course, as were all primitive religions and cultures. Its animism followed the usual pattern of development out of ancestor worship. That is, the early Chinese believed that the souls of the departed had entered into natural objects, making them sacred and supernatural and therefore evoking an attitude of awe. So when the Chinese crossed the threshold of history we find them offering sacrifices to rivers, mountains, stars, and other "inhabited" objects of nature. When nature became overpopulated with ancestral souls, then the latecomers apparently had no more objects to enter and so had to hover about while waiting for the attentive ministrations of their children. Meanwhile only the great could lay claim to having ancestors whose souls were expansive enough to enter into the entire sky, or into the wide earth. Thus it came about that the Chinese Emperor offered sacrifices to his ancestors, Heaven and Earth.

Man and Nature

The ancient Chinese, prior to Confucius, conceived of a certain regularity in the behavior of nature. It seemed obvious that strong, great spirits inhabited the sun and the moon, for their regular paths were never seriously interfered with. Many demonic spirits aspiring to greatness caused disaster from time to time, but on the whole the cycle of day and night, and the seasons of the year, continued despite all occult opposition.

Among the presiding forces of nature were, for the pre-Confucian Chinese, the *Yin* and the *Yang*. At least the Chou Yü (I, 10) reports that in the year 780 B.C., when three river valleys experienced earthquakes, it was explained by the theory that the *Yin* and *Yang* forces had become confused. "When the *Yang* is concealed and cannot come forth, and when the *Yin* is repressed and cannot issue out, then there are earthquakes."[4] Apparently these two forces were conceived to be exceptions to the rule of direct control by ancestral spirits. In a crude way, the *Yin* and the *Yang* represent the begin-

Ancient Chinese symbol of Yang-and-Yin, rhythmic alternating life force.

ning of Chinese philosophy. Other instances of skeptical thought prior to Confucius are cited by Fung Yu-lan.[5] The *Yin* and the *Yang* dramatized the operation of the *Tao,* that is, the "Way" which Heaven followed in its rule over the affairs of man and nature.

Much older than either Confucianism or Taoism is the ancient Chinese idea of the *Tao*. Literally meaning a "way," or a "path," or the "channel" of a river, the Chinese used this word also to describe nature's harmonious manner of behavior, as well as the proper kind of conduct for human beings. When men follow the *Tao,* then there is harmony between heaven and earth, and all things are well. This was especially true of the ruler, the Son of Heaven, who was the natural link in the chain connecting earth and heaven. Based on this insight, it was believed that when the ruler followed the *Tao,* there would be peace and prosperity in his realm. Conversely, if peace and prosperity were not achieved, that was perfectly good evidence that the ruler was not in the right path and should therefore be replaced by another. This philosophy was essentially similar to our Old Testament philosophy that God blessed Israel or Judah under a pious king, but sent calamity when the king was impious.

Chinese animism was most extreme. The "Mounds of Yin" at Anyang, known since 1079 A.D., have produced ample evidence that during the Shang Period, a thousand years before Confucius, people were sacrificing to their ancestors and to the spirits of fields, mountains, rivers, wind, earth, and heaven. One god was called "Emperor;" to him all kinds of problems were addressed.[6] People prayed to "Grandmother Yi" for rain. Animal sacrifices were cooked and served to the spirits. There were processions to the place of sacrifice, accompanied by the music of flutes, drums, and bells. There was ceremonial dancing and the singing of odes such as are preserved in the classic *Book of Poetry*.[7]

An interesting detail of the ancient Chinese religion was its use of "oracle bones." Some of these were found in the mounds at Anyang, and were used for divination during the second millennium B.C. They contain the earliest writing known in the history of Chinese culture. Questions which were addressed to deities and ancestral spirits were sometimes written on the oxbone or tortoise shell. Heat was then applied to the bone or shell, and the way in which it cracked was supposed to give the answer to the question, written or spoken. "The question was often as simple as 'Will it rain tonight?' and on a bone where this interrogation was recorded there was also a later notation, 'It really didn't rain.' Other queries concerned sacrifices, trips, wars, hunting, farming, illness, and all kinds of miscellaneous subjects."[8] Ancestral spirits were certainly expected to know much more in death than they knew in life.

Ancestor Worship

From ancient times until today the Chinese have practiced some form of ancestor worship. This may therefore be described in the present tense. Sometimes a wealthy family or clan has a temple in which ancestral spirits are worshiped. But the average family conducts its worship in the home. In either case there is always an altar holding the tablets on which appear, in chronological order, the names of the deceased ancestors. There is no professional priesthood in China. The father is the priest and leads in the rites of sacrifice, chanting, singing, and prayer. He speaks the recorded ancestral names, as if expecting some response. Then the food which has been offered to the spirits is returned to the living members of the family, who eat it in the spirit of communion. The ancestors are informed of the principal events having taken place in the family recently, and the family is reminded of the notable deeds of ancestors when they were in the flesh.

The Chinese family took on tremendous importance through these rites. In the first place the family was a much larger unit than it is with us. The Chinese family, living together as a group, was like a perpetual family reunion in America. Furthermore, each member of the family, living and dead, fulfilled an important function. The dead spirits were dependent upon the living for whatever happiness they might enjoy in heaven and in the clan's geographical environment where the spirits also roamed. In turn, the living were dependent upon the dead for numerous blessings and favors. An unfaithful family could make an ancestor become a homeless wanderer. But the forlorn spirit, on his part, could also bring all kinds of calamity upon the faithless family. This belief insured that the Chinese family would enjoy an unusual solidarity. The loyalty of all members of the family was greatly encouraged by this means. This was why, in Chinese custom, the family's interests normally came ahead of the concerns of the state.

Like the spirits of one's own ancestors were the good spirits and the bad spirits, unattached to any family but likely to be associated with lonely places and to bother travelers when darkness fell. China has a tradition of belief in dragons and demons in addition to the local spirits inhabiting geographical and natural objects. Some of the earliest ornamented pottery of the ancient Chinese displays the peering eyes of dragons and other imaginary spirits. But this is the story of animism which is already familiar, and may have emerged out of early ancestor worship. The animistic outlook characterizes the religion of the ignorant masses, rather than of the Chinese intellectuals, of course. Now that the Chinese intellectuals are writing excellent English, we are learning about many misconceptions which were conveyed to us in the past, such as the idea that the "shen" were good spirits, while the "kwei" were the bad ones referred to above. These have in reality turned out to be concepts related to the *Yang* and the *Yin*, and are given interesting interpretations by modern Chinese philosophers.[9]

Among the spirits of nature, two were especially important. They were earth—"she"—and heaven—"ti." The worship of the earth deity was an agricultural rite which, in Chou times, was performed in connection with a mound of earth in every village.[10] The sacred mound was the center of village life.

The heaven deity was in Shang times known as Ti, or as Shang Ti. Christian missionaries adopted "Shang Ti" as the best translation into Chinese of the idea of an exalted personal god. The words seem to mean literally "the Ruler Above."[11] Ti may also mean Emperor, and may originally have referred to the deified ancestral spirit of the founder of the Shang dynasty. Then when the Chou conquered the Shang around 1100 B.C. they brought with them their chief deity T'ien. The evidence indicates that T'ien was composed of the spirits of several former kings who collectively were called T'ien. This might be translated as the "council of the gods," and is often translated by the word "Heaven," used in an impersonal sense, or by the word "Providence." From Chou times the Emperor has been referred to as the "Son of Heaven," or the Son of T'ien, showing the element of ancestor worship involved in the state cult. Eventually the word T'ien came also to mean the visible heaven. But in the evolution of Chinese religion, the Chou kings merged Shang Ti with T'ien, sometimes using one name and sometimes the other. The introduction of T'ien tended to impersonalize the chief deity. It became customary for the Emperor to conduct the official worship of Heaven, his special ancestor. He was the "father" of the Chinese people and so acted as priest in the official worship of his ancestors. For this reason the Chinese religion—meaning this particular phase of it—is sometimes described as a state religion.

Because of the centrality of ancestor worship, Chinese religion has been fundamentally conservative. Maintaining reverence and respectful relations with one's ancestors necessarily entailed the observance of the old, time-honored customs. This has kept Chinese society more stable and unchanging, probably, than any other society on earth. Ancestor worship has also kept China poor, burdening families with the duty of staging elaborate funerals in honor of the deceased, and for conducting costly sacrifices.

The most horrifying aspect of ancestor worship was the human sacrifices which, in times past, it sanctioned. There is definite proof of human sacrifices on a large scale during Shang times. "The practice continued under the Chou and is referred to at least twice in the *Book of Poetry* and some eleven times in the *Tso Chuan*. Of the instances of human sacrifice mentioned in the latter work, three took place during Confucius' lifetime, one in the state of Lu itself. Mo Tzu, just after Confucius, declared that those who advocated elaborate burial wanted large numbers of men, as many as hundreds in the case of an emperor, killed to attend important persons in death."[12] In 210 B.C. the Ch'in emperor was buried and many of the women of his harem were killed to accompany him in death. In the first century B.C. sixteen slave musicians were forced to commit suicide in order to join their dead prince of the Han dynasty. But Confucianism effectively put a stop to human sacrifice.

The popular horror at human sacrifice was reflected in an ode in the *Book of Poetry* referring to one of the victims buried in 621 B.C. with Duke Mu of the state of Ch'in:

> Who followed Duke Mu to the grave?
> Tzu-ch'e Chen-hu.
> And this Chen-hu
> Could withstand a hundred men.
> But when he came to the grave,
> He looked terrified and trembled.[13]

Historical Periods

The political background of Chinese culture begins with the Hsia Dynasty, so far as tradition is concerned. This may not have been a dynasty in the modern sense of the word. But the tradition is that it began in 2205 B.C. and ended in 1765 B.C. Actually it may have been about two hundred years more recent. Following Hsia came the historical Shang dynasty. During this period the transition was made from stone to bronze, and the decorations on its bronze objects and oracle bones indicate the beginning of writing. According to the traditional chronology the Shang Dynasty ruled from 1765 to 1122 B.C. The latter date may be about one hundred years too early. Then came the Chou Dynasty. The Western Branch of this dynasty ruled until 771 B.C., and the Eastern Branch from 771 to 256 B.C. The latter also was divided into two periods, that of the "Spring and Autumn Annals," lasting until about 478 B.C. when Confucius died, and the "Warring States Period" lasting from then until 256 B.C.

The empires of the several Chinese dynasties usually comprised not the whole of China but only the territory adjacent to the Yellow River. As such they were not well organized political units, but rather were feudal in nature. Considering the manner of travel and communication in those times, it was almost impossible for one person, no matter how powerful, to govern a large territory consisting of several states.

The usual pattern of empire in China began with armed invasion of a territory governed by corrupt and degenerate politicians. The victorious commander became the new Emperor and established the new dynasty, but parceled out to his relatives and military aides the several states comprising the empire. After centuries of rule corruption again became customary, and a new conqueror arose to enforce the "decrees of Heaven" and establish a new and more vigorous rule. This concept contributed an element of morale to each new conqueror. When Confucius was born the Chou dynasty had been in power from 1122 to 551 B.C. The political situation was quite unsettled in Confucius' day. Subsequently no one seemed to have enough power to maintain peace in the empire. That condition brought about the "Warring States Period."

With this brief glance at the historical background we may pass to a discussion of the philosophy of Confucius.

XVIII. CONFUCIAN HUMANISM

Confucianism, according to Professor Fung Yu-lan, is not a religion at all but only a philosophy.[1] This semantical problem hinges on one's definition of religion and of philosophy, as Professor Fung admits. But it also depends upon one's definition of Confucianism. One may well be justified in holding, for example, that Confucius' attitude was philosophical rather than religious. Yet in the course of the centuries Confucius came to be more and more revered and worshiped as a god and in that phase Confucianism definitely became a religion. Furthermore, Confucius himself had a philosophy of religion which should be noted as we review the works of the great prophets of mankind.

The purpose of the present chapter is to discover, so far as possible, what were the original teachings and attitudes of the man, Confucius. What happened to those teachings as legend took hold of them will be the subject of later chapters. According to the legend, for example, Confucius was of noble birth, having kings as his ancestors. But Confucius' own words were, "When young, I was in humble circumstances."[2]

Our most reliable source of information concerning the real Confucius is the *Analects*. This is a collection of the sayings of Confucius. "The first collection was probably made, not by Confucius' disciples, but by some of their disciples."[3] This was not so long after Confucius as to distort the picture of his real personality. But even so we must beware of the interpolations and additions of later centuries. A large amount of critical scholarship has been devoted to the study of Confucius during the past several decades, both by Confucians and by non-Confucians. As a result we were able recently, for the first time since the *Analects* were written, to reconstruct a true picture of the man Confucius and of what he said and did. And it is a picture worth striving for.

Other sources of information should be mentioned, at least. There was, for example, the *Tso Chuan,* a historical work dating from about 300 B.C. in its present form. This is a rather disconnected record of important or striking events in the state of Lu between 722 and 468 B.C., including the years of Confucius' life. The fact that Confucius is mentioned so seldom in the *Tso Chuan* is evidence that he was not nearly so important as later tradition makes him out to be. The *Book of Mencius,* his follower and apostle in the fourth and early third centuries B.C., is a fairly reliable source of information about Confucius, and generally agrees with the *Analects.* The other main source, the *Historical Records,* was written around 100 B.C. Practically all later biographies of Confucius were based on it. But the *Historical Records* is confused and self-contradictory, and certainly contains a large element of the legendary. The three works just named are used by Confucian scholars to the extent to which they agree with and help to explain the *Analects,* our primary source.

On the strength of such evidence we may assert that Confucius was born about 551 B.C. in the state of Lu and in the town of Tsou (or Chou), which is in the southwestern part of the modern province of Shantung. His parents were certainly not wealthy, although the family was probably of aristocratic descent. Confucius became an orphan at an early age. Possibly he was looked after by his uncle, or by his elder brother, since his niece is mentioned in the *Analects.* At any rate, he received an education from which he profited greatly, qualifying himself to become one of the greatest teachers in the history of the human race.

Confucius married and had a son and a daughter. His son's death occurred before his own. The later story that Confucius was divorced within a few years after his marriage may or may not be true, but certainly he lived a life free from family entanglements. From this his disciples were to profit.

The greatest ambitions of Confucius lay in the field of politics. But in this he was woefully unsuccessful, primarily because he was unwilling to flatter those who were in authority. He had definite ideas about governmental reform, and expressed them so readily that no one seemed willing to give him an important political appointment. For one thing, he argued that government should be administered by experts who had been trained for their jobs, rather than by conquerors or their relatives. This doctrine was to have a great influence on Chinese history, but it did not help Confucius get any important positions for himself.

Many of his students were more successful than he in securing governmental positions. At least ten of them held important posts at one time or another, as revealed in the *Analects*. Some of these positions were secured through the efforts of Confucius. The appointments were made, however, not so much out of courtesy to Confucius as because the rulers realized that a scholar trained by Confucius was a real asset in the government of a state. Typical positions filled by Confucius' disciples were in diplomacy or management.

It is probably true that Confucius held several very insignificant political jobs early in his career. But legendary were the stories about him holding high positions in the state of Lu. One legend asserts that he was minister of crime there, in which capacity he is supposed to have caused people to be executed for such mild offenses as "inventing unusual clothing."[4] This is not at all like the Confucius about whom we read in the *Analects*.

The one position of any importance held by Confucius was as an employe of the Chi family in the state of Lu. He was about fifty years old when he accepted an advisory position which turned out to be without power. His hopes of bringing about significant reform, therefore, were doomed, and about a decade later he resigned from a position which had all the while been merely honorary. At the time of his resignation he was confident that some other ruler would hire him and provide him with genuine opportunity. In fact he set out on a journey which was to take him far in search of his goal. But his ambition was never realized.

As he traveled about he was honored by the heads of the states. It seems that his travels were even subsidized at times by the states which he visited. And occasionally a minor position was offered him. His students occupied positions in some of these states, which may help to explain the courtesies to Confucius.

The Teacher

The net result of these fragments of Confucian biography is to confirm the fundamental fact that Confucius spent most of his life as a teacher and a scholar. In both of these capacities his interests were not theoretical but practical. Like Plato, he was interested in governmental reform. Like Plato also he prepared his pupils to serve the state. But unlike Plato, he believed that the ideal state was a definite possibility, not merely an idea that was "laid up in heaven" and unrealizable on earth.

A teacher is known through his students. Mencius said that Confucius had seventy students in his life time. From the *Analects* we learn of perhaps twenty-two personalities who might be called his students. His oldest student was probably Tzu-lu, a disciple who was critical both of himself and, on occasion, even of his master. The latter happened, for example, when Confucius once interviewed the Duchess Nan Tzu who was notorious for her immoral character. Confucius in turn criticized Tzu-lu for his tendency to be over-enthusiastic and courageous to the point of indiscretion. Yet master and pupil were very fond of each other and always most loyal and considerate. Tzu-lu met his death trying loyally to defend the Duke of Wei, in whose service he had been employed. He might easily have escaped with his own life, but refused to do so.

Another disciple, Jan Ch'iu, was the opposite of Tzu-lu in that he coolly calculated all of his actions. He was shrewd particularly in politics, and proved to be very successful in holding a good job. Jan Ch'iu once ingratiated himself with his political superior by devising means of increasing the already heavy load of taxation. For this Confucius refused to admit that Jan Ch'iu was his disciple.

Tzu-kung was one of Confucius' most admirable disciples. He was eloquent, diplomatic, and at the same time committed to the Confucian principles of integrity. He ably served the Chi family, and may have been one of the chief donors to Confucius' financial needs from time to time.

A great favorite with Confucius was Yen Hui, for reasons which are hard to understand. Apparently he was very intelligent but lacked something in the way of personality. He was always docile, agreeable, and close to poverty. He seems never to have secured a political job. But he lived an exemplary life. His early death distressed Confucius greatly.

Like those already mentioned, Tsai Yu seems to have been among Confucius' earlier disciples. His character is revealed in his teacher's appraisal: "There was a time when I merely listened attentively to what people said, and took for granted that they would carry out their words. Now I am obliged not only to give ear to what they say, but also to keep an eye on what they do. It was my dealings with Tsai Yu that brought about this change."[5]

The later disciples seem to have been the ones who carried on the Confucian mission. One of these was Tzu-yu, accomplished both in politics and in education. Apparently he organized an educational program on an unusually democratic basis in the town which he governed. Another disciple, Tzu-chang, became a successful teacher. He was exceptionally ambitious and prudent. Tzu-hsia also was a successful teacher and politician. He earned a reputation for being somewhat pedantic, but this may not do him justice. Tseng Shen, another successful teacher, exemplifies the tendency of the later disciples to emphasize filial piety, a quality which has been prominent in the history of Confucianism. Confucius' own son may also be counted among his later disciples, but in him Confucius seems to have been greatly disappointed.

These are only a few of his disciples. But they show such a variety of personality and character that we can well believe the report that Confucius accepted as disciples all who came to him, regardless of rank or wealth. All that he demanded of them was the ability to learn and a willingness to work.

The Curriculum

As an educator Confucius started something really new in China. The most reliable sources reveal that before Confucius there were just three types of education. (1) There were schools of archery, mentioned in the inscriptions on early bronze vessels. (2) There was the customary tutorial instruction for young princes preparing to rule a state. (3) Minor governmental officials were trained as apprentices to their political superiors. The Confucian education differed from all of these in breadth and purpose. For example, Confucius included in his curriculum character training and music. Courage and sincerity can hardly be considered prerequisites to political success, but Confucius required them of his disciples. He and his pupils also studied the best in literature, with emphasis on poetry. But with Confucius the most important object of study was life itself. Such study was to be critical and constructive. For Confucius expected his disciples above all to learn to be gentlemen in the truest sense of the word—men whose inner experience was cultivated and mature, and whose outward behavior gave suitable expression to that gentility of soul.

Confucius, himself accomplished on the lute and in song, regarded music as an important part of the curriculum. But, like Plato, he regarded it as a means rather than an end. He believed that music could motivate people to good or bad behavior, depending on what kind it was. Therefore, like Plato, he would have music controlled by the state. The psychiatrist's use of musical therapy today is in harmony with the basic Confucian concept of its function.

As for the goal of education, Confucius would be satisfied with nothing less than the reform of government. He expected his disciples to be civil administrators. But he would have them not merely carry on the traditional type of government. They must improve upon the customary to bring about the happiness of the people, for whom government existed. This was revolutionary doctrine, but it was what Confucius taught. He was training men for real life. He insisted that they should contribute to the real improvement of human society.

At the very heart of the Confucian curriculum was character education. His ideal of the gentleman was nothing superficial. The true gentleman (chun tzu) was not such by heredity but only through self-discipline and achievement. One must learn skill in the use of language. But Confucius feared eloquence as greatly as the inability to express oneself. So we come back to the ideal of sterling character, simply and sincerely expressed in words, attitudes, and deeds. Said he, "I do not know how a man without truthfulness is to get on. How can a large carriage be made to go without the cross bar . . . ?"[6] "The gentleman does not mind not being in office," he said; "all he minds about is whether he has qualities that entitle him to office. He does not mind failing to get recognition; he is too busy doing the things that entitle him to recognition."[7] Again, "A gentleman is ashamed to let his words outrun his deeds."[8]

Confucius has been misunderstood concerning his doctrine of *li.* This word has been translated as "ritual," or as "the rules of propriety." Its original meaning was "a sacrifice." This is still one of its meanings. It is true that later Confucianism overstressed ceremonial and rules of propriety, but such was not Confucius' attitude. He insisted on sincerity and graciousness of heart. Said he, "Ritual performed without reverence, the forms of mourning observed without grief—these are things I cannot bear to see."[9] At another time he exclaimed, "Ritual, ritual! Does it mean no more than presents of jade and silk? Music, music! Does it mean no more than bells and drums?"[10] Yet, for Confucius, *li* demanded that individuals observe the outward form as a suitable expression of the inward grace. Said he, "Courtesy not bounded by the prescriptions of ritual becomes tiresome. Caution not bounded by the prescriptions of ritual becomes timidity; daring becomes turbulence; inflexibility becomes harshness."[11] Again, the gentleman is one "who takes the right as his material . . . and ritual as the guide in putting what is right into practice."[12] And, "Only when ornament and substance are duly blended do you get the true gentleman."[13] *Li* was a means of disciplining the emotions and the intellect in such a manner that the gentleman was always in command of himself, while at the same time properly disposed toward others. Confucius insisted on being the gentleman regardless of how difficult the situation might be.

Apparently Confucius did not teach classes or conduct examinations. He taught one pupil or just a few at a time, fitting his instruction to the needs of each. He would inspire his disciples to do independent study and solve original problems. He did not set himself up as an infallible teacher but only as a counsellor, a loyal friend, and a source of inspiration and helpful criticism. At times he found himself sincerely admitting that his students were right and he was wrong when disagreements arose. Only a teacher with sterling character could be so humble, or rejoice when his disciples were far more successful than he in civic achievements. His pupils learned humility by observing his deportment, althought the master was always prepared to make the stinging remark. Once he noticed that "Tsu-kung was always criticising other people. The Master said, 'It is fortunate for Tsu he is so perfect himself as to have time to spare for this. I myself have none.' "[14]

Confucius the Scholar

As a scholar Confucius is traditionally credited with having edited or written the Five Classics. This tradition is now regarded with great skepticism. A reexamination of all the available data seems rather to lead to the conclusion that Confucius may not have edited or written anything whatsoever. A reading of the Five Classics leaves one with the inescapable impression that a man who had written or edited them could scarcely be one such as the *Analects* reveals.

It is most likely that very little of the so-called Five Classics of Confucianism existed in Confucius' day. One classic which did exist before Confucius was the *Shih Ching,* or *Book of Poetry*. Confucius once said to his disciples, "My children, why do you not study the *Poetry? The Odes* serve to stimulate the mind. They may be used for the purpose of self-contemplation. They teach the art of sociability. They show how to regulate feelings of resentment. From them you learn the more immediate duty of serving one's father, and the remoter one of serving one's prince. From them we become largely acquainted with the names of birds, beasts, and plants."[15]

It is possible that part of the *Li Chi—Records on Ceremonial*—also existed prior to Confucius, or if not, then something like it did. To it Confucius also referred, urging his disciples to study *li.* The older "classic," the *Book of History,* is of little value. And so the most that we may say with any assurance about Confucius as a scholar is that he probably made some minor alteration in the *Book of Poetry,* and that he referred to documents with which we are no longer familiar. When he urged his disciples to study, he meant that they should study life itself, quite as much as any documents. The practical side of Confucius' teaching is evident in that study of all sorts was intended by him to produce practical results such as political reform and social happiness.

Religious Philosophy

Confucius' philosophy of religion is of particular interest to us. What evidence do we find in the *Analects* which will show reliably what he believed about religion?

That Confucius approved of the traditional religious ritual is quite evident.[16] He urged his disciples to go in mourning for three years after the death of their parents.[17] Probably he believed in the survival of the soul after death, but thought that it was wrong to subordinate the welfare of the living to that of the dead. His humanistic emphasis is seen in two passages from the *Analects*. Replying to Tzu-lu's question on how to serve the spirits he said, "Till you have learnt to serve man, how can you serve ghosts?" In the same conversation he tried to turn Tzu-lu's mind away from the problem of death. "Till you know about the living, how are you to know about the dead?"[18] Apparently he felt that the ancestral spirits should require no more solicitude in death than they had in life, and that one should be satisfied with showing due respect for them without becoming the victim of superstitious fear and anxiety.

On another occasion Confucius was critically ill and Tzu-lu wanted to pray for him. "Is it done?" asked Confucius. Tzu-lu replied that it was customary. But still Confucius was not convinced that it was desirable. "My kind of praying was done long ago," said he,[19] referring no doubt to the fact that his whole life had been lived in an attitude of respect for the Good and the True as revealed in life's deepest experiences.

The positively expressed religious attitude of Confucius, so far as the *Analects* reveal, has to do with his faith in T'ien—Heaven, or Providence. There is no indication in the *Analects* that he thought of God intimately and personally. But he certainly believed in Providence as a divine power in his life. Like Socrates, he felt that he was obeying the heavenly voice within him as revealed in the nature of things. Confucius was not so simple as to believe that there was a one-to-one correspondence between the will of Providence and the blessings or cursings which followed from obedience or disobedience. But he did have faith in the Good as the Way of Heaven. He believed that men should follow the Way not for a reward but just because it was the Way. And he felt that generally speaking, at any rate, the good life resulted in true happiness while the life that was out of harmony with the cosmic Good must tend toward unhappiness.

There is nothing fatalistic about Confucius' philosophy, although such has erroneously been charged against it. He did say, "Death and life are the decree of heaven; wealth and rank depend upon the will of Heaven." But the context shows that he meant what everyone must agree to, that when death comes to some and life to others, there is little that we can do to alter that accomplished fact. What we can do in such circumstances is what should concern us, as the remainder of the quotation indicates: ". . . a gentleman attends to business and does not idle away his time . . . he behaves with courtesy to others and observes the rules of ritual."[20]

So important was the *Tao* in Confucius' philosophy that he said, "In the morning, hear the Way; in the evening, die content."[21] The *Tao* (Way) of Heaven, as understood by Confucius, was the Way of a cooperative, peaceful world, in which every one did his own duty instead of complaining that others shirked theirs. It was the Way in which the family was recognized as the most important unit of society. If one did not learn loyalty and cooperation in the family relationship, certainly one could not learn to cooperate as a loyal citizen.

A Way of Life

Although the ancient Chinese family was organized on the monarchic principle, which Confucius approved, yet there is little doubt but that family affection enforced a practical democracy. In the same way Confucius conceived of the social order, or the divine *Tao,* as based upon democratic experience. No doubt it was Confucius who told Tzu-hsia that "all within the Four Seas are . . . brothers."[22] If so, then Confucius was truly cosmopolitan in his outlook. And when he insisted that the purpose of the state was to make its people happy he showed a remarkable anticipation of democratic theory. He even insisted that education should be for all the people. Said he, "When the man of low station is well instructed, he is easily ruled."[23] As always he conceived of education as the cultivation of virtue, such as "loyalty, sincerity, good faith, justice, kindness, accord with li."[24]

If one should have to choose between following the *Tao* and following the ruler, one ought always to choose the *Tao*. Knowing that he is right is better than riches and honor: "With coarse rice to eat, with water to drink, and my bended arm for a pillow, I have still joy in the midst of these things."[25] And there is that quotation already cited, which shows Confucius teaching that success is of less importance than integrity.[26] The supreme worth of individual integrity was understood by Confucius: "If, on self-examination, I find that I am upright, I will go forward against thousands and tens of thousands."[27] Thus the Confucian *Tao* conceived in terms of personal integrity does not conflict with the *Tao* conceived in familial and political terms. But that is because character and duty come first in Confucianism. "You may rob the Three Armies of their commander-in-chief, but you cannot deprive the humblest peasant of his opinion."[28]

Confucius gave his disciples a technique by which to determine how far to go in the application of the principle of benevolence, and it was a technique remarkably similar to the Golden Rule of Jesus. Said Confucius, "What you do not want done to yourself, do not do to others."[29] This has been called the Silver Rule of Confucius because it is expressed negatively, making it less valuable than the positive rule of Jesus. But Confucius had the positive concept of duty also, and should be so interpreted. For he also said, "Now the man of perfect virtue, wishing to be established himself, seeks also to establish others; wishing to be enlarged himself, he seeks also to enlarge others. To be able to judge of others by what is nigh in ourselves,—this may be called the art of virtue."[30]

The humanism of Confucius is seen in that he regarded human nature not as fixed or fated but as most plastic in quality. Said he, "It is only the very wisest and the very stupidest who cannot change."[31] Apparently he thought that original human nature was neither good nor bad but only neutral, with capacities for either good or evil. "By nature, men are nearly alike," he said; "by practice they get to be wide apart."[32]

Legendary is the story that Confucius urged his disciples to pattern their lives after the ancients and to study the Classics in order to find an anchor for right belief. Nor did he regard himself as an infallible teacher. Such views of Confucius are entirely out of harmony with what we have found by looking into the *Analects* as seen through the eyes of the historical scientist.

It is really not easy to think of Confucius as a religious prophet in the light of his simple modesty as revealed in the *Analects*. "There were four qualities from which the Master was entirely free: he had no foregone conclusions, he was not over-positive, not obstinate, and never saw things from his own point of view alone."[33] Confucius himself said, "The superior man, in the world, does not set his mind either for anything, or against anything; what is right he will follow."[34] Among other things, this principle involves judging truth in terms of its context. Confucius never felt that to admit having made mistakes was a sign of weakness. "To be mistaken, and yet not to change; this is indeed to be in error," he said. And his disciple, Tzu-kung, made the point dramatic when he said, "The faults of a gentleman are like eclipses of the sun or moon. If he does wrong, everyone sees it. When he corrects his faults, every gaze is turned toward him."[35] ("All men look up to him," reads another translation.)

All of this sounds more like the ideal teacher or tutor than like the religious prophet. And such, in fact, is exactly what Confucius was. Yet we must remember that some of our greatest religious prophets regarded themselves as teachers, while later generations turned them into infallible avatars or incarnations of deity.

Undoubtedly Confucius found great satisfaction in being a teacher, as any one must in order to remain a teacher. And yet, as hinted earlier, Confucius' main ambition in life was to transform government so as to make it the instrument of happiness. So long as his opportunity to do this did not arrive, he undertook to train disciples to be prepared to do likewise. When his own opportunity finally arrived but proved to be a disappointment he returned to teaching, but again with a primary interest in political reform as a path to social reform.

Confucius was not the only great teacher or prophet to be interested in political and moral reform. We have only to think of

Socrates and Plato—or even Jesus. The latter realized the unhappy predicament of Judaism and sought to establish the Messianic Kingdom, with some supernatural help. Many argue that the social gospel is the most vital aspect of Christianity even today.

The view that Confucius was a political and moral reformer at heart is really revolutionary. Most books on Confucianism have simply followed the Confucian tradition which pictures the master as a lover of the ancients and as an advocate of the observance of time-honored custom. But recent scholarship has shown how and why such a tradition arose. And by restoring the *Analects* to its rightful place, minus its glosses, scholarship has established the more genuine view of Confucius as primarily a reformer, and hence as the very opposite of the reactionary or conservative. A great student of Confucian and Chinese culture summarizes the views of Confucius on government and education as follows:

> The proper aim of government is the welfare and happiness of the whole people.
>
> This aim can be achieved only when the state is administered by those most capable of government.
>
> Capacity to govern has no necessary connection with birth, wealth, or position; it depends solely on character and knowledge.
>
> Character and knowledge are produced by proper education.
>
> In order that the best talents may become available, education should be widely diffused.
>
> It follows that the government should be administered by those persons, chosen from the whole population, who prove themselves to have profited most by the proper kind of education.[36]

Because of the philosophical opposition of Confucius to the hereditary aristocracy, his followers were referred to by the aristocrats as "the weaklings." Used first as a term of derision, it was later taken up by the Confucians themselves. In the course of time it became popular for a king to engage Confucian scholars as his ministers. Eventually these scholars seem to have put the "rulers" in their place by taking over the actual government. So it might be said of such rulers that they "reigned but did not rule." But success was something Confucianism could not bear. This story will be told after our account, in the next chapter, of Taoism, the second indigenous religion of China.

Religious Maturity of Confucius

By capturing Confucianism at its source we may do the best job in evaluating it. And as we reflect upon Confucius himself we are amazed at his personal freedom from magic, mythological literalism, and the conservative attitude of traditionalism. He was deliberately committed to the truth wherever he might find it, and presupposed a rationalistic view of the universe, even though it was prescientific in many respects. He also had a sound concept of mental health and human nature, and worked toward the goal of a well adjusted personality in a world of peace and human happiness. He even appears to have had a certain mystic sensitivity which he expressed through his faith in providence and his respect for the dead. Remarkably enough, his mystic sensitivity was restrained by a wholesome measure of skepticism and a practical insistence on humanistic values and progress. He was a teacher and a reformer at heart, not a prophet.

The ritual which Confucius practiced was essentially twofold. First, he offered the traditional sacrifices to ancestral spirits, but as we have seen, this was primarily humanistic in intent. Second, he insisted on observing the proper forms of human relationship, not perfunctorily but as an expression of social and personal realities. This twofold ritual was mutually complementary and dramatizes, in a sense, the religious or cultural maturity of the man, Confucius.

Among the great religions, Confucianism is most often referred to as primarily a system of ethics. Confucius' preoccupation with problems of personal conduct and social and political reform supports this classification and witnesses to the fact that Confucianism was unusually mature ethically when it came from the mouth of the master. His universalism is attested by the fact that the great modern European philosophers hailed him when he became known to them.

XIX. TAOIST MYSTICISM

Taoism, like Confucianism, was originally a philosophy rather than a religion. As a philosophy, however, Taoism had more religious significance and lent itself more naturally to religious development than Confucianism. In the present chapter we shall describe the character of early Taoist philosophy. A later chapter will relate the story of the development of Taoism as a religion.

The historical problem is greater in the case of Taoism than with Confucianism. There is no doubt about the historicity of Confucius, nor about the essential reliability of the *Analects* as revised in the light of critical scholarship. But the "great prophet" who is supposed to have been the founder of Taoism, Lao Tzu, may be only a myth. If he was a real person, then Lao Tzu most certainly was not his real name. That he wrote the Taoist Classic, the *Tao Te Ching,* is doubtful, to say the least. And if he lived at all, it is not known when he lived. Was he the founder of Taoism, as tradition asserts? Or was Yang Chu the founder, while Lao Tzu was the second great Taoist, as some have maintained?

The Taoist Philosophers

Fung Yu-lan's present position on this issue is that there really was an historical person who came to be called Lao Tzu, and that he probably was an older contemporary of Confucius, but that the book which is sometimes called the *Lao-tzu* and at other times the *Tao Te Ching* was not composed until after the times of Yang Chu. He admits, however, that the *Tao Te Ching* may contain some of Lao Tzu's sayings.[1] This historical problem is neither solved nor stated by Finegan, probably because he regards its solution as hopeless.[2] On the other hand Lin Yutang reverts to the traditional view that Lao Tzu was an historical person, born about 571 B.C. and living to an unusually old age; that he was for a time the keeper of the imperial archives and that he was the primary author of the Taoist Classic.[3] Lin makes a plausible case for his view.

Without dogmatism let us simply assume that Lao Tzu lived, that he was a senior contemporary of Confucius, and that some of his sayings are found in the *Tao Te Ching*. What more can we say about him and his teachings? And who else contributed to early Taoist philosophy?

According to the *Historical Records* of Ssu-ma Ch'ien, written c. 100 B.C., Lao Tzu was an acquired name—we might call it a nick-name—his real name being Li Erh. "His given name was Erh, his style was Tan, and his family name was Li," wrote Ssu-ma Ch'ien. He is sometimes referred to as Lao Tan. But he is best known as Lao Tzu, just as Gautama Siddhartha is best known as Buddha and Jesus is known as Christ. Literally Lao Tzu means "Old Master." I shall refer to him as Lao Tzu, and for the sake of convenience shall speak of him as the author of the sayings of the *Tao Te Ching*. The legends about the precocity of his childhood, the excessive age to which he lived, and the off-hand manner in which he wrote the *Tao Te Ching* on reaching the border of Chou for retirement, are all incredible and irrelevant.

A second main contributor to Taoism was Yang Chu. In the late fourth century B.C. Mencius complained, "The words of Yang Chu and Mo Ti fill the world." But Mo Ti, or Mo Tzu, had not mentioned Yang Chu when he wrote a century earlier. We judge, therefore, that Yang Chu lived between the times of Mo Tzu and Mencius, in the early and middle fourth century. He wrote nothing which survives, so all that we know about him is what others say of him.

The third main contributor to Taoist philosophy was Chuang Tzu, a contemporary of Mencius. His approximate dates are 369-286 B.C. He is said to have written the book which is known as the *Chuang-tzu*. It is certain, however, that some of the *Chuang-tzu* was written later than his time, since there are references to people who lived later. Some of it was probably written before his day. Possibly the book was compiled in its present form by Kuo Hsiang, "Chuang Tzu's great commentator of the third century A.D."[4] All scholars admit that chapters 28-31 were written later than Chuang Tzu's day.[5]

The Taoist point of view in general was known to Confucius and his disciples, according to the *Analects*. Chuang Tzu even relates stories of conversations between Confucius and Lao Tzu, or between Confucius and his disciple Yen Hui, in which Confucius is represented as having become, late in life, a disciple of Lao Tzu. All scholars recognize, however, that the stories are imaginary. They may be regarded as a literary device used by a Taoist to show the superiority of Taoism over Confucianism.

The Taoists, or pre-Taoists, of Confucius' day were recluses whom Confucius described as obscurantists and escapists.[6] These recluses were cynical about the possibility of improving the human situation. They thought Confucius ought to know better than to try to reform political society, describing him as "the one who 'knows it's no use, but keeps on doing it.' "[7]

Yang Chu's Individualism

Among the early Taoists, Yang Chu was probably the best representative of the point of view of the recluse. The essentials of his philosophy may be summed up in two brief epigrams: (1) Let each one look out for his own interests. (2) Life is worth more than possessions and honors. In the third century A.D. some one misinterpreted Yang Chu as a kind of Epicurean, describing his philosophy in a chapter which is translated as "Yang Chu's Garden of Pleasure."[8] But this does not do justice to Yang Chu and the early recluses. The truth seems to be that these people were cynical even about the value of sense pleasures. We can best understand them if we think of them as extreme individualists. Mencius wrote, "The principle of Yang Chu is: 'Each one for himself.' Though he might have profited the whole world by plucking out a single hair, he would not have done it."[9] Two centuries later some one wrote, "Preserving life and maintaining what is genuine in it, not allowing things to entangle one's person: this is what Yang Chu established."[10]

Yang Chu's philosophy was obviously opposed to that of Confucius. The latter was keenly interested in human welfare, and dedicated his whole life to the service of man. But Yang Chu was sure that society could not be saved. If every one contented himself with looking after his own interests and did not try to busy himself with the welfare of others, all would be as happy as possible. The folly of entering into the service of the state was twofold: to do so was useless, to do so was dangerous, for one might easily lose one's life and honor by such means. Political service really was dangerous in those days. Courtiers were in danger of being killed by a victorious invader or by their own superiors. All were in danger of assassination and intrigue. Under such conditions the early Taoists preferred to stay out of politics and to find satisfaction in undisturbed contemplation. This was the character of the "first phase of Taoism," as represented by Yang Chu, according to Fung.[11] But this point of view is also found in the *Lao-tzu* and in the *Chuang-tzu*.

A writer in the third century B.C., Lü-shih Ch'un-Ch'iu, reflected the individualistic phase of Taoism in his chapter (1.3) on "The Importance of Self." Said he, "Our life is our own possession, and its benefit to us is very great. Regarding its dignity, even the honor of being Emperor could not compare with it. Regarding its safety, were we to lose it for one morning, we could never again bring it back."[12]

So far Taoism seems a reasonable philosophy. Its individualism is at least tenable, even if not ultimate. But from this point onward we find ideas which are not easy either to understand or to defend. Taoism is thus seen to be mystical and paradoxical. Some of it, however, is both valid and significant.

Of first importance is the problem of defining the *Tao*. The primary meaning of the word is simple: It denotes a "road" or a "path." The *Tao* is usually translated into English as "The Way," signifying the way of life, or the way of nature. The *Tao Te Ching* may be translated as "The Classic of the Way and Its Power." The primary meaning of *Tao* is, of course, not absent from its derived meaning in Taoist philosophy. But this is only the beginning of understanding it.

Taoist Mysticism

In fact, one striking doctrine of Taoism is that the real *Tao* is nameless. Some see the influence of the "School of Names" in this doctrine, but that seems irrelevant and unimportant except for dating purposes. Thus Lao Tzu says in his first chapter, "The *Tao* that can be comprised in words is not the eternal *Tao;* the name that can be named is not the abiding name. The Unnamable is the beginning of Heaven and Earth; the namable is the mother of all things." Later, in chapter thirty-two, he writes, "The *Tao* is eternal, nameless, the Uncarved Block. . . . Once the block is carved, there are names."[13] In chapter twenty-five he says,

> Something there is, whose veiled creation was
> Before the earth or sky began to be;
> So silent, so aloof and so alone,
> It changes not, nor fails, but touches all:
> Conceive it as the mother of the world.[14]

In chapter twenty-one of the *Lao-tzu* we read,

> The Way itself is like some thing
> Seen in a dream, elusive, evading one.

That he is speaking about the ultimate principle of all Being is perhaps best evident from the concluding part of chapter twenty-five:

> Man conforms to the earth;
> The earth conforms to the sky;
> The sky conforms to the Way;
> The Way conforms to its own nature.

Fung Yu-lan tries his hand at interpreting these dark explanations. He writes, "If we analyze the existence of things, we see there must first be Being before there can be any things. *Tao* is the unnamable, is Non-being, and is that by which all things come to be. Therefore, before the being of Being, there must be Non-being, from which Being comes into being. What is here said belongs to ontology, not to cosmology. It has nothing to do with time and actuality. For in time and actuality, there is no Being; there are only beings."[15] Does this make the mystery still deeper? Or was it as obscure as it could get when Lao Tzu finished with his explaining?

The Harmony of Nature

Not quite so difficult is the Taoist doctrine that the course of nature is the course of perfection and harmony. That is so because nature is based on the *Tao,* which is wonderfully smooth, invariable, and just. We may ask, how can one know this about the *Tao* which is nameless, dark, silent, isolated, elusive, and evasive? Well, perhaps pragmatically we know simply because nature, based on the ultimate *Tao,* is smooth and invariable, and because he who puts his life in tune with the *Tao* as thus felt, lives a life that is deeply satisfying. This is the perennial mystic's approach to the problem of immediate, intuitive knowledge which cannot be conveyed by means of logic but only through the assurance of personal experience.

Not only is *Tao* the source of harmony in nature and man; that harmony is also a rhythmic movement which inevitably comes full-circle back to its origin, thereby identifying the end with the beginning. This process, which is not necessarily physical, is called reversion. It all takes place silently, without grandiose announcement or ceremonious accompaniment. The very perfection of the *Tao* lies in the fact that without action it nevertheless accomplishes all things. This is the Taoist doctrine of "inactivity," with its implications for human conduct. In turn it gives rise to the Taoist paradox of the unity of opposites. These several doctrines call for illustrative quotations from the *Lao-tzu* and from the *Chuang-tzu.*

The pervasive, harmonious, but unostentatious harmony of *Tao* is reflected in chapter thirty-four of the *Tao Te Ching:*

> O the great Way o'erflows
> And spreads on every side!
> All being comes from it;
> No creature is denied.
> But having called them forth,
> It calls not one its own.
> It feeds and clothes them all
> And will not be their lord.

The relation between inaction, harmony, reversion, nature, and the *Tao* may be seen in chapter sixteen of *Lao-tzu,* where the reader is advised to be still and seek emptiness, thus reverting to his roots.

> All things work together . . .
> though you die,
> You shall not perish.

The Sage senses the cycle of action and repose in the whole universe, and finds peace and fulfillment in his own life.

Chuang Tzu once offered some parabolic advice in the form of a conversation between the Spirit of the Clouds and the Vital Principle. The question was how to restore harmony that had been lost through "the fault of government."

> "But what am I to do?" exclaimed the Spirit of the Clouds.
>
> "It is here," cried the Vital Principle, "that the poison lurks! Go back!"
>
> "It is not often," urged the Spirit of the Clouds, "that I meet with your Holiness. I would gladly receive some advice."
>
> "Feed then your people," said the Vital Principle, "with your heart. Rest in inaction, and the world will be good of itself. . . . Spit forth intelligence. Ignore all differences. Become one with the infinite. Release your mind. Free your soul. Be vacuous. Be nothing!
>
> "Let all things revert to their original constitution. If they do this, without knowledge, the result will be a simple purity which they will never lose."[16]

The Taoists admitted that temporary success might follow the actions of those who do not live according to the *Tao.* But the principle of reversion is inherent in the nature of reality; it cannot long be ignored.

Often quoted is chapter nine of the *Tao Te Ching,* which shows how inevitable it is that the strong become weak and the rich become poor. Voluntary acquiescence is Heaven's Way. Be satisfied not to be the top person in your group, or to own more wealth than others. Such ambitions only lead to worry and insecurity. Do your proper work and then retire.

> When fame and success
> Come to you, then retire.
> This is the ordained way.

Ethics of Taoism

Humility and selflessness are strange yet natural lessons of the *Tao*. So the *Lao-tzu* says, in chapter seven:

> The Wise Man chooses to be last
> And so becomes the first of all.

The unselfish person is the one who best realizes his self. This is scarcely in harmony with Yang Chu's individualism, unless we figure a way to unify even these opposites of selflessness and self-seeking. Yet the emphasis on selflessness is such that we cannot regard this doctrine as accidental in Taoism. In chapter thirteen Lao Tzu insists that the stress upon self is what causes anxiety. One who would rule the world should love mankind as he loves himself. Only then is he worthy to rule mankind.

The most serious fault of Taoism is its nihilism. Thus both Lao Tzu and Chuang Tzu condemn knowledge and civilization as superficial and pernicious. Says Lao Tzu in chapter nineteen:

> Get rid of the wise men!
> Put out the professors!
> Then the people will profit
> A hundredfold over.

The writer seems even to suggest that the teaching of morals and law does more harm than good. Let people be good by themselves, he urges.

It seems utterly paradoxical to follow Chuang Tzu in his critique of civilization. Said he, "If we thrashed the Sages and let the brigands and assassins go, there would soon be peace and order. . . ."[17]

Chuang Tzu also tells how householders use locks and ropes to make their wealth secure. "But suppose real brigands come. They will snatch up the boxes, hoist the sacks, carry away the big trunks on their backs, and be gone; only too glad that the locks are solid and the ropes strong."[18]

Our most natural reaction to such nihilism is to condemn it, for we are inclined to fear any philosophy that leads to the denial of a real difference between true and false, or between good and bad.

But the Taoist prophet was not writing without experience. Too often in history the rulers really are little more than successful gangsters. Too often a superficial wisdom is worse than ignorance. And force sometimes makes wrong appear to be right and vice versa. No doubt Lao Tzu and Chuang Tzu had witnessed enough examples of these things to feel quite justified in what they wrote. Much sad experience probably underlay Lao Tzu's insight in chapter thirty-one, which might still be worth contemplating:

> Weapons are tools of bad omen,
> By gentlemen not to be used;
> But when it cannot be avoided,
> They use them with calm and restraint.
> Even in victory's hour
> These tools are unlovely to see;
> For those who admire them truly
> Are men who in murder delight.

Perhaps what Chuang Tzu was really aiming at was neither anarchy nor ignorance. Said he,

> Get rid of small wisdom, and great wisdom will shine upon you. Put away goodness and you will be naturally good. A child does not learn to speak because taught by professors of the art, but because it lives among people who can themselves speak.[19]

It seems that Lao Tzu was inculcating genuineness or naturalness of character in chapter thirty-eight when he described the degeneration which takes place whenever man loses that feeling for reality and sinks to mere formality:

> Truly, once the Way is lost,
> There comes then virtue;
> Virtue lost, comes then compassion;
> After that morality;
> And when that's lost, there's etiquette,
> The husk of all good faith,
> The rising point of anarchy.

The Doctrine of Inaction

The Taoist doctrine of inaction may seem nihilistic and absurd. But something should be said for it. First, *wu-wei,* generally translated as "inaction," means literally "not to do anything for." "Lao Tzu uses the phrase . . . for an unassertive, effortless behavior which actually accomplishes much more than blustering, violent effort. Hence *wu-wei* really signifies something like simplicity, spontaneity, or naturalness."[20]

As Lao Tzu saw it, the Sage was not a busy-body, an everlasting do-gooder, but one who governed least in order that the realm might be governed best. By not trying to interfere with the operations of human nature, the Sage best promotes righteousness, since nature is basically good.

> So long as I do nothing, the people will work out their own reformation. So long as I love calm, the people will right themselves. If only I keep from meddling, the people will grow rich.[21]

Wealth and happiness are best earned by the least effort or anxiety. The ambitious are never satisfied. And when they attain wealth and honor, then they will be anxious not to lose either. They will never be secure. Let them learn a lesson from nature.

> The softest of stuff in the world
> Penetrates quickly the hardest;
> Insubstantial, it enters
> Where no room is.[22]

According to Lao Tzu it is unnecessary to travel far for wisdom. Inaction is more effective:

> The world may be known
> Without leaving the house. . . .
> The further you go,
> The less you will know.[23]

The real classic on inaction seems to be chapter forty-eight, where the paradox seems insurmountable:

> The student learns by daily increment.
> The Way is gained by daily loss.
> By letting go, it all gets done.

Some light is thrown on this paradox by chapters sixty-three and sixty-four:

Requite anger with virtue. . . .
Take hard jobs in hand
While they are easy. . . .
Establish order before confusion sets in. . . .
A nine-storied terrace began with a clod.
A thousand-mile journey began with a foot put down.

Taoist Generosity

It has often been said that Taoism teaches generosity rather than strict justice. This is partly due to Ch'u Ta-Kao's translation of chapter seventy-nine. According to him, this chapter begins with:

Return love for great hatred.
Otherwise, when a great hatred is reconciled, some of it will surely remain.
How can this end in goodness?[24]

Apparently, however, this translator supplied the most important first line, no doubt on the theory that it was the sense of the whole. This may be true. But a more restrained translation shows that Lao Tzu was really trying to say that too often the effort to settle a dispute only leads to further anger. The whole thing is a matter of attitude, he said in effect. The smart person will hold the left-hand part of a contract tally—a Chinese sign of inferiority—and will not try to place the blame on others. What is to be gained by insisting "It was your fault." Truly the spirit of generosity shines through these lines even as thus rendered. They picture the Sage, or virtuous man, as anxious to cancel all hate, and as humble enough to refrain from insisting that the other party is the guilty one even when that is so. Chapter sixty-three, quoted above, reveals the same generous attitude.

Lao Tzu's readiness to redeem the sinful by treating them with respect and confidence is seen in chapter forty-nine:

Alike to good and bad
I must be good,
For vitue is goodness.

The passage just quoted sustains the doctrine of generosity. In fact, Legge's translation of the same passage definitely makes it mean generosity, although the accuracy of the translation may be questioned:

> To those who are good to me I am good; and to those who are not good to me, I am also good;—and thus all get to be good. To those who are sincere with me, I am sincere; and to those who are not sincere with me, I am also sincere;—and thus all get to be sincere.[25]

The doctrine of generosity reminds us, of course, of Jesus. The lofty heights of the Old Testament prophets in like manner are suggested in the ethical reflections of chapter fifty-three. Here the contrast is pictured between the neat and shining prosperity of rulers and rich men, and the hunger and poverty of the poor. Such conditions remind the mystic not of the Way but of gangsters and brigands.

Remarkably enough, we find in Lao Tzu the principle of finding one's life by losing it. The Sage serves others, not himself.

> Having given all he had,
> He then is very rich indeed.[26]

The "three jewels" or virtues emphasized most by Taoism are gentleness, frugality, and humility. "Be gentle, and you can be bold; be frugal, and you can be liberal; avoid putting yourself before others, and you can become a leader among men."[27]

Humility

We come back again, therefore, to humility, one of Taoism's most characteristic virtues. Water is used as a striking symbol of humility because it always seeks the lowest places. As Lao Tzu says,

> The highest goodness is like water, for water is excellent in benefiting all things, and it does not strive. It occupies the lowest place, which men abhor. And therefore it is near akin to Tao.[28]

But water is also a symbol of that kind of weakness which is stronger than the strongest. Its lessons are suggested in chapter seventy-eight:

> Nothing is weaker than water
> But . . . nothing will alter its way.[29]

Consistently with such ideas, Lao Tzu taught that moral power is greater than arms and armies. This is seen in chapter thirty, for example, where we are told that the mystic frowns upon the use of armed force as a means of realizing the *Tao*. Chuang Tzu adds a note of deep insight regarding armaments. He pointed out that when an army is handy, it is just natural to use it.[30] Elsewhere, he said, "Appeal to arms is the lowest form of virtue. Rewards and punishment are the lowest form of education. Ceremonies and laws are the lowest form of government. Music and fine clothes are the lowest form of happiness. Weeping and mourning are the lowest form of grief."[31]

All of these citations constitute evidence that the mystic is likely to have a certain practical good sense. His ultimate goal is union with the One. That mystic unity is the negation of all individuality and separate qualities. But even the most dreamy mystic realizes that he cannot live in the world of the Absolute all the time. So long as he lives the life of a human organism he must engage in activities that are relative, since his body is relative and has relative needs. But while he lives in the relative world of time and space he is inspired by the irrepressible intuition that God alone has absolute being, and that all things are one in Him. So the paradox of the mystic's life is expressed in Lao Tzu's chapter fifty-six, where we read that the talker is likely to be one who does not know, while the wise man does not talk. The solution is:

> Keep the mouth shut, close the gateway of sense, and as long as you live you will have no trouble. Open your lips and push your affairs, and you will not be safe to the end of your days.[32]

Salvation is to be found in the mystic unity in which form and color, words and noises, are known to be merely the surface. Reality is far deeper than the objects of sense. Not that the mystic is weak in mind or body, or confused in sense perception. By not cluttering his sensibilities with sights and sounds he perceives more clearly than others. Such is the Way of Heaven.[33]

In other words the mystic, because he realizes the relativity of all things, quietly waits for the Absolute to envelope his being. Then he is able to see more clearly than ever the real nature of the relative. To the ordinary, hard-headed rationalist the Absolute has no meaning; it seems empty. But to the mystic it is inexhaustible. This is the meaning of chapter four:

> The Way is a void,
> Used but never filled.

One who is on intimate terms with the Absolute does not fear death. For death, like birth, belongs to the relative world of time and space. When one has transcended the relative world through his intuition of the Mystic One, he is superior to both death and life. So in chapter fifty we read that life and death belong to the same cycle. With this knowledge the Sage so lives that he never meets tigers or buffaloes. He is safe from attack by man or beast.

> Why so? In him there is no place of death.

The above is one of the very few passages in which Lao Tzu refers to death at all. But these words were interpreted literally by later Taoists, contributing to the magical phase of this religion.

Chuang Tzu shared the philosophy of Lao Tzu and was its greatest interpreter. He believed that life and death are inseparable phases of the process of nature, and that both may be transcended in the mystic Unity. The story is told that when Chuang Tzu's wife died a friend, Hui Tzu, went to comfort him. The vistor was astonished to find him singing, accompanying himself by drumming on a basin. Naturally this called for an explanation.

> When she died I was in despair, as any man well might be. But soon, pondering on what had happened, I told myself that in death no strange new fate befalls us. In the beginning we lack not life only, but form. Not form only, but spirit. We are blended in the one great featureless indistinguishable mass. Then a time came when the mass evolved spirit, spirit evolved form, form evolved life. And now life in its turn has evolved death. For not nature only but man's being has its seasons; its sequence of spring and autumn, summer and winter. . . . She whom I have lost has lain down to sleep for a while in the Great Inner Room. To break in upon her rest with the noise of lamentation would but show that I knew nothing of nature's Sovereign Law. That is why I ceased to mourn.[34]

This same point of view, looking upon nature's phases as relative, and upon life and death as of equal value, is expressed in the following selection:

> The pure men of old did not know what it was to love life or to hate death. They did not rejoice in birth, nor strive to put off dissolution. . . . Cheerfully they played their allotted parts, waiting patiently for the end. This is what is called not to lead the heart from Tao. . . .[35]

Chuang Tzu's imagination reaches truly poetic heights in some of his references to death. One such passage is found in chapter twenty-two:

> Man passes through this sublunary life as a white horse passes a crack. Here one moment, gone the next. . . . One modification brings life; then another, and it is death. Living creatures cry out; human beings sorrow. The bow-sheath is slipped off; the clothes-bag is dropped; and in the confusion the soul wings its flight, and the body follows, on the great journey home.[36]

So life comes and goes in its elusive beauty. But what is life and what is death? That is the problem. Which experience is most characteristic of the soul?

> Once Chuang Tzu dreamt that he was a butterfly. He did not know that he had ever been anything but a butterfly and was content to hover from flower to flower. Suddenly he woke and found to his astonishment that he was Chuang Tzu. But it was hard to be sure whether he really was [Chuang] and had only dreamt that he was a butterfly, or was really a butterfly, and was only dreaming that he was [Chuang].[37]

Summary of Taoism

We may leave Chuang Tzu in his confusion over things that are relative, and summarize the truly amazing teachings of early Taoism.

1. Taoism is essentially a form of mysticism. Like all mysticism, Taoism teaches that the world of the senses is relative. The real world is not a world apart from nature, and yet the particularities of nature are a source of error. For the real is the One and the all, combining life and death, joy and sorrow, wisdom and ignorance in a higher unity. This higher unity, the *Tao,* is known not through reason but through the intuition, a kind of spiritual perception.

2. Taoism is also a Way of Life. As such it seems most paradoxi-

cal, rejecting learning while embracing wisdom, spurning pleasure while nourishing peace of soul, condemning force but approving true strength. Taoism's condemnation of learning seems odd, since it is always exalting the ideal of "the Sage." The sayings and example of the Sage are always represented as pointing the way to shrewd and successful living. So with all its scorn for the relative point of view, somehow early Taoism takes pride in the success with which it surmounts the problems of life. Prudence turns out to be one of its most prominent ideals, although it is not mentioned as such.

3. In political and social relations Taoism taught that Nature, reflecting the *Tao,* would work out its beneficent purposes best if left alone. Therefore its political ideal is *laissez faire,* and its ethics likewise is built upon individualism. Yet while rejecting anything approximating political totalitarianism, at the same time it embraces a kind of cosmic totalitarianism in which the individual is absorbed in the mystic Unity of all things.

4. Finally, to point up its real nature, we may say that in a deep sense Taoism was the antithesis of Confucianism. The latter was intensely this-worldly, common-sense, and practical. Confucius took no special delight in paradoxes. And he was certainly far removed from the way of mysticism. In contrast, Taoism was dreamy, otherworldly, and mystical. Its ideal of sageliness was based on a nihilistic attitude toward knowledge and government. While Confucius counseled a kind of humanistic devotion to the ideal of postive government and the matching of formality and genuineness in social relations, Taoism always sought the "higher" point of view which, in effect, tended to negate the human concern over right and wrong, truth and falsehood, and even life and death. The struggle between Confucian and Taoist philosophy was to occupy the cultural stage in much of the subsequent history of China. To this and other issues we shall turn in the next chapter.

Religious Maturity of Early Taoism

Having described the religion of Confucius as mature in many ways, may we do likewise for early Taoism, which was the antithesis of early Confucian philosophy? Paradoxically, yes, though Taoism had a different kind of maturity.

Early Taoist philosophy reflects the maturity of mysticism, while Confucius shows the maturity of rationalism. Confucius was remarkably mature precisely because of his exceptional rationalism. Taoism was mature because of its coherent mysticism. Early Taoist mysticism is comparable with Upanishadic mysticism.

On the basis of our simplified criteria, Lao Tzu and Chuang Tzu were relatively free from magic. They both appealed to myth, but always in a dreamy, poetic frame of mind. They knew how to use myth as intuitive symbols having no literal value.

The early Taoist appeal to sageliness shows a virtual commitment to the requirements of truthfulness. Perception of the rhythm of nature and the unchanging character of basic human relations were insights of Taoist philosophy, showing maturity and depth far beyond the ordinary. Willingness to accept the paradoxes of life without being overwhelmed by them proved to be a source of great spiritual strength and health in early Taoism.

Like Confucianism in one respect, early Taoism was largely free from religious ritualism. They were free for different reasons, nevertheless free. That is why we call them philosophies rather than religions. Yet Confucius practiced an enlightened kind of state religion involving reverence for ancestors and the use of sacrifice. There is little to guide us in evaluating Taoism on this point, but it is likely that Lao Tzu and Chuang Tzu were freer than Confucius from any concern with ritual. They were more the Quaker type. As representing this type, they too were mature.

Certainly Lao Tzu and Chuang Tzu were mystically sensitive—supremely so. This was their greatest strength, showing their genius for tapping the universal sources of spiritual power. The vitality of early Taoism is quite evident, and surely flows from its mature apprehension of the mystical, if paradoxical, character of the universe.

XX. EARLY CONFUCIAN APOSTLES AND RIVALS

CONFUCIUS died in 479 B.C., at the age of seventy-two. His death occurred at Chufou (also spelled Ch'u-fou, Ch'u-fu, Kufow), not far from where he was born. Near Chufou he was buried, and his tomb stands there until this day. Ssu-ma Ch'ien describes the ceremonial grief which his disciples expressed for Confucius over a period of three years—some even for six years. Many built houses near his grave, in order to cultivate his memory and his influence. If Ssu-ma Ch'ien's story is correct, the practices of the Chinese in reverencing the souls of their ancestors were applied to Confucius by his faithful followers, as if he were their real father.

Ssu-ma Ch'ien reflects the attitudes and practices toward Confucius which had become customary by 100 B.C. when his *Historical Records* were composed. He explained how in the province it had long been customary to offer sacrifices regularly at Confucius' grave. Festivals and archery contests were engaged in by scholars there, and the school room of Confucius' pupils was transformed into a temple and then into a sacred museum to display the master's possessions. This continued, wrote Ssu-ma, for more than two hundred years. Then the Han emperor, on passing through Lu, set an example followed by many of offering sacrifice to Confucius.

Ssu-ma goes on to tell what a deep impression had been made on him when he read the master's writings, and what deep reverence he felt on visiting the shrine at Confucius' grave. Considering how democratic and simple Confucius had been, it amazed Ssu-ma Ch'ien that his fame should be so great and so lasting, and that princes and emperors should learn from him.[1]

In front of the grave of Confucius stands a ritual stone tablet on which is written the simple inscription, ANCIENT, MOST HOLY TEACHER.[2]

How long before 100 B.C. the situation described above developed we are not sure, since Ssu-ma Ch'ien was not a critical historian in the modern sense of the word. Even Ssu-ma Ch'ien related how Confucianism became divided and weak after the death of Confucius in the "Warring States Period."

One of the voices raised in protest against Confucius, yet echoing many of his teachings, was that of Mo Ti, or Mo Tzu ("Master Mo"), who lived sometime between 480 and 390 B.C.[3] He wrote a book which is called the *Mo Tzu,* containing fifty-three chapters in its present form. Part of it represents additions by his disciples, some even by his opponents.

Moism

It is probable that Mo Tzu was a Confucian as a young student. Certainly he knew Confucianism. But he founded his own school in opposition to it, and proposed his own unique philosophy. Moism, as it is called, may even be classed as a religion in certain of its aspects, and Mo Tzu may be thought of as a prophet. Says Professor Fung, "Confucius was a refined gentleman, while Mo Tzu was a militant preacher. A major aim of his preaching was to oppose both the traditional institutions and practices, and the theories of Confucius and the Confucianists."[4]

Moism was authoritarian, like some brands of other religions. He was so sure that he held the solution to the ills of the world that he proceeded to lay down the dogma which his followers were required to believe. Said he, "My teachings are sufficient. To forsake my teachings and try to think for one's self is like abandoning the crop and picking up a few grains."[5] Not only was his teaching authoritative, but also his school was organized on the principle of authority and discipline. The leader of the Mohist school got his position by inheritance, and is believed to have held the power of life and death over its members. Furthermore, Mohism taught the principle of political authoritarianism. Poverty, lawlessness, and war could be abolished if each would accept the authority of his leader and he, in turn, of the next higher leader. "What the superior thinks to be right, all must think to be right; what the superior thinks to be wrong, all must think to be wrong."[6] In such a system a tremendous responsibility, of course, rests upon "der Fuehrer." If the supreme leader is wrong, what happens? Mo Tzu had an answer. If the Son of Heaven failed to keep in tune with Heaven, then all sorts of calamities were showered on the sons of men. Mo Tzu cited what he believed to be historical instances of this sort of thing, such as the time when "it rained blood for three days," and "dragons appeared in the temple."[7] No doubt he was citing folklore rather than history. But in later centuries even the Confucians accepted this theory of divine retribution for the failure of the ruler to keep in harmony with Heaven.

Mo Tzu was opposed not to war as such, but only to offensive war. In fact, Fung identifies the Mohists with a class of people known as *hsieh,* or *yu hsieh,* that is "knights-errant"—professional soldiers who in the Warring States Period hired themselves to whoever could pay for their services. But the Mohists would not fight for a prince who waged offensive war. The story is told that the prince of Ch'u planned to attack the state of Sung with a new weapon. Mo Tzu went to Ch'u and tried to convince the prince by means of a miniature demonstration, that even with his new weapon he could not conquer Sung. The prince hinted that if Mo Tzu were murdered the attack might be successful, since Mo was the defending General. But Mo Tzu replied that his followers in Sung were well enough organized to carry on without him, and that they were well prepared. So the attack was called off. Nine chapters of the Mo Tzu discuss tactics of defensive warfare.[8]

Much more positive, yet perhaps not so effective in a realistic world, was Mo Tzu's declaration in favor of the principle of all-embracing love. This principle he developed by applying three "tests of judgment" which probed "its basis, its verifiability, and its applicability." A right principle is "based on the Will of Heaven and of the spirits and on the deeds of the ancient sage-kings." It is verified by the sense experience of the common people. And it is applicable in political and social relations. Judged by these tests, Mo Tzu proves that the principle of discrimination is harmful whereas the principle of all-embracing love is beneficial to all. Discrimination leads to war and crime, while love leads to peace and good citizenship.[9]

It would be naïve to insist that Mo Tzu's doctrine of love was identical with that of Christianity. The latter may properly be characterized as an emotion of brotherliness applied to the whole human race. But Mo Tzu's doctrine was primarily intellectual, and may well be paraphrased as "enlightened self-interest," as Creel points out.[10] Emotion as such, he held, must be superseded by iron-clad policy that is logical and successful.

Thus rationalizing on the basis of utilitarianism, Mo Tzu concludes in the spirit of the Old Testament prophets and Jesus—or perhaps we should say of Jeremy Bentham—that all-embracing love will work if it is tried. "Thus the aged and widowers will have support and nourishment with which to round out their old age, and the young and weak and orphans will have a place of support in which to grow up."[11]

The main defect of the Mohist doctrine of all-embracing love is the obvious difficulty of getting men to practice it. But this difficulty applies to the Christian and Buddhist teachings on love as well as to the Mohist. Many may profess it, but few truly live it.

Mo Tzu attacks the problem of motivation by trying to prove the existence of spirits—ancestral and otherwise—and of God. God loves mankind and wants men to love one another. He and the good spirits bless those who love, and punish those who discriminate. Not that all suffering is the result of sin; but at least sin does cause some of the suffering. If everyone believed that, the world would benefit, argued Mo Tzu.

The above argument was purely utilitarian, as can easily be seen by comparing it with other words which he wrote. "Whoever loves others is loved by others." And again, "How can there be anything that is good but not useful?"[12]

It seems certain that Mo Tzu believed in a personal supreme God—Shang Ti—and in spirits, ancestral and otherwise. He criticized the Confucians for not believing in God and the spirits, "with the result that God and the spirits are displeased."[13] He was only partly right in this judgment of Confucians. For we recall that Confucius held to an impersonal view of God, as "Heaven." And he insisted on observing the customs regarding ancestor worship although this seems to have been for the purpose of cultivating filial piety, as we have seen. Certainly his emphasis was humanistic,[14] whereas Mo Tzu, although utilitarian, was nevertheless supernaturalistic in his outlook.

Another significant difference between Mo Tzu and Confucius was in regard to the value of music and the role of the emotions. According to Mo Tzu music was bad because it stirred up the emotions, whereas conduct should be intellectually determined. Besides, music absorbed too much of one's time and was wasteful of wealth. "Joy and anger, pleasure and sorrow, love [and hate], are to be got rid of," said he. "What is it that causes rulers to neglect government and common men to neglect their work? Music. Therefore, Mo Tzu says, 'It is wrong to play music.' " Contrast this with the Confucian attitude: "Music produces pleasure, without which man's nature cannot do."[15]

The third principal Mohist criticism of Confucianism was of its acceptance of fate. In this criticism Mo Tzu was unjust. For Confucius had never advised a lazy resignation to fate. Confucius believed in doing everything possible to make the world a happier place. In fact he was ridiculed for trying to change things even when they appeared hopelessly unchangeable. But when one has done all that and still the undesirable happens, it should be accepted as the inevitable. This was what was meant when the Confucians spoke of "knowing *Ming*" (fate, destiny, decree).

Finally, Mo Tzu condemned the customary Confucian expenditure of wealth, time, and energy in elaborate funerals and a three year period of mourning. Such practices impoverish families and leave the whole population in a dejected state. Actually, Confucius no more approved of extravagant funerals than Mo Tzu did. It is probable, however, that the Confucians of Mo Tzu's day practiced an excess of mortuary ritual.

Mo Tzu had many devoted disciples, and Moism as a school became a principal rival of Confucianism. Their common interest in eliminating human discord was overlooked because of their differences as to the means to be used. But Confucianism outlasted Moism. The latter completely disappeared from the historical scene sometime during the first century B.C.

Mencius, Apostle of Confucianism

One basis for the persistence of Confucianism was the effective work done by the zealous and able Mencius, whose dates are probably 372-289 B.C. Mencius (Meng Tzu, or Meng K'o) was said to have been tutored by disciples of Tzu Ssu, the grandson of Confucius. The book called *Mencius* was probably put together by his own disciples, but seems to be accepted generally by scholars as faithfully representing the teachings of Mencius. The work is prolific, judged by the standards of his day. Unfortunately it is also misleading in that it developed some doctrines of Confucius along original lines which were taken by later scholars to be the teachings of Confucius himself. On the whole, however, Mencius was truly Confucian and ably defended Confucianism against Moism and Taoism.

In many ways the life of Mencius parallels that of Confucius. Ssu-ma Ch'ien states that he was born in Tsou, Confucius' birthplace, but this is slightly in error.[16] Like Confucius, Mencius was a real scholar. He sought an influential position in government, and in this aim he was only somewhat more successful than Confucius had been. He also traveled from capital to capital, accompanied by his disciples and maintained in great style by his hosts. His success in this respect was greater than that of Confucius. But this was because the ideal of scholarly advisement to rulers had already been sold to the princes by Confucius and his followers. Thousands of scholars, including non-Confucians, reaped the reward. Like Confucius, too, Mencius was democratic and sought to improve the human lot through expert governmental administration. He was not so humble as Confucius, however. And he was committed to a system which he sought to defend. Thus his starting point in an argument was somewhat more prejudiced than that of Confucius. Mencius seemed never willing to admit that he was wrong, as Confucius did.

Mencius was quite bold in asserting the real superiority of the scholar over the hereditary rulers. The princes might possess a human nobility, but scholars had a divine nobility. He exalted the scholars in the following terms: "To dwell in the wide house of the world, to stand in the correct seat of the world, and to walk in the great path of the world; when he obtains his desire for office, to practise his principles for the good of the people; and when that desire is disappointed, to practise them alone; to be above the power of riches and honours to make dissipated, of poverty and mean condition to make swerve from principle, and of power and force to make bend:—these characteristics constitute the great man."[17] To such scholars, said Mencius to the King of Ch'i, the government should be entrusted, with no interference by the hereditary rulers. For this reason Mencius came very close to getting into real trouble with the king. But he managed to talk himself out of his trouble with rare diplomacy and truthfulness.

Mencius expressed some really remarkable ideas on political and economic theory. He insisted that the morale of the common soldiers was more important than their armor. He proposed a redistribution of land in order to group farm families into villages for certain cooperative purposes. He even proposed public education very soon after Plato had elsewhere in the world.[18]

The later Confucian emphasis on antiquity and tradition may be laid at the door of Mencius. The *Analects* shows Confucius making a fresh approach to human problems, attempting to solve them on the basis of present experience. Mencius, however, lays down easy rules to follow, such as imitating the ancient sage-kings. Many documents were forged in Mencius' times, in order to prove that antiquity was thus and so, constituting the pattern for all time. While Mencius was critical of the pseudo-histories, he nevertheless acquiesced in the idea that the past was perfect, and that the farther back one went, the better the example.

Somewhat at variance with this was his doctrine that human nature is good. If so, why are not moderns as perfect as the ancients? Mencius is quite explicit in affirming the natural goodness of man:

> If men do what is not good, the blame cannot be imputed to their natural powers. The feeling of commiseration belongs to all men; so does that of shame and dislike, and that of reverence and respect, and that of approving and disapproving. The feeling of commiseration implies the principle of benevolence; that of shame and dislike, the principle of righteousness; that of reverence and respect, the principle of propriety. . . . [These virtues] are not infused into us from without. . . . "Seek and you will find them. Neglect and you will lose them."[19]

Mencius seems to have taught that human personality is a miniature cosmos. "All things are already complete in us." "Knowing his nature, he knows Heaven."[20] Meditation thus came to be of much greater importance with Mencius than with Confucius. The unconscious influence of Taoism on Confucianism may be recognized at this early point.

One object of Mencius' criticism was the utilitarian ethics of Mo Tzu. He believed that not mere utility, but genuine virtue was what one should be concerned with. Book I of the *Mencius* begins:

> Mencius went to see King Hui of Liang. The king said: "Venerable sir, since you have not counted it far to come here . . . may I presume that you are likewise provided with counsels to profit my kingdom?" Mencius replied, "Why must your majesty use that word 'profit'? What I am 'likewise' provided with, are counsels to benevolence and righteousness. . . . If your majesty say, 'What is to be done to profit my kingdom?' the great officers will say, 'What is to be done to profit our families?' and the inferior officers and the common people will say, 'What is to be done to profit our persons?' Superiors and inferiors will try to snatch this profit the one from the other, and the kingdom will be endangered. . . . There has never been a man trained to benevolence who neglected his parents. There has never been a man trained to righteousness who made his sovereign an after consideration."[21]

Creel points out that Mencius actually anticipated Freud in his analysis of human nature. Whereas Mo Tzu would suppress desires and emotions, Mencius advised people to limit and control them rationally. The emotions are not bad. But they need integration according to a rational principle. Every act tends to form character.[22]

Hsün Tzu, Unorthodox Confucian

Shortly after Mencius another Confucian differed sharply with him concerning human nature and certain other issues. This was Hsün Tzu, who lived near the end of the Warring States period. Probable dates for his life are 320-235 B.C. He was born in the northern state of Chao but migrated to Ch'i where he received political appointment. But he gave this up, according to Ssu-ma Ch'ien, because of the corruption of the government and the people. This may not have been the real reason, for he seems to have had to leave Ch'i. He also held office in Ch'u with some success as well as with some disappointment. He traveled and taught and wrote the book which is called *Hsün-tzu,* although parts of it were completed by his disciples.

Hsün Tzu was undoubtedly the greatest scholar of his day. And although he differed from both Confucius and Mencius in certain respects, yet he influenced Confucianism for centuries to come. One lasting influence of Hsün Tzu lies in the fact that the *Li Chi,* or *Records on Ceremonial,* was partly made up of long excerpts from the *Hsün-tzu.* Since tradition assigned the authorship of the *Li Chi* to Confucius, the latter was credited with the doctrine of the *Hsün-tzu* and the *Li Chi* regarding the importance of ceremonialism in the life of man. Later Confucians recognized Hsün Tzu's disagreement with original Confucianism and tended to minimize his importance, with the result that most people today are unaware of his contributions to Confucianism.

One of the soundest of Hsün Tzu's teachings was his theory of language. Words are tools for communication, said he. They are agreed upon by convention, and have no other connection with the objects or ideas which they symbolize. Names are convenient devices by which to group objects by similarity and difference. They summarize the experience of the senses. The best "names" are those which are "simple and direct, easily understood, and not confusing."[23] Confucians and others would have done well to heed his advice about the use of language. In it he was close to the spirit of Confucius.

But his doctrine that human nature is bad was thoroughly out of harmony with the Confucian tradition. Probably Confucius would have disagreed with Mencius' view that human nature is good; but he would have differed still more with Hsün Tzu's view. No doubt both extremes have some basis in actual human experience, and it depends on what type of experience we have as to whether we shall be optimists or pessimists.

Quite emphatic was Hsün Tzu's argument in the chapter entitled "The Nature of Man is Evil":

> Men are born with the love of gain; if this natural tendency is followed they are contentious and greedy, utterly lacking in courtesy and consideration for others. They are filled from birth with envy and hatred of

others; if these passions are given rein they are violent and villainous, wholly devoid of integrity and good faith. . . .[24]

The only way for men to become good is through the influence of good teachers, said Hsün Tzu:

It is essential that men be transformed by teachers and laws, and guided by *li* and justice; only then will they be courteous and co-operative, only then is good order possible. . . .[25]

The role of *li* and of teachers becomes tremendously important, therefore, in the Confucianism of Hsün Tzu. One might raise the question as to how good manners arose in the first place if men were naturally bad. And if the only way by which men can become good is through good teachers, how did the first teachers, who themselves had no teachers, ever get to be good? Hsün Tzu asserts, in reply to these objections, that the sage-kings instituted *li,* that is, courtesy or ceremony. It was they who made good laws and taught people to restrain their evil tendencies. Thereafter there were always teachers and traditions to make others good. This still does not solve the problem, for how did the sage-kings become good if human nature is evil? Yet it probably answers it as well as Thomas Hobbes answered it in western philosophy. He explained that although man is naturally selfish and warlike, yet he is also rational, and it was his reason that led him to see that he cannot have security without forming a political society to restrain the evils of human nature. Corresponding to that rationality of Hobbes was the sageliness of the sage-kings of Hsün Tzu. He drags his argument on further, but with no material improvement in the situation.

The role of the teacher is emphatically stated by Hsün Tzu in these words: "Thus a teacher and precepts are the most important treasures a man can have; to be without a teacher and precepts is the greatest of misfortunes."[26] This was an emphasis which was to characterize Confucianism and China for centuries to come.

Most influential of all of Hsün Tzu's teachings was his view regarding the curriculum. According to Hsün Tzu the scope of education was to be limited to the study of "the classics." Hsün Tzu seems to have been the first to use this designation, and scholars still are not sure what he meant by it. Yet from then on Confucians laid unique emphasis on book study, contrary to the teachings of Confucius, and in particular exalted the books which came to be known as the "Confucian Classics." Furthermore Hsün Tzu's exaltation of the teacher and of *li* led to the authoritarian quality of Confucian education and the ceremonialism of Chinese society.

Yet there was much that is strikingly sound in Hsün Tzu's insights. For instance, although he was wrong in holding that all are created equal, yet he recognized the fact that mature human beings actually differed in abilities. He also insisted, quite democratically, that people should be allowed to rise as high in society as their abilities justified. Furthermore he understood that there is an intrinsic quality in wisdom which needs no extrinsic reward to enhance its value. Most value, too, said he, belonged to the things of the spirit rather than to material things. Some of his words are so admirable that we must quote them:

> Those who regard moral principles lightly always attach great importance to material things. And those who externally attach great importance to material things are always inwardly anxious. Those who act without regard for moral principles are always externally in a dangerous position. And such persons are always inwardly afraid. . . . Even if all the pleasant things in the world were offered to one in this state, he could not be content. . . . This is what is called making one's self a servant of material things.
>
> When a man's mind is peaceful and happy, then even sights below the ordinary will satisfy the eye; even sounds below the ordinary will content the ear; coarse rice, vegetables, and soup will be enough for the mouth; clothing of coarse cloth and sandals made from rough cords will give comfort to the body; a hut of straw, with a mat on the floor and a battered stool to lean against, will suffice for the form. . . . This may indeed be called . . . making material things one's servant.[27]

Hsün Tzu's ideas on the religion of his day were strictly rationalistic. They closely resemble the Deism of eighteenth century Europe. God, i.e., Heaven, was identical with Nature. Miracles did not occur. Heaven is orderly. Nature is uniform. "If men pray for rain and get rain, why is it? There is no reason," he explains. "If they hadn't prayed it would have rained anyway."[28] Rheumatism will not be cured by beating a drum; this just wears out the drum. Nor are there ill omens in nature. Bad omens may be found only by looking into the manner in which government is conducted, to see if it is for the people or merely for the rulers' profit. Furthermore, there are no such things as ghosts. A lively imagination accounts for their "appearance." Sacrifices to ancestral spirits or gods have only a social and psychological value.

But ceremony and sacrifices (the original meaning of *li*) do have most important human value. The Sages invented *li* realizing its usefulness to man. Without it society would break down. (Hsün Tzu thought society was even then disintegrating, so he was urging *li* as a desperate remedy.) *Li* required a stratification of society, in order that some might command and others obey. Only so would there be order and prosperity. But Hsün Tzu did not approve of hereditary caste. Ability and gentlemanly or scholarly conduct were for him the true marks of aristocracy. Evil rulers should be disobeyed and even dethroned. Good rulers would always employ scholars as their chief officials. Thus *li* would be preserved and the people would be happy.

The chief fault of Hsün Tzu was that he was not willing, as Confucius had been, to trust the intelligence and good will of the common man. Hsün Tzu prescribed an authoritative state, supported of course by scholarly officials, but nonetheless based upon the disciplinarian ideal. And rather than let the average man think for himself, he insisted that all should follow the customs which the ancient Sages had initiated. These principles were held to be for the good of the people. But Confucianism and China suffered from their influence.

Rise of Legalism

The immediate sequel to Hsün Tzu was the rise of the "Legalist School"—although in fact there was no such school, but only a number of scholars whose doctrines tended to favor the centralization of political power, the undermining of feudal disunity, and a general antagonism to Confucianism. The Legalists might better be called Authoritarians or Totalitarians, since they did not emphasize the role of law but only the universal sovereignty of the Emperor. It was through the advice and encouragement of the Legalists—for I must still call them by their traditional name—that the Duke of Ch'in rose to the position which he himself designated as that of First

Emperor—Shih Huang-ti. His idea was that his successors should be numbered as Second Emperor and Third Emperor—on up to ten thousand!

The chief Legalists were two of Hsün Tzu's pupils, Han Fei Tzu and Li Ssu. Han Fei Tzu was a prince of Han, which bordered on the state of Ch'in. He was credited with writing the book called *Han Fei Tzu*, parts of which seem genuinely to have originated with him. When the Duke of Ch'in read his essays he was greatly impressed and wished to meet him. When Han Fei Tzu went to Ch'in as Ambassador from Han the Duke had his opportunity. Meanwhile Li Ssu had entered the service of the Duke of Ch'in. Realizing his intellectual inferiority to Han Fei Tzu, whom he had known as a fellow-student of Hsün Tzu, Li Ssu plotted against him as a rival. When the Duke offered the Han Ambassador a position in his own government, hoping to profit by his ruthless advice on how to succeed as an autocrat, Li Ssu managed to sow suspicion and bring about his rival's arrest. Subsequently he connived against him and brought him to the point where he committed suicide.[29] Then Li Ssu himself advised the Duke as he rose to become the First (Ch'in) Emperor, with all of China under his sway.

Han Fei Tzu was undoubtedly the most notable of all who were called Legalists. His philosophy is more Machiavellian than Machiavelli. He blamed "useless scholars" for the world's disorders, because they undermined authority with all their talk and failed to perform any productive labor. Let us stop coaxing the people to cooperate with the government, he said, and put fear into their hearts through a system of spying and reporting, rewards and punishments. Human nature is wicked, unreliable and treacherous. Education cannot change it. Rulers would do well not to trust it. Let the people see the power of the ruler, and they will then obey. Virtuous scholars cannot rule by their virtues. What government needs is expertly trained technicians. And the state needs laws that are objective and unvarying. Only thus can order be maintained and the people themselves be happy. The welfare of the people seemed an afterthought, for Han Fei Tzu's outlook was almost wholly that of the ruler. He was as totalitarian as any twentieth century dictator. Said he, "All speech and action which is not in accord with the laws and decrees is to be prohibited."[30]

It is said that the First Emperor, following the bloody policy of Han Fei Tzu and Li Ssu, once caused the massacre of 400,000 soldiers who had surrendered. In 221 B.C. all China was brought under the rule of Ch'in.

Uniformity in everything characterized the "Legalist" rule of the First Emperor. "Laws and regulations were made uniform, weights and measures standardized, cart wheels spaced the same distance apart, and the forms of written characters made uniform,"[31] wrote Ssu-Ma Ch'ien. He used forced labor in large quantities for public works and royal projects, building the first Great Wall of China, hundreds of royal palaces and a fabulous royal tomb. The displaced feudal lords were frightened into docility. But many scholars criticised him and broke his command not to "use the past to discredit the present." So he publicly burned all the Confucian books that he could find and in 212 B.C. he caused 460 scholars to be buried alive. Some of the "scholars" were in truth merely magicians, but some also were true Confucians.

The First Emperor died in 210 B.C., taking with him to the tomb his childless concubines and the workmen who might know the secrets of the tomb's wealth. Confusion followed. Li Ssu was executed by a fellow-conspirator in 208 B.C.

Confucianism was both harmed and helped by the persecution of the First Emperor. It was helped in the manner in which persecution and martyrdom always help a cause. It was harmed to the extent to which legalist and authoritarian influences entered into it at that time. Confucian texts were altered so as to make them seem to agree with Legalism. This may have been done in part by Legalists and in part by Confucians who were gradually becoming more and more authoritarian. Certain it is that Confucianism was undergoing changes which were to be most significant, as we shall see.

XXI. EMERGENCE OF NEO-CONFUCIANISM

In 207 B.C. Han Kao Tzu, a peasant who joined—and then led—the outlaws after he had unwittingly broken a Ch'in law, brought order out of anarchy by founding the Han dynasty. Realizing the popularity of Confucianism because of its antagonism to the Ch'in tyranny, Kao Tzu sought to gain the support of the Confucians. He tried to pacify as many groups as possible, and gained friends by his leniency. Even the people of the Ch'in capital were spared in his hour of military triumph.

Kao Tzu probably never did become a sincere Confucian, but he catered to Confucianism while tolerating other philosophies and religions. He asked the Confucians to draw up a simplified program of court ritual by which some of his rude democratic associates might be guided, he himself not being exempt from the need of such guidance. In 196 B.C. he directed that imperial officials recommend scholars in order that the Emperor might duly honor them. Recommendations were made on the basis of competitive examinations. Thus was taken the first definite step toward the Confucian examination system leading to governmental appointment. Yet Kao Tzu continued to employ many of the experienced advisers and officials who had served the former Ch'in Emperor. And although he sought advice and wide support, he kept power in his own hands.

Han Confucianism

Emperor Wen, the fourth Han sovereign, ruling from 179 to 157 B.C., was a model of Confucian perfection. Having the welfare of the people primarily in mind he brought about many reforms stressing governmental economy and integrity, civil liberties, and a kind of social security. Personally superstitious, he nevertheless cultivated tolerance between the schools of thought.

But policy was radically changed by the Emperor Wu Ti, sixth of the Han dynasty (140-87 B.C.), whose subtle influence on Confucianism has been inestimable ever since. It is customary to say that Wu was a great patron of Confucianism. This is erroneous in essence but true in form. His acts and policies were totalitarian and legalist in spirit. His rule was harsh and tyrannical, and his most honored advisers were Legalists. He had been inclined toward Confucianism upon his accession at the age of fifteen, but soon reversed this tendency. However, realizing the popularity of Confucianism, he cultivated the illusion that he followed its principles. He even appointed Confucians to high positions, but without any power attached. One famous Confucian scholar, Tung Chung-shu, who fearlessly criticized Wu in writing his civil service examinations, was virtually banished by being given an appointment to a provincial position in the court of one of Wu's barbarous brothers. When Tung was successful there the Emperor appointed him to a still more difficult position from which he soon retired. Still the Emperor honored him in a conspicuous manner by sending messengers to ask his advice, to which no attention was paid.

Another young Confucian scholar, Kung-Sun Hung, wrote his civil service examination under Wu Ti using Confucian terminology but subtly expressing the substance of Legalism. The examiners placed his name in last position on the eligible list, but the Emperor was so pleased with him that he changed it to first place and proceeded to make him Prime Minister. In this way Wu earned the erroneous reputation of being a great patron of Confucianism, which was precisely what he wished. Through his policy of choosing "Confucian Legalists" he encouraged scholars to pay lip service to Confucius while they interpreted Confucianism legalistically.

Another subtle move on the part of Emperor Wu Ti was the founding of an imperial university where classes of fifty students were admitted and subsidized while studying the so-called Confucian Classics. Since the choosing of students was ultimately the privilege of the Emperor, he used this means of influencing the development of Confucianism. He also encouraged the scholarly interest in recovering the texts which had been burned under the Ch'in dynasty.

Tung had pointed out to the Emperor that "the teachers of today have diverse Ways . . . Hence . . . the rulers possess nothing whereby they may effect general unification. . . . All not within the field of the Six Classics should be cut short . . ."[1] So Emperor Wu made Confucianism, with its "Six Classics," the official state teaching. Of course the Confucianism which resulted was not the genuine thing. For one thing, the emphasis upon the classics was really quite un-Confucian, since Confucius' first interest was the reform of government. But the official policy at least gave the appearance of honoring Confucius.

About this time also many commentaries were written adding myth to Confucian legend. The net result was that a new kind of Confucianism emerged which placed emphasis upon tradition, erudition, ceremonialism, and authority, and eventually raised Confucius to the pinnacle of divinity. One new (Han) text commenting on the *Spring and Autumn Annals,* for example, teaches that Confucius was the son of a god, the Black Emperor, and tells of miracles occurring in his life.

It was in Han times that the *Book of Changes* came to be regarded as one of the Confucian classics. Confucius and his early followers had no use for divination, but his Han followers made it appear otherwise. They even wrote ten appendices to the *Book of Changes,* very much in the spirit of Taoist mysticism, and tried to make it appear that Confucius himself was their author. "The great mass of Confucians wanted Taoism, they wanted divination, and they wanted the blessing of Confucius on these things. In the appendices to the *Book of Changes* they got all three."[2]

The *Records on Ceremonial* (*Li Chi*) were also compiled about this time. This "Confucian Classic" also is unreliable, for even though parts of it may have existed soon after Confucius, none of it remained in its original character. The section called the *Doctrine of the Mean,* and another called the *Great Learning,* obviously date from Ch'in times or later, yet eventually they gained recognition as two of the "Four Books of Confucianism," along with the *Analects* and the *Mencius*. Taoist and Legalist influences abound in the *Li Chi.*

Also composed at about the time of Wu Ti were the *Historical Records,* written by Ssu-ma T'an and his son, Ssu-ma Ch'ien, both of whom were court officials of Wu Ti. The only systematic ancient biography of Confucius is contained in this work. It has been suggested that Ssu-ma T'an may have been trying to undermine the Confucianism of his day, by making Confucius out to be the kind of "flattering Confucian" whom he knew at the court of Wu. Ssu-ma T'an is known to have been a Taoist; it is not known what Ssu-ma Ch'ien was.

It is no wonder, therefore, that Confucianism took on an entirely new character during the Early Han Period. Culturally this era is sometimes called the Age of the Eclectics, because discordant ideas were chosen from different sources and woven loosely together in the same works. For example the *Records on Ceremonial,* revered by Confucians as a classic but probably compiled in the first century B.C., has elements of Confucianism, Taoism, Legalism, *Yin* and *Yang* metaphysics, and the theory of the five forces.

Tung Chung-shu, the Confucian candidate for public office whom Wu Ti tried to outsmart, taught the theory of the five forces. In his work entitled *Luxuriant Dew from the Spring and Autumn Annals,* Tung says:

> Heaven has five forces, namely, wood, fire, earth, metal, and water. . . . Thus wood receives from water, fire from wood, earth from fire, metal from earth, and water from metal. As transmitters they are all fathers, as receivers, sons. Constantly to rely upon one's father in order to provide for one's son is the way [*Tao*] of Heaven. . . .
>
> Fire delights in wood and nourishes it by means of the *Yang* [solar?] power; water overcomes metal [its father], yet mourns it by means of the *Yin* power. Earth, in serving Heaven, shows the utmost loyalty. Thus the five forces provide a pattern of conduct for filial sons and loyal ministers. . . .
>
> The sage, by understanding this, is able to increase his love and lessen his severity, to make more generous his support of the living and more respectful his performance of funeral rites for the dead, and so to conform with the pattern established by Heaven.[3]

Tung's Confucianism may thus be seen to contain eclectic elements. His effort in the *Luxuriant Dew* was to analyze the *Spring and Autumn Annals,* erroneously attributed to Confucius, so as to see the relation between the acts of rulers and the acts of nature which were regarded as punishment or reward for the ruler's actions.

Human nature is not good, said Tung Chung-shu, although he admitted that the controversy on this point was largely a matter of the definition of terms. The people are dependent upon the ruler, the Son of Heaven, to make them good, said he. If the ruler is negligent of this duty, then Heaven sends calamities. Such a theory constituted a superstitious kind of check on the ruler, but it also viewed the ruler as the divinely approved sovereign of men so long as calamities did not come.

The *Yin-Yang* school of the fourth or third century B.C. had already taught that there is a correlation between the five forces and the periods of history, and that the ruler who is wise will understand the prevailing force of his period and will pattern his rule after it. The alternation of these forces was thought of as the expression of *Yin* and *Yang*, periods of creativity or achievement (*Yang*), and periods of passivity and depth (*Yin*). "The *Yang* and the *Yin* came to be regarded as two cosmic principles or forces," writes Fung, "respectively representing masculinity, activity, heat, brightness, dryness, hardness, etc., for the *Yang*, and femininity, passivity, cold, darkness, wetness, softness, etc., for the *Yin*. Through the interaction of these two primary principles, all phenomena of the universe are produced. This concept has remained dominant in Chinese cosmological speculation down to recent times."[4]

During the Early Han Period, Confucians divided into the Old Text School and the New Text School. The Old Text School arose as a reaction against the extravagant eclecticism that characterized Confucianism during the Han Period. Such eclecticism was associated with the "new texts"—copies in the New Script of the texts which the First Emperor had burned. Writing was greatly facilitated by the use of the New Script which the First Emperor had decreed. As the texts were copied, new glosses were easily added while appendices and commentaries multiplied, creating the new kind of supernaturalist Confucianism with its doctrine of *Yin* and *Yang* and its belief in the five forces. The Old Text School deplored such absurdities and insisted on going back to the rare old texts, written in the older Chinese characters but possessing purity and freedom from the late accretions.

Wang Ch'ung: Old-Text Confucian

The best representative of the Old Text School was Wang Ch'ung, whose dates are from 27 A.D. to about 97 A.D. The Early (Western) Han Period had ended in 9 A.D. and the New (Eastern) Han Period was to last from 25-220 A.D. Wang received a governmental appointment early in life, but was forced to resign because of his tendency to point out the mistakes and shortcomings of his superiors and associates. His most significant writing was the *Critical Essays*. In them he criticized contemporary Confucians for parroting the past while having no ideas of their own. While history has its uses, said he, it also has its abuses. It is just as important to know the present as the past. Nor should one accept as history all that purports to describe the past. Furthermore the honored past turns out, on careful examination, to be less worthy of reverence than it is usually thought to be. Even the great Confucius was imperfect, obscure in language, inconsistent in his beliefs, and improper in his acts. Maybe if his students, instead of holding him in superstitious awe, had criticized him, they might have helped his cause. That is the way pupils should behave toward their teachers, said he. Accept nothing on authority. As he put it:

> The Scholars at the present day have a passion for believing that what their teachers say is [genuinely] old, and they regard the words of worthies and sages as all of the very essence of truth.[5]

Wang sounds ultra-modern, urbane, and incredulous. He rejects supernatural causes for natural events. By way of illustration, it was —and still is—popularly believed that the bore, or abrupt rushing wave regularly flooding the mouth of the Ch'ien-t'ang River, was caused by the vengeful ghost of an official who had been killed and his body cast into the river five hundred years earlier. Wang ridiculed this explanation, and correctly guessed that the bore was caused by the tide entering a narrowing channel. The tides, in turn, he believed to be related to the moon's phases.[6]

In fact, Wang rejects the whole fabric of Chinese belief in ghosts.

> The common idea is that the dead become ghosts. . . . [I maintain that] the dead do not become ghosts, have no consciousness, and cannot injure people.[7]

Another passage from Wang Ch'ung well worth quoting deals with popular superstitions:

> At the height of summer, thunder and lightning come with tremendous force, splitting trees, demolishing houses, and from time to time killing people. The common idea is that this splitting of trees and demolishing of houses is Heaven setting a dragon to work. And when the thunder and lightning rush on people and kill them, this is described as due to hidden faults, for example, people eating unclean things, and so Heaven in its anger striking them and killing them. The roar of the thunder is the voice of Heaven's anger, like men gasping with rage. . . . This is all nonsense.[8]

Wang Ch'ung regarded nature as ruled by chance and mechanism, not as designed to reward and punish man. Man in nature had no more influence over universal forces than a flea or a louse under a man's jacket has over the behavior of man, he said.[9]

It will come as a surprise to learn that Wang, despite his modern skeptical attitude, nevertheless accepted many of the traditional stories of the miraculous. We must remember, however, that even Roger Bacon spoke modern words while still believing many medieval superstitions. Wang's significance lies in the fact that he offered negative criticism of many contemporary superstitions such as the belief in ghosts, the interpretation of natural events as signs from Heaven, the practice of divination, and the use of pills to gain youth and immortality. Wang was certainly in the minority, and his essays were scarcely known for centuries after his death.

The Syncretistic Movement

It was probably during Wang Ch'ung's liftetime that Buddhism was introduced into China. Throughout the following centuries it had a wide appeal, at first to the common people and later even to the literati. Some of the emperors became Buddhists. Taoism, too, spread during these early centuries of the Christian era, first as a philosophy and then as a popular religion. In the eyes of many Chinese there was little or no difference between Buddhism and Taoism. For that very reason the two religions at times developed an intense rivalry. On the whole, however, Taoism and Buddhism were mutually tolerant.

Upon the fall of the later Han dynasty there ensued the period of the Six Dynasties (220-581 A.D.). Some refer to this period as China's "Dark Ages." For only twenty-four years during this entire period was China united. The rest of the time she was divided into three states, or at times into a larger number of small warring states. Barbarians from the north took advantage of the confusion to invade and conquer parts of China. During such a period of outward turmoil it should not be surprising that men turned from a philosophy of formalism and this-worldliness to a religion of mysticism and escapism. Such a trend was noticeable as early as 184 A.D., when the masses under Taoist leadership staged a momentarily successful rebellion characterized by the "Yellow Turbans." A few decades later the Taoist, Mou Tzu, fled to southwestern China and became a Buddhist monk, devoting his life to the quiet pursuit of reading the scriptures, performing religious ritual, and meditating. He defended his actions by citing both Taoist and Confucian scripture, and indeed regarded himself as a good Confucian all the while.[10]

A sympathetic appraisal of the influence of Buddhism on Chinese culture is made difficult by the incidence of idolatry. The normal Christian reaction to Buddhist and all other idolatry is to condemn it as wholly depraved and inexcusable. Yet Buddhist idols in Chinese culture went through an artistic cycle which in one sense may justify their existence. At its best, Chinese Buddhist sculpture was expressive of the spiritual ideals of universal love, moral achievement, and serenity of heart. The sensitivity of spirit thus expressed was compatible with the richest qualities of scholarship and gentility. The eminent American authority on Chinese culture, Professor H. G. Creel, says of Kuan Yin, the Chinese Buddhist "goddess of mercy," that "some of the small representations of this goddess, exquisitely rendered in wood, ivory, or porcelain, are so beautiful and appealing as almost to convert me to Buddhism."[11]

Mutual influences among Chinese Buddhism, Taoism, and Confucianism were so complex that it seemed not at all incongruous that many should be at once Buddhist, Taoist, and Confucian. In such a situation, there was as much cooperation as rivalry between the religions. Taoism was the first to try to embrace the other two religions. It reached out for Confucianism quite early when Chuang Tzu told his legends of how Confucius made a pilgrimage to sit at the feet of Lao Tzu and learn true wisdom from him. It sought to encompass Buddhism by relating how Lao Tzu had once traveled to India to impart his wisdom to the Buddha, thus leaving Buddhism in the position of being little more than an extension of Taoism. Buddhism in turn gave approval to Confucianism by accepting Confucius as a Bodhisattva. It is reported that at one time there was in Shantung a Buddhist temple dedicated to Confucius.

Three examples will suffice to show how a syncretism of the "Three Religions" tended to develop toward the end of the period of the Six Dynasties, and during the Sui (581-618) and T'ang (618-906) dynasties. About the sixth century the Taoist, T'an Ch'iao, insisted that the three religions shared a common foundational belief in the *Tao*. Near the end of the same century a Buddhist, Li Shih-ch'ien, declared that Buddhism was the sun, Taoism the moon, and Confucianism the five planets. Still later a Buddhist monk succeeded in convincing many of his contemporaries that it was proper to place side by side on the altar images of Buddha, Lao Tzu, and Confucius. Even the Confucians encouraged the syncretism, as in the case of Wang T'ung (583-616), who proposed that the three religions had a common core in the doctrine of the golden mean. There was, in fact, a good deal of truth in these observations, but this was emphasized at the expense of many important differences, such as the conflicting interpretations of the *Tao*, and the contrast between Buddhist-Taoist mysticism and other-worldliness on the one hand and Confucian rationalism and humanism on the other. Even the tendency on the part of both Taoists and Confucians to think of Confucius as a Sage represented really a tendency to obscure his hard-headed practicality and to picture him as substantially a Taoist.

But in the same centuries as those just reviewed there were a few small groups who maintained their aloofness from any and all of the three described above. One such group, called "The School of Pure Speech," tried to escape at once the involvements of politics and the superstitions of the three religions by focusing their attention on nature, poetry, and wine. Another group, the so-called "Seven Sages of the Bamboo Grove," gleefully ridiculed Confucians and politicians while they, too, escaped from their own sorrows through wine and poetry. Fung Yu-lan seems to classify the Seven

Sages (or "Worthies") of the Bamboo Grove as Neo-Taoists of the Sentimentalist variety—perhaps corresponding to our class of Romanticists.[12]

A lone dissenter from both syncretism and romanticism was the more traditional type of Confucian, Han Yü (767-824 A.D.). To him belongs the honor of having boldly protested when the T'ang emperor, Hsien Tsung, made a great show of ceremoniously accepting from some Buddhist monks a "bone of Buddha." The emperor accepted the bone but not the protest and banished the protestant to south China. Han Yü also protested against the superstitious form of Taoism then current. In his essay on "The Origin of the *Tao*," he argued that the Taoists had corrupted the meaning of the *Tao*, which in ancient times signified a way of virtue and of service to one's fellow man, not a way of monkishness, mystery, and miracle.

Not long after Han Yü's death there developed the most serious persecution of Buddhism that China ever experienced.

Neo-Confucianism

The Sung Dynasty (960-1279 A.D.) witnessed the rise of Neo-Confucianism—a movement designed to combat all forms of irrationalism and to revive a purer kind of Confucianism than that which had thus far developed. But ironically even the Neo-Confucians were affected by Taoism and Buddhism in ways too subtle to sense easily. Two of the earliest and greatest of the Neo-Confucians were thus affected: Wang An-shih (1021-1086 A.D.) and Chu Hsi (1130-1200 A.D.). Wang An-shih was a great statesman and reformer who became one of the "saints" of Confucianism. His commemorative tablet was to be found in Confucian temples next to that of Mencius. He was deeply distressed by the current interest of scholars in Buddhism and Taoism. Yet his own son was soon to find solace and inspiration in the two religions which he himself scorned. Even the great Chu Hsi, founder of recent Confucian "orthodoxy," admitted that scholars in his day were finding it necessary to look to Buddhism and Taoism for moral and religious inspiration.[13]

One clue to the nature of the subtle influence of Buddhism on Confucianism may be found by comparing Ch'an (Zen) Buddhism with Neo-Confucianism. Ch'an Buddhism was quite philosophical, for one thing. It emphasized the importance of meditation and humanistic achievement, teaching that man naturally possesses the resources of his own happiness. Neo-Confucianism, too, laid great emphasis on meditation—much more than Confucius had done. Neo-Confucianism insisted that by meditation one became not a Buddha but a Sage—in this respect showing an affinity with Taoism also.

The Confucian rivalry with Buddhism and Taoism in T'ang and Sung times also spurred Confucians to develop an elaborate cosmology and a canon of sacred scriptures similar to those of the other religions. The Confucian scriptures were coming to be recognized as the "Four Books," namely, the *Analects,* the *Mencius,* the *Great Learning,* and the *Doctrine of the Mean.* To these were soon added the *Book of Changes,* together with its *Appendices.* The metaphysical and religious cosmology resulting from this growth is known historically as Neo-Confucianism. Apparently the least important element of Neo-Confucianism was the humanistic insights of Confucius. More important were the speculations of the *Book of Changes* and its *Appendices,* and the ideas of Mencius and later Confucians.

From the *Book of Changes* the Neo-Confucians derived the cosmological concept of the mystic influence of the hexagrams. In this they differed little from the Taoists. The hexagrams are individually composed of six solid and broken lines in varying combinations, sometimes arranged in rows and concentric circles exhibiting rhythmic developments:

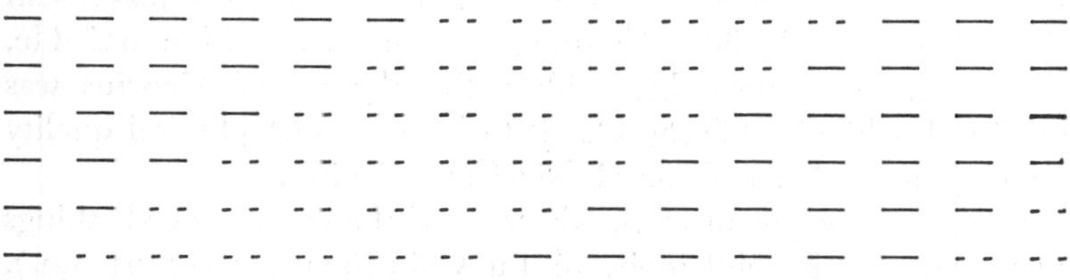

The Neo-Confucians taught that the various seasons of the year, as well as the stages of universal evolution, are governed by the hexagrams. Taken in sequence, these mystic symbols dramatized the rhythm of the *Yin* and the *Yang.* The Neo-Confucian Shao Yung (1011-1077 A.D.) was especially ingenious in his explanation of the mystic symbolism governing the succession of the seasons and the universal cycles of creation and decay.

Metaphysics of Neo-Confucianism

An important development in Neo-Confucianism was the doctrine of *Ch'i.* Chang Tsai (1020-1077 A.D.) was indebted to the *Appendices* of the *Book of Changes* for the cosmological theory which he based upon the *Ch'i.* By the *Ch'i,* Chang Tsai meant physical matter which individuates all things. He taught that the *Ch'i* is influenced by the rhythm of the *Yin* and the *Yang* to form and to dissolve the worlds. Yet by the "dissolution" of the worlds he did not mean the emergence of non-being, but only the periodic quiescence of reality. Thus Chang Tsai guarded against the radical mysticism of Taoism and Buddhism. In another respect he approached the rational universalism of Stoicism by teaching that since all things in the universe are made of one body, the *Ch'i,* therefore we should regard Heaven and Earth as we do our parents, and should think of all men as our brothers. In truth, he taught, we honor our universal parents when we serve our fellow men.

The doctrine of human brotherhood was further developed by Ch'eng Hao (1032-1085 A.D.), friend of Chang Tsai. According to Ch'eng Hao, the individual is essentially one with the universe. He needs to realize this in order to grow naturally with the universe. Ch'eng Hao taught that the virtue of "human-heartedness" (*jen*) is best realized when the individual *feels* wholly at one with the universe. He who realizes this will act accordingly. We may recall that Mencius had said, "All things are complete within us." He, too, emphasized human-heartedness. But the *jen* of Mencius was empirical, while for Ch'eng Hao it took on the metaphysical quality which was so characteristic of Neo-Confucianism.

Further development of the doctrine of the oneness of all things took place in the philosophy of Lu Chiu-yüan (1139-1193 A.D.). Wrote he, "The universe is my mind; my mind is the universe."[14] Thus the Stoic-like materialism of Ch'eng Hao became a vivid monistic idealism in Lu Chiu-yüan. This point of view was brilliantly worked out by the later Neo-Confucian, Wang Shou-jen (1472-1528 A.D.).

Meanwhile Ch'eng Yi (1033-1108 A.D.), brother of Ch'eng Hao, proposed a theory having some of the characteristics of Platonic idealism and of Aristotelian realism. The same theory was further perfected by Chu Hsi (1130-1200 A.D.), who is called the father of recent Confucian "orthodoxy." According to this theory the universe results from the concentration of *Ch'i* (matter, substance, or perhaps Aristotle's "potentiality") according to the *Li* of each species of thing. The *Li* in this case is not at all the same as the *li* about which earlier Confucians talked. The earlier *li* meant "sacrifice," "ritual," or "ceremony." The later *Li*, pronounced the same but formed by different Chinese characters, meant "principle," or "principles." The Neo-Confucian *Li* is similar to the concept of *Tao* derived from the Appendices of the *Book of Changes*. As the mystic *Tao* is empty and meaningless apart from the concrete world, so the *Li* can function only through *Ch'i*. But the *Li* seem to be logically prior to the *Ch'i*. The *Li* are timeless, but become concrete actuality only in combination with *Ch'i*. This is somewhat like the Platonic Ideas, or like Aristotle's forms.

As in Plato individual forms were conceived to be a part of the supreme Idea of the Good, so in Chu Hsi the *Li* were conceived to be a part of the "Supreme Ultimate." Not only was the *Li* realized in each individual, but the Supreme Ultimate itself, being one with each species of *Li*, was also present in each individual. How the Supreme Ultimate could be in each individual without being divided was a problem which Chu Hsi solved only by analogy. Said he, "It is like the moon shining in the heavens, of which, though it is reflected in rivers and lakes and thus is everywhere visible, we would not therefore say that it is divided."[15]

Just as Plato insisted that the state reflects its own archetype in varying degrees of imperfection, so Chu Hsi maintained that the *Li* constituted the ideal which the state ought to embody. Both philosophers regarded the political ideal as perfect and eternal, independent of human thought and practice. Chu Hsi differed from Plato in teaching that the ancient Sage-kings did perfectly conceive and practice the ideal state. But he was like Plato in insisting that, since those good old days, no one had ever come close to the ideal. He believed government was successful only as it tended to conform to the perfect type. One of the characteristics of perfection, said he, was government according to the principle of the well-being of the governed. The ruler who follows such principle will most surely be successful, Chu Hsi insisted.

So with regard to all things, there is one right way (*Tao*) to succeed. That is the way of the golden mean, which was fully realized only by the ancient Sages. Scholars and philosophers should be absorbed in the "investigation of things," by means of which they may learn the nature of the *Li*. Enlightenment in this enterprise comes not gradually but quite suddenly, as when all things are seen to fit together into a single whole. In this view of enlightenment we again recognize the influence of both Taoism and Buddhism.

The two main schools of Neo-Confucianism may be seen most clearly by summarizing the philosophy of Chu Hsi and that of Wang Shou-jen (also known as Wang Yang-ming). Chu Hsi tried to show the imperfections of Taoism and Buddhism, in contrast with the progressive and practical character of Confucianism, by proving that the universe is essentially rational and pluralistic. His point of view was much more metaphysical than that of Confucius or of Mencius. And it was less mystical than either Buddhism or Taoism. The cosmos-forming pair of *Li* and *Ch'i* he conceived to be related in a system of mutual dependence. The *Li* was nothing apart from *Ch'i*, nor the *Ch'i* from the *Li*. In contrast with Chu Hsi's metaphysics, the Buddhist cosmic essence was the absolutely and independently real substance—the emptier the realer. And the *Tao* of Taoism, too, was real because it lacked individual or specific character. But for Chu Hsi the universe was made up of an infinite number of real things, through the combination of form (*Li*) and matter (*Ch'i*). The "investigation of things" which the ancients encouraged and Chu Hsi approved, meant for him the investigation of the rational nature of the universe. It meant the silent contemplation of nature until the rational in nature spoke to the rational in human nature, leaving the student in a state of knowledge and peace. Even human-heartedness (*jen*) or love, as it is sometimes translated, is to be found in nature as in man. "Heaven and Earth," said Chu Hsi, "has for its purpose the creation of matter (*Ch'i*). All matter, including human beings, have in them the same purpose as that of Heaven and Earth. . . . This purpose, to summarize, is Love (*jen*). Love is behind all creation. Were we able to recognize its meaning and keep it, we would be in possession of the source of goodness and the foundation of living."[16]

For Wang Shou-jen, on the other hand, the physical universe was a neutral sort of thing, having no rationality in itself. The only meaning which the universe has, said he, is the meaning which it has for man. And that meaning is put into the universe by man, not vice versa. The anecdote is told that Wang earnestly tried to let the objective meaning of the universe seep into his mind and vivify it, as Chu Hsi had advised. For his experiment, at the age of twenty-one, he sat in a bamboo grove continuously for three days (seven days says one account), waiting for the light of universal reason to break in upon his soul. But the light never came. Instead, he caught a universal cold, and had only sorrow for all his efforts. This sad experience was sufficient to convince him that reason was not communicated by external things to the mind; instead, the mind communicates reason by external things to the universe. The order of the universe is really the order of our minds.

Wang Shou-jen's philosophy included the Socratic doctrine of the natural goodness of the rational man. He who knows the good will act accordingly, said both Socrates and Wang Shou-jen. One does not need to be taught to avoid bad odors nor to perform rational acts. And rational acts are good acts, Wang continued. "There has been no one who really has knowledge and yet fails to practice it."[17] Furthermore, real knowledge is intuitive, as when one sees a child about to fall into a well. His first impulse is to save the child. If he does not act immediately on the principle of intuitive knowledge, he may begin to rationalize that it is the child of his enemy, or that if he tries to save the child he himself may be killed. His unstudied intuition is true, while rationalization is artificial.

As between Chu Hsi and Wang Shou-jen, modern Chinese Confucianism tends to follow the former rather than the latter, which is really a kind of continuation of Ch'anism, according to Fung.[18] Shryock agrees essentially with Fung, but points out that both Wang Shou-jen and Chu Hsi are still influential, and that the tablets of both will be found in a Confucian temple.[19]

XXII. TAOISM, CONFUCIANISM, AND MODERN CHINA

SINCE THE RELIGIOUS CULT of Confucius was, in important respects, inspired by the influence and rivalry of Taoism and Buddhism, I shall in this chapter survey first the development of religious Taoism and then consider the growth and decay of the Confucian cult. After that I shall discuss Chinese religion and culture today.

A most peculiar development in Taoism was its increasing play upon the human desire for immortality. Now we must admit that early Taoist philosophy was individualistic in that it upheld the ideal of independence of one's environment. But the typical Taoist point of view as reflected in the *Tao Te Ching*, was that the relative being of the individual was merged in the absolute being of the *Tao*. Like all mysticism, Taoist philosophy sought to transcend individuality. It was one of the ironies of history, therefore, that Taoism should have led the Chinese to the most intense and superstitious striving for the immortality of the individual human organism. In fact, such was the Taoist emphasis upon immortality that it absorbed into itself other mystery cults, such as the one based on the myth that the immortals dwelt among the mountains of central Asia, ruled by the Queen of the West, Hsi Wang Mu. There grew in her garden a peach tree bearing fruit once in a thousand years. Whoever ate of the peaches would never die. Several such myths contributed to the growth of Taoist superstition.

Magic and Immortality

The First Emperor himself (221-207 B.C.) had been a Taoist, it is said, partly because Taoism taught the doctrine of inactivity which, if practiced by everyone, would make his absolutism much easier to enforce. But he was a Taoist also because he was naturally superstitious and eager to believe the promises of Taoism regarding immortality. Even the historian, Ssu-ma Ch'ien, seriously tells of the "Isles of the Immortals" where a wonder drug was to be found. People in ancient times succeeded in reaching the isles and finding the youth-giving drug, said he; but modern attempts had all failed. Ships might get close enough to see the paradise, but then a wind always blew them away. The First Emperor once organized a naval expedition to go in search of the paradise. But its leader landed with thousands of assistants, young men and women, on an attractive spot and made himself king. Still the emperor did not give up. He spied from high mountains and from the sea shore, but discovered nothing that tempted him to exchange his kingdom for it. So as we might expect, he too died.

A legendary Taoist, Lieh Tzu, is said to have acquired the powers of levitation. According to Chuang Tzu "he could ride upon the wind and travel whithersoever he wished, staying away as long as fifteen days."[1] A book called the *Lieh-tzu,* originating in the Han Period, tells of "a man who emerged out of a solid rock cliff and hovered in the air amidst flames and smoke; of a magician who carried a king of Chou high into the sky to see his aerial palace; and of another wonder-worker who successfully constructed an automaton which could walk and sing."[2] One chapter in the same book is entitled "Yang Chu," and is translated by Anton Forke as "Yang Chu's Garden of Pleasure." It advises man to live in harmony with his own reason and impulse, not according to the customs and morals of the time.[3] This seems an odd combination of rationalism and superstition. Apparently, however, it represents the views of the *Lieh-tzu* well enough, but not quite the attitude of Yang Chu.

The Han Emperor, Wu Ti, alongside of his Confucian patronage and his Legalist tendencies had also found Taoism attractive, as explained in the last chapter. He listened to advice on how to gain perpetual youth, and earnestly tried to do so.

Then in the first century A.D. one Chang-ling—better known as Chang Tao-ling—founded a tradition. His followers formed a sect which came to be called the Wu Tou Mi Tao, or "Five Pecks of Rice Way," because all who joined and sought the chief's "medical" advice were required to pay five pecks of rice. He was also called "Rice Thief." Yet his followers later made him a god and gave him the name "Celestial Teacher," saying that Lao Tzu had appeared to him and ordained him for his holy task of discovering the formula for the elixir of immortality. The story concludes that Chang Tao-ling went directly to heaven, somewhat as Elijah is said to have done, riding a tiger from the top of the Dragon-Tiger Mountain in Kiangsi. This is said to have taken place when he was already one hundred and twenty-two years old.

Throughout the centuries which followed the "ascension" of Chang Tao-ling, a long line of successors have maintained headquarters on Dragon-Tiger Mountain (Lung-hu). In 748 A.D. Hsuan Tsung (712-756), T'ang emperor, gave official recognition to the family of Chang Tao-ling as the head of the Taoist religion. The Taoist "Heavenly Teacher"—falsely called a "Pope," since he controlled no ecclesiastical organization—maintained a magical reputation among the superstitious Chinese, whose Sung emperor Chen Tsung (998-1023 A.D.) provided support. So long as there were Chinese who believed in demons and hobgoblins, the Taoist pope was ever ready to obey the first chief's command to "kill demons, chase off hobgoblins, protect the kingdom, bring peace to the people, and let my dignity pass from father to son without ever leaving my family." Finegan (1952) states that the Taoist society and its "pope" are still active, but Noss (1949) states that the "popes" have recently been driven off, "probably never to return."[4] "The family of Chang was dispossessed by a communistic section of the National Army in 1927," states Lewis Hodous.[5] Wing-tsit Chan states that the present "Heavenly Teacher" is an opium addict and pleasure-seeker; that he is now an exile from communist China, in Macao, where he has finally decided to read some books.[6]

But other Taoist sects arose, notably the one following the tradition of Chang-Chiao, a descendant of Chang Tao-ling. This sect attempted a rebellion (Yellow Turbans) in the second century A.D., and for a time gained control over the Yellow River basin.[7] The Taoists continued to entertain serious political ambitions in later centuries, on the theory that their rule would be the best for mankind, since it sought harmony with Heaven.

Taoist Geomancy

One noteworthy Taoist was Kuo P'o, who, around 300 A.D., applied the ancient pseudo-science of Wind and Water (*feng-shui*) to the problem of the proper location of graves. According to *feng-shui* the contour of the land, the flow of streams, the position of the heavenly bodies, and other factors influenced the forces of wind and water, which in turn represented the *Yin* and *Yang* principles of the universe. The geomancers of *feng shui* claimed to know how to locate houses, temples, and graves in order to profit most from the mysterious cosmic influences. With the aid of a tortoise shell Kuo P'o is said to have placed his mother's grave dangerously close to a river, but his insight was "proved" to be correct when sand was washed up over the area for several miles, transforming the wet ground into fertile land for fruit and agriculture. Tradition makes Kuo P'o the author of the *Book on Burial,* which for centuries has been used to locate graves in China. Superstitions of the Chinese have kept the Taoist geomancers busily employed for many centuries.

Another Taoist geomancer was Ko Hung, born in Kiangsu around 300 A.D. He is also known as Pao P'u-tzu, author of a book by that name. Ko Hung has left us a solemn account of the breathing exercises—reflecting Hindu Yogism—and other practices designed to give one magical powers and immortality. A special diet was prescribed to enable one eventually to live on dew and air alone, and thus to be immune to illness. One of the goals of alchemists was to make gold edible, and thus attain immortality. As Ko Hung put it, if salt preserves dead meat, surely something could be found which would preserve live flesh eternally. Ko Hung told of persons who had discovered the formula which gave them immortality, but each one had entered into immortality without revealing the secret to others. He himself spent his last years on Lo-fu Mountain trying desperately to discover the precious formula. There is a story that at the age of eighty-one he invited a friend to visit him, but when the friend arrived he found nothing but Ko Hung's empty clothes. The implication was clear. Ko Hung had gone to be with the immortals. The ambiguity never has been cleared up as to exactly what was immortal. The expectation seemed to be that one's body would perpetually renew its youth through the correct magical practices. But the only instances of having attaind immortality appear to be persons whose living bodies are said to have disappeared into a different world.

Ko Hung's magical preconceptions are easily seen in the charms which he described. Some charms were to be swallowed, some to be worn as ornaments, while others were to be spoken. By these means one could make oneself immune to weapons, invisible when in danger, or capable of assuming different shapes, of flying through the air, or of walking on water. One charm when "impressed on the dust or mud, prevents ferocious beasts or malignant goblins from passing. The same, placed on the doors of storages and stables, protects the provisions and the animals."[8]

That Ko Hung was not solely a magician whose interests were devoid of any religious or philosophical quality may be seen from the fact that he sought to realize the Three Original Principles of Taoism, namely, Essence, Vital Force, and Spirit. The reason he elaborated the techniques of alchemy was to realize this traditional goal of Taoism. And he "incorporated Confucian ethics into Taoist philosophy" for the same reason.[9] His alleged authorship of the *Biographies of the Gods* proves, if true, that he was much interested in Taoist theology and in the folklore of Chinese religion.

Biographies of the Gods

The facts are that some of the Taoist gods were once human, that some were acquired from primitive Chinese lore or from Buddhism or Confucianism, and that others were deliberately invented.

The best example of a Taoist god who had once been human is Lao Tzu—assuming, of course, that he did live, as tradition insists. A landmark in his deification was the imperial decree of 165 A.D. ordering that sacrifices be offered to him and that a temple be built in his honor. The decree alone was scarcely enough to insure Lao Tzu's worship by the masses. Yet five hundred years later we find the full fruit of historical growth in that Lao Tzu was fully recognized as a god and worshiped in Taoist temples. In the fullness of time this cryptic philosopher was made a member of the Taoist Holy Trinity, called the Three Pure Ones. The first member of the Trinity was the Jade Emperor, jade being the symbol of purity. This deity embodied the First Principle of the universe in the cosmogony of Ko Hung. He was believed to reside in the highest heaven, sitting upon a throne on the Jade Mountain. Second in rank was Tao Chun, or Ling Pao T'ien Tsun, whom we may call "Honorable Tao," or "Heaven's Mystic Jewel." He dwelt in the middle heaven and manipulated the *Yin* and *Yang*. In the lower heaven dwelt Lao Tzu, expounding the doctrine of "Honorable Tao." Suitable gods, saints, and immortals or genii accompanied the Trinity in their hierarchical order, from highest heaven to lowest hell. The nature deities were acquired from primitive Chinese folklore, which in turn probably originated from animism and ancestor worship by a long process of cultural evolution. Many of the Taoist gods thus arose.

One incident in the history of Chinese culture shows that not all the accretions of Taoism from Buddhism and primitive Chinese mythology entered into it without deliberate deception. The incident occurred during the reign of Chen Tsung—also known as Chao Heng, 998-1023 A.D. According to Giles[10] the Emperor, Chen Tsung, was deceived into believing that he had received a divine revelation. But according to Wieger[11] the emperor deliberately took part in the fabrication of the hoax. The latter version of the incident pictures Chen Tsung as seeking to recover the prestige which he had lost when in 1005 A.D. he was forced to make peace with the invading Kitan Tartars by ceding to them much of north China. He sought the advice of the Taoist magicians. At that point his minister, Wang Ch'in-jo, suggested that he concoct a divine "revelation" to impress the people with his supernatural sanctions. When the Emperor expressed surprise Wang Ch'in-jo countered, "Bah! the Ancients had no such scruples. Each time the need was felt the Sages caused Heaven and the spirits to intervene in order to bring their policy into popular favor. It is precisely in this that their wisdom consisted."[12] The Emperor was easily convinced and soon, with the aid of willing scholars, staged a divine revelation. Telling his ministers that he had dreamed that Heaven was trying to send him a message, he went personally to receive a "twenty-foot-long letter written on silk," floating down from a cornice of the "Gate of Heaven." The letter purported to be congratulations from Heaven upon the justice of his rule and the prosperity of the kingdom. Its contents were spread abroad, and other revelations followed. Soon the Emperor let it be known that his heavenly scribe was none other than Yu Huang Shang Ti and the Divine Most High Jade Emperor himself.

It is easily seen how all this mythology, in part deliberately invented and in part unconsciously creeping into Taoism from folklore and other religions, resulted in a philosophy far different from that attributed to Lao Tzu. But it was exactly this change that made Taoism popular with the superstitious classes of Chinese. Scholars might protest, as the one who deplored the transparent hoax of Emperor Chen Tsung and said, quoting Confucius, "I have heard that God does not even speak; how then should he write a letter?"[13] But the scholars were relatively few in number, and the credulous were many. Apparently they loved it when Chinese folklore was incorporated into an increasingly magical type of religion, such as Taoism came to be.

One reason for the popularity of the Taoist magician-priests was that they affirmed the popular belief in the several types of Heaven and Hell, and offered—quite advantageously to themselves, no doubt—to secure the release of dear ones from the torments of Hell. It seems likely that the concepts of Heaven and Hell, not being original with Taoism, were borrowed principally from Buddhism which, in its Chinese Mahayana form, provided thirty-three heavens and eighteen hells. But in taking them over, Taoism insisted on outdoing the Buddhists by offering eighty-one heavens and supplying the priests who possessed the necessary qualifications for rescuing the souls of the deceased from the Buddhist hells.

In a popular Taoist publication originating in the Sung Period (960-1279 A.D.) a very naive theory of rewards and punishments was expressed. "According to the lightness or gravity of his transgressions, the sinner's term of life is reduced . . . poverty also strikes him . . . he perishes." The writer seemed to know precisely how much reward or punishment would follow a specific type of behavior.

Even so, a noble standard of human values shone through the popular superstitions which Taoism encouraged.

Do not sin in secret. . . . First rectify thyself and then convert others. Take pity on orphans, assist widows; respect the old, be kind to children. Do not call attention to the faults of others, nor boast your own excellence. . . . Extend your help without seeking reward. . . ."

As for evildoers,

Though they know their mistakes they do not correct them. . . . Improperly they have grown rich, and withal they remain vulgar. . . . They crush what is excellent in others. . . . They shorten the foot, they narrow the measure, they lighten the scales, they reduce the peck. . . . With the members of their own family they are angry and quarrelsome. . . . They spit at falling stars and point at the many-colored rainbow."[14]

One of the most vivid examples of the Taoist appropriation of non-Taoist mythological figures occurred in the case of the "Eight Immortals." These divinities, long adored by the Chinese masses, had become definitely a part of Taoism by the time of the Yüan dynasty (1279-1368 A.D.). They are believed originally to have been human beings who in some manner or other achieved immortality of both body and soul. (1) Chung-li Ch'uan, whose symbol is his fan, was thought to have found the formula for transmuting metals and thus to have become immortal during the Han dynasty. (2) Lü Yen, whose symbol was a sword, became immortal through scholarly and ascetic practices. (3) Chang Kuo was a magician who rode a donkey which he could fold up like a piece of paper when not needed. (4) Lan Ts'ai Ho, usually seen as a woman, entertained the other Immortals by playing her flute. (5) Han Hsiang is usually pictured with a basket of peaches, the fruit symbolizing immortality. (6) Ts'ao Kuo-chiu is usually seen with castanets. (7) Ho Hsien Ku, originally a shopkeeper's daughter, became immortal by living on "powdered mother-of-pearls and moonbeams. . . . She sometimes appears to men floating on the clouds."[15] Her symbol is a lotus blossom or sometimes the peach of immortality. (8) Li T'ieh-kuai is pictured as "a beggar with an iron staff."[16]

Other mythological creatures of religious Taoism are the God of the Hearth, the Guardians of the Door, and the City God.

The God of the Hearth was revered by Han Wu Ti as the spirit of the alchemy-furnace. Known as Tsao Shen, he is feared by superstitious Chinese as the kitchen spirit hiding in the chimney corner to see what the members of the family say and do. Children are warned that Tsao Shen is watching them. Once a year food offerings are made to his paper image. Then the image together with paper money and paper horses are burned and Tsao Shen goes flying up the flue to report to heaven on the family deportment.

The two Guardians of the Door, represented by paper images, are placed on the front door at New Year with suitable weapons. This ceremony is supposed to keep evil spirits away during the following year.

Worship of the City God, Chen Huang, was until quite recently observed unofficially in almost every city of China and still is in many cities. In the City Temple the devotee is reminded, by signs and symbols, of the certainty of rewards and punishment, for good and bad deeds respectively.

Too numerous to mention are the spirits of nature, the patron deities, the exalted saints, and such mythological creatures as dragons and unicorns taken over from Chinese lore by religious Taoism.

This story of Chinese folk religion and Taoist superstition would be incomplete without mentioning the development of the scientific outlook and the decline of superstition.[17] No new temples are being built in China nowadays, and many of the old ones are being appropriated to non-religious purposes. Magic and geomancy are being abandoned in favor of experimental methods. Yet the old ideas cling, and it will be long before they have disappeared from Chinese culture.

Confucian Cult and Legend

Although Confucianism supplied the hard core of critical rationalism throughout China's history, it was not entirely immune to popular superstitions and mythology. Seeing the popularity of the Buddhist and Taoist superstitions, the Confucians themselves gave in and began to tell or retell legends of Confucian miracles and heavenly signs. The Taoists did not challenge this tendency; in fact they were often the intiators of the legends, as was the case with Lieh Tzu and Chuang Tzu. For the most part the Confucian legends are of late origin. Typical among them are the stories such as the one about a unicorn that appeared before Confucius' birth. Confucius' mother is said to have tied a ribbon on its horn. She is also said to have made a pilgrimage. And a piece of jade was seen with an inscription announcing Confucius' birth. On the night he was born "two dragons appeared, and the five planets drew near in the shapes of interested old men."[18] As music drifted gently from the heaven to earth a voice was heard to say, "Divine harmony strikes the ear, because Heaven has caused a saint to be born. His doctrine will be the law of the world."[19] "Other stories, circulated perhaps by the Taoists before the Confucianists themselves believed them, told how when Confucius was dying a meteor descended and turned into an inscribed jade tablet; and how when Shih Huang-ti (the First Emperor) ordered his soldiers to open Confucius' tomb, they found within it a written prophecy of this very event and a prediction of the death of the First Emperor, which was later exactly verified."[20]

On the whole, however, Confucianism was inclined toward rationalism and skepticism. And in view of the Confucian enlightenment it is not easy to understand why a Confucian religious cult should have emerged at all and in such close association with the schools. Of course the proper key to an understanding of this phenomenon is the Chinese institution of ancestor worship, in which the ancestor or other hero is not really regarded as a god but only as a departed spirit whose consciousness demands reverent remembrance by the living.

The Confucian cult began inconspicuously when the K'ung family and the Confucian disciples revered the departed master in the ancestral house at Chufou. This is the story which was told so impressively by Ssu-ma Ch'ien, cited in Chapter XX.

Subsequent events have undoubtedly been misinterpreted and exaggerated in importance. For example, when in 195 B.C. the first Han Emperor, Kao Tsu, offered the first royal sacrifice at the tomb of Confucius, this probably had no more significance than when a foreign dignitary visits Washington's home at Mount Vernon and lays a wreath upon his tomb, or when a pilgrim prays at the shrine of Thomas á Becket at Canterbury. It is generally admitted that Han Kao Tsu was not sincerely a Confucian, but only tried to curry favor with the Confucian scholars because of their known popularity.[21] No other Early Han emperor is said to have visited Confucius' tomb or to have offered sacrifices to his memory. It is true that the Early Han Emperor, Wu Ti (141-87 B.C.), made Confucianism the official philosophy of the state, but this is not the same as making Confucianism the state religion, which Finegan and Hodous apparently do not perceive.[22] Even Han Wu Ti connived to effect a legalistic modification of the official state philosophy that was called Confucianism.

It is recorded that the Early Han Emperor, P'ing Ti, in 1 A.D. repaired the ancestral temple at Chufou, and that he conferred the posthumous title of Duke upon Confucius. He also conferred lesser titles upon living descendants of both Confucius and the Duke of Chou, for the purpose of insuring the continuation of sacrifices in the line of their royal families—Confucius now being considered as a descendant of the Shang kings. But this was not so much to honor Confucius as to honor the Shangs.[23] It was not until 739 A.D. that Confucius was finally elevated to the rank of "wang" (king or prince).

In 37 A.D. for the first time there is an indication of an official cult of Confucius. This occurred when Kuang Wu, founder of the Later (Eastern) Han Dynasty, ennobled certain descendants of Confucius in order to insure the continuation of sacrifices to Confucius. These sacrifices continued to the end of the Han Dynasty in 220 A.D. Being performed because of state decree and administered by political officers, they should be regarded as a part of the state religion.[24] Even so, however, the rites were probably performed at the ancestral temple at Chufou and were essentially a form of ancestor worship.

How or when the religious cult of Confucius arose in the schools is not known. In the course of the first century A.D. we find historical references to some kind of religious ritual being performed in the schools. The most significant reference was an imperial decree of Ming Ti which in 59 A.D. ordered sacrifices to both Confucius and the Duke of Chou, to be conducted annually by the schools in the larger cities.

By the end of the first century A.D., therefore, we recognize two types of Confucian cult. One was the simple cult of ancestor worship carried on primarily by the descendants of Confucius in the ancestral shrine. The emergence of official state support in 37 A.D. did not alter the fact that it was still essentially ancestor worship. Nor did the sacrifices performed by later Han Emperors in 72, 85, and 124 A.D. at the ancestral temple conflict with the fact that they were really participating in the family ceremonies honoring a great ancestor. The other type of Confucian cult was a kind of hero-worship, conducted in the schools by the teachers themselves.

The next development in the Confucian cult was largely a product of Buddhist influence. As Buddhism spread, Confucian thought was for a time overshadowed and neglected. Confucian scholarship became mediocre while the appeal of Buddhism and of its twin, Taoism, became great. Many Chinese tried to be Buddhist, Taoist, and Confucian at the same time, and some leaders tried to organize a combined cult. The masses were inclined to accept Confucius as a god possessing the usual divine powers of magic. It is said that a decree was published about 500 A.D. forbidding women from praying to Confucius for children.[25] No doubt scholars inspired the decree, but at least it shows the light in which Confucius was then regarded by the ignorant many.

The Confucian schools after the first century A.D. suffered not only from the tendency to become weakened but also from occasional persecution. At one time, in 601 A.D., Confucian schools were closed by decree of Sui Kao Tsu ("Yang Chien"). But the next emperor, Yang Ti, in 605 A.D. restored and strengthened the Confucian schools.

There seems little doubt that, so long as Confucian schools were allowed to exist, they had observed religious rites in honor of Confucius since the first century A.D. These rites were emphasized at certain times more than others, as when the Northern Chi dynasty (550-577 A.D.) ordered an increase in the frequency of the ceremonies, placed shrines inside the school properties, and prescribed punishment for students who absented themselves from the religious ceremonies. In 619 A.D. the T'ang Emperor Kao Tsu ordered that a temple be built in the capital and dedicated to both Confucius and the Duke of Chou. At that temple T'ang Kao Tsu offered sacrifice in 624. His successor, T'ai Tsung, established more schools and endowed one of them with a library of 200,000 books. He withdrew the name of the Duke of Chou from the imperial temple, leaving Confucius to be its unrivaled deity. In 630 A.D. he decreed that temples to Confucius be built in all districts (like our counties) of the empire, and that sacrifices be offered by state officials. Thus Confucianism grew more and more into a state religion, with temples and schools everywhere. Its priests were not a separate class, but simply the scholars and teachers of the schools.

The imperial and provincial temples in time developed into national halls of fame, honoring not only Confucius and his disciples but also great scholars since those early days. For in 647 A.D. T'ai Tsung ordered that tablets honoring twenty-two Confucian scholars be placed in these temples. From time to time thereafter the list of twenty-two scholars was revised, some names being withdrawn and some added, the honors always going to orthodox Confucians by the judgment of a Board of Rites.

Rise and Fall of Confucian Image-Worship

The use of images in Confucian temples tended once more to minimize the difference between Confucianism and Buddhism. It seems quite likely that in the seventh century, perhaps earlier, wooden images of Confucius and his disciple, Yen Hui, were a regular part of temple furniture. But from 720 A.D. onward there is no doubt about the use of images. In that year the emperor decreed that ten seated images should be added to those of Confucius and Yen Hui, and that the seventy disciples and twenty-two scholars should have their pictures placed on the walls.[26] In 960 clay images were substituted for wood. This situation continued until 1530 when all images were replaced by wooden tablets bearing the names of the Confucian saints and heroes.[27] From 720 until 1530 the images were grouped around the temples in a manner closely paralleling the grouping of images in Buddhist temples.

That Buddhist influences affected Confucianism does not mean that significant differences ceased to exist. One such difference was the Confucian emphasis upon the civil service, with its orientation toward the present world, and the ever-present school of government and the classics, associated always with the Confucian temple. Undoubtedly it was this orientation that was responsible for the elimination of the images in 1530 and the restoration of the more simple

Confucian humanism. Meanwhile the Neo-Confucian schools of philosophy had done their work.

In 1370 the first Ming emperor, Hung Wu, demoted all the national gods except Confucius himself. This was an indication of the growing influence of the Confucian rationalism, as well as of a Confucian reluctance to apply their own enlightened principles to their chief divinity, Confucius. As if to atone for the loss of some traditional religious elements, the cult of Confucius allowed the sacrificial rites to become more and more elaborate, and more rigidly regulated by imperial decree. Musicians, dancers, sacrifices, and temples were multiplied. But finally in 1530 Ming Chia Ching ("Shih Tsung"), heeding the advice of the enlightened and honest Confucian scholar, Chang Tsung, simplified the sacrifice, destroyed all the images, and demoted Confucius himself from the ranks of royalty. Some of the scholars protested in vain. But the Board of Rites upheld the actions of the emperor and recommended that to Confucius should be restored the simple title, "Master K'ung, the Perfectly Holy Teacher of Antiquity."[28] It is somewhat ironical but irrelevant that the emperor, Chia Ching, later in life became a Taoist and sought diligently to secure the pill of immortality. On his deathbed he repented and confessed his errors.[29]

The humanization of Confucius and the simplification of the ritual did not mean the complete abandonment of the cult of Confucius. It did change the character of the cult to such an extent that the Jesuits, on entering China as missionaries a few decades later, ruled that Confucians did not regard Confucius as a god, and therefore, that a Chinese could properly be a Confucian and at the same time a Christian.

The Jesuit missionaries to China made a twofold contribution to philosophy. One was calling the attention of Chinese Confucians to the fact that even Neo-Confucianism was considerably different from the philosophy of the humble Confucius himself, and in particular contained elements of Buddhism. In this their contribution was very effective. The other was their communication to the western world of the thoughts of Confucius and other elements of Chinese culture. Such European scholars as Leibnitz, Voltaire, Quesnay, Oliver Goldsmith, and many others were influenced by the Jesuits' reports, and even the equalitarian ideas of the French

Revolution were inspired or reinforced by Chinese Confucianism.[30] Actually, Chinese culture began spreading to Europe as early as the Mongol dynasty (1280-1386 A.D.). In this period China's civilization was more mature than that of Europe. During the fifteenth century European civilization profited by its new acquaintance with the Chinese inventions of printing, gunpowder, and the compass, and out of this developed European science.[31] The Chinese classical type of education prevented the Chinese from making the progress which some of their own contributions inspired in Europe.

Although both the Mongols (1280-1386) and the Manchus (1644-1912) were foreign dynasties ruling over China, nevertheless they outdid native dynasties in promoting the cult of Confucius. In fact it was their foreign character that led them to do so, in their efforts to win the good graces of the powerful Confucian literati. It was the native Ming dynasty (1368-1643) that put an end to the use of images in Confucian temples and demoted Confucius from royal rank to that of a humble teacher. Typical of the Manchus, on the contrary, was K'ang Hsi's edict in 1684 requiring the worshiper at the Chufou temple to kneel three times and kowtow nine times. The government also prescribed the official music.[32] In 1729 by imperial decree and subsidy the temple at Chufou was reconstructed and embellished. The Manchus did resist in 1747 the move to restore Confucius to the place of a nature-god. But when in 1906 the tottering Manchus fully realized their insecurity they issued an edict decreeing that the sacrifices to Confucius be made equal with those to Heaven and Earth.[33] This was an act of political desperation which failed to save the dynasty.

A brief description of the Confucian sacrifice as it was conducted in the temple at the Mongol capital suggests that the cult was then at its height religiously. In use at the temple were 686 bronze, 384 bamboo and wooden, and three porcelain vessels and 632 pieces of cloth, probably silk, for veils or covers. In the service incense was used, and music—instrumental and vocal—helped to coordinate and inspire the ceremonies. Sacrificed were an ox, five sheep, five pigs, two kinds of wine, and other specially prepared food. The animals were inspected and killed before the sacrifice. Three celebrants sacrificed in the same extended ceremony, accompanied by officials robed in scholar's gowns, and assisted by many attendants.

The sacrifice began in mid-afternoon and reached a climax hours after midnight. Elaborate dress was resorted to by all who participated. In the depth of the night a melodious bell broke the silence, announcing the dramatic moment for the actual offering of the sacrifice. Music and marching, kowtowing and dancing, kneeling with incense before the image of Confucius and many other symbolic acts took place.

The first part of the actual sacrifice consisted of a piece of silk containing the full title of Confucius, and a screen inscribed with a prayer. Then the silk and the screen were ceremoniously buried in the temple court. Inscribed on a screen used in the Manchu sacrifice was this prayer:

> O great teacher, thy virtue surpasses that of a thousand sages, and thy way excels that of a hundred kings. Rivaling the sun and moon, thy light shines forever. Truly there is none like thee among us.
>
> The time is here for us to observe the rules of propriety and to make music. Beating the bells and drums of the P'i Yung college, we offer to thee in the *pien* and the *tou* sacrificial vessels.
>
> Now it is spring (or autumn), wherefore we respectfully offer thee this sacrifice according to the ancient rites. The reverent and constant observance of thy moral teaching is the expression of our gratitude to thee. Mayest thou enjoy this sacrifice.[34]

After the sacrifices were made the spirits who had been called up to witness the ceremony were dismissed, and the victims were carved and sent to those whom the emperor wished to honor.

Such was the character, also, of ancestor worship when conducted by the king. Lesser officials and heads of families conducted their sacrifices less lavishly. Of course the day-to-day reverence for Confucius in the shrines and halls of the temple schools was relatively simple, varying from age to age. But for the emperor . . .

> The great drum boomed upon the night, . . . flutes sounded, and the chant rose and fell. . . . "Pai," and the officials fell to their knees, bending forward till their heads touched the ground.
>
> "Hsin," and they were erect again.
>
> Within the hall, the ox lay with his head toward the image of Confucius. The altar was ablaze with dancing lights, which were reflected from the gilded carving of the enormous canopy above. Figures moved slowly through the hall, the celebrant entered, and the vessels were presented toward the silent statue of the sage, the "Teacher of Ten

Thousand Generations." The music was grave and dignified, and the sound of the harsh Mongolian violin was absent. The dancers struck their attitudes, moving their wands tipped with pheasant feathers in unison as the chant rose and fell.[35]

Coming only twice a year, and then performed only by the emperor or his representative, the ceremony as described was perhaps not too elaborate for the adoration of a glorious divinity. Yet we can easily imagine with what scorn and derision the humble Confucius would have spoken of such goings-on. Confucius was always more concerned about honoring the living than trying to please the dead.

Recent Changes in China

The Chinese Republic tried to steer a diplomatic—some would say opportunistic—course in its attitude toward Confucianism. The Republic was organized in 1911 and the emperor abdicated in 1912. The monarchy in 1905 had abandoned the old system of classical education and classical examination for the civil service. This modernizing policy was confirmed by the Republic. In order to avoid offending the popular religious sensibility, however, the Republic approved the continuation of the Confucian cult in modified form. The President or his representative was to perform the modified Confucian rites in the capital, while ranking officials were to do likewise in the districts. But the real support of the cult had ceased when the monarchy fell; consequently the kind of Confucianism celebrated by the Republic was not entirely sincere, and it was bound to come to an end. This happened in 1928 when the government ordered the sacrifices to Confucius to be abandoned. The decaying temples had already fallen by default to the practical uses of the workers. So a remarkable tradition seemed ended.

But then when Japan undertook the conquest of Manchuria and north China in 1931 the Chinese Republic realized its need of a unifying symbol. So in 1934 the leaders of the Kuomintang took the initiative in conducting the Confucian rites at Chufou. There and elsewhere Confucian temples were repaired at government expense. The fictitious birthday of Confucius, August 27, was declared a national holiday. Living descendants of Confucius were again sought out and honored with new titles. At the same time Confucianism was reinterpreted harmoniously with the principles of democracy and scientific rationalism.

With the triumph of the Chinese Communists in 1949 Confucianism entered upon a still newer phase. Confucianism is too deeply embedded in the Chinese culture to be ignored. Hence although the Communists have rejected the Confucian cult, along with all other religion, they have reinterpreted Confucianism as a political and economic philosophy. The Confucian stress on the leadership of the literati easily lends itself to the Communist policy of relying on the leadership of the intellectual liberals, as they say. Then there was the *Li* of Neo-Confucianism—the "supreme principles of the ultimate." This was adapted to the Communist concept of the eternal truths of Marxism and Leninism.

Mao Tse-tung has insisted, however, that China must effect a genuine synthesis of Marxism with Chinese revolutionary principles. Wrote he, "In the past China has suffered greatly by accepting foreign ideas simply because they were foreign. Chinese Communists should remember this in applying Marxism in China. We must effect a genuine synthesis between the universal truth of Marxism and the concrete practice of the Chinese revolution. Only after we have found our own national form of Marxism will it prove useful."[36] Whether such statements are sincere or are made only for opportunistic purposes is a matter for further observation. But the same general point of view apears in the work of Lin Shao-ch'i, a Chinese Communist philosopher.[37] It is quite clear, therefore, that Communism in China is trying to use Confucianism to promote its goals. Whether the Communists are distorting Confucius any more than he has been distorted in the past is a real question. I have a strong feeling, however, that China today would greatly profit by knowing the real teachings of Confucius, and by having complete freedom to apply his teachings to all phases of life. It seems likely that the Way of Confucius would not be far removed from the Way which a man of Nazareth once taught, whose cult is also condemned by those now in power in China. The Confucian and Christian emphasis is upon individual liberty, moral responsibility, and family loyalty.

Evaluation of Chinese Religion

There has long been, in China as elsewhere, a contrast between the magical religion or culture of the unenlightened and the rational ideal of those who have achieved the best education available. No doubt this situation exists in China today.

It is interesting to note, however, in the case of Taoism and perhaps even Confucianism, that the most mature religious philosophy was that of the founder or founders of the tradition already evaluated. It should be obvious that Taoism since its early beginning has become more and more superstitious and magical in its outlook, while Confucianism went through a period of "dark ages." Both Taoism and Confucianism in their popular practice have interpreted their myths literally. Both have had accompaniments of social-ethical values that have shown certain mature characteristics. But in general, it is not difficult to determine the relative maturity of Confucianism versus Taoism, since the latter has not been motivated by the ideal of commitment to truth. Taoism never developed a cult with mature symbolism. Its strongest appeal during its centuries of experience on the popular level, has been its mystic sensitivity. But that has been derived almost exclusively from its animism and magic rather than from its mystical philosophy.

Confucianism, on the other hand, has always been primarily in the keeping of the most scholarly class in China. Moism may be viewed as a rather unique development of or reaction from Confucianism, while Mencius and Hsun Tzu were both in a direct line of development. Mo Tzu's authoritarianism, animism, and magic must be viewed as departures from maturity, while his doctrine of all-embracingness shows a large measure of maturity. Hsun Tzu's authoritarianism and ceremonialism were likewise less than mature, while his rationalism showed remarkable qualities of maturity. Mencius was rather faithful to the original pattern and spirit of Confucius.

After the "dark ages" the Neo-Confucians tried to rescue Confucianism from syncretistic influences but were not altogether successful. The cult of Confucius continued to evolve. Partially interrupted during the years of the Republic, it had meanwhile attained a high degree of maturity in its recognized symbolism, its beauty, and its devotion to the truth. But as of today we are in a position of trying to evaluate a religion which may no longer exist under Communism.

As to the extent to which Confucianism does exist in Communist China, or in Nationalist China, or elsewhere, we may be sure of one thing—it is based on an implicit commitment to truth in all fields of human experience. As such it may have a great vitality and may accomplish much among the Chinese masses in cooperation with other mature world religions. It may free many from magic and literal myth and lead to healthy personal experience and social-ethical relationships.

Chinese Buddhism would be close to Confucianism in certain respects, in its potentialities for popular influence and religious maturity. It would be less intellectually orientated than Confucianism but better suited to awaken the soul to mystic sensitivity, although the latter characteristic is by no means absent from modern Confucianism—thanks to the influence of both Buddhism and Taoism in Neo-Confucianism.

XXIII. SHINTO, THE JAPANESE RELIGION

When the Japanese suffered military defeat in 1945, one author quickly wrote a book[1] in which he warned that military defeat was not enough, that the only way to insure that Japan would remain harmless would be to conquer Shinto, the religion of the people. The sequel to—though not necessarily the effect of—that book was the disestablishment of Shinto in December, 1945, and the ban on its official propagation or support by the state or the schools. The Emperor promptly renounced his traditional claim to divinity and declared that his rule was based solely on the will of the people.

In the light of these events, Shinto becomes more rather than less interesting. Why have Westerners felt that Shinto was dangerous to the peace of the world? Were their fears really justified? Was Shinto really used as a means to promote warlike ends? How popular is Shinto today? Is peace still in danger because of the prevalence of Shinto among the Japanese masses? Was state Shinto a religion, as some maintain, or only a vehicle of expression for Japanese patriotism? Was it possible to be a Christian and a Shintoist at the same time?

That Shinto is not a dead religion is proved by the fact that quite apart from state Shinto, sectarian Shinto numbered something over seventeen million members (followers) in 1940, and today claims 70,044,623 adherents.[2] Whether this figure is accurate or not, there is no doubt that Shinto is numerically one of the major religions of the world; therefore it cannot be ignored.

There are other factors than numbers of adherents which make our study of Shinto important. For example, Shinto has never progressed beyond the stage of primitivism. Therefore in studying Shinto, we shall be viewing a religion analogous to that of our Teutonic ancestors of prehistoric times. This is a rare opportunity.

Furthermore, Shinto is a unique religion in that it has remained nationalistic throughout its history, while most other living religions have become universal. The national religion of ancient Rome is dead. Christianity, by a special definition, is the national religion of certain states like England and Norway. But only one of the living religions is national in the sense of being the aboriginal religion of a single nation, remaining still in that position after more than two thousand years. That religion is Shinto, and it deserves our careful study because it is the single exception to the rule of universality.

Japanese Origins

Since Shinto can truly be understood only in the light of its history, we must look at the Japanese people who gave it birth. Who are the Japanese? How did their nation come into existence? What sort of culture did they develop? Many have said that Shinto has made the Japanese chauvinistic. Is that true? Or is it true, as others insist, that the Japanese are the most peaceful nation on earth, and wanted only to be left alone? When this became impossible, then (it is said) they tried to defend themselves by attacking before they were attacked. These are interesting questions which need to be answered.

The earliest inhabitants of Japan, as far as we know, were the Ainus, whose descendants now live on the northern island of Hokkaido. If they were the Neolithic people whose "kitchen middens," or shell mounds, are scattered by the thousands along the coasts of the islands, then they were in the Japanese islands as early as the third millenium B.C. But where did the Ainus come from originally? Anthropologists classify them as probably Caucasoid. They lived as most Neolithic peoples lived, using tools of stone and bone, and subsisting by hunting and fishing. They made and decorated pottery. Their religion was animistic nature-worship. It is interesting to learn that Mt. Fuji bears an Ainu name signifying the fire-goddess.* We may infer that the Ainus revered Mt. Fuji, the volcanic embodiment of the spirit of fire and the highest (12,461 feet) mountain in Japan.

Then came the conquering Japanese, some few centuries before

* Fuji literally means "ancestress," but was understood to designate the fire-goddess.

the beginning of the Christian era. It was a gradual and a mixed invasion in which there were probably some Malaysians, Melanesians, and Polynesians, while the dominant racial strain was Mongoloid from the Asiatic mainland. The invaders had already reached the cultural level of the Iron Age. Relics of the centuries-long invasion include axes, chisels, swords, daggers, bits, and stirrups—the latter indicating that the domesticated horse was an important ally of the conquerors.[3] With their Neolithic weapons the Ainus were defenseless against iron and cavalry. In the course of the centuries some of the Ainus were assimilated, while many more retreated northward as the invaders continued to stream across the Korean Strait, or drifted northward from southern seas. The result was that the island culture scarcely knew a Bronze Age at all, but passed from the Neolithic Age of hunting, fishing, and crude agriculture to the Iron Age of true agriculture and domesticated animals.

The earliest references to the Japanese are contained in a geographical treatise originating in China during the third or fourth century B.C. At that time the Japanese were mentioned as the Wo people, south of Korea, in the region of Ye-ma-t'ai (Yamato, the name adopted by the Japanese).[4] The island of Kyushu is south of Korea, of course.

Other references to the Japanese occur in later Chinese literature. But in these early centuries of migration and conquest there was no Japanese literature, since as yet the Japanese were illiterate. Their myths, reflecting certain things in their legendary background, were handed down by word of mouth and modified in the process, as we shall see.

The name "Japan" is a corruption used only by occidentals. The name first met with in earliest Japanese literature was "The Country in the Midst of Luxuriant Reed-Plains,"[5] or "This Luxuriant-Reed-Plain-Land-of-Fresh-Rice-Ears."[6] A shorter name used by the Japanese after the great prehistoric migration was Yamato. Some centuries later it became "Hi-no-moto" or "The Source of the Sun" ("Land of the Rising Sun"). Chinese characters for "Hi-no-moto" confused this name, resulting in the pronunciation "Nippon." Marco Polo reported this last form to Europe, but spelled it "Jipangu," and the West has since called it Japan.[7] Japanese school children apparently are familiar with all of these names except "Japan."

As China expanded into Korea and Japan sent military expeditions into the same peninsula, their cultures gradually made contact. The Japanese were the ones who profited most from this, since the Chinese were culturally advanced far beyond them. The art of writing was practiced in China nearly two thousand years before the Japanese invented their system. And when the Japanese did invent a script, it was by borrowing Chinese characters. In doing so, however, the Japanese merely used Chinese characters as convenient symbols of Japanese sounds or words. This led to some confusion, as when the Chinese sign for Hi-no-moto was later interpreted phonetically and so came to be pronounced Nippon. Some of the earliest Japanese literature was written simply in Chinese, such as the *Nihongi* (Japanese Chronicles) in 720 A.D. The first known writing which used Chinese characters to express the Japanese language was the *Kojiki* (Ancient Chronicles), in 712 A.D.[8] Both the *Kojiki* and the *Nihongi* showed much Chinese influence. The very different *Kujiki,* written in 620 A.D., did not survive—although there are extant spurious "copies" of it in Chinese. Neither the contents nor the form of the original is known.[9]

The *Kojiki* is our best source of Japanese mythology and tradition. The *Nihongi* repeats much that is found in the *Kojiki,* but adds variations to the tales and brings the Japanese record more nearly up to date. The *Nihongi* mentions some documents from which its chronicles were derived, thus witnessing to an earlier Japanese use of writing—probably in Chinese. Other early Japanese literature includes the *norito,* or ritual prayers, contained primarily in the *Engi Shiki,* and the poems of the *Manyoshu.* Some of the *norito* were probably composed in the sixth and seventh centuries, but the compilation was made in 923 A.D.[10] The *Manyoshu* poems date from about the eighth century, and relate to a variety of humanistic topics, such as the seasons, love and loyalty, suffering and happiness, patriotism, legend, and allegory.[11]

Origins and Meaning of Shinto

The myths related in the *Kojiki* and the *Nihongi* include the most primitive traditions of the Japanese people. As such, since the Japanese are of mixed blood, we should expect their myths to be a mixed collection. Such, indeed, seems to be the case. Some of the myths appear to come from a people who worshiped sea-gods, some from those who most feared the storm-gods, while the central-core myths belong to people who adored the sun-goddess. The Japanese people, by unifying their mythology, helped to unify themselves.

The word "Shinto" was a late accretion to the already old Japanese religion. It is not the native name of their religion. The adoption of the name Shinto reveals a climax of Chinese influence in Japan, since the word is really a combination of two Chinese words with which we are already familiar: "shen" and "tao." "Shen" means "heavenly spirits,"[12] while "tao" is most simply, but inadequately, translated as the "way." Shinto is thus often translated as "The Way of the Gods." This is misleading for two reasons. First, the gods suggested by the early Chinese "shen" were too personal to meet the total requirement of Shinto. And second, the "tao" meant much more than a "way." Lao Tzu would not have been satisfied with this definition of "tao." Nor would Confucius. *Tao* is "the Great Principle with which everything in the universe should be in accord," as Holtom[13] summarizes it. Like the mystic Absolute, *Tao* is rationally unknowable and inexplicable. But it may be known through intuition by the simplest of good men. He who lives in accord with it is supremely happy and good. But this makes Shinto seem more mature than it really was. In truth, the relative maturity suggested by its Chinese name was due to the influence of the relatively mature Chinese Buddhism and Confucianism. If Shinto were to mean "the principle of godly living," we could not ask for more maturity. But this is not the case.

The meaning of Shinto is better seen in its Japanese equivalent, *Kami no Michi*. In this phrase *Michi* corresponds to the Chinese *Tao*, while *Kami* is fairly similar to *shen*. The *no* signifies the possessive case. So *Kami no Michi* appears to mean just what Shinto means. But let us go deeper.

Kami is the word which will lead us to the heart of the matter. It is more revealing than the Chinese *shen*, in the first place, because its reference to divinity was more primitive than the Chinese word. *Kami* has recently been compared with the Melanesian concept of *mana*, with which Bishop Codrington dealt at great length in his anthropological studies.[14] Before *mana* was discovered, western scholars were confused about *kami*. Even the leading Japanese scholars at times despaired of identifying its real meaning. When they did try to explain it, they seemed to be contradicting one another. Motoöri, one of Japan's greatest scholars in the eighteenth century, after first confessing, "I do not yet understand the meaning of *kami*," proceeded to enumerate the things denoted by the word:

> . . . deities of heaven and earth that appear in the ancient records and also the spirits worshiped at the shrines . . . human beings . . . birds, beasts, trees, plants, seas, mountains . . . anything whatsoever which was outside the ordinary, which possessed superior power or which was awe-inspiring. . . . Evil and mysterious things, if they are extraordinary and dreadful . . . successive generations of sacred emperors . . . far-separated, majestic and worthy of reverence . . . thunder . . . called "sounding-*kami*" . . . dragons, the echo, and foxes. . . . In the *Nihongi* and the *Manyoshi* . . . are further instances in which rocks, stumps of trees and leaves of plants spoke audibly. These were all *kami*. There are again numerous places in which seas and mountains are called *kami*. This does not have reference to the spirit of the mountain or the sea, but *kami* is here used directly of the particular mountain or sea. This is because they were exceedingly awe-inspiring.[15]

Considering the many varied meanings assigned to *kami* in the quotation above, it is no wonder that scholars were mystified. But when the meaning of the Maori word *mana* became known, it was clear that *kami* was its Japanese equivalent. As such it connoted the magical power that was believed to dwell in objects of nature and of imagination which enabled them to do awe-inspiring things. Thus filled with *kami* were "fearful animals," "mysterious and awe-inspiring natural phenomena," magical artifacts, vital organs, demons, spirits, powerful ancestors and living men, and gods.[16]

In the light of the citations above it is clear that Shinto or *Kami no Michi* cannot properly be translated simply as "The Way of the Gods." A more accurate and more pregnant phrase might be "The Principle of Mysterious Power." As the summation of such an ultimate principle, Shinto from ancient times was always a challenge to the individual's absolute loyalty to whatever had *kami*-quality. For the primitive Japanese today, this means a kind of dread of, or dependence upon the powers of nature, the deities of heaven and earth, ancestral spirits, the life-force of phallicism, the magic of charms and fetishes, and the inherited *kami*-power of the emperor. Judged by these characteristics, Shinto is just as primitive as the religion of the Melanesians, or of the prehistoric Saxons and Celts.

This is not to say that all Shintoists are, or have been, superstitious and immature. The "modern educated Japanese," says Holtom, "finds nothing of the feeling of the 'holy' [*kami*] in the fear of the wolf or the magical fertility of the phallus. He finds his sacred world in the values of moral living. He discovers his holy, *kami*-relationships in the highest interests and supreme personages of the national life, in the deep emotions that they call forth, and in his participation in the powerful sentiments and habits that are associated with tried and true tradition."[17] In other words, an enlightened Japanese takes the essence of Shinto to be its insistence upon loyalty to Japanese political and cultural values. Like the classical Greeks, the enlightened Japanese have outgrown the morals of their myths, as may be seen from the fact that at the end of the last century the Japanese government removed the old phallic symbols from public places, in the interest of "morals and decency." The religion of enlightened Japanese may not be as mature as the universal religions, and yet it is probably as free from magical concepts as that of many westerners.

Nevertheless, the Japanese common folk today, as two millenia ago, may think of *kami* as a magical power. We must therefore tell the story of the myths which formed the basis of Shinto throughout the ages, and are still the basis of its practice today.

Amazing Myths of Shinto

Shinto myths are not easy to relate. Found fascinatingly in the *Kojiki,* they are the most amazing myths of mankind in that their very extravagance is beyond civilized imagination. The primitive lack of inhibition was almost complete when it came to telling details which would be revolting in modern polite society—or even in impolite society. Some of our contemporary novelists may approximate their candor without matching their imagination. At least in the case of the primitive Shinto myths, there is good reason to tell the story, which always has an ulterior meaning in human experience.

Amazing is the myth of how the Japanese islands were formed from divine materials. First of all, chaos yielded to the ordered separation of heaven and earth, apparently by spontaneity, in the process of which three gods were born. Six generations of gods ensued, gods with names more fanciful than those of some American Indians. Such were Deity Master-of-the-August-Center-of-Heaven, Pleasant-Reed-Shoot-Prince-Elder-Deity, Deity Mud-Earth-Lord, and Deity Oh-Awful-Lady.[18] Then the seventh-generation deities were Deity the Male-Who-Invites (Izanagi-no-kami) and Deity the Female-Who-Invites (Izanami-no-kami). These seem to be the first really important deities to be born, and are familiarly known simply as Izanagi and Izanami. Apparently they were the first deities to have sex or sexual relations. The "births" of the earlier gods were a more mysterious "coming into being." But with Izanagi and Izanami things really began to happen. "Hereupon all the Heavenly Deities commanded the two Deities His Augustness the Male-Who-Invites and Her Augustness the Female-Who-Invites, ordering them to 'make, consolidate, and give birth to this drifting land.' Granting to them a heavenly jeweled spear, they thus deigned to charge them. So the two deities, standing upon the Floating Bridge of Heaven [rainbow?], pushed down the jeweled spear and stirred with it, whereupon, when they had stirred the brine till it went curdle-curdle, and drew the spear up, the brine that dripped down from the end of the spear was piled up and became an island. This is the island of Onogoro."[19] The spear is generally interpreted as a phallic symbol of creativity, as is also the "august central pillar" around which they went to meet each other and be united in wedlock, in the newly created island. Perceiving that their bodies were different, they reasoned what to do about it.[20] After some trial and error they learned the correct procedure for procreation, with the result that the eight larger islands of Japan were born, the divine offspring of these two heavenly deities.[21]

Then Izanagi and Izanami set an example by continuing to give birth to a number of deities. At last Izanami bore "the Fire-Burning-Swift-Male-Deity, another name for whom is the Deity Fire-Shining-Elder." But this birth proved tragic, for in it "her august private parts were burnt, and she sickened and lay down. The names of the Deities born from her vomit were the Deity Metal-Mountain-Prince and Metal-Mountain-Princess."[22] Numerous other deities were born from other types of bodily-elimination from the ill goddess. Angered at the child whose birth had caused Izanami's fatal illness, Izanagi drew his "ten-grasp sabre" and cut off the child's head. (Author withholds comment.) But still other deities were born from the drops of the child's blood and the parts of his body.

Now follows the Japanese equivalent of the mystery myths of West Asia and Egypt, Greece, and Rome. Izanami died and descended into the underworld. But Izanagi mourned for his sister-wife and followed her below. Making a light with a tooth of his comb, he gazed at her as she (consciously!) rotted and decomposed. From the parts of her rotting body were born eight Thunder Deities. The whole thing repelled and frightened Izanagi and he turned and fled. Izanami burned with shame and anger to be viewed in this condition, so she sent the "Ugly-Female-of-Hades" in pursuit of him. He in turn threw down first his headdress and then his comb. The former turned to bamboo sprouts, and the witch was so intrigued that she stopped to eat. After this Izanami sent the "eight Thunder Deities with a thousand and five hundred warriors of Hades to pursue him." He fought them off with his "ten-grasp sabre" and threw at them, from Hades Pass, three peaches—"Japanese symbol of the female sexual organs."[23] When all else failed, Izanami herself took up the pursuit. But Izanagi lifted a rock which would have required the strength of a thousand men, and "blocked up the Even Pass of Hades."[24] Then he paused to exchange with his sister-wife, on the opposite side of the rock, angry words of love.

Birth of the Sun Goddess

Having escaped from the foul land of death, Izanagi proceeded to purify himself by bathing in a small river, thus setting an example of purity which has become traditional in Japanese culture. Deities were born from each article of clothing or adornment as he disrobed. Even more wonderfully, others were born from the filth which he washed from the various parts of his body. Most amazing of all was the birth of the Heaven-Shining-Great-August-Deity, Amaterasu Omikami, as he washed his left eye. He gave to her his jeweled necklace as a token of her right to rule the Plain of High Heaven.

This seems a rather casual way in which to create the sun-goddess and endow her with the grandiose function of ruling the day-sky. But Izanagi went on bathing and soon, as he washed his right eye, he gave birth to His Augustness Moon-Night-Possessor, who was to rule the night-sky. Then, on washing his nose, he produced the arch mischief-maker, His Brave-Swift-Impetuous-Male-Augustness, the storm-god, Susa no Wo. To him Izanagi gave the rule over the islands.

Let us keep in mind that all of the life-giving deities, who were born from the soiled robes and from the filth which was washed from his body, owed their being to the substance of decay and death brought back from Hades. It is a unique version of the old story of a dying and resurrected god, as in the mystery religions already studied. While Izanami herself did not return to life, yet her dying substance gave birth to sun and moon and other deities, suggesting the cycle of life and death.

But to go on with our story, Susa no Wo became dissatisfied and asked to be allowed to go to his mother in Hades. Izanagi angrily expelled him from the islands, and sent him up into heaven. As he ranted around between heaven and earth[25] he caused storms and quakes in the islands. When he reached heaven, Amaterasu feared what her storm-god brother might do. He swore that his intentions were good, so they agreed to produce children. Result: eight more deities. After all, it does require the cooperation of sun and rain to produce life.

But Susa no Wo got heady with success and started making mischief. He "broke down the divisions of the rice fields, laid out by Amaterasu Omikami, filled up the ditches, and moreover, strewed excrement in the palace where she partook of the great food." This was really no more than what one should expect of a storm-god, playing havoc with the efforts of the sun. Amaterasu should have known what to expect. (Still, there is no meaner trickster in all literature.) But that was not all. "As Amaterasu Omikami sat in her awful weaving hall, seeing to the weaving of the august garments of the Deities, he broke a hole in the top of the weaving hall, and through it let fall a heavenly piebald* horse which he had flayed† with a backward flaying."[26]

* I.e., of two or more colors. † I.e., skinned.

Now that was the last straw. In terror Amaterasu fled to the Heavenly Rock-Dwelling and fastened the door. This, of course, threw the world into complete darkness. The "eight hundred myriad" deities met together to take counsel on how to get the sun-goddess to come out again. Adopting a plan, they set night birds to singing; they made a matchless mirror and a long string of jewels. They hung their offerings near the Dwelling on a Sakaki tree—the most sacred tree in Japan, even today. They recited a grand liturgy in mighty unison. Then Her Augustness Heavenly-Alarming-Female, on an inverted tub, in front of the door of the Heavenly Rock-Dwelling, noisily performed a ribald dance that brought heaven-shaking laughter from the eight hundred myriad deities.

By this time Amaterasu's curiosity was getting the better of her, and she opened the door slightly and demanded to know why they were laughing, since it was so dark. The Heavenly-Alarming-Female replied, "We rejoice and are glad because there is a Deity more illustrious than Thine Augustness." Some one coyly held the mirror before her and apparently the sight made her jealous of the person whom she saw in it. So she took a step farther through the half-open door and another deity took her hand and pulled her through, while still another tied a rope behind her so she could not retreat. So the heavens and the islands again had light.

Divine Japanese Conquest

Meanwhile things were not going well in the islands. For one thing, Susa no Wo—His Brave-Swift-Impetuous-Augustness—had been sent back to earth for all his mischief. There he tried to redeem himself by heroic deeds. One act of heroism occurred when he killed an "eight-forked serpent" which had terrorized a poor, divine family. From one of its tails he had taken a miraculous sword.

But by now there were numerous other power-seeking deities in the land, and tumultuous disorder arose. So Amaterasu determined to send "her son, His Augustness Truly-Conqueror-I-Conquer-Conquering-Swift-Heavenly-Great-Great-Ears"[27] to rule. But his heart failed him when he looked down from the Floating Bridge of Heaven and saw the violence in the land. So in his stead, after some delay, they sent *his* son, His Augustness Heaven-Plenty-Earth-Plenty-Heaven's-Sun-Height-Prince-Rice-ear-Ruddy-Plenty. (Ni-ni-ji, part of the Japanese equivalent, often designates him.) Thus the land was subdued—reflecting, no doubt, the fact underlying the legend, that the Japanese invaded and conquered Kyushu first, on which Prince Rice-ear-Ruddy-Plenty is said to have landed. There Amaterasu's grandson established his peaceful rule. He was given the string of jewels, the sword which had been taken from the serpent, and the mirror, as symbols of his divine sovereignty. The mirror, most especially, was to remind him that his ancestress was the sun-goddess. "Regard this mirror exactly as if it were our august spirit, and reverence it as if you were reverencing us," he was told.

The simple mirror, regarded not as the sun but as its reflection, became Japan's most popular symbol of deity.

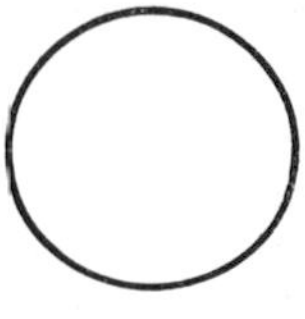

Prince Rice-ear-Ruddy-Plenty (for short—or Ni-ni-ji for shorter) married Princess Blossoming-Brilliantly-Like-the-Flowers-of-the-Trees, whose father was the Deity Great-Mountain-Possessor. After three more generations and many strange adventures two brothers, great-grandsons of the grandson of Amaterasu, took counsel on where to carry on the government of the Empire. "It were probably better to go East," they concluded. So leaving Kyushu they undertook military campaigns on Honshu lasting many years. Just one brother survived: His Augustness Divine-Yamato-Ihare-Prince. He "subdued and pacified the savage deities and extirpated the unsubmissive people," and set up the first Japanese government on Honshu. It is generally thought that Prince Yamato-Ihare was a real human being, who led the Japanese on their invasion of Honshu. Certainly Japanese tradition regards him as real (though divine), and as having been the first to rule the Japanese empire from Honshu. Eight hundred years later they bestowed a new name on him: Jimmu Tenno, meaning Emperor Jimmu. From him they date the empire at 660 B.C. Scholars place the date at about 40 B.C.[28]

The moral of all this mythology is that the Japanese emperor is the lineal descendant of the sun-goddess, the Japanese people are descendants of lesser deities, and even the land of Japan was born of the gods. Shinto commentators have added that other lands were later created out of seafoam and mud, and were inferior to the Japanese islands, which consisted of divine substance.[29]

Significant is the fact that the story of Izanagi and Izanami is analogous, down to many details, to the world-wide myths which were intended to account for the changes of the seasons—decay and death in the fall and winter, and rebirth in the spring. Izanami's death by the burning of the Fire Deity symbolizes the burning of the food-bearing earth by the summer heat. When Izanagi hacked up the infant with his sword, producing the lightning, thunder, and rain deities, that represents the coming of the rain-storms to relieve the drought and burning of summer. I have already commented on the descent of Izanagi into Hades and his triumphant return, which resulted in the springtime revival.[30]

But the Shinto myths are not simple. In them is far more than a reflection of the central theme of the mystery cults. Struggle between sun-deity and storm-deity may be seen as an independent myth suggesting cosmic dualism. And the trouble which arose between Amaterasu and the prankster storm-god, Susa no Wo, is thought also to symbolize the struggle between the sun-people of Kyushu and the storm-people of Izumo, immigrants competing for primacy.[31] The sun-clans were ultimately victorious, partly because they sold their antagonists on the idea that their chief was the lineal descendant of the sun-goddess. They apparently had vivid and aggressive imaginations, and may have gained their ascendancy partly by being the first to combine the myths of the several clans into a kind of symbolic unity. Thus were won the Kyushu clans, who worshiped the gods of the sea, and the Izumo clans who, on eastern Honshu, worshiped Susa no Wo, the storm-god.[32]

Three Stages of Shinto

It is said that there have been three main stages in the history of Shinto: first, primitive Shinto; second, Shinto mixed with Buddhism; and third, "Pure Shinto," best seen in the Restoration period beginning 1868 A.D. This scheme oversimplifies the case, but offers a general plan.

The first stage is described as "primitive nature worship or polydemonism." At this stage the worshiper made no distinction between fire and the fire-god, or between the storm and the storm-god. The fire was holy because it was permeated by *kami*-power. The echo was holy because it was mysterious, *kami*-natured. It was only in a later phase of this stage, it is said (by Kato and by Holtom, e.g.),[33] that the worshiper conceived of *kami*-spirits—or demons—dwelling in the fire, the storm, and the echo. Some of these spirits were thought to be good and some bad.

The analysis of the first stage into its two phases betrays the usual preconception that dynamism always precedes animism and ancestor worship. No evidence is cited, nor can it be cited in the nature of the case. After all, the Japanese scriptures are of late origin and cannot tell us in what order primitive Japanese ideas arose. All that we can be sure of is that when the Japanese crossed the threshold of history they were already worshiping ancestors, both real and imagined; they were worshiping spirits or souls in nature, some conceived to be good and some malicious; and they revered the objects of nature which exhibited *kami*-power.

But besides these three there was a fourth phase of the first main stage, namely, that in which the worshiper conceived of gods as transcending the natural objects through which they manifested themselves. This phase may be regarded as transitional to the second main stage of Mixed Shinto, and belongs perhaps more truly to it than to the first main stage. We can discern it in the earliest of the Japanese scriptures. But we must remember that the *Kojiki* and the *Nihongi* were not written until the eighth century, whereas the more advanced culture of the Chinese, as revealed in their own writings, had been in close contact with the Japanese since the third century A.D.[34] Chinese influence grew over the next two or three centuries, resulting in the introduction of Buddhism, Confucianism, and much Chinese literature.

Transition to Second Stage

The impact of Chinese on Japanese culture was probably at its height during the fifth century A.D. The transformation which took place at that time in Japanese culture is often referred to as "the first great transformation of Japan."* The Buddhist influence will be discussed shortly. Through the influence of Confucianism as it was then understood, ancestor-worship and the ideal of filial piety were magnified, along with other elements of spiritual culture. And in the field of material culture the Japanese, always efficient adapters, learned the Chinese techniques in "pottery making, metal working, wood carving, farming, horticulture, gardening, silkworm culture, road and bridge building, and canal dredging."[35]

Then in the sixth century Buddhism was formally introduced in Japan by way of China and Korea. This took place in 538 A.D., says Anesaki (some say 552 A.D.).[36] Chinese refugees and scribes had come to Japan in the earlier waves of Chinese influence. Now a delegation including Buddhist monks came carrying with them "statues of Buddha and his saints, copies of scriptures, banners and other ceremonial articles."[37] With them came also Chinese medicine, astronomy, and other sciences and arts, including the art of writing (in Chinese, of course). It was all very impressive. Yet many Japanese were strongly opposed to this "foreign intervention" and to the introduction of foreign gods.

A cultural struggle ensued which lasted about fifty years, accompanied by some violence. The imperial family led the way to the acceptance of Buddhism, and others followed. Throughout the struggle, and even more so at its conclusion, other Buddhist missionaries came to Japan bearing more gifts from Chinese culture. One of the greatest gifts was the vision of all mankind united in brotherhood, with special reverence for a certain Indian who had pointed the way to salvation through contemplation, moderation, and human compassion. The anti-foreign Japanese party especially needed that vision.

One product of the opposition to foreign influence was the putting into writing of the Japanese myths and traditions. The *Kujiki*, in the seventh century, and the *Kojiki* and *Nihongi* in the eighth, presented the "pure Japanese" versions of cultural rectitude. Other Japanese literature followed. But the interesting thing is that even in the Japanese literature we find traces of Chinese influence—even of Buddhism. One such trace, cited above, was the Chinese and Buddhist concept of personal gods transcending the objects of nature

* In contrast with "the second great transformation" in 1868 A.D.

through which they manifested themselves. A related influence is seen in the very name "Shinto," as already explained. A distinctly Chinese idea is also found in the Preface of the *Kojiki* itself, when it refers to the need for "trusting the former sages."[38]

Buddhist Shinto

The net result of Chinese-Buddhist influence was the second main stage in the history of Shinto. This stage is called by various names: Ryobu Shinto, Mixed Shinto, Buddhist Shinto, and even Shintoist Buddhism. "Ryobu" means "twofold." Therefore Ryobu Shinto might be translated as "The Twofold Way of the Gods," referring to the combined ways of Shinto and Buddhism. It was about this time that the Chinese term "Shinto" arose as a sophisticated substitute for the Japanese *Kami no Michi*. When that happened, Shinto had already advanced to the stage where the "shen" or "kami" were viewed as personal deities. This concept did not displace the earlier views, but existed along with survivals of the more primitive ideas, even in the same people.

In my discussion the term Buddhist Shinto is adopted as being more descriptive than the indefinite terms Ryobu Shinto and Mixed Shinto. It is better, too, than the term Shintoist Buddhism, for throughout the history of Shinto there was a core of the aboriginal tradition which preserved its identity.

Buddhist Shinto, then, came into existence during the eighth and ninth centuries, but not without the active help of Buddhist monks and laymen. Even nature lent a helping hand by sending a smallpox epidemic to the Japanese capital in 735 A.D. The common people in that crisis turned to the old Shinto gods for help. But the Emperor Shomu proposed to escape the plague by erecting a huge statue of Buddha. So "the Buddhist patriarch Gyogi was sent to the Shrine at Isé to seek the blessing of the sun-goddess for the emperor's project. The oracle was favorable, and the succeeding night the emperor himself experienced a dream in which Amaterasu declared herself identical with Vairocana, a great Buddha of the Mahayana."[39]

Thus Shinto, at first a religion whose only idolatry was the worship of fetishes, at length through Buddhist influence carved anthropomorphic representations of the gods.* In 750 A.D. we find a statue of the Shinto war-god, Hachiman, being taken from his shrine at Usa on Kyushu to the great Buddhist Central Cathedral in Nara, to demonstrate his high regard for the Buddha's "bronze statue more than fifty feet in height, seated on a gigantic lotus pedestal."[40] In this way Buddhist Shinto added the whole Buddhist pantheon to its own recently humanized deities.

Noteworthy in fashioning Buddhist Shinto was Kukai, also known as Kobo Daishi (774-835 A.D.), one of the founders of the mystical Shingon sect of Buddhism. Like Brahman, Kobo's Buddha included all things in his Buddha-nature. Yet he is within our own souls, as Kobo put it:

> The Buddhas in the innumerable Buddha-lands
> Are naught but the Buddha within our own soul;
> The Golden Lotus, as multitudinous as the drops
> Of ocean water, is living in our body. . . .
>
> In realizing all this every one shall attain
> The glories of being, even in this corporeal life.[41]

As a young man Kobo received an education with Confucian background. Dissatisfied with Confucianism, he turned to Taoism, and from that to Buddhism. His restlessness was ended when he had a vision of a Buddhist saint. Subsequent visions guided him in his efforts to find the unity of all religions. The unifying principle he found to be Buddhist revelation, which represents "the wisdom and the mercy of the central Buddha—the wisdom which illumines us in the truth of universal communion and represses folly and subjugates vice, and the mercy which includes all beings in the all-embracing love of the cosmic Lord."[42]

Kobo's most significant vision, for Buddhist Shinto, came during a week of seclusion at the great shrine of Isé. In his vision he learned that all of the Shinto deities are but avatars, or incarnations, of the Buddhas. Amaterasu, said he, was the manifestation in Japan of Amida Buddha.[43] Kobo was probably as sincere as he was earnest in his conviction that all religions find their ground in Buddhism.

With the example set by the emperor himself, and the leadership

* It will be remembered that Buddhist influence led to the use of images in Chinese Confucianism about this same time.

of prophets like the great Kobo Daishi, it is no wonder that the Japanese should have added Buddhism to their Shinto. But let us not expect too much in the way of real synthesis. In the era of Buddhist Shinto, illiteracy prevailed generally. Philosophical understanding was rare, even among the literate. Most people all the while were attracted to Buddhism for two reasons: first, its assurance of immortality; second, its challenge to higher moral living. People wanted the promise of heaven, but they also needed the assurance of local gods that their crops would grow and their children be safe. In order to get both, they became Buddhists without ceasing to be Shintoists. That was the beauty of the new doctrine.

So mixed was Shinto with Buddhism that an inner sanctuary within the Shinto shrines was provided for Buddhist worship, with the assistantance of Buddhist priests preaching Buddhist sermons. Buddhist ritual and architecture more and more characterized Shinto, and their priests exchanged duties. (Would that we had that much cooperation among Christian sects today!)

In view of the popularity of Buddhism and the strong Buddhist influences in Shinto, it is understandable that some scholars have characterized Japan as a Buddhist nation during this period.

Though Shinto was overshadowed or infiltrated by Buddhism, it was not without its purists and jealous defenders. Generally speaking, the motivation of Pure Shinto lay in the spirit of nationalism. Yet it cannot be said that only Pure Shinto contributed to Japanese nationalism. Certain Buddhist sects were also influential in the development of nationalism. A new class arising at this time, the Samurai, was also very important.

Steps toward Nationalism

There is no simple explanation of the evolution of Japanese nationalism. This can be understood only in the total background of the history of Japanese culture, domestic politics, and foreign policy. Since nationalism is so prominent in modern Japan, it is important that we understand how it came about.

During the Heian period (794-1185 A.D.) in which Buddhist Shinto was perfected, it became customary for the emperor to abdicate in favor of his successor, and to retire to a Buddhist monastery. This tended to weaken the monarchy, since the retired monarch still wielded much influence on account of his added holiness.

Strife among the feudal lords and great families also caused a decline of the state. The three great families of the period were the Taira, the Minamoto, and the Fujiwara. From the Minamoto later came the Tokugawa family which held the Shogun dictatorship from about 1600 to 1867 A.D. The Fujiwaras were cultured statesmen who claimed divine descent from a close relative of Amaterasu. They gained control over the imperial court and intermarried with the imperial family. But the Tairas and Minamotos had the armies, and while they contended with each other for military dominance the power of the emperor was reduced to the area of the capital, Heian-kyo—later called Kyoto. Competing with the armed power of the two families, paradoxically, were the Buddhists—apostles of love! Irritated by the unfavorable land-policies of the government, armies of priests attacked the capital itself, and also fought each other on occasion. Such was the confusion of the times, and the imperial power was too weak to counteract it.

The Kamakura era (1185-1333 A.D.)[44] was ushered in by the triumph of the Minamotos over the Tairas. Yoritomo then secured from the emperor the title of Shogun ("Armed Leader"), and from his own capital, Kamakura, ruled Japan. Thus was established the office of shogun, with imperial sanction, which made a puppet of the emperor most of the time from 1185 to 1867 A.D. It is said that during this era the emperor reigned, while the shogun ruled.

The Shogunate and the Kirishitan Mission

It is significant that the shoguns retained and protected the imperial family. This was due in part to their reverence for the direct descendants of the sun-goddess. Partly also, it was due to the shogun's need for a symbol of his authority. As long as the emperor lived in his palace, surrounded by his functionless courtiers, the people would be more likely to obey the emperor's shogun. Meanwhile, however, the imperial line was being preserved in a "lineal succession unbroken for ages eternal."[45] This made possible the cultivation of emperor-worship, with its nationalistic accompaniments in modern Japan.

Inward corruption weakened the Kamakura shogunate, and the imperial party brought it to an end in 1333 A.D. The victory of the emperor was short-lived, however, for in 1336 the dynasty was divided in two, one part insisting on direct rule and the other relying on feudal support, headed by the Ashikaga family. The latter was descended from the Minamotos. The Ashikaga established their capital at Kyoto, and at the end of fifty-six years of struggle (1392 A.D.) nominally reunited the dynasty. But the dynasty was a puppet of the Ashikaga, who in turn were subject to feudalistic control. The result was an era of strife and discord. The Ashikaga shogun was able to stay on top, but it was rough riding. One example of the turmoil was the violent destruction in 1467 of the capital city, Kyoto. The city was lavishly rebuilt, but the strife continued until 1573, when the Ashikaga regime was supplanted by the Taira shogunate of Nobunaga.

The arrival of Francis Xavier in 1549 signalized a new source of strife, with the establishment of the Kirishitan* mission.[46] The enterprise was phenomenally successful from the first. Its "preaching and education were reinforced by works of charity; churches, colleges, hospitals, leproseries were established."[47] Under the conditions of the times, each feudal territory posed its own problems of favor or opposition. When in 1569 Nobunaga put an end for a while to the confusion of the times, he gave his blessing to the mission. Thousands of converts had already been won, including the Takayama and other noble families. Then in 1573 Nobunaga supplanted the Ashikaga after the latter had proved ineffective for more than two centuries. Under the new regime the church prospered, achieving a membership of 150,000 up to the death of Nobunaga in 1582. By 1605 the membership is estimated to have reached 750,000[48]—a larger percentage of Japanese than has been Christian at any time since.†

* The name Kirishitan was a Japanese corruption of Christian, and is used by historians to designate this Roman Catholic mission.

† In a later work Anesaki reduces the number to 500,000, while Noss quotes it at 300,000. The number of Japanese Christians in 1934 is given as 311,000. See p. 377.

Nobunaga never succeeded in bringing more than half of Japan under his sway. But when he was assassinated one of his generals, Toyotomi Hideyoshi, gained control and brought all of Japan under his power by 1590. He continued Nobunaga's Kirishitan policy until 1587 when suddenly he ordered preaching stopped and all foreign missionaries expelled. But the order was not enforced. In 1597, however, Hideyoshi caused the crucifixion of twenty-six missionaries and converts.[49]

After succeeding at home, Hideyoshi sent his troops to Korea and China and wrote a letter to the Spanish governor of the Philippines threatening war unless he quickly submitted to Japanese rule. His foreign conquest, he said, "is not actuated by our own inclinations, but is taken in pursuance of a heavenly command."[50] This threat was never carried out, though it showed that Amaterasu's command to Jimmu Tenno to bring the whole world under his rule ("all the world under one roof") was taken seriously, at least by one militarist. Hideyoshi died in 1598, leaving an infant son and a precarious succession.

In 1600 occurred probably the most significant event since the establishment of the first shogunate in 1185. Iyeyasu won a decisive battle among the contenders for power, and instituted the Tokugawa shogunate which was to last until 1867.

The Kirishitan mission came to disaster under Iyeyasu. This shogun, called a tyrant by most writers but defended by some, adopted a policy of opposition to any religion showing a spirit of independence or of loyalty to a foreign power. In 1614 he issued a proclamation[51] ordering the expulsion of missionaries and the suppression of Christianity. This step may have been caused in part by the arrival of contending Catholic orders and by an indiscretion of shipwrecked Spaniards. The policy was continued throughout the Tokugawa shogunate. Up to 1633, when the identity of faithful Christians was discovered they were executed by being burned alive. Thereafter execution was by being suspended in a pit.[52] It is really amazing that under such conditions some Christianity survived until the policy was finally reversed in the last century.

On only one occasion did the Kirishitans, joined by others, rise in revolt against intolerable tyranny, in 1637-38. After temporary success the rebellion was crushed and thirty thousand men, women, and children were massacred. Mainly as a result of this experience Japan systematically isolated itself from the rest of the world, allowing only a few Dutch and Chinese traders to touch Japanese shores from that time until the forcible visit of Admiral Perry in 1853 and 1854. This story is too well known to need retelling.

Transition to Meiji Era

It is true, as all will admit, that the opening of Japan to the West was motivated from within as well as from without.[53] The oppression suffered by most of the classes in Japan was becoming more and more unbearable. Unlike the preceding shogunate, that of the Tokugawa was a purely autocratic regime. The Tokugawas ruled despotically, resorting to devices such as hostages, spying, and the requirement that all feudal lords, in order to retain their estates, visit the capital at stated intervals. No time was left for rebellion.

Culturally the Tokugawa period was progressive, since the one great gift that the Tokugawas bestowed was peace. In religion Buddhism was favored both on account of its great adaptability and because it could be counted on to keep watch against Christianity. In ethics the Shushi (Chu Hsi) school of Confucianism was officially endorsed because of its Stoical tendencies and its conservative emphasis on tradition. The professional military caste, the Samurai, adopted a modified Confucian ethics, while relying on Buddhism for religious motivation. Paradoxically an alliance developed even between Shinto and the ethics of Confucianism, as we shall explain.

Unfortunately for the shogunate, there was leisure for scholarly research. And scholarship showed that the Confucianism which strengthened the power of tradition was not at all the philosophy of Confucius. Historical studies also made it clear that the shogun had usurped the emperor's functions. Such considerations were reinforced by economic conditions such as the impoverishment of the Samurai caste, who had no alternative but to starve rather than change occupations. In fact the whole social system of Japan was a caste system. The system was ready to erupt. Occasional rebellions were attempted, but proved abortive.

Then when Admiral Perry forced Japan to permit the return of the Occident, the Tokugawas were virtually finished. The very title on which their function was based was "Generalissimo for Expelling Foreign Barbarians." Since this plank was taken out from under them they had to fall. The nobles flocked to the standard of the emperor, pledging him their all. The shogun in 1867 relinquished his title and his power.

The emperor resumed rule in his own right in 1868. He was careful to nourish the tradition of his sacred person, his descent from deity, and his divine commission to govern. But he was unable to go backward to a condition of the past. New things were taking place, among which was democratic government. So missions were dispatched to learn about western constitutions. In 1889 the new Japanese constitution was adopted, providing for a parliament to discuss and enact laws, subject always to divine imperial guidance and approval.

The Emperor Meiji* ruled until his death in 1912. By 1931 the emphasis upon the divine destiny of Japan had worked so sufficiently into the hands of the militarists that any peaceful intentions which Emperor Hirohito may have had were necessarily overruled. Meanwhile Europe and America had been sucked into the whirlpool of a war between "Christian" states, in which Japan unluckily joined the losers. It seems that the "Christian" West ought to be somewhat charitable toward a "pagan" nation newly aroused from feudalistic isolation. Nor is this meant to excuse the Japanese militarists from their responsibilities. It does, however, justify the reopening of the case of Japanese nationalism in its cultural and religious setting. This is the problem of the next chapter.

* A title meaning "Enlightened Government," applied first to the new era and, posthumously, to the restored monarch.

XXIV. RELIGION AND NATIONALISM IN MODERN JAPAN

SINCE FOR MANY CENTURIES there has been a strong Buddhist element in Japanese religion and culture, our first concern in this chapter will be to describe the relationship between Buddhism and Japanese nationalism.

Many regard Japan as having been a Buddhist nation from the ninth to the sixteenth century. The same view is held of Japan today. In 1940 a census showed 45,000,000 Buddhists in Japan, as compared with 17,000,000 Shintoists (sectarian) and 311,000 Christians. The Japanese Ministry of Education in 1953 estimated that since disestablishment there remained a total of 70,044,623 Shintoists, compared with 43,637,000 Buddhists and 415,081 Christians. These figures for Shinto and Buddhism are admittedly erroneous,* but they witness to the continued strength of Buddhism without even suggesting the strong Buddhist influence in Shinto. Many are of course at the same time both Shintoists and Buddhists, and many more are Shintoists who do not realize their debt to Buddhism. This being the case, should we expect Japan to be as chauvinistic as we have understood it to be? This calls for a careful scrutiny of Japanese Buddhism.

Growth of Buddhism

Modern Buddhism grew out of medieval Buddhism by a perfectly natural process. After the government ceased to control Buddhism,

* "Buddhist totals usually represent the number of households whose ancestral graves or tablets are in a temple's custody, multiplied by five. Shinto shrines generally base their reports on such factors as the number of charms and amulets sold." Oguchi, "The Religions of Japan," *The Atlantic,* Vol. CXCV (Jan., 1955) 122.

probably the most momentous event was the establishment of a hermitage by the monk Saicho (Dengyo Daishi, 767-822) on a mountain peak, Hiei-zan, near Kyoto. To him came many disciples and he built a dormitory alongside the chapel. Others came, and more dormitories were built. Thus was founded what came to be known as the Tendai sect of Buddhism, noted for its learning and its faithfulness to the spirit and practice of the Buddha himself. Tendai was one of the most broadminded of all Buddhist sects.

When conditions grew congested and spirits overflowed on Hiei-zan, monks would move away to found other hermitages. Thus the Tendai continued to grow.

But some who studied with the Tendai later went forth to found new hermitages with distinctive doctrines or practice. Thus arose some of the sects which have proved to be the most vital in Japanese Buddhism, most of them founded by monks who got their inspiration at the top of Mount Hiei. Jodo was founded by Honen, who left Hiei in 1173. Yeisai left in 1200 and founded Rinzai Zen. Shinran, a pupil of Honen, left in 1201 to found Shinshu, the largest Japanese Buddhist sect in existence today and allegedly the most vital. Later in the same century Dogen founded Soto Zen and Nichiren founded Hokké, which I shall call simply Nichiren.

There are six principal sects of modern Japanese Buddhism which may be classified according to size and relevancy to modern culture. In 1934 Jodo Buddhism claimed 3,646,000; Shinshu 13,160,000; Nichiren 3,381,000; Tendai 2,149,000; the Shingon group 9,527,000, and Zen 9,475,000. Other Buddhists numbered 539,000, making a total of 41,877,000.[1] These figures are said to include only "priests, nuns, and novices." The inclusion of laymen would apparently swell the Buddhist following considerably, though the statistics are confused.

Tendai is now the smallest of the six main sects and allegedly it has lost much of the spiritual power of its early mission. This may be seen by a visit to Hiei-zan, the mountain peak where still stand the many buildings erected during its heyday. Says Anesaki, "Occasional services are still held by the priests and monks, but very few laymen attend them. Besides these temples there are a number of monastic buildings on Hiei-zan, but they are almost as silent as dead, each being inhabited only by a head and a handful of novices. And this is all that remains of the famous Hiei-zan, once the greatest center of Buddhist learning and discipline."[2] The primary service of Tendai today is that "here is handed down a precious lineage of Buddhist learning, besides works of art, books, and manuscripts. Yet they have little relation to the religious life of the people today."[3]

Comparable with Tendai in certain respects is Shingon. For centuries the only real rival of Tendai, it surpassed it in membership. But its relevance to modern culture seems even less than that of Tendai. A visit to Mount Koya, near Osaka, will demonstrate this. Here on the peak of Koya-san in the ninth century Kobo Daishi* taught the unity of all religion under Buddha-Vairocana, whom all people worship under various names. Where Kobo once invented sacramental rites designed to reveal the heart of all religions, there today we find little besides extreme mystification. It is

> quite a city of temples, chapels, monasteries, tombstones, and memorial tablets, all interspersed among the rocky heights and hillsides and surrounded by great trees. All these buildings contain altars, platforms, statues, pictures, banners, and symbolic utensils for the performance of the different sacraments, embracing between them every possible variety. The statues, for example, are of Buddhas, celestial beings, monsters, demons, and human persons. Bells resound at morning and evening, chanting and music are everywhere heard, sacrificial fires are burning, whilst the officiating priests in brilliant robes are continually occupied in mysterious manipulations of hands and fingers, reciting mystic formulas, pouring oil and perfume into this vessel and that, burning incense, striking on plates, shaking little bells, swinging mystic rods that symbolize thunderbolts, and many other ways. There may be a few worshipers besides, most of whom, being quite ignorant of the meaning of all these performances, can only sit and gaze. The attendance of laymen at these sacraments is not so much regarded as an expression of belief and devotion as an occasion for becoming absorbed into the mysterious atmosphere of the ritual.[4]

Besides gaudy-robed priests and "pious pilgrims in white robes, chanting their diverse formulas . . . there are also many who are simply curious visitors. In fact the whole precinct of Koya-san is now regarded as a summer resort, with its cafes and restaurants, and even dubious houses of pleasure."[5] One of the chief uses of the area is as a cemetery for aristocratic bones.

* Pp. 370-371.

Zen Buddhism

In remarkable contrast to Shingon is Zen Buddhism, more like Quakerism than anything else in western religion. The founder, Dogen (1200-1253), studied under a master in China to which it had come from India as *dhyana* Buddhism, or meditation Buddhism. Dogen finally settled at Eihei-ji, near Fukui.

The meditation encouraged in Zen is not to be interpreted as rationalistic or discursive thinking. The Zen monks are taught to rely on intuition rather than logic. Many are the stories told to illustrate the fact, how the disciples have been subjected to slaps, knocks on the head, and other indignities designed simply to make them conscious of their own intuitions. Many have regarded Zen Buddhism as the most distinctive development in Japanese Buddhism. Anesaki, however, classes it with those forms of Buddhism which have little relevance to modern culture and its problems.

The character of modern Zen may be seen by exploring the establishment which is still found at Eihei-ji. The buildings are situated on a hillside and in a valley. The first is "a plain temple, wherein a statue of Buddha [stands behind] a sober-looking altar. [Behind this] *Butsu-den,* or Buddha Hall," is a larger building furnished with a high platform and simply decorated. In this assembly hall a small congregation of monks and novices in black robes, "and maybe some lay brothers as well," stand waiting for the master to enter. When he arives on his platform he waves his *hossu,* or duster, "and then, after a silent interval, he will open his lips to deliver what is called a sermon or an instruction . . . [which is always] terse and incisive, and may be only a few sentences or a verse."[6] Then the meeting is over, the monks go to their rooms, and the novices go to labor or learning.

In the gloomy hall below, the "Meditation Hall," studious novices sit working on problems assigned by the master. When the disciple has solved enough problems, with the approval of his master, he becomes a Zen monk.

Theologically Zen may be regarded as having restored something of the spirit of the Buddha. Gautama Siddartha's refusal to commit himself on any metaphysical or theological issue was made a fundamental principle of Zen. Silence was often the best answer.

Another virtue of Zen was its unique policy of discipline and a readiness of courage which appealed to the Samurai. "Being peculiarly suited to the life and spiritual needs of the *Samurai*, or warrior class, who in the thirteenth century had the government of the country, Zen came to be adopted as the religion of the *Samurai*, in contrast to Shingon . . . the religion of the sentimental nobles of the court." In the next centuries "Zen exerted its purifying and tranquilizing influence upon the feudal lords and retainers" who contributed liberally to "the foundation of thousands of Zen monasteries and smaller institutions."[7] The Zen "combination of moral life with the sense of beauty was the basis of Bushido, the 'Way of the Warrior'; serenity and simplicity, calm resignation and bold idealism, these permeated more or less the life of the people through the influence of the warrior class."[8]

Zen Buddhism today is largely a survival of its feudal prosperity. "Nevertheless, the spiritual influence which Zen exercises upon the men of today, chiefly among the military and intellectual classes, is still a factor to be reckoned with, to say nothing of its pervasive influence in the daily life and artistic taste of the Japanese people."[9]

Nichiren

The fourth type of Buddhism, Nichiren (Hokké), arose from an impassioned protest against all false forms of Buddhism (meaning all but Nichiren), and against the sinfulness of the Japanese nation. Nichiren's intolerance of all Buddhist sects but his own naturally made him the object of persecution. The same consequence flowed from his fearless criticism of Japanese decadence in general.

Nichiren (1222-1282) claimed to have received a revelation for the degenerate people of the "latter days." He taught that the Buddha Shakyamuni was truly revealed only in the "Lotus (Hokké) of Truth," where he is pictured as the eternal Lord of the world, the very essence of the life of the universe. Nichiren taught that sin was basically an estrangement from the gospel of the *Lotus* and from the intuitively known mystic unity of all life which it taught. But there was nothing sentimental about this message. His was a stern call to discipline and heroism. Sentimental types of Buddhism received his worst condemnation. His own life was filled with the extremes of frustration and triumph. He was sent to lonely exile for predicting a foreign invasion, but was recalled when the Mongols twice attempted the invasion of Japan (1274 and 1281). He was even condemned to execution but escaped as if by a miracle.

No one was more patriotic or nationalistic than Nichiren and his followers. The judges of the Old Testament are comparable in their devotion to Israel. This patriotism and the disciplinary ideal of Nichiren ultimately appealed to the militarists. The three vows of the Nichiren are: "I will be the Pillar of Japan; I will be Eyes to Japan; I will be a great ship for Japan." Nichiren himself believed that Japan would become the center of the universal type of Buddhism which he preached. Although the militarists and nationalists long rejected his gospel, which for centuries nurtured primarily the lower middle class, finally in the twentieth century the militarists, nationalists, and intellectuals of Japan recognized its usefulness and sought to promote it.

The universal value of Nichiren was to be found in its insistence that all Buddhists should take on the ideal of the Bodhisattva, refusing to withdraw into a life of contemplation or the pursuit of Nirvana until all had heard the truth. The missionary spirit of Nichiren was remarkable.

Today? Observe the annual ceremony commemorating Nichiren's death, which occurred in the early morning of October 13, 1282. This event took place at Ikegami, then several miles from Tokyo, but now within its city-limits. To it, on October 12, moves a great procession of people carrying small drums and lighted lanterns, with banners and quotations from the *Lotus*. The multitude loudly chants its sacred formulas. On reaching the temple where stands a statue of Nichiren the pilgrims continue to beat drums and shout through the night until finally the bell rings, signalizing the moment of the prophet's death. This brings a veritable roar from the throng which is swept away in its fervor for their prophet.

Few groups are more fanatical than Nichiren. Yet it possesses certain assets, such as missionary zeal, discipline and selfless devotion to mankind's salvation, and potential universality. A fresh interpretation of its mission by an educated Nichirenite church could make a positive spiritual force of it.

Jodo Sects

The two other main sects of Buddhism are Jodo and Shinshu. These are so much alike that they may be treated together. Honen founded Jodo at the end of the twelfth century, while Shinran, his pupil, founded Shinshu at the beginning of the thirteenth century.

Shinshu may be defined as "Genuine Teaching of the Pure Land," while Jodo means simply "Pure Land." The term Jodo may be used to denote both churches. They are said to be the closest to Christianity of any of the forms of Buddhism.[10] Shinran required the complete surrender of the self to Amida Buddha who, said he, had made a vow to save all who put their trust in him and called upon his name. Salvation seems to have meant the safe arrival of the soul at the western Paradise, which by faith would provide a sense of immediate security. Certainly salvation was made easy, since one need not perform good works in order to attain it. All that was necessary was to call upon Amida and he would save. Other forms of Buddhism required enlightenment, wisdom, or good works, but not Shinshu. Common people who knew nothing about the principles of meditation, nor had time for it, felt attracted to this form of Buddhism. Honen, founder of the related Jodo sect, demanded exclusive faith in Amida Buddha.

For Jodo life was burdensome and worthless, but heaven was glorious beyond conception. Honen explained how to gain the reward of heaven:

> The method of salvation which I have taught is neither a sort of meditation such as that practiced by many scholars in China and Japan in the past, nor is it a repetition of the Buddha's name by those who have studied and understood the deep meaning of it. It is nothing but the mere repetition of the name of Buddha Amida, without doubt of his mercy, whereby one may be born into the happiest land of the Buddha.[11]

Even the celibacy of the priesthood is unnecessary to salvation in Amida Buddhism[12]—as also in Zen.

The political and social unrest of the twelfth and thirteenth centuries may have contributed to the success of the Amida sects, which provided a strong tower in the storm. Even when the Tokugawa regime brought social stability, Jodo pietism continued to spread. It appealed to the lower middle class, the farmers, and even some of the higher classes. At one time armed conflict developed between Nichiren and Shinshu, in which, paradoxically, the gentle Shinshu was the winner.

The younger men in Jodo today are tending to reinterpret their tradition as minimizing moral judgment and exalting vital instincts. This is alleged not to encourage immorality, but rather to display the natural goodness of man. It has been noted that donations in the Amida sects have fallen off in recent years. Yet there is a great deal of genuine piety among these sects, in which laymen form such a large part, attending church services and maintaining their private home-shrines. Attending a church service in the Hongwan-ji in Tokyo one would hear frequent quiet murmurings from the congregation, "Namu Amida-Butsu," meaning "Praise to the Infinite Buddha." This reminds one of the fervent "Amen, Praise the Lord," which once characterized certain Christian churches.

Education is carried on today by the various Buddhist sects from kindergarten to college, designed to fit persons to meet the problems of life. Many types of social service also are conducted. Some of this has been inspired through contact with Christianity, yet much of it also is indigenous, and will develop as enlightenment grows. We should keep in mind that Japan has become one of the most literate countries in the world.

Taoism and Confucianism

Not only Buddhism, but also Taoism, came to Japan from China. Taoism as an organized religion never appeared in Japan. But the concepts of popular Taoism, such as sorcery and the various types of magic, were current in Japan even prior to the coming of Buddhism. There may in fact be an ethnic kinship between primitive Shinto and continental Shamanism, which is virtually the same thing as popular Taoism. In any case, such popular superstitions passed very naturally from person to person and penetrated the Japanese culture. As the centuries passed, Taoist books, poems, and paintings were circulated in Japan. The Taoist feeling for nature may have had some influence in the kindred feeling developed by Zen Buddhism.

Far more important, but still less conspicuous than Buddhism, was the part played by Confucianism in Japanese religion. It would be impossible to estimate the degree to which Confucianism has penetrated Japanese culture generally. But there is much truth in the saying that the Japanese entrusted their earthly interests to Shinto deities, heaven to the Buddha, and morality to the guidance of Confucius. Long before the Tokugawa regime officially endorsed Confucian ethics, the Japanese had experienced its influence. Zen monasteries systematically cultivated Confucian ethics in order to fill a gap in their own teaching. Emperor Meiji recognized Confucianism in his Rescript on Education in 1890, mentioning the five great relationships of life: ruler and subject, parent and child, elder and younger brothers and sisters, husband and wife, and friend and friend. These—particularly the first two—were felt by the Japanese to be more important than the abstract Confucian virtues, such as justice and courtesy.

It is important to note that the Confucianism in Japanese culture was not that of Confucius, but of Neo-Confucianism. As such it stressed civic loyalty and obedience to prince and parents, and served as a conservative factor. Progressive Confucianists and others arose ineffectively. The only element of both original and neo-Confucianism which was anathema in Japan was the doctrine of the propriety of revolution when the ruler fails to rule well.

Confucianism was used during the Tokugawa shogunate as a tool for combatting Buddhism. Later it was used to combat both Buddhism and Christianity, but was ineffective on both.

The most conspicuous role of Confucianism was in its contribution to Bushido, the code of the Samurai.

Bushido: Way of the Warrior

The West needs to understand the Japanese ideal of Bushido, the principles of the Samurai caste. The "do" in Bushido is the same as the "to" in Shinto, and may be translated simply as "way." And since the Samurai were quite similar in many ways to the Christian knight of medieval chivalry, we may translate Bushido as the "way of the knight, or warrior."

The Samurai caste was formed during the period when the Minamoto and Taira clans were struggling for supremacy. A man, having chosen the profession of warrior and attached himself to some feudal lord, was committed to remain such forever, and his children after him. When death or other accidents left him without a lord, he offered his services elsewhere, but always remained a warrior.

As a warrior, the Samurai was meticulous in observing the proprieties of his profession. In this respect, as in other more specific ways, he owed much to Confucianism. It is said that the Bushido code was derived from Confucianism by Yamaga Soko (1622-1685) who applied its principles to the life of the soldier. Soko's lecture notes outline the elements of Bushido:

I. The fundamental principles: Fidelity to vocation; an earnest desire to carry out the Way [of the Warrior; i.e. Bushido]; efforts devoted to its practice.
II. Training of the mind; Composure of mind; Magnanimity; Purity of sentiment; Gentleness; Refinement, etc.
III. Training in virtues and the perfection of ability.
IV. Self-introspection and self-restraint.
V. Mindfulness of dignity and propriety; Self-respect and gravity; Vigilance in seeing and hearing, etc.
VI. Vigilance in daily life; Daily life and its surroundings; the use of wealth and its significance in life, etc.[13]

The western student may be surprised at the idealism of Bushido. Certainly the Samurai chose the best that was in his culture and made it an integral part of his practical life. It is clear that he was inspired not only by the Confucian ideal of propriety, but also by Buddhist (Zen and Nichiren) ideals of thoughtfulness, meditation, and discipline. So comparable was his mode of life to that of the medieval Christian knight that one wonders if there was not some influence. It is significant that a number of Samurai were among the first Kirishitan converts. Take the Bushido code of virtues as listed by one writer: loyalty, gratitude, courage, justice, truthfulness, politeness, reserve, honor.[14] The Christian need not take credit for contributing these ideals to the Samurai, but he does need to recognize their Christian quality, derived no doubt from the best in Japanese culture.

It should be noted that the Samurai code is expressed in terms of the spirit, and not of mere ritualism. For example, the "purity" which in Shinto tradition may be interpreted to mean physical cleanliness, or ritual purification, or purity of heart, is definitely interpreted by Bushido as primarily the last (in Section II *supra*).

Not all of the Bushido code, of course, was like that of the Christian knight. Honor, courage, and reserve, for example, were interpreted somewhat differently. Honor, to the Samurai, meant that death was better than saving one's own life by disloyalty or blundering behavior. "The knight always carried two swords, a long one to fight his foes, a short one to turn upon his own body in the case of blunder or defeat."[15] Courage was expressed in such extreme form as to mean not merely that the warrior was unafraid to die, but rather that he feared to die in bed without having had the chance to die for his lord in battle. Reserve meant the suppression of feeling. This is not a Christian ideal, although it is Stoicism, which had some influence on Christianity. Nor does Christianity approve of suicide, even when it is performed with such religious ritual and unselfishness as Bushido requires.

Since "harakiri"* was so characteristic of Bushido, we must add at least one illustration, showing how loyalty, honor, reserve, and politeness—even to one's enemy—belong to the warrior. No story of harakiri is told more often than the one about the "Forty-seven Ronins." A ronin was a feudal retainer deprived of his fief. A large number of ronins were deprived of their fiefs when their lord was condemned to commit harakiri because he had attacked his overlord, who had insulted him. The ronins petitioned the government to restore the confiscated estate of their dead lord, while the guilty overlord lived in affluent retirement. The ronins bound themselves in a plot to avenge their lord's death. It took two years to bring the plot to fruition, during which time some of them fell away and some turned traitor, while the enemy spied upon them. When the leader of the plot feigned drunkenness and profligacy the overlord relaxed his heavy guard, thinking that the ronins had lost their spirit. Then one night while it snowed they stormed the castle and captured its lord. Treating him with the utmost respect

* Anesaki uses the term *seppuku,* and refers to *harakiri* as "the vulgar term" (meaning colloquial). *JR,* p. 280.

and politeness, they explained the whole situation. Asking him to acknowledge the justness of their cause, they suggested that he atone by committing harakiri himself. Trembling and speechless, he could not act. Therefore the leader of the ronins attacked him and cut off his head with the very dagger which his lord had used to commit harakiri. Without further secrecy the ronins presented the enemy's severed head ceremoniously at their lord's grave and went about their business. They presented their case again to the government and "waited in noble calm the decision of the authorities."[16] The decision was that they, too, must commit harakiri. Forty-seven of them had stuck together to the very last, and all forty-seven committed harakiri by the prescribed ritual of self-disembowelment, rehearsed in imagination from childhood till death.

The sequel is still more important. The people of Yedo, following the course of events like modern newspaper readers of a sensational trial, were thrilled on hearing of the success of the ronins in January 1703. Soon the entire city was repeating the story. Later when the heroes were buried in the cemetery near their lord, the people crowded around the graves with flowers and incense and great mourning. Short stories and dramatizations became very popular, showing that the Samurai who lived the ideals of Bushido were the idols of Japan.

The fanaticism of Japan's soldiers in every recent war has become proverbial.* There is no doubt about the fact that this aspect of Bushido permeated the fighting forces and was approved by public opinion. Yet it also seems true that such fanaticism is a perversion of the original Bushido. The purpose of harakiri in original Bushido was to afford an honorable way out when the goals of the warrior were frustrated on an important assignment, especially when his own blundering was the cause.

As an element of the code of Bushido, vengeance seems rather far down the scale of cultural progress. Nor does honor, as they interpret it, seem a high ideal. Yet the selfless devotion of a vassal to his lord is a quality which commands our respect. The rest of the Bushido code, though less spectacular, is worthy of the most advanced culture. It certainly was not the cause of Japanese nationalism.

* "Kamikaze" pilots who gladly died in a suicidal bombing attack were following the Samurai ideal. "Kamikaze" means "divine wind."

Up to this point it has seemed right to eliminate each suspect as the specific root of Japanese nationalism and imperialism. It is easy enough to see how some of them may have contributed to the cause. This we may say of Bushido only to a slight degree, and of the professional military caste, the Samurai. It is also true in some degree of Zen Buddhism and Confucianism, both of which contributed to Samurai morale and purpose. Nichiren also played a part in the twentieth century. Christianity even played a part by complicating the cultural situation in the seventeenth century, and also more recently, leading to the Japanese reaction. In the seventeenth century this brought about Japanese isolation and the expulsion of western influences. Recently it led to a supreme effort to escape from the domination of western powers and western culture.

The one remaining suspect, of course, is Shinto. Does it end our search?

The Shinto Revival

I believe that too much importance has been attributed to Shinto as a cause of Japanese nationalism and imperialism. Nationalism is an outgrowth of the very natural sentiment of patriotism. The Shinto myths were an expression of the sentiment rather than the cause. Once created, of course, Shinto could thereafter be used to fan the nationalistic sentiment, or to justify imperialism. The latter happened when Hideyoshi sent troops to Korea and China and wrote an imperious note to the governor of the Philippines.*

Buddhism, by its universalistic tendencies, threatened to destroy Japanese nationalism by becoming the dominant religion of Japan and by modifying even the native Shinto. This was the occasion when patriotism led some to fight the universalistic tendency by stressing the principles of original Shinto. Since Buddhism had diluted old Shinto, they sought to restore "Pure Shinto" for the sake of Japan.

Shinto ideas were debated by Buddhist sects and others in the fourteenth century, while in the fifteenth some small progress was made in the organization of Shinto theology. In the syncretism of re-

* See p. 374.

ligion Shinto was declared to be the center by Chikafusa (1293-1354) and Kanera (or Kaneyoshi, 1402-1481). The many gods are, metaphysically speaking, really one, said Kanera. Said both, the imperial insignia symbolize the unity of divine virtues with the divine Japanese nation: the mirror is truth, the jewels are love or mercy, and the sword is justice. A Shinto nation must aim at the realization of these virtues. The destiny of Japan lies in communicating these virtues to mankind.[17] The element of enlightened nationalism in these two imperial courtiers became an inspiration to the later Shinto Revivalists. Nothing so significant as their work occurred again until the seventeenth and eighteenth centuries.

In the seventeenth century Keichu (1640-1701), a Buddhist monk, prepared for the Shinto revival by philological studies in the Manyoshu, written in archaic characters about the ninth century. Earlier in the same century the Confucian scholar, Soko, made an outstanding contribution to Bushido by systematizing its ethics.

In the eighteenth century Mabuchi (1697-1769), reading the archaic Japanese poetry, was fired by zeal for pure Japanese civilization as he conceived it to be before foreign influence corrupted it. Historical studies also were showing that the divine emperor should not be in second place in the nation. Mabuchi, thoroughly acquainted with early Shinto texts and with Chinese philosophy as well, attributed the decline of the emperor to the influence of Chinese thought. Yet he reflected the thinking of Lao Tzu in advocating the return of the emperor to simplicity of life and to direct rule. He also answered the charge that China had produced an ethics while Japan had none by saying that the Chinese needed one, while the Japanese are just naturally good and have no need of ethical philosophy.[18]

Motoöri Norinaga (1730-1801), a pupil of Mabuchi, seconded everything that his teacher had said and added more of his own. Some say that Motoöri was Japan's greatest scholar. A philologist and patriot, he wrote a truly significant commentary on the *Kojiki* and other ancient writings. He insisted that the primitive Japanese exemplified the pristine purity of human nature. They needed no Confucian system of ethics. Furthermore, the emperor was divine and divinely commissioned to rule. He denounced the Confucian doctrine that the emperor was to be obeyed only so long as he was a good ruler.[19] The divinely instituted Japanese state is superior to all others, and is destined to receive their homage and tribute, said he.

We may say that Motoöri's scholarship was well founded, but the superstructure was rather fanciful. By way of contrast his contemporary, Ichikawa Tatsumaro, was a rationalist who showed the absurdity of Japanese mythology as a serious basis for political or natural science. He wrote:

> The gods in heaven make no difference between races of mankind, who are formed into separate nations by the seas and mountain ranges which divide them off from each other, and the sun shines equally over all.[20]

Tatsumaro flatly denied the divinity of the Mikado and the Japanese people and asserted that if they were not descended from men, then they probably came from birds or beasts.

The third Pure Shinto Revivalist belongs primarily to the nineteenth century: Hirata Atsutane (1776-1843). An enthusiast for the system of Motoöri, he insisted that Shinto was pure knowledge, beyond which it was unnecessary to go. He was the most chauvinistic of all the revivalists, trying to apply his theory to concrete situations in religion, politics, and foreign affairs. His followers continued to do likewise. Unfortunately they seemed to be more numerous than the followers of Tatsumaro.

Shinto Sects

Playing a part in the Pure Shinto Revival were the sects which arose mostly in the nineteenth century. Some of the sects are prophetic in character, indicating a high degree of enlightenment. One such, which may be called Isson (apparently the same as Remmonkyo in Young's list[21]), "The Unique Reverend," was founded by a woman teacher, Kino (1756-1826). In 1802 this peasant servant received a revelation announcing her mission. Her message was to all mankind who were lost in sin and needed a savior. Her cosmology may have been influenced by the Kirishitan tradition which it resembled. Her way of life idealized simplicity, community of possessions, and faith in the founder. The sect had little in common with Shinto, but illustrates how the common Japanese peasants sought a more mature religious experience.

The Tenri Kyo is one of three "faith-healing sects," and is often referred to as the Christian Science of Japan. It, too, was founded by a woman, Miki (1798-1887). At first an Amida-Buddhist, she received in 1838 a revelation from the "Lord of Heaven" calling for the commitment of life and substance to the salvation of mankind. To be a worthy instrument of God one must be pure and merciful. She also practiced healing by faith. The sect was persecuted under both the shogunate and the emperor; nevertheless it grew. Like Isson, Tenri Kyo was universal in its outlook and prophesied the transformation of the world in the age that was soon to begin. Before 1867 people were longing for a new era, so Tenri Kyo was welcomed by many.

The third sect was founded by Kurozumi (1780-1850), a pious peasant who approached monotheism. His deity was the one exalted sun-goddess. Communion with her was the source of cosmic vitality, healing, and goodness. He taught his followers to face the sun and pray, inhaling deeply; good health would be sure to result. This sect revealed a closer connection than the first two with the Shinto tradition but, like them, interpreted religion in terms of piety and brotherhood.

The sects arising out of peasant experience and founded by peasant men and women are remarkable in that they have succeeded in freeing many ignorant people from the superstition of magic. "Their founders, despite their association with such dubious quasi-religious ideas and practices, gradually emerged out of them and transformed them into a purer faith verging on ethical theism. . . . Their popular theism amounts to a faith in one all-pervading life, a divine power to be realized in human life, the fundamental condition being to make oneself a receptacle of divinity by cleansing himself of all selfish motives and passions. . . . 'Brush away all the stains from the heart, then divine power will pour into it,' says Miki. 'To be of one heart with the Great Divinity is to live fully and forever,' says Kurozumi."[22]

Thirteen sects in all were recognized by the government of Meiji, some of which are less patently Shintoist than others. The thirteen sects may be classified in three groups: (1) Mountain sects, including Jikko, Fuso, and Ontake; (2) Popular Theism, including Kurozumi, Tenri, and Konko; (3) Churches with a political background and occult practices, including Honkyoku Shinto, Misogi, Shinri, Taishi, Shusei, Taisei, and Shinshu.[23] One writer divides the sects into five types, the first of which is classified as Pure Shinto, the second as Confucian, the third as Mountain, the fourth Purification, and the fifth Faith-healing.[24]

The three Mountain sects stress the divinity of certain mountains, or of the divinity dwelling therein. Two of them think Mount Fuji is the "soul of the earth," and pilgrims who climb its slopes feel closer to their god than anywhere else. These sects share with Shinto the belief that Japan is divine because its sacred land is filled with gods. This, of course, engenders or expresses patriotism and nationalism.

The Confucian sects of Shinto accept the elements of Shinto tradition, but add Confucian morality and common sense to these elements. Shusei and Taisei are the recognized Confucian sects.

Purification sects stressed the Shinto tradition of physical and spiritual purity, and may have been inspired by Buddhism. Some of their purification rites are reminiscent of Hindu practices, such as breath-control and walking on live coals. The Ten Precepts of Shinshu Kyo seem generally quite practical, though less than universal.[25]

The Pure Shinto sects attempt to interpret the old traditions in terms of present experiences. Shinri Kyo counsels piety toward gods, ancestors, and the state, and reminds one that fortune and health derive from divine sources. "Do not forget that the world is one great family," states another precept—no doubt referring to the destiny of Japan therein. Yet it is a precept which can be reinterpreted, like much of Shinto, in terms of human brotherhood.

The principal worth of the Shinto sects lies in their initiative in interpreting Japanese traditions. Most of them contain superstition, but so do other religions. The hopeful thing is that they also contain ideas which can be expanded to express universalism, leaving the primitive ideas by the wayside. A few educated prophets would help at the present time. Enlightened and sympathetic Christian missionaries would also help.

State Shinto

Had it not been for the action of the Meiji government making Shinto the official Japanese faith, sectarian Shinto might have evolved more rapidly than it did. But the new government saw the propaganda value of Shinto and acted thereon. With the state behind Shinto, powerful propaganda and a tax-supported system of shrines and priesthood tended to keep all Japanese in the groove of tradition.

The official doctrine that State Shinto was not a religion but merely a patriotic instrumentality was interpreted with skepticism. It was felt by impartial observers that State Shinto was introduced in this manner to counteract the inevitable influence of the Occident in reopening to it the gates of Japan. Christianity had to be tolerated, yet Shinto had to be the religion of all the Japanese. Therefore by the expedient of a simple definition, the new government tried to make Shinto compatible with any foreign religion. At the same time they hoped that Pure Shinto would make Japanese see the incompatibility of foreign faiths. It seems clear that the definition of State Shinto as secular was a ruse. Anesaki displays considerable embarrassment in trying to maintain the official doctrine.

One strong evidence that State Shinto was religious and not merely patriotic, was the part played in it by emperor-worship. Holtom[26] cites an outstanding Japanese authority on Shinto who insists that the emperor is regarded by Japanese as Jehovah is by the Jews. Obeisance before the imperial palace and, by school children, before the emperor's portraits were some of the customs established to insure emperor-worship.

Another evidence lies in the policy of requiring the schools to teach *saisei-itchi*—the "Way of the unity of religion and government."[27]

Now that the state has withdrawn support from the Shinto shrines, they are operated privately and supported by popular offerings. Meanwhile sectarian Shinto has a freer hand to develop its adaptations to modern needs. Yet there are clouds on this horizon, since sectarian Shinto, like "popular" Shinto, is declining among educated Japanese. Of course, as long as a large section of the

Japanese population remains unsophisticated, many of the old ideas will persist, such as the worship of local deities and fetishes. "Tree worship, phallicism, worship of the mountain and forest gods, are all parts of popular Shinto, to some or many features of which almost all Japanese, whether they are members of Shinto sects, Buddhists, or even Japanese Christians, subscribe. The practice of keeping 'god shelves' for the spirits of ancestors in every Japanese home, and making offerings to them, is within the realm of popular Shinto."[28] But with education comes skepticism. In a student poll at the University of Tokyo in 1920, it was learned that out of 4,618 who answered the questionnaire 2,989 declared themselves to be agnostics, while 1,511 listed themselves as atheists. Only 118 claimed that they believed in Christianity, Buddhism, or Shinto.[29] That is slightly more than 2 per cent.

In 1938 there were a hundred and ten thousand state shrines served by sixteen thousand priests. Many of these were simply unpainted archaic houses, in a natural woodland setting. The shrine was set off by a sacred fence and entered through a gate. The gate also is sacred and has great traditional significance. Following the path through the gate one comes to the outer shrine which contains the customary bell beneath its eaves. The worshiper now pauses to purify himself by washing hands and mouth. Then stepping forward he claps his hands to tell the gods he is there. He bows, rings the bell, bows again. Kneeling, with head to the floor, he worships, prays, places an offering, bows again in worship, and withdraws. Meanwhile he has not reached the inner shrine where the *shintai* or god-body (fetish) is housed. He knows it is there, and it makes him reverent as he pauses at a respectful distance. What is the god-object? Sometimes it is an image,[30] reminiscent of the Buddhist influence. But it is more likely to be the traditional mirror, sword, jewel, or scripture. Also mentioned are "an odd-shaped stone, a phallic emblem, a lock of human hair, or a paper wand . . . a living tree or even a mountain [outside] . . . a sanctuary."[31] Except for such *shintai* as a tree or mountain (perhaps also the image), the object is always covered several times, rarely moved, and then only by priests in religious festival.

Anesaki calls attention to the fact that Shinto shrines are everywhere, and are often maintained commercially. He pictures one which exists "on the roof garden of a modern department store, Shirokiya, in Tokyo. The same roof has another dedicated to Kwannon, long inherited by the Shirokiya family."[32]

There were just a few really great shrines, such as the one at Isé, dedicated to Amaterasu. It was the center of pilgrimage for most Japanese for centuries. It constituted an inner shrine connected by a long avenue of cryptomeria trees with an outer shrine dedicated to the Food-goddess—of great importance to any people. These shrines are also built of unpainted wood, with typical thatched roof, ridge planks, and jutting logs. In the inner sanctuary of Amaterasu were enshrined the imperial insignia, making this shrine especially important. Priests and state officials alone were allowed in the inner shrine. At times the emperor himself entered the inner shrine. The outer shrine of the Food-goddess was open to all. Now that state shrines are no longer official, there is no distinction between them and sectarian holy places.

One of the holy places to most Japanese is the god-shelf in each home, where objects of sacred import are kept. The degree of enlightenment determines the nature of those objects and their interpretation. The institution of the god-shelf takes on an aesthetic quality for many who are too enlightened to share the naive fetishism of primitive Shinto.

Typical of Shinto worship is the experience of a Japanese woman whose husband became a Christian. She herself found Christianity unsatisfying, so she returned to her old practices. Whenever she feels the need of inward strengthening she goes down the street to the little shrine, walks along its shaded path, passes through the gate, purifies her hands and mouth with holy water, claps her hands, rings the bell, and kneels and prays. When she receives the needed peace and strength, acquired no doubt through the intuition that the spirit or spirits of Japan are with her, she returns to her work.*

Aside from individual worship, the main use of the sectarian shrine is in connection with its festivals. These are colorful occasions which historically have given rise to Japanese art forms.

One accompaniment of traditional Shinto festivals has been the Kagura, a pantomimic dance. It is "performed at this day to the

* This story was told by a Fulbright Fellow who lived at her house, Professor Harold Wren, then of the University of Mississippi.

sound of fife and drum at Shinto festivals, on a platform provided for the purpose. The antiquity of the Kagura may be inferred from the fact that when the *Kojiki* (A.D. 712) and the *Nihongi* (A.D. 720) were written, there was already a myth current which was intended as an explanation of its origin."[33] The myth referred to was that of the fantastic dance performed by the Terrible Female of Heaven as she stood on an inverted tub outside the cave where the sun-goddess was hiding. The infernal noise and mimicry brought her out as desired.

Growing out of the Kagura about five centuries ago was the No, a libretto for dialogue to be spoken with the dance. In its origin it was religious, and probably was written for the most part by Buddhist monks for the purpose of arousing piety. Typical themes developed by some of the best examples of the No are patriotism, nature's beauty, hospitality to priests, the sin of killing, the uncertainty of life, glorification of some deity, and any of the Japanese or Buddhist myths. After a time the No developed independence of the religious festivals. They ceased to be written after the sixteenth century, but are still performed to select audiences.[34]

Prospect and Evaluation

When Christian missions returned to Japan last century they met with much official opposition and with popular reception. Gradually the official attitude changed, with diplomatic pressure, and the device was adopted of making State Shinto a required ritual, secular by definition.

The Kirishitan mission was, of course, Roman Catholic. Since the return of the West, Christian missions have been predominantly Protestant. The 1953 census showed 171,785 Roman Catholics, 32,889 Greek Orthodox, 32,000 Episcopalians, and 167,407 members of the United Church of Christ. Since the victory of the democracies in the last war Japan appears to have gained a new respect for western culture. Christian opportunity today is great. Its reinforcement of the principles of individual freedom and responsibility is most strategic in Japan today.

Where does this place Japanese religious tradition? What value shall we place upon its past, and what of its future? Certainly Pure Shinto in the naive traditional sense can have no future as Japan goes forward in cultural maturity. With the initiative regained by sectarian Shinto today, however, it seems entirely possible that the universal elements, which have been noted in passing, may be reinterpreted and emphasized. Those Japanese who are not able to embrace a foreign religion may find joy and peace as enlightened human beings through such an approach. The resources of Buddhism and Confucianism in Japanese culture may be added to those of Shinto.

As we think back over the religious history of Japan, in terms of our criteria of maturity, certain judgments appear necessary. First, magic is the essence of primitive Shinto. Second, the highly imaginative mythology of early Shinto, while assuming a magical cosmology, is non-committal as to whether the myths are to be regarded as literal or as symbolic. Historically they came to be regarded literally, the Emperor being conceived of as having descended biologically from the sun-goddess. Such literal interpretations committed a nation to a cosmology and a social science at variance with the truths of nature and human society.

Despite its limitations, Shinto and its accretions from Buddhism and Confucianism developed respectable forms for the expression of human aspiration, as in Bushido and in the Shinto sects. Universality was in the realm of the possible in the evolution of Japanese religion, and still is.

In any case, our hope for Japan is that their deepest commitments will always be to the universal in human nature, and to the divine as revealed therein. Japan was by accident brought into the current of world wars. She sought to be left alone, but we insisted on contact. Perhaps our insistence was wise in a sense, for no people can live long to themselves. But the point is that Japan must not permanently be branded as an intrinsically warlike nation. The outlook of peace and brotherhood is there today.

PART FIVE

Zoroastrianism

XXV. ZOROASTER, PROPHET OF IRAN

AMONG THE WORLD'S GREAT LIVING RELIGIONS, Parsiism is numerically the smallest of all. With few more than one hundred thousand refugee survivors in India today, and eighteen thousand still remaining in Muslim Iran, its numbers are insignificant. And yet historically Parsiism, or Zoroastrianism as it is better known, is of great importance. Judaism and Christianity are heirs to some of its ideas. No complete Christian philosophy can be adequately formed without considering the relation between these three religions.

Since Zoroaster was a prophet aiming at the reformation of the traditional Persian religion, it is well to look briefly at what Zoroaster inherited before we consider his reformation. First of all let us look at the land and its people.

Ancient Iran

Iran is the modern—and ancient—name of the land traditionally called Persia. The Ionian Greeks formed the word *Persai,* referring to the inhabitants of Parsa (Fars) in southwestern Iran. Since the time of Cyrus II the Great, when the Persians gained control of Iran and the Near East, all Iran has been popularly called Persia. The name officially became Iran (Aryan Land) in 1935, as it had been of old.

Modern Iran has virtually the same boundaries as did ancient Iran, consisting of the high plateau between the Mesopotamian valleys on the west, the Indus River (now in Pakistan) and Afghanistan on the east, the Persian Gulf on the south, and the Caspian Sea and Russia on the north.

Prehistoric Iran is comparable with prehistoric Mesopotamia, which was touched upon in Chapter IV. The discovery of *homo sapiens* in the fossil remains of Hotu Cave near the Caspian Sea recently gave rise to the theory that the cradle of modern man is in Iran. Professor Carleton Coon of the University Museum, the University of Pennsylvania, is inclined to date his fossils at about 75,000 B.C.[1] Thus in Iran there lived, as contemporaries of the less advanced Neandertal Man of western Europe, a race which was comparable in bone and brain structure with Cro-Magnon man later in France and Spain. These Iranians were hunters of the Old Stone Age, and were perhaps the first human beings to engage in agriculture and to settle in village communities. Villages have been discovered, dating perhaps from 5000 B.C., which were too large to be supported except by agriculture. Susa was founded about 4000 B.C.

In these labyrinthine villages of stamped-earthen buildings were found objects which were probably used in worship, such as the usual "mother-goddess," and a demonic humanoid figure. In proper order is found the normal cultural cycle here as elsewhere: Paleolithic, Neolithic, Chalcolithic, Bronze, and Iron Ages. The Chalcolithic Era began sometime during the fifth millenium and the Bronze about 2200 B.C.

The coming of the Aryans—or Aryan-speaking peoples—about the fifteenth century was soon followed by evidences of Iron Age culture. The earliest migrant Aryans are believed to have continued moving, some to the west and others to the southeast. Hittite inscriptions reveal their presence in Asia Minor about 1400 B.C., and in India about the same time or earlier. Other Aryans stayed in Iran, to cultivate traditions similar to those of their cousins east and west.

Two of the tribes to settle in Iran were the Medes, in the Northwest, and the Persians, or dwellers in Parsa, in the southwest. The Medes, long subject to Assyrian control, joined with Babylon to destroy Nineveh in 612 B.C. But in 550 Cyrus II, known as Cyrus the Great, King of Persia (Parsua), captured Ecbatana (Hamadan), the Median capital, and dethroned its king. Cyrus was a descendant of Achaemenes, founder of the Achaemenid dynasty (c. 700 B.C.). He proceeded to conquer Babylon and the west as far as Asia Minor, and to bring all Iran under his control. Cyrus reigned c. 559-530 B.C., and Cambyses 530-522. So great were the successes of the Persian kings that the whole land of Iran came to be known as Persia.

Succession troubles arose in 522 B.C., and rebellion broke out in the subjugated provinces. At this juncture Darius I the Great, 522-486, representing a collateral line, became king and saved the empire from collapse. Darius was a Zoroastrian, as can be seen from his inscriptions on the Rock of Behistun. Furthermore, his father's name was Vishtaspa (Greek, Hystaspes), and that is the name of the king whom Zoroaster is said to have converted. Was he the same king?

Since our main source of information from here on will be the Zoroastrian sacred writings, let us pause to describe them.

Zoroastrian Scriptures

The original writings of Zoroastrianism are called the Avesta. The word Avesta is asserted by one author to mean "original text," while another conjectures that it meant "knowledge"[2]—thus making it cognate with Veda and wissen.

Another term, the Zend-Avesta, is used to refer to the Avesta plus its commentaries or interpretations in later centuries. "Zend" means "interpretation."

The original Avesta, as we now have it, consists of five principal parts, besides fragments of the much larger part of the lost Avesta. Of the five parts only one is complete. Tradition has it that the rest was destroyed by Alexander the Great.

The Avesta was written in what is called Avestan, in different stages of development. Its most archaic form, found in the Gathas and some of the Yashts, is very closely akin to the archaic Sanskrit in which the Vedas are written. The "interpretations" which were added later are written in a modified Old Persian.

As the language of the people evolved, the Old Persian of the Avesta became largely unintelligible. Therefore the priests of Zoroastrianism made a new version in the language of their day, the Pahlavi. This was accomplished in the fourth to sixth centuries A.D. Sometimes the new version was a loose paraphrase of the original, while at other times explanatory comments were inserted.

In the course of the next few centuries there arose an extensive literature, in Pahlavi, dealing with topics arising out of the Avesta and the religious experiences of the Zoroastrians. These writings may also be regarded as a part of the Zoroastrian sacred literature. Much of the Pahlavi literature was in turn lost or destroyed by the Muhammadans. Some was saved by being carried by the Parsi refugees to India.

A summary of the important Zoroastrian scriptures follows.

(1) The Yasna is a liturgical book from which the Zoroastrian priests read while celebrating the Yasna ritual, honoring all the deities whom the later Zoroastrians recognized as such—a digression from Zoroaster's monotheism, as we shall see. The introductory chapters (1-27) are mostly invocations of the deities, although some of these are Yashts or "hymns of praise," such as those to Haoma (9 and 11). One (Chapter 12) is a summary statement of the ancient Zoroastrian creed, no doubt repeated from very early times. In the concluding chapters of the Yasna are found "the prayer to fire (62), and the great liturgy for the sacrifice to divinities of the water (63-69)."[3]

(2) The Gathas form the central part (28-54) of the Yasna. They are far too important to be regarded as subordinate to it. If Zoroaster wrote any part of the Avesta, it was certainly those Gathas in particular which are written in archaic Avestan. They do not reflect the ritualism of a later time, but are concerned with praising Mazda alone, setting forth the nature of the universal struggle between good and evil. The Gathas are arranged in five groups according to the meters used.

(3) The Vispered may best be understood as a kind of liturgical appendix to the Yasna. Its name means "all the lords," and refers to the heavenly beings who are addressed.

(4) The Vendidad is a priestly code of ritual purifications and taboos, in which the Parsi cosmology and way of life are detailed.

(5) The Yashts, or "hymns of praise," are similar to those found in the Yasna. Some of them are very old, and constitute an excellent source of Iranian mythology and legend. They are like the Rig Veda in Hinduism. "The most important of all, the nineteenth Yasht, gives a consecutive account of the Iranian heroic saga in great broad lines, together with a prophetic presentment of the end of this world."[4]

(6) The Khordah Avesta, or "little Avesta," consists of short prayers for the use of laymen and priests alike in meeting the problems of living.

After the Middle Persian or Pahlavi version of the Avesta was made, men of the Sassanian Period (229-651 A.D.) and later, produced supplementary works in Pahlavi, the most important of which are: (1) the Bundahish, treating of cosmology, mythology, legend and history; (2) the Dinkard, detailing certain matters of tradition, custom, history, literature, and doctrine; (3) miscellaneous works like a catechism, an apologetic, letters and essays, a collection of laws and customs regarding sin and impurity, and mystic literature describing supernatural visions. Some of this literature—perhaps most of it—was composed as late as the ninth century A.D.

Iranian Religion before Zoroaster

Almost all that we know about Iranian religion before Zoroaster comes from references to it in the Avesta. These allusions are always prejudiced, even though much of the earlier religion crept back into the later Avesta. The inscriptions of the Achaemenid dynasty, soon after Zoroaster's day, add nothing except to confirm the data gleaned from the Avesta.

The ancient Iranians were polytheists at the time of Zoroaster's birth. It has been noted that many of their gods formed a common heritage among the Indo-Aryan peoples, but that the Iranian mythology underwent a unique development. A few examples follow:

The word "deva," common to the Indo-Aryans, took on opposite meanings in the two groups. To the Hindus the "devas" were "shining ones," divine beings worthy of worship. Before Zoroaster the Iranians also worshiped the devas, but Zoroaster's teachings reversed this, making them devils, or demons. In English we use the word in both senses (devil and divine).

The god Indra underwent similar change before Zoroaster. Known to the Iranians as Indara, Intar, or Andar, he changed from a beneficent rain god into a mischief-maker, a special creature of the Lie Demon. In most cultures the storm god is pictured as a mischief-maker.

In reverse fashion, in India the "asuras" were viewed as demons, whereas in Iran the "ahuras" (same word) were thought to be gods.

An almost identical myth is shared by the Iranians and Hindus, namely the myth of the first man. Called Yama in India, he was known as Yima in Iran. Being the first man to live, he was also the first to die. Thus in both cultures he became the god (or king) of the dead, presiding over the destinies of Hades.

Among the Iranian deities one of the greatest was Mithra, god of light. "Like the Indian Mitra, he was first and foremost the god of loyalty (*mitra* means 'a treaty')."[5] But he was also the god of war

> to whom the princes pray when they go forth to battle against the bloodthirsty hosts of the enemy, those who gather themselves together in battle array. . . .[6]

Against the evil hordes of deceivers, men of bad faith, Mithra causes that

> the steeds of the deceivers refuse to bear their riders; though they ride they make no progress, though they ride in their chariots they gain no advantage; backward flies the lance hurled by the enemy of Mithro. Even if the enemy throw skillfully, even if his lance reach his enemy's body, the stroke does not hurt. The lance from the hand of Mithro's enemy is borne away by the wind.[7]

The Iranian Mithra was shared, as Mitra, with the Hindus and as Miidraashshiill with the Aryan Hittites and Mitanni of Asia Minor. He was the Mithras of Mithraism, the mystery religion which rivaled Christianity in the Roman Empire. The Romans thought he was a sun god.

A strange thing occurred in the career of the heavenly twins, the Nasatya or Asvins, called Nashaadtianna in the Hittite inscription. The Iranians reduced them to a single god and regarded him as demonic.

But the case of Ahura Mazda was still different. "Ahura Mazda" is thought to mean "lord of light." Since light is a symbol of knowledge, he may also be thought of as "lord of knowledge." This was a descriptive term which the Iranians applied to the god whom the Indians called Varuna and the Hittites called Uruwanaashshiel.[8] The same god the Greeks called Ouranos, god of "heaven." The original name was lost by the Iranians, who called him by the more descriptive term. Zoroaster's clan regarded him as its special god, and Zoroaster exalted him to monotheistic status.

Another god, Haoma, was the same as the Indian Soma, and was worshiped by both groups originally. Haoma was an intoxicating juice pressed from the stems of a plant belonging to the genus Ephedra.[9] At times reverence was expressed toward the beverage itself, conceived as divine because intoxicating, i.e. god-filling. This impersonal power was at other times conceived as personal. Zoroaster prohibited the worship of Haoma, although it returned later like many other things. Today haoma is produced ritually by Parsi priests, but laymen no longer "take the cup." That is reserved for the priests.

There is evidence, supported by Greek writers, that the primitive Iranians revered fire, earth, water, and animals. The Greeks tell us that the Persians offered their animal sacrifices by laying them on soft grass or clover, and that the priests sprinkled haoma juice on the grass surrounding the sacrifice and touched the votive flesh with thin "rods," sturdy twigs conveying the magic of trees. The Avesta reveals also the later use of twigs in the sacrifice. All of this is evidence that the elements of nature were regarded with reverence. The Zend Avesta clearly supports this view, as we shall see.

Ancestor worship was also practiced in early Iran. The primitive concept of the *fravashi* reveals this. Possibly the presence of ancestral *fravashi* in the objects of nature was what made them awe-inspiring. The *fravashi* later came to mean guardian spirits, or the ideal essence of one's personality, possessed by both men and gods. But at first they were simply the "fathers," or their guardian spirits guiding and protecting but expecting reverence in return. It is noteworthy that the Iranian concept of *fravashi* is closely akin to the Roman "genius."

Fire worship was another aspect of primitive Iranian—and Indian—religion. Special priests in both cultures—called Atharvan in India and Athravan in Iran—were responsible for attending the sacred fire.[10] Zoroaster prohibited its worship, but reinterpreted it as a symbol of deity. He is said to have been officiating at the sacred fire when he was assassinated. The Parsis of India today keep fires burning continually in rooms especially reserved for that purpose. Five times daily, with prayers and other rites, the fire is replenished with incense and sandalwood. A modern Parsi daubs his forehead with ashes as he leaves the fire.

The early Iranians also had the concept of Asha, or Arta, corresponding to the Rita of the Vedas. Rita survives in our English word "right." Like Asha, it referred to the truth and justice which seemed to them to be the basis of order, in nature as in the great society of men and gods.

Ancient Iran was overburdened with a priesthood too numerous to support in a hard land. The Magi, a Median tribe, was just one of the groups of priests who for some time opposed the new religion. Not only were the priests unproductive, but also they were a stubborn force standing in the way of progress. Or so it seemed to Zoroaster, whose life now becomes our interest.

Early Life of Zoroaster

The name Zoroaster, as used in the English language, is derived from the Greek and Latin form. The other form, Zarathustra, is more nearly like the Avestan. Except in quotation I shall follow the English custom.

Zoroaster is a name compounded of two words. The latter part of the Avestan form means camel: "ustra." The first part, "Zar," is obscure. The compound word may mean "One whose camels are old (or fierce)."[11]

Another name, sometimes combined with Zoroaster and sometimes used alone, is Spitama. This seems to be his family or clan name, meaning "of the Whites." So "Zoroaster" was probably meant to be some kind of camel operator belonging to the White family. Later Zoroastrian tradition traces his ancestry to an ancient royal line and ultimately to the Iranian Adam. According to tradition also he had four brothers, three wives, and several sons and daughters.

The dates of Zoroaster are still controversial. Those who favor an early date, such as 6000 B.C., were apparently misled by a simple confusion in the Dinkard, which referred not to his birth in the flesh but to his preexistent spiritual body. The suggestion of 1000 or 900 is just slightly more conservative. The dates most generally accepted until recently were 660-583, ably defended by Jackson.[12] But the most reasonable dates seem to be 570-493, as supported by Finegan.[13] All the circumstantial evidence fits together beautifully in this theory, and identifies Vishtaspa (Hystaspes), father of Darius the Great, as the Vishtaspa whom Zoroaster converted.

If Zoroaster was born 570 B.C., that rules out the possibility that Cyrus the Great, conqueror of Babylon and liberator of the captive Jews, was a Zoroastrian, as has often been assumed. There is no mention of Ahura Mazda or Zoroaster in his inscriptions, nor do any of the ancient writers state that he was a Zoroastrian. Since Zoroaster did not begin to preach until the age of thirty, and had only one convert after ten years—his own cousin—this would bring us down to 530. But Cyrus had already taken Babylon in 540 or 539 and died in 530 or 529. Cyrus' statesmanlike treatment of Jews can easily be accounted for without resorting to his alleged Zoroastrianism. Nor did he favor the monotheistic Jews any more than he did the polytheistic Babylonians. Instead of displaying the conqueror's usual vengeance wherever he was victorious, he granted political and cultural autonomy and retained local statesmen in his newly organized government. On the cylinder recording his conquests we see reflected his statesmanlike policy in that Babylon is said to have fallen "without a battle and without fighting." "He came as a deliverer rather than a conqueror, and accepted the throne as a gift of Marduk."[14] This surely does not reflect Zoroastrianism.

Zoroaster's birthplace was probably in the neighborhood of Azerbaijan, near Lake Urmia west of the southern part of the Caspian Sea. This was near the Median stronghold in northwestern Iran. His missionary journeys seem to have taken him to northeastern Iran, to the court of Vishtaspa at Balkh in Bactria. He traveled elsewhere in Iran, but certainly did not carry his gospel to distant lands like India and Tibet, as tradition asserts.

The scriptures of Zoroastrianism assert that predictions were made of the coming of a great prophet. This occurs in the Avestan Gathas (Yasna 29:8) as well as in the less restrained Pahlavi texts.[15] Taking the two sources together we learn about the royal-priestly Glory which was to be combined with the fravashi and the body of the prophet to form a threefold perfect nature. The Glory even descended upon his mother prior to her own birth (the "immaculate conception"), and remained with her for fifteen years until Zoroaster was born (a young mother!). The mother's womb was sanctified, and other miracles attended pregnancy and birth. For example, Zoroaster's body was not composed of sinful sex-made substance, but of plants that entered into virgin cows and became milk which Zoroaster's parents drank. This pure, uncontaminated substance became the material part of Zoroaster. Demons were continually plotting to prevent the prophet's birth and health, never ceasing until his death. At his birth all nature thrilled; "a divine light shone round the house; and a shout of joy arose when life triumphed." The infant babe laughed aloud at his birth, for the Lie Demon had been confounded. His birth was in answer to his father's prayer to Haoma.

Then sorcerers and messengers of the Lie Demon plotted to destroy the child. Once he was suckled by a lamb, unharmed in a wolf's den. The Pharaohs and Herods of Iran failed to effect his death. Instead the child grew and at the age of seven pointed out the errors of the mighty priests, like Christ in the temple.[16]

There is very little real history in all this. But without a recorded history of the times to rely on, we may infer from chance allusions in the Gathas and the Texts that the times were bad. There was devil-worship, wolves were abroad, slaughter and abuse of cattle were common, and people were deceitful, dishonest, impure and immoral. There was plenty of work for a prophet to do. Zoroaster came of age at fifteen by donning the sacred girdle, which put a temporary end to the black magic.[17]

Then followed fifteen years of preparation. There is evidence that he attained such education as the times allowed. More importantly, his character matured in manly traits. He practiced generosity—like giving away fodder in times of famine—and showed sympathy for all. At twenty he wandered in search of opportunities to serve. There is a tradition that he spent seven years silently in a mountain retreat, where God's glory was felt in the lightning, the sunshine, the stars and the dew. There he worked out his system and plan.

Zoroaster's Mission

At thirty came the climax, in the form of his first visions. The Archangel Vohu Manah (Good Thought) ushered him into the presence of Ahura Mazda himself. So surrounded was he by effulgent beings that, as he noticed, he cast no shadow. This does not seem so strange, since it was his soul, or spiritual body, which had come into the presence of Ahura Mazda. What happened to his body when his soul was in the presence of Mazda is not explained. Presumably it was fixed in a trance. The vision was three times repeated the same day.

After his first great vision, wandering about like a dervish, Zoroaster sought to convert all who would hear. He tried to win to his cause the ruling heretical priests, telling them to worship only Ahura Mazda and his angels, and to give up demon-worship. But the priests were incredulous and hell-bent. As we read in the Gathas,

> The Kavis and the Karpans have united themselves with power
> For destroying the life of man by their evil deeds;
> But their own soul and their religion will make them howl
> When they come where the Bridge of the Accountant hereafter is,
> To be inmates for ever and ever in the House of Falsehood
> (i.e. Hell)![18]

Elsewhere in the Gathas we find terrible curses upon all rich and proud unbelievers, who certainly included the reigning priests.

Tradition takes the prophet even into Turan, land of a Mongoloid people. If he did have any success there, which is doubtful, he certainly had none in Iran. Discouraged, the prophet turned homeward.

Then came more visions, two years after the first one. But none was quite the equal of the first. The other six visions seem like ordinary reasoning compared with the poetry of the first. In the second vision Archangel Good Thought (Vohu Manah), in individual conference, counsels him to care for the useful animals. The third vision enjoins the care of the sacred fire, and of all fires, sacred and secular. The Archangel Asha Vahishta, or Best Rightness, was the counsellor in this vision. The other four visions were conferencess with the archangels Khshathra Vairya (Desired Dominion), Spenta Armaiti (Holy Piety), Haurvatat (Welfare), and Ameretat (Immortality), respectively. The burden of their several counsels was the care of metals, the making of boundaries and settlements, the care and reverential use of water, and the proper treatment of plants. There were other unclassified visions, such as the earliest of all, revealing a great army to support him, with his cousin at its head;[19] and another in which he saw Haoma rising out of the sacrifice on the altar.[20] Certainly no other saint or prophet can claim more dramatic visions than Zoroaster.

But after the visions came the temptation. Ten years of visions might be expected to make a man too good to have temptations. Well, Zoroaster was good enough and great enough to withstand the temptations. But he gained his strength, it is said, by concentrating on the law and repeating the creed made famous by his religion. The Lie Demon offered him a worldly kingdom if he would renounce Ahura Mazda. Zoroaster's insight was too keen for Ahriman. In another temptation even a false priest was made to seem alluring, but again Ahriman's deceit was recognized and the good triumphed. Then as a reward for his steadfastness the prophet gained his first convert, his cousin Medyomah (Maidhyo-maungha), the object of the prophet's earliest vision.[21]

At one place the prophet is found complaining that he had preached for ten years, finally gaining only one convert. But instead of remaining discouraged he raised his sights, and determined to visit the court of Vishtaspa. No doubt there was much basis for the story that the king's court suffered from an atmosphere of magic and superstition, controlled by scheming Karpans (priests). It was Zoroaster's task to challenge their authority.

There is a legend that Zoroaster met two kings on his way to Vishtaspa's court. He sought to convert them, but they were unbelieving. So like Elijah he prayed to God and God destroyed the kings, but in a most unusual manner. He sent a great wind which lifted them into the air, suspending them there while vultures ate their flesh until finally their bones dropped to the ground. This seems out of character for Zoroaster.

At Vishtaspa's court the priests connived against him, led by the evil Zak, even planting false evidence against him in his room. He was jailed. But then the king's black horse suddenly lost the use of its legs. This seemed the judgment of God. Zoroaster then sent word that he would restore the animal if the king would grant a boon for each leg. When this was agreed to, the king accepted the new faith when one leg was restored; he consecrated his own son as a crusader when the second leg became normal; the privilege of converting the queen was granted for the third leg, and this was accomplished; for the fourth, the names of the plotters against the prophet were revealed, and they were properly punished.

We may gather from such legends the underlying historical reality that Zoroaster did go to Vishtaspa's court, that he encountered opposition from a superstitious and entrenched priesthood, and that he won the king to his reformed faith. After that the queen and the court followed his example. The king turned out to be the prophet's most important convert not only on account of his example, but also because he was zealous in supporting the propagation of the faith. If he was the father of Darius the Great, as I believe, then it seems that much of the success of the conqueror may have been due to his having inherited from his father the new faith when it was freshest and most inspiring. For Zoroastrianism was a nationalistic and a militant faith.

The success of a prophet depends in part on how ready his people are for his message. In Zoroaster's case it seems that the country had long felt the need of his message in certain respects. They needed to rid themselves of the burden of animal sacrifices. They were oppressed by priest-encouraged superstitions regarding magic, demonism, luck, and ritualism. And they needed a vision of their cultural integrity and national destiny. Spurred by the example of a king and his court, the people also responded. Seistan in southeast Iran was noted for its early converts to the faith. Not all of Iran could be reached at once, but in the course of some years practically all of Iran professed faith in the reformed religion.

Zoroaster was perhaps forty-five when he felt that his work at Balkh was finished. He then turned to more wandering. In the course of his preaching mission one legend tells how at one time he healed a blind man by dropping the juice of a plant into his eye. This story may at least indicate that his intentions were practical. He earned a reputation for scientific knowledge, as even the Greeks believed.[22] His Gathas reflect a high regard for wisdom and for common sense living.

As the high priest of the new faith, Zoroaster founded temples in many places, and carried the sacred fire from one to the other, symbolizing the eternal presence and inspiration of the true God in their midst.

But the most spectacular results of Zoroaster's preaching lay in the inspiration of morale which he breathed into his countrymen, moving them to resist the Turanian oppressors from the north. These nomads raided the well-cultivated fields of the peaceful and industrious Bactrians, taking from them the produce which they desired and destroying much else. In addition they exacted tribute from the king of Bactria, who at this time was Vishtaspa. This story forms the introduction to the following chapter.

XXVI. DESTINY AND DECAY OF ZOROASTRIANISM

Opposition to the new faith was like the anvil on which the sword was forged. What could be better proof of the truth of the doctrine than that the evil ones lined up against it? The jealous priests of the old religion, within Iran, were aided by foreigners without. Tradition is supported by the Gathas in witnessing to the conflict which developed into violent fury between Bactria and Turan. The leader of the Turanians is referred to as King Arjasp, or Arejat-aspa. We know that Bactria had been paying tribute for some time to these raiding nomads, whose primitive religion Zoroaster had denounced. The new faith had given such morale to the Bactrians that they now dared to withhold tribute and shout defiance at their Mongoloid neighbors. When the messenger of war arrived at Vishtaspa's court in Balkh he cited the withholding of tribute as a *casus belli*. But there was far more to it than that. It was that two ways of life were in deadly conflict—the way of peace, agriculture, and industry as over against the way of the restless nomads, parasites on the good community. Both groups knew the issues involved. The thing that moved the peace-loving Bactrians to fight, however, was the fire of a new faith, the inspired conviction that God was on the side of law and civilization, and that war was better than enslavement to uncivilized tyranny.

The Holy War

On two occasions Turan invaded Iranian Bactria, aiming at the capital city of Balkh. Each time the Iranians responded to the call to arms with religious fervor. There seemed no doubt on their part but that the infidel Turanians were strictly allied with the Lie Demon and all his helpers. Zoroaster himself is said to have taken a commanding part, along with Vishtaspa's son, in directing the defense of Balkh. The enemy's fury was fast and devastating, forcing the Bactrians to fall back. But after initial defeats the Zoroastrians were victorious. So holy was their cause that their strength was increased supernaturally. One warrior is said to have killed ten infidels every time his sword struck down, and eleven every time he drew it back. Tradition states that in the first war 100,000 of the enemy were slain and 30,000 Iranians. This is probably an exaggeration, but gives some idea of the spirit of the war.

The second war repeated the pattern of the first. The Turanians invaded and won early successes. But there was the factor of morale on the side of the Iranians, this time as before. As they surged back to victory they carried the fighting into the enemy's territory, captured its king and executed him. The spirit of the Iranians, once aroused, was far more invincible than the enemy had dreamed.

The first Iranian victory had established Zoroastrianism as a national force. The second victory set it on its course of destiny. Already the Iranian Medes had teamed up to destroy Nineveh in 612 B.C., and Cyrus II the Great, king of the Persians, c. 540 B.C., captured Babylon after first having conquered Media. Thereafter he united all of Iran under the Persians at just about the time when Zoroaster was winning his auspicious convert, King Vishtaspa. The stage was thus being set for Persian destiny.

Unfortunately Zoroaster lost his life in the second Turanian war. He is said to have been assassinated in the opening year of the war, while the Turanians were enjoying their short-lived success. Tradition insists that Zoroaster died by the hand of a Turanian, and that at the time he was officiating before the sacred fire in the temple at Balkh. If this was the way it happened, it is no wonder that the faithful fought with supernatural strength to avenge their holy prophet.

Subsequently Iran went through an age of glory, followed by decay within and finally conquest from without. Zoroaster died when he was seventy-seven years old. If our reckoning is correct this was in the year 493 B.C. At that rate, Vishtaspa had died about seven years before Zoroaster. But Vishtaspa's son Isfendiyad, or Isfendiar, or Asfandiyar (i.e. Darius the Great), had become king in 522, about six years after Vishtaspa's conversion. Darius, coming to the throne of Persia when the Iranian provinces were revolting, saved the empire from collapse and moved in conquest across Asia Minor into Greece proper. He was defeated at Marathon in 490, and his son Xerxes was defeated by the Greeks at Salamis in 480. Darius in his inscriptions shows himself to be a fervent Zoroastrian, a worshiper of Ahura Mazda and a follower of the prophet. The same was true of Xerxes, who succeeded Darius in 486, and of Artaxerxes who succeeded to the Persian throne in 465. Before the fifth century was over, the descendants of Darius I the Great were introducing the worship of strange gods and images.

Then in 331 B.C. Alexander the Great conquered Persia and introduced Hellenism. Although the Zoroastrians hated the Greek conqueror, yet they were inevitably influenced by Greek ideas. And Alexander's conquest was after all a kind of delayed response to the attempted conquest of Greece by Darius and Xerxes a century and a half earlier. The Seleucid (Greek) rule of Persia began to break up about 250 B.C. It was followed by the native rule of the Parthians, during which there was still no cultural freedom from Hellenism. The Sassanian period however (c. 229 A.D.-651 A.D.) was more anti-Hellenistic, and saw a revival of Zoroastrianism. It was during the Sassanian period that the Pahlavi version and texts were written.

Then came Islam and the gradual end of Zoroastrianism, except for a few thousand brave souls who stayed and endured persecution while most of their brethren migrated to India. Today in India there are few more than 100,000 Parsis.

Original Teachings of Zoroaster

It has often been noted how much more optimistic and nationalistic the Iranians were than their Indo-Aryan cousins. Some have attributed this difference to climate, since India was hot, humid, and enervating whereas Iran was a climate of extremes—hot in summer and very cold in winter. This theory is incapable of proof. Furthermore we must not neglect the causative influence of a great personality who aroused in his countrymen enough morale to defy Turan, unify Iran, and conquer the entire Near East. This difference between the Iranians and the Hindus is worthy of note, but its explanation is primarily personal or spiritual.

The greatness of Zoroaster's teaching, in the background of his times, is most remarkable. In the midst of polytheism, animism and magic, Zoroaster asserted the doctrine of monotheism; he insisted that religion was essentially based on moral principles rather than magical rites, and that the cosmic order held man responsible for his acts; he denied that God's power was either arbitrary or infinite; and he emphasized the goals of the good society. It is not necessary to maintain that Zoroaster was completely consistent in all of these respects. Consistency is hard to find even among our present-day enlightened thinkers. Zoroaster's greatness is rather to be found in the greatness of the ideas which he created with little help from his environment.

Light and fire combined as the symbol of Mazda's purity, knowledge, and goodness.

Personally humble, like all great prophets, Zoroaster attributed his notable ideas not to his own inventiveness but to revelation from the one true God, whom he called Ahura Mazda. Even the name, descriptive of his God, means "lord of light," that is "lord of knowledge." Descriptive originally of the Aryan sky-god, Varuna or Ouranos, Zoroaster proposed a completely spiritualized concept of the one God. Ahura Mazda, contracted later to Ormuzd or Ormazd, was conceived to be a God whose brilliance informs the intellect while it quickens the will.

So when Zoroaster had his first great vision, it was introduced by Good Thought, or "Archangel Vohu Manah." This may be interpreted allegorically to mean that visions really come to people who prepare for them by sincere, courageous and progressive ("good") thinking. In no other way can creative, intellectual discovery take place. At the very time when the vision takes place, it may come without effort and seem like a free revelation. But people do not receive such revelations unless they have prepared for them by struggling with the issues involved, and making a sincere effort to dispose of them satisfactorily.

Some have suggested that the archangels with whom Zoroaster had conferences, one of whom ushered him into the presence of Ahura Mazda, were the equivalent of gods, and that therefore we should not say that Zoroaster was a monotheist. But this is unjust. An angel, even conceived as an individual personality having a (spiritual?) body, still is not God if he is not worshiped. Zoroaster did not worship the archangels. To him they were God's ministers and messengers, who tried to bring men into a direct awareness of God's holy presence. Worship was reserved for God alone.

But it is even questionable whether Zoroaster thought of the archangels as individual personalities. When we consider the names of the angels and what they mean, it seems highly probable that he used them as figures of speech, to be interpreted allegorically. So the one true God comes to be known through the medium of Good Thought, True Law, Pure Power, Piety, Prosperity, Immortality. These ideas lead us to a knowledge of the true nature of God. In that sense they are properly called in the Gathas God's sons and daughters, or his messengers. These particular angels or qualities of God are together called the "Immortal Beneficent (or Holy) Spirits," the "Amesha Spentas." There were others besides these six, such as Sraosha (Obedience), Spenta Mainyu (Holy Spirit—perhaps meant merely to describe Ahura Mazda in contrast with Angra Mainyu, the Evil Spirit), and Geus Urva (the Ox-soul or Ox-creator, the spirit that protects cows). This last is somewhat hard to reconcile with an allegorical interpretation, yet it is not impossible. Considering how important cows were in the Iranian way of life, God's spirit would consecrate any mode of living that would protect them. So the originally animistic Ox-Angel could well be allegorized by Zoroaster as a sacred way of behavior.

Harmoniously with his fundamental monotheism Zoroaster describes God's nature and work in one of the most beautiful passages in all literature. Found in the second Gatha, it is fully as beautiful as a similar passage in Job. Says Zoroaster:

This I ask thee, tell me truly, Ahura. Who is by generation the Father of Right, at the first? Who determined the path of sun and stars? Who is it by whom the moon waxes and wanes again? This, O Mazdah, and yet more, I am fain to know.

This I ask thee, tell me truly, Ahura. Who upheld the earth beneath and the firmament from falling? Who made the waters and the plants? Who yoked swiftness to winds and clouds? Who is, O Mazdah, creator of Good Thought?

This I ask thee, tell me truly, Ahura. What artist made light and darkness? What artist made sleep and waking? Who made morning, noon, and night, that call the understanding man to his duty? . . .

This I ask thee, tell me truly, Ahura. Who created together with Dominion the precious Piety? Who made by wisdom the son obedient to his father? I strive to recognize by these things thee, O Mazdah, creator of all things through the holy spirit.[1]

In the first Gatha (Yasna 30) we read how "the holiest Spirit chose Right, he that clothes him with the massy heavens as a garment."[2] Thus God is conceived to be immanent within his universe, as in the theistic Upanishads and the Book of Job.

Also in the first Gatha (Yasna 28) Zoroaster recognizes Mazda as the source of all good:

With outspread hands in petition for that help, O Mazdah, first of all things I will pray for the works of thy holy spirit, O thou of the Right, whereby I may please the will of Good Thought and the Ox-soul.

I who would serve you, O Mazdah Ahura and Good Thought—do ye give through the Right the blessings of both worlds, the bodily and that of Thought, which set the faithful in felicity. . . .

Grant, O thou the Right, the reward, the blessings of Good Thought; O Piety, give our desire to Vishtaspa and to me; O thou, Mazdah (Wise One) and Sovran, grant that your prophet may perform the word of hearing.[3]

As in the nineteenth Psalm, so in these Gathas God is conceived of as the author of two kinds of law, the natural and the spiritual. He creates nature, his splendid garment; and he establishes the spiritual laws of piety by which the son obeys his father and the herdsman is kind to his cattle.

Cosmic Dualism and the Universal Battle

Thus Ahura Mazda, revealing himself through the good spirits, proves to be the creator of all that is good, but not of the bad. In saying this, however, we run into the problem of the limitation of

God. God is limited, that is, opposed, by Angra Mainyu—often contracted to Ahriman or Aharman. Zoroaster seems to have believed that Angra Mainyu could do things contrary to the will of Ahura Mazda, that he was solely responsible for the evil in the world, and that God did not create Angra Mainyu in the first place. This doctrine constitutes history's best example of cosmic—and moral—dualism.

There is some disagreement as to exactly what Zoroaster himself taught regarding the origin of evil and the limitation of God. It is my personal belief, however, based on the information supplied by the Gathas, that Zoroaster did not make Mazda responsible for evil. Mazda did not create the Evil Spirit, Angra Mainyu, nor does he tempt man to do evil. Nor can God prevent the presence of evil in the universe or in man's moral struggle. The existence of evil eternally—whatever that means—is just one of those hard facts of life which, though undesired and ultimately irrational, are nevertheless here for us to deal with. Since evil is here and must be disposed of in some manner, it is well that God is at our side ready to help us if we call upon him. Furthermore God is more powerful than evil, as truth is more powerful than falsehood. We should never forget that the God of might is on our side as we struggle against evil within our own breasts and in human relations. With God's help we are bound to win. And as we need God's cooperation, so he depends on ours. This seems to me to be the essence of Zoroaster's original doctrine.

In the second Gatha we read that the Good Spirit (Spenta Mainyu, meaning Ahura Mazda) said to the Evil Spirit (Angra Mainyu):

> Neither our thoughts, doctrines, plans
> Beliefs, utterances, deeds,
> Individualities, nor souls agree.[4]

This situation is dramatized still further in the opening hymn of the first Gatha:

> Now the two primal Spirits, who revealed themselves in vision as Twins, are the Better and the Bad in thought and word and action. And between these two the wise once chose aright, and the foolish not so.
>
> And when these twain spirits came together in the beginning, they established Life and Not-Life, and that at the last the Worst Existence

shall be to the followers of the Lie, but the Best Thought to him that follows Right. . . .

Then truly on the Lie shall come the destruction of delight; but they that get them good name shall be partakers in the promised reward in the fair abode of Good Thought, of Mazdah, and of Right.[5]

It is probably unfair to regard such dramatizations as Zoroaster's literal beliefs. Viewing the early Gathas as a whole, it certainly seems that Zoroaster was merely describing poetically how in our own lives we are confronted by good and evil, both natural and moral, but that God is too wholly good to send evil upon us. Therefore evil just naturally arises out of the nature of existence, out of the nature of our struggle for the best. The dramatis persona responsible for the evil is called Angra Mainyu, in contrast with Spenta Mainyu. But to take this literally and conclude that therefore Angra Mainyu is an eternal Evil God, existing as long as has Ahura Mazda, is perhaps being too literalistic. Yet it is convenient to use the designations of his dramatis personae in discussing the cosmic and moral struggle.

The moral struggle in which man finds himself engaged requires decision of character and steadfastness of principle. Nor are these requirements abstract or intangible. They relate to the common experiences of life, which to the Iranians meant diligence in tilling the soil, irrigating water-hungry ground, feeding the cattle, refraining from plunder, deceit, lying, sorcery and demon-worship, and granting freedom to one's associates. He who diligently supports the forces of civilization is cooperating with Ahura Mazda. Those who resort to lying, robbing and demon-worship are followers of Angra Mainyu.

The Rewards of Good and Evil

All will be rewarded according to their deeds. Along with Angra Mainyu, his followers will journey in darkness and eat foul food. Mazda's companions will enjoy the fellowship of righteousness for ever. This is rendered beautifully in a free English translation:

> I ask thee, O Ahura, what shall be the punishments
> Of them that serve the Evil One,
> Of them that cannot make their living

Save through violence to cattle and herdsmen.
O Ahura Mazda, I ask thee whether the well-disposed,
The one who strives to improve the houses,
The villages,
The clans and provinces,
Through justice,
Can he become at all like thee?
And when?
And by what deeds? . . .

(And Ahura Mazda answered:) O well-disposed believer,
Hearken not to the followers of the Evil One,
For these seek to wreck houses,
Raze villages,
Despoil clans and provinces;
They can cause only disaster and death.
So fight them with all your weapons!

The righteous alone shall be saved
From destruction and eternal darkness,
From foul food and the worst curses,
At the time of the End of Days.
But ye wicked ones, beware,
For to these will ye be delivered,
Because of your evil spirit!

He who serveth Ahura Mazda in mind and deed,
To him shall be granted the bliss of divine fellowship,
And fullness of Health,
Immortality,
Justice and Power,
And the Good Disposition.

The man who is well-disposed, he comprehends this,
Even as does Mazda, who is All Wise.
It is such a one who weds justice to authority,
It is the well-disposed man who most surely prospers,
And is a companion to Ahura Mazda.[6]

In these words of Zoroaster we find a truly mature concept of rewards and punishment. Zoroaster's cosmic dualism was essentially the dualism of the moral struggle, linked with the principle of human accountability. His picture of heaven was as a "House of Song," where dwells "the best thought" and all good companionship. Hell was conceived to be the dwelling of "the worst thought" and of the loneliness of each individual who by his anti-social behavior cuts himself off from all good companionship. Such an idea may be found in Yasna 46.11:

> Their own Soul and their own Self [*daena:* conscience?] shall torment them when they come to the Bridge of the Separator. To all time will they be guests for the House of the Lie.[7]

The practical common-sense nature of Zoroastrianism may be seen in the inscriptions of Darius I the Great, the son of King Vishtaspa. The religion at that time still remained in its pristine purity. In his Behistun inscription he expresses pious devotion to Ahura Mazda, and gratitude for his help in overcoming the revolution of the Magi. The latter were a priestly tribe of Media who apparently were still opposed to the new faith, but who soon afterward adopted it and propagated it, modifying it in the process. Darius labels these and other enemies as ones who are followers of the Lie and the enemies of civilization.

In the inscription on his tomb Darius reviews his achievements and evaluates his own character. His standard of values is obviously harmonious with the ideals preached by Zoroaster, as may be seen from the following quotation:

> A great god is Ahuramazda, who created this excellent work which is seen, who created happiness for man, who bestowed wisdom and activity upon Darius the king.
>
> Says Darius the king: By the favor of Ahuramazda I am of such a sort that I am a friend to the right, I am not a friend to wrong; it is not my desire that the weak man should have wrong done to him by the mighty; nor is that my desire, that the mighty man should have wrong done him by the weak.
>
> What is right, that is my desire. I am not a friend to the man who is a Lie-follower. I am not hot-tempered. What things develop in my anger, I hold firmly under control by my will-power. I am firmly ruling over my own [impulses].[8]

Pahlavi Parsiism

The religion was not to remain like this for long. When we read the commentaries and modifications of Zoroastrianism in the Pahlavi version and texts, we see that much is altered.

One remarkable change in the religion was the development of an attitude of reverence toward the person of Zoroaster. The most implausible myths were related about his supernatural birth and life, as noted above. Fantastic miracles which he performed were described, as when he first visited the court of King Vishtaspa. We are told that he floated down through the roof which parted to admit him. Immediately thereafter people noticed that "in his hand was a cube of fire with which he played without its hurting him."[9]

From the Farvardin Yast we quote a paragraph which is quite clear in its implications:

> We worship Zarathustra, the lord and master of all the material world, the man of the primitive law; the wisest of all beings, the best-ruling of all beings, the brightest of all beings, the most glorious of all beings, the most worthy of sacrifice amongst all beings, the most worthy of prayer amongst all beings, the most worthy of propitiation amongst all beings, the most worthy of glorification amongst all beings, whom we call well-desired and worthy of sacrifice and prayer as much as any being can be, in the perfection of his holiness.[10]

That Zoroaster, the monotheist, should have been changed into a god seems as unfitting as most other such deifications. None was more humble or human than he.

But his monotheism suffered also in other respects. Vohu Manu, the personification of Good Thought, became an agricultural deity such as the Aryans had earlier worshiped, protecting the cattle and their food. Asha, who personified Justice, assumed the role of god of fire, and Khshathra (Power) became the god of metals. The other Amesha Spentas became goddesses, Armaiti (Piety) of the soil, Haurvatat (Prosperity) of water, and Amertat (Immortality) of vegetation.

Other deities, more distinctly Aryan than these, also came back into the house that had been swept clean of polytheism. Sometimes they tended even to overshadow the typical Zoroastrian "Amesha Spentas." We now meet with Ushas, goddess of the dawn, and Vayu, wind-god, and above all Mithra.

The case of Mithra becomes most interesting. He had been replaced in Zoroastrianism by Ahura Mazda in a special sense, since each was regarded as a god of light. Many of the common people were especially devoted to Mithra and probably never did become reconciled to the new views. So when Mithra was reintroduced into Parsiism, even though he was represented in the Pahlavi texts as subordinate to Ahura Mazda, the people probably exalted him above all others. In one of the texts Ahura Mazda is even represented as offering sacrifices to Mithra—usurper of Mazda's functions! The Hymn to the Sun found in the Khorshed Yast is addressed to Mithra. Ahura Mazda is placated somewhat by the proviso that "he who offers up a sacrifice unto the undying, shining, swift-horsed Sun . . . offers it up to Ahura Mazda, offers it up to the Amesha-Spentas, offers it up to his own soul." But the next declaration is: I will sacrifice unto Mithra, the lord of wide pastures, who has a thousand ears, ten thousand eyes.[11]

Another god of the Parsi restoration was Haoma, who returned to the fold in the role of life-giver, death averter. And from a foreign source came Anahita, goddess of waters and of fertility, love, and childbirth. She was made on the pattern of Ishtar of Babylonia.

The old animism of ancient Iran seems thinly veiled in the following passages from the Farvardin Yast:

> We worship this earth; we worship those heavens; we worship those good things that stand between the earth and the heavens and that are worthy of sacrifice and prayer and are to be worshiped by the faithful man.
>
> We worship the souls of wild beasts and of the tame.
>
> We worship the souls of the holy men and women, born at any time, whose consciences struggle, or will struggle, or have struggled, for the good. . . .
>
> The Fravashis of the faithful, awful and overpowering, awful and victorious; the Fravashis of the men of the primitive law; the Fravashis of the next-of-kin; may these Fravashis come satisfied into this house; may they walk satisfied through this house![12]

The doctrine of rewards and punishment also was changed from maturity to superstition. The Good Spirit and Evil Spirit were made into willful personalities fighting a long and heroic war of the worlds. Ahriman created all the diseases of man, in fiendish glee, and invented frostbite, heat, drought, serpents, ants, lust, and disbelief. He was also the author of death. And he was assisted by numberless other fiends like himself.

On the judgment day, according to the Pahlavi texts, every soul must walk across the Chinvad bridge (or Bridge of the Separator).

The good souls manage to cross, while the evil ones fail to reach the Paradise yonder.

As it were that bridge is like a beam of many sides, of whose edges there are some which are broad, and there are some which are thin and sharp; its broad sides are so large that its width is twenty-seven reeds, and its sharp sides are so contracted that in thinness it is just like the edge of a razor. And when the souls of the righteous and wicked arrive it turns to that side which is suitable to their necessities, through the great glory of the creator and the command of him who takes the just account. . . .

And he who is of the righteous passes over the bridge, and a worldly similitude of the pleasantness of his path upon it is when thou shalt eagerly and unweariedly walk in the golden-coloured spring, and with the gallant body and sweet-scented blossom in the pleasant skin of that maiden spirit, the price of goodness. He who is of the wicked, as he places a footstep on the bridge, on account of affliction and its sharpness, falls from the middle of the bridge, and rolls over head-foremost. And the unpleasantness of his path to hell is in similitude such as the worldly one in the midst of that stinking and dying existence, there where numbers of the sharp-pointed darts are planted out inverted and point upwards. . . .[13]

Heaven is said to be a "place" filled with "all comfort, pleasure, joy, happiness, and welfare . . . and there is no want, pain, distress, or discomfort whatever in it. . . ." Hell, in contrast, "is sunken, deep, and descending, most dark, most stinking, and most terrible. . . . And in it is no comfort, pleasantness, or joy whatever; but . . . stench, filth, pain, punishment, distress. . . ."[14] As vivid as Jonathan Edwards!

With like vividness the resurrection of the dead is described. At that time "all men stand up; whoever is righteous and whoever is wicked, every human creature, they rouse up from the spot where its life departs. . . .

"Then is the assembly of the Sadvastaran, where all mankind will stand at this time; in that assembly every one sees his own good deeds and his own evil deeds; and then, in that assembly, a wicked man becomes as conspicuous as a white sheep among those that are black."[15]

Zoroaster himself apparently taught that a general resurrection of the dead would take place at the end of the present age. At that time, he said, fire would test the quality of men's deeds, good ones not being consumed thereby. But in later Zoroastrianism a general resurrection is made more picturesque and withal more terrible. The resurrection will occur after damned souls have already suffered untold torment. A scheme of ages was worked up by ingenious theologians. A Messianic era was even included. In the end Ahriman and all evil souls would be consumed, says one account, while good adults would forever remain forty years old and children fifteen.[16]

The Magi, who finally accepted the religion and undertook its promotion as a nationalistic faith, probably contributed a large share of the magical element which also returned to Parsiism. They gained a wide reputation in the ancient world from their "magic," which of course was named after them. The old magical concepts of ceremonial impurity and purification thus quite naturally returned to Parsiism. Ritual was conceived to be efficacious of itself.

Instructions were given on how to use lovely passages from the Gathas as a sure cure for certain ills. The haoma sacrifice is still used by the Parsis for magical purposes. Ways were detailed for ridding oneself of pollution from having touched a dead body. Corpses were so defiling that they must not be allowed to touch the divine earth, water or fire. So burial and cremation were ruled out, as well as burial in the sacred water. All that was left was to build the "towers of silence"—still visible in India and Iran—where the corpse might be exposed above the earth and the vultures come to devour them. Spitting and exhaled breath also are defiling, and ceremonial cleansing become necessary.

More philosophical was the theory proposed by the Magi to the effect that Ahura Mazda and Angra Mainyu emerged simultaneously from Zervan, a unitary principle of space-time. Thus both were co-eternal, and the cosmos was an eternal battle of wills, good against evil. Even so, however, they anticipated the final victory of Mazda.[17]

Practical Values of Parsiism

Whether early or late, enlightened or magical, the Zoroastrian religion has always cultivated values which were appropriate in a land of hardship. The great strength of Zoroastrianism, the secret of its real success over the centuries, lies in the fact that it lined up with the forces of civilization, stability, and social order in a settled community, and condemned nomadism, robbery, violence, and laziness, the enemies of civilization.

The emphasis in Zoroastrianism was upon a happy combination of thought, word, and deed, as in the Mazdayasnian Confession which concludes: "A Mazda-worshiper am I, of Zarathustra's order; so do I confess as a praiser and confessor, and I therefore praise aloud the well-thought thought, the word well spoken, and the deed well done."[18]

Even in the late Pahlavi texts, when the ritualistic side of religion was emphasized, we still find a practical trend of thought, as in the following passage on the "five dispositions" and the "ten admonitions" for priests:

> Of those five dispositions the first is innocence.
>
> The second is discrimination among thoughts, words, and deeds. . . .
>
> The third is authoritativeness. . . .
>
> The fourth is to understand and consider the ceremonial as the ceremonial of Ahura Mazda, and the essentials with all goodness, beneficence, and authority; to be steadfast in his religion, and to consider the indications of protection which are established for this religion. To maintain the reverence of the emanations from the six archangels, be they fire, be they earth, or be they of bodily form, and of the creatures which are formed by them; also the pure cleansing from dead matter, menstruation, bodily refuse, and other hurtfulness. . . . and all life long not to depart from steadfastness, nor allow your proper duty to go out of your hands.
>
> And the first of those ten admonitions is to proceed with good repute. . . .
>
> The second is to become awfully refraining from evil repute . . .
>
> The third [I like this one especially!] is not to beat your teacher with a snatched-up stick, and not to bring scandal upon his name, for the sake of annoying him, by uttering that which was not heard from your own teacher.
>
> The fourth is that whatever is taught liberally by your own teacher you have to deliver back to the worthy . . .
>
> The ninth is to fully understand the forward movement of the religion, also to keep the advancing of the religion further forwards, and to seek your share of the duty therein . . .[19]

Note the idea of a progressive, evangelistic religion in the ninth admonition.

The Iranians, both before and after Zoroaster, revered the earth as divine. This reverence is understandable, for the earth was the source of their sustenance. Religion as the endeavor to conserve values encouraged, for the Iranians, a very practical relationship with mother-earth. So in the Vendidad we read that the earth is "most happy" in five places:

(1) . . . the place whereon one of the faithful steps forward; (2) . . . the place whereon one of the faithful erects a house with a priest within, with cattle, with a wife, with children, and good herds within, and wherein afterwards the cattle continue to thrive, virtue to thrive, fodder to thrive, the dog to thrive, the wife to thrive, the child to thrive, the fire to thrive, and every blessing of life to thrive; (3) . . . the place where one of the faithful sows most corn, grass, and fruit, O Spitama Zarathustra! where he waters ground that is dry, or drains ground that is too wet; (4) . . . the place where there is most increase of flocks and herds; (5) . . . the place where the flocks and herds yield most dung.[20]

In no religion is the value of the dog recognized with such fine appreciation as in Zoroastrianism, whose shepherds needed a faithful dog to protect their flocks, and a house dog to warn them of robbers.

Whosoever shall smite either a shepherd's dog, or a house-dog, or a Wohunazga dog, or a trained dog, his soul when passing to the other world, shall fly howling louder and more sorely grieved than the sheep does in the lofty forest where the wolf ranges.

No soul will come and meet his departing soul and help it, howling and grieved, in the other world; nor will the dogs that keep the Chinvad bridge help his departing soul howling and grieved in the other world.[21]

It was the religious duty of whoever was near at hand to give protection and aid to a bitch about to give birth to puppies.[22]

Survival and Influence

Eleven thousand Gabars have survived Mohammedan rule in Iran, and over a hundred thousand Parsis live in India or Pakistan today. There they worship in their unpretentious fire temples, sacrifice haoma, purify themselves ceremonially, and form a prosperous and respectable part of the larger community. Suffering from a multitude of taboos, they have found the business world least offensive, and have made the most of their opportunities therein. Their practicing priests are said to be too ignorant to understand most of what they recite from the archaic language of the Avesta in their sacred services. Some of the ruling priests, however, are said to be highly educated. They hold the people in the palms of their hands, directing their habits and their worship.

Zoroastrianism is a religion of one prophet. It has sorely needed new prophets and reformers; but no St. Benedict, no Luther or Wesley has appeared. So superstition and ritual magic remain as the legacy of a religion which began auspiciously and flowered for a time magnificently. As Zoroaster himself taught it, there has never been a better expression of the great ideas which have made it a religion long to be remembered. In truth, we may say that its great ideas are more alive today in the three religions which it influenced than in Parsiism. Those religions are Judaism, Christianity, and Islam, which form our next interest. In them the most spectacular legacy from Zoroastrianism is probably the element of cosmic and moral dualism, and the doctrines of the resurrection of the dead and a last judgment.

The Standard of Maturity

On the basis of our adopted criteria we may conclude that Zoroaster was quite mature religiously in that, first, he opposed the magic of the traditional priesthood. Second, he rejected the established, literal interpretation of Iranian mythology, and proposed a spiritualized conception of one God who may be known to man by such means as good thought, good living, an orderly society, and immortality. His great emphasis was upon social and moral values, and his challenge was to his countrymen, urging them to resist nomadism and disorder. He appealed to men's reasonableness as the best means of cooperative progress in civilization. His idea of a physical resurrection and a judgment day were harmonious with the cosmology of his day, and his cosmic dualism was not without its justification. At least it recognized the fact of conflict in human experience, and the apparent inability of even a divine power to eliminate evil completely. His mystic sensitivity is recognized by all, and the symbolism of his fire-ritual showed beauty and symbolic insight. Considering the stage of culture in his day, we must judge his religion as remarkably mature and in essence universal. The pity is that magic and mythological literalness returned, and that he himself was worshiped along with many other gods. While Parsiism never became wholly immature, especially with regard to its social-moral values, yet its degeneration from maturity was marked, and no prophets appeared to rescue it. Its potential universalism was realized only in the religions which Zoroaster influenced.

PART SIX

The Religion of Israel

XXVII. EARLY HEBREW TRADITION

JUDAISM, CHRISTIANITY, AND ISLAM, the three religions yet to be described, all developed out of a common background. The origin and development of this common tradition took place in and around the Arabian desert, in the experiences of Semitic peoples. Christianity is built upon Judaism, while Islam is built upon both Judaism and Christianity. Therefore in giving the story of Judaism we are, up to a certain point, giving the story of all three religions.

Not only do the three religions have a common origin; they also have many common beliefs and a common missionary spirit. All teach the unity and providence of God and the moral responsibility of man. All seek disciples over all the world. Because of the ritual requirements of Jewish discipleship, Judaism has succeeded least in its missionary endeavors. But what it lacks in numbers is surpassed by its contribution to the foundations of Christianity and Islam.

Judaism, Christianity, and Islam, claiming together almost a billion followers, have exerted a mighty influence on mankind. The succession of their prophets, the universality of their appeal and the flexibility of their cultures have been important factors contributing to human maturity. However, not all is on the credit side of any religion. It would seem that the sincere cooperation of almost a billion men of goodwill ought to bring peace and happiness on earth. That has not come to pass. Wars have even been fought in the name of the Christian church, as was the case with the crusades. Lest we be too sure of our own religious rectitude, therefore, let us reappraise our total situation with regard to the origin and development of our Semitic-Christian set of values. An objective appraisal will be more difficult here than heretofore, since we are now dealing with traditions touched with our own emotions. We must realize, though, that it is more important to be cosmopolitan in our insights than to resort to prejudice in order to justify our own tradition.

Sumero-Babylonian Religious Influence

An unmistakable influence in the Hebrew tradition was the myths of Sumero-Babylonia. We have already examined the religion of the ancient Sumerians, Akkadians, and Old Babylonians.* There we found a nature religion based on dynamism, animism, and the worship of local deities. The orientation of the Mesopotamian Semitic religion was mainly this-worldly, with emphasis on the values of prosperity for this the only life which man would ever live. Fertility gods and goddesses figured largely in it, guaranteeing good crops and many children.

The influence of the Mesopotamian tradition is seen most clearly in two places. The first is Genesis 2-11, which parallels myths already cited from Sumeria and later Babylonia. The second is the Mosaic code (Exod. 21-23), closely paralleled by the code of Hammurabi and its antecedents.

Genesis 2-11 has been called "S" because it entered the Hebrew tradition from Seir, south of Israel; it originated in Mesopotamia. It represents a variety of individual sources and was worked into the narrative by the writers of Genesis. The "S" hypothesis was proposed by Robert H. Pfeiffer,[1] but has not met with general acceptance as yet. My use of the symbol does not imply acceptance of the theory.

The parallels between Babylonian myths and Genesis 2-11 should

* Chapter IV *supra.*

not be pressed too far. There are enough similarities to prove a common origin, but the differences are as significant as the likenesses. The Babylonian myths, for example, are found to depend largely on accident or the caprice of the gods. In the case of Genesis, however, each story has a moral.

One of the parallels between Babylonian traditions and Genesis lies in the human character of their deities. In the Babylonian tale the gods are motivated like human beings. One god, Utnapishtim, is represented as the deified ancestor of Gilgamesh, presiding over the realm of the dead in very human fashion. So also in "S" we find a human sort of Lord who fashions man as a sculptor would, and then miraculously brings him to life by breathing into his nostrils. Like a gardener he "planted a garden in Eden." He presided over the paradise where he placed man, giving him orders what to do and not do. As overseer he went out only in the "cool of the day."

Another parallel lies in the hero's loss of immortality in both traditions. In the Babylonian, Gilgamesh found the herb of immortality and was on his way home when the serpent robbed him of it and became immortal, sloughing off his old skin. In Genesis the serpent "beguiled" Eve and she enticed Adam, so both disobeyed. Thus the serpent robbed them also of immortality. The Genesis account is an epic of human morality, while the Babylonian sees merely an accident of chance.

In the incident of the tower of Babel the Genesis writer tries to explain the origin of different languages. God up in heaven saw men building the tower. So the Lord said, "Come, let us go down, and there confuse their language, that they may not understand one another's speech." "So the Lord scattered them abroad from there over the face of all the earth" (Gen. 11:5-8). This was supposed to teach men not to aspire to divine powers and honors. We may note also the suggestion that in the original tradition more than one god in heaven agreed to go down to Babel: "Let us go down." This shows how ancient was the source.

In the Sumero-Babylonian tale a god revealed to Utnapishtim the intention of the other gods to destroy mankind by a flood. To him exact instructions were given on how to build an ark. Into the ark with him he took his family, his cattle, and "beasts of the field." When the flood subsided he sent forth first a dove, then a swallow, and then a raven. The last did not return, so he knew that it was safe to land. Noah's experience paralleled each of these events. In the Genesis account, however, the flood came because of man's sin, while in the Babylonian the divine motive seems capricious. Two accounts of the flood are readily distinguishable in Genesis, but both are moralistic.

The parallels of sacrifice are also significant. The Babylonian hero of the flood sacrificed to the gods after being delivered from death. Since sacrifices had ceased when the flood began, this was the first time the gods had been fed for a long time. So they "gathered like flies" when they "smelled the sweet savor," and apparently forgot that their intention to destroy all mankind had been thwarted.[2] Ishtar scolded Enlil for his responsibility in bringing the flood, and Enlil seemed to acquiesce in her judgment. At any rate, all the gods were appeased and pleased, now that Utnapishtim (or Ziusudra, or Xisuthros) was saved. So also when Noah offered his sacrifice, Yahweh "smelled the pleasing odor" (Gen. 8:21) and was appeased and pleased. The Genesis account is monotheistic and more dignified in its treatment of deity than the Babylonian, even though Yahweh is still conceived as very human.

There is enough similarity between the two sets of myths to prove that they both had a common origin among the Semites and Sumerians. But the Hebrew account was modified as it was passed on from generation to generation, conforming more and more with the Hebrew religious enlightenment. While "S" is one of the most primitive elements of the Pentateuch, yet it is far advanced over the Babylonian account in concept and significance.

General Semitic Religious Influence

Besides the specific Sumero-Babylonian influences on the Hebrew religion, there was the common heritage shared by all Semites. This was the heritage of animism, magic and fetishism, universal among primitive peoples. Belief in local deities was in turn a product of animism and ancestor worship. Primitive also was religious totemism.

There are reasons for believing that totemism was practiced among the primitive Semites and Hebrews. Some of the names of the Hebrew tribes suggest a totemic origin. Simeon was a "hyena" and Levi was a "wild cow." And place names were reminiscent of animals: Aijalon of the stag, Ephron of the antelope, Thalbim of foxes. Related to Old Testament lore and worship were goats, bulls, calves, and serpents.

That Abraham's kinsmen worshiped fetishes, ancestral spirits and local deities is borne out by the Biblical tradition itself. Embedded in one of the early documents is the statement of Joshua: "Thus says the Lord, the God of Israel, 'Your fathers lived of old beyond the Euphrates, Terah, the father of Abraham and of Nahor; and they served other gods'" (Josh. 24:2). When later Jacob went back to Paddan-aram beyond the Euphrates to marry one of his cousins, Rachel refused to leave home without carrying with her the "household gods" of her father Laban (Gen. 31:14, 30-35). Abraham's own household most likely sheltered such fetishes and revered local deities. The common use of household gods (teraphim) and images in later times is reflected in the stories of the Judges of Israel (Judges 17:5; 18:14-20f). Even David's household had its wooden images, for Michal snatched one up and put it in bed, disguising it to look like David asleep, whereupon David escaped from Saul (I Sam. 19:11-17).

Abraham himself is said to have chosen one local deity and revered him above all others. Here was a budding monotheism in the Hebrew tradition. The story usually refers to Abraham's God as Yahweh, but in Exodus 6:3 we find Yahweh admitting to Moses that he had been known to Abraham, Isaac and Jacob as El Shaddai, literally the Mountain God. So the name Yahweh did not come into the Hebrew tradition until Moses' day, and it was Moses who discovered him on the mountain in Midian, as another local deity. El Shaddai is believed to have been the local deity of the mountains (or a mountain) near Haran, where Abraham first heard his call to adventure. There El Shaddai chose Abraham and Abraham chose El Shaddai. Abraham became the "friend of God." Even after Abraham had reached Canaan El Shaddai's spirit appeared and spoke to him and to Isaac and Jacob. Later Moses on "the mountain of God" communed with its deity who revealed himself to Moses by the name Yahweh.* Moses, or the historian who wrote the story,

* Hebrew JHVH, no vowels being used in ancient Hebrew; probably pronounced Yahweh.

then identified Yahweh as the same God as El Shaddai, though known by a different name.[3] At best the patriarchal view was not monotheistic but henotheistic. That is, they may have believed that El Shaddai or Yahweh was the greatest God, but not the only God. The trend was toward monotheism, but it was only a trend, not a fact, in patriarchal times.

Comparable with Yahweh (translated "Lord") is the Hebrew word "Adonai." When the later Jews came across the word Yahweh in a text, it was thought to be too sacred to pronounce. So they substituted the word "Adonai," which is cognate to the Greek Adonis. The Hebrew "adon" means "lord."

Another name by which God was called among the Hebrews and other Semites was "El" and its related "Elim," or "Elohim." El is singular while Elim and Elohim are plural in form. By these words the Canaanites, Arabians, and other Semites meant the numerous spirits and sometimes even the high gods, individually or collectively. As prophetic insight developed there was a tendency to think of all the deities together as being not multiple but the one and only real God. So the term Elohim in the Old Testament is interpreted as referring to the one high God. Yet there are reminiscences of plurality, as when God (Elohim) said, "Let us make man in our image." Then after the fall God said, "Behold, the man has become like one of us. . . ." (Gen. 1:26; 3:22). The author of these passages probably thought of Elohim as singular, but it is likely that the original tradition which he reported intended it as plural.

Other words designating gods among the Semites were Malak (Moloch; Hebrew Melech), meaning King; Baal (Bel) meaning Lord, or Lord of the Land; and Rabb (Rabbi) meaning Master.

The Semitic concept of local deities extended to other things than mountains. Among the sacred places were springs, wells and oases, where supernatural power seemed so obviously to manifest itself. Semitic wanderers from the desert would naturally place a high value on the sources of water. In the Biblical narrative springs and wells assumed great importance, and angels were sometimes seen there.

Common among the ancient Semites, including Hebrews, Canaanites and Arabs, was the belief in angels and demons. The

Arabian desert was peopled with a goodly number of fairies and jinn who roamed around to bless and to curse. The angels in Jacob's dream were very real to him. Abraham was visited by angels, as were many Old Testament characters. An angel of the Lord (or the Lord himself) had a long and serious conversation with Gideon (Judges 6:11-21). Angels and demons survived even in the New Testament, where illness is sometimes described as possession by devils, particularly in the case of mental illness.

Although the monotheistic tradition goes back to Abraham and Moses, we must raise the question to what extent the advanced idea was realized by them or how far it affected the average Israelite. The complete answer to this question must wait upon our story of Israel. Here we may anticipate merely by saying that it took many centuries and the efforts of the great prophets to bring about a general acceptance of the full implications of the monotheistic idea. Even the patriarchs and Moses did not deny the existence of other gods than El Shaddai or Yahweh, but merely scorned their worship since they were so inferior to their chosen deity. The patriarchs seem to have tolerated the presence of "household gods," or fetishes. We must not expect of the patriarchs and their families too much enlightenment. Indeed, some higher critics question whether Moses was the author of the first two or more commandments, since there is so much evidence of the reverence of images and local deities in the early Old Testament.

Religion of the Canaanites

More specific than the general Semitic influence, and more continuous than the Babylonian, was that of the Canaanitic religion. These natives of Palestine among whom the Israelites settled were typical representatives of the Semitic culture, like the Israelites themselves. The significant theological difference between the Canaanitic Semites and the Israelitic Semites was the fact that the Israelites cultivated a religious epic of their tribal history and eventually identified one spiritual God with their destiny, whereas the Canaanites were satisfied with the nature religion which they inherited from the desert. This contrast was not too strong, however.

and the common Israelite in the era of the monarchy was subject to the influence of his Canaanitic neighbor just as much as the neighbor was subject to the Israelitic influence. The conqueror has often been assimilated by the conquered.

Besides the theological difference was the difference of *mishpat*, or economic justice. The Canaanites had a custom of buying and selling land, along with other merchandise. Consequently the rich *baalim*, or landlords, gravitated toward the strong walled cities where they lived as aristocrats while slaves tilled their fields. The Joseph tribes, however, living among the "hills of Ephraim," held to the *mishpat* of the inalienability of the land. When Naboth refused to sell his land to Ahab and Jezebel it was not because he was stubborn but because the custom in Israel was thus. The landlords of Ephraim were *adonim* (lords) from whom the land was inseparable, in contrast with the Canaanitic *baalim* (lords). It may have been this difference, more than any other, which caused the ultimate triumph of Yahweh over Baal.

From two primary sources we learn much about the Canaanitic religion. One is the archaeological discoveries at Ras Shamra (Ugarit) north of Palestine. The other is the Old Testament narrative itself, which shows how the Canaanitic religon paralleled the popular Hebrew ideas.

The tablets found at Ras Shamra were written in Ugaritic, which has been deciphered and identified as a Semitic language closely akin to Canaanitic and Hebrew. These Ugaritic inscriptions reveal that there were many baals in Canaan, local deities who presided over the fertility of the fields and of men and animals. Over the local deities was a chief, sometimes called simply Baal and sometimes called Zabul, meaning Prince. It was on him that King Ahaziah called when he was ill. Ahaziah "sent messengers, telling them, 'Go, inquire of Baal-zebub, the god of Ekron . . .' " (II Kings 1:2). This same god has survived in the Beelzebub of the New Testament (Mark 3:22). Above Baal were his father and mother, El and Asherat. Baal was the manager, as it were, of the local baals. As the storm god he hurled the thunderbolt and sent the rain. His father and mother were the source of his power. Asherat is represented as a sea goddess, and El as the "source of the two deeps." As we have seen, the name El passed into accepted usage in the Old

Testament as one of the names of God. Even El Shaddai is mentioned in Canaanitic inscriptions as referring to the high god, perhaps to be identified with El and Elohim. This identification is confirmed in our Biblical tradition in Numb. 24:16.

Old Testament clues to the Canaanitic religion are manifold. A good summary is found in the Judaic author's report summarizing Moses' sermon to the Israelites recounting God's commands:

> These are the statutes and ordinances which you shall be careful to do in the land which the Lord, the God of your fathers, has given you to possess, all the days that you live upon the earth. You shall surely destroy all the places where the nations whom you shall dispossess served their gods, upon the high mountains and their altars, and dash in pieces their pillars, and burn their Asherim with fire; you shall hew down the graven images of their gods . . . (Deut. 12:1-3).

We see from this quotation that the Canaanites were accustomed to building their altars on top of the hills and mountains, on the assumption that the gods were nearer to them there than in the low places. They also revered evergreen trees as bearers of continuing life. And they practiced phallicism, like most primitive peoples, in the worship of stone pillars. As always, the pillars symbolized the power of fertility. When Jacob and Laban set up a stone pillar and a heap of stones (Gen. 31:44-49) they showed their sympathy for the phallic symbol as a boundary marker similar to its use by the Greeks.* The word *gilgal*, a place name in Palestine, originally meant a circular enclosure of stone pillars, suggesting the possibility that the primitive Hebrews also worshiped the life force symbolized by the pillar.

Ever present was the danger that the invading Israelites would lose their identity as they lived in the midst of the Canaanitic culture. That would have been unfortunate, for fertility cults such as that of the Canaanites are likely to encourage impurity and the practice of magic. And the local deities of Canaan tended to retard the emergence and growth of the Hebrew monotheism. Israel was counseled to remain a distinct people, ritually separate from the Canaanites. This, however, was a counsel of perfection which was in fact far from realization, particularly in the era of the Hebrew monarchy when Canaanites and Israelites commingled. In those

* See Chapter V, p. 79.

days whenever a Canaanite's crops prospered while a neighboring Israelite's crops failed, it was probably interpreted to mean that the local baal had helped those who had called upon him and had brought disaster to others. Even when the crops of both Israelite and Canaanite failed it might be interpreted as a sign of the baal's displeasure at the presence of impious foreigners in their midst. Many Israelites yielded to such arguments. There was so much of phallicism, fetishism and the worship of local deities in their own tradition that it was easy to fall into these same practices of the Canaanites. This will be evident as our story continues.

Divine Possession of the Prophets

In another respect the ancient Semites held to a common religious concept, namely, in the divine possession of the prophets. Strange behavior was interpreted as signaling the indwelling of a supernatural spirit. Epileptics, on losing control of their own bodies, were thought to be under the control of a supernatural being. The epileptic is often a person of high intellectual ability, and his discreet acts outside the periods of seizure may support the belief that he is acting from supernatural motives.

It is said of Saul, after he was selected to be king, that "God gave him another heart. . . . When they came to Gibeah, behold, a band of prophets met him; and the spirit of God came mightily upon him, and he prophesied among them. And when all who knew him before saw how he prophesied with the prophets, the people said to one another, 'What has come over the son of Kish? Is Saul also among the prophets?' " (I Sam. 10:9-11). Regardless of the critical question as to the historicity of this story, it reveals the then-current concept of the nature of the prophet.

During his kingly career Saul developed what we might today call melancholia, and with David's rising popularity he became jealous. The Spirit left him, and he sent messengers to capture David. When the messengers "saw the company of the prophets prophesying, and Samuel standing as head over them, the Spirit of God came upon the messengers of Saul, and they also prophesied. When it was told Saul, he sent other messengers, and they also prophesied. And Saul sent messengers again the third time, and they also prophesied." Finally Saul himself went, "and the Spirit of God came upon him also, and as he went he prophesied, until he came to Naioth in Ramah. And he too stripped off his clothes, and he too prophesied before Samuel, and lay naked all that day and all that night" (I Sam. 19:20-24). The last verse clearly shows the then-current conception of the nature of the prophet as a person who is possessed by a supernatural force or being, and who in that frenzied state utters words not his own but of that divine power. Withal, however, the primitive Hebrew prophets were agents of democracy and patriotism. They were devoted to Israel and to the ideal of liberty. Kings who developed autocratic tendencies were denounced by the prophets who at times even resorted to tyrannicide. Out of crude beginnings the institution of Israelitic prophets eventually developed into the enlightened moral and spiritual concepts of Isaiah, Micah, Amos, and Jeremiah.

Origin of the Hebrews

It is said that the Hebrews belong to the Semitic race. The most obscure problem of anthropology, however, is race. In this case all that we really know is that a group of ancient peoples spoke related languages. These languages together are called Semitic. "By the term Semites we must understand not a race but many races that adopted a Semitic language."[4] This represents an extreme position. For it is probable that there was a common ancestry of most Semitic peoples, although in some cases the Semitic race was mixed with others. For example, one author states flatly that the so-called "Semitic features (of the Jews), including the prominent nose, are not Semitic at all. They are exactly the characteristics which differentiate the Jew from the Semitic type and evidently represent an acquisition from early intermarriages between the Hittite-Hurrians and the Hebrews."[5] The same writer asserts that there is a common ancestry of all the Semitic peoples, who emerged at various times from the Arabian peninsula, "the Babylonians, the Assyrians, the Chaldeans, Amorites, Aramaeans, the Phoenicians, Hebrews, Arabians and the Abyssinians. . . . Here they lived at some time as one people."[6] In this list we certainly should include the Canaanites, frequently called Amorites.

That the Semites all originated in Arabia is only one among several theories. Other hypotheses are that they came originally from central Asia; Babylonia; Amurru, between Syria and Mesopotamia; or Africa.[7] Professor Della Vida, with his characteristic agnosticism, confesses that we are completely in the dark as to Semitic origins. Yet a few pages later he seems to know that wave after wave of Semites emerged from Arabia into various parts of the "fertile crescent"—i.e., the crescent-shaped area extending northward between its two tips, the Mesopotamian delta and southern Palestine.[8] Perhaps Della Vida meant that he did not know how the Semites got into the desert in the first place. That is a real problem.

There seem to have been three main migrations of Semites about four thousand years ago. First the Akkadians broke out from Arabia into southern Mesopotamia, spreading through the river valleys and gaining control over their Sumerian predecessors. Later the Amorites (Amurru) moved in two directions, taking over Mesopotamia from the Sumero-Akkadians and moving westward into Syria and Palestine. The Amorites gave Hammurabi to the world. The third wave of migration moved in both directions as the one before it had, but its main strength was westward. This group is identified as Aramaic-speaking, and it is to them that the Israelites persistently refer as their ancestors or kinfolk. The Aramaeans were also the ancestors of the Canaanites, between whom and the Israelites there were closer ties of blood and culture than is usually supposed.[9]

When we first meet with the Hebrews we find them in "Ur of the Chaldeans" about the twentieth century B.C. It was during this century that the Elamites captured Ur, the capital city of the Sumero-Akkadian Empire of Ur. The Amorites, too, played a part in the military and political changes of that century, and later established the Old Babylonian empire about 1830 B.C. The Akkadians and the Amorites were Semites, as was Abraham.

Living in Mesopotamia during this period were a people called Habiru. From inscriptions of Hammurabi's day (c.1728-c.1676 B.C.) we learn that Habiru referred not to a race but to a low social status attached to a migrant people. Some of the Habiru entered voluntarily into slavery to the established classes.[10] Such were some of the disabilities operating on Semitic emigrants from the desert, former nomads who had found that Arabia could not support all whom it produced. If the Habiru were indeed Semites, they represented only a small portion of the Semitic world of that day.

Since the origin of the word Hebrew is otherwise unknown, we may assume that it is identical with Habiru, as in fact it is phonetically. So when we find references to the Habiru in its various forms, in Egyptian inscriptions and elsewhere, we may identify them as belonging to this group. Such a group, though indefinite in extent, is obviously much larger than merely the clan of Abraham.

One writer suggests "outsiders" as a synonym for Habiru. Possibly Max Weber has something like this in mind when he refers to the ancient Jews in Palestine as "pariahs," by which he means that they were considered as a guest people—ritually separate from the rest of the population.[11]

The Tradition of Abraham

Of course not all the "outsiders" in Mesopotamia were unfortunates. One migrant clan which settled at or near Ur was headed by the patriarch Terah. The Biblical patriarchs may be thought of as bedouin sheikhs who with their clans left the desert without forgetting its nomadic habits. The word patriarch means literally "father-king." As ruler of his clan Terah was the one who made the decision to move on, this time toward the west. Nomadism had not disappeared from the old patriarch's heart. Nor was his clan impoverished or dependent on the charity of the local citizens. Probably nevertheless he felt, as many who move to a new community have felt, that being "outsiders" they were not accepted. So Terah moved his clan toward Canaan, as later generations told the story.

While Canaan was the alleged goal, yet the first generation failed to reach it. Instead they stopped at Haran, a town having the same name as that of Abraham's brother who had died at Ur (Gen. 11:27-32). Haran is located on the upper Euphrates River, perhaps five hundred miles from Ur by caravan route. For a clan to move that far in those days, with the aged, the mothers and their children, their goods and their cattle, was an undertaking calling for both faith and courage. We must realize, too, that such a clan consisted not only of all the living descendants of the patriarch but also of its servants and its fighting men. Of course people with nomadic traditions knew how to subsist on the land through which they moved. And the servants (slaves) would be more of a help than a hindrance.

After Terah died the clan split up into those divisions headed by the new patriarchs. Abraham seems to have headed the most powerful clan. Lot, the son of Abraham's deceased brother, headed the smaller clan (Gen. 12:4, 5). Then when Abraham resumed the trek westward Lot "went with him." The journey was not quite so long as before, though the terrain was more difficult. On arriving at Shechem Abraham is said to have built an altar to God as he did also at Bethel and at Hebron. The tradition goes on to say that Abraham heard God's voice telling him that this great land wherein the Canaanites then dwelt would some day belong to his descendants. The promise was repeated and enlarged until it included everything between the Euphrates and the "river of Egypt" (Gen. 15:18-21). The variety in the statement of the promises is partly due to the fact that they came from different traditions such as the Ephraimitic and the Judaic, as will be explained. They may have represented the aspirations of later times.

After descending into Egypt to escape a famine, on their return Abraham's clan and Lot's clan went their own ways. Lot chose the fertile Jordan valley, leaving the rough hill country for Abraham. The separation showed Abraham to be magnanimous while Lot sought personal gain. Later, however, a coalition of eastern kings, including "Chederlaomer king of Elam," raided the rich cities of the valley and captured Lot, taking all his goods with them. When Abraham heard what had happened he loyally led his "three hundred and eighteen fighting men" in pursuit. With smart tactics he divided his men and attacked the enemy at night from two sides. He was victorious, rescuing both Lot and his goods (Gen. 14:1-16). It is evident from this that Abraham was no recluse whose interests were impractical and other-worldly. He showed the cunning, courage, and loyalty of the bedouin sheikh, whose tradition he embodied. We may state this without exaggerating his might in meeting the coalition of eastern kings, whose raid was a small thing compared with later warfare and even then was probably a kind of "border incident" carried on by obscure soldiers of the kings named.

Some have suggested that the story of the eastern kings was the invention of a later age.[12] Albright asserts on the contrary that the language of the story is archaic and exhibits signs of authenticity. It is rather puzzling, however, to find the narrator saying that Abraham pursued the kings as far as Dan, whereas we learn from a later narrative that Dan was not in existence in Abraham's day. When the Danites many centuries later migrated from the south to the north of Ephraim to escape the Philistines, they destroyed the town of Laish and then rebuilt it, calling it Dan.

Uses of Tradition

Other stories relating to the patriarchs were patently inventions of later ages. They reveal more about the experiences and motivations of the later age than about early history. Certainly the story of the origin of the Moabites and the Ammonites was such an invention, typical of the manner in which such explanations were fitted to the needs of each situation. According to this story Lot's two daughters connived to make their father drunk in order to commit incest with him, "that we may preserve offspring through our father" (Gen. 19:30-38). This explanation is too simple to be true, and may easily be explained as the effort of later tradition-makers to show the depravity of their neighboring enemies, the Moabites and the Ammonites. Similar is the story according to which Abraham became the father of Ishmael by Hagar, the Egyptian slave of his wife, Sarah. The tradition notes that Ishmael became the father of a great nation, which has been taken to refer to the Arabs. This is obviously mythical, intended to account for the existence of the desert nomads, whose character is well stated in the sentence describing Ishmael: "He shall be a wild ass of a man, his hand against every man and every man's hand against him; and he shall dwell over against all his kinsmen" (Gen. 16:12).

The stories of Isaac, Esau and Jacob suggest some theories concerning their late composition by Ephraimites and Judaites. Esau is said to have been the father of the Edomites, whom Judah enslaved. Their degradation was justified according to one story because Esau had "despised his birthright," selling it to his younger brother for a mess of pottage (Gen. 25:29-34). Another justification was invented, it is said, when Jacob, the younger son, gained his father's blessing through deception (Gen. 27:1-29). A third story is that Jacob's hand grasped Esau's heel as he was being born, foreshadowing his role as a supplanter (Gen. 25:24-26). Even while the twins were in the womb the mother is said to have complained of the commotion within her. She was then told by Yahweh that

> Two nations are in your womb,
> and two peoples, born of you, shall be divided;
> The one shall be stronger than the other,
> the elder shall serve the younger (Gen. 25:21-23).

When Esau later begged for his father's blessing he was told that Jacob had already been made his lord. After Edom had revolted from Judah the prophecy added, "You shall break his yoke from your neck" (Gen. 27:30-40. Cf. II Kings 8:22).[13]

In like manner the stories about the sons of Jacob are said to be legends invented by Ephraimites or Jews in later ages, reflecting contemporary events and issues in the lives of the venerable patriarchs.[14] Accordingly in Genesis 33 the men of Shechem willingly sell land to Jacob, contrary to the Israelitic custom which forbade the alienation of land from a family. Then in Genesis 34 Simeon and Levi and their brothers are said to have destroyed the family of Hamor and Shechem after the latter had had sexual relations with Jacob's daughter, Dinah, whom he loved. It was through treachery that the Jacobites did this, for Shechem and his fellows had agreed to be circumcised according to the Hebrew custom. On the third day after circumcision, when the Shechemites were in no condition to fight, the Israelites perfidiously attacked and killed them and looted the houses of their city, taking Dinah away with them. Jacob is then made to say to Simeon and Levi, "You have brought trouble on me by making me odious to the inhabitants of the land, the Canaanites and the Perizzites. . . ." (Gen. 34:30).

When the Joseph tribes occupied the hill country south of Esdraelon they did not try to take the Canaanitic cities in the plain, and even left Shechem standing in the midst of their hill country. After Gideon's death the Shechemites made Abimelech their king, a son of Gideon by a Shechemite concubine. It seemed like a diplomatic move on the part of the Shechemites. They showed their conciliatory spirit in this way, taking one of Gideon's seventy sons by his many wives and concubines, and making him their king. In reality this was a subtle move to win the Ephraimites over to the basic economy of the Canaanites. Hence the legend took shape that Jacob had willingly bought land and traded peacefully with the Shechemites, later to repudiate that compromise and destroy the city. The patriarch was too venerable to be condemned for such an act. But if he did so, why should not his descendants? This is exactly what happened in the time of Gideon, long after settlement in Canaan, when Abimelech turned against his benefactors in Shechem and led in its destruction. The Canaanitic walled cities in the valley of Esdraelon, north of Ephraim, must have regarded this act of the Josephites as unjustified and sinister. In terms of Israelitic safety and cultural purity it seemed necessary to destroy the one walled city of the Canaanites remaining in the Ephraimitic hill country. The legend of the sons of Jacob treacherously destroying Shechem, in Genesis 34, was proposed as a kind of allegory justifying the later actual destruction.

Similarly the legend of Sodom may have been told as a kind of allegory to justify the later Israelitic destruction of Gibeah. Sodomy (so-called because of the Sodom incident) was the intended crime in both cases, while its execution was prevented by the master of the house offering female substitutes. Sodom was destroyed by divine fire and brimstone, while Gibeah, south of Ephraim, where "Benjamin" was now growing into a tribal unit, was destroyed by Israelites fighting against Benjaminites who allegedly were responsible for the moral outrage. It is said that this situation, in turn, was created partly in order to descredit the house of Saul, a native of Gibeah. David's Judah, a late-comer among the tribes of the Hebrews, was made the main hero of this tale, composed by a Judaic author after the destruction of the northern kingdom.

Some scholars regard all the stories of the Pentateuch thus as reflections of events happening at the time the stories were written, one story growing out of another until the Pentateuch was the result. This is a radical view of tribal tradition, and would seem to be unique among ancient cultures if true. It hardly seems credible that it should all have arisen in such a manner. I shall assume that there is a basic core of history underneath the accumulation of tradition, and that both history and tradition have their uses.

XXVIII. FROM EGYPT TO CANAAN

When Moses was born we find the Hebrew tribes in some kind of bondage in Egypt. Many historical problems are involved in this situation. Was Moses a man or a myth? If the Hebrews were in bondage how did they get into it? How many tribes were there? What was their religion? How did they become Yahweh worshipers? What historical core underlies the legends of escape from Egypt, wilderness wandering, and conquest of Canaan?

The traditional number of tribes is twelve, but then twelve is a magical number in the Bible and is a norm rather than a fact. Twelve was the number of sons not only of Jacob, but also of Nahor (Gen. 22:20-24), of Ishmael (Gen. 17:20), and of Esau (Gen. 36:15-19), to say nothing of the twelve apostles in the New Testament. Saul knew of no twelve tribes when he cut his yoke of oxen in pieces (I Sam. 11:7), according to the Ephraimitic narrator. The later Judaic tale of the Levite, who cut his concubine's dead body in twelve pieces, fell under the spell of the magic number twelve (Judges 19:29). When the prophet Ahijah incited Jeroboam to rebel against Solomon he tore a cloak into twelve pieces and told Jeroboam to take ten of them (I Kings 11:30f.). One tribe he kept for Solomon, for David's sake. Now ten and one do not make twelve, but the number had to be twelve anyhow.

It is plausibly suggested that only the Joseph tribe or tribes—one or two—descended into Egypt and settled in the border area of Goshen, still following the customs of semi-nomads. How large they were is not agreed by the traditions. One strand states that they were "few in number," comprising only seventy persons in all. Two midwives were sufficient to care for all the births of Hebrew babies, even at the time of the oppression.[1] In another tradition Jacob refers to his armed forces as if they were large.[2] Abraham is said to have had three hundred and eighteen fighting men in his household. The number of Habiru migrating to Canaan was certainly augmented *en route,* as will be seen.

The invasion of Canaan may have occurred over centuries. Albright holds that the two Joseph tribes—Ephraim and Manasseh—entered Canaan in the fourteenth century, whereas Joshua's invasion occurred a century later.[3] My study has led me to believe that the Josephites were the nucleus of the Biblical Hebrews, and that they left Egypt and entered Canaan somewhere around 1250 B.C.

Escape from Bondage

When the Josephites settled in Goshen their presence was agreeable to the Egyptians, who at that time were ruled by the Hyksos, a north Semitic people (it is now thought) who were masters of Egypt from about 1750 to 1560 B.C. The patriotic eighteenth dynasty, which expelled the Hyksos pharaohs, and the succeeding nineteenth dynasty, did not get along so well with the Hebrews.

Three different pharaohs have been named as the possible pharaoh of the oppression.[4] They were Thutmose III (c. 1490-1436 B.C.) of the eighteenth dynasty, and Seti I (c. 1319-1301 B.C.) and Ramses II (c. 1301-1234 B.C.) of the nineteenth dynasty.

The presumed reason for the enslavement of Joseph was the deterioration of foreign relations. Egypt had long been a great empire; but as early as the reign of Ikhnaton (c. 1377-1360 B.C.) when the Tell el-Amarna tablets (found in 1887) were being written, it is evident that Egypt was in trouble. The motive for the oppression as suggested in Exod. 1:10 was probably the real one: fear lest the numerous Hebrews on the border of Egypt might join with Egypt's enemies, the rising Hittites, and conquer the land.

The historicity of Moses is well attested. This does not mean that the details were as cited. For example the story of his being found in the bulrushes and adopted by Pharaoh's daughter is a tale which with varying details went the rounds in the ancient Near East, being told of a number of great men.* Yet he was evidently a Hebrew of broad experience and high achievement, very possibly reared in the royal palace. Even his name witnesses to his historicity, for the essence of the name, Moses, is found to be a part of Thutmose,

* See Chapter IV, p. 61.

Ahmose, and Ramses, and as such was a popular name among the royal princes of the eighteenth and nineteenth dynasties.

Moses was probably responsible for one of the most significant developments in the history of Israel, namely, for learning to know Yahweh and interpreting him to his fellow Hebrews. Upon killing an Egyptian taskmaster for beating a Hebrew he fled to the land of the Kenites (Midianites) at Kadesh. There he married a daughter

Originally a mountain god, sending storms and giving success in battle, Yahweh went along with the Josephites into Canaan where the prophets transformed him into a god of ethical universality.

of one of the Kenites, who already were worshipers of Yahweh. Since Moses adhered to the nomadic tradition, it was natural enough for him to feel at home with the semi-nomads of Kadesh. As a shepherd he must have found himself often alone with nature. Meanwhile his father-in-law commended to him the chief local deity, Yahweh, a war god ("Yahweh of Hosts"). The legend of the burning bush dramatizes the deep emotional experience of the Hebrew shepherd when he became aware of the divine presence on the holy mount, the home of Yahweh. Nor was the experience a purely individualistic one. For the experience of God's presence, no matter by what name he is called, is likely to carry with it a moral mission. For Moses this mission was to return to Egypt and free his people from bondage. Tradition tells that Moses felt too clumsy to undertake such an assignment. But he was sure that someone must do it, and since Yahweh told him to do so he decided to try, with God's help.

How desperate was the enslavement and how hard it was to escape cannot be determined. Certainly the finished tradition pictured it as humanly hopeless. The mildest interpretation of the core experience must regard the Hebrews as a nomadic tribe that wished further adventure but was forbidden by the Egyptian border guard to leave Egypt. They had proved themselves too useful in Egypt to be allowed to go without protest.

There are conflicting traditions as to where the Hebrews were when they decided to escape from Egypt. One strand pictures the Israelites as shepherds in Goshen, on the border of Egypt, dwelling in complete separation from the Egyptian population.[5] The other envisages the Hebrews as mixed with the general Egyptian population. They seemed to be so intimate with their Egyptian neighbors that when on the eve of the exodus they asked to "borrow" jewels of silver and gold they could not be denied. They were such close neighbors that the only way in which the angel of death could distinguish between an Egyptian and a Hebrew household was by the blood of the lamb on the doorpost.[6]

One account is filled with supernatural intrusions into nature and history, while the other suggests merely providential factors. Many are the survivals of magic in the titanic struggle between Pharaoh's magicians and Moses and Aaron. Then when the exodus finally occurred, according to one account when the Israelites reached the Sea of Reeds it was Moses' magic wand which caused the waters to stay apart just long enough to save them and drown the Egyptians. But the other explanation was that a providential east wind caused the sea-bed to become dry. The Song of Miriam, expanded by a later poet, stresses the providential element.[7]

The purely secular explanation for the escape of Joseph may well lie in the fact that at that very time Egypt was busy defending itself against the New Hittite Empire. The basic fact of history is that Israel did escape from Egypt, probably against the will of the Egyptians, and were led by Moses to the holy mount where he had already met Yahweh.

Home in the Wilderness

If the holy mount was near Kadesh, as suggested in several Biblical passages, then we shall have to revise the traditional account of the descent to Sinai and the miraculous events of revelation there. Even the tale of the forty years of wandering in the wilderness turns out on this theory to be not history, but reflections of later experiences (the oppression of Ephraim by Judah under David and Solomon?). The Judaic and Priestly traditions might be expected to provide a convenient opportunity in the wilderness wherein Yahweh could reveal the intricate details of late ritual and also emphasize the importance of Judah, such as did not exist until later times.

The tendency of recent historians is to picture the Joseph tribes as making a fairly quick journey to Kadesh, an oasis described as "the city of palms." Says one account, "When they came up from

Egypt, Israel went through the wilderness to the Red Sea and came to Kadesh" (Judges 11:16). There they tarried long enough to get organized for the invasion of Canaan. An important part of their preparation was morale building. For this purpose it was only natural that Yahweh, whose help had enabled them to escape from Egypt, should now loom larger and larger in their estimation, and that they should take vows to be faithful to such a great deity. This further strengthened them for the task still to be accomplished.

Kindness of the Kenites

The Kenites were remembered in later times for having done a great kindness to Israel. Since a crucial problem of religious history is involved in the nature of this kindness, I shall pause to discuss it here.

The word used to denote the Kenite kindness to Israel was *hesed.* This word has connotations of a special type of service, a divine sort of kindness, or steadfast love.[8] Thus Saul gave the Kenites in his day special consideration, "for you showed kindness (*hesed*) to all the people of Israel when they came up out of Egypt" (I Sam. 15:6).

Could it be that the special kindness of the Kenites consisted in their hospitality and cooperation with the Josephites? Not only did they give them sanctuary in the wilderness, but they also joined in the invasion of Canaan. "And the descendants of the Kenite, Moses' father-in-law, went up with the people of Judah from the city of palms [Kadesh] into the wilderness of Judah, which lies in the Negeb near Arad; and they went and settled with the people" (Judges 1:16). Some of the Kenites settled farther north, in the plain of Esdraelon, where Jael, wife of Heber the Kenite, dwelling in a tent, killed a Canaanitic captain after a crucial battle (Judges 4:11; 5:24). The Kenites were a highly respected part of the Judaic community even in Jeremiah's day (Jer. 35).

Important as the Kenites' political cooperation with Israel was, it does not rate the quality of *hesed.*[9] The special kindness of the Kenites was to introduce the Israelites to Yahweh and teach them his *mishpat,* first through Moses and later face to face. Late authors of the Pentateuch did not understand this. They developed stories which culminated in the divinely ordered slaughter of the entire male population of the Midianites, who were substituted in their story for the sub-tribe of Kenites (Num. 31:7). The amazing thing to a modern reader, seeing the various stories juxtaposed in our Bible as they were not originally, is to learn in Judges 6 and 7 that the Midianites, after being exterminated in Numbers 31, were somehow resurrected later, causing Gideon and his fighters a good deal of trouble.

The suggestion may be elaborated that Israel was still pagan before coming to Kadesh. Even the late Priestly tradition admits that Yahweh was not known as such prior to Moses: "And God said to Moses, 'I am the Lord [Yahweh]. I appeared to Abraham, to Isaac, and to Jacob, as God Almighty [El Shaddai], but by my name the Lord [Yahweh] I did not make myself known to them.' "[10] Add to this evidence the statement of Joshua, from the Ephraimitic tradition: "Now therefore fear the Lord [Yahweh], and serve him in sincerity and in faithfulness; put away the gods which your fathers served beyond the River, and in Egypt, and serve the Lord [Yahweh]" (Josh. 24:14). These passages make it clear that the earliest traditions regarded the ancestors of the Mosaic tribes as pagans who first came in contact with Yahweh, the divine benefactor of Joseph, through the instrumentality of the Kenites.

That Ephraim (and Manasseh) learned the Law of Yahweh at Kadesh is further witnessed by specific references. This core experience is reflected in the enlarged traditions regarding the encampment at Sinai. A secondary name for Kadesh was En-mishpat. Kadesh means "Holy Place," and En-mishpat means "Center of Justice," and these two terms were regarded as synonymous. "Then they turned back and came to En-mishpat (that is, Kadesh)" (Gen. 14:7). It was there, through the kindness or steadfast love (*hesed*) of the Kenites, that Joseph learned the *mishpat,* or justice, of Yahweh. Here was a semi-nomadic people like the Joseph tribes who had a culture similar to that of Joseph. Moses had synthesized the two cultures in his retreat there before returning on his mission to Egypt. Then on organizing the tribal exodus he brought them to the same holy place and taught them the sacred law at headquarters.

That the wilderness experience was much simpler than is indicated by the Judaic and Priestly accounts, or even the edited Ephraimitic and Deuteronomic accounts, is clear for several reasons. For example, the ark did not originate in the wilderness as alleged, for it does not accompany the tribes in their first attack on Canaan. Nor is it mentioned in the account of Deborah and Barak, not even in the primitive poetic source, the Song of Deborah. Judge Ehud did not take it on the attack against Moab, nor Gideon against the Midianites, nor Jephthah against Ammon.[11] The priestly hierarchy, too, originated not in the wilderness but in post-exilic times. Samuel, who was an Ephraimite, not a Levite nor a descendant of Aaron, was the attendant of the holy ark which apparently was first enshrined at Shiloh. There is conflict among the traditions as to priestly priorities and ritual organization even in the wilderness. While the Priestly tradition gives an ecclesiastical monoply to Aaron and his sons, and locates the ark at the center of the camp in the wilderness, the Ephraimitic account places the sanctuary outside the camp and names as priests Moses and his sons and miscellaneous young men of Israel. The Priestly account, produced by priests of Judah after surviving the Babylonian captivity, aims at two main goals: to show the greatness of Judah over Ephraim, and to establish the priestly ritual as an ancient and venerable tradition. On this theory the confusions can easily be understood, and we may discount the story of how Yahweh prescribed an elaborate ritual for temple worship in the wilderness.

That Yahweh ordered no ritual or burnt offerings or sacrifice prior to the conquest of Canaan is stated by Jeremiah. "Thus says the Lord of hosts, the God of Israel: 'Add your burnt offerings to your sacrifices, and eat the flesh. For in the day that I brought them out of the land of Egypt, I did not speak to your fathers or command them concerning burnt offerings and sacrifices'" (Jer. 7:21, 22). Jeremiah further witnesses to the first love and the marriage of Israel and Yahweh in the wilderness, where he represents the Lord as saying:

> I remember the devotion of your youth,
> your love as a bride,
> how you followed me in the wilderness,
> in a land not sown.
> Israel was holy to the Lord,
> the first fruits of his [Yahweh's] harvest (Jer. 2:2, 3).

Deuteronomy, too, asserts that Israel and Yahweh met in the wilderness:

> For the Lord's portion is his people,
> Jacob his allotted heritage.
> He found him in a desert land,
> and in the howling waste of the wilderness;
> he encircled him, he cared for him,
> he kept him as the apple of his eye" (Deut. 32:9, 10).

The Mosaic Law

It is most unlikely that all of the decalogue originated in the wilderness experience. The *mishpat,* or nomadic folk-justice which the Israelites learned—or relearned—from the Kenites, was the core around which the enlarging law of Israel gradually coalesced. Fundamental was the principle of the sacredness of the family inheritance. Land which was owned in common by nomadic desert clans became, on settling down to an agrarian economy, inalienable from the family unit. This was the opposite of the Canaanitic custom.

The earliest form of the decalogue, as we now have it, was probably that given in the Ephraimitic tradition in Exodus 20. More ritualistic was the Judaic version of Exodus 34, evidently of later origin. The decalogue as found in Deuteronomy 5:6-21 was composed in the mid-seventh century B.C., and represents a compromise between prophetic and priestly religion which was even then developing.

The most primitive code on which the Josephites relied forbade theft of property. Covetousness, the twin of thievery, was eventually forbidden also though perhaps not as soon as the account would have it. The code also forbade putting Baal, or any other inferior god, ahead of Yahweh. And it certainly condemned falsehood and murder.

Thus we find a basis in Israelitic experience for the first commandment (against other gods), the sixth (against murder), the eighth (against theft), the ninth (false witness), and perhaps the tenth (covetousness).

The seventh commandment, against adultery, may have been enunciated in the wilderness, but if so its interpretation was far different from ours today. A careful and critical analysis of Israelitic experience makes one suspect that loose sexual relations were regarded as normal. Women customarily were thought of as man's property. The "man servant" and the "maid servant" were really not "free" servants but slaves owned by the master, the "adon." And the many "wives" possessed by the ancient Hebrews were not wives in our sense, or even in the Muslim sense. The Hebrew word which is translated "wife" is really just the word for "woman," who was regarded as man's property. The injunction not to covet another man's property included the command not to covet his "women," i.e. his female property. The context is entirely clear on this point for any one who will read. In Exod. 22:16, 17 we read, "If a man seduces a virgin who is not betrothed, and lies with her, he shall give the marriage present for her, and make her his wife [i.e., his woman]. If her father utterly refuses to give her to him, he shall pay money equivalent to the marriage present for virgins." It is evident that he would thus be making an economic payment for his adultery merely by passing money amounting to the marriage present over to the father. It was purely a financial transaction. The many "wives" and "concubines" of David, Solomon, and many other early Old Testament characters, show that the position of women as the property of man did not change quickly. The patriarchs not only had several "wives" but also slave women. The ease with which Gilead, Samson, and others went to harlots is also indicative. Jephthah, son of Gilead by a harlot, played an important role as a Judge of Israel. Samson's role as Judge and hero seems to have been unspoiled by his resort to harlots and other women whom his fancy desired. In earlier times Judah is said to have gone in to a harlot who turned out to be his own daughter-in-law. His embarrassment was caused merely by the fact that he did not know until later that it was his daughter-in-law (Gen. 38). The story of Joseph's chastity in Pharaoh's household is a reflection of the morals of a much later age.

As to the second commandment, it seems that Israel did not generally understand that they were to use no "graven images." For they were commonly used by the best of people in Israel until the prophets enunciated the doctrines of monotheism and the spirituality of God.

Even the fourth commandment seems to have been a late addition to the Mosaic code. The observance of the sabbath received support by the prophet-priests of the seventh century, as when they wrote Deuteronomy. But the great prophets had nothing to say about the customary failure to observe the sabbath until after the exile.

In any case, the commandments which Moses sanctified in the wilderness must be understood as having a much different orientation than they acquired later. One thing which many today do not realize, for example, is that slavery was an established institution in ancient Israel. The *mishpat* which was so sacred in the economy of Israel applied only to free men. The women purchased as slaves had fewer rights than those women who were purchased from free fathers. And the men-slaves (called men-servants in our translations) were chattels like anything else. Even the poorest of free Israelites had slaves. Said Gideon, "My clan is the weakest in Manasseh; and I am the least in my family" (Judges 6:15). Yet Gideon had many slaves, from whom he selected ten for a certain task.

The great thing accomplished by Moses in the wilderness, with the aid of the Kenites, was to bring the Josephites into a covenant relation with Yahweh, and to give sanction to a way of life which the Israelites learned at Kadesh in the school of the Kenites. This was the germ of a spiritual life which grew in the new environment of Canaan, as prophets and leaders gained insight into the nature of man and God. The end product was the Mosaic decalogue as we now have it, plus the visions of the prophets and the sentiments of the Psalms.

In at least one case we have good evidence that a rite originated at Kadesh which is stated elsewhere in the Bible as having had an earlier origin. That was the rite of circumcision. In Gen. 17:10 God instructs Abraham to initiate the rite as a part of his covenant. In Exod. 4:24-26 a different and more interesting account is given, such as would attract the interest of a modern anthropologist. The account of Genesis 17 appears to be a pious effort to link circumcision with the oldest Hebrew tradition. Exod. 4, however, seems to be the innocent record of an old superstition, modified by interpretation and passed on to the Hebrews.

The thing which most surprises one in Exod. 4:24-26 is the statement that as Moses was on his way to Egypt to carry out Yahweh's commands "the Lord met him and sought to kill him." Now why would Moses' precious Yahweh seek to kill him? The explanation lies behind the following verses: "Then Zipporah took a flint and cut off her son's foreskin, and touched Moses' feet with it, and said, 'Surely you are a bridegroom of blood to me!' So he [Yahweh] let him [Moses] alone. Then it was that she said, 'You are a bridegroom of blood,' because of the circumcision." All of this goes back to a primitive Semitic superstition that on the wedding night a demon would seek to slay the groom unless the bride's father performed on the groom the rite of circumcision, touching his feet with the foreflesh in order to give him a magical immunity to the power of the demon. The use of flint knives testifies to the antiquity of the rite and the superstition.[12] The preservation of this bit of folklore applied at this juncture suggests that Israel learned the rite of circumcision from the Kenites (or Midianites). The fact that it was Moses' son instead of Moses who was circumcised merely shows that the editors were trying to do something reasonable with an ancient and misunderstood tradition. And the fact that it was Yahweh instead of a demon who sought to kill him shows that the editors were putting all power into Yahweh's hands, as happened also in the case of Gen. 38:7, where Yahweh that time succeeded in slaying someone. The wholesale circumcision of the Hebrews on entering Canaan (Josh. 5:2ff.) was an evidence that the rite did have its inception at that time in the Hebrew tradition.

Hebrew Culture a Continuous Development

The decalogue must be regarded as a late product, in its present state. Some of its elements were far older than Moses, while some must have arisen later than Moses. The same is true of the ordinances following the decalogue in Exod. 21f. Much of it, for example, applies only to an agrarian economy and should be regarded as a product of Hebrew experience in Canaan. Practically all of the Mosaic code was anticipated by the code of Hammurabi, and has its parallels in other ancient codes, the oldest of which were the Sumerian and Akkadian codes of the nineteenth century B.C. or earlier. I do not mean that the Mosaic—or post-Mosaic—code copied the earlier codes. Their provisions were generally known throughout the Semitic East, and probably inspired Israel's formulation while in

Canaan. Codification may not have been completed until during or after the Babylonian captivity.

There was cultural continuity also in the tribal movement into Canaan. When in the thirteenth century B.C. the Josephites left Kadesh and began fighting for a place in the more fertile land of Canaan, they were joined by the Kenites and possibly other Hebrew groups. Some of the Habiru had already infiltrated into Canaan, as witnessed by the Tell el-Amarna letters a century earlier. Now the Josephites became the nucleus of a spirited new anti-urban culture based on a covenant with the rural war god, "Yahweh of hosts." How much greater than a war god Yahweh was to become, Joseph at that time simply could not imagine. It all came about so gradually that people could not see it taking place, until the prophets dramatized it. Finally, though, it seemed so significant that oral traditions took shape and many writers composed their varying epics trying to describe and explain how it had happened. The result was the literature of our Old Testament. Meanwhile some tribes gradually accepted Joseph's cultural leadership, while the Canaanites eventually gave way to the political power of Israel and partially accepted its culture.

So far as we know, there were just two divisions of Josephites: Ephraim and Manasseh (or Machir). It is held that Manasseh was the older of the two tribes, and took the initial leadership, but that Ephraim grew stronger than Manasseh and in time usurped the first place. In the end both were referred to as one group, namely, Ephraim, or sometimes Joseph, or just Israel.

On leaving Kadesh Ephraim circled unfriendly Moab and Ammon (according to one tradition) and pierced directly into the heart of Palestine. The conquest of the pleasant hill country south of the valley of Esdraelon might reasonably be expected to have taken place by way of Jericho, as the book of Joshua relates. Substantially this is true, but here as elsewhere the reader must beware.

Conquering Canaan

The flaw in the Jericho stories consists in the archaeological discovery that Jericho was destroyed during the fourteenth century and not rebuilt until the ninth century B.C., during the reign of Ahab.

Therefore the Israelites could hardly have been the agents, unless indeed some of them arived in Canaan during the fourteenth century. It is more likely that the tradition of Jericho's destruction by non-Israelites was told and retold until finally it was incorporated into the Joshua tradition as an exploit of his fighters.

The magical fall of Jericho was like the magical crossing of the Jordan, which in turn paralleled the supernaturalistic version of the crossing of the Sea of Reeds. Beneath the crust of tradition we may perceive that Ephraim did cross the Jordan by means which at the time seemed providential, and ascended to Bethel. The tradition interposes Ai between Jericho and Bethel, but here too archaeology sheds light. Ai was utterly destroyed about 2200 B.C. and was never rebuilt until after Israel had occupied the land, and then only as a mere village. Probably the conquest of Ai, as told in Joshua, should be taken as describing the destruction of Bethel, which archaeology shows to have occurred about 1250 B.C.

After capturing Bethel the Ephraimites were ready to strike into the heart of Palestine, which was their goal. They abandoned any idea of capturing the walled Canaanitic cities in the plain of Esdraelon, but instead entrenched themselves in the hill country to the south. There was one formidable walled city in the highlands, namely, Shechem. This, too, they bypassed until a later time. Meanwhile everywhere they went they killed the inhabitants of the land and appropriated their property including their slaves. Yahweh himself is represented as saying, "Its spoil and its cattle you shall take as booty" (Josh. 8:2). The hardy Ephraimites, toughened by the desert experience and subsquent successes, spread over the highlands and put their newly acquired slaves to work for them while they organized for its defense. When they were not fighting they worked democratically alongside their slaves.

The Joshua story of the complete conquest of Canaan is proved untrue in the light of Judges and Samuel. But if its essential story is applied to the hill country of Ephraim, it seems to be substantially true. No mercy was shown to the inhabitants of the hills. Eventually even the walled city of Shechem was captured, as we shall see.

Entrenched in the highlands, the Ephraimites spearheaded the movement of the newcomers to resist the urban culture of the Canaanitic walled cities. It is not necessary to conceive that the rest of the newcomers were descendants of Abraham or of Jacob or Israel —and some think that the latter were two different persons. What happened was that other tribes, Habiru or otherwise, who were unhappy about the dominance of the Canaanitic aristocracy, joined with Ephraim in resistance. Gradually the idea took root that the several tribes belonged together as a large common family. The physiological fact of descent from a common patriarch was not so important as the belief that they were so descended.

From our most primitive source, the Song of Deborah, plus the supplementary narratives, we learn much about early Israel in Canaan. Benjamin was most probably a colony branching off from the tribe of Ephraim about 1200 B.C. The name means literally "son of the south." As Ephraim became secure in the central hills its numbers grew. Since the fortified Canaanitic cities in the plain of Esdraelon discouraged northward expansion, it was only natural that growth should have occurred southward, and the result was Benjamin, who is represented in legend as the younger brother of Joseph (Gen. 35:16-18). These two patriarchs are said to have been Rachel's only sons (Gen. 35:24). Manasseh and Ephraim, in turn, are represented as Joseph's two sons. That these were the original tribes of Israel may be conjectured from the formation of the name Israel, "Ish-rachel," or "man of Rachel," referring to Israel's legendary love for her.[13] Rachel's descendants turn out thus to be the historical nucleus around whom Israelitic expansion gradually took place.

Drawn into the Israelitic expansionist movement were certain other tribes for whom legends were duly provided. In the twelfth century B.C. those tribes were three, namely, Issachar, Naphtali, and Zebulun. Issachar lived in the valley of Jezreel, at the eastern end of the plain of Esdraelon. The men of Issachar were peasant-farmers enslaved by their Canaanitic masters. They were represented as having been descended from Jacob by Leah, who by deceit became the mother of Jacob's oldest son. Naphtali, from the hills north of the valley, was represented as a son of Jacob by Rachel's slave girl, Bilhah. Zebulun came to be regarded as descended from Leah. This tribe, like Naphtali, inhabited the northern hills. Joseph needed the help of these northern tribes in order to overcome the Canaanitic cities of the plain of Esdraelon. In return for their cooperation they would gain freedom from Canaan's urban aristocrats.

Other groups were referred to bitterly in the Song of Deborah (Judges 5) for not having come to the help of Ephraim. However, there were good reasons why some of them did not cooperate. The Danites, southwestward toward Philistia at that time, were too afraid of their closer enemy, the Philistines. Asher, near the Phoenician coast, was blocked by the large cities of the plain. Reuben and Gilead were east of the Jordan, and their homes would have been exposed to danger from the desert by their participation in a western war. Reuben was made a sort of renegade Israelite by Leah. He seduced Rachel's slave girl, Bilhah, and earned the contempt with which the Ephraimites looked upon him. Gilead remained uncooperative and hostile toward Ephraim, and never attained Israelitic descent in the Ephraimitic legends, although the Judaic Priestly narrative changes that situation (Numb. 26:29; I Chron. 2:21; 7:17).

The most surprising thing about the Song of Deborah was its silence about Judah. Certainly if Judah had cooperated with Joseph that would have been mentioned. And if there had been a good excuse for non-cooperation, such as separation from Joseph by Jebus (Jerusalem), an unconquered Canaanitic city, it should have been mentioned just as Asher and Dan were. Silence probably means that no such tribe was known at that time. Likewise Simeon and Levi were unmentioned in the poem, or elsewhere in the Hebrew history of Canaan. Levi finally figures as the progenitor of a subordinate priestly group. Gad was the other name used to make up the magical number of twelve for the sons of Jacob.

The motivating force in the formation of the Hebrew tradition was the success of the Yahweh people. The Joseph tribes, including Benjamin, were the nucleus of the new order in Canaan. As they were joined by Issachar, Naphtali, and Zebulun, and later by other tribes, they all shared in the *mishpat* ideal of Yahwism and were subject to the rising influence of the Hebrew prophets and other leaders.

Battle of Esdraelon

One of the decisive battles of history was fought on the plain of Esdraelon about 1150 B.C. Ephraim had been promoting a war against the fortified Canaanitic cities for a long time, secretly sending agents and arms to Issachar and the northern hill tribes. Finally about 1150 the crisis arrived. Deborah, an Ephraimitic "Judge," and Barak, a natural-born military genius from Issachar, inspired and organized the expedition. The cities of the plain represented the old order, and the hill people stood for the new order. The urbanites had chariots of iron—nine hundred of them—and masses of infantry. Against ten thousand Israelites (Judg. 4:6; forty thousand are mentioned in 5:8) the Canaanitic chariots and weapons might well have won the battle. But a sudden rain mired the chariots in mud, and Jabin, king of Canaan, and Sisera his captain, were thoroughly defeated. Yahweh gained a reputation that day as rain-maker outranking the Canaanitic Baalim.

It was when Captain Sisera fled that Jael, the Kenite woman, lured him into her tent and killed him by piercing his head with a tent spike. Sang Deborah,

> So perish all thine enemies, O Lord!
> But thy friends be like the sun as he rises
> in his might. (Judges 5:31).

By this time Israel was beginning to think of itself as master of the land, ready to defend it against all comers. So when the nomadic Midianites and Amalekites from the desert tried to despoil the tribe of Issachar, up rose a new "judge" or leader of the Yahweh people, Gideon the Ephraimite. The battle cry now was "A sword for the Lord and for Gideon" (Judges 7:20). To his leadership rallied not only the Josephites but also men from Zebulun, Naphtali, and even Asher. Men of Issachar joined, no doubt, if in the first attack they had not already perished. There are parallel stories as to exactly what happened, but at any rate a small company of brave men claiming Yahweh as their leader defeated and destroyed the Midianites and their allies. This is believed to have happened about 1125 B.C.

It is related that Gideon made a golden image ("ephod") through which he might learn the will of Yahweh, and that he had many wives and slave girls, and many sons ("seventy" in Judges 8:30). But the people of Joseph and his allies accepted him as a Yahweh leader or "judge," and he defended the land against Canaanites within and nomads without.

A strange compromise may be seen, however, in Gideon's relationship with a "concubine" in the Canaanitic city of Shechem. The Shechemites chose as their king Gideon's son by this concubine. Abimelech accepted the honor but later perfidiously joined the Israelites to destroy Shechem. Supposing that it was impossible to convert the Shechemites to the Ephraimitic *mishpat,* and that to compromise with them otherwise would have been cultural catastrophe, there probably was no alternative but to destroy the Canaanitic fortified city in the heart of Ephraim. Still it is hard to give complete moral assent to it, even considering the times in which they lived. Diplomatically it had two effects. First, it destroyed the absentee urban landlord class and rewarded many Ephraimites with additional land and other property. Unfortunately, however, the people of the remaining walled cities, as in Esdraelon, who had perhaps begun to regard the Israelites as protectors against foreign invaders, now began to look upon them with a new suspicion.

Shortly a new danger arose from the Moabitic nomads east of the Dead Sea. "Judge" Ehud delivered the Benjaminites from this threat. And "Judge" Jephthah, a Gileadite of ill repute who possessed much military skill, delivered Gilead from the attacks of the Ammonites. Later Jephthah offered his only child, a daughter, in tragic sacrifice. This story was told to explain the origin of a custom in mourning.

The Philistine Menace

Southwest of Benjamin were the Danites, a kind of buffer tribe between Ephraim and the Philistines. The latter were Mediterraneans of Lycian-Carian origin who wandered along the Asia Minor coast as a result of the Phrygian invasion (c. 1300) until they settled in Palestine about 1200.[14] Their importance is reflected in the fact that they gave their name to Palestine, which is a corruption of Philistine. The rustic Danites certainly showed more kinship toward the Josephites than toward the Philistines, who possessed iron tools and weapons and harassed the hill people of Benjamin and Dan.

The collection of short stories about Samson illustrates the frustrated life of the Danites. Samson himself was a Danite, we are informed. The Samson sagas were told at rustic gatherings, not for the entertainment of nobility. "Always brawling and excelling all rivals in muscular strength, this uncouth fellow is no match for feminine wiles. But under the rough exterior there is a witty if untutored mind, quick at repartee, an instinctive devotion to his own people, and a dogged determination in avenging wrongs, which culminates in a self-inflicted heroic death."[15]

Samson set out to marry a Philistine woman. Killing a lion on the way, he later found the carcass infested with bees. He proposed a riddle to the thirty wedding guests, who secured the answer through his girl. Samson was thus forced to pay the forfeit, in the form of clothing which he obtained by killing thirty Philistines. The girl's father then angrily gave her to one of the guests. Samson was so incensed by this that he tied torches to foxes' tails and set the foxes loose in the harvest fields. Once he killed thousands of his enemies with a simple weapon—probably not the "jawbone of an ass." After an affair with a harlot of Gaza (in Philistia) Samson escaped by carrying off the city gates. In a later series of episodes Delilah's cunning secured from him the secret of his strength, and brought about his tragic downfall.

The Samson folklore as we have them are substantially in the form in which they came from the Judaic narrator, displaying Judaic prejudices.

When the Danites finally wearied of being the brunt of the Philistine forays upon Israel, they gathered up their possessions and migrated to the far north, beyond Zebulun and Naphtali.

Story of Two Levites

An interesting insight into the culture of ancient Israel is afforded by the brush between the migrating Danites and Micah, an Ephraimite who maintained a temple of images and other ritualistic items. Two images of silver were designed as aids to the worship of Yahweh. Aware of the religious values of Micah's collection, the Danites used strong-arm methods to get what they wanted. From the collection they "took the graven image, the ephod, the teraphim, and the molten image." To Micah's priest they said, " 'Keep quiet, put your hand upon your mouth, and come with us, and be to us a father and a priest. Is it better for you to be priest to the house of one man, or to be priest to a tribe and family in Israel?' And the priest's heart was glad. . . ." (Judges 18:18, 19, 20). Micah was powerless to prevent this act, since the Danites had "six hundred men armed with weapons of war" (18:17). Arriving at the northern city of Laish, they captured it, killed the inhabitants, rebuilt it and called it Dan.

The priest who was kidnaped by the Danites was said to be a Levite, a descendant of Moses. Another Levite whose story appears in Judges reflects infamy upon Ephraim. However, the story is so fantastic that its moral serves primarily to identify its author as late Judaic, who tried to bring disrepute to Gibeah, the home of Saul. Judaic authors trying to glorify David and his dynasty were always on the alert for any such opportunity. Scholars are disagreed as to what portion of Judges was originally contributed by Ephraimitic writers. There can be no disagreement, however, as to who wrote the story of Gibeah, or who did the final editing of the entire book.

The Levite from Ephraim went down to Bethlehem-Judah to secure a concubine. On his journey home he arrived at Gibeah of Benjamin late in the day and was invited to spend the night with a kind man. Before bedtime the men of the city surrounded the house and demanded that its master surrender his male visitor for the purpose of sodomy. As in the story of Lot (Gen. 19:4-8), the master offered his own daughter and the concubine as substitutes for the Levite. The concubine was accepted in this case and killed through abuse during the night. The Levite later cut her body in twelve pieces and sent them to arouse Israel to vengeance. In the ensuing epic Judah played the heroic part. The Judaic author thus atoned for the absence of Judah otherwise from Judges, and placed a black mark on Gibeah and its famous native, King Saul.

Thus legend brings us to the end of the period of the Judges, and to the beginning of the monarchy, when more organized action was taken by the growing Israelitic group for national independence and safety.

XXIX. RISE OF THE HEBREW MONARCHY

If we date the exodus from Egypt at about 1250 B.C., and the invasion of Canaan a very few years later, then we may believe that soon after mid-century the Josephites gained control over the hill country south of the plain of Esdraelon, killing off the free population and taking over its slaves. In the course of the next half-century expansion had taken place southward, and the sub-tribe of Benjamin was born. Unable to push farther south because of the Philistines, who had settled there about 1200, Ephraim tried driving northward. He gained the cooperation of Issachar, Naphtali, and Zebulun who assisted in defeating the alliance of the cities of the plain. This occurred about 1150. Within about fifty more years the Canaanitic city of Shechem, in Ephraim's hill country, was destroyed. Meanwhile Gideon, Ehud, and Jephthah had led in the defense of Israelitic tribes against their nomadic neighbors.

To Israel the worst threat of all was from the Philistines to the southwest. The rustic Danites, southwest of Benjamin, developed a fundamental feeling of kinship for Ephraim because of the enmity of their coastal neighbors, the Philistines. When the Danites in desperation migrated to the far north they left Israel's southern flank exposed. Their continuing sympathy for Ephraim, however, encouraged the strengthening of Israel through consolidation northward. The Israelitic aristocracy, united in its loyalty to Yahweh and his *mishpat,* inevitably developed a broad national consciousness and soon recognized its need for monarchy. Nothing less than monarchy would take care of the Philistine threat.

The first effort toward national monarchy came from Ephraim. Only later did Judah emerge as a significant tribe. Still later Ephraim was destroyed, and Judah lived on, ultimately to go into exile itself. When Judah found itself the sole bearer of the Hebrew national tradition, there were strong reasons why its prophets and writers should have exalted Judah at the expense of Ephraim. The books of Samuel and Kings were written during the exile, by Judaic writers drawing upon earlier sources. The Judaic bias was inevitable. The new material which they introduced denied the more primitive sources and reflected unfairly on the first Ephraimitic monarch, a native of Gibeah in Benjamin.

Ephraim Elects Saul

Saul's first opportunity came when messengers from Gilead hurried to Gibeah and reported that the Ammonites were making savage threats against the Gileadites. Gilead had always been cool to the idea of union with Israel, but now there was good reason for the change of policy. When Saul heard the story which the men from Gilead told, he took a yoke of oxen and cut them in strips, sending them by messengers to all parts of Israel with this challenge: "Whoever does not come out after Saul and Samuel, so shall it be done to his oxen!" (I Sam. 11:7). The Judaic editor cites the fantastic number of 330,000 men who responded, emphasizing the presence of Judahites. More credibly the account elsewhere suggests three thousand as the number who turned out and delivered the Gileadites, as in the days of the Judges (I Sam. 11:8-11; 13:2). Because of Saul's vigorous leadership on this occasion he was elected king of Israel, which at that time meant Ephraim and associated tribes of the north.

It was about 1015 B.C. when Saul was made king by popular election at Gilgal "before the Lord," i.e., in front of Yahweh's altar (I Sam. 11:15). The people offered sacrifices of thanksgiving, showing no awareness of a need for priests to officiate for them in such ritual. As Saul himself said, ". . . today the Lord has wrought deliverance in Israel" (I Sam. 11:13).

While Saul and his men were fighting for Gilead to the northeast, the Philistines attacked from the southwest and established garrisons designed to bring about military control. This placed upon the new king a much greater responsibility than he had bargained for. He was courageous, however, in accepting the new and greater tasks.

It may be that the Ammonites had been deliberately used in Gilead merely to distract while the Philistines in the south did the real damage. But one thing by this time was clear, namely, that the disorganized Israelites under the Judges had been unable to meet the Philistine threat. Now the question was, could the nation united under a monarch meet it?

King Saul was never able to secure a clear-cut victory over the Philistine menace. Once his noble son, Jonathan, with the cunning and courage of youth, and without his father's knowledge, ambushed some Philistines at Michmash Pass. Saul with six hundred men followed up the ambush and defeated the Philistines in that particular battle (I Sam. 14:2, 23, 31, 46). The over-all picture, however, is well described in I Sam. 14:52, "There was hard fighting against the Philistines all the days of Saul; and when Saul saw any strong man, or any valiant man, he attached him to himself."

A careful reading of the record will yield interesting insights into Israel's culture about 1000 B.C. For one thing, we learn that it was customary to worship Yahweh at any shrine which might be set up for that purpose. There was no prohibition against local centers of worship. One of the most important of those local shrines was then at Shiloh. Even when Jeremiah was prophesying early in the sixth century B.C. it was generally understood that Yahweh had been very properly revered at Shiloh until that shrine was destroyed—probably by the Philistines during the early monarchy, according to archaeological evidence. Said Jeremiah, "Go now to my place that was in Shiloh, where I made my name dwell at first, and see what I did to it for the wickedness of my people Israel" (7:12).

Also significant is the appearance of an "ark" or box containing holy articles. What its real origin was is not known, but in I Samuel where it first appears in character, it was a kind of fetish. When the Israelites were defeated by the Philistines they hastily sent to Shiloh for the ark in order to improve their luck (I Sam. 4:2-4). The expected magic did not appear, and the Philistines, far from being defeated next time, captured the ark itself (4:5-11). Stories are then added which describe all the black magic which the ark worked among the Philistines (I Sam. 5:1-6:11). When the Philistines frantically returned it to Israel the box continued to make magic (6:12-19). After this the ark was left with Abinadab, a

Gibeonite of Kirjath-jearim, until David brought it to Jerusalem (I Sam. 6:20-7:2; II Sam. 6:2-3).

Rise of David

David first came in contact with King Saul as a musician, brought in to soothe his melancholia. But the young musician also had sex appeal and before long had put himself in line for the kingship by marrying Michal, Saul's daughter.

The Judaic writers and editors, in the cases of both Saul and David, inserted stories of how Samuel the prophet selected and anointed the king. A careful reading of the texts, however, will reveal the natural manner in which the kingship of Israel evolved. Samuel's name was often glossed into the text where it did not belong. Saul became king by popular approval, after the incident of the Ammonites and the Gileadites. Samuel's later intervention to make David king in Saul's place was intended by the Judaic priestly writers to teach that certain unorthodox ritualistic practices of Saul had offended Yahweh, as judged by the norms of later Judah (I Sam. 13; 15; 16). But the facts of the case seem clear. Judah was not a part of Israel at the time when David came in contact with Saul. If David got royal ideas when he was at Saul's court, he went back to Judah to begin his ambitious climb from his own isolated hills. There we find him using six hundred fighters as protection for his hill people and their neighbors (I Sam. 23:13; 25:13). He attacked and defeated the Philistines who were threatening the fortified Canaanitic city of Keilah—one of many such cities which Joshua had never conquered (I Sam. 23:1-5). When Saul heard that David was protecting Keilah, even though he too was fighting the Philistines, he tried to capture him. Saul really feared a strong and independent Judah, as the territory of David came to be called. It was also a known fact that David was friendly with Nahash, king of the Ammonites, whose threat to the Gileadites had aroused Saul in the first place (I Sam. 11:1; II Sam. 10:2). Perhaps Saul had visions of David allying with the Ammonites to conquer the Philistines. In this way Ephraim would be completely surrounded by enemies. So it was not mere jealousy that caused Saul to set out to capture David. Nor was it mere piety which caused David to contend against Saul. It was personal ambition, among other things.

When David heard that Saul was on his way to Keilah to capture him, he showed the stage of his culture by consulting the ephod, or image of deity, in order to learn what to do. In answer to alternative questions, the ephod answered in the same way as a tossed coin would answer. In the case of the ephod, however, the "answer" was supposed to reveal the will of Yahweh. This time the ephod indicated that Saul would indeed come down after him, and that the people of Keilah would betray David. On one occasion David had a very narrow escape with his life (I Sam. 23:6-29).

David's protectorate of his own people and neighbors was not always accepted with enthusiasm. One of his unwilling wards was an Edomite, Nabal, a man of great wealth. When Nabal refused his protection David sought to purge him on account of his insulting behavior. Then Nabal's wife heard about it and made a dramatic effort to end the matter peaceably. David was pacified and incidentally also attracted by Nabal's pretty wife, Abigail. Shortly afterward Nabal died, and David promptly married Abigail and also another woman of the south. Meanwhile Saul reclaimed his daughter Michal and gave her to another suitor (I Sam. 25).

Although it is necessary to see through the mask of perfection which the Judaic writers placed upon David, yet there seems no doubt that David was the more capable of the two military-political leaders. David certainly meant to rule both Israel and Judah, but he knew that he could not do so until King Saul was out of the way. So when Saul unmistakably showed murderous intent despite David's generosity in sparing Saul's life when he might easily have killed him, David took his six hundred men and joined the Philistines, making an alliance with Achish, king of Gath. If we had to regard Judah as a traditional part of Israel at this time, then it would be necessary to say that David betrayed Israel. But Judah was not a part of Israel as yet. Nor did his marriage to Michal obligate him to strict loyalty to Saul or Israel. He was also married at the same time to another princess whose father was king of Geshur, a Canaanitic city in the north (II Sam. 3:3), and that did not obligate him to loyalty to Geshur.

Loyalty and suspicion played alternating parts in David's early career. The king of Gath seems to have trusted him implicitly, and was willing to take him along with the federated Philistine forces when they attacked Saul from the plain of Esdraelon. And David was willing to go along. But the confederates were suspicious of David and insisted on sending him home, lest he change sides during battle. Reluctantly Achish sent him back. Luckily David and his men arrived soon after some Amalekites had looted and burned Ziklag. After consulting the ephod again David decided to pursue the Amalekites. His band overtook them and recovered the loot. Instead of returning the booty to Ziklag, however, he sent some of it to the towns of Judah where his men had been stationed. Perhaps this was intended to show those towns how fortunate they would be to back David and share in his booty from time to time.

David's diplomacy is evident in what followed. The Philistines badly defeated Israel in the battle of Mount Gilboa in 1008 B.C. Saul and his sons perished. When David heard about this he took his men up to Hebron, about twenty miles south of Bethlehem. There the men of Judah made him king. That David was not a mere freebooter, devoid of deep feeling, is shown by the sincere but unaffected poem—assumed to be authentic—in which he laments the death of Saul and Jonathan (II Sam. 1:19-27). David then sought the succession to Saul's kingship over Israel, but found that he had to fight for it, since Ishbaal (changed to Ishbosheth in later texts), a surviving son of Saul, had already been crowned. Some hard fighting and hard diplomacy finally won for David the crown of all Israel. The elders of Ephraim came to Hebron and elected him as their king. This was after seven years as king over Judah alone (II Sam. 5:1-5).

David's Regnal Policies

David's strategy in defending all Israel soon became plain. It was to be a policy of conciliation between Israelites (rural aristocracy) on the one hand and Canaanites (urban aristocracy) on the other. He saw that the only way for Israel to be secure against the Philistines was to weld into one nation all the inhabitants of the land, to make Israelites out of the urban Canaanitic Amorites, and from the fortified cities to defy the Philistine terror. This policy had its dangers as well as its merits. By accepting the Canaanites—the original inhabitants of the land—into the unified nation, the Israelites would run the risk of being absorbed by them. This meant that there was danger that the Israelites might become Canaanites rather than *vice versa*. For the first time since the "conquest" such a danger became genuine. Later Judaic writers and editors projected this danger back into the earlier history of Israel.

On becoming king of all Israel about 1001 B.C. David proceeded with his bold plan to win the cities by conquest or diplomacy. Most important of all those cities was Jebus, or Jerusalem, which had long been a stumbling block in the free expansion of Israel southward. It is suggested that David's town five miles south of Jebus, sometimes called Bethlehem-Judah and sometimes Bethlehem-ephratha, was one of the first colonies of Ephraim beyond Jebus. Its relative safety, separated thus from Ephraim, was due to its position among high hills. David was under no illusions as to the hazards of the situation, however, and set out to take Jebus and make it the capital of a united nation. He first tried diplomacy on the Jebusites. They were defiant and haughty. With consummate military skill, therefore, he proceeded to do what no Ephraimitic conqueror or judge before him had been able to do—or perhaps even had the courage to think. He captured the citadel and turned it into an Israelitic stronghold.

When the Philistines learned that David was no longer their ally or deputy, but instead a greater ruler than Saul had ever been, they sent military forces toward Jerusalem. Instead of waiting for them, David quickly occupied the fortress (not "cave") of the Canaanitic city of Adullam, directly in the path of their advance. There he inflicted a decisive defeat upon the Philistines. He was generous toward the Canaanites of Adullam, thus earning favor with urban Canaanites everywhere. Then he helped the inhabitants of Gibeon to avenge themselves on Saul for his still-remembered attack on Gibeon (not Gibeah). The savage manner in which this was done is scarcely creditable to David, but he put the responsibility upon Yahweh who, he let it be known, was displeased with the Israelitic deed. Other Canaanitic cities became more and more inclined to look upon David as their friend, while Israel had to wonder what was to come of it all.

Another deliberate policy of David was the promotion of intermarriage between Hebrew and Canaanite. David himself was a master of the art of marrying non-Hebrews, and we may be sure that his example was widely followed, although most Israelites could not afford plural wives as David could. In this manner the Canaanites as a group disappeared, causing later generations to assume that their ancestors were all Hebrews, and that the Canaanites or Amorites had all been destroyed.

The new policy of cultural integration in Israel was rather successful, socially and politically. Religiously speaking, however, it left the nation with a split personality. Yahweh was the predominant symbol of deity for the nation, but there was also a consciousness of many local baals. The inherited custom of worshiping Yahweh at local shrines was easily confused with the Canaanitic custom of worshiping local baals and other deities. The prophetic institution, originating in Ephraim where the Yahwist tradition was stronger than elsewhere, arose largely out of this confusion which the prophets sought to rectify.

David tried to make Jerusalem both the political and the religious capital of Israel. He brought the ark from the obscure house of Abinidab to a tent especially designed to shelter it in Jerusalem. The ark he regarded as a magical instrument which should be housed in Jerusalem for the sake of any benefits which it might bring. Israel had not yet matured in its use of symbolism. Nevertheless the priestly writers of the Old Testament magnified David for making Jerusalem the city of Yahweh.

Not only was David's Canaanitic policy successful in unifying the entire land of Israel; he was also successful in gaining military control over neighboring enemies. He enslaved the Edomites (II Sam. 8:14) and Moab (II Sam. 8:2; cf. II Kings 3:4). A like fate overtook Syria (II Sam. 8:6. The word "servant" should be translated "slave" in all these instances). His defeat of the Philistines insured that there would be no more trouble from that quarter.

The reign of David was financed by levying tribute upon Israelites in the form of forced labor and military service. Some revenue also came from tithes of certain crops (I Sam. 8:11-17). In addition he requisitioned private property whenever it was needed for his own personal use or for the use of his friends and officials (II Sam. 14:30).

An immense amount of wealth also came to his treasury in the form of tribute from neighboring tribes and from caravans passing through Palestine by way of Esdraelon's plain.

David's Fall

As Israel became well organized politically and militarily David tended to leave things in the hands of trusted officials. This was not wise, for beneath the disciplined uniformity there was much unrest. And where there is much unrest there is also opportunity for intrigue and insurrection, which took place among David's officers and in even his own family.

Absalom's rebellion was more of a social uprising than is generally realized (II Sam. 15:2-6). Absalom was a handsome prince, the son of David by the daughter of the king of Geshur. Undoubtedly personal ambition played a large part in his scheme, as he stopped visitors to the capital and not too subtly suggested that if he were their judge they would receive complete justice in their complaint. Now politicians cannot lead people astray unless there is some cause which a demagogue can play up. There must have been much disaffection among the people. Certainly the Ephraimites were alienated by his fiscal policies, by his disregard for their inheritance rights, and by his compromises with the Canaanitic urban aristocracy. Even the men of David's Judah were offended when he moved his capital from Hebron to Jerusalem.

So nearly successful was Absalom's rebellion that David and his court fled, while Absalom gained control over Jerusalem and the palace. By some well-timed deception David caused Absalom to delay action until his own forces could rally. The result was the defeat and death of Absalom.

The failure of Absalom did not mean the failure of the cause. His successor in rebellion was Sheba ben Bichri. This rebellion did not last as long as Absalom's, but did reveal a continuing determination in Ephraim to be free from Judaic control. Men close to David apparently sympathized with Ephraim. This may explain why Amasa delayed the attack upon Sheba. Thereupon Joab killed Amasa and made himself general in his place, while David did nothing about it (II Sam. 20).

It has been justly said that David's greatest failure was moral. That he possessed traits of nobility and strength is not denied. He was generous toward some of his enemies, though not toward all. At times his patriotism toward Yahweh's people rose to great heights, while at other times his conduct was indefensible. But the nadir of his whole moral career was his adultery with Bathsheba and his indirect murder of Uriah, her husband. The story of his penitence may be a later idealization. "The alleged penitence of David cannot be linked with Psalm 51, which is a post-exilic prayer of contrition."[1] No doubt his murder of Uriah alienated much of the Canaanitic portion of the population. The extent of David's impiety should not be minimized. Even the Judaic authors who glorify him were honest enough to report his wickedness.

David's deterioration toward the end of his life is evident in the intrigue for the succession. Adonijah was his oldest surviving son and would naturally have expected to inherit the throne, although the monarchy was not constitutional and thus far the king had always been elected. But Bathsheba had captured David's favor, and she wanted her son, Solomon, to be the next king. When Adonijah sensed the situation he planned a private coronation party for himself. Bathsheba learned of the plan and promptly thwarted it by having Solomon crowned, with David's approval. When Adonijah heard the people shouting "Long live the king!" he knew that his chance had vanished. He vanished too, until "all was forgiven." I suppose the fact that there were three contenders for the throne among David's sons was really not remarkable, considering how many wives and sons he had.

Solomon's Reign

Solomon was far less statesmanlike than his father had been. Born in a Canaanitic city—Jerusalem—of a Canaanitic mother, and knowing only regal surroundings all his life, Solomon was out of touch with Israelitic sentiment. Instead of being elected, as David and Saul had been, he was proclaimed king, sometime between 973 and 955 B.C.[2] His visions of grandeur exceeded those of his father. The Judaic writers, desiring to magnify Judah where his dynasty continued to reign, no doubt exaggerated his grandeur. They praised him most for building a splendid temple for Yahweh, and even included a list of his splendid palaces of administration and domestic bliss. In one palace he housed his "thousand wives and concubines" —if we may believe these figures. Another he built for his most honored wife, a daughter of the Egyptian Pharaoh. There seemed no limit to his personal indulgence or governmental extravagance, so long as he could secure the necessary revenue.

Bathsheba's son was magnified by the Judaic writer for three main things: first, his wisdom; second, his riches; and third, the splendor of his buildings, in Jerusalem and elsewhere. There is little doubt about his riches and his splendor, although whether he should be praised on account of them is questionable. About his wisdom there is more doubt. The story of the two harlots who claimed the same child, and Solomon's shrewd decision, was probably an oriental folk-tale ascribed to Solomon.[3] And the proverbs certainly were not coined by him; probably most of them were unknown to him.

David's fiscal oppression was as nothing compared with that of Solomon (I Kings 4:1-28; 5:13-17). It was merciless outside as well as inside Israel. Solomon continued the enslavement of Edom, where copper mining was done on a huge scale by slave-labor for the royal masters of Israel. Luxury commerce on the high seas was conducted by Solomon from Edom's port on the Red Sea. Israel was earning a reputation among the nations, though some of the nations may have thought it not an admirable one. Nor were the oppressed classes in Israel greatly pleased with the magnificence of Solomon's city. Common folk looked on it with pride only in retrospect. The stability of his reign is to be explained largely by the fact that an effective police and military system had been bequeathed to him by his father.

Two cases of foreign revolt are cited in the narrative. The first was that of Edom under Hadad, who had fled to Egypt while David was alive but returned after his death (I Kings 11:14-22). The other was that of Rezon of Damascus and Syria (I Kings 11:23-25). The revolts probably occurred early in Solomon's reign, and reveal his incompetence, though the narrator cites them as having occurred later and as proving Yahweh's judgment on Solomon for his foreign wives and their foreign religions.[4]

Renaissance of Ephraim

Only one instance of open domestic rebellion is cited during the reign of Solomon. That was the one attempted by Jeroboam. When it collapsed, Jeroboam fled to the protection of Shishak of Egypt. As soon as Solomon was dead, however, Jeroboam returned about 922 B.C.[5] to head a new rebellion against Solomon's son, Rehoboam. The success of this rebellion is characterized by the Judaic authors as a calamity which was justified only by the lack of statesmanship on the part of Rehoboam. From the point of view of Judah it was, of course, a calamity. But from the point of view of Israel it was a renaissance of the ancient *mishpat* and a return to the earlier spirit of Yahwism. The cultural unification of urban Canaanites and rural Israelites which had taken place during the reign of David and Solomon could not very well be undone now. The prophets and leaders of Israel, however, viewing all the inhabitants of Israel as Israelites, sought strenuously to bring them into the cultural bonds of Yahwism. This was a difficult task, made still more difficult by the tendency of Israel's kings to marry foreign princesses in order to promote good international relations.

The separation of Israel and Judah left both nations weaker than the combined nation had been before. It is alleged that war continued between the two nations under Jeroboam and Rehoboam. After five years of this Shishak I of Egypt invaded Palestine and collected tribute from the weakened cities of both north and south. Jerusalem was robbed of much of the wealth which David and Solomon had amassed. Thereafter Judah had neither the prestige nor the resources which it had enjoyed as the capital of Israel. Since the narrative of the divided kingdoms is told by Judaic authors, however, we are led to believe that Judah was as great as Israel, or even greater. The facts are otherwise. Israel was far larger and stronger than Judah, and still retained the initiative in Yahwist culture. A principal reason why Israel fell in 721 B.C. while Judah lasted until 587 is that Israel was strong enough to be feared by Assyria, while Judah could be ignored.

The prophets, champions of Yahwism in Israel, had their rise not in Judah but in Israel. Elijah and Elisha were both Israelites, and the "sons of the prophets," or prophetic schools in the days of Elijah and Elisha, were also northern in origin. They were largely a patriotic institution dedicated to making known the will of Yahweh with regard to political and religious matters. In matters of religion the prophets fought especially hard against the tendency of Israelites to conform to the cultural patterns of the Canaanites whom David had taken into the Hebrew commonwealth.

One real disadvantage which the north suffered was the fact that it had no recognized dynasty. The dynasty of David continued in little Judah down to the end of that kingdom in 587 B.C., while in Israel there was not even an established policy with regard to the succession. Sometimes a military rival would assassinate the ruling monarch in order to become king himself. At other times a prophet of Yahweh would anoint some one to assassinate a "wicked" king and replace him. Only ten out of the nineteen kings of Israel were legitimate dynastic successors. The other nine were cases of violent succession.

According to the Judaic authors, the worst sin of Jeroboam I was preventing Israelites from going down to Jerusalem to worship. The fact is, however, that they never had practiced such a custom. Solomon's temple had been in existence for only a short time, and even then was not conceived as a center for national religious assembly. One Judaic editor condemns the idolatry at Dan and Bethel (II Kings 17:7-17; cf. 17:18, 21-23). Such idolatry was not abnormal even at this time, however. There was as yet an approved tradition of using images of bulls or of man as symbols of Yahweh. Yahwism was still in a primitive state in Jeroboam's day. Nor was it destined to improve rapidly. Jeroboam probably ruled Israel well, despite the censure of later enlightened but prejudiced writers. He died about 901 B.C.

Military tension continued between Israel and Judah until Omri, about 876 B.C., established the fourth dynasty to rule Israel in less than fifty years. With his accession came peace and strength. The Moabite Stone, found in 1868, reveals that Omri reconquered Moab and collected heavy annual tribute from it.

Omri was really a great statesman and a great soldier. He displayed vision in transferring his capital from Tirzah to the hill of Samaria, which withstood a siege of three years before it fell to Assyria in

721 B.C. When Omri had trouble with Syria he formed an alliance with Ethbaal, king of Tyre. Omri's son, Ahab, then married Jezebel, princess of Tyre. This entailed the building of a temple for the national god of Jezebel's Tyre, Baal-Melkart. Trouble was to come to Israel from Jezebel (Isabel) and her religion.

Nor was Ahab quite the rascal that the Judaic account pictures. Coming to the throne about 869 B.C., he was even more successful than his father in foreign relations. Omri had been forced to pay tribute to Syria but Ahab's military skill broke that bond. In the last year of his life Omri joined neighboring kings in paying tribute to the rising power of Assyria. Ahab, however, joined a coalition to resist Assyria. At Karkar on the Orontes the coalition defeated the Assyrians about 853 despite Shalmaneser's vain boast to the contrary. Ahab also gained the friendship of Jehoshaphat, king of Judah, whose son married Athaliah, daughter of Ahab and Jezebel. Ahab persuaded Jehoshaphat to join him in his new war with Syria, and probably would have won had he not lost his own life through sheer chance.

Ahab's success in foreign affairs was in part purchased at the expense of domestic peace. For the wife whom he married to bring Tyrian support to Israel proved a great handicap domestically. She was strong of intellect and will, and loyal to Baal-Melkart. Since Baal-Melkart was the national god of Tyre, that meant that her first loyalty was to Tyre. Apparently she was trying to make Tyrians out of Israelites in order to enlarge Tyre's influence and control. The extent of her influence over Israel, however, is exaggerated by the Judaic narrator, who reports that most of the Israelites flocked to her god. Even Ahab is censured long after the event for collaborating with Baalism. Yet the honest reporter notes that Ahab consulted Yahweh's prophets, whom he liked to have close at hand. The "seven thousand who have not bowed the knee to Baal" must have been a very partial census. One unintended service which Jezebel performed for Yahwism was to arouse the prophets of Yahweh to heroic efforts, which resulted in the triumph of spiritual monotheism in Israel and Judah and in much of the world afterward.

XXX. LEGACY OF ISRAEL

One of the most dramatic portions of the Bible is that in I Kings where three characters play against one another: Ahab, Jezebel, and the prophet Elijah. It is dramatic because a real crisis in Israel came to a head with them. Yahweh had come with Israel from the desert as a war god whose moral standards were relatively high. After settling in Canaan the Josephites, as farmers, tended to transform Yahweh into an agricultural deity. At the battle of Esdraelon Yahweh outfought Baal by sending rain at the right time. This was long before Israelites and Canaanites began to fraternize. When David coordinated the Canaanitic cities with rural Israel, it became a kind of scramble between the Canaanitic baals and Yahweh. In the confusion which resulted it became hard to distinguish between a local altar to Yahweh—which was common and proper—and a Canaanitic shrine to a local baal. Then when Jezebel introduced the worship of her particular Baal-Melkart, she in effect reenforced the Canaanitic influence by enticing the Israelites to participate in her agricultural fertility cult. Elijah, the eccentric prophet from Gilead, felt the crisis burn deeply upon his heart. He dared to do something about it, around the middle of the ninth century.

Elijah as a Symbol

Legendary is the story of Elijah and the priests of Baal on Mount Carmel. Yet there is essential truth in it. Picture Elijah with his hair and beard grown long, wearing a rough sheepskin cloak, meditating in the wilderness of Gilead. Yahwism was suffering under Ahab, through Jezebel's influence. One day Elijah stood before the king and announced that Yahweh would withhold both dew and rain except by the prophet's word. As proof of Yahweh's power and displeasure, Elijah called for no rain. While Ahab sought him, the prophet hid here and there, performing miracles of various kinds. Eventually he challenged the prophets of Baal to meet him on Mount Carmel. Four hundred and fifty showed up against the one lone Yahwist. Numbers were unimportant, however, for it was a contest between Baal and Yahweh. Which god would send the fire to devour the sacrifice? Which would send the rain? The legend has Baal turn out to be impotent while Yahweh triumphs on both counts. The story is fascinatingly told, and well symbolizes the fierce struggle between Baalism and Yahwism in Israel. The contest turned out to be gladiatorial in that it was a life-and-death struggle, for the triumphant Yahwist prophet brought the prophets of Baal "down to the brook Kishon, and killed them there" (I Kings 18:40) "with the sword" (19:1). Thus Yahweh triumphed over Baal-Melkart as he had over the Canaanitic baals at the battle of Esdraelon in 1150 B.C. He was reaching a place of such supreme power as almost to erase all other gods in a triumph of monotheism.

The story of Naboth's vineyard still further points up the struggle between Yahwism and Baalism. Here the issue was *mishpat*. Naboth refused to sell his family inheritance to anyone, least of all to a king whose wife favored the Canaanitic policy of selling land as if it were merchandise. The ancient Ephraimitic *mishpat* was sacred to him. Human character is portrayed as Jezebel goads Ahab to action. She herself enters into a plot which ends in the "judicial" murder of Naboth. The king got the coveted land, but in the process had aroused the indignation of Israel, as personified in the prophet Elijah. Speaking for Israel, Elijah accused Ahab of murder and announced Yahweh's judgment: his whole family would be wiped out (I Kings 21:15-26).

The deadly serious nature of the struggle against Baal is reflected also in Elijah's divine commission to anoint Jehu to be king over Israel, in order to destroy the house of Ahab (I Kings 19:15-17). It was not Elijah nor even Elisha, but "one of the sons of the prophets" who finally anointed Jehu for this task (II Kings 9:1ff.). The assignment was vigorously carried out and Jehu became king.

Meanwhile Elijah on two occasions called down fire from heaven to devour a company of fifty soldiers who had come to capture him (II Kings 1). His mantle became a wand of Moses as it magically parted the waters of the Jordan (II Kings 2:6-14). Finally as Elijah commissioned Elisha to be his successor in the struggle, "a chariot of fire and horses of fire separated the two of them. And Elijah went up by a whirlwind into heaven" (II Kings 2:11). The cosmological assumption here, of course, is that the earth is the lower part of Yahweh's universe, while heaven is up yonder in the sky—not more than a few miles, at most. So we must write this story off as untrue literally, though the fiery nature of the prophet who started the purging flames which led to spiritual monotheism is truly presented. His discouragement when persecuted by Jezebel symbolizes the spiritual plight of Israel during its struggle with baalism.

Elisha has a more prosaic nature than his prototype. It is unworthy of a prophet that he should become indignant at "some small boys" as he came into town. The boys were mere children who jeered, "Go up, you baldhead!" But Elisha cursed them in Yahweh's name. "And two she-bears came out of the woods and tore forty-two of the boys" (II Kings 2:23, 24). Other acts are merely marvelous, such as bringing back to life the son of the Shunammite after he had been dead for many hours (II Kings 4), curing Captain Naaman of leprosy (II Kings 5:1-14), and making an iron axe head float magically upon the waters of the Jordan (II Kings 6:5-7). The truth-value of the Elisha legend is that it dramatizes the continuing struggle between Yahwism and baalism. One striking difference between Elijah and Elisha was the greater sociability of the latter. He was the center and inspiration of the "sons of the prophets," and the confidant of kings. All of this means that the cause of Yahweh was making some progress.

We read of two other prophets of Yahweh, Obadiah (I Kings 18:7-16) and Micaiah ben Imlah (22:8ff.). But there were many more in Israel who were aroused by the threat of Baalism and moral laxity (22:6). The persistence of these Yahwists led finally to the spiritual monotheism and ethical insights of Amos, Hosea, Isaiah and Micah in the eighth century, and others who followed. The stress of these prophets was not upon miracle or magic, but upon genuine justice and mercy between man and society.

End of Israel

The dynasty founded by Jehu lasted from about 842 to 745 B.C., during which petty local wars prepared the way for victory by Assyria. Jehu himself submitted to Shalmaneser III and paid tribute to him, as proclaimed in the conqueror's black obelisk erected at Nimrud about 825. Damascus remained stronger than either Samaria or Jerusalem in foreign affairs, dominating both Israel and Judah when Assyria was quiescent. Jehoash (801-786), grandson of Jehu, and Jeroboam II, great-grandson of Jehu, reigning from about 786-746, recovered some of Israel's lost territory and brought Judah again into temporary subjection to Israel (II Kings 13:25; 14:23-25). Then in 745 the house of Jehu was ended by assassination. The assassin reigned for a month and then he too died violently. His assassin, Menahem, paid tribute to Assyria during his short reign. Israel was thoroughly demoralized. When Hoshea, the last king, refused to pay tribute to Assyria, he was captured in 724 and Samaria, after standing siege for over three years, fell in 721. Thus ended Israel.

During the last century of Israel's existence the common man suffered most. The king would require tribute from his nobles with which to satisfy the foreigner. They in turn would raise the tribute booty from the farmers and consumers. This gave rise to the socio-economic condition described by Amos, Hosea, Micah, and Isaiah, who reinterpreted Yahweh's evident displeasure with Israel—and Judah—as due not to some dynastic failure to destroy "high places," or to failure to worship at Jerusalem, but to a moral perversity in the matter of simple justice and mercy. So evolved the spiritual religion of the prophets of Judah.

Judgment of Judah

Between 922 and 721 B.C. in Judah there occurred many political, economic and religious developments parallel with those of Israel. Like the Israelitic kings, those of Judah too were judged by the deuteronomistic formula of having done good or evil and been rewarded or punished accordingly. While Israel's kings never did seem to please Yahweh in the final analysis, because of idolatry, high places, and other things, some of Judah's kings were accorded Yahweh's approval. Unfortunately, however, the formula did not always work, for some of its good kings suffered reverses and some of Judah's bad kings brought unusual prosperity and happiness to the kingdom.

The narrative asserts that both Rehoboam and his son Abijam did evil before Yahweh by letting "high places and pillars" stand —even as Yahweh shrines. Asa, Rehoboam's grandson (c. 913-873 B.C.), was the first king of Judah to do "what was right in the eyes of the Lord." This was because he "put away the male cult prostitutes out of the land, and removed all the idols that his fathers had made. . . . But the high places were not taken away" (I Kings 15:11-14). Such a reserved endorsement was made also in the cases of Jehoshaphat, Jehoash (Joash), Amaziah, Azariah (Uzziah), and Jotham. Only Hezekiah and Josiah gained unreserved deuteronomistic approval. Of Hezekiah it was said that he "removed the high places, and broke the pillars, and cut down the Asherah. And he broke in pieces the bronze serpent that Moses had made, for until those days the people of Israel had burned incense to it" (II Kings 18:3,4). This is a strange and unintentional commentary on David, Solomon, Asa, and other "good kings" who saw nothing amiss in letting the bronze fetish be housed in the holy places. To us, if not to the narrator, it proves that spiritual monotheism did not truly emerge until Amos and his successors set forth the new doctrine.

One must withhold judgment concerning the historicity of the religious reforms of Asa around 900 B.C. His reign, however, was peaceful and prosperous, and such a fact could easily have given rise to the deuteronomistic judgment in the absence of negative evidence. However, the only prophetic activity of which we have knowledge prior to Amos, around 750, was in the northern kingdom, and this casts suspicion on the report that Judah began its religious reform before Israel did. Nor does Jehoshaphat's tragic death conform to his alleged piety.

On the contrary Manasseh (c. 687-642 B.C.) was the most mercilessly condemned among the kings of Judah. That he sought

Assyrian approval by cultivating Assyrian religion is well known. By all standards of the deuteronomist, he should have experienced misfortunes throughout his reign. Instead he actually had a long and peaceful reign, bringing prosperity to the upper classes.

After the fall of Samaria in 721 B.C. and the scattering abroad of its leaders, Judah carried on the Hebrew tradition under the shadow of Assyria. Sargon II came to the Assyrian throne just before the fall of Samaria, while Ahaz was king of Judah. Hezekiah succeeded Ahaz in 715, and Sennacherib succeeded Sargon in 705. The Assyrian invasion of Judah about 701 frightened Hezekiah, while the prophet Isaiah comforted him by saying that Jerusalem was Yahweh's city and could not be taken by the heathen. Hezekiah's apostate son, Manasseh, after a reign of forty-five years, was taken prisoner by the Assyrian king in 642. Two years later the young Josiah became king. He was greatly influenced by the newly written book of Deuteronomy, which in 621 became the pattern of reform for the future as well as of judgment on the past. Nineveh, the Assyrian capital, fell in 612, whereupon the New Babylonian Empire arose.

Under the pressure of international politics little Judah soon lost its life. Josiah resisted the Egyptian drive on Palestine and was killed in battle in 609 B.C.—scarcely a fitting reward for his piety. One of his sons, King Jehoahaz, was taken to Egypt as a captive three months later, and another son, King Jehoiakim, changed loyalties between Egypt and Babylon as international power swayed back and forth. He died in time to escape deportation to Babylon, but his son, Jehoiachin, was deported three months later by Nebuchadrezzar* along with other leading citizens of Judah about 598. Finally in 587 Jerusalem and the temple were destroyed and Zedekiah, the last king of Judah, was blinded and deported after his children were executed. Many were allowed to remain in Judah, but colonists settled among them, as had happened in the case of Israel in 721. Henceforth the entire geographic area was orientated toward Babylonia. The real Jewish culture went along with the exiles to Babylon.

* Nebuchadrezzar is now the preferred form. Cuneiform inscriptions give an *r*, not an *n*.

Birth of Judaism

In the last deportation the exiles carried with them all that they could salvage in the way of literary and other works of Hebrew culture. With no temple, and apparently forsaken by their conquered God, they reinterpreted their religion under the leadership of priests and prophets who now said that Yahweh was not defeated by foreign gods, since there really was no god but Yahweh. It was he who had used foreign nations to punish Israel and Judah for their sins. So they built synagogues and used them for worship and education. Judaism had been born as a world religion. The Hebrew Bible was mostly written during the next three centuries, some of it based on pre-exilic sources and some of it collected from pre-exilic times, such as Deuteronomy and certain prophetic writings.

The Jews fared well in captivity. Their relative freedom was large, allowing them to engage in business enterprises of their own, or farming, and to form their own peculiar culture. Some of them deflected to Babylonian culture, while some Babylonians were proselyted to Judaism.

Then in 539 B.C., less than fifty years after the final deportation, Cyrus the Persian conquered Babylon and a new empire controlled Mesopotamia and the Near East. Cyrus was a liberal administrator and encouraged all subjugated peoples to live their own lives. In keeping with that policy the Jews were allowed to return to Jerusalem. Some of them went back in 537. Disappointment met them, however, for the land was now poor and inglorious. The Davidic prince, Zerubbabel, inspired them for a time to rebuild the temple, but that undertaking lapsed and was not finally completed until about 516. Nehemiah about 445 led in the rebuilding of the walls of Jerusalem and the reconstruction of an exclusive cult which frowned on fraternization between "pure Jews" and "Samaritans." Priestly organization and influence tended to become top-heavy.

When Alexander conquered Persia and founded the Hellenistic empire in the latter part of the fourth century B.C., the Palestinian Jews faced another trial. This time it was a vital struggle against Hellenization. The Seleucid kingdom in Palestine was determined to benefit the Jews by making Greeks of them. The struggle was intensified under Antiochus III who ruled Palestine 198-187, and Seleucus IV, 187-175. It came to a crescendo under Antiochus IV Epiphanes ("God Manifest") 175-163. He appointed as high priest a man who promised to Grecianize the Jews. Greek dress, Greek games and dramas, and even Greek religious practices soon became popular. The Law was publicly burned, and circumcision was prohibited. In 168 Antiochus set up an image of Zeus in the Jewish temple and ordered the priests to sacrifice swine to it. A terrific struggle ensued, during which a comparative handful of desperate Jews in the wilderness maneuvered the overwhelming Greek forces into unfavorable positions time after time, and defeated them. So in 165 Judas Maccabeus cleansed the temple (December 25). Hanukkah, the Feast of Dedication (our Feast of Lights), was then instituted in honor of this great event, and has since been observed in the sacred calendar of Judaism. Antiochus died in 163 while en route to punish the Maccabeans. This gave Judas an opportunity to extend his control over all of Palestine, so that the new kingdom virtually equaled that of David. Shortly afterwards circumstances made it advisable for the Greeks to withdraw. But the struggle was taken up again, and Judas was killed in 161. His brother Jonathan then led the cause until he was assassinated. Simon, another brother, then took over and paved the way for formal recognition of Jewish political independence in 143.

The Hasmonean dynasty, as it is called, degenerated in the course of the next century. Pharisees (orthodox) and Sadducees (pro-Greek party) contended with each other, and murder, assassination and exile followed for many, until finally in 63 B.C. Pompey conquered Palestine for Rome. The politics of Rome thereafter determined the course of affairs in Palestine. Finally an Idumean, Herod, was appointed king of Judea, securing his title in 37.

Herod the Idumean was unpopular with the Jews. However, he bought tolerance by building probably the greatest temple which the Hebrews had ever seen. He was married to a descendant of the Maccabean or Hasmonean family, and one of his sons might have been expected to succeed him in the Roman protectorate of Judea. However, as he grew older he became insanely suspicious and had three of his sons murdered. He himself died in 4 B.C. History has called him Herod the Great, because he brought a kind of peace to Judea, built a great temple, and forbade any political practices by the Pharisees and Sadducees, thus insuring their devotion to purely religious interests.

Herod's kingdom was divided among his three surviving sons, Archelaus inheriting the Judean nucleus. He was called ethnarch rather than king and after ten years of ineptitude was replaced by a Roman procurator. Pontius Pilate held this position from 26 to 36 A.D. There were two kings called Herod Agrippa, one (I) over Judea from 41-44, the other (II) beyond the Jordan when St. Paul was being tried for treason.

Finally in 66 A.D. the Jews rebelled against Rome. Rome put down the rebellion in 70, but not until after Titus had caused death and destruction on such a wholesale scale that not even the fanaticism of the Jews beleaguered in Jerusalem could stand it any longer.

After such destruction one would hardly have expected another revolt. But in 132 A.D. Bar Kokba proclaimed himself to be the messiah, and was joined by many fanatics. The rebellion was provoked when the Roman Emperor Hadrian proposed to rebuild Jerusalem as a typical Roman city honoring Roman gods. He also forbade the "mutilating" rite of circumcision. These edicts inflamed the Jewish people into one last, bitter insurrection. This time Hadrian suppressed the rebellion after more than three years, and all of Judea again was in ruins. Judah had to learn that her gift to the world was to be not a model state but a religious idea.

Meanwhile the Jewish scriptures had been pronounced complete and perfect in 90 A.D. by a group of rabbis at Jamnia (Jabneh), in Palestine, and Jewish culture was spreading around the world through little colonies which had been forming here and there since the beginning of the sixth century B.C. At that time large colonies existed at Babylon and in Egypt. The colony at Elephantine, on the Nile, probably antedated the exile. Gradually the Jewish reputation declined through Christian influence until, in late medieval and modern Europe the Jews were confined to the unprivileged parts of towns and cities, in districts which came to be known as ghettos. Jews were persecuted in the Spanish inquisition beginning in 1480, and banished from Spain along with the Muslims in 1492. They migrated from land to land, meeting with persecution nearly everywhere. Probably papal Italy and Muslim Turkey were the least inhospitable to the Jews in these years of suffering. We may argue that it was not really Christianity that caused their suffering, but simply human ignorance, superstition, and selfishness. Certainly Jesus would never have approved of the behavior of his professed followers.

Judaism has furnished one of the oldest continuous traditions of the human race. If we may assume that there is a core of truth in the patriarchal tradition, we may date its beginning at about 1700 B.C., perhaps earlier. The sojourn in Egypt probably ended about 1250, followed soon by the invasion of the hill country by the Joseph tribes. After some expansion and foreign contacts the kingdom of Saul was established about 1015. The Judaic remnant of a kingdom came to an end in 587, but was revived again briefly under the Maccabeans in the second century B.C. Meanwhile the formation of a body of immortal literature had taken place, which was supplemented by writings concerning a Jewish Messiah during the first century after Christ.

Growth of the Talmud

Jewish scholarship and culture did not end with the formation of the Bible and the dispersion of the Jewish people. In fact a large body of oral tradition had been accumulating for a long time, while the Bible itself was being written. In the last generation before Christ there lived two great scholars who carried in their memories these oral traditions. One was Shammai, the Palestinian literalist. The other was Hillel, said to have been a native of Babylon. When Jesus a generation later taught his disciples the golden rule and the doctrines of love and humility, he was repeating what Hillel had already said. Hillel developed a fruitful method for interpreting the scriptures, and helped to organize the principles around which the oral traditions could be grouped for memorization and exposition. Hillel and Shammai were followed by Johanan ben Zakkai and other great rabbis—including the heretical Jesus of Nazareth.

When Jerusalem was destroyed in 70 A.D., its survivors were again scattered. Some surviving scholars formed a kind of Jewish deliberative council at Jamnia under the leadership of Johanan, which decided between rival doctrines such as those of Hillel and Shammai and adopted the final canon of the Hebrew Bible.

Most of the rabbis tried to reconcile the Jews to the need for settling down to a religion of the spirit. But Rabbi Akiba supported the messianic claims of the Zealot Kokba, involving Palestine in its last Jewish insurrection, which Hadrian suppressed. When peace finally came again, Rabbi Meir quietly carried on the work of codifying the tradition. Then Rabbi Judah, building on the work of his predecessors, laboring throughout his lifetime with the help of many assistants, about 220 A.D. completed the codification of the Palestinian Mishnah. The tradition regarding the interpretation of the Torah was thus established under such headings as agricultural laws, justice for the poor, the observance of Jewish holy days and holidays, marriage and divorce, civil and criminal laws, temple rites (then non-existent), and purification of various sorts. Formed over a period of almost six centuries, the Mishnah reflected the changing life of the Jewish people. The makers of the Mishnah represented all classes of Jews. Its completion marked an era in Judaism. The Mishnah

> was never intended to be authoritative legal code, but in effect it became just that. Even the obsolete laws . . . became sacred and were discussed and expounded as if they still had vitality. . . . and what some of the rabbis had feared came true. The great compilation tended to overshadow the Scriptures which it was created to expound.[1]

"Even yet the Mishnah was not committed to writing," states Rabbi Sachar. Solomon Grayzel, however, states that "Judah wrote the Mishna in Hebrew."[2] Says A. Cohen, "Scholars are still in disagreement, but the weight of opinion is gradually accumulating in favour of the view that it was issued in the form of a written code" by Judah.[3]

Throughout the following two centuries Palestinian scholars discussed the Mishnah, carefully preserving in their memories the results of their discussions until they were finally codified in the Palestinian Talmud in 390 A.D. Meanwhile Jewish culture had declined in Palestine, and Babylon was becoming a new Jerusalem. The Palestinian schools had been given a sort of official recognition when the Roman Emperor appointed their leader as Patriarch of Judaism. Even this practice was discontinued in 425. In the meantime the Jewish population of Babylon continued to increase until it surpassed a million, it is said. This large group, composed of farmers, merchants and scholars, was accorded virtual autonomy through the recognition of an exilarch.

Babylonian scholars built upon the results of Palestinian efforts. Samuel in the mid-third century accepted the Mishnah of Judah, and ably expounded it. Abba Arika, better known as Rab, surpassed Samuel in versatility and insight.

Things might have gone on in this manner in Babylon for many centuries had not the Sassanian dynasty come into power. The Sassanians were Zoroastrians whose regard for the sacred fire was so fanatical that they prohibited its use in the synagogue. And they forbade the burial of dead bodies in the sacred earth. Persecution of the Jews mounted, causing the removal of a school of learning from Nehardea to Pumbedita. So Ashi, head of the Sura Academy late in the fourth century, began to codify the results of centuries of oral discussions of the Mishnah. As persecution increased, the need for written records became imperative. Rabina II, head of the Sura Academy, undertook to reduce the Gemara to writing, with the help of many scribes. His death occurred in 499, and the Gemara was completed very shortly afterward. Added to the Mishnah, this formed the Babylonian Talmud, which has been accepted basically as the Talmud of all Judaism. This does not mean that discussion and new applications of old laws ceased. For commentaries then grew up on the Tadmud. In fact, Jewish scholarship still continues in the Talmudic tradition, as in all other lines. Many great men have influenced Jewish thinking in the framework of that tradition, bringing it up to date in the light of new discovery. Charming bits of ancient lore, myth, and history exist side by side with the fundamental law or Torah in the Talmud and its commentaries. Anecdotes, illustrations, parables and poetry vitalize the Talmud sufficiently to make it a living book even today.

Three other terms need explanation. Halakah is a term used to designate those parts of the Talmud, wherever found, which make clear the nature and demands of the Torah. The Haggada ("narration") clarifies the law by illustration, or brings comfort, inspiration and even entertainment by means of legends, allegories, poems and historical facts. It can scarcely be maintained that the two types of literature or tradition do not overlap or merge with one another. The third term is midrash, which is essentially an exegesis or exposition of a Biblical text for edification or instruction. Many a midrash crept into the Biblical text before the canon was completed. Midrashim have been collected since the conclusion of the Talmud, and even today continue to grow.

One quotation from the haggada of the Talmud, more or less at random, illustrates the attractiveness of the corpus even for a modern reader:

> In their intercourse with Gentiles, the Rabbis were sometimes challenged to demonstrate that the God they worshipped, an invisible deity, was actual. It is recorded that the Emperor Hadrian said to R. Joshua b. Chananya: "I desire to behold your God." "That is an impossibility," he replied. The emperor persisted; so the Rabbi bade him face the sun, it being the time of the summer solstice, and said, "Gaze at that." "I cannot," he answered. Whereupon the Rabbi exclaimed: "You admit that you are unable to look at the sun, which is only one of the attendants upon the Holy One, blessed be He; how much more beyond your power must it be to look at God Himself!" (Chul. 59b *et seq.*).[4]

In the later history of Judaism no greater name is known than Moses Maimonides—"the second Moses." Born in Cordova in 1135, he migrated to Palestine and Egypt where he became famous as a physician and a scholar. He tried to relate Jewish tradition to the best traditions of the Greeks and Arabs. His *Guide to the Perplexed* became almost as important as parts of the Talmud for a long time. Maimonides died in 1204.

Spirit of Judaism

Judaism has revealed its human weakness along with its strength. There have been quarrels within and intolerance without. One of the greatest Jews of history, aside from Jesus, was Spinoza, who was excommunicated and hunted by his Jewish persecutors, as he was anathematized also by Christians. Today Jews are divided into orthodox, conservative, and liberal groups. Many are Jewish only for the sake of social relationships, having no faith in the essence of Jewish teachings. They look for a rabbi only in times of special emergency.

There are as many political and economic views among Jews as among Christians. Some modern anti-Semites would have us believe that all Jews are communists, while others assert that they are capitalists whose only aim is to make money. The truth is that most Jews, like most Christians, try to govern their lives according to their great traditions, and generally succeed quite well.

Zionism arose since the World Wars primarily as a practical answer to the wave of anti-Semitism in Europe. While it helps to solve some vital problems it also creates problems in world tension. It is quite certain that many Jews in America, like their counterparts in ancient Babylon, have no personal interest in political Zionism, and prefer to maintain Judaism as a religion of the spirit, based on the law which has traditionally been ascribed to Moses, on its interpretation in the Talmud and living midrash, and upon the insights of the ethical prophets who probably constitute the greatest legacy of Judaism to mankind.

Jewish Customs Today

Jews are differentiated from Christians today by their refusal to regard Jesus as the divine Son of God. However, the liberal Jew is proud of Jesus as a representative of his race, and thinks of him as one of the greatest of the prophets. His synagogue is his church. In it the ark as a symbol plays a part as important as the cross or the altar in Christian churches.

Since Jewish holidays interest most non-Jews I shall briefly outline their nature. The minor feasts, Purim and Hanukkah (Dedication), are dealt with elsewhere.* Besides these we may mention the sabbath, the days of awe, and the major festivals.

The Jewish Sabbath begins at sundown on Friday and lasts until sundown on Saturday. One of the practical compromises which Judaism has made with Christian civilization has been to do their worshiping at the beginning of their Sabbath, that is, on Friday evening, since Saturday is the big business day for Christians.

* See p. 488, also p. 526.

Then inasmuch as Sunday is a day free from business responsibilities in our Christian culture, Jews have come to utilize it for religious education and other social and religious purposes. As for the degrees of strictness or enlightenment in sabbath observance, this depends on the spiritual insight of the Jewish groups, just as among Christians.

The days of awe, or most solemn days, include Rosh Hashanah and Yom Kippur. Rosh Hashanah is the Jewish New Year, beginning in September or early October according to the variations in the Jewish calendar. It is a most solemn day for Judaism, not a day of merrymaking. And Yom Kippur is their Day of Atonement, on which they remember their sins and also their dead. This day occurs ten days after Rosh Hashanah.

The three Jewish festivals are Pessach, Shabuoth, and Sukkoth. Pessach is the Passover feast, coming in the spring of the year and historically associated with the Christian Easter. Its agricultural meaning attaches to the sowing of seed in the springtime, when all nature seems to come alive again. In its derived meaning, it celebrates the Israelitic deliverance from slavery in Egypt and the birth of the nation. Shabuoth is the Feast of Weeks, coming seven weeks after Pessach and culminating in Pentecost. This is the feast of the first fruits of harvest. The rabbis also have given it significance as commemorating the giving of the law, which has come to be its primary meaning. Sukkoth is the Feast of Tabernacles or Booths. Like the other two feasts this also is agricultural, reminding Israel of its debt to God for the ingathering of the harvest. It is the Jewish Thanksgiving holiday.

Modern Judaism is like Muhammadanism and Christianity in insisting on the oneness and spirituality of God. Like Muhammadanism also, Judaism rejects the divinity of Jesus. In fact, the Jews are likely to feel less admiration toward Jesus as a prophet than the Muhammadans, because the age-long recital of how the Jews were basely responsible for the crucifixion of Jesus has, naturally, antagonized them. Yet many modern Jews are proud of Jesus as a truly great representative of their race, and try humbly and truly to embody in their daily lives the principles which he taught. Orthodox Judaism inclines toward the narrower view, while liberal Judaism is tending to comprehend the teachings of Jesus.

Judaism emphasizes the sanctity of the family relationship. The religion might have perished ages ago had it not been for the strictness with which Judaism supervises family relationships, marriage and individual social problems. Many of the ceremonies of Jewish feasts and holy days are performed by the father and mother in the home.

Judaism stresses the necessity of keeping the law, the centrality of love to God and man, God's mercy, and the instrumentality of Judaism as a people chosen to reveal God to the world. Orthodox and conservative Jews retain the strict forms and traditions of ceremonial Judaism. Reformed Judaism has modified some of those forms while retaining their essence, meanwhile preserving the association with more conservative Jews.

If Jews are clannish, that is partly to be explained by the fact that the customs of conservative Jews have made their association with non-Jews difficult. Jewish clannishness can also be partly explained by Christian intolerance and persecution. In self-defense, Jews must stick together. It is high time that Christians cease to vilify today's Jews for the crime of crucifying Jesus—a crime with which they have no moral connection whatsoever. It would be well for us to make the acquaintance of some of the great and noble rabbis in our communities, and of their spiritually minded followers.

PART SEVEN

Hebrew-Christian Scriptures

XXXI. THE JEWISH TORAH

THE WHOLE WORLD owes a profound debt to Judaism for its Bible. On it were nourished the spirits of Jesus and his disciples, as well as the leaders of Christian history. The Bible of Judaism, inherited by the Christians, takes its place alongside the greatest literature of all traditions.

It is just as tragic to be ignorant of the contents and value of the Bible as to be superstitiously in awe of it. Unfortunately many are at the same time superstitious regarding its authority and ignorant of its essential contents. The Bible is not a sort of fetish having a magical power to bless or curse, according to one's attitude. It does, however, have depths of meaning and value for those who approach it intelligently for whatever it is worth.

It used to be thought that everything stood or fell with the traditional view of the authorship of the books of the Bible. Tradition taught that Moses wrote the Pentateuch and David wrote the Psalms; Solomon wrote the Proverbs, the Song of Solomon, and Ecclesiastes. When the schools of historical criticism arose, the faithful feared that the disproof of traditional authorship and date might mean the collapse of Christianity. So they resisted the arguments of the critics, hoping thereby to preserve their precious faith.

Two things need to be said concerning this attitude, which is by no means a thing of the past, although it is in process of passing. First, if the ascertainable facts of history should lead logically to the abandonment of the faith, then it were better to know the truth than to persist in being fooled. Second, the new views of date and authorship have not led to the collapse of faith. What difference does it make who wrote what or when? The important thing is what they said, and what it meant in terms of human experience. The message of the Bible has intrinsic worth independent of traditional notions of date and authorship. In fact, the more we learn through historical science about the real date and authorship of the Biblical documents, the more meaningful do they become.

Was Moses an Author?

Here is a brief summary of the case for the Mosaic authorship of the Pentateuch. Basic is the fact that there is no claim of Mosaic authorship in the Pentateuch itself, consisting of Genesis, Exodus, Leviticus, Numbers, and Deuteronomy. In several places we are told that Moses wrote, but that is always in the third person. We are never told that Moses wrote precisely what we are reading. "And Moses wrote all the words of the Lord," states the author of Exod. 24:4. Similar statements are found in Exod. 34:27, Numb. 33:2, and Deut. 31:9. It seems obvious that some one other than Moses is here writing the story of Moses.

It was not until Chronicles, Ezra, and Nehemiah were written about 250 B.C. that the Mosaic authorship was assumed for the entire Pentateuch, as in such expressions as "the law of Moses" (II Chron. 23:18; 30:16; Ezra 3:2; 7:6; Neh. 8:1), and "the book of Moses" (II Chron. 35:12; Ezra 6:18; Neh. 13:1). This evidence was a thousand years after Moses, and according to elementary principles of historical science it cannot be trusted as authoritative. The writer of Ecclesiasticus, the classical writers Philo and Josephus, and the writers of the Talmud and the New Testament all regard Moses as the author of the Pentateuch. But from the point of view of historical science these are all late witnesses and as such have no authority. It would be absurd to accept uncritically all the statements of these documents removed by over a thousand years from the events themselves.

The evidence gleaned from the Pentateuch itself is overwhelmingly against the Mosaic authorship. As Spinoza realized as long ago as in 1670,[1] Moses could hardly have written the account of his own death, as he must have if he wrote all of Deuteronomy. Even if we concede that God might have "inspired" him to write the account of his death in advance, still he would certainly not have written: "and he buried him in the valley in the land of Moab opposite Beth-peor; but no man knows the place of his burial to this day" (Deut. 34:6).

Another proof that Moses did not write the Pentateuch is the recurring expression of the author unwittingly revealing that he resided on the west side of the Jordan River, where Moses never set foot. Usually when Moses is pictured as giving directions, his geographical references are properly oriented as "beyond Jordan," meaning west of the Jordan, and "this side of Jordan," meaning the east side. But occasionally in explaining general locations the author lapses into the habitual expressions which identify the west side of the Jordan as "this side of Jordan," and the east side as "the other side of Jordan." So in Numb. 35:14 we read, "You shall give three cities beyond the Jordan, and three cities in the land of Canaan, to be cities of refuge." Likewise in Deut. 4:41 we are told, "Then Moses set apart three cities in the east beyond the Jordan." The same orientation is indicated in Deut. 4:46,47, and in Josh. 1:15, 2:10 and elsewhere. These expressions identify the author as an inhabitant of the land west of Jordan at a late time when the expressions had become habitual.

One more indication of non-Mosaic authorship is the appearance in the Pentateuch of differing accounts of the same events. Spinoza noticed that Gen. 21:31 explains the origin of the name Beer-sheba in one way, attributing it to Abraham, while Gen. 26:33 assigns the naming to Isaac for certain reasons. These two accounts must have been written by two different persons, said Spinoza.

Equally convincing is the casual remark in Gen. 12:6, "At that time the Canaanites were in the land." The clear implication is that at the time when the passage was written the Canaanites no longer were the inhabitants of the land, but had been superseded by the

Israelites. Of course when Moses was alive, the Canaanites were still in the land, and the Israelites had not yet crossed the Jordan. Nor were the surviving Canaanites assimilated into a united nation until David's day.

Again, could Moses have written (Numb. 12:3), "Now the man Moses was very meek, more than all men that were on the face of the earth." It would seem like bragging about his own meekness, which would have been more than paradoxical. Furthermore the statement is in the past tense.

Father Richard Simon in 1678 called attention to the parallel stories appearing in the Pentateuch. By separating and classifying them according to vocabulary, style, ideas and attitudes he suggested how it was possible to arrange two complete and independent accounts of the same series of events. Subsequently on this theory it turned out that there were not merely two but four or more main narratives, at first independent, going to make up the Pentateuch.

The theory of the multiple authorship of the Pentateuch was developed by several scholars since the seventeenth century, but was set forth most effectively last century by K. H. Graf (1865) and Julius Wellhausen (1878). The theory has been modified somewhat since then, but its main features remain the same. Oral tradition has been recognized in recent scholarship as having as much value as written documents once had.

Four Main Traditions in the Pentateuch

It is believed that there were four main authors of the Pentateuch, whose names of course have long since been lost but who are referred to by the symbols J, E, D, and P. There are very good reasons for using these symbols. J was chosen to symbolize the one tradition because its sources and channel were obviously Judaic, and also because it referred to God by the name Yahweh—spelled JHVH, with no vowels indicated in old Hebrew. Those scholars who still speak primarily in terms of "documentary" or written sources insist that there was not merely one J, but two or more. These are symbolized as J^1 and J^2. E symbolizes the second tradition because its sources and locus were originally Ephraimitic, and also because it used the word Elohim to refer to God. When Ephraim was destroyed, Judah inherited E, probably in written form by this time. Naturally Judah did some editing of E. D symbolizes the Deuteronomist, the seventh century Judaic author of original Deuteronomy (mainly chapters 5-26 and 28). This writer shared the point of view of the seventh century prophets who lived during the reign of Manasseh, the apostate king of Judah. The polytheism of old Canaan and of Assyria was threatening Yahwism at that time, and the surviving prophets fought bitterly against the inferior religions. D pictured Moses as ruling that all worship should take place at one central shrine. This was D's plan for getting rid of the many false gods. Finally, P symbolizes a priestly tradition which was reduced to writing by a Judaic priest in the fifth century B.C. It reveals the priestly interest in ritual, priestly prerogative, and the authority of the ritual law.

The picture is perhaps not quite so precise as Wellhausen and his disciples have tried to make it seem. For one thing, since Wellhausen, oral tradition has come to be regarded as much more reliable than it was formerly thought to be. There is no doubt but that authors, like Homer of the Greeks, took earlier traditions and wove them together. In such cases it is impossible to know exactly what they did with the earlier traditions. So in the case of the Pentateuch, we know very little about the actual work of each author and editor.

The traditions grew and crystalized according to the needs of each group and each age. By studying their characteristics we can tell which ones crystallized earlier or later. For example, when D pictures Moses as insisting that all worship be carried on at one sanctuary, that dates D in the seventh century or later. Since P assumes the basic premise of D, it must be later than the seventh century. In the earlier narratives there was no one exclusive sanctuary. The Ephraimitic prophet Samuel sacrificed at Ramah, Mizpah, Bethlehem, and Gilgal (I Sam. 7:17; 9:13; 16:4-5; 10:8). Elijah knew no restrictions on place of worship. So it was in all the early sources.

According to the Graf-Wellhausen theory, the earliest of the four traditions to be put into writing was J, about the middle of the ninth century. Then about a century later E, the more mature Ephraimitic tradition, is said to have been written. This theory of the priority of J has been questioned by some scholars recently. There is no doubt that J is more primitive in conception, but this may be due to the fact that the culture of Judah was more primitive than that of Ephraim, who by some is regarded as the original bearer of the Hebrew tradition. Nor does it matter greatly which was reduced to writing first, since oral tradition is very persistent, and the final editor of the combined traditions colored the whole with his views. Since Judah fell heir to E and much besides from its northern parent on the fall of Samaria in 721 B.C., it was inevitable that the Judaic point of view should prevail in the whole.

There are certain differences between J and E which every student of the Bible should understand. I have mentioned the difference in their names for God and in their partiality toward Judah or Ephraim. J asserted that Yahweh was known by that name almost from the beginning (Gen. 4:26). E was the one who asserted that Yahweh was revealed to Moses in the wilderness and was unknown to them before that. Thereafter E also uses Yahweh as a name for God much of the time. In J Sinai is the name of the mountain on which Yahweh revealed the Law to Moses; in E it is Horeb. In J "Israel" is the favored name of the patriarch who fathered the twelve tribes, while in E the name Jacob is preferred. J called the prior inhabitants of Palestine Canaanites, while E called them Amorites. In J God appeared physically to certain persons, whereas in E he appeared only in dreams and visions or through angels. Numerous other differences may be observed, such as J's use of the phrase "took him a wife," and E's characteristic reference to "the man Moses." When all of these peculiarities vary together from one passage to another, there can be no reasonable doubt as to the original integrity of J and E as independent traditions. Similarly D and P have their own peculiarities and characteristic contributions.

There are interesting contrasts between the same stories as told in the different strata. In J we read that Abram (*sic* in J) lied about Sarai (*sic* in J) being his sister instead of his wife (Gen. 12:10-20). E tells the story also, but tries to save Abraham's integrity by explaining that Sarah really was his half-sister (Gen. 20). The same story is told of Isaac and Rebekah in Gen. 26:6-11.

Then there is the story of Hagar. In the J account Abram is like putty in Sarai's hands, forcing pregnant Hagar out into the desert alone (Gen. 16:1-6). E, however, makes Abraham out to be more humane, though he still sent Hagar into the desert with their son (Gen. 21:2-21).

From these typical stories of J and E it seems that J's cruder account represents the folktales at an earlier stage than E. The cruder culture of Judah in the eighth century can account for that, however, without insisting that J was written first.

Even though J and E may have been reduced to writing by some "inspired" contemporaries of Amos, they still were not regarded as holy scripture. Inspired communications from God to men in those days were believed to be through priests by oracle, or through prophets by word of mouth, not by pen.

The First Holy Scripture

The distinction of being the first "scripture" to be regarded as holy, that is, as containing an authoritative message from God, awaited D, which consisted of most of Deuteronomy. This was an underground protest of the prophetic school against the heathenism and idolatry of Manasseh, and was written about 650 B.C. When the pious king Josiah later ordered the temple repaired, this book was "found" as if long neglected, covered with cobwebs and dust. Josiah was greatly impressed by it and executed a reformation along the lines suggested by the "Book of the Law." The Law or Torah as thus recorded required the closing of all shrines except the central one, thus insuring that only Yahweh would be worshiped and only his Torah would be taught.

Deuteronomy was really a dramatic statement of the program of the prophetic reform party in Judah, put into the mouth of Moses as he rehearsed the great principles of Yahweh's revelation on the eve of the assault on Canaan and of his own death. The Torah as here set forth was much more mature than that evidenced by J and E. It was now brought up to date by being applied to contemporary problems. It asserted that those kings of Judah who obeyed the Law would be rewarded by Yahweh with happy reigns. Those who did not obey would bring disaster on themselves and the nation. The deuteronomistic theory of rewards and punishment became a norm which was applied in retrospect to the kings and "judges" of the past, and continued to be applied henceforth.

The requirement of the closing of all shrines except that at Jerusalem was far from being in accord with Law or custom in Ephraim or Judah. But because of the religious confusion brought about by David's political unification of Canaanites and Israelites, because of the failure of many to distinguish between local deities and Yahweh at local shrines, Yahwism needed Deuteronomy. The authors of Deuteronomy meant to give a true interpretation of Yahwism in terms of contemporary needs. Deception was not their aim.

Verses, Curses, and Codes

Besides the four main traditions there are other elements helping to make the Pentateuch. In most cases these additional elements were appropriated by one or another of the main traditions. They are easily recognized nevertheless, and deserve to be pointed out.

First of all should be mentioned the very oldest survivals of Hebrew lore. These are not the four major traditions, but bits of poetry found in the Pentateuch and historical books, or Former Prophets, preserved in common memory for thousands of years. Such are the Song of Lamech (Gen. 4:23), the Well Song (Numb. 21:17,18), the Song of Miriam (Exod. 15:21), and the longer but probably authentic Song of Deborah (Judges 5), composed about 1150 B.C. Probably very ancient also were some proverbs and riddles (I Sam. 24:13; Judges 14:14-18).[2] When they were first recorded no one knows. Writing was probably unknown among the Palestinian Hebrews (the Canaanites were culturally more mature) prior to the tenth or ninth century. Maybe these fragments were first recorded when the major traditions absorbed them.

A number of independent legal codes are also to be found in the Pentateuch, woven into the tradition at one stage or another. They now appear mostly in Exodus or Deuteronomy. First is the Covenant Code, closely resembling the Code of Hammurabi* (Exod. 20:22-23:33). Hammurabi's code had been promulgated many centuries earlier, and was common knowledge in the Near East when the

* See p. 69.

Covenant Code was drawn up. It is also true that there are remarkable parallels between Israel's legal literature and the Assyrian and Hittite laws,[3] proving merely that the Biblical legal debt is not simple.

The Ritual Decalogue (Exod. 34:10-16; 22:29b-30; 23:12, 15-19) in its earliest form, is believed to be the original nucleus around which developed the Covenant Code and other legislation of the Jewish Torah.[4]

The Twelve Curses may also be identified as a primitive legal code (Deut. 27:14-26). It is legislation against sins which are secret, known only to God, and unpunishable by the community. That is why they are curses, referred to a higher power for enforcement.

Of course there is the code known simply as the Decalogue (Exod. 20:1-17; Deut. 5:6-21). Even here we have not the simple original commandments, but an accumulation of motivation and wisdom-reasoning, characteristic of late Palestinian times.[5] Some of the commandments were themselves added, in the course of the centuries, to what Moses the Lawgiver provided.*

The Deuteronomic Code (Deut. 12-26) was the reformulation of older laws so as to meet modern needs, as already explained. The book of Deuteronomy as we have it is post-exilic (Deut. 30:1), but the code as more precisely defined arose in the milieu of seventh century Judah.

The Priestly document, P, is usually called the Priestly Code, because it was primarily interested in justifying the ritual aspects of Judaism. It is found in two forms. One is simple narrative in which a story clearly illustrates why a certain commandment or rite must be observed. So Gen. 1:1-2:4a tells the story of creation and explains that God rested from his creative work on the seventh day. Therefore we should rest on the sabbath day. The priestly narrative also describes the origin of circumcision (Gen. 17; 21:4), the Passover (Exod. 12:1-20), and the priesthood (Levit. 8-10; 16-18). These stories are to be regarded, of course, not as scientific history but as a kind of preaching. More purely legislative material of P may be found in Exod. 25:1-31:18 and Numb. 1:1-10:10. In these passages Yahweh shows his great concern for the smallest details of the forms of worship, citing the precise dimensions of the

* See pp. 455-459.

sanctuary and the minutiae of its construction. He directs how to furnish a sanctuary, who shall be its priests, what shall be their vestments, duties and privileges. He dictates to Moses a most elaborate ritual for the purification of a woman who has been sexually defiled, or whose husband's jealousy and suspicion practically necessitate her ritual purification. It is amazing how priestly and Judaic Yahweh seems to be in this stratum of the Pentateuch.

The Holiness Code (Levit. 17-26), symbolized as H, originated in Babylonia with the first generation of exiles. Its author insisted on ritual holiness such as might be required by a holy God. Its ideas were characteristic of the priest-prophet Ezekiel. The requirements were a development beyond those of D two hundred years earlier. Generally those extra requirements were ritualistic, based on the holiness concept. Yet H contained some of the elements of prophetic religion such as that laid hold of by Christianity: "You shall not hate your brother in your heart, but you shall reason with your neighbor, lest you bear sin because of him. You shall not take vengeance or bear any grudge against the sons of your people, but you shall love your neighbor as yourself: I am the Lord" (Levit. 19:17-18).

The scroll of the law signified that God had made permanent his message to man.

The climax of this story of the Pentateuch was its canonization about 400 B.C. We may complain because the priests of Judah, in the Pentateuch and elsewhere, favored Judah and the priesthood. But after all we would probably not have had either Judaism or Christianity had it not been for the priestly zeal for the Torah, for Yahweh, and for Judah. Some of the prophets introduced the idea of a supranational God, but the idea was too advanced for most of the priests and prophets. It was probably a priest who combined J E about the time (650 B.C) that D was written also by a priest-prophet. J E D was probably combined by a priest about 550. And of course the final stratum and editing was done by P, producing the Pentateuch. Without the strong nationalistic bent to the Torah with its emphasis on the glorious destiny of Judah it seems unlikely that the Jewish culture would have survived. Poverty and discouragement were crushing in the times of Nehemiah and Ezra, and Judah needed the Torah. More discouragement was experienced subsequently. Finally, when Greek culture was presented in all its glory, it was resisted only through the strength of the conviction that Yahweh lived, that he was partial to Judah, and that Judah had a great destiny. Thus Judah survived and bore Christianity.

Progress on the Bible

Between 400 and 200 B.C. much of the Bible of Judaism was written. Then about 200 another step was taken in canonization. This was the recognition of the authority of the prophets. For Judah the prophets are the "former" and the "latter." The "former prophets" are the narrative books of Joshua, Judges, Samuel and Kings. The "latter prophets" are Isaiah, Jeremiah, Ezekiel, and "the twelve"—whom Christians call the minor prophets. Considerably more than this had been written before 200, but these alone were elevated at that time to the same status as the Torah. I shall discuss the prophets before turning to the other "writings."

XXXII. THE PROPHETS

THE JUDAIC DISTINCTION between "former prophets" and "latter prophets" was not accepted by Christianity. The former came to be classed as books of history, while the latter alone were recognized as prophecy. The Jewish usage, however, is sound. The stories of Joshua, Judges, Samuel and Kings are told for a purpose. In many cases it is to show Yahweh's special concern for Israel. In others it is to demonstrate that Yahweh rewards the nation of Israel when it is faithful and punishes it when unfaithful to Yahweh. This is the deuteronomistic theme. It is an important part of the story of Israel in the times of the judges, and in the latter part of Samuel and in Kings. Its centrality has been over-emphasized by the higher critics until recently. Many of the stories used by the compilers carried no special moral. The compiler's introductions and conclusions provided the morals, making the books as a whole deuteronomistic. The morals were a kind of preaching. So they were prophetic, in the Judaic sense of that word.

Former Prophets

The first of the Former Prophets is the book of Joshua, traditionally written by the "prophet" Joshua. However, the book lacks unity, just as the Pentateuch does. It tells of the death of Joshua, as Deuteronomy does of Moses. And there are strata of tradition in it, as in the Pentateuch.

Some have insisted that Joshua is a unit with the Pentateuch, making the whole a Hexateuch.[1] It is true that the promise of success in Canaan is both implied and asserted in the Pentateuch, making Joshua a necessary complement to it. Yet the continuity of traditions or authorship cannot be demonstrated. Some say that P is easily recognizable, and others that D is clearly there, as well as J and E.[2] These problems are relatively unimportant, in view of the lack of sufficient evidence.

The important thing to note about Joshua is its obvious legendary quality. Impossible sequences are given. The Israelites crossed the Jordan on the 10th of the month (4:19). On the 13th a mass-circumcision was conducted. The next day—the 14th of the month—they celebrated the passover (5:10). Health reasons alone would show this to be unrealistic. Not only in details, but on the whole, Joshua is legendary. Claims are made of smashing victory through the length and breadth of the land of Canaan. Victory is through supernatural means, as when the priests blew the trumpets and Yahweh caused the walls of Jericho to fall. I have already shown the historical discrepancies in these claims.* The book was written to show that if Judah obeyed Yahweh's law, he would miraculously give them Canaan. Some have suggested that the reason why Joshua was not included in the Torah in 400 B.C. was because the helpless citizens of Judah knew that such a doctrine was untrue.

The book of Judges is deuteronomistic as a whole, but its separate legends often show incoherence with such character. That it was written after the exile began is seen in 18:30 where we read that Moses' (and Gershom's) descendants "were priests to the tribe of the Danites until the day of the captivity of the land." The deuteronomistic bias is expressed in the formula that when the children of Israel sinned they were punished by a foreign oppressor. Then they repented and Yahweh sent a deliverer who drove out the oppressor. But when the deliverer died they sinned again and the whole process was repeated. Yet in the case of Gideon we find a clue to his motivation in his duty of blood-revenge (8:18).[3] The later author-editor used a non-religious tale and gave it a religious setting, in order to drive home a lesson that was dear to him, especially in view of later catastrophes of Israel. The Song of Deborah taken alone suggests no deuteronomistic motive (5). Nor does the fable of Jotham (9:7-15).

Judges is more reliable than Joshua. Despite the deuteronomistic editing and late accretions, its gems of ancient tradition shine

* See pp. 459-460.

through to give an insight into the adventures of Israel as it emerged into the light of history. From it we learn how hard and slow was Canaan's conquest. Samuel was regarded traditionally as the author of Judges—a very poor guess.

Samuel—only one book originally—takes up the deuteronomistic thread, applying it with some reservations. Traditionally attributed to Samuel, last of the "judges," it also turns out to be a compilation of traditions and documents. The book itself refers to one source, the Book of Jashar (II Sam. 1:18). There are two different traditions of how David came to Saul. One tells how Saul developed a mental illness, and they brought in David to play the lyre. Here David is represented as a mature man, a warrior (I Sam. 16:14-23). In the next chapter when David first meets Saul he is a mere boy (I Sam. 17:1-18:2). There are also two stories of the slaying of Goliath, the first time by David (I Sam. 17:1-18:2), and the second time by Elhanan (II Sam. 21:19). There are two accounts of the origin of the monarchy. One shows Yahweh as antagonistic to the idea of kingship (I Sam. 7-8, 12), the other shows him as approving, since monarchy would be good for Israel (I Sam. 9-11).

Some maintain that the oldest written part of the Bible is the story of the succession of David in II Sam. 9-20, together with I Kings 1-2.[4] Probably written about the middle of the tenth century or earlier, perhaps by one who knew David personally, it antedates by many centuries the historical writings of Herodotus. It is a fascinating, well-written story portraying both David's virtues and his faults.

One motive of the Judaic writer-editor of the David-story was to show that David was the rightful successor to King Saul. Thus King Saul had to be portrayed as Yahweh's anointed, in order that David might have a worthy tradition to follow. Yet there was obviously an intense political rivalry between David and Saul, and between Judah and Ephraim. These two strands are to be found in the books of Samuel, along with other strands which are hard to reconcile.

The most definitely deuteronomistic of all the Former Prophets is the book of Kings—now divided into two books, like Samuel. Here Solomon makes his mistakes and brings punishment upon Israel for his sins, especially in the division of the kingdom. Solomon permitted the shrines to continue in the "high places," and indulged his foreign wives' predilection for foreign worship. These were the crucial sins for which, according to this historian, Israel was punished. Then in describing the achievements of the kings of Judah and Israel after Solomon, the same norms were used.

In its present form Kings was written after the release of Jehoiachin in 561 B.C. (II Kings 25:27-30). The author looked back over the panorama of Israelitic history and applied the norm of D to all the kings, from Solomon to Jehoiachin. Some of the stories are told, however, not in order to illustrate the norm, but to glorify Judah, such as the stories of Solomon's wealth, wisdom and splendor. His dream at Gibeon was originally told for this purpose (I Kings 3:3-15). Later editing added the norm even to this story, since Gibeon also was a "high place."

So we find different strata in the books of the Former Prophets. They may all have undergone a final—or intermediate—editing by the same Judaic priestly redactor. Certainly there is a wealth and variety of interesting material gathered together in these books of the Bible, which may carry their own intrinsic messages to the reader. In this way, as books of the prophets, they reveal God's will.

Latter Prophets

The books of the "latter prophets" begin with Isaiah. Since the earliest of the latter Prophets, however, was Amos, I shall begin with him. Amos was composed about 750 B.C. This was just about the time E was put into writing, ultimately surviving as a part of the Pentateuch. Amos survived on its own merits for about 550 years before it was canonized along with the other prophetic writings about 200 B.C.

Beginning with Amos a new kind of prophetic office emerged. Before him the prophets were ecstatic seers who told fortunes and accepted fees for a living (I Sam. 9:7-8). Elijah and Elisha had influenced the development of the new institution but, so far as we know, neither wrote anything. When Amos prophesied he wrote his message which was thus preserved for future generations.

Amos was a poor Judean farmer who went north to Bethel, in Ephraim, on business. There at the shrine he observed the worship of Yahweh, and noticed the injustice and unconcern of the priests and people. Everyone seemed to assume that if they followed the traditional modes of worship and sacrifice, Yahweh would protect them from all harm. Now Amos was probably fully aware of the threatening behavior of Assyria. So he spoke to the Israelites who would listen to him about their way of living, and announced that Yahweh would reward them not according to their ritual but according to their morals. And their morals were bad. They had indulged in the orgiastic practices of the Canaanitic fertility rites. They had taken to drinking immoderately. They had abandoned the traditional *mishpat* which forbade the alienation of land, and the rich were adding farm after farm to their possession while the poor were starving. Urban business practices were unprincipled and oppressive. Judges accepted bribes, and priests were growing rich on fees. So they had better watch out for Assyria, the whip of Yahweh, unless they mended their ways. Amos reported Yahweh's message:

> I hate, I despise your feasts,
> and I take no delight in your solemn assemblies.
> Even though you offer me your burnt offerings and
> cereal offerings
> I will not accept them,
> and the peace offerings of your fatted beasts
> I will not look upon.
> Take away from me the noise of your songs;
> to the melody of your harps I will not listen.
> But let justice roll down like waters,
> and righteousness like an everflowing stream (5:21-24).

Amos had unknowingly established a new school, that of the ethical prophets who insisted that Yahweh was not a magic-god who saved a nation merely because it observed the magic-ritual. On the contrary, Yahweh's only real interest was justice.

Within a decade after Amos visited Bethel an Israelitic prophet, Hosea, announced to his countrymen that Yahweh would bring judgment upon them for their immoralities. Assyria was being readied for Yahweh's visitation, said he. They were turning to Egypt for help, but that would do no good; it would only make matters worse. Then came Hosea's message of God's love. He himself had married a woman who turned out to be a harlot. Nevertheless he loved her and tried to woo her back to righteousness and pure, true love. So Yahweh would do to Israel, said Hosea, if only they would repent and turn to Yahweh.

Hardly more than another decade had passed when Assyria did, as predicted, attack and destroy Samaria, the capital of Ephraim. Somehow Hosea's message was preserved, along with that of Amos, long enough to find a place in the Bible.

Just before the fall of Samaria a third prophet, Micah, began to preach in Judah. His message was much like that of Amos, but was delivered to the people of Judah. When Samaria fell in 722 B.C., shortly after the fall of Damascus, capital of Syria, Micah had more fuel for the fire of his message. The Ephraimitic hill fighters had successfully fought off invaders from the plains for centuries. But Yahweh had forsaken them at last, it seemed, and would also forsake the inhabitants of Judah if they too relied on ritual and sacrifice instead of doing justly. Micah names the Assyrians by name (5:5).

The moral quality of Micah's message is best illustrated in 6:6-8:

> With what shall I come before the Lord,
> and bow myself before God on high?
> Shall I come before him with burnt offerings,
> with calves a year old?
> Will the Lord be pleased with thousands of rams,
> with ten thousands of rivers of oil?
> Shall I give my first-born for my transgression,
> the fruit of my body for the sin of my soul?
> He has showed you, O man, what is good;
> and what does the Lord require of you
> but to do justice, and to love kindness,
> and to walk humbly with your God?

Isaiah

Contemporary with Hosea and Amos was Isaiah, one of the greatest of the Old Testament prophets. He felt the prophetic call about 740 B.C. ("in the year that King Uzziah Died"), and was still preaching after 700 B.C.

Isaiah was apparently a citizen of Jerusalem and possibly a relative of the royal family. He was intensely interested in politics throughout his career. Like Amos, Hosea, and Micah, Isaiah decried ritualism and religious formality. He differed from them, however, in that he came to believe that Yahweh took so much pride in Jerusalem that he would not let it fall to a heathen invader. Yet Judah had certain responsibilities which it must fulfil, on its part.

Isaiah dramatized the role of the prophet several times during his career. The first time was when Israel and Syria, fearing Assyria, tried to force King Ahaz of Judah to join them in defiance of their overlord. Isaiah was opposed to any such alliance, and he advised Ahaz to resist his northern neighbors when they came to attack Jerusalem. Ahaz was skeptical of Isaiah's promises, so the latter gave him a "sign" from Yahweh. "Behold, a young woman [i.e., a woman who at that time was young, or virgin] shall conceive and bear a son, and shall call his name Immanuel. He shall eat curds and honey when he knows how to refuse the evil and choose the good. For before the child knows how to refuse the evil and choose the good, the land before whose two kings you are in dread will be deserted" (Isaiah 7:14-16). Isaiah was indeed a keen observer of the international scene. His prediction came to pass. For he made his prophecy in 734 B.C. and by 721 Assyria had destroyed both Ephraim and Syria. His dramatic illustration about the young woman came later to be twisted into a prediction of a far-off virgin birth of the Messiah. Isaiah's purpose was simply to convince the king of Judah that Yahweh was the best protection he could have.

King Ahaz was far from Isaiah's ideal, however, for after Judah was delivered from neighboring enemies and brought back under the "protection" of Assyria, Ahaz visited the Assyrian emperor's headquarters and returned to Jerusalem filled with foreign culture. He provided for the worship of Assyrian deities in the very temple of Yahweh (II Kings 16). Thereupon Isaiah cooperated with others to form a "prophetic party" of protest against the current paganism.

The next king, Hezekiah, was courted by Egypt and by Babylon, both working against Assyria. Isaiah urged faithfulness to international commitments and resistance to international intrigue, since Yahweh would protect. Early in Hezekiah's reign Israel was destroyed by Assyria. Only Judah remained to carry on the Hebrew tradition.

A story has survived that Isaiah became a martyr under Hezekiah's successor, Manasseh, who turned to Assyrian paganism and persecuted the prophets of Yahweh.

In certain respects it seems that Isaiah's message was more political than that of Amos, Hosea, or Micah. Yet Isaiah had no use for ritualistic religion. The way to earn Yahweh's approval was not through sacrifices and festivals (1:12-15), but by living good lives:

> cease to do evil,
> learn to do good;
> seek justice,
> correct oppression;
> defend the fatherless,
> plead for the widow (1:16-17).

Isaiah realized that there can be no separation between religion on the one hand, and moral and political life on the other.

It was during the reign of Manasseh, the apostate king, that the prophetic group, working in the "underground," produced Deuteronomy. Then when Josiah succeeded his grandfather, the "book of the law" was left in the temple, to be found by zealous workers. Although the Pentateuch is classed as law, Deuteronomy was originally intended as a book of prophecy, that is, preaching.

Zephaniah, Nahum, Habakkuk

Shortly before the book of the law in 621 B.C. was found in the temple, the prophet Zephaniah[5] was predicting that the warlike Scythians, wild barbarian invaders from the north, would be used by Yahweh to scourge and purify Judah. The Scythians did not do as Zephaniah expected. Yet his moral insights were wholesome, and that is all that matters. His fault was nationalism.

After the reforms of Josiah, the prophet Nahum wrote his short book which some interpret as a pageant designed to dramatize the fall of Nineveh. Most critics date it just prior to the fall of Nineveh.[6] This Assyrian capital was destroyed in 612 B.C. Nahum taught that Yahweh was the real ruler of world events. More and more, the religion of Yahweh took on universal significance.

A difficult problem then arose for the prophets to solve. The good king, Josiah, faithful to his international commitments, and to the policies advocated by the prophetic party, fought against the efforts of Egypt to recapture its old control over Palestine, since Assyria had fallen. Instead of being rewarded for his piety, however, he was killed in battle. And little Judah, faithful to the program of the prophetic party, was for a time enslaved by Egypt and then became a vassal of Babylonia. Why should righteousness be so rewarded?

One prophet's answer to this question was that faith brings its own reward. Said Habakkuk:

> Behold, he whose soul is not upright in
> him shall fail,
> but the righteous shall live by his faith (2:4).

No one really knows when Habakkuk lived.[7] But a plausible theory is that he was alive when Josiah was killed in battle. His little book fits into the picture of those times as well as any other. Evidence from the recently discovered Dead Sea Scrolls supports an early date for Habakkuk.

Jeremiah

Another prophet who faced the problem of God's reward for righteousness was Jeremiah. He is believed by many to have been the greatest prophet in Hebrew history. He was born about 645 B.C. and began his ministry in 627, "the thirteenth year of (Josiah's) reign" (1:2). His father was a poor priest of Anathoth near Jerusalem. He saw the Scythian threat arise and disappear. His ministry was hardly begun when the "book of the law" was found in the temple and forthwith applied by Josiah. He heard the news of the fall of Nineveh and saw Egypt and Babylon contend for power when Assyria was gone. He lived to see Josiah killed in battle, Jerusalem destroyed and its leading citizens taken into captivity. His own personal life was tragic in many ways. What kind of faith, or what kind of explanation, came out of such experiences?

For one thing, Jeremiah was not optimistic as some of his predecessors had been. Isaiah had tried to bolster the faith of Ahaz and

Hezekiah by reminding them that Jerusalem was Yahweh's holy city, and that he would not easily abandon it. In contrast, Jeremiah predicted the fall of Jerusalem, reminding its inhabitants that their wickedness was an open invitation to Yahweh to abandon it.

There was really much agreement between Jeremiah and the other prophets. He accepted the democratic spirit of the law which Josiah had put into effect. He was on the side of the oppressed, and opposed the landlords and unjust judges. Probably the greatest difference between Jeremiah and the other prophets was that, whereas for them Yahweh's relationship was with the Hebrew nation, for Jeremiah it was with individuals. Furthermore Jeremiah lived to see the reforms of Josiah come to failure. The Deuteronomic decrees that money should be loaned without interest, and that loans were to be canceled after seven years if the borrower had been unable to pay them back, proved to be impracticable. And the Deuteronomic provision allowing pilgrims to the central sanctuary to convert their sacrificial animals into money before leaving home, then to travel to Jerusalem and buy the sacrificial animal, was in effect making money-changers out of the temple priests. So Jeremiah must have realized that no really great reform had been accomplished, and that Yahweh must have been unimpressed.

International events seemed to point only in one direction for Judah. Josiah died in battle while opposing Egypt's bid for power, after the fall of Assyria. Then for a few years Egypt held control of Judah. Soon this ended, however, and Babylonia appeared from the east and wrested away that control. The battle of Carchemish in 605 B.C. signalized that fact. So long as the reigning king of Judah was obedient to the dominant power, all was peaceful outwardly. But inwardly this meant that tribute had to be raised with which to pay the tyrants. The burden of the tribute money always fell on the poorest class, while the wealthy merely transacted the business details, a phenomenon common in the history of many lands. This meant ferment within, which led ultimately to the withholding of tribute. When this occurred in 598, the Babylonian king captured Jerusalem, took many citizens into captivity, and forced the extortion of more wealth. The same cycle was repeated about a decade later, at which time Jerusalem and the temple were utterly destroyed and thousands were deported.

Jeremiah's part in all these events was unpopular. He had realized how superficial the Deuteronomic reforms really were, and how little the most zealous were able to accomplish. So he turned pessimist and, most of the time, kept saying that Judah must fall. Once his scroll of prophecy was burned by the angry king. He was imprisoned and abused. He was accused of impiety toward Yahweh and toward his holy temple and city. He lost the confidence of the prophetic party, which supported the government that had carried out its program even superficially. Nevertheless what he predicted did actually come to pass. Many superstitious people believed that he was a kind of wizard whose black magic caused the awful events that he had predicted. Jeremiah, however, was just a little more penetrating and honest in his insights than the false prophets were. He was realistic enough to advise the king of Judah to be obedient to that foreign power whose control was undisputed.

Seeing the inevitability of national destruction, Jeremiah was driven to the inward religion in which Yahweh dealt directly with each individual. He did not abandon the concept of God's dealing with nations, but insisted that the personal relation was a new and more important development in Yahwism. Foreseeing a chastened and faithful remnant, Jeremiah predicted an ultimate restoration of Judah, as a means whereby Yahweh would win the loyalty of all people.

Jeremiah was left in Jerusalem in both deportations, but in a later emergency was forcibly taken to Egypt by emigré Jews.[8] There he completed the writing of his book, the first great exposition of a personal religion.

Ezekiel

Ezekiel, the next great prophet, was like Jeremiah in combining the offices of prophet and priest. His priestly ministry was barely initiated when he was taken captive to Babylon in 598 B.C. There he performed a great service to his fellow captives by helping them to organize Yahwism on a community basis, transferring their religious customs from temple to synagogue. His faith in the future of Judah was not destroyed, and he encouraged his exiled compatriots to dream of returning someday to Jerusalem to rebuild the city and temple.

Ezekiel helped his fellows to make the transition from a national to a personal religion (18:20), a transition anticipated by Jeremiah. Hitherto the gods were always attached to a particular nation. When that nation was conquered or destroyed, its gods were believed also to have been conquered or destroyed, while the victor nation displayed greater gods. But beginning in 593 B.C. Ezekiel had visions, in a background of Babylonian symbolism, proving to him that Yahweh still lived. The Jews were captives not because of Yahweh's weakness but because they had sinned and were being punished by him. In fact, the rest of the nation was destined to be destroyed before any improvement could begin, he declared. After long suffering and genuine repentance Yahweh would restore Jerusalem and the temple.

When the final docm of Jerusalem fell in 587 B.C. Ezekiel began preaching the destruction of other nations whose sins also were great: Moab, Edom, Tyre, Egypt (Ezek: 25-32). Then he began encouraging the exiles. His vision of dry bones joined together again to form new life, was an allegory teaching that Judah would be restored (37:1-14). Yahweh was still in full control of the world.

Ezekiel's elaborate visions contain more mystery than inspiration, and his outlook was still essentially nationalistic and Judaic. He had no message of hope for Judah's enemies. Yet he helped to preserve the faith of Jewish exiles until a larger vision could be created. He made elaborate though conservative plans for the restoration of the temple and its ritual.

Nameless Prophets

There were other prophets who ministered to the Jewish exiles in Babylonia, whose names we do not even know. Portions of Isaiah, for example, were obviously not written by Isaiah, although they are now a part of his book. Long before the prophetic books were regarded as sacred scripture they were owned by private individuals, who used the blank spaces of the scrolls on which to copy significant messages. Such must have occurred in the case of Isaiah 13:1-14:23, where Babylon and Media are referred to, and where Israel is pictured as in exile but destined to return again to Palestine. Obviously Isaiah could not have written this.

The author of Isaiah 40-55 is now usually referred to as Deutero-Isaiah, or Second Isaiah, while Isaiah 56-66 is said to have been written by Trito-Isaiah, or the Third Isaiah.

Deutero-Isaiah addressed his inspiring message to the disillusioned exiles in the decade 540-530 B.C.[9] Chapters 49-55 may have been aimed at Jews everywhere, in Babylonia, Egypt, and even those few remaining in Jerusalem. The Dead Sea Scrolls offer some evidence that Isaiah 52:13-53:12 may have been written as late as 200 B.C. (See Dupont-Sommer, *The Dead Sea Scrolls,* pp. 22-23.)

Reading between the lines it is easy to see that the exiled Jews had no easy time in Babylonia. They competed with native labor for jobs, and were envied when they were successful and ridiculed when unsuccessful. In order to avoid social stigma many Jews patronized Babylonian shrines and set up Babylonian images in their homes. Under such circumstances the Ephraimitic exiles a century and a half earlier had failed to maintain their cultural identity. But by the sixth century Isaiah, Zephaniah, Habakkuk and Jeremiah had done their work, and Ezekiel and Deutro-Isaiah labored in Babylonia. The result was that the Jews were molded into a unified people, the heart of whose culture was religious, monotheistic, and highly moral. It is maintained by some that Deutero-Isaiah was the first Hebrew prophet who was completely monotheistic.

It was Deutero-Isaiah's purpose to comfort and inspire the Jews. To do so he interpreted their suffering as having already atoned for their sins. Their present suffering was for the purpose of saving others. Israel as Yahweh's "suffering servant" (Isa. 53; 41:8; 44:1,2; 49:3) was to reveal God's true nature to all mankind (49:6). Yahweh would use Cyrus, the Persian king, as his "messiah" to bring about the destruction of Babylon and the restoration of the exiles in Jerusalem (45:1ff.; 47:1ff; 43:14; 46:1, 48:14). God's character as reflected in the poetry of Second Isaiah was one of mercy, love, and justice. Ritualism finds no place in Deutro-Isaiah, and nationalism disappears in the kingdom of God.

The Third Isaiah (56-66) may be regarded as an interpretation of Second Isaiah to a later generation, probably between 450-350

B.C.[10] It shows some compromise with ritualism and Jewish nationalism, and on the whole does not display the fine sense of God's mercy and universal evangel as does the Second Isaiah.

Between the Second and Third Isaiahs came certain other prophets with a variety of messages. In the meantime Cyrus the Persian had conquered Babylon in 539 B.C. and two years later had sponsored the return of thousands of Jews to Judah. But prospects in Palestine were discouraging. In these circumstances arose the prophet Haggai, who about 520 told the Jews that before they could prosper they must rebuild the temple. Yahweh would send them supernatural help if they would only try, said Haggai. They did try, but the supernatural help did not come. Haggai promised the Davidic heir, Zerubbabel, that he would become a great ruler.[11] Though his messages were unfulfilled, his brief book was incorporated later into the sacred scriptures.

Most familiar symbol of Judaism is the six-pointed star of David, symbolizing the revival of Jewish culture and influence.

Zechariah then told the Jews that they must repent and live righteously. Then if they rebuilt the temple as an outward sign of their renewed spiritual life, Yahweh would fill the land with people and happiness. His book (chapters 1-8) was completed about 518 B.C., and the temple is believed to have been finished two years later. Chapters 9-14 do not belong to Zechariah.[12]

The book of Obadiah—consisting of twenty-one verses—is thought to have been written in this same general period. It is bitterly aimed against Edom, whose people were inhospitable to the Jews when they were driven from their homes by the Babylonians. The book has little value.[13]

About 450 B.C. or earlier Malachi was written.[14] The name means "my servant." What his real name was no one knows. He found the people complaining that Yahweh still had not rewarded them for their efforts. But Malachi explains that their burnt offerings are often second rate, and they fail to bring in their tithes. Furthermore divorce had become common among them, and they were marrying outside the faith.

The last of the Old Testament prophets was not Malachi, whose small book is the last in the Old Testament collection, but Joel. This last of the prophets probably wrote about 350 B.C.,[15] and thought of Israel as Yahweh's favorite among the nations, since Israel (Judah) alone possessed the holy law.

The last book of the "latter prophets" to be written, about 300 B.C., was Jonah. This is a short story about a prophet who lived in Israel during the reign of Jeroboam II (786-746).[16] It tells of Jonah's call to preach to the Ninevites, Jonah's resistance to the divine commission, and the miraculous way in which nevertheless the prophet was induced to go to Nineveh. He preached to the Ninevites, they repented as he commanded, and Yahweh withheld destruction.

If we were to regard Jonah as history, it would seem rather strange that by just a little preaching the whole big city of Nineveh (about thirty miles wide according to the author of Jonah) should have been converted so quickly. The prophet seemed to be disappointed, for he really relished the idea of non-Jews being destroyed. But God taught Jonah the lesson of his fatherly love for all people, Jewish or Gentile. This was a rather unique book even for those late times. The book still gives much trouble to those who solemnly believe that everything found written in the Bible is to be regarded as inerrant historically and otherwise. Jonah was evidently written to oppose the nationalistic point of view which had developed out of the period of the restoration of the Jewish nation.

The prophetic books were canonized around 200 B.C. The Law and the Prophets were the only fully recognized parts of the Jewish Bible even in Jesus' day. The "Writings," constituting the remainder of Judah's Bible and the Christian Old Testament, were growing sacred through use, but were not canonized until 90 A.D., after most of the New Testament had been written. We turn now to the Writings.

XXXIII. "THE WRITINGS"

MOST OF THE WRITINGS, or Hagiographa ("Sacred Writings," so called in the Greek translations) came into existence after the Law and the Prophets. This rule is far from absolute, but is a general guide. The Writings include the books of poetry and philosophy, the books of fiction (Ruth and Esther, but not Jonah), an apocalypse (Daniel), and a late Jewish version of tradition and history (Chronicles-Ezra-Nehemiah).

Daniel's Apocalypse

The one "prophetic" book in the Christian Bible which was written after Jonah was not prophecy but apocalypse. This was the book of Daniel, written between 168 and 165 B.C. to encourage the Jews to resist Hellenization under Antiochus IV Epiphanes. Its historical errors concerning the events of the sixth and seventh centuries B.C., the use of the term "Chaldeans" to refer to astrologers (customary in the second century), the employment of late Hebrew, and of Aramic (2:4-7:28), and the failure to include Daniel among the Latter Prophets in the canonization of 200[1] show that this was a late book. It heartened an oppressed people at a time when a Greek tyrant tried to force the Jews to desecrate their temple and substitute Greek customs. They resisted the Greeks until the Maccabees were able to rally enough fighters in the Judean hills to defeat the Syrian mercenaries.

Daniel was designed in a manner to suggest that it had been written by Daniel in the sixth century B.C., soon after the end of the Babylonian captivity. This was the apocalyptic style which was so popular during the second century. Some of the other apocalypses were included in the Old Testament Apocrypha.

The first six chapters of Daniel are stories of how he and his friends remained true to their religion despite persecution. Daniel and his three friends, Jewish captives in Babylon, were educated at court for the royal service, but refused to violate the Jewish dietary laws (Dan. 1). Daniel then interpreted Nebuchadrezzar's dream of a great image: the golden head represented Babylonia, the silver chest and arms Persia, the brass abdomen Media, the iron legs Macedonia, and the feet and toes represented the divided kingdoms of Alexander's Hellenistic successors. For interpreting the dream Daniel and his friends were given high political appointments (Dan. 2). Then Nebuchadrezzar, insincere in his praise of Daniel and his Yahweh, set up a golden image for all to worship. When Daniel's three friends refused to bow down they were thrown into an intensely heated furnace but were not harmed. Again they were given political promotion (3). After another dream and its interpretation by Daniel, Nebuchadrezzar became insane for seven years and upon his restoration sang Yahweh's praises (Dan. 4). Then came Belshazzar's feast, the handwriting on the wall, Daniel's interpretation and honor, and the victory of Darius (5). The latter appointed Daniel as a high official, but his jealous fellow-officials secured a royal decree forbidding for a month any petitions to gods or men except Darius. Daniel disobeyed by petitioning Yahweh as usual and was thrown in the lions' den, only to triumph again (6).

These stories, of course, were clear in their implications. The Greek tyrants were trying to make their Jewish subjects change their customs and worship strange gods. But if Yahweh saved Daniel and his friends for their piety, he would also save them. It is apparent that the author of chapter 2 was familiar with the pattern of history from Nebuchadrezzar to Antiochus IV, with much greater accuracy and detail as he gets down into the second century. There he identifies Antiochus as the "one who makes desolate," or the "abomination that makes desolate" (9:27; 11:31; 12:11). The alleged ability of an ancient prophet to predict such events as these must have been a great reassurance to the pious that Yahweh would give them the victory.

We must not judge the apocalyptic author harshly, as we would some one who might write under false pretense today. In principle, D had used the same device in the seventh century to put sermons into the mouth of Moses. In the second century B.C. such a device was traditional, and was employed for a purpose which was harmonious with its supernatural assumptions. The preservation of the Jewish way of life was thus secured, with certain promises of a universal divine kingdom on earth and future bliss for those who died in the faith. Messianic ideas and the doctrine of the resurrection of the dead were also formative in Daniel, contributing to concepts which were prevalent when Christianity emerged from Judaism.

Daniel was not written in time to be grouped with the "latter prophets" in the Jewish Bible. So it was placed among "the Writings," as were the two short stories which have not yet been mentioned. One of these was Ruth and the other was Esther.

Two Short Stories

The story of Ruth could conceivably have been written early or late in Old Testament times. But its topic, the problem of mixed marriages between Jews and neighboring peoples, was one which was being discussed around 400 B.C. The story concerns the emigration from Judah, in time of famine, of Elimelech and Naomi, and their settlement in Moab. Their two sons married Moabitic women, but both sons died. When Naomi decided to return to Judah she was telling her Moabitic daughters-in-law good-bye when one, Ruth, eloquently insisted on going along with her to Judah. There later she was married to Boaz and bore a son, Obed, whose grandson was David. Without pointing out the moral, the story beautifully suggested that mixed marriages could not be all wrong, and might turn out to the glory of God.

The other story, Esther, was almost certainly the last book of the Old Testament to be written, probably about 125 B.C. It is a nonreligious story of Jewish persecution and vengeance, but proved to be too popular to be excluded from the sacred Writings.

According to the story Esther was a Jewess married to a Persian king—whose identity is uncertain but irrelevant anyhow. Her nationality was supposed to be a secret from the king, yet all her associates well knew that Mordecai, her uncle and guardian, a daily visitor at the palace, was proudly Jewish. He once reported a plot on the king's life, but the service was forgotten. When Mordecai would not bow to Haman, the grand vizier, he became a marked man. Haman then secured from the king authorization to exterminate a large number of "disloyal non-Persians," slyly aiming at the Jews. But Mordecai learned of the plot and appealed to Esther. The queen risked her life in order to plead for her people. She invited the king and the vizier to a dinner, and then to another, during which everything worked out beautifully. In the sequel Haman was hanged on the gallows which he had built for the execution of Mordecai. And instead of a Jewish pogrom, the Jews were authorized to slay those who had intended to kill them. The slaughter could not be finished in one day, so was extended into the second. As a short story Esther shows emotional suspense and depth, but certainly adds nothing to Christian literature. Modern Jews have regarded the book highly, and celebrate the Feast of Purim in memory of their "deliverance" from Haman's intended pogrom. Considering the number of pogroms which Jews have experienced, they may perhaps be forgiven for taking delight in a story which turns the tables on their persecutors.

Chronicles—Ezra—Nehemiah

Four books of historical tradition and several books of poetry and philosophy complete the Writings of the Jewish Bible.

The first books of historical tradition are the Chronicles, originally one book but, like Samuel and Kings, conveniently divided into two volumes. The Chronicles take up the story of sacred events where P leaves off in Joshua, and carry it down to Nehemiah. Ezra and Nehemiah then complete the story in the same priestly spirit. The Chronicles probably were written during the first half of the third century, perhaps close to 250 B.C. One reason for this date is that the author cites Samuel and Kings as sources for numerous statements, but takes liberties with his "authorities." This shows that the Chronicles were written after the completion of the "former prophets" but before their canonization around 200, after which no liberties might be taken. There are other specific reasons for this date.[2]

In the Chronicles we find that the holy people are no longer

Israelites but only Jews, and that the events of sacred history are brought about not by natural causes but supernaturally.[3] The supernatural causation may be detected in the manner of describing the use of armies. As P made Jericho fall supernaturally, so the Chronicler sees armies as phantoms playing no real part in the destinies of peoples.

The difference between Chronicles and Kings may be seen in their accounts of the reign of Abijam, son and successor of Rehoboam king of Judah. The author of Kings of course favored Judah, but not so fanatically as the Chronicler. In I Kings 15:1-8 we read the whole story of Abijam, whose sins are said to have been like those of his father Rehoboam. Yahweh was good to him, however, for David's sake. The continued warfare between Israel and Judah is barely mentioned. The Chronicler, however, assigned fantastic numbers to their armies: 400,000 for Abijah (his name and mother differ in the two accounts) against 800,000 for Jeroboam (II Chron. 13:3). Then instead of describing the warfare the Chronicler quotes a sermon which Abijah piously delivers to his enemies from a mountain, explaining why they are in the wrong. They are rebels against the legitimate line of David, and against Yahweh, whereas Judah follows David's line, accepts Yahweh, employs only the sons of Aaron and Levites as priests, and follows the prescribed ritual (II Chron. 13:4-11). Abijah concludes his sermon by asserting, "Behold, God is with us at our head, and his priests with their battle trumpets to sound the call to battle against you. O Sons of Israel, do not fight against the Lord, the God of your fathers: for you cannot succeed" (II Chron. 13:12). Then the miracle happens. Jeroboam, unimpressed, begins the battle in orthodox military manner by sending troops to fight Judah's army from front and rear. But that made not a bit of difference, for the priests of Judah blew the trumpets and the disheartened army became inspired and killed 500,000 Israelites. That was more than sixty percent of the Israelites killed in a single battle. "And when the men of Judah shouted, God defeated Jeroboam and all Israel" (II Chron. 13:15). Just like the walls of Jericho.

The character of the book of Ezra is revealed when we note that the last two verses of II Chron. (36:22-23) are repeated verbatim in Ezra 1:1-3. The author was certainly the same. Furthermore Ezra and Nehemiah were originally undivided. Hence we may conclude that the whole of Chronicles, Ezra, and Nehemiah were originally a single work. When we analyze it we find the same point of view prevailing throughout, and the same policy followed in the use of sources. We can hardly expect the writer to be more faithful as an historian in Ezra and Nehemiah than he was in Chronicles.

Among the sources used by the author were the memoirs of Ezra and of Nehemiah. As to the historicity of Nehemiah and the genuineness of a part of his memoirs there seems to be no doubt. But as to the reliability of Ezra's memoirs, or even his existence, there is much controversy. Ben Sira in 180 B.C. did not know any Ezra.[4] If Ezra was a real historical character and not an invention used by the Chronicler to put across some ideas, then it is likely that he brought the book of the Law to Jerusalem not before Nehemiah but afterwards, in 397.

Nehemiah visited Jerusalem in 444 B.C. with the approval of the Persian king in whose service he held high position. He engineered the rebuilding of the walls of Jerusalem within the brief period of fifty-two days, and the restoration of an *esprit de corps* to its dejected inhabitants. In this manner Judaism came to have an intolerant attitude toward the Samaritans and frowned on mixed marriages. These attitudes may now be condemned, but we might never have inherited Judaism and Christianity without them.

We may think of the author of Chronicles—Ezra—Nehemiah as a priest of the third century B.C. who was not trying to write history in the modern scientific sense, but who was trying to emphasize the priestly and scribal point of view in history. Many of his sermons (perhaps he preached in the synagogue) were put into the mouths of historical characters. Many of them were developed from historical situations imaginatively told for a reason. His writings must be accepted for what they are worth. Certainly they do not teach the same simple lessons about the universality of God's nature and power that we find in Amos, Jeremiah, and the Second Isaiah.

The poetic and philosophical books of the Jewish Bible also turn out, on occasion, to be less than universal in their theology. These books, belonging like Chronicles to the Writings and produced largely about the same time, constitute some of the most valued part of the Bible. In many cases they have gained universality through interpretation and use.

Job

One of the most universal of all the poetic books was Job. It is not an easy book to interpret. An ancient folktale appears in the prose introduction and conclusion of the book. Substantially the same tale is told in ancient India, Egypt, Babylonia, and Edom.[5] The folktale describes how perfect had been the behavior of the hero—in this case Job. Yet he was visited with suffering and calamity When he refused to curse God for his injustice, God finally rewarded him for his piety and steadfastness.

The poem itself, of later origin and great beauty, describes the efforts of Job's friends to get him to admit his secret sins, in order that God's character might be justified. Eliphaz, Bildad, and Zophar accepted the orthodox view that all suffering was the result of sin. But Job knew his own heart and was sure that he did not deserve to suffer while wicked men went free. So he held that God was arbitrary and unjust. If only God would grant him an audience that he might present his case, as before a just judge! Then the great event did indeed happen: God appeared to Job in the whirlwind. Firing at Job question after question which he could not answer (38ff.), God implied that Job was not wise enough to pass judgment on God's justice. God never insinuated that Job was suffering justly for sins which he would not confess. The whole matter was thus left in a state of agnosticism.

Some later poet was dissatisfied with the poem's conclusion, so he inserted his explanation between Job 31 and Job 38. These chapters 32-37 really add nothing new to the argument, however, serving primarily to interrupt the natural sequence of the original poem. Other additions to Job are the poem on the origin and place of wisdom (Job 28), and the poems on the ostrich, the hippopotamus, and the crocodile (39:13-18; 40:15-41:34).

Some writers regard Job as the work of a non-Jewish author—perhaps an Edomite, since the places named are in Edom.[6] Clues are meager as to both date and authorship. Some critics think that Job influenced the author of Deutero-Isaiah on the Suffering Servant. If so, Job was in existence early in the sixth century. Others think that the Suffering Servant passages influenced Job. This matters little. It is one of the greatest pieces of literature in the world, and its place in the Bible was won despite its unorthodoxy.

Ecclesiastes

Even more unorthodox than Job was Ecclesiastes. Its popularity won for it a place in the Writings, especially since Solomon's name was associated with it—falsely, of course. It was probably written sometime in the late fourth or the third century, from the evidence afforded by the Dead Sea Fragments.

At the heart of Ecclesiastes is the view that human life is futile. His recurring theme is,

> Vanity of vanities! All is vanity (1:2).

Human life is one round of futility, and there is nothing new under the sun.

> All things are full of weariness;
> a man cannot utter it;
> the eye is not satisfied with seeing,
> nor the ear filled with hearing.
> What has been is what will be,
> and what has been done is what will be done;
> and there is nothing new under the sun (1:8-9).
> . . . all is vanity and a striving after wind.
> What is crooked cannot be made straight (1:14-15).

Even the life of pleasure is unsatisfying. Ecclesiastes had tried it and found it lacking (2:1-11). "And whatever my eyes desired I did not keep them from; I kept my heart from no pleasure. . . . Then I considered all that my hands had done and the toil I had spent in doing it, and behold, all was vanity and a striving after wind, and there was nothing to be gained under the sun" (2:10-11).

Riches also are futile, "seeing that I must leave it to the man who will come after me; and who knows whether he will be a wise man or a fool? Yet he will be master of all for which I toiled and used my wisdom under the sun. This also is vanity" (2:18-19). Even while a man is working for his riches he is not satisfied: "For all his days are full of pain, and his work is a vexation; even in the night his mind does not rest. This also is vanity" (2:23).

With some inconsistency Ecclesiastes frequently recurs to the theme that the role of practical wisdom is to be happy while one can. "There is nothing better for a man than that he should eat and drink, and find enjoyment in his toil" (2:24). "I know that there is nothing better for them than to be happy and enjoy themselves as long as they live" (3:12). "And I commend enjoyment, for man has no good thing under the sun but to eat, and drink, and enjoy himself. . . ." (8:15). There is no logic or consistency about making happiness the aim of life. But in the absence of any other meaning for life, we may as well aim at pleasure, it seemed to Ecclesiastes.

The theme of enjoying life while you can comes to a crescendo with the advice:

"Rejoice, O young man, in your youth, and let your heart cheer you in the days of your youth; walk in the ways of your heart and the sight of your eyes." Then follows some advice wholly outside the spirit of the entire passage and of the whole book, but which helps to account for the ultimate inclusion of the book among the sacred Writings. It is an excellent illustration of how an annotated gloss was edited into the text. It reads: "But know that for all these things God will bring you into judgment" (11:9). Then the original author continues:

"Remove vexation from your mind, and put away pain from your body;" (adds the orthodox annotater, "for youth and the dawn of life are vanity. Remember also your Creator in the days of your youth") (11:10-12:1a). And the original author takes up from where he left off in 11:10, "before the evil days come, and the years draw nigh, when you will say, 'I have no pleasure in them' " (12:1b). The rest of this passage displays exquisite beauty. His statement that "man goes to his eternal home" (12:5) is an Egyptian manner of referring to death, thus revealing some Egyptian influence. The rest of the passage refers to age as the prelude to death. Two editors added their comments (12:9-11 and 12:12-14), restoring some piety to the whole.

Much of the pessimism of Ecclesiastes seems to stem from his disbelief in immortality. Men in reality, says he, "are but beasts. For the fate of the sons of men and the fate of beasts is the same; as one dies, so dies the other. They all have the same breath, and man has no advantage over the beasts; for all is vanity. All go to one place;

all are from dust, and all turn to dust again" (3:18-20). It is no use to wait for justice in a future life, for there is none, he says in effect.

Even in this life, however, there is cause for pessimism. There is no justice even here. All is vanity, "since one fate comes to all, to the righteous and the wicked, to the good and the evil, to the clean and the unclean" (9:1-2). Even so, it is better to be alive than dead, for "he who is joined with all the living has hope, for a living dog is better than a dead lion. For the living know that they will die, but the dead know nothing, and they have no more reward; but the memory of them is lost" (9:4-5).

One of life's irritations is apparently caused by God's deliberate design: he has put order in the universe (3:1-8), but chooses thereby to vex man's mind by withholding the wisdom necessary to understand it (3:9-11). God "has put eternity into man's mind, yet so that he cannot find out what God has done from the beginning to the end" (3:11).

Ecclesiastes is grouped with the wisdom literature, produced in an age when such literature was popular. In Ecclesiastes we find contrary attitudes toward wisdom. On the one hand he teaches that "he who increases knowledge increases sorrow" (1:18), and that the wise man is no better off than a fool since "one fate comes to all of them" (2:14). Yet even this is an insight of wisdom, and the author does include many gems of wisdom in his book, usually in the form of proverbs. Who would not recognize these:

> Cast your bread upon the waters,
> for you will find it after many days (11:1).

> Whatever your hand finds to do, do it with your might; for there is no work or thought or knowledge or wisdom in Sheol, to which you are going (9:10; we seldom hear all of this one).

> Again I saw that under the sun the race is not to the swift, nor the battle to the strong, nor bread to the wise, nor riches to the intelligent, nor favor to the men of skill; but time and chance happen to them all (9:11).

Like all proverbs, these do not cohere with one another in a system. Considering the purpose of Ecclesiastes, however, that is hardly a fault.

Proverbs

The book of Proverbs completes, with Job and Ecclesiastes, the "wisdom literature" of the Bible. Of the three books, it alone is orthodox in the sense of agreeing with the prevailing philosophy of the Old testament that suffering is the result of sin and that goodness is divinely rewarded with happiness.

Proverbs, like Ecclesiastes, is traditionally associated with the name of Solomon, and with no more plausibility. A comparison of Prov. 1:1; 25:1; 30:1; 31:1 reveals that the book is a collection of sayings, wise and otherwise. The last chapter contains an alphabetic acrostic poem on the ideal wife and mother (31:10-31). The early part of the chapter is attributed (31:1) to Lemuel, king of Massa (or to his mother). The preceding chapter reports "the words of Agur son of Jakeh of Massa" (30:1). In Prov. 22:17-24:22 are found some simple adaptations from *The Wisdom of Amenemope,* an Egyptian book dated between 1000 and 600 B.C. Others are taken from the *Sayings of Ahikar,* an Egyptian writing discovered among the papyri at Elephantine.

The theme of the first collection of proverbs is that wisdom begins in piety:

> The fear of the Lord is the beginning of knowledge (1:7; 9:10).

The second collection (10:1-22:16), called "The Proverbs of Solomon," is too miscellaneous to have a unifying theme. In form almost all the proverbs in this group consist of two rhythmic statements, the second one repeating or developing the first, or presenting its antithetical complement:

> When the wicked dies, his hope perishes,
> and the expectation of the godless comes to nought (11:7).
> Whoever loves discipline loves knowledge,
> but he who hates reproof is stupid (12:1).

The third collection (22:17-24:22), containing Egyptian material, is composed mostly of longer sections. These passages advise young men on how to succeed as public officials, and warn against liquor, sex, and the subtler sins. Especially vivid is the portrayal of the perennial alcoholic whose "eyes . . . see strange things," who is "like one who lies down in the midst of the sea, like one who lies on the top of a mast."

> "They struck me," you will say, "but I was not hurt;
> they beat me, but I did not feel it.
> When shall I awake?
> I will seek another drink" (23:29-35).

The fourth collection is brief (24:23-34), concluding with an interesting description of the sluggard's field.

The fifth collection reveals a contrast between a secular type of wisdom (25-27) which commends good manners but condemns folly, slothfulness and the evil tongue, and proverbs of piety (28-29) which teach that the judgments of God are experienced in the present life.

The royal proverbs of the sixth and seventh sections (30:1-31:9) are of mixed value. But the eighth section of the book (31:10-31) in praise of the ideal wife is both vivid and true.

Love and Desolation

The Song of Solomon, or Song of Songs, is unique in the Bible. Like Proverbs and Ecclesiastes, it is assigned to Solomon, with equal implausibility. In one verse the poet even exults that he would not exchange his estate for Solomon's:

> My vineyard, my very own, is for myself;
> You, O Solomon, may have the thousand,
> and the keepers of the fruit two hundred (8:12).

This would hardly be written by Solomon! It probably was composed about 250 B.C., although some of the poems which are found in it are older. In part it is an anthology of erotic poems of Judah and other Semitic peoples. Egyptian influence is also discerned. In part it is the work of a nameless artist who put the poems together with some expert editing. It has been suggested that some of the poems lent themselves to dramatization, since there is a good deal of conversation in them. But the poems are truly great for intrinsic reasons. There is no suggestion of religious motivation. Allegorical interpretations have often been proposed. But to interpret the poems so is to miss the real value of the poetry, which as love verse is unexcelled.

Another book of poetry in the Jewish Bible is Lamentations. It consists of poems composed in bitter recollection of the siege and fall of Jerusalem and its subsequent desolation. May Yahweh so treat their enemies! And may he look upon Jerusalem in her sorrow. The lament was completed before the rebuilding of the temple in the mid-sixth century. In course of time it was most naturally attributed to Jeremiah, the "weeping prophet."

The Psalms

The most inspiring book of poetry in the Old Testament undoubtedly is the Psalms. Christians and Jews alike derive inspiration from reading them, publicly and privately. Here, too, their value depends not on who wrote them or when, but on what they say.

The problem of authorship of the Psalms has proved less controversial than in the case of the Pentateuch and certain other scriptures. For while the Psalms as a whole have traditionally been ascribed to David, yet many of them are specifically described as having arisen otherwise. Typical is Psalm 44. "To the choirmaster. A Maskil of the Sons of Korah." After describing how God had fought for the fathers, this Psalm goes on to say,

> Yet thou hast cast us off and abased us,
> and hast not gone out with our armies.
> Thou hast made us turn back from the foe;
> and our enemies have gotten spoil.
> Thou hast made us like sheep for slaughter,
> and hast scattered us among the nations (44:9-11).

It is evident that these verses were written after the Babylonian captivity had begun. It may even refer to the later national suffering when Greek tyrants had driven the loyal Jews from Jerusalem, to dream in exile of their holy city, or perhaps to organize under the Maccabeans for a successful fight about 165 B.C.[7]

If there had been a liturgical psaltry in use prior to 400, this fact would certainly have been mentioned by P in the Pentateuch, produced about that time. Judging individual Psalms by their style, vocabulary, and scanty clues to historical setting, it seems necessary to conclude that most of the Psalms were written between 400 and 200 B.C. Almost all the Psalms were certainly written between 500 and 100.[8] The poetry of II Isaiah set the new literary style before 500, which was followed by the Psalmists. God is referred to as king of all nations, and devotional ideas useful in personal religion are expressed in elaborate rhythmical phrases. A very few Psalms afford specific clues. Such is the case in Psalm 2, the acrostic of which indicates that it was written in 103 to celebrate the marriage of Alexander Janneus to Alexandra. Also "the acrostic in Ps. 110:1-4 (sm'n, Simeon), conjointly with the contents of the Psalm, shows the poem to have been the oracle by which Simon Maccabeus was solemnly confirmed in the office of leader and high priest in 141 (see I Macc. 14:41)."[9] Many of the Psalms refer to "the law of Yahweh," or "thy law." This is taken to refer to the Pentateuch, canonized about 400; such Psalms must have been written after that date. Psalms 89 and 132 reveal that the Davidic dynasty had ended long before. Possibly Psalm 24:7-10 and Psalm 45 were the only ones in existence prior to the exile. The former is brief like all early Hebrew poetry, and may have been used liturgically on bringing the ark from Shiloh to the temple of Solomon at Jerusalem. Psalm 45 seems to have been written on the occasion of the marriage of a king of Israel or Judah to a foreign princess. It is really improbable that any of the Psalms were written by David.

One of the most frequent themes in the Psalms is that of the greatness of God, who is usually called Yahweh ("the Lord"), but in one whole series of Psalms was called Elohim. Psalm 19:1-6 and Psalm 104 are noteworthy in relating nature to God. The latter shows dependence on Ikhnaton's "Hymn to the Sun." Psalm 82 asserts God's preeminence among all the gods:

> God has taken his place in the divine council;
> in the midst of the gods he holds judgment (82:1).

God's greatness is in contrast to the weakness of man, God's handiwork.

When I look at thy heavens, the work of thy fingers,
  the moon and the stars which thou hast established;
What is man that thou are mindful of him,
  and the son of man that thou dost care for him?
Yet thou hast made him little less than God,
  and dost crown him with glory and honor (8:3-5).

God is the judge of human behavior, the ruler of mankind.

Let the nations be glad and sing for joy,
  for thou dost judge the peoples with equity
  and guide the nations upon earth (67:4).

He is not only just, but also merciful.

He does not deal with us according to our sins,
  nor requite us according to our iniquities.
For as the heavens are high above the earth,
  so great is his steadfast love toward those who fear him;
as far as the east is from the west,
  so far does he remove our transgressions from us.
As a father pitieth his children,
  so the Lord pities those who fear him.
For he knows our frame;
  he remembers that we are dust (103:10-14).

Some Psalms showed bewilderment regarding God's justice, in view of the prosperity of the wicked and the suffering of the good. But such Psalms did not go so far as did Job.

Some Psalms express confidence that God will help those who trust in him. Such is the character of Psalm 23, no more so however than of Psalm 91. Similar are 16, 27, 34, and 42 and 43; the latter together form a single poem. Others teach that religion consists in living blamelessly, as in Psalm 15. Another example of the latter is Psalm 1, which is prose rather than poetry, and was added as a kind of preface to the entire Psalter when it reached its final state.

Other Psalms had definite liturgical use. Such was Luther's Psalm 46. Also the Maccabean complaint in Psalm 79 was used congregationally. Even the "imprecatory psalms" came in for collective use, such as Psalm 109.

The titles of the Psalms are of course untrustworthy, since they were added by later editors who knew less about the actual writing of the Psalms than do modern scholars who are using scientific techniques.

The division of the Psalter into five books or collections is partly historical and partly artificial. The editors insisted on making five divisions to correspond to the five books of the law. There is evidence of smaller collections in the larger ones, and there is no doubt that certain groupings of psalms were used for congregational or temple worship, or for personal devotion. Singers' guilds had their special collections. The Elohistic Psalter (42-83) for some reason was changed to make the text read Elohim instead of Yahweh about four times out of five. In the rest of the Psalter Yahweh occurs twenty times to one for Elohim.

It is interesting to trace the origin of the "sons of Korah," who formed one of the singers' guilds. Korah was originally a clan of Edomites but eventually joined Judah (Gen. 36:5,14,16,18; cf. Exod. 6:18,21,24, where their Edomitic origin was erased). Other singers' guilds came out of Edom also.[10]

The use of the Psalms in personal devotion and in the synagogue was a primary purpose. The numerous cases where "I," "me," and "my" are used may witness to this fact, without however excluding the Psalm from liturgical use later. The personal nature of religion is, in fact, one characteristic which identifies the Psalms as late.

The religious imperfections of many of the Psalms merely demonstrate their origin in the experiences of a people in their search for God. Some Psalms showed great maturity while others were relatively defective. Some were too smugly convinced of the continued exclusiveness of Yahweh's concern for Judah. Some even called passionately on Yahweh to destroy their enemies.

In many cases the "enemies" railed against in the Psalms are themselves Jews who taunt the faithful by reminding them that Yahweh has not shown special interest in Judah, or in individual faithful Jews. If the faithful fared less well than the unfaithful, what did that prove? The implication was atheism, and it is no wonder that the faithful composed passionate psalms directed against them. Thus a poet wrote:

> It is not an enemy who taunts me—
> then could I bear it. . . .

But it is you, my equal,
  my companion, my familiar friend.
We used to hold sweet converse together;
  within God's house we walked in fellowship.
Let death come upon them;
  let them go down to Sheol alive;
  let them go away in terror into their graves (55:12-15).

In other cases the "enemies" are foreigners. The beautiful 137th Psalm is marred by extreme bitterness in its conclusion:

O daughter of Babylon, you devastator!
  Happy shall he be who requites you
  with what you have done to us!
Happy shall he be who takes your little ones
  and dashes them against the rock!

The Christian anthem based on this Psalm properly omits the expression of this sentiment. Yet it is understandable, since in Christian America the savagery of the war a century ago is still rehearsed, lest any one should forget.

Even in the "imprecatory" Psalms, however, we find mature sentiments. So in 55:22 we read:

Cast your burden on the Lord,
  and he will sustain you;
he will never permit
  the righteous to be moved.

The truthful character of the latter couplet may be questionable, in the light of Job and much human experience. But there is at least a sense in which it can be made to come true if we will claim the promise.

The common men in Judaism and Christianity, like Jesus and his disciples, received much of their spiritual food from the Psalms. But they were also creative, and refused to let their experiences remain in the stage represented by some of the Psalms. They also had the prophets and the great rabbis to guide them. Through the latter Judaism produced its living commentary in the Talmud and later literature, which has already been noted.

Apocrypha

The Christian sect of Judaism, like other Jews, was also indebted to the literature which is sometimes referred to as the Apocrypha. The books of the Apocrypha belong to the same movement as those of the Writings. It is a little difficult to explain in some cases why one book got into the canon and another did not.

Technically the difference between the canon and the Apocrypha[11] lies in the fact that the former consists of books included in the Hebrew text, while the Apocrypha was a broader collection in other languages. The Jews of the Dispersion were more easily satisfied than the Palestinian Jews. Then when the Rabbinical school at Jamnia in 90 A.D. passed judgment on the books worthy to be included in the Jewish sacred literature, those which were excluded but still popular came to be called Apocrypha. Another term needing explanation is Pseudepigrapha.[12] In it are included books which some churches approved but which were excluded from both the Hebrew canon and the Apocrypha.

Among the Apocrypha are the following books of note. III Esdras supplements Ezra with some interesting legends, most important of which is that of the three boys in the service of King Darius. The three books of Maccabees are of unequal value. The first two relate to the Maccabean struggle against Antiochus IV Epiphanes. Tobit is the story of miracle, demons, and angels in the case of a pious man, Tobit, who is alleged to have been deported to Nineveh in 721 B.C. His sight is restored. His son, Tobias, plays the hero. The father, Tobit, gives some sage advice, reflecting the age of the wisdom literature. In Judith we find a heroine, the wealthy widow Judith, single-handedly saving the Jews from destruction by Holophernes, leader of the forces of Nebuchadrezzar, who is here said to have been king of Assyria. The story is gory and, of course, supernaturalistic.

Also in the Apocrypha are the Prayer of Manasses, the Additions to Daniel (The Song of Azariah and of the Three Men, Susanna, Bel and the Dragon), the Additions to Esther, the Book of Baruch, the Epistle of Jeremiah, the Book of Sirach, and Wisdom of Solomon. One of the best known among these is the story of Susanna, related to the Daniel legend. The pure Susanna was condemned to death for adultery, whereas the elders were the really guilty connivers. The wisdom of the boy Daniel saves her. The Book of Sirach is perhaps better known as Ecclesiasticus, by Jesus ben Sirach. It is typical of the wisdom of the second century B.C., when it was written, and compares with Proverbs in some respects. The Wisdom of Solomon is still another example of late wisdom literature, coming more than a century after Ecclesiasticus.

Among the Pseudepigrapha[13] the only one referred to in the New Testament is the book of Enoch. Like some of the Apocrypha and more of the Pseudepigrapha, this may be described as an apocalypse. It tells of the fall of the angels and God's punishment, and of strange journeys of Enoch through earth and hell. He gained great wisdom through walking with God, and finally went bodily to heaven.

Although there is high quality in some of the non-canonical Jewish literature and certainly a gradation of value among the canonical books, yet in general it can be understood why the learned rabbis refused to admit more than they did to the body of sacred literature. Our debt to them is great, both for what they excluded and for what they included. Their action helped to preserve permanently a great body of literature.

Jewish Maturity

We can hardly expect any religion to be born fully mature, like Athena born from the head of Zeus. A normal person is born as a baby and necessarily goes through a maturing process. The simile is imperfect, of course, but may be fruitful.

At its birth as a free religion in the sixth century B.C., Judaism was not without a variety of antecedents. As spiritual monotheism it was non-magical. It had become freed from the concepts of a fertility cult, such as Baalism was. The influence of Elijah and Elisha was in principle opposed to magic and fertility, although the legendary contest on Carmel over the power of the contending gods to bring rain and fire was still magical. Then when Amos, Hosea, Micah and Isaiah expressed their inspirations, it became more clear that the test of divine approval was not ritual-magic but social-ethical behavior. Yet even Isaiah clung to the magic of the inviolability of Yahweh's holy city. It remained for the Second Isaiah, singing his refrains in Babylon, to become more completely spiritual. He saw Israel as the suffering servant who was to bring divine redemption to the world through his moral and spiritual experiences.

Israel was nourished by the Torah, with its elements of primitive tradition, its background of Mesopotamian magic and polytheism, and its traditions of Yahwism from Kadesh to Canaan. The Torah in turn was reenforced by the Former Prophets who moralized on Israel's proud political and cultural achievements, and by the Latter Prophets who went more directly to the heart of Yahwism. Some of the Latter Prophets saw more clearly than others the nature of true religion. After the Second Isaiah had reached the heights of universalism, some of his successors descended to the plains of particularism. Haggai exalted Judah and the supernatural. Obadiah blamed the Edomites. Joel revered the Torah and its favored possessor, Israel. Even these prophets had their spiritual greatness, and the author of Jonah rose again to the heights of universalism.

Among the Writings, the Psalms have had a mighty influence on Jews and Christians. Some Psalms have encouraged universalism (Psalms 8 and 19), some particularism (Psalms 137 and 147); some have nourished notions of magic—intentionally or otherwise (Psalm 91). Job and other wisdom literature have shown complete spirituality and universality. Daniel may be viewed as magical if interpreted literally, or as using myth in a mature manner if otherwise interpreted.

As Judaism grew into a world religion, though small in numbers, it had the complex background which we have described. It had resources of greatness, but accompanying elements of magic, literalism, and particularism. It should not be surprising, therefore, to find that Jewish history is many-sided. In Christ's day Judaism earned the just condemnation and the worthy praise of its greatest prophet. It was condemned for its literalness and praised for its spirituality. Both qualities characterized it then, and in varying degrees have characterized it ever since.

Some of the magical influences in Judaism have been its tendency to trust in a holy city, or in a holy code of laws or in ritual and tradition. Its myths also become magic when taken literally and made a condition of salvation.

Nevertheless the traditions and cult of Judaism culminated in a beautiful religion. When interpreted symbolically, socially, and ethically, in harmony with its prophetic insights, Judaism became one of the most mature religions of man. Its mystic sensitivity, as seen in the Psalms and in its greatest prophets, could not be more genuine or more soundly based in human experience. Its confidence in a friendly universe and a universal God is a long step toward psychological health. Throughout the centuries, as its rabbis have sought to interpret first the Bible, and then the Talmud, in the light of human experience, Judaism has broadened its commitment to the truth in science and human relations.

With such a complex background of tradition, history, and inspiration, it is no wonder that we find representatives of a religion such as Judaism who are less than mature, as well as those who are fully mature as judged by our tentative criteria.

XXXIV. BEGINNING THE NEW TESTAMENT

So CRUCIAL, for most of us, are the issues involved in the next chapters that we must proceed with great care. Before we can profitably discuss the nature and work of Jesus it is necessary that we reexamine the Christian sacred literature.

The first Christians had no New Testament. What sacred scriptures they had were thought of as Jewish, as they themselves were —Jews who had had the thrill of sharing the experiences of one whom they expected to be king over a supernatural kingdom. Their thrill was turned to mourning through the passion of Christ, but was renewed when they were led to believe that he lived again and momentarily might return with angelic armies to establish the kingdom.

We who have learned to rely on the New Testament may feel puzzled as to how there could have been any real Christianity without an authoritative book. This is a natural first reaction to such a startling thought. Yet we are also accustomed to thinking of the first Christians as of a higher order, somehow, than we today. While this is not a necessary or logical assumption, yet it would be just as unwarranted to suppose that, because there were no scriptures, the first Christians were of a lower order. Perhaps a more logical assumption than either of these alternatives would be that later generations have acquired the custom of unduly revering the Christian scriptures once they were accepted.

Our problem now is to see the New Testament in its true light, to learn why its books were written, to inquire into their sources, and to ponder their value for us today. When we know its sources and understand why a book was written, we have gone a long way toward appreciating its present value.

Since the Dead Sea Scrolls were first discovered in the caves near Qumran in 1947, much light has been cast on the immediate background of the origin of Christian ideas. Besides making copies of Old Testament manuscripts, the New Covenanters at Qumran produced original works which seem to relate that sect to the Jewish Essenes, who were described by the Jewish philosopher Philo, the Roman historian Pliny, and the Jewish soldier-historian Josephus. The original manuscripts include a Commentary on the book of Habakkuk, a Manual of Discipline, the Damascus Document, The War of the Sons of Light with the Sons of Darkness, and Thanksgiving Psalms.[1] A careful reading of these manuscripts has revived an old theory that Christianity grew out of Essenism.[2]

Recent studies have made it clear why the various New Testament books were written. In no case was a book written to serve as authoritative sacred scripture. Other writings of early Christian times throw light on the New Testament, while revealing some intrinsic merit of their own.

Besides the writings of the New Testament one should mention those of the "apostolic fathers" and their successors, the apologists and the historians.[3] Clement of Rome wrote about 95 A.D. Ignatius of Antioch wrote c. 110-115; Polycarp of Smyrna c. 115; the so-called Barnabas c. 130-135. Papias, whose writings we know only through the quotations made by Eusebius in his *Church History*, c. 325, was writing c. 140. The Second Epistle of Clement to the Corinthians was written c. 150. Justin the martyr wrote c. 150-160. Tatian, a pupil of Justin Martyr, was writing c. 170. Irenaeus wrote *Against Heresies* between c. 175-189.

The Shepherd of Hermas was adopted for Christian use c. 130-140, and the Didache, or Teaching of the Twelve Apostles, c. 150, although since the discovery of the Dead Sea Scrolls we realize that both of these were originally Jewish—probably Essenian. Similar is the Testament of the Twelve Patriarchs, fragments of which have been found in the Qumran caves. This scripture anticipated Christian sentiments and ideas.[4]

Marcion, later regarded as a heretic, was the first to suggest a canon of authoritative Christian writings c. 144. He saw the need for settling controversy by an appeal to writings recognized as authoritative. He approved of a modified Luke and ten letters of Paul. The Muratonian canon, expanding this list as viewed by the Roman church, was drawn up c. 185-200. It approved of the four Gospels, Acts, thirteen letters of Paul (adding the pastoral epistles to Marcion's ten), Jude, I and II John, Wisdom of Solomon, Revelation (John's), Revelation of Peter, and recommended the Shepherd of Hermas for private reading but not public ritual.

Besides the writings of Christian partisans there were also references to Christianity by secular writers. Such occurred, for example, in the exchange of letters between Pliny, governor of Bithynia-Pontus, and the emperor Trajan (111-113 A.D.).[5] Tacitus (c. 52-117) gave similar witness, commenting especially on the effort of the emperor Nero to divert suspicion from himself to the Christians for having set fire to Rome in 64 A.D. Tacitus' comments were made long after the event—perhaps 114 A.D.—but have a certain historical value.[6]

These sources of Christian history have made their several contributions to our understanding of the origins of Christianity.

Paul's Early Letters

Recent New Testament scholarship tends to regard Paul's letter to the Galatians as the first New Testament book to be written. This took place most probably in 49 A.D., at Antioch in Syria. The letter was addressed to "the churches of Galatia," referring probably to those which Paul had founded and then visited in Perga, Antioch of Pisidia, Iconium, Lystra, and Derbe, all in the Roman province of Galatia.[7] In the short time required for a boat trip back to Antioch of Syria, Paul learned that Judaizers had visited the Galatian churches and insisted that his Gentile converts observe all the Jewish customs, including circumcision. Paul's soul was filled with consternation, causing him to write the most heated letter of his whole career. He invoked a curse on his enemies and even hoped they would go so far as to mutilate themselves (1:8, 9; 5:12). He made a strong defense of his apostolic position.

Paul's message is historically significant in that it reveals a rift between himself and Peter (2:11-14). We have somehow acquired the idea that the early Christians knew exactly what they must believe on all points, and that there was unanimity among all. The fact is that Christian doctrine grew out of experience in which at first there was much uncertainty and disagreement—even bitterness at times. Without an authoritative church organization or body of literature the early Christians had to discover the true doctrine for themselves through whatever means of divine guidance they could conceive.

The message to the Galatians is therefore first of all a defense by Paul of his apostleship which, in the controversy, had been questioned. He established that point clearly by describing how independent of the apostles had been his call and Christian preparation (1:15-2:2) and how he had defended his mission to the Gentiles before the other apostles (2:2-14). Paul then went on to state his famous doctrine of justification by faith, apart from customary Jewish observances such as circumcision, sabbath rules and festive ritual. These are the "works of the law" to which he refers (2:14-16, 20-21). That Paul regarded the Christian life as morally above reproach is easily seen in his insistence upon love as the fulfilment of the law, and the underlying principle of living by the spirit (5:13-6:10). The motivation of the law is negative and self-frustrating, while the motivation of the spirit is positive and triumphant. Despite Paul's invectives against those who with apparent malice tried to undo what he had done for the Galatians, there shines through this spontaneous letter to his spiritual children (4:19, 20) a passion of tenderness and an insight into the need for witnessing to Christ through guileless living. Wrote he,

> But I say, walk by the Spirit, and do not gratify the desires of the flesh. . . . Now the works of the flesh are plain: immorality, impurity, licentiousness, idolatry, sorcery, enmity, strife, jealousy, anger, selfishness, dissension, party spirit, envy, drunkenness, carousing, and the like. I warn you, as I warned you before, that those who do such things shall not inherit the kingdom of God. But the fruit of the Spirit is love, joy, peace, patience, kindness, goodness, faithfulness, gentleness, self-control; against such there is no law. . . .
>
> Brethren, if a man is overtaken in any trespass, you who are spiritual should restore him in a spirit of gentleness. Look to yourself, lest you too be tempted. Bear one another's burdens, and so fulfil the law of Christ (5:16, 19-23; 6:1-2).

The modern Christian is not bothered by the specific problem which motivated Paul's writing of Galatians. Yet we can understand how Christianity was being fashioned in this concrete situation. Had Paul not won his point then, it is improbable that Christianity would have survived in any form. What then would have happened to Judaism? or to Islam?

After Galatians was written late in 49, Paul journeyed to Europe for the first time. He established Christian communities at Philippi (Acts 16:12f.) and Thessalonica (Acts 17:1f.). Passing on, he stopped at Athens (Acts 17:16f.) and then proceeded to Corinth (Acts 18:1f.). From there he wrote his first letter to the Thessalonians during the spring of 50 A.D., after Timothy had arrived with news good and bad concerning the Thessalonians.

Besides the perennial problem of how to inspire his followers with the spirit of Christ, Paul faced the special problem in this letter of comforting those whose loved ones had died before the return of Christ, still momentarily expected. So he assured them that "we who are alive, who are left until the coming of the Lord, shall not precede those who have fallen asleep" (4:15). The "dead in Christ" will not lose out in the anticipated kingdom, but "will rise first; then we who are alive, who are left, shall be caught up with them in the clouds to meet the Lord in the air; and so we shall always be with the Lord. Therefore comfort one another with these words" (4:16-18). His message dramatizes the belief of the primitive Christians that Christ would return to set up the kingdom while his apostles still lived, as he promised and as Paul obviously expected. Some of the Thessalonian Christians were so sure of the speedy coming of Christ that they gave up jobs and possessions, and just waited. So Paul advised the more level-headed to "admonish the idle, encourage the faint-hearted, help the weak, be patient with them all" (5:14).

That Paul was working against some personal opposition in Thessalonica is seen in 2:3-6. The idolatrous and immoral background of some of his converts is reflected in 1:9 and 4:3-7. Paul's devotion to them all in the spirit of Christ is revealed in 2:17-20 and 5:13, 15.

Still at Corinth two or three months later, Paul heard further reports of conditions at Thessalonica. So he immediately wrote another but briefer letter, Second Thessalonians, emphasizing what he had said in his first and shifting his attack on certain problems. The Thessalonians had received a letter supposedly written by him stating that "the day of the Lord has come" (2:2). Such a false letter served only to increase the despondency of some, while encouraging the idleness of others. So Paul expressed the apocalyptic ideas which had gained currency since Maccabean times, meanwhile assuring all that nothing was of greater value in the Christian life than reliability in vocation and spiritual attitude (2:15; 3:7-8, 10-15).

It is apparent that the Thessalonian correspondence has not the universal value of Galatians, nor the latter's passion. It does reveal the concern of the first great missionary for the Christian growth of his early converts. Paul's Christian spirit is of course evident, though some question the genuineness of Second Thessalonians.[8]

Corinthian Correspondence

When we come to the Corinthian letters, we find Paul's ministry maturing. Certain universal ideas are brought out through the particularities of his pastoral problems.

A critical reading of the Corinthian letters leads one to the conclusion that they constitute not two letters but four. The first three were written probably from Ephesus between the end of 53 and summer of 55 A.D. The earliest to be written, referred to in I Cor. 5:9, seems to have been II Cor. 6:14-7:1—probably only a fragment of the original, written early in 54 and preserved by being combined with Second Corinthians by a later editor. Shortly after Timothy left with this earliest letter, crucial news arrived from Corinth requiring an urgent answer. So First Corinthians was then written and hurriedly sent by direct route before Pentecost of 54 (I Cor. 16:8). Probably that fall Paul visited Corinth but failed in his mission (II Cor. 2:1-5; cf. 12:14; 13:1). He returned to Ephesus and, probably in the spring of 55, wrote his third letter, which is believed to be preserved in II Cor. 10-13, referred to in 2:4 and 7:8. The third letter was harsh, designed to accomplish what his early milder letters and his "painful visit" (II Cor. 2:1) had failed to accomplish. His fourth letter was probably written during his journey from Ephesus to Corinth in the fall of 55, after Titus had met him to convey the good news that the harsh letter had been successful. The fourth letter constitutes II Cor. 1-9, excepting 6:14-7:1, and shows a happier tone.

Paul's first letter to the Corinthians, characterized in I Cor. 5:9 and preserved in II Cor. 6:14-7:1, counseled his converts not to "be mismated with unbelievers" (II Cor. 6:14). His advice was subject to misunderstanding, however, and required a second letter —our First Corinthians. This second letter contains the cream of the Corinthian correspondence. It is a mild and reasonable presentation of Paul's gospel in the light of the particular needs of the Corinthian Christians. The third letter, II Cor. 10-13, is polemical and heated, showing Paul's reluctant resolve to deal with the Corinthian offenders through the use of his apostolic authority if necessary. The fourth one adds nothing really new except the biographical-historical climax of success and harmony, effected by his third letter.

The first problem of First Corinthians was factionalism:

> What I mean is that each one of you says, "I belong to Paul," or "I belong to Apollos," or "I belong to Cephas," or "I belong to Christ." Is Christ divided? Was Paul crucified for you?" (1:12,13).

This was an early display of denominationalism, which Paul roundly condemns. Christian ministers should be regarded merely as "servants through whom you believed" (3:5), "stewards of the mysteries of God" (4:1).

Paul next elaborates his earlier theme on associating with unbelievers (5:1-13). He has heard that a man in the Corinthian church is "living with his father's wife" (5:1). "And you are arrogant! Ought you not rather to mourn? Let him who has done this be removed from among you" (5:2). What problems the apostle had to meet in this Corinthian crossroads of the world!

The matter of Christians going to pagan law courts to settle their quarrels Paul next discusses (6:1-11). "To have lawsuits at all with one another is defeat for you. Why not rather suffer wrong?" (6:7). He then deals with such matters as prostitution (6:12-20).

The rest of the letter is devoted to problems raised by inquiries from Corinth (7:1). First, should one marry? Says Paul, preferably not, since "the appointed time [for Christ's coming] has grown very short" (7:29). Yet the married should stay married, even to unbelievers, if it is possible to do so in Christian charity. Nor is it wrong to marry, he concedes.

As for meat offered to idols and later sold in the market, Paul dismisses all notions of magical contamination, showing his good common sense. Yet so pagan was Corinth, and so recently converted were many of its Christians, that their consciences bothered them. So in Christian charity Paul counseled the Corinthians to regard the consciences of others tenderly (8:12; 10:29).

Paul shows less than universal insight in discussing the Corinthian problem of the place and conduct of women, a problem greater there than elsewhere because of the independent, religious prostitutes in service at the Temple of Aphrodite (11:2-16). Modern Christian women have finally been emancipated from Paul in the matters of dress, hair-style, and relation to husband. In the observance of the "Lord's supper" Paul counseled courtesy and decorum, remembering the gravity of its symbolism (11:17-34).

The most universal element of First Corinthians is the chapter on Christian love—*agape* (13). Many are unaware, however, that this is merely a part of his larger discussion of spiritual gifts (12-14). Apparently some of the Corinthian brethren had gone wild in exercising the "gift of prophecy" by speaking in unintelligible tongues—a remarkable instance of exhibitionism in church. Paul puts a quietus on this kind of behavior by stating that "there are varieties of gifts but the same Spirit" (12:4), and that the gift of tongues is least important of all, especially in its public use (14:4, cf. 27, 28). Paul, a linguist of wide experience, could say:

> I thank God that I speak in tongues more than you all; nevertheless, in church I would rather speak five words with my mind, in order to instruct others, than ten thousand in a [foreign] tongue.
>
> Brethren, do not be children in your thinking; be babes in evil, but in thinking be mature (14:18-20).

These are important words to remember when a discussion arises as to the Christian attitude toward the traditional Greek virtue of wisdom.

Paul's greatest gem of wisdom, however, is his contrast of other spiritual gifts with the gift of love—*agape*. This is the climax of the three chapters under discussion (12-14):

> Are all apostles? Are all prophets? Are all teachers? Do all work miracles? Do all possess gifts of healing? Do all speak with tongues? Do all interpret? But earnestly desire the higher gifts.

And I will show you a still more excellent way.

If I speak in the tongues of men and of angels, but have not love, I am a noisy gong or a clanging cymbal. And if I have prophetic powers, and understand all mysteries and all knowledge, and if I have all faith, so as to remove mountains, but have not love, I am nothing. If I give away all I have, and if I deliver my body to be burned, but have not love, I gain nothing.

Love is patient, and kind; love is not jealous or boastful; it is not arrogant or rude. Love does not insist on its own way; it is not irritable or resentful; it does not rejoice at wrong, but rejoices in the right. Love bears all things, believes all things, hopes all things, endures all things.

Love never ends; as for prophecy, it will pass away; as for tongues, they will cease; as for knowledge, it will pass away. For our knowledge is imperfect and our prophecy is imperfect; but when the perfect comes, the imperfect will pass away. When I was a child, I spoke like a child, I thought like a child, I reasoned like a child; when I became a man, I gave up childish ways. For now we see in a mirror dimly, but then face to face. Now I know in part; then I shall understand fully, even as I have been fully understood. So faith, hope, love abide, these three; but the greatest of these is love.

Make love your aim, and earnestly desire the spiritual gifts, especially that you may prophesy (12:29-14:1).

Paul's final topic is the resurrection. His discussion of Christ's resurrection is the first Christian record of that event and is intended to bolster the Christian faith in the resurrection of "those who sleep." Paul himself still expected to be among the living at the return of Christ, when "we shall all be changed, in a moment, in the twinkling of an eye, at the last trumpet. For the trumpet will sound, and the dead will be raised imperishable, and we shall be changed" (15:51-52).

As the earliest Christian record of Jesus' resurrection from the dead, it may be significant that Paul does not mention the empty tomb, and that he regards the appearances of Jesus as visions, not physical but spiritual. Paul apparently believed that Christ had been raised a "spiritual body," for in describing his appearances to the disciples and others he goes on to say, "Last of all, as to one untimely born, he appeared also to me" (15:8). But Christ's appearance to Paul had already been described as a mystical vision. A little later he teaches that the believer's body "is sown a physical body, it is raised a spiritual body" (15:44). If Paul was mistaken in his expectation of escaping death, he might also have erred in his interpretation of the resurrection of a (spiritual) body—whatever that can mean. This is a difficult transition for many Christians to make, but it is perfectly logical, and may leave us free to spiritualize the Christian message, as Paul did despite his retention of the apocalyptic views of the Pharisees and the Essenes. His doctrine of love as the greatest of the Christian virtues contributed to such spiritualization.

Paul's Letter to the Romans

To the best of our knowledge, Paul's next letter was written to the Christians at Rome. He had gone to Corinth in the fall of 55 A.D. and had stayed there for about three months on that visit. Either then or soon afterwards he wrote Romans. He had wanted to go to Rome at that time in order to make sure that the Christians there possessed the spiritual gifts which he had so successfully communicated to others (1:11-13). He felt that his work in the east had been brought to a climax, and wished to go westward as far as Spain, enlisting the aid of the Roman Christians on the way (15:17-24). But instead he decided to go personally to Jerusalem with the "aid for the . . . poor among the saints at Jerusalem" (15:25-26). While there he would incidentally have his best opportunity to confer with the leaders at Jerusalem and perhaps check at its source the trouble which had spread dissension among his missions in the form of Judaistic legalism. Meanwhile he wrote his letter to the Roman Christians forcefully stating his view of the gospel of salvation by faith in Christ. No doubt he hoped that his letter would save him much time and effort when he did finally arrive at Rome, and thus speed his mission to Spain. We see then that even the letter to the Romans was written with specific purposes in mind. It was not at all a general letter intended to be read as holy scripture, although it was later circulated with references to Rome omitted, as proved by some ancient manuscripts. It is most likely that Chapter 15 was originally a part of Romans, but that in the changes Chapter 16 was erroneously added. Romans 16 seems originally to have belonged to an epistle to the Ephesians.

In the Roman letter Paul becomes very systematic, in order to carry conviction to his readers. He first presents his apostolic credentials and summarizes his gospel (1:1-17). Then he forcefully states his brief for the doctrine of justification by faith, carefully explaining what he means by justification (1:18-5:21). A modern psychologist may accuse Paul of rationalizing, but all must admit that it was a courageous and creative step which Paul took to free the Jesus-messianists from all the crippling formalities of orthodox Judaism while still retaining the spirit of the Israelitic traditions. The significant addition was, of course, the spirit of Jesus. And this is exactly what he meant by his discussion of the mystical union with Christ (6:1-8:39). Dying with him, we rise also with him from the dead. "So you also must consider yourselves dead to sin and alive to God in Christ Jesus" (6:11). This is dynamic. It might be traced to the Hellenistic mystery cults which some discern in Paul's philosophy. "For the law of the Spirit of life in Christ Jesus has set me free from the law of sin and death" (8:2). Paul interjects his lament for Israel (9:1-11:36). Finally he points out the practical consequences of the Christian faith (12:1-15:33). Mystical union with Christ implies union with all believers (12:5).

> Let love be genuine; hate what is evil, hold fast to what is good; love one another with brotherly affection; outdo one another in showing honor. Never flag in zeal, be aglow with the Spirit, serve the Lord. Rejoice in your hope, be patient in tribulation, be constant in prayer. Contribute to the needs of the saints, practice hospitality.
>
> Bless those who persecute; bless and do not curse them. Rejoice with those who rejoice, weep with those who weep. Live in harmony with one another; do not be haughty, but associate with the lowly; never be conceited. Repay no one evil for evil, but take thought for what is noble in the sight of all. If possible, so far as it depends upon you, live peaceably with all (12:9-18).

The gospel of Christ does not teach lawlessness or disobedience. Christians should obey the laws of the state (13:1-7). At the time when Paul was writing, Nero was doing a statesmanly job of governing the empire, and Paul saw no conflict between the temporal and the spiritual or supernatural. In any case, let the Christian show forth the spirit of Christ. "For salvation is nearer to us now than when we first believed; the night is far gone, the day is at hand. Let us then cast off the works of darkness and put on the armor of light" (13:11-12). Also let the strong help the weak (14:1ff).

The Philippian Letters

Paul's letter to the Philippians probably combines two letters, the second one ending at 3:1 and the first beginning with 3:2. The earlier letter may have been written from Ephesus in the spring of 55 A.D., at about the time when he was writing a similarly sharp letter to Corinth. The later letter was written during an imprisonment, most likely from Rome about 60.[9] He hoped to send Timothy to them "just as soon as I see how it will go with me; and I trust in the Lord that shortly I myself shall come also" (2:23-24). The first letter reveals the recurrence of interference by the legalists. The second letter is primarily personal, and is intended to accompany Epaphroditus on his journey home. His sympathy for the latter shows Paul's Christian character as he tries tenderly to save the feelings of his friend, who was ill and homesick on his visit (2:25-30). His counsel to the Philippians is that they let their "manner of life be worthy of the gospel of Christ, so that whether I come and see you or am absent, I may hear of you that you stand firm in one spirit, with one mind striving for the faith. . . ." (1:27). The letter is an eloquent plea for displaying the mind of Christ, whose proud position never affected his humility (2:1-11). Paul is ready to die, if necessary, for such a savior (2:17).

Colossians—Philemon

Colossians and Philemon need to be considered together. They were both addressed to the same situation in one very important respect, and were probably written at the same time and sent by the same messengers to neighboring churches—the former to Colossae, the latter to Laodicea. The authenticity of both letters has been questioned, probably unjustly.[10] Place of writing most likely is Rome, in the year 61 or 62. Colossians has a wider subject-matter than Philemon, for reasons which will be explained. Philemon seems to be the letter to which Paul refers in Col. 4:16, 17:

> And when this letter has been read among you, have it read also in the church of the Laodiceans; and see that you read also the letter from

Laodicea. And say to Archippus, "See that you fulfil the ministry which you have received in the Lord."

Now what was the ministry which Archippus had received in the Lord? Almost certainly it was that he free Onesimus, the runaway slave whose owner he was (rather than Philemon; see Philem. 1, 2). The "church in your house" was no doubt the church of Laodicea, meeting in the house of Archippus, a wealthy land-owner and slave-owner, whose Christian pastor and his wife were Philemon and Apphia (Philem. 1, 2).[11]

The human-interest story leading to this complex situation seems to be that while Paul was awaiting imperial trial at Rome he converted Onesimus, who became both dear and useful to him. It was probably Epaphras who precipitated the crisis. Paul was personally unacquainted at Colossae and Laodicea (Col. 1:4, 8, 9; 2:1), but had sent Epaphras there as a missionary (Col. 1:7; 4:12, 13; Acts 19:1, 8-10). Then when some practical and theoretical problems arose, Epaphras sought Paul's counsel in Rome. While there he found Onesimus, and of course recognized him. The story of Onesimus' flight and transformation had to come out; as did also Paul's two letters with all their human interest, the one supporting the other.

That Colossians refers to the same human situation may be seen in Paul's discussion of the family and master-slave relations (3:18-4:1). This passage deserves careful restudy, especially the mutual responsibilities of masters and slaves, wives and husbands, children and parents. The passage is in turn introduced by a prior consideration:

> Put on then, as God's chosen ones, holy and beloved, compassion, kindness, lowliness, meekness, and patience, forbearing one another and, if one has a complaint against another, forgiving each other; as the Lord has forgiven you, so you also must forgive. And above all these put on love, which binds everything together in perfect harmony (3:12-14f.).

In the letter to Colossians Paul mentions Onesimus: "I have sent (Tychicus) to you. . . . that you may know how we are and that he may encourage your hearts, and with him Onesimus, the faithful and beloved brother, who is one of yourselves. They will tell you of everything that has taken place here" (4:8-9). No wonder Paul wanted both letters read to both churches, in these towns eleven miles apart. No wonder Paul says to the Colossians, "And say to Archippus, 'See that you fulfil the ministry which you have received in the Lord'" (4:17). As he says to "Archippus our fellow soldier, and the [Laodicean] church in your house" (2),

> I preferred to do nothing without your consent in order that your goodness might not be by compulsion but of your own free will.
>
> Perhaps this is why he was parted from you for a while, that you might have him back for ever, no longer as a slave but more than a slave, as a beloved brother, especially to me but how much more to you, both in the flesh and in the Lord. So if you consider me your partner, receive him as you would receive me. If he has wronged you at all, or owes you anything, charge that to my account. I, Paul, write this with my own hand, I will repay it—to say nothing of your owing me even your own self (Philemon 14-19).

These were bold words, a personal message for two whole congregations to read. Paul was counting on the grace of Christ to do its work in the heart of Archippus, who probably had not carried his Christianity over into the master-slave relation any more than some of us do, I fear, in race relations and business. The sequel to this story will be suggested when we discuss Ephesians.

The rest of Colossians is devoted primarily to answering the theoretical questions brought to him by Epaphras. It concerns the Hellenistic viewpoint which became a serious heresy known as Gnosticism, especially in Asia Minor. Even in Paul's day the syncretistic movement was affecting Christianity, suggesting that God is far off and needs many mediators, and that Christ might well have been one of those mediators. Apparently such a view was proving popular at Colossae, Laodicea and Hierapolis, and Epaphras had sought Paul's advice on how to deal with it. Wrote Paul:

> See to it that no one makes a prey of you by philosophy and empty deceit, according to human tradition, according to the elemental spirits of the universe [the demiurges of Plato and Neo-Platonism—mediators between gods and men], and not according to Christ. For in him the whole fulness of deity dwells bodily. . . . (2:8-9). Let no one disqualify you, insisting on self-abasement and worship of angels, taking his stand on visions, puffed up without reason by his sensuous mind, and not holding fast to the Head. . . . (2:18-19).

Paul was not an untutored charlatan, but was well versed in Jewish tradition and in Greek philosophy. He quoted Stoic poets and philosophers at Athens (Acts 17:28). As a young man he had studied at Jerusalem with Rabbi Gamaliel (Acts 22:3). He ably synthesized both traditions, but stressed the value of the Christian experience. To him the Christian needed no other interpreter of God than Christ. Gnosticism and Neo-Platonism seemed to him superstitious and fantastic by introducing angels and sub-deities to reach from God to man when, after all, man had reached God immediately in Christ, whose spirit was the perfection of divine quality available to all, not to just a few great philosophers. This view of Christ seems so advanced as to suggest that Colossians might have been written not by Paul but by some one around the end of the century. But the personal elements of the letter, and its publication with other letters of Paul around 95 A.D., witness to Pauline authorship. His theological views were a synthesis of his education and his Christian experience.

In conclusion, we see that every letter which Paul wrote was addressed to specific situations and intended to solve specific problems arising among those Christians to whom it was addressed. There was no thought that these letters would some day be gathered together and become authoritative in all situations of life. Paul would have been amazed to learn that eventually his homely letters became holy scripture and were treated legalistically—practically revered by many.

Paul probably was martyred in the Neronian persecution of 64 A.D., at about the same time as Peter also was killed, according to tradition. This left the church without its two greatest leaders. Still it had no recognized scriptures and little organization. It seems a miracle that it survived.

XXXV. THE GOSPELS AND ACTS

THE FASCINATION of the Gospels and Acts lies in their subject matter. In the case of Paul's epistles we are intrigued by the personal response of the great missionary to the problems of the people in the churches which he established. In the case of the Gospels and Acts we know so little about who wrote them that their authorship becomes relatively insignificant. Their greatest value lies in the story which they tell.

Yet the authorship and date of the Gospels are important, as are also the sources from which their contents were derived. These are crucial considerations for a Christian philosophy of religion, so far as they can be ascertained. New Testament scholarship has progressed enough to tell us many interesting and valuable things in these respects. We know, for example, that the Synoptic Gospels and Acts were the next books of the New Testament to be written after the letters of Paul. We also know much that will explain why they were written and what were their sources.

The Gospels and Acts are usually classified as biography and history; but this is misleading. The Gospels deal with the life and teachings of Jesus, and the Acts with some items of early Christian history. These facts, however, do not explain why they were written or what was their essential nature. In reality, they all arose as a kind of preaching, not in order to serve as objective biography or history. We shall misunderstand these important books unless we first understand this primary purpose of them all.

Another important fact is that the Gospels and Acts were not generally known or used until long after they were written. In this respect they were like the letters of Paul, which were written before he was martyred about 64 A.D. but did not begin to circulate until near the end of the first century. The Gospels and Acts were written between 65 and 115, while the fourfold Gospel canon was not formed until about the middle of the second century.[1] Meanwhile the church was without a recognized set of scriptures and was getting along pretty well. Perhaps we today overemphasize the authoritative character of the scriptures, while neglecting more important things.

In stating that the Gospels did not exist and were not generally known throughout much of the first century, we must remember that the power of tradition was strong. We have already noted that oral tradition antedated the written documents and books of the Old Testament by centuries. The same thing happened in Talmudic tradition and writing. These events are paralleled in the traditions and scriptures of other religions and cultures, and were repeated in the case of Christianity. The Christian Gospels were not invented by the imaginations of men, but were compiled from traditions, both written and oral.

The story runs somewhat as follows. After the crucifixion of Jesus his disciples returned to their homes in Galilee. What then happened can never be fully reconstructed, since the accounts differ in many details. Yet we do know that a strong tradition arose that Jesus was brought back to life and appeared to his disciples. Certainly Jesus had made such an impression on his disciples that they told and retold the stories of his deeds and his words. Others hearing these stories repeated them. In harmony with the Galilean background, where Jewish messianic expectations were strongest, the tradition soon developed into an expectation that the risen Christ had gone up into heaven and would soon return at the head of heavenly armies to establish his kingdom and transform human society.

Since there is much agreement between the Synoptic Gospels upon what Jesus said and did, it is reasonable to suppose that the traditions upon which these Gospels drew were in the first place inspired by the very "heralds" whom Jesus himself had trained to spread his messianic movement during his own lifetime. The stories were therefore well founded from the beginning, but suffer from the tendency of all oral traditions to grow with retelling, and to be accepted somewhat uncritically by a homogeneous cultural group. For example, the Galileans and other Jews and non-Jews shared a common cosmology. They thought it not at all strange that miracles should occur, or that the dead should come back to life under some circumstances. Early preaching and missions consisted of telling the traditions, with inevitable embellishment which caused their gradual growth.

References to the oral traditions may be discerned in various parts of the New Testament. Peter is probably reciting an oral tradition, which he undoubtedly helped to form, in Acts 10:34-43. Luke made use of both oral and written accounts in his narrative (1:1-4), late in the first century, incidentally noting that many others had been doing the same sort of thing. Paul and Mark also used oral traditions and may have had some written records to draw upon even at that early time. When Paul was bidding farewell to the Ephesians he reminded them of "the words of the Lord Jesus, how he said, 'It is more blessed to give than to receive'" (Acts 20:35). Certainly he was not quoting any Gospel that we know, nor could he, since none of them had yet been written. He was also assuming that his hearers knew Christ's words, and needed only to be reminded of them. That Paul was using oral Christian traditions is witnessed by the fact that he uses the same word to describe them as he used in referring to the oral tradition of the Jewish scribes:

> I commend you because you remember me in everything and maintain the traditions even as I have delivered them to you (I Cor. 11:2).
> . . . and I advanced in Judaism beyond many of my own age among my people, so extremely zealous was I for the traditions of my fathers (Gal. 1:14).

As time went on and the expected kingdom did not come, the oral tradition congealed somewhat differently in different Christian communities. Only gradually was it reduced to writing. When it was recorded it was in Greek rather than in Aramaic, since by that time the Christian groups everywhere had become primarily Hellenistic rather than Jewish. These records, variously symbolized as Q, L, and M, together with still other unrecorded traditions, became the sources of the four Gospels. No great Christian center continued long after the first generation without its own cultivated traditions, all of them oral at first, but partially reduced to writing in the course of time. The Christian churches which cultivated them antedated the work of Paul, for he had been their persecutor. Such churches existed in Caesarea, Syrian Antioch, Damascus and Jerusalem. Before long a Christian community was in existence at Rome.

Mark—Q—M—L

If we take Mark's Gospel and omit the editorial connecting-links in the narrative, we may be getting close to the traditions, written and oral, which Mark used in his earliest of all the Gospels. In that case we find the traditions to be small fragments—originally unorganized collections—of sayings and stories of Jesus. Such was the character of what Mark found at Rome, where he is supposed to have lived. How the traditions got there, or how the Roman church was founded in the first place, is not known. There was, of course, much travel between all the provinces and Rome, and Christians would have been among those who traveled. The later theory that Peter founded the Roman church is without basis. Since Mark's Gospel confines Jesus' ministry mostly to Galilee, we infer that the primitive Galilean tradition was influential at Rome. According to Mark the disciples after the crucifixion fled to Galilee, where the risen Christ was present to meet them when they arrived (14:50; 16:7). Mark also reflects the Galilean expectation of an imminent supernatural manifestation of the kingdom. These strong Galilean influences probably reached Rome—and Mark—by way of Syria.

Much has been written about Q—a symbol derived from Quelle, the German word for "source."[2] No one knows exactly or fully what it was, but the general theory is that before any of the Gospels were written Q had come into existence in some form. At first it was oral tradition in Aramaic, then it was translated into oral Greek and used in preaching to the Gentiles. Between 50 and 65 A.D. it probably assumed written form. It is doubtful that Mark knew of the existence of Q which, by definition, consists of most of those Synoptic passages shared by Matthew and Luke but not present in Mark. In Luke it is said to comprise 252 verses or partial verses relating four parables, some sermons, a little narrative, but no miracles. All of Q was used for preaching purposes, and may be traced to the heralds (disciples) of Jesus who memorized these sayings of the master even during his lifetime in order to help him proclaim the nature and nearness of the kingdom. Oral Q was thus more primitive than Mark or even Paul's writings. Originating in Galilee, it is believed to have evolved into its written form in Syrian Antioch.

A third important source has been called M, to symbolize the special material used by Matthew but not by Luke or Mark. It, too, was Syrio-Palestinian in origin, but was modified by a later development of the tradition than the Q. M reveals characteristics of the legalistically-minded Christians of Jerusalem, who may have fled to Syria to escape persecution. It is thought that Matthew wrote his Gospel in Antioch of Syria, where he combined Mark, Q, and M into a fascinating story. His account has been regarded as the most complete of all the Gospels, and certainly became the most popular one in the course of time.

The fourth principal source is called L, to symbolize Luke's special source. Probably still in oral form when Luke used it, L is said to have been the product of Christian witness at Caesarea. The suggestion has been made* that Q and L were combined with the Passion Story to form the first version of Luke, and that when Luke learned about Mark's Gospel he incorporated it in his finished work mainly in five large blocks. The theory is interesting but not too convincing. Luke was also influenced by the Jerusalem tradition, though not so strongly as John was.

The elements from which the traditions were composed are classified most simply by Taylor and Barnett.[4] These are: pronouncement stories, miracle stories, sayings, and simple narratives.

The pronouncement story always has as its climax a saying of Jesus, and the story itself is subordinate to that saying. The saying was preserved on account of its bearing on the Christian life and its first-century problems.

The miracle story is told in order to portray some quality of Jesus such as his human sympathy or his divine quality. The historicity of the miracle stories cannot, of course, be investigated now. The cosmology of that day viewed miracles as intrinsically credible, whereas modern cosmology does the opposite.

The sayings of Jesus were incorporated in the several traditions

* By Streeter and Taylor, and apparently accepted by Barnett. The theory is unacceptable to Gilmour, writing for the *Interpreter's Bible*.[3]

as isolated aphorisms and parables, and as groups of sayings and parables. A brief saying, as finally preserved, may represent a much longer discourse originally, while a collection of sayings such as the "sermon on the mount" may well have been culled from many separate discourses.

The simple narratives are told to illustrate the significance of his nature and work, as in the birth stories, the stories of his baptism and temptation, and the passion stories.

The first of all the stories to congeal into an accepted pattern forming a longer continuous narrative was the passion story, it is held. This story of his death and resurrection was told in anticipation of his return to inaugurate the kingdom. It was the core around which the other stories and sayings grew, finally forming the Gospels and Acts. The Galilean traditions in turn probably became the core around which the other traditions grew. In time there developed a special Judean form of the passion story which changed the locale of Jesus' resurrection appearances from Galilee to Jerusalem and its environs. Both John and Luke were influenced by this, and Luke (in Acts) proceeded to locate the earliest Christian activity and influence in Jerusalem, whereas in reality it was more likely in Galilee.

It is clear that we have nothing like historical records to guide us in reconstructing early Christian history. The Gospels and Acts, written generations after the events, embodied traditions arranged topically for inspirational or apologetic uses, and connected by skilful editing.

From these sources, then, the four Gospels and Acts were formed. Naturally therefore the Gospels have much in common, but they also differ. The most obvious difference is between the three Synoptics and John. The Synoptic* Gospels are so called because they report many of the same sayings and deeds of Jesus—often in identical words. As we have noted, Matthew and Luke report some things which are not found in each other's books or in Mark or John. John's material seems almost entirely new. Statistics indicate that "only 8 per cent of the materials of the Fourth Gospel are found to be coincident with materials in one or more of the other three, whereas the coincidence of contents for the other Gospels amounts to 93 per cent for Mark, 58 per cent for Matthew, and 41 per cent

* Synoptic" means literally "seeing together."

for Luke."[5] These data reveal the nature of the original problem of the sources and interrelations of the Gospels. On the Gospels, together with Acts and Paul's letters, we are dependent for our knowledge of the origin of Christianity.

The special values and problems of the Synoptic Gospels and Acts may now be dealt with briefly.

Mark

The earliest specific reference to Mark's Gospel is by Papias, writing about 140 A.D. and quoted by Eusebius (Eccles. His. 5.8.3) in 325. Papias in turn quoted a nameless "elder" who "used to say:"

> Mark, indeed, who became the interpreter of Peter, wrote accurately, as far as he remembered them, the things said or done by the Lord, but not however in order.

Commenting on this quotation Papias went on:

> For he [Mark] had neither heard the Lord nor been his personal follower, but at a later stage, as I said, he had followed Peter, who used to adapt the teachings to the needs of the moment, but not as though he were drawing up a connected account of the oracles of the Lord. . . .[6]

There are important clues in this earliest of all specific references to any of the Gospels or Acts. First, the narrative is "not . . . in order." Any effort to reconstruct a modern type of life of Christ must for ever be conjectural in that respect. Second, Mark wrote "accurately" only "as far as he remembered (the oral traditions)." Third, even the words of Jesus which Mark heard Peter report were not intended to be verbatim, since Peter "used to adapt the teachings to the needs of the moment, . . . not as though he were drawing up a connected account of the oracles [sayings] of the Lord." This, indeed, was the custom of the ancient world, as when Thucydides "quoted" the great oration of Pericles.* Fourth, Mark was entirely dependent upon the traditions, written or oral, since "he had neither

* Thucydides I, 22, 1: "It was in all cases difficult to carry (the speeches) in one's memory, so my habit has been to make the speakers say what was in my opinion demanded of them by the various occasions." So Plato did for Socrates.

heard the Lord nor been his personal follower, but at a later stage . . . had followed Peter." So Papias wrote, about 140 A.D. The "presbyter" whom Papias in turn quoted may have been a second century Christian who did not know Mark personally.

The Mark who is reported by Papias, seventy years after the event, to have written the earliest Gospel, was probably a young Hellenistic Christian living at Rome in the sixties.[7] More sentimental than factual is the theory, still defended by Barnett and others, that the author of the second Gospel was none other than John Mark, Paul's early but unstable traveling companion (Acts 12:25; 13:13).[8] Certainly the book itself does not tell us who wrote it. Whoever did so is obviously trying to explain Jewish customs and Aramaic expressions to non-Jews whose common tongue was Greek. Some of his explanations are such as no Palestinian Jew would have suggested. At least one scholar finds "an undeniable element of anti-Judaism in Mark, partly due to the circumstances under which the gospel tradition was handed down, but partly due to Mark himself . . . and perhaps his Roman environment. Slight as this trace is, Mark can hardly be the work of a Palestinian Christian."[9]

More important than authorship is the purpose for which it was written. And the purpose in writing Mark was evidently to encourage the Roman Christians who had just recently passed through the Neronian persecution in which Paul and Peter are believed to have met the martyr's death in 64 A.D. In this persecution of the Christians at Rome, as Tacitus describes it (*Annals,* IV, 44),

> . . . insults were added to their death, in that, clad in the skins of wild beasts, they perished through being mutilated by dogs, or, attached to crosses, as the day declined, they were burned for the purpose of illumination. Nero offered his own gardens for the spectacle and put on a show after the manner of the circus, in the costume of a charioteer either mixing with the people or driving in a chariot. . . .[10]

For a martyr church, "for Christians who themselves may soon be called to enter the arena,"[11] Mark wrote his gospel. The Jewish war of 66-70 A.D. was probably in progress and may have offered promise of the fulfilment of messianic expectations. Their hopes were fanned by the inclusion of the "little apocalypse" in Mark 13. Their will to endure necessary persecution was strengthened by such teachings as Mark 8:34-9:1,

And he called to him the multitude with his disciples, and said to them, "If any man would come after me, let him deny himself and take up his cross and follow me. For whoever would save his life will lose it; and whoever loses his life for my sake and the gospel's will save it. For what does it profit a man, to gain the whole world and forfeit his life? For what can a man give in return for his life? For whoever is ashamed of me and of my words in this adulterous and sinful generation, of him will the Son of man also be ashamed, when he comes in the glory of his Father with the holy angels." And he said to them, "Truly, I say to you, there are some standing here who will not taste death before they see the kingdom of God come with power."

Dramatically, Mark's first words were,

The beginning of the gospel of Jesus Christ, the Son of God (1:1).

He wasted no words in presenting his account of the traditions. His first statement was not even a complete sentence, but merely a topic. That topic contained three important terms: (1) "gospel," meaning a story containing good news; (2) "Jesus Christ," an expression which a generation earlier had been used cautiously but by 70 A.D. had become a meaningful name familiarly spoken; (3) "Son of God," indicating Mark's theological commitment at this early date in the development of Christian doctrine. Being a Hellenistic Christian, as even Paul was, Mark was thoroughly familiar with the mystery cults' doctrine of a dying and resurrected God. Mark indulged in no theologian's explanations, but proceeded to illustrate by citing the traditions.

From here on we find the simplest narrative of Jesus' deeds and sayings to be found in any of the Gospels. The chronological order is admittedly uncertain but reasonable, and the other synoptics accepted it as basically sound. No more reasonable reconstruction of Jesus' ministry has been devised.

Papias, in the statement previously quoted, went on to say:

For he had only one object in view, namely to leave out nothing of the things which he had heard [oral traditions], and to include no false statement among them.

Without elevating Papias to a place of ultimate authority, we may nevertheless believe that the above quotation is true. Mark omitted nothing—not even the birth and childhood stories, which apparently had not arisen by that time. And he falsified nothing. He reported just what he had heard—that is, the oral traditions—so far as he remembered. Therefore we have the Christian traditions in Mark in their earliest known form, joined together and explained in Mark's fascinating style.

Mark's first story is of John's ministry, and the baptism and temptation of Jesus. It is all very brief, showing the stage of the traditions in his day. Then Mark tells of John's imprisonment and the end of his ministry before that of Jesus began (1:14). The "gospel of God" which Jesus proceeded to preach was that "the kingdom of God is at hand; repent and believe in the gospel" (1:15). This was worth recalling in 65-70 A.D., and was a principal motive of Mark's writing to keep alive that original anticipation of a supernatural kingdom. The spirit of Christian piety and devotion was preserved in the admonition to repent and believe in the gospel of the coming kingdom.

One indication of the adaptation of a Jewish messianic gospel to a Hellenistic world at this early date was Mark's insistent stress upon the exorcism practiced by Jesus. This was a custom familiar to the Greek world and could be used to explain to them why the Jews had not accepted Jesus as their messiah. It was because Jesus had wanted his kingdom to be world-wide. Therefore his messiahship was hidden from the Jews, and even from his own disciples. But the demons recognized him as the divine messiah and obeyed his authority. When the demons which Jesus cast out revealed their knowledge, Jesus commanded them to be still (1:24-28, 34, 39; 3:11, 12), lest the plan of God be thwarted. It was God's plan that he should die and rise again before the kingdom could come. That was why he died. That was why the Jews rejected him—because God so intended it (4:11, 12; 8:31).

Mark tells of the choosing of twelve disciples (1:16-20; 3:13-19). Whether this tradition was based on the magic number twelve, or rests upon fact, can never be settled nor need be. The Gospels differ in naming the disciples, and we never hear of some of them again. The historic core, however, is that some of his followers were more constantly with him than others, and those he tried to prepare as heralds of the coming kingdom. To them he taught the new laws which should govern men's hearts and actions in that realm of

God. The idea of apostolic authority plays no part in Mark. Indeed the word apostle occurs only once in the whole narrative (6:30). In Mark they are "learners" of Jesus and simple heralds of the kingdom.

Jesus' early ministry, assisted by his heralds, was confined to eastern Galilee (1:14-7:23). After that he is said to have gone to the "region of Tyre and Sidon" where he ministered to non-Jews (7:24, 26). To Mark this was significant, since it anticipated the later development of a Gentile church. Stories of faith and power are related, drawn from different sources. This section ends with 9:50. Chapter 10 makes the geographical transition to the environs of Jerusalem as the setting for the passion narrative.

Mark's story of the "triumphal entry" (11:1-10) gives no clue as to the day of the week. Other miscellaneous stories follow, such as the cursing of the fig tree and its subsequent withering (11:12-14, 20-24)—originally a parable which we can literally witness turning into a miracle story (cf. Matt. 21:18-22 and Luke 13:6-9). Some of the ensuing stories are more relevant to the passion narrative than others. Some recall the messianic problem—why the Jews rejected Jesus, why the kingdom had been so long delayed, what should be the Christian attitude and expectation. Many apocalyptic sayings and their interpretation were gathered together in 13:1-37.

Then in 14-15 comes the passion story, with simple embellishment and interpretation. Jesus is perfumed by an unnamed woman (14:3-9). He eats the passover meal with his disciples (14:12), suffers in Gethsemane, is betrayed and arrested (14:12-52). There is an interlude of trial before the Jewish Sanhedrin, at which no disciple was present (so how did this story ever get started and acquire its details?) (14:53-72). Finally comes the trial before Pilate, the pressure of Jewish instigators, and his crucifixion (15:1-47). The story of his resurrection is brief and dramatic.

Much controversy has arisen over what may have happened to the "original" ending of Mark. Scholars are agreed that 16:9-20 is spurious, an addition of a later hand. A shorter "ending" than this appears in some manuscripts, and is equally spurious. What, then, happened to the original ending? One strong possibility is that there never was one. If Mark closed his narrative with 16:8 it would be no more abrupt than his opening was. He leaves no doubt about his belief in the resurrection, but merely alludes to post-resurrection appearances without describing them. Possibly this was the stage of the traditions with which Mark was acquainted when he wrote, just as no birth and childhood stories had appeared then either. We will recall that Paul described post-resurrection "visions" of Jesus but was apparently unacquainted with any birth or childhood stories. Thus there was a fundamental agreement between our earliest sources.

Matthew

A tradition dating back to Irenaeus (175-189) views Matthew as the earliest of the Gospels to be written. This tradition, arising a century or more after the event, is certainly mistaken. It is a proven fact that both Matthew and Luke used Mark as a verbatim source. Other evidence, such as the allusion to the destruction of Jerusalem (22:7), date the Gospel after 70 and prior to 100 A.D. Between these dates recent scholarship varies widely. I am convinced of a late date, perhaps 95 A.D.[12]

The date of writing and other considerations clearly indicate that Matthew the apostle could not have been its author. As in the other Gospels, here too there is no claim of authorship. The earliest reference to Matthew's having written anything at all comes from Papias, about 140 A.D., when he says, "Matthew composed the oracles [sayings] in the Hebrew language, but everyone interpreted them as he was able."[13] This report is ambiguous and untrustworthy, and in turn was the authority for later assertions of Matthew's authorship. The simplest argument against apostolic authorship is that the book is a compilation of sources, obviously dependent upon Mark, Q, and other documents and traditions. Furthermore Matthew was almost certainly written originally in Greek, not in "Hebrew" (Aramaic)[14] as the apostle would have written it.

Another mistaken tradition is that Matthew is a Jewish Gospel, written from the point of view of the Judaizers, as if the writer were aiming to convert the Jews to Christianity. The fact seems to be that Matthew had given up hope of ever reaching the Jews, and was trying to show how they had been abandoned to their fate by God while the Christians have become the true heirs of Israel. He points out that even John the baptizer had warned the Pharisees and Sadducees not to

> . . . say to your selves, "We have Abraham as our father"; for I tell you, God is able from these stones to raise up children to Abraham (3:9).

In the same spirit Jesus said to the chief priests and elders,

> Truly I say to you, the tax collectors and the harlots go into the kingdom before you. For John came to you in the way of righteousness, and you did not believe him, but the tax collectors and the harlots believed him; and even when you saw it, you did not afterward repent and believe him (21:31-32).
>
> Therefore I tell you, the kingdom of God will be taken away from you and given to a nation producing the fruits of it (21:43).

Similar sentiment is to be found in 22:1-14; 23:33-38; 27:25.

There are, it is true, some passages in Matthew which reflect the point of view of Judaism or of Judaistic Christians. These passages, however, reflect the views not of the author but of the M source which only Matthew used, consisting of twelve parables and additional sayings (13:24-30, 36-53; 18:22-35; 20:1-16; 21:28-32; 22:1-14; 25:1-46).[15] The stress in Matthew, the passages into which the author projects himself, is un-Jewish or anti-Jewish. Such is the following bitter passage:

> Thus you witness against yourselves, that you are sons of those who murdered the prophets. Fill up, then, the measure of your fathers. You serpents, you brood of vipers, how are you to escape being sentenced to hell? Therefore I send you prophets and wise men and scribes, some of whom you will kill and crucify, and some you will scourge in your synagogues and persecute from town to town, that upon you may come all the righteous blood shed on earth, from the blood of innocent Abel to the blood of Zechariah the son of Barachiah, whom you murdered between the sanctuary and the altar. Truly, I say to you, all this will come upon this generation (23:31-36).*

The real motive of Matthew seems to have been to explain to a Hellenistic Christian church how and why Christianity came into

* The reference to "Zechariah the son of Barachiah" is incorrect. Such designation applies to the prophet whose book appears in the Old Testament (Zech. 1:1), who dates himself in "the second year of Darius." It was Zechariah the son of Jehoiada the priest who was thus slain two centuries earlier (II Chron. 24:20-22).

being, how it differed essentially from both Judaism and paganism, why the kingdom had been delayed so long and when to expect it, what the authority of the church was (18:15-20), and what was the basic code of Christian conduct. Matthew was probably intended for local use where it arose—perhaps in Antioch[16] of Syria, to which the M source may have been brought by Jewish Christians fleeing from persecution at Jerusalem.

One of the major stresses of Matthew is on the new law of Christianity. Jesus is regarded by Matthew as the Moses of the new era, giving the law which must be obeyed by his followers (5:21-48; 19:8-9; 28:19-20). The old law was not negated but fulfilled by the new law. That is, the old law was "filled" with a newer and fuller meaning which had not become apparent until Jesus explained it to his disciples. Said he, "Therefore every scribe who has been trained for the kingdom of heaven is like a householder who brings out of his treasure what is new and what is old" (13:52). This means that new and better scribes—makers of traditions—were to be trained to replace the blind Jewish scribes in the messianic kingdom.

In our terminology, Jesus "reinterpreted" the old law and scribal traditions. As thus reinterpreted, the new law became as fundamental and binding as the old. It forbade retaliation, swearing, sexual impurity and divorce. This was churchly law, not civil law of course. It was the law of the kingdom, which Matthew began to identify with the church, since its members were to constitute the kingdom on its appearing. Mark's report of Jesus' saying about divorce knows no exception (Mark 10:2-12). Matthew's report made an exception when the other party had committed adultery (5:31-32; 19:8-9). Paul's teaching about divorce (I Cor. 7:12-15) seems to be unknown to the Gospel writers. Likewise the Gospel writers seem totally unaware of Paul's teaching about the antithesis between law and grace, indicating that Paul's letters were not in circulation as yet. In this blissful unawareness Matthew presents the concept of a new and binding law to replace the old.

The concept of the law is reflected in the structure of Matthew. The author introduces the sayings of Jesus into his narrative in five major groups, corresponding to the five books of the Pentateuch (5:1-7:29; 9:35-11:1; 13:1-58; 18:1-19:1; 24:1-26:2). These sayings become a nucleus for the fivefold division of the book's message, beginning respectively at 3:1; 8:1; 11:1; 14:1; and 19:1. The prologue is prior to 3:1 and the epilogue consists of 26-28.

By representing Christianity as a religion founded on the true law, Matthew tried to show that Jesus was indeed the true Messiah, rejected by his own people who thus earned their rejection by God (22:6-7; 23:33-35). Thus Christians were to understand their place in the heavenly kingdom as the heirs of Israel.

Besides the Christian law, a second major stress of Matthew was on the church as an interim institution. It was vested with great authority and grave responsibility. Matthew is the only Gospel that uses the word "church" (16:18; 18:17). This church was to have ultimate authority which extended into the realm of eternity (16:19). Certainly it included the power to discipline its own members (18:17). With that power, however, went the responsibility for extending the good news of the kingdom to all parts of the earth (28:18-20). This, then, was the reason why the kingdom had been delayed, because the Christian evangel had not yet reached the ends of the earth:

> And this gospel of the kingdom will be preached throughout the whole world, as a testimony to all nations; and then the end will come (24:14; cf. 20:1-16).

Christians should not be discouraged because the kingdom has not come. Let them make perfect their obedience to the kingdom's law, thus proving themselves worthy of their inheritance. And let them carry the gospel to the ends of the earth. Suffering and death may be expected (10:16-39), but the reward is infinitely great (10:40-42).

Late traditions such as the birth and childhood stories of Matthew (1-2), the dream of Pilate's wife (27:19), and the dead leaving their tombs (51-54), were included in order to add weight to the Christian belief in the divine nature of Christ and the supernatural power of his kingdom. The stories fulfilled their purpose in an age when a supernaturalistic cosmology was taken for granted. Today they are a stumbling-block for many who are unable to reinterpret the Christian traditions harmoniously with present knowledge and experience, as Jesus did with the traditions which he inherited.

Of most permanent value in Matthew is his story of the Sermon on the Mount (5-7), regarded by many as the greatest words ever spoken by man. The beatitudes (5:3-12), taken together with their climax—"Let your light so shine. . ." (5:16)—have been characterized as a Christian decalogue. Their relation to the Mosaic-scribal law is indicated in 5:17-20. Said Jesus:

> I have come not to abolish . . . but to fulfill. . . . Whoever then relaxes one of the least of these commandments and teaches men so, shall be called least in the kingdom of heaven; but he who does them and teaches them shall be called great in the kingdom of heaven.

Not less but more is required in the law of the new kingdom than before:

> . . . unless your righteousness exceeds that of the scribes and Pharisees, you will never enter the kingdom of heaven.

Some have described the Sermon on the Mount as impractical idealism because of its pacifism, its teaching of non-resistance, its apparent prohibition of all sexual feeling for any but purely functional purposes, and its insistence on moral and spiritual perfection.

Star of Bethlehem symbolizes the birth of Christianity's great son of David.

One thing is certain: our "Christian" civilization is not based on these principles. Some justify the non-observance of the sermon's precepts by explaining that they were meant for the kingdom, and that Jesus expected the kingdom to manifest such supernatural power as to make it possible then for everyone to be meek and peaceful. Others justify its non-observance by saying that Jesus should not be expected to know the principles of psychoanalysis any more than he should know that the earth is round or that illness is caused not by demons dwelling in one's body but by biochemical processes. Still others explain that it is necessary for each new generation of Christians to reinterpret the whole Christian message in the light of its own experience and knowledge. All will admit that the peaceful, kindly spirit which permeates the sermon, its lofty goal of perfection and its view of God as a heavenly father, have permanent value. The golden rule, the counsel not to worry or to judge others harshly, and the spiritual depth and sincerity to be found in it have helped millions of human beings. What more could we demand?

One of the most significant contributions of the M source is the parable of the talents (25:14-30). Its relevance to the kingdom is developed in succeeding verses. Its permanent message is its ideal of social service, motivated by loyalty to the messiah, the great teacher of Galilee:

> I was hungry and you gave me food, I was thirsty and you gave me drink, I was a stranger and you welcomed me, I was naked and you clothed me, I was sick and you visited me, I was in prison and you came to me. . . . Truly, I say to you, as you did it to one of the least of these my brethren, you did it to me (25:35-40).

When our beloved teacher thus identifies himself with the earth's unfortunates, making service to them a condition of loyalty to himself, who would not be moved? Whatever the theological or cosmological implications, I say that this special report by Matthew of the words of Jesus has brought untold comfort to the world's poor, and blessings to the generous. Another great teacher, unremembered until the Dead Sea Scrolls recently brought him to light, anticipated Jesus' teachings by perhaps a century, almost word for word.[17] This fact can never diminish the glory of Jesus who made good his merciful intent.

With this tribute to Matthew—whoever he was—and to his Christ, we turn briefly now to the special contribution of Luke.

Luke-Acts

Luke is of one piece with Acts. The two should be treated as one. They were originally together and were separated when the Fourfold Gospel was formed about 150 A.D. The separation was unfortunate, for the same theme runs through both, and is not always understood since their separation. The unity of Luke-Acts is further attested by their common dedication to Theophilus, by unity of style and vocabulary, and by the purposes which they reveal.

Said Jerome in the third century, Luke "of all the evangelists was the most polished in his use of the [koine] Greek language."[18] When Luke copied Mark he often chose to use Greek equivalents of Mark's Aramaic words, thus avoiding the need for explaining. The Hebraisms in the Magnificat and certain sermons in Acts may indicate translations from early Aramaic originals.

Who wrote Luke-Acts? The two most plausible answers are: (1) Luke, the companion of Paul, whose identity is confirmed by a comparison of Paul's letters and the "we" sections of Acts; (2) a later writer who used Luke's diary without changing the "we." If it was the latter, why was he so successful in imposing his style elsewhere without so much as altering the "we" of Luke's diary? Possibly it was to give the impression that it was, indeed, Luke who wrote it. Scholars are divided.[19]

The most likely date of writing was 95 A.D., or just prior to that, both because the author shows ignorance of Paul's letters, published just about that time, and because in the early 90's when the emperor Domitian was encouraging a general persecution of Christians, other Christian writers as well as Luke sought to prove that Christianity was not subversive, either in its foundation or in its expansion. Luke personalized his arguments by addressing them to Theophilus, but he must have expected and hoped that his treatise would also be read by other local Christians who thereby would be strengthened in the faith in times when martyrdom was not uncommon. Who was Theophilus? The name means "beloved of God" and may have been used as a general term. More likely he was a Roman official, possibly a convert, whose influence at Rome was considerable. "Most excellent Theophilus" was an address comparable with that to Felix (Acts 23:26; 24:3) and Festus (Acts 26:25).

Luke dates Christian events according to the Roman reckoning, stresses Jesus' loyalty to Caesar, the responsibility of the Jews rather than Pilate for his crucifixion, Christ's innocence as viewed by the centurion, Paul's Roman citizenship and loyalty, his exoneration by numerous Roman judges (the jailer at Philippi, Claudius Lysias, Felix, Festus, Herod Agrippa and Bernice, the centurion Julius), and his virtual freedom at Rome. Delicately he refrains from mentioning Paul's martyrdom, probably in the Neronian persecution, and so brings his Book II to a close. Some think Theophilus was a member of the royal court at Rome, thus placing the origin of Luke-Acts at Rome.[20] Others are unconvinced, preferring to think of Theophilus as a representative of Rome at Ephesus.[21]

In support of his first aim Luke also wrote to show that Christianity was the true heir of Judaism, which had rejected its rightful messiah. "The crowd" had welcomed Jesus (8:40), but their leaders had caused his crucifixion. Since the Christians accepted him they should be regarded as the true Israel and given their free status in the empire.

In carrying out his primary theme of the rise and expansion of Christianity Luke shows, by tracing his ancestry (through Joseph!) all the way back to Adam, that Jesus belongs not just to the Jews but to all mankind. Simeon is made to predict his mission to the Gentiles (Luke 2:25-32). Jesus counseled his worshiping disciples at the moment before his ascension that his message must be preached to all nations, beginning at Jerusalem (24:47-48). The kingdom was not really being postponed; its fulfilment was waiting on the preaching mission. Christ promised his spirit as a witness of his presence (24:49). The spirit (or Spirit) of Christ is mentioned only six times in Mark, in contrast with seventeen times in Luke and fifty-seven times in Acts.[22] The book of Acts traces the expansion of Christianity under the spirit's leadership until, from Jerusalem, it reaches all Palestine, then Syria, then Asia Minor, Europe, and finally Rome.

Significant passages in Acts reveal the author's careful adherence to his theme, showing how Christianity became a world-wide non-Jewish religion. There is the story of Peter and Cornelius, the Roman centurion at Caesarea whose vision was in no uncertain terms. Peter's vision in turn led him to Cornelius, to whom he said:

> Truly I perceive that God shows no partiality, but in every nation any one who fears him and does what is right is acceptable to him (10:34-35).

At Pisidian Antioch Paul and Barnabas were cordially received by the multitudes.

> But when the Jews saw the multitudes, they were filled with jealousy, and contradicted what was spoken by Paul, and reviled him. And Paul and Barnabas spoke out boldly, saying, "It was necessary that the word

of God should be spoken first to you. Since you thrust it from you, and judge yourselves unworthy of eternal life, behold, we turn to the Gentiles. For so the Lord has commanded us, saying, "I have set you to be a light for the Gentiles, that you may bring salvation to the uttermost parts of the earth" (13:45-47).

Paul said to the Athenian philosophers:

> And he made from one every nation of men to live on all the face of the earth, having determined allotted periods and the boundaries of their habitation, that they should seek God, in the hope that they might feel after him and find him. Yet he is not far from each one of us, for "In him we live and move and have our being"; as even some of your poets have said, "For we are indeed his offspring." . . . he has fixed a day on which he will judge the world. . . ." (17:26-28, 31).

Finally Paul carried the gospel as far as Rome, where he declared to the Jews who, as always, were incredulous:

> Let it be known to you then that this salvation of God has been sent to the Gentiles; they will listen (28:28).

Luke's special contribution, as revealed in the L passages of his Book I, stressed the part that women played in the drama of Christ's ministry, magnified the miracles of the master, told certain matchless parables, noted the quality of Christ's compassion, brought out the power of persistent prayer, and taught stewardship. Eschatology, or the attempt to predict the time of the coming of the kingdom, is almost entirely absent from L.[23]

Only Matthew and Luke supply stories of the birth and childhood of Jesus. The two accounts differ regarding the Galilean origin of Joseph, the royal lineage of Jesus, and the events of Jesus' infancy. Luke's story is more elaborate than Matthew's. He adds a tradition of John's supernatural birth, has an angel appear more often and to other persons than in Matthew, repeats the poetry inspired by the divine events or sung by heavenly choirs, and even tells about Jesus' boyhood in Nazareth. Luke knows nothing about wise men, the slaughter of the innocents, or the flight to Egypt.

The sermon on the mount is scattered somewhat in Luke, and differs from Matthew by favoring the poor. The beatitudes in Luke read, in part:

> Blessed are you poor, for yours is the kingdom of God.
> Blessed are you that hunger, for you shall be satisfied. (6:20-21).

Luke's love of the poor is further evident in the sequel:

> But woe to you that are rich, for you have received your consolation.
> Woe to you that are full now, for you shall hunger (6:24-25).

The parable of the rich fool, from the L source, further illustrates Luke's point of view (12:13-21), as does that of the rich man and Lazarus (16:19-31).

Besides lesser ones, we find in Luke alone the two priceless parables of the good Samaritan (10:25-37) and the prodigal son (15:11-32). The former is an example of Christian conduct; the latter illustrated God's love and mercy toward all his children. The latter tale might more appropriately be called the parable of the lost son, following as it does the two about the lost sheep and the lost coin (15:3-10). Jesus becomes the embodiment of God's love seeking those who are "lost." Other parables of L include the story of the importunate friend (11:5-8f.) and the one about the widow and the judge (18:1-5), both of which illustrate the power of persistent prayer. The parable of the pharisee and the tax collector dramatizes the Christian virtue of humility (18:9-14). Luke's parable of the barren fig tree (13:6-9) seems to have used this particular tradition in its most primitive stage, before it had turned into a miracle.*

I have tried to show how the unitary treatise of Luke-Acts carries out the essential theme and its related aims. The treatise may have been prepared over a period of years, and published in two instalments. The traditions used in Book I were naturally richer and more abundant than those available for Book II. Yet Book I was less important in one respect than Book II, for the simple reason that Book I repeated much that had already been recorded by Mark and Matthew—assuming that Matthew was written earlier than Luke. Acts, on the other hand, proved to be the only canonical record of the post-resurrection growth of the church. As such it came to have much greater value than its author ever intended or imagined.

Both Luke and Acts must be viewed, like most of the New Testament books, as having been produced for local use for certain rather

* See p. 569.

definite purposes. All the Gospels and Acts were intended to be used for didactic purposes rather than as scientific treatises on biography and history. As such they are, of course, still used today, which fact attests to my point. The relevance of the didactic uses in today's world is far different from what it was in the world of Jesus and his followers in the first century. But that relevance becomes greater as we cease to view these valuable books as works of scientific history and accept them for what they were intended to be, namely, lessons for late-first century Christians who were facing rather definite problems and needed some help. We need to reinterpret them in terms of our needs today, just as they did for their needs in their day.

The later New Testament books were produced for a variety of reasons and with a variety of results and values, as we shall now see.

XXXVI. THE LATER NEW TESTAMENT

THE LAST DECADE of the first century was rich in the production of Christian literature. First to be produced was Luke-Acts. This may have been a contributing factor in the production of Ephesians and the general circulation of all of Paul's known letters. Then came Hebrews, Revelation, and First Peter, not necessarily in that order, and around the beginning of the next century probably the Gospel of John and then the epistles of John. James and Jude were in existence by the middle of the second century, after which it is believed that Second Peter, Timothy, and Titus were written.

No single explanation can be given for the outburst of Christian literary production around the end of the first century. Yet one circumstance which figured largely as a common motivation was the general persecution of the Christian church during the reign of Domitian (d. 96 A.D.). The persecution under Nero in 64 had been a purely local matter. But by the time of Domitian the Roman authorities took cognizance of the fact that here was a new and healthy religion, spread widely across the empire. Earlier Christianity had been noted merely as a strange sect of Judaism, and as such tolerated in accordance with the Roman policy. The split with Judaism became irreconcilable when Christianity insisted on the divinity of Jesus. Now in the nineties Domitian required divine honors for himself, and when the growing church refused him such honors, preferring to give them to Jesus instead, it was persecuted. Trajan (98-117), replying to an inquiry from Pliny, governor of Bithynia-Pontus, made clear that imperial policy was not to seek out Christians systematically, but to prosecute known cases of Christian subversive activity. Each governor could follow his own discreet policy. So the worst period for the church seems to have been in the early and middle nineties. It was then that books multiplied rapidly, most of them (by Christians) designed either to defend Christianity from the charge of subversion or to inspire and console Christians in their hour of trial. So Luke-Acts had been motivated, among others.

A second motivation during this same period was the rise of heresy. Most prominent among the heresies of this era was Christian Gnosticism. This strange doctrine was a form of Neo-Platonism adapted to a kind of cosmic dualism and the Hebrew-Christian tradition. It followed the usual pattern of syncretism in the Hellenistic world, combining a bit of this and that in the search for truth and salvation. Christian Gnosticism professed loyalty to Jesus as the divine revelation of God, the mediator between a lofty, remote deity and earthly man. Other mediators and angelic beings formed a kind of ladder reaching up to God, who was conceived to be far different from the Yahweh of Judaism. Even Jesus, who appeared in the form of man, did not actually live in the flesh, since flesh and matter were thought to be too evil to house the divine mediator. He merely appeared to be human, while actually he was divine. Jesus was never really born in the flesh, nor crucified on the cross. However, as the Gnostics saw it, this was a philosophy which only a few select minds could understand. The many were too ignorant to appreciate this secret wisdom.

Another heresy which received recognition about this time took the form of a sect which followed the messianic traditions of John the baptizer. In this sect John occupied a place analogous to that of Jesus in Christianity. This movement figured in some Christian literature.

Judaism as such was practically forgotten. Of course Christians never forgot that they were of Jewish origin, but they had long ceased to try to win Jews to the Christian faith. Turning to the Gentiles had saved Christianity from extinction, but it had in effect produced a Hellenistic religion, a movement having a strong element of Jewish tradition plus certain Greek cultural features.

In the pages which follow, we shall see how these various strands were woven into the fabric of Christian experience, as reflected in the later New Testament literature. I shall note each book briefly, in order to see how it was affected.

Ephesians

The sequel to Luke-Acts is not John's Gospel, as one might suppose, but Ephesians. The brilliant work of Luke, in his second volume, served to awaken new interest in the life and work of Paul. We may suppose that Luke-Acts, whether produced in Rome or in Ephesus, had such influence locally that it began to circulate more widely. That the other Synoptics were becoming well known is implied by Luke himself (1:1-2). Then as Luke-Acts circulated and vivified the interest in Paul, his genuine letters were reexamined wherever they could be found. That they had not been in circulation before is attested by Luke's apparent ignorance of them, since his story does not always agree with data derived from the epistles. Beginning in 95 A.D., Paul's letters are reflected in new Christian writings.

Ephesians comes into the picture not because Paul wrote it, as tradition has it, but in order to ride the crest of Paul's wave and to adapt Paul's message to the current generation. Some scholars go so far as to say that Ephesians was written by an admiring disciple as an introduction to the works of Paul, which were then circulated as a unified corpus. The suggestion is even made that Onesimus may have been that writer-editor-publisher.[1] The theory is plausible but not too probable.[2]

Ephesians is strongly reminiscent of Colossians, repeating some of its expressions almost *verbatim* (cf. 6:21-22 with Col. 4:7-8). This is one reason why some have thought that Paul wrote both letters, the one so closely following the other that the apostle used many of the same words, phrases, and ideas in both.[3] A more likely explanation, however, is that a later writer, on finding that Colossians was in part concerned with Gnosticism as it arose locally at Colossae, adapted its message to the church generally when Gnosticism became a menace to the whole church. By using much of Paul's language, together with his ideas and his name, the writer would make his message more effective. Whoever wrote it was personally unknown to his readers (1:15; 3:2). It is now known that the letter was not addressed to the Ephesians, since they are not mentioned in the earliest manuscripts. Its intended general circulation was a purpose which Paul never displayed in any of his letters, and would scarcely have proposed in this case without far more explicit reference to such purpose, together with a justification in terms of the demands of some special situation. Reference to the "holy apostles and prophets" as the foundation on which the church was built, also rules out Paul as the author (2:20; cf. I Cor. 3:11).

Regardless of who wrote it, however, Ephesians has much value both traditionally and in its relevance to today's needs. Throughout the centuries it has been one of the most popular books of the New Testament. What are some of its values?

First, Ephesians disposes of Gnosticism by stating that God

> has made known to us in all wisdom and insight the mystery of his will, according to his purpose which he set forth in Christ as a plan for the fullness of time, to unite all things in him, things in heaven and things on earth (1:9-10).

Thus the divine wisdom was not for just a few sophisticated believers. Nor was Jesus a subordinate mediator, nor one whose function was purely spiritual. It was cosmic in scope, uniting all things in the universe. The triumphant Christ reconciled in himself all opposition of angelic beings, demiurges, universal forces. This is also seen in that God

> raised him from the dead and made him sit at his right hand in the heavenly places, far above all rule and authority and power and dominion, and above every name that is named, not only in this age but also in that which is to come; and he has put all things under his feet and has made him head over all things for the church, which is his body, the fulness of him who fills all in all (1:20-23; cf. Col. 1:19).

Earthly rulers and heavenly powers are thus relegated to their proper places in the divine order. This exaltation of Christ to cosmic significance was not intended to remove him from human contact but just the opposite:

> that you, being rooted and grounded in love, may have power to comprehend with all the saints what is the breadth and length and height and depth, and to know the love of Christ which surpasses knowledge, that you may be filled with all the fullness of God (3:17-19).

God's fulness is available to us in present experience through Christ, not merely in some divine far-off heaven. The essence of that fulness is God's wisdom and his love, seen perfectly in Christ. He who wears "the whole armor of God" will be victorious in contending

> against the principalities, against the powers, against the world rulers of this present darkness, against the spiritual hosts of wickedness in the heavenly places (6:12).

These references can be understood only in the background of Gnosticism and Roman emperor worship.

One characteristic of Ephesians is its insistence on the unity and value of the church as a self-conscious organization. The church has become the true Israel, heir of all God's promises (3:6), and was eternally destined to fulfil the purpose of saving the Gentiles (3:10-11). It is an organism, being the body of Christ who is its head (4:15-16; 5:23, 27, 30, 32). As one body it should not be divided into schisms or credal sects. Christians should lovingly be

> eager to maintain the unity of the Spirit in the bond of peace. There is one body and one Spirit, just as you were called to the one hope that belongs to your call, one Lord, one faith, one baptism, one God and Father of us all, who is above all and through all and in all (4:3-6).

This unity does not rule out diversity, since

> his gifts were that some should be apostles, some prophets, some evangelists, some pastors and teachers, for the equipment of the saints, for the work of ministry, for building up the body of Christ, until we all attain to the unity of the faith and of the knowledge of the Son of God, . . . no longer . . . tossed to and fro and carried about with every wind of doctrine (4:11-14).

This consciousness of credal heresy and the need for church unity became characteristic of the church from the end of the first century.

The relevance of Ephesians to today's needs lies in its practical motivation to

> lead a life worthy of the calling. . . . forbearing one another in love (4:1-2).
>
> Let all bitterness and wrath and anger and clamor and slander be put away from you, with all malice, and be kind to one another, tenderhearted, forgiving one another, as God in Christ forgave you.
>
> Therefore be imitators of God, as beloved children. And walk in love. . . . (4:31-5:2).

Such practical motivation need not be overshadowed by the background of first century cosmology, wherein Jesus is represented in Ephesians, for the first time in New Testament writings, as descending into Hades (4:9-10). This, of course, is comparable with the view of his ascent to God's right hand in a heavenly place (*idem* cf. Acts 1:10-11). The sanction of slavery and of wifely obedience to one's husband (5:22-23; 6:5-8; cf. 6:1) is interpreted in the light of mutuality, at any rate (5:25, 28, 33; 6:4, 9). There is no New Testament injunction against growing into a greater perfection than that which could be conceived in terms of first-century cosmology and mores.

Ephesians scarcely refers to the apocalyptic hope, stressing rather the present experience of salvation, against a background of Hellenistic thought.

Hebrews

Our next topic is the so-called "Letter to the Hebrews." This title was not a part of the book originally. Nor was it added before the third century.[4] The editor's guess in this case was mistaken, for the book was certainly meant for non-Jewish Christians, probably at Rome, who were facing persecution under Domitian. The author was writing from somewhere outside of Italy, for in his conclusion he adds, "Those who come from Italy send you greetings," referring perhaps to a group of Christian exiles (13:24). Who was the author it is impossible even to guess, since its style, vocabulary, and content distinguish it from any literature which we possess, and there is no slightest hint in its thirteen chapters as to who it might have been. That is unimportant.

The date of composition must have been 95 A.D., since Clement of Rome used the book in 96 and since the author shows ample acquaintance with Paul's writings.[5] This date fits in with the orientation of the entire book of Hebrews. The early use of the book by Clement and the Shepherd of Hermas supports the view that its destination was Rome.

The reason why some editor gave the book its misleading title is because the writer tries to show that Christianity is superior to

Judaism. The natural inference was that he wanted to win the Jews to Christianity or that he wanted to prevent Jewish Christians from lapsing back to Judaism. It is true that the author compares Christianity and Judaism at great length, but not for that purpose. What he really did was to show that Christianity was the best of all religions, and since Judaism was its only real rival he proved his point by showing that Christianity was even better than the next best. The lapse that he feared was not to Judaism but still worse, to paganism.

It is evident therefore that the primary aim of this letter was didactic. In the absence of face-to-face contact some great leader chose to write a sermon and send it to Rome, in order to strengthen a group of Christians there to endure suffering and stand firm in the faith. He had in mind a little band of learners preparing for Christian leadership.

> Therefore, holy brethren, who share in a heavenly call, consider Jesus, the apostle and high priest of our confession (3:1).
>
> For though by this time you ought to be teachers, you need some one to teach you again the first principles of God's word (5:12).

The theme of Christian leadership and its responsibilities runs through the entire book.

> Who were they that heard and yet were rebellious? Was it not all those who left Egypt under the leadership of Moses? (3:16).
>
> For God is not so unjust as to overlook your work and the love which you showed for his sake in serving the saints, as you still do (6:10).
>
> Remember your leaders, those who spoke to you the word of God; consider the outcome of their life, and imitate their life. Jesus Christ is the same yesterday and today and for ever. Do not be led away by diverse and strange teachings (13:7-9).

As time went on and Christ did not return, some gave up hope and reverted to paganism or indifference. This tendency was accentuated by the renewal of persecution. So the preacher wrote,

> But recall the former days when, after you were enlightened, you endured a hard struggle with sufferings, sometimes being publicly exposed to abuse and affliction, and sometimes being partners with those so treated. For you had compassion on the prisoners, and you joyfully accepted the plundering of your property, since you knew that you yourselves had a better possession and an abiding one. Therefore do not

throw away your confidence, which has a great reward. For you have need of endurance, so that you may do the will of God and receive what is promised.

> "For yet a little while,
> and the coming one shall come and shall not tarry;
> but my righteous one shall live by faith,
> and if he shrinks back,
> my soul has no pleasure in him."

But we are not of those who shrink back and are destroyed, but of those who have faith and keep their souls.

Now faith is the assurance of things hoped for, the conviction of things not seen (10:32-11:1).

Here follows the famous faith chapter, full of examples of fine old heroes whose reward was only then being fulfilled. For they themselves

did not receive what was promised, since God had foreseen something better for us, that apart from us they should not be made perfect (11:39-40).

The point of the comparison of Judaism and Christianity lies in the superiority of Jesus over prophets, priests, and angels, who in Judaism revealed God but not so perfectly as did Jesus. The exaltation of Jesus is typical of Christian theology at the century's end, as time was running out:

In many and various ways God spoke of old to our fathers by the prophets; but in these last days he has spoken to us by a Son, whom he appointed the heir of all things, through whom also he created the world. He reflects the glory of God and bears the very stamp of his nature, upholding the universe by his word of power. When he had made purification for sins, he sat down at the right hand of the Majesty on high, having become as much superior to angels as the name he has obtained is more excellent than theirs (1:1-4).

Jesus is superior to human priests because he united God and man in himself, being divine yet being tempted as man.

For because he himself has suffered and been tempted, he is able to help those who are tempted (2:18; cf. 2:5-18; 4:14-15).

Much of the glory of Jesus lies in the fact that as a son he learned to obey his father (5:7-9). So we must be obedient to our leaders

(13:17). We must persevere as he and the great exemplars of faith did (12:1-4). We must not be satisfied with elementary principles, but must go on to maturity (5:12-6:2). Above all, let us not lapse into paganism; that would be the state from which we could never again be renewed in the faith (6:4-6). This doctrine of an "unpardonable sin" has been a needless stumbling-block to many.

Hebrews shows a Hellenistic background in its doctrine of two worlds, the invisible eternal world, and the visible world of change. The latter is a copy of the former (9:24). Jesus is far superior to an ordinary priest since he has entered the invisible Holy Place (8:1-2; 9:11-12). The visible priest repeatedly offered the same sacrifice, whereas Christ made his self-sacrifice once and entered the invisible temple whence he will in due time appear for the judgment (9:24-28). Without abandoning the apocalyptic hope, the author of Hebrews nevertheless makes salvation a present experience by uniting us with the eternal invisible world (10:19-20).

All of this, however, has a very practical purpose, namely, to inspire faith, love, good works, and regular habits of worship (10:21-25). The author can hardly write a paragraph of doctrine without digressing to exhort his readers to live the Christian life. Love, hospitality, kindness, faithfulness in marriage, and contentment are commended in one such brief interlude (13:1-5).

Revelation

This is a unique book in the New Testament, an apocalyptic writing comparable only with Daniel in the Old.* Although tradition identified John, its author, with the apostle, as early as 150-160 A.D., yet other external and internal evidence shows that it cannot be. What John it was we cannot know. We can know that he was suffering persecution along with those Christians whom he addressed in order to console and inspire (1:9). And he must have been a churchman of broad experience, in order to know so intimately the conditions existing in the seven churches addressed (1:4-3:22).

Specifically addressed were "the seven churches that are in Asia" (1:4), namely, those at Ephesus, Smyrna, Pergamum, Thyatira,

* Cf. Chapter XXXIII, p. 523.

Sardis, Philadelphia, and Laodicea (1:11). In highly symbolic but forceful language he wrote as a prophet concerning events not in some distant era but which were soon to happen (1:1; 2:16; 3:11, 20; 14:15; 20:6-7, 10, 12, 20). All the data indicate that Revelation was written by one whose name and authority were recognized by those to whom he wrote, and that the occasion was the persecution of the church under Domitian. The date was probably 95 A.D. The place was probably Ephesus, a center of Christian literary activity at that time.[6] His visions took place in the small barren island of Patmos, where he had apparently been an exile. But that was a thing of the past when he wrote (1:9-10).

John was aware of two dangers facing the church. One was the outward danger of persecution because Christians refused to worship the "beast." The other was inward and more serious, for the church would survive if its inward life were refreshed, despite all outward events (2:4-5, 9-10; 3:16-19, 21).

Specifically predicted by John was the destruction of Rome, which he cautiously called Babylon. There is no doubt about who was meant, for he described her as "the great harlot who is seated upon many waters, with whom the kings of the earth have committed fornication" (17:1-2), and as "the great city which has dominion over the kings of the earth" (17:18). Again he describes her as the "beast with seven heads," and then says, "This calls for a mind with wisdom: the seven heads are seven hills on which the woman is seated" (17:3, 7, 9). No one had any doubt about who was intended, or of the prediction that Rome was soon to be destroyed (16:19; 17:16-18; 18:2, 9-10, 21). The message had the one ill effect of convicting the Christian church of subversion. Other Christian leaders arose to oppose this antagonistic spirit. Among them was the author of First Peter.

First Peter

This book may have been written during Domitian's persecution, or during the milder persecution of Trajan—more likely the latter. This could be one reason why he modifies the message of Revelation, preferring Christian patience and eventual exoneration from charges of subversion. The date would be the late nineties. Peter is most probably a pseudonym used in the ancient manner to gain a wide hearing. His humility, patience, and love are qualities beautifully expressed, and the great apostle of Christ would doubtlessly have approved every word which was written in a Greek more flawless than he could have penned.

Peter's is a call to piety and harmlessness.

> So put away all malice and all guile and insincerity and envy and all slander (2:1).

Prominent among the virtues of the Christian life is that of obedience to officials of state. Peter would have none of that subversive spirit which John had encouraged. Peter's spirit is much closer to that of the master than is the spirit of Revelation.

> Be subject for the Lord's sake to every human institution, whether it be to the emperor as supreme, or to governors as sent by him to punish those who do wrong and to praise those who do right. . . . Honor the emperor (2:13-17).

Significant is his attitude toward suffering.

> For one is approved if, mindful of God, he endures pain while suffering unjustly. For what credit is it, if when you do wrong and are beaten for it you take it patiently? But if when you do right and suffer for it you take it patiently, you have God's approval. For to this you have been called, because Christ also suffered for you, leaving you an example, that you should follow in his steps. He committed no sin; no guile was found on his lips. When he was reviled, he did not revile in return; when he suffered, he did not threaten; but he trusted to him who judges justly (2:19-23).

This sort of counsel is reiterated as in 3:8-18. Note especially the advice:

> Always be prepared to make a defense to any one who calls you to account for the hope that is in you, yet do it with gentleness and reverence; and keep your conscience clear. . . . (3:15-16).

Reference to unjust suffering makes it clear that this letter was written in a time of persecution. That it was not the Neronian persecution at Rome is seen in that the letter is addressed

To the exiles of the dispersion in Pontus, Galatia, Cappadocia, Asia, and Bithynia (1:1).

The recipients of the letter were finding their faith tried by the ordeal of fire (1:6-7; 4:12-16). The gospel of patience in unjust suffering is preached in all five chapters. It is even recalled that

the same experience of suffering is required of your brotherhood throughout the world (5:9).

Reflecting full knowledge of the antagonistic spirit of Revelation, and still posing as the apostle Peter whom tradition even then associated with Rome, the writer closes with the message,

She who is at Babylon, who is likewise chosen, sends you greetings; and so does my son Mark (5:13).

The lateness of the letter is also reflected in its reference to Christ's descent to Hades (3:19). Also in I Peter the Gentiles are always referred to as non-Christians, not non-Jews (4:3).

Peter is confident that the kingdom is coming very soon (4:7). But his emphasis is on the Christian attitude of patience in persecution, and the living of exemplary lives in order that conscientious governors such as Pliny, in Pontus and Bithynia during Trajan's reign, might find no just cause for prosecuting Christians. Addressing the same Christian community as Revelation did, Peter's impersonator must have hoped to check the influence of John the Elder. We do know that the church continued to thrive under persecution, and the attitude of I Peter seems a proper one for the suffering Christians to assume, in faith that a glorious reward awaited them soon.

The Gospel of John

John is generally dated between 100 and 115 A.D.* It represents

* The possibility of its earlier composition, in the light of the Dead Sea Scrolls, may be admitted without essentially changing the picture. The Johannine type of literature included among the scrolls was as distinctly Hellenistic as the Gospel of John. "There is no danger . . . that our understanding of the New Testament will be so revolutionized by the Dead Sea Scrolls as to require a revision of any basic article of the Christian faith," says Burrows, *op. cit.*, p. 327; cf. pp. 338-339, 390ff.

a distinct growth in the direction of Hellenistic Christianity. The synoptic gospels, as we have seen, embody much growth of Christian tradition as it suited the needs of a Gentile church. This was far more true of John, in which Christ's Thucydidean discourses have ceased entirely from being short aphorisms, and have become long philosophical teachings, supplemented by comments of the narrator whose remarks are sometimes indistinguishable from the discourse he is reporting. It is believed that John was written in Ephesus and was originally meant to contribute to the growth of a group of philosophical Christians in that community.[7]

The value of John's Gospel lies in its interpretation of the messianic message in terms of the needs and background of Hellenistic Christians. This in no way discredits the Gospel. Making allowances for its supernaturalistic cosmology, we can still see through its eyes the wonders of Jesus reflected in the lives of his followers in John's day. We can understand the problems which confronted them and trace the course of Christian development.

John opposes two heresies. First is that of the sect of John the baptizer, whose disciples at Ephesus had posed a problem even in Paul's day (Acts 19:1-7). Eventually the baptist sect came to believe that John was the true messiah. They regarded Jesus as originally one of John's disciples and therefore inferior to John.[8] This view John opposes by making John speak of himself as the forerunner of the messiah, 'the thong of whose sandal I am not worthy to untie" (1:27; cf. 1:20-26, 29-36; 3:30).

The second heresy which John opposed was Gnosticism. This had become a major threat in Christian circles of Asia Minor by John's time, and he met it on firm philosophical grounds. Replying to the Gnostic tenets that the Christ had not actually been in human flesh and that the divine wisdom was unavailable to the many, John made his famous statement of the "logos doctrine," following it up immediately by his doctrine of the incarnation.

Regarding the logos John taught that it existed in the beginning, and that it was divine.* Wisdom is God and God is wisdom. And that wisdom was completely embodied in the flesh of God's Son, Jesus the Christ (1:1-18).[9]

John did not realize it, but in the logos doctrine he was supply-

* Cf. *Manual of Discipline,* Closing Psalm. See Burrows, *op. cit.,* pp. 338, 388.

ing Christianity with a means of infinite growth. For if God is logos, that is, if he is the fulness of truth and wisdom, then whenever we discover new truth and new wisdom we need not fear it since it is a part of God's very essence, progressively revealed to us as our experience is enlarged. It was expressed fully in Jesus in that his concept of the values of life was perfect. Men will never fully realize the infinitude of Christ's love and goodness. In him it is dazzlingly bright, as God's own nature is likewise.

Besides replying to two heresies, John is concerned over the increasing antagonism of the Jews. He often refers to "the Jews" as enemies of Jesus—not just a few conniving leaders of the Jews. And the reason why they are his enemies is because he claimed to be God's Son. He claimed equality with God; indeed he claimed identity (5:18; 10:30). John's Thucydidean reports of Jesus' speeches represent him as repeatedly making great claims about his divine nature—a situation strikingly at variance with the Synoptics in which the most that Jesus does is cautiously to sound out his disciples' views of him (Mark 8:27-30; Matt. 16:13-20; Luke 9:18-21). We today do not notice this, for after reading John we then have acquired the habit of reading him back into the Synoptics.

One of the outstanding qualities of John is seen in his reports of the "I am" discourses, in which Jesus makes one claim after another. First was his forthright claim to being the messiah, in his conversation with the Samaritan woman (4:25-26). Earlier in the same conversation he had claimed to be the water of eternal life (4:14; cf. 7:37). Then he claims to be the one whom the scriptures had predicted (5:39). After feeding the multitude he claims to be the bread of life (6:35, 51). In the same connection he claims to be the blood of life (6:53-58, 63). Next he says, "I am the light of the world" (8:12). This passage logically belongs at the end of chapter 9, with which it may have originally been associated. His healing of the blind man was intended to teach a lesson, as John brings out. Again, Jesus asserts his very eternity: "Truly, truly, I say to you, before Abraham was, I am" (8:58). He also says "I am the good shepherd" (10:14); "I am the Son of God" (10:36); "I am the resurrection and the life" (11:25); "I am the way, and the truth, and the life" (14:6); "I am the true vine" (15:1).

Another quality of John is its use of miracles. In the Synoptics the miracles were a climax to faith and when people had not eonugh faith Jesus confessed that he could perform no miracle. Miracles were never used to arouse faith. The opposite is true of John. Like the Essenes before him, he regards the miracles as having occurred in order to inspire faith. In the Synoptics miracles also revealed the compassion of Christ; in John they were performed to teach some great lesson, as if they were to be regarded as allegories. For example, when Jesus healed the blind man he answered the query of his disciples by explaining, "It was not that this man sinned, or his parents, but that the works of God might be made manifest in him" (9:3). The story became the occasion for teaching, "I am the light of the world (9:5; cf. 8:12). So the miracle of feeding the multitude was used as an allegory teaching that Jesus is the bread of life, and the raising of Lazarus became an allegory teaching, "I am the resurrection and the life." Lazarus' death was a means intended to glorify God's Son (11:6). Jesus deliberately delayed going to where Lazarus lay in the tomb, until he had been dead four days, in order to make the miracle more wonderful (11:6, 14-15, 17, 24-27, 41-45).

Because John regards Jesus as the incarnation of the divine logos, the complete expression of the wisdom and love of God, he had no need of the story of a virgin birth, found no fitting place for his baptism, and mentions no transfiguration. It is not that he was ignorant of these traditions, for he shows familiarity with Mark, Matthew, Luke-Acts, and Paul. Rather, since Jesus embodied the fulness of God, it seemed inappropriate that he should have to be virgin-born, or baptized by John, or transfigured from human to other-worldly form. He did not deny these traditions; he merely ignored them. He wanted to preach his own sermon about the nature and meaning of Jesus, so we fell heir to the Gospel of John.

The Jesus of the Fourth Gospel appealed to the Hellenistic world through his bold mysticism. He brought God down into their very midst in his own familiar person. Man's longing for fulness of life was satisfied by this intermediary between man and God. Yet there were dangers in John's bold interpretation. Most notable was the danger that Jesus, the flesh-and-blood deity who brought the almighty, ineffable God down to earth, would himself grow more remote and need other intermediaries, such as the Mother-of-God or the saints. Mark's earliest of the Gospels still conceived of Jesus as human, and as sharing the limitations of other human beings. Luke and Matthew, particularly in the temptation and Gethsemane experiences, retain that human personality with its approach to the kingdom through ethical perfection. But in John Jesus is too divine to be tempted, and too omniscient to need to be told anything (1:47-51; 2:24-25; 7:15). When he went to the cross it was with an iron will that was calm and completely undisturbed (18:4-11). Gethsemane was so out of harmony with this conception that it was wholly omitted. Christ's death and resurrection became incidents in the divine drama which was understood by the chief actor before the worlds began. Such a lofty view of the Christ led to the exaltation and dehumanization of Jesus, and to credal struggles over the problem of how to reconcile the human and the divine.

Yet the Fourth Gospel has a real value in presenting to us the meaning of Christ in the experience of some great mystic who had no inhibitions against the miraculous. For in John we see God as perfect wisdom, love, and service as exemplified in one man's life. John's Christ approached the kingdom not through ethics but through mystical union with God. Yet the kingdom was not to be realized apart from the good life. Ethics needed the motivation of love and the indwelling spirit. With all his divine qualities the Son of God "girded himself with a towel . . . and began to wash the disciples' feet" (13:4-5). This, said he, was "an example, that you also should do as I have done to you. Truly, truly, I say to you, a servant is not greater than his master" (13:15-16). Paradoxically, like a true mystic, the master a little later is made to say that "he who believes in me will also do the works that I do; and greater works than these will he do" (14:13). After all, Christ the mystic was one with the Father, as his followers are one with Christ and, like him, divine, sharing in the wisdom, love, and service that is the essence of deity (17:23). John dared his readers to think of God not merely as fatherly but as Christlike—something more than fatherly. There can be no jealousy in such a God, who is always overjoyed when his disciples surpass him in good works or spiritual insight.

In John the kingdom is no longer a future event, forever bafflingly postponed. It is a present experience. "And this is eternal life, that they know thee the only true God, and Jesus Christ whom thou hast sent" (17:3). The only way to gain access to any future kingdom is by way of present experience of that which is in its essence eternal. That way is Christ, or the truth with which he boldly identified himself (14:1-7). Christ's "second coming" is a spiritual experience that does not wait even until death (14:3, 15-18). It need not be miraculous, for even John's supernaturalism was tempered by his earthly insistence on service and love as the true way of life. It was purely an accident that John's mysticism happened to be expressed through the supernaturalist cosmology of his day. Far more essential to John's mysticism was his sense of the unity of God and man through the intuitions of loving service and creative progress through divine wisdom—down-to-earth wisdom that allows no prejudice or malice.

John's Letters

There has been much controversy over the authorship of the letters of John: whether they were all by the same author, or whether I John was from a different hand from the other two; and whether one or all are by the author of the Fourth Gospel. The tendency today is to regard the three letters as by one author, but perhaps a different author from that of the Gospel. All four "books" seem to have originated at Ephesus.

In any case, the three letters were produced within a decade or so after the Fourth Gospel, and I John seems almost like a continuation of the Gospel. It is aimed against Gnosticism by insisting that Christ came in the flesh. It stresses the mystical experience of the union of God and man, identifying God not as something ineffable but as something as familiar as love. To have love *(agape)* in the heart is to have God in the heart.

> If any one says, "I love God," and hates his brother, he is a liar; for he who does not love his brother whom he has seen, cannot love God whom he has not seen" (4:20).

If any one wants to take the Bible literally, let him begin with I John 4:8, "God is love." This reduces mysticism to an insight which even the simplest can understand. It is really all the theology that any one needs to know. Even if one's cosmology is primitive, if his heart is mature in its apprehension of the love that is God, he is as truly Christian as the most sophisticated. If sophistication leads to pride it is likely to crowd out the love that is even more important than all the sophistication in the world.

The reiteration in I John that Jesus Christ has come in the flesh is to be understood not in terms of a theological issue today, but in terms of the spread of speculative gnosticism among Christians in John's day. It is well for us today to realize that this insistence of John was in order to hold fast to the original Christian tradition that Jesus was truly human, not just a divine mediator who merely "seemed" to be human.

Thus John insisted on correct doctrine, but even more so on Christian piety by living the life of love.

The Letter of James

It is nearly certain that the letter of James was not written by an apostle, and that it was written quite late. Its canonical acceptance did not come generally until c. 400 A.D. What evidence we have leads to the conclusion that James was produced between 125 and 150 A.D. as a tract for general Christian reading. Its pseudonym and its address "To the twelve tribes in the dispersion" support this reasoning. Its Greek composition and its relevance to Christian experience in these times are factors in such judgment.

James is one of the most prosaically practical books of the New Testament. Its over-all aim is to counteract the false interpretation of the doctrine of justification by faith by pointing out that the only way to prove faith is through works (2:14-26). Equally memorable is his definition of pure religion:

> to visit orphans and widows in their affliction, and to keep oneself unstained from the world (1:27).

He counsels his readers to be patient in trials (1:12), slow to anger (1:19), without favoritism for the rich (2:1-9), peaceable (3:6-4:11), and humble (4:14-5:6). James appears harsh in his judgments of the rich, who are likely to set their hearts on their riches and forget the finer qualities of Christian service (5:1-6; 2:1-7). The expectation of the coming kingdom has, in James, settled down to a continuing hope, with faith that this present age must surely be superseded some day by the era of universal righteousness (5:7-11).

Jude and II Peter

No book of the New Testament is so insistent on its apostolic origin as II Peter. One might say of it, he "doth protest too much methinks." Differences of style and vocabulary prove that I and II Peter could hardly be by a single author, and internal and external evidence virtually rule out apostolic authorship of either.

The little book of Jude is virtually reproduced in II Peter 2:1-18. Which copied the other, or whether both copied from a common source, is unimportant. Both were produced probably between 125 and 150. The writers of both assumed pseudonymns in order to fight unorthodox tendencies arising within the church. Both condemned the scoffers who ridiculed the return of Christ. Both appealed to the prophets and apostles as authorities in matters of orthodoxy.

Timothy and Titus

These "pastoral letters" of Paul are now believed by many scholars to have been written during the third quarter of the second century.[10] Although opinion is not at all unanimous, yet it seems reasonable to believe that these letters were composed in order to reinstate Paul's genuine writings after they had become somewhat unpopular through their abuse by such heretics as Marcion. Marcion himself did not mention the pastorals, though he mentioned the others about 140 A.D., in his first effort to set up scriptural authority for the Christian faith.

Again, it matters little who actually wrote a book. Its genuine value is all that matters. In this respect the pastorals have mixed value today. Certainly they accomplished their purpose historically by uprooting the Marcionite tendency to antinomianism and other heresies. Yet each of the books contains passages which are most useful in modern settings. The reference to bishops (I Tim. 3:2; Titus 1:7) dates these letters long after Paul, yet their descriptions of the proper character of a bishop are timeless (I Tim. 3:1-7; Titus 1:7-8). Related verses which follow seem almost superfluous in our day, since we take their advice largely as a matter of Christian common sense and decency. Likewise the reference to holy scripture is post-apostolic (II Tim. 3:15-17). Yet its advice to the pastor is good. There is the inevitable reference, characteristic of the times, to the scoffers about the return of Christ (3:1ff.).

It is difficult to dissociate intimate passages of personal devotion, such as II Tim. 4:6-8, from the historical Paul. Yet such a passage could have just as much value by showing what Paul's self-sacrifice had come to mean in later Christian experience. Nothing has any vital meaning apart from its relevance to present experience, in any case. Only by reinterpreting the writings of our New Testament in terms of the experiences which gave rise to them can we derive from them their true value for us today.

XXXVII. THE CONTINUING CHRISTIAN TRADITION

Concerning the life and times of Jesus we can, strictly speaking, know very little. That Jesus was born is certain, for he did live. How he was born we cannot know. We do know that primitive cosmology favored the cultivation, in the course of time, of a tradition of virgin birth, while modern cosmology is definitely opposed to the miraculous.* The annunciations and childhood stories are likewise favored by the primitive cosmology, and regarded sceptically in the modern. Since all religions used these forms to enhance the persons of their founders, the stories can be understood as reflections of the esteem in which the founders were held by their devoted followers.

When Christian tradition is related to Roman chronology we conclude that Jesus was born in Bethlehem about 5 B.C., and that he was reared in a carpenter's home in Nazareth.† There he probably witnessed the destruction of nearby Sepphoris in 8 A.D. as a result of Zealot violence, and may have helped to rebuild it later. He surely acquired Jewish culture and habits from the local synagogue.

All evidence indicates that Jesus was essentially Jewish in his cultural outlook. He accepted the traditions of Moses and the Prophets, and enjoyed the Writings with which he was familiar. Although the Old Testament canon had not been completed by the rabbis, Jesus probably knew all the books which were finally approved, and other Jewish literature besides. The fact that he wrote nothing does not prove that he could not have written. Very likely he refrained from writing because of his expectation that the messianic kingdom was

* It is asserted that virgin birth by parthenongenesis is scientifically possible in the human species. This, however, is applicable only to female offspring.

† It is questionable if Nazareth existed as a village in Jesus' day. We assume that it did.

imminent. He probably could converse in the *koine* Greek used in the Greek cities of Palestine, where he journeyed according to tradition. He was fully aware of the political situation also, and of the political-cultural issues between Judea and Rome. In these matters he sided with Judaism as against Hellenism and Rome.

Judaism was not united in its cultural attitudes. There were differences between Sadducees, Essenes, Pharisees, Zealots, Herodians, and the followers of John the baptizer. As a follower of John, Jesus was of course opposed to the Herodians. He was closer to the traditions of the Pharisees and Zealots than to those of the Sadducees. The discovery of the Dead Sea Scrolls in 1947 has revived a theory that he may have been sympathetic with the Essenes and the New Covenanters (New Testamenters) of Qumran.

The five groups just named have been variously called Jewish sects and Jewish political parties. They were neither in any strict sense, yet were both in a general way. An important issue on which they differed was in their interpretation of the Jewish messianic expectation.

Messianism

Ever since their return to Jerusalem from Babylonian exile many Jews had cultivated the hope or expectation that a Jewish state would be reestablished in a form comparable with that of preexilic times or, still better, with the age of David and Solomon. They hoped for a strong and independent state which preferably would be ruled over by some legitimate descendant of David, founder of the dynasty. Soon after the decree of Cyrus in 537 B.C., some had hoped that Zerubbabel, a prince of the Davidic line, would work a miracle and become the messiah, that is, the one "anointed" (Greek "Christ") to rule. This was an unrealistic dream and the pious patriots were doomed to disappointment. Nor did any great hopes materialize through the works of Nehemiah or Ezra.

In the middle of the second century B.C. the Maccabean state became a reality, although no descendant of David ever ruled over it. Even so, a state which began gloriously turned out to be weak and inglorious through the corruption of the Hasmonean dynasty. A century later Rome fell heir to Palestine in 63 B.C., and in 40 B.C.

installed as a puppet king Herod, a non-Jew (an Idumean) who had married a Hasmonean Jewess. Herod sought the favor of the Jews by lavishly rebuilding their temple. He died soon after Jesus' birth, and the Herodians of Jesus' day favored the broadening of the authority of a later Herod whose rule over Judea had been replaced by that of a Roman procurator.

Because of the continued delay in the coming of the messianic kingdom, and because of the position of mighty Rome standing squarely in the way of any attempt to set up an independent Davidic kingdom, popular imagination turned to the miraculous as a way of escape. Daniel 7:13, 14, written in the tense days of the Maccabean struggle, was one basis for their miraculous hopes.

> I saw in the night visions,
> and behold, with the clouds of heaven
> there came one like a son of man,
> and he came to the Ancient of Days
> and was presented before him.
> And to him was given dominion
> and glory and kingdom,
> that all peoples, nations, and languages
> should serve him;
> his dominion is an everlasting dominion,
> which shall not pass away,
> and his kingdom one
> that shall not be destroyed.

A similar passage in the apocalyptic book of Enoch, in the Pseudepigrapha, may have been even more influential than Daniel in creating the miraculous concept of the coming of the kingdom. Also the concepts of the Essene-Qumran sectarians favored a supernaturalistic messianism.

The group most influenced by the miracle concept was the Zealots. They thought they knew why Yahweh had not sent the messiah. It was because the people lacked courage to support their faith, they said. Let the people really believe that Yahweh is with them; then let them supplement their faith with courage to shoulder arms and attack the Roman legions, despite any odds. Yahweh could not let such faith go unrewarded. He would intervene miraculously by sending to their aid the heavenly hosts, led by the messiah, who would thereupon establish his glorious kingdom. Harmoniously with their faith, the Zealots organized a considerable group of followers, and made several attempts to force Yahweh to intervene. But Yahweh did not come miraculously to the rescue on any of these occasions.

The Sadducees frowned upon the Zealots. They were satisfied with things as they were. The messiah had already arrived in the form of the Roman Empire. At last Israel had obtained peace and prosperity, under the stabilizing influence of the *pax Romana*. Had not the prophets foretold such an age of universal peace? So the Sadducees did not want revolution. As a matter of fact, the Sadducees as a class were pretty well established economically. Most of the priests were Sadducees. The successful are seldom on the side of revolution. Suppose Rome should lose patience with a rebellious Judea? The priests and bankers would lose their fine incomes. It is not strange that the Sadducees should frown upon Jesus when he seemed to be preaching revolutionary doctrine, similar to that of the Zealots.

The Pharisees, however, were different. They were looking for the messiah. They believed that Yahweh would send the messiah miraculously from heaven whenever they really observed the whole law. That was why they were so zealous in trying to enforce the letter of the law of Moses, as supplemented and interpreted by the scribes, a class of lawyers. In an effort to save Yahweh's face (and their own) when the kingdom failed to come, they raised the legal requirements from time to time until it was impossible to fulfill the law. Yet they wanted to seem to observe it, so they devised all kinds of subterfuges. This brought the scathing rebukes from Jesus. But their underlying motive seems to have been to help bring in the messianic kingdom. They would not accept Jesus as the messiah, because he opposed their view of how the kingdom was to be brought in, namely, by legalism.

New light has been thrown upon the Essenes by the discovery of the Dead Sea Scrolls. There is a strong tendency to identify the community at Qumran as Essenes—perhaps as their most distinguished representatives.[1] Writes Dr. Cross, "Thanks to a combination of literary evidence, not least that of the adjacent caves, and spectacular archaeological data, the identity of the site as the Essene community center or 'city in the wilderness' has been established beyond reasonable doubt."[2]

The Essenes practiced baptism and other lustrations, symbolizing repentance from sins and purification of soul. They objected to the use of oaths as superfluous when a good man's word and reputation were sufficient guarantee of his truthfulness. The Qumran sect and Essenes generally held all things in common. They were ascetically inclined, and opposed war except when it might lead to the coming of the messianic kingdom. They were dualistic in their view of the universe as a scene of conflict between the forces of darkness and of light. They also believed in the immortality of the soul. Closely relating them to the Judean Christian community, the Essenes also practiced a communion meal which clearly anticipated its fulfilment in the messianic kingdom. (Cf. Mark 14:25; Luke 22:14-19; I Cor. 11:26.)

In the light of these facts it is understandable that scholars have recently revived the theory of Renan that Christianity grew out of Essenism. The Essenes were that Jewish sect which most specifically anticipated the character and teachings of John the baptizer and of Jesus. This does not mean that John and Jesus had no originality, but only that their teachings were more an outgrowth of Essenism than of any other form of Judaism. Many of the Christian traditions were enigmatic before this theory was understood. Now they have become clear. Even the Qumran sect's Teacher of Righteousness was revered as an authoritative teacher and as a Messiah who after his (violent?) death was expected to return. There is some uncertainty as to the interpretation of the Essenes' messianic teachings, but they seem closer to those of the Christian tradition than do the messianic doctrines of the other Jewish sects.

John's Preaching

In the midst of this situation appeared the dramatic figure of John the baptizer. Possibly a member of the Essene sect, he is described as preaching in the Judean wilderness—a setting which could very easily be identified with the area of Qumran. His practice of baptism, his ascetic habits, his utter devotion to righteousness and his anticipation of the messiah, all point to an association with the Essenes. Yet he was also like the Pharisees in believing that the messianic kingdom would come when men lived the right kind of lives. But he differed profoundly from the scribes and Pharisees as to what constituted the right kind of lives. Do not try to purify the well by painting the pump, he said in effect. Make your motives right, and you will not need to stress the outwardness of legal forms. Yahweh would send the messiah whenever the Jews repented and lived lives of purity and kindness. He believed that the messiah was close at hand. Let all Jews get ready for the kingdom!

Great crowds came to hear him. Many were convinced and joined his group. Then one day Jesus came to hear him. The meager account does not explain to what extent Jesus was already familiar with the work of John. Nor can we know where tradition and history part company. The later followers of John witness to an independent tradition. And we may be sure that Jesus had long been pondering the problem of the messianic kingdom. He had observed the Zealots at work. The attitudes of the Essenes, Sadducees and Pharisees were very likely well known to him. And he had heard enough about John's preaching to want to hear him. That the heavens literally opened and a voice spoke, however, is an incident arising from a devlopment of tradition with the background of ancient cosmology. Aesthetically this story, like others, is worthy of being retained and treated in a symbolic sense, but regarded literally it is of doubtful value.

Now if Jesus was baptized by John it is most likely that he did so because he felt a strong conviction of the truth of John's message. It may even be the case that Jesus regarded his baptism as the entrance into the communion of the Essenes, as some have recently suggested. Undoubtedly his emotions and will were deeply touched by the experience of contact with the wilderness prophet. And as he looked back over it he felt that the heavens had been opened and God had spoken to him. What is time in a case like that? The ultimate meaning of the experience is all that is really important. Jesus certainly pondered the significance of Jewish life and traditions, and concluded that his life was destined for something in keeping with his awakened insights and powers. These reflections constituted his temptations, his own wilderness experience as the traditions came to formulate them in terms of later preaching.

Learners naturally gravitated around such a prophet-rabbi as Jesus proved to be. It was not such a formalized drama as later writers made it, but we do know that he had disciples. And if he had disciples, then he must have taught them something. What did he teach? A difficult question, but it can be answered in principle.

Short sayings, most easily memorized by the learners, are to be regarded as the most primitive. How original they were in each case, cannot be determined. We surely understand how the later traditions expanded on the earlier ones, turning simple aphorisms into long discourses, and passing from the originally modest attitude of Jesus toward himself to grandiose "I am" sermons in the late Johannine doctrines. Therefore we conclude that the man, Jesus of Nazareth, originally was convinced only—as John the baptizer was—that the messianic kingdom was about to come, and that people should make ready for it. That he expected it to be manifested with supernatural power after the manner of Daniel's phrases, we may well assume. Jesus' significance, however, lies not in his consent to the cosmology of Daniel or the Essenes, but rather in his insistence that the way to prepare for the kingdom was by living perfect lives such as the kingdom would require—and make possible. So he taught the Christian decalogue of beatitudes. He taught his disciples the "Lord's prayer"—minus its emotionalized ending. He taught his disciples to think of God as father, and of one another as brothers. At least in principle, Jesus taught the fatherhood of God and the brotherhood of man.

From here on the mixture of original and later traditions becomes indistinguishable. How many of the parables were his and how many arose to interpret him it is impossible to say. The parables belong to the tradition, and that is enough. That they interpret him truly is all that we need to know. God through him was seeking to save the lost—the lost son, the lost sheep, and the lost coin. God is interested in man, the crown of his creation, and his love is vicariously expressed. So Jesus was sacrificed for our sins and for our redemption. Most of these ideas were added by his followers, but they are true in terms of our Christian experience.

How long his ministry lasted we cannot know. The synoptics mention only one passover, suggesting that it was very brief indeed. John mentions three passovers, but we have learned to put small confidence in John's account of historical facts.

Jesus himself was probably too human not to be disappointed

when the kingdom did not materialize as he expected (Matt. 10:23; cf. Luke 10:18, 20).[3] When the kingdom did not come, it seems likely that he revised his schedule and, when his death seemed imminent, remained unshaken in his faith. His lone retirement to Tyre and Sidon was in order to reflect on its postponement, not to foreshadow the mission to the Gentiles.[4] The kingdom would come in the near future, after his passion. And he would be among the angelic hosts who would come with the clouds of glory to establish it. So his predictions of his survival of death and his return to life with the manifestation of that kingdom form a natural development, in his own thinking and in the continuing Christian tradition. Visions of him were seen after his death. Time means little in the formation of the resurrection traditions. The Christian experience was a reality and saved the remnant of his survivors for posterity.

The Latin cross, since Constantine, came to symbolize a sacrificial death and the triumph of life over death.

The daily expectation of the kingdom settled down in time to the formation of a church, with its leaders and their evolving creeds. Eventually the divisions and sects required authoritative scriptures, so apostolic authorities were found and, by 400 A.D., the New Testament scriptures became canonical authority.

There were a few important steps in the formation of the New Testament canon. First came Marcion's appeal to apostolic authority about 140 A.D. He proposed that the church read the ten letters of Paul and the Gospel of Luke instead of Old Testament scriptures. About mid-century the Fourfold Gospel was published and used with the Old Testament. Near the end of the century the Roman church approved most of the books of our present New Testament and some not in it. Origen in the third century approved our present New Testament adding two books not in it. The West was slow to accept Hebrews until Hilary did so in 367; Jerome included it in his Latin Vulgate version a few years later. Revelation came to be accepted slowly in the East. Differences of opinion continued into the fifth century, although agreement was reached for the most part by 400 A.D. There has never been any formal action on New Testament canon. It has grown up in response to Christian needs.

The "continuing Christian tradition" is an expression which I have used to indicate that the church continued to live and therefore to adapt its heritage to new situations as it had done from the beginning. Even its founder had adapted his concept of the kingdom to the stubborn fact that the kingdom had not come as expected.

Continued postponement of the kingdom required new interpretations of the church's experience as time went on. First came the experience of the presence of the living Christ in the hearts and minds of those who waited for his appearing. Then came the preaching of his presence and the recall of his teachings. With the growing emphasis on his resurrection and exaltation came the alienation of the Jewish nation and the success of the gentile mission.

As the gentile mission continued, the character of the church grew and required new interpretations of the traditions. Paul's work is significant as it contributed to the new needs by insisting that gentiles were acceptable to God without first becoming Jews. When it became clear to Roman officials that Christianity was not a mere sect of Judaism but a vigorous young religion of importance to the empire, its political status had to be determined. The church had to feel its way through this crisis in its growth. Recognition of the legitimacy of Christianity did not occur officially until early in the fourth century. Before that century was over Christianity came to be regarded as the religion of the Roman empire, while paganism was banned.

The influence of Hellenistic thought on Christianity has already been noted in New Testament writings. In his sermon to the philosophers at Athens Paul quoted a Stoic poet (Acts 17:28). As a native of Tarsus it is not strange that Paul should be familiar with Stoic philosophy, since a famous school in that city was headed by a distinguished Stoic.[5] Certainly Paul's writings expressed Stoic doctrines which now are indistinguishable from Christian doctrine, such as God's unity and fatherhood, human independence of environment, and the foreordination of God. Others besides Paul in the New Testament showed Hellenistic leanings, notably John.

Logos Christianity became popular among Christian leaders in the second and third centuries. Justin Martyr was followed by Clement and Origen of Alexandria, and they were followed by Augustine, in reflecting Neo-Platonism and other Hellenistic influences.[6] This does not mean that Neo-Platonism displaced the Christian tradition, but only that certain values of Platonic tradition were woven into Christian doctrine. A part of the influence of Neo-Platonism on Christianity, in fact, consisted in the reaction of Christian leaders against heretical elements in Neo-Platonic thought as it arose in the form of Gnosticism. A similar development took place in respect to the mystery cults. The similarity has often been noted between the dying and resurrected god of the mystery religions and Christian tradition. Are we then to understand that the Christian story of the death and resurrection of Jesus was a simple adaptation of Christian tradition to pagan needs and habits?

It is not that simple. Even the Jewish tradition cultivated, in the Passover, a special form of the universal human celebration of the spring rites. The Christian tradition of Jesus' passion and resurrection was closely associated with that celebration, though more closely perhaps with the Essenian love feast. This tradition was the most primitive in Galilean Christianity. Its inception did not depend on the gentile mission. Yet as the tradition continued it stressed the uniqueness of Jesus and his exaltation until virtually the whole of Jewry was alienated by the tendency to deify the hero of the Christian spring rites. It was this very tendency to deify its Lord that made Christianity so popular among the gentiles, with their background of mystery cults. Certainly, therefore, that tendency did not grow less as the Christian traditions were taken over and further cultivated by the gentiles. Even the tendency to exalt the mother of Christ was reinforced by the prevalent myths of the mystery cults, whose mother goddess rescued the dying god from death. The pagan pair of the mother goddess and the resurrected god could make an easy transition to the immaculate Mary and her triumphant son Jesus.

The point is also made that Roman emperor worship influenced the Christian tradition by substituting Christ as king of kings and lord of lords in place of the earthly Roman emperor. Jesus as Christ was expected, on his return, to rule over all earthly kingdoms. The original Christian tendency to exalt and deify its king was reinforced by a similar concept in Roman emperor worship, but was not a direct transfer. The concept merely found a fertile field in which to develop in the Roman world.

A more definite Roman influence over the young church may be said to be the Roman genius for organization. In the course of time the church, instead of following the Hellenistic pattern of breaking up into schools of philosophic thought, was organized into an empire-wide institution. When the empire ceased to exist as such, the church took over some of the functions of the state, and the Roman pope strove to become the successor to the Roman emperor. The tendency to organization, encouraged by the Roman environment, may have had something to do with the survival of the Christian church in circumstances where pagan schools of thought died a natural death. This explanation, however, is secondary rather than primary. It was an inward vitality which perpetuated Christianity, perhaps despite its organizational uniformity.

Ascetic Influences

The fact that Christianity was at first a persecuted religion has had something to do with its present character. It was partly on this account that the ascetic strain in Plato found such ready acceptance by Christianity. Our New Testament writings have been based to some extent upon the concept that Christian character is developed through persecution. That was one way of rationalizing the persecutions which were being experienced. The practical effect has been that real consolation is offered to any who are unjustly oppressed. They find companionship with those who before them have been persecuted for righteousness' sake. When we think back upon the experience of the martyrs, we are impressed with the triviality of most of our own troubles.

If, as seems likely, Christianity was a more vital offspring of that form of Judaism known as Essenism, that is another reason why it should have fostered an ascetic strain.

The monastic movement was an outgrowth of the persecutions. This movement found expression in two ways, namely, the eremitic type of monasticism in the hot east, and the communal type in the north and west. In Syria and to some extent in Egypt the monks did not form communities, since they were able to live alone. Sometimes they built themselves pillars and stayed on top of them indefinitely. They spent all their time in meditation and prayer, and depended on the piety or curiosity of their fellows for their daily bread. Such is the story of Simon Stylites, who is said to have spent thirty-seven years on top of a pillar.

In the west, however, the monks formed communities in order to provide for their mutual needs in the form of shelter and sustenance. They shared the view that there was virtue in repressing the ordinary instincts of life, and that it was more important to meditate and pray than to do anything else. In the course of time, they proposed to work for their living, as well as for the good of their souls. At first their work was of a merely physical nature, but later it took on the character of intellectual and social work. Prayers alternated with farming, teaching and social service. So the monasteries served many needs in the middle ages. They supplied an instrument for copying and preserving many valuable manuscripts, for developing better libraries and facilitating the development of culture, and for establishing hospitals and other institutions for social service. From the monasteries came some of the greatest teachers of the church. They handed on to the German barbarians the culture of Greece and Rome, as well as the Hebrew-Christian tradition.

The monasteries have cultivated an austere view of life. Yet it may be that some such reminder has value in the midst of a life in which the sufferings of a savior and the need for sacrifice are likely to be forgotten. Puritanism in America and England has in a sense followed the spirit of the monastic tradition. The tradition of austerity, however, has little encouragement in our contemporary society, surrounded as we are by innumerable invitations to luxury and ease. The average Christian is much more likely to be suffering from the popularity complex, becoming a Christian because he inherited his Christianity, than from the persecution complex.

One phase of the continuing Christian tradition has been the growth of doctrine, both orthodox and heterodox. Orthodoxy has never been a simple norm, even at the beginning. Conflicts were inevitable and actually occurred among the disciples, as ever since. Yet the effort was made to keep the tradition "pure" by some sort of test. When there were as yet no creeds or scriptures the apostles appealed to their own experiences as reflecting the spirit of Jesus. This left Paul in a position of having to defend his apostleship from time to time. Then after the apostles had died it became increasingly customary to appeal to the traditions or to the writings which came into existence.

In addition to the books of the New Testament, the church formulated its creeds as new crises developed. Such was the case when the so-called Apostles' Creed came into existence. Most of this creed was formulated between 160 and 175 A.D., though it was not completed until the sixth century.[7] As an answer to Marcion, this creed was probably formulated at Rome and expressed the orthodoxy that was conceived there, especially as it referred to the Marcionite Gnosticism.

Prominent in the Marcionite controversy was the problem of the nature of Christ. The question was, as with earlier Gnosticism, whether Christ was so exalted as to be unhuman. The creed denied that degree of exaltation.

The problem nevertheless continued. One group—the "dynamistic monarchians" or "adoptionists"—held that Jesus, virgin-born, had become divine through a power that bound him together with God. Another group—the "modalistic monarchians" or "patripassians" —believed that God assumed three modes of being, Father, Son, and Holy Spirit. Sabellius and Sabellianism taught a form of this unorthodox view, which tended to make Christ so completely divine that he ceased to be human. If Jesus was God, then God suffered on the cross and raised himself from the dead. The theologians were deadly serious in debating such issues. Tertullian, the North African theologian (c. 160-c. 222 A.D.), became involved in a primitive movement—Montanism—in reacting against a more rationalistic Platonic Christianity. He was willing to let the mystery of Christ's nature remain a mystery. Clement of Alexandria (c. 150-c. 213) and his successor, Origen (c. 185-c. 251), were somewhat naive in their interpretation of the Logos doctrine.

The controversy regarding Christ's nature became heated when Arius (256-336) in 318 accused his bishop, Alexander, of incoherence in teaching that Christ was the Son of God and that, like God, he existed eternally. If he was a Son, then he must have come into existence at some time, when the Father created him. Yet Arius believed that Christ preexisted for ages before his human birth, having a soul that was superhuman. The emperor Constantine called Christian leaders together from East and West at Nicea in 325 to settle the controversy. At this first of the so-called ecumenical councils of the church, the majority agreed that the Son was uncreated and eternal with the Father. The decision was far from unanimous, and after a brief exile both Arius and Bishop Eusebius were recalled while Athanasius, their chief opponent, was later banished. This seems a strange way for Christians to behave, but it illustrates what happens when creeds come before Christian experience.

In 381 a council at Constantinople further developed the so-called Nicene Creed, clarifying the nature of the Trinity, with special attention to the place of the Holy Ghost therein. Other councils followed, such as the one at Ephesus in 431 dealing with the place of Mary as "mother of God."[8] The council at Chalcedon in 451 affirmed the unity of Christ's nature without yielding his unity with both God and man. Another at Constantinople in 680-681 debated whether Christ had one will or two—a human and a divine. The latter was its enlightened conclusion, which many sincere Christians must still reject.

The need for church conferences ceased when Roman leadership became strong enough to enforce uniformity by unilateral action. It was perfectly natural that a large metropolitan church should acquire a place of leadership. In order to settle matters of orthodoxy the Roman church reinforced its natural prestige by appealing to Peter as its founder, thus contributing to a feeling of the power of magic which came to be associated with his name. The lack of historical proof meant little so long as people were willing to accept the tradition which was cultivated. Once this was accepted, it became possible to develop the doctrine of the superiority of church over state. In the eleventh century the pope succeeded in deposing an emperor. Abuse of papal power led to the conciliar movement and the Protestant reformation. The counter-reformation reestablished a strong centralized ecclesiastical system within the remnants of Roman Catholicism, resulting in the assertion of the monarchical doctrine of the infallibility of the pope.

The medieval split between Greek Orthodoxy and Roman Catholicism was one price paid for Rome's insistence on its formal claim to primacy. In principle this schism was not different from others occurring in the primitive church or between Protestant and Roman Catholic more recently.

The Protestant schism was by no means sudden. The Cathari and the Waldensians in the twelfth century lacked the support of nationalistic sentiment to give them conditions of success. Wyclif and Huss led Protestant movements which proved abortive for lack of political powers to support strong bids for independent religious thought. Luther and Calvin were not more vigorous than their predecessors; they lived in times which supplied more of the conditions of success. The same is true of the rise of Anglicanism. In the course of time Methodism branched off from Anglicanism, and other "isms" branched off from Methodism.

Roman Catholicism has been able to point to the sectarianism which has characterized the Protestant movement. It is true that the divisiveness of Protestantism has been bad, yet not all bad. Ultimately it led to mutual toleration and a truly wholesome approach to Christian unity based on the spirit of the master rather than on some formal autocratic principle. Denominations are still immensely important to many small people. When thought gains a sufficient sweep to see the rise of religion and Christianity in perspective, denominational considerations turn out to be inconsequential in themselves. The spirit of Christian unity and human brotherhood is of real importance. An understanding of the reason for the rise of the sects contributes to one's perspective. If we had time and space we should be well repaid for surveying the rise of denominations. As it is we shall have to be satisfied to bring our story of the continuing Christian tradition to a close, and turn to the one remaining world religion not yet touched upon, namely, Islam, which is far more significant than most Christians are inclined to believe.

Christian Maturity

Most difficult is the task of evaluating and reinterpreting our own traditions. There should be more gain than loss in this task, however, so long as one's loyalty is to the truth as we find it.

The first test of maturity is the absence of magic. Are there magical elements in Christianity? The answer to this depends in part on what we mean by Christianity. If by this we mean the sum total of what Jesus believed and taught, then we should probably have to admit that there was something like magic in it. When Jesus accepted the popular Jewish messianic cosmology and looked for the supernatural coming of the kingdom while he yet lived, and then changed to the belief that the kingdom would come soon after his death and ascension, there was evidence of an element of magic. But by insisting that the messianic kingdom was essentially an inward or spiritual experience, and that preparation must be made for it by accepting the beatitudes as basic principles of the divine kingdom, he transformed a primitive magical concept into a thoroughly mature religion.

We must also distinguish between what Jesus actually taught and what the traditions eventually represented him as teaching. If Jesus believed in demons, that illness was demonically caused, and in his supernatural power to drive them out by uttering certain words in Hebrew or Aramaic there seems to be, again, evidence of magic. This is not to deny the healing power of mind over body, which Jesus probably did possess.

And what of the allegorical miracles of the fourth gospel, such as the raising of Lazarus after he had been dead for four days? This story certainly does not go back to primitive tradition. Belief in it is like belief in magic.

So the whole complex of later beliefs by the professed followers of Jesus is subject to evaluation. The question here is not what did Jesus believe and teach, but what do his followers believe? And is it mature? Do we believe that by submitting to certain rites we can assure our entrance into heaven? By refusing to submit, do we earn eternal condemnation? By repeating credal formulas do we insure our soul's salvation? By saying certain words, does the priest change bread into individualized flesh, and wine into a certain person's blood? Does a certain kind of prayer, properly spoken, guarantee the acquisition of the object for which one prays? What could this be but magic?

Very few, if any, of the great prophets were free from the tendency to interpret literally the traditional mythology. It remained for their followers in the "latter days" of historical science to reinterpret myth in terms of simple symbolism. The mid-twentieth century has seen a return to the great myths of the Hebrew-Christian tradition not as history but as symbols of truth which cannot be conveyed in logical propositions. Even the tradition of Christ's divinity may be maintained as pointing to the fact that God enters into the life of man, while man in turn enters into the life of God. Other religions have insisted on this same essential insight.

Commitment to the truth is a moral experience, and in terms of such experience Jesus was perfectly mature. It was an accident of history that the science which he knew was the science of the first century, not of the twentieth or even the seventeenth. But Jesus demanded perfection both of his followers and of himself, and that perfection necessarily included loyalty to the truth. There could have been no intellectual dishonesty in his thinking, so far as he was informed concerning nature and history.

Furthermore the teachings of the Johannine traditions imply the absolute demands of truthfulness. First was the Logos doctrine of John I, making truth divine. Then came Jesus' bold identification of himself with the truth: "I am the way, the truth, and the life" (John 14:6). We have nothing to fear from the divine truth. Ultimate reality is good, and we can entrust our very souls to that good. The holy spirit is the "Spirit of truth" (John 14:17). According to the Johannine tradition, "you will know the truth, and the truth will make you free" (John 8:32). There is great stress upon truth in the Christian gospel, and we do no violence to the essence of Christianity by insisting on intellectual honesty and personal commitment to the truth in science, cosmology, history, sociology, or wherever the truth is found. It is not necessary that we believe in first century cosmology just because we want to be Christians. That Jesus did not ride a bicycle is no reason why we should not.

Likewise Jesus was committed in principle to a realistic concept of human nature. His view of sex was not in harmony with twentieth century views, but that is not entirely a fault. The general trend of his teaching in Matt. 5:27-30 is negative and repressive, whereas the modern view of psychological health, while perhaps erring in the opposite direction, yet points to the need for normal emotional expression tempered by sublimation. As we compare the general attitude of Jesus, however, with that of John the baptizer, or with the stricter Essenes, we find that Jesus was not the ascetic. He associated freely with all kinds of men and women, and found joy in their presence. He was no kill-joy. He did have a fundamental purpose in life and tried to influence others to find a similar purpose. The happiest person, said he, was he who lost himself in a worthwhile task.

Essentially the religion of Jesus was an ethical way of life in which love, service, and the forgiving spirit were absolutes, a way in which fulfilment was better than suppression. His ideal was that of the "abundant life" which found its full realization in the kingdom of God. For him as for the ethical prophets, religion was essentially a life of goodness in social relationships. In this his followers have most often fallen short by failing to love, serve, and forgive. Instead we have hated and killed and sought personal advantage.

Jesus did not condemn the ritual of synagogue or temple. He did demand that the forms of worship should be symbolic of spiritual reality, and that reality was to consist in love and service to one's neighbor. The cult may well be beautiful, but it must first of all be symbolic, and the symbolized experience must be ethical. Herein lies the greatest maturity of the Christian religion: its absolute commitment to the way of love, service and humility in a true democracy wherein God is our common father. Can religion be more truly universal?

Little need be said about Christian maturity according to the test of mystic sensitivity. So far as Jesus himself is concerned, the most elementary Christian traditions witness to his sensitivity to God's presence and will. Prayer as communion and as a strengthening experience was his constant habit. When he was disappointed he was always able to find the needed spiritual resources to overcome despair and strive again to do his father's will.

Because of our deep emotional attachment to him, we are apt not only to love him, as we should, but to rob him of his true humanity by denying his human limitations. Our loyalty to ritual merely because it is traditional, our mystic sensitivity to the idols which hold first place in our affections, and our tendency to interpret religion magically, all endanger our quest for religious maturity. We must remember that real loyalty to Jesus is conditioned by our commitment to his way of love, service, and the forgiving spirit. This is mature religion.

PART EIGHT

Islam

XXXVIII. THE RELIGION OF MUHAMMAD

THE PROPER NAME for the religion of Muhammad is Islam, not Muhammadanism (or Mohammedanism). The latter name is repugnant to a Muslim, whose tradition is opposed to the worship of any man or any creature. Islam means "submission." A Muslim is "one who submits."

There may, of course, be some justification for calling this religion Muhammadanism, since despite the tradition Muslims do nevertheless revere their prophet deeply. I have observed that Muslims, in talking about Muhammad and his message, exhibit the same emotional response which Christians do in speaking of Jesus. This may justify us in calling the religion Muhammadanism, but it does not seem courteous on our part, when they prefer to call it Islam.

Islam is the one religion, next to Judaism, in which Christians should be most interested, since its traditions and doctrines are shared with both Judaism and Christianity. Paradoxically it is probably for this very reason that Christians have not been interested in Islam, since it seems to be merely a spurious brand of Christianity's essence. The Christian's attitude toward Islam may well be regarded as a test of his catholicity and insight into the real meaning of the message of Jesus.

As a missionary religion Islam has proved to be the most serious rival of Christianity. After the decline of the missionary spirit of early Christianity, Islam outdid its rival in appealing to all races and nations until the nineteenth century revival of Christian missions. Today there are over 100,000,000 Muslims in India and Pakistan, of whom about ninety percent are in Pakistan. In Malaya and Indonesia are another 70,000,000. In the Arabic Near East,

Star and crescent, symbol of Islam's rise and destiny.

Egypt, and North Africa are about 65,000,000, while Turkey has another 20,000,000. In Russia and China are perhaps 30,000,000, while Africa south of the Sudan has an additional 25,000,000. Iran and Afghanistan have nearly 30,000,000 more. This makes a total of about 340,000,000 Muslims.[1]

Semitic Background

At the time of Muhammad's birth Arabia harbored the traditional Semitic culture. In this culture animism was prominent, with its beliefs in spirits, angels, and demons roaming the desert to bless or to curse. Some of the spirits had reached the status of deity, making Arabia polytheistic. Among its deities were three goddesses who were especially popular: Manat, goddess of fate and fortune; Allat, a kind of mother-goddess such as is found often in fertility cults; and El 'Uzza, somewhat similar in character to Allat. Some scholars believe that Muhammad in an early stage of his monotheism regarded the three goddesses as intercessors with God.[2] Idols and fetishes were also objects of Arabian worship. There is really not much difference between the worship of a fetish in the form of a meteorite—a messenger from heaven—and reverence for a spring made sacred by the presence of a spirit which dwells there to bless man.

Famous in Arabian tradition are the black meteorite at Mecca, and the well of Zemzem nearby. The small black meteorite is housed in the kaaba or cube-like building, and is regarded as a gift to Abraham by the angel Gabriel. It surely should be understood as a fetish in pre-Islamic culture, when it was the main object of the customary pilgrimage to Mecca. Muhammad finally found a way to reconcile it with his sincere monotheism, thereby giving a certain continuity to his native culture as he sought to change it. The well of Zemzem, in turn, was sacred on account of its animistic associations. In Arabian and Islamic tradition the legend arose that the well sprang forth when Hagar was taking Ishmael through the desert, wandering as a refugee from Abraham and Sarah. Ishmael was about to die of thirst when a miracle happened causing the well to bubble up.

Such elements of animism and fetishism were not all that local Semitic culture contributed to Islam. There was also a pre-Islamic belief in "Allāh" as a high god. This was not monotheism, of course, but it had the potentialities of monotheism. Muhammad brought out those potentialities.

Other Influences

How may we explain the fact that Muhammad alone, among the Arabs, perceived the superstitions of animism, idolatry and polytheism, and brought about a significant reform? To this question recent scholarship supplies a reasonable answer. The answer essentially is that Judaism and Syrian Christianity awakened in him a new insight into religious maturity. Of these two influences, the more important seems to have been that of Syrian Christianity. He learned from Christians that the desert jinn were not friendly spirits but demons, and that idolatry was wicked. Arabian Judaism and Christianity both suggested monotheism. The kind of Christianity which was available to him in Arabia also suggested to him his ideas of the resurrection and the judgment day, of Heaven and Hell, and of the kind of rewards which the righteous might expect in a sensuous type of paradise. Like the Koran is the Syrian Christian Afrem's *Hymns of Paradise,* which describe the rewards of piety thus:

When they lie at the table the trees offer their shade in the clear air. Flowers grow beneath them and fruits above. . . . Swift winds stand before the blessed, ready to do their will. One of them wafts appeasement, another causes drink to flow. . . . Think, O aged one, of Paradise! When its aroma refreshes you and its pleasant odours renew your youth, your blemishes will vanish in the beauty which surrounds you. . . . Whoever has abstained from wine on earth, for him do the vines of Paradise yearn. Each one of them holds out a bunch of grapes. And if a man has lived in chastity, they (feminine) receive him in a pure bosom, because he as a monk did not fall into the bosom and bed of earthly love.[3]

It is not maintained that Muhammad had read the writings of the Syrian fathers, or that he knew the Bible at first hand. His contacts with Jews and Christians, however, had brought to him such information and suggestions as to influence his own thinking. Possibly he had heard Syrian Christian monks preach or teach. His Koranic style resembles the pattern of development found in a number of sermons by Syrian monks.[4]

Little is known of Muhammad's life prior to the period of his revelations. Tradition places his birth-date at 570 A.D., and this is at least approximately correct. His family was poor but respected, belonging to the Koreish* tribe which ruled Mecca. He was left an orphan at an early age and reared by an uncle. He became engaged in caravan trade for a rich widow named Khadijah, whom he married even though she was his senior by fifteen years, according to tradition. It seems quite certain that he was monogamous so long as she lived, although Arabian custom permitted polygamy. He was loyal to her and she was most sympathetic to him in the early uncertain stages of his career as a prophet. We can also be sure that Muhammad was oriented toward city life and that he was not the nomadic bedouin type. Mecca, the city of his birth, was an important center of trade. Most of the traffic between the Indian Ocean and the Mediterranean passed through Mecca. It was an object of religious pilgrimage long before Muhammad. Nomads, merchants, natives and foreigners came and went. A higher culture was thus stimulated, in which wickedness also grew.

* Sometimes spelled Quraysh.

Muhammad as a Prophet

What entitles Muhammad to be called a prophet of God to men? Assuming the possibility of revelation, did Muhammad show signs of sincerity and genuineness? Or was he an imposter, deliberately trying to fool people and get a following? When the question is put in this way, we must answer that he was sincere and that he showed the usual marks of the mystic. The revelation came to Muhammad as a surprise.

> Thou didst not expect that the book of the Koran should be delivered unto thee.[5]

The voice which he heard, and which he attributed to the angel Gabriel, instructed him not to make any effort of will to memorize it, since that would be taken care of divinely.

> Do not move thy tongue thereby to hasten it. It is for us to collect it and to read it.[6]

This insistence of Muhammad that he spoke not of his own will but of God's is to be tested in only one way: what was his message? Did the message have a coherent content which witnessed to the prophet's sincerity?

Andrae classified Muhammad as the mystical type that hears voices rather than sees visions. He did have two visions near the beginning of his prophetic career, but his revelations were mainly by heavenly voices rather than visions.[7] The traditions are unreliable in describing the manner in which the revelations came to him. Judging by the indirect evidence of the Koran, our primary source, we must conclude that Muhammad sincerely believed that he was the recipient of a significant message from God to man. His first revelation is believed to have come to him at the age of forty, which would have been about 610 A.D.

Certainly any theory about the the revelation which came to Muhammad must account for the secondary nature of its content. On this score it is a well known fact that Muhammad's message was in part an erroneous relay of the Jewish and Christian scriptures and traditions. In reporting the Christian tradition he even fell into the error of the Gnostics and Manicheans by insisting that Jesus was not crucified:

> "Verily we have killed the Messiah, Jesus the Son of Mary, the apostle of God," . . . But they did not kill him, and they did not crucify him, but a similitude was made for them.[8]

He even confused Mary with Miriam, the sister of Moses. The Jews of Medina were so horrified and amused by the errors in his recitals of Jewish traditions that they ridiculed him, causing such resentment as later to bring about the destruction of one whole clan of Jews in Medina.

But a prophet does not need to have an entirely new message. Nor must he be free from errors of cosmology or history. His message need not be one of absolute perfection. The only real test of a prophet is, does his message fit the needs of his times and their specific cultural problems. In terms of this criterion we may therefore assert that Muhammad was indeed a prophet to the Arabs of his day and, indeed, to all people of all time in respect to the heart of his message.

The Koran

The heart of Muhammad's message may be found in the words of the Koran.* These are the words of the prophet himself, more truly than in the case of any other sacred scriptures. They were revealed to him orally in relatively short sections, called "suras" or "chapters." There are 114 suras, some of them combinations of shorter revelations. As they stand in the Koran, they are arranged according to length, the longest ones coming first and the later ones decreasing in length. The one exception is the first sura which serves as an introduction:

> In the name of God, the Compassionate, the Merciful.
> Praise be to God, Lord of the worlds!
> The compassionate, the merciful!
> King on the day of reckoning!
> Thee *only* do we worship, and to Thee do we cry
> for help.

* Sometimes spelled Qu'ran in order to suggest its correct pronunciation.

Guide Thou us on the straight path,
The path of those to whom Thou hast been gracious;
with whom thou art not angry, and who go not astray.[9]

It will be noted that there are seven verses in this sura. Also each verse ends with a rhyme. Every sura is introduced by the formula, "In the name of God, the Compassionate, the Merciful."

Each revelation made such an impression on the prophet that, without effort, he remembered it distinctly and in detail. His first revelations he repeated to his most intimate friends—his wife and an uncle, and a widening group of disciples. Then with courage he repeated his revelations to incredulous Meccan citizens, pilgrims, and visiting merchants. His first revelations came spontaneously to him, causing in him an ecstatic experience of communion with the divine. Such were the suras revealed to him while he remained a citizen of Mecca. When he removed to Medina and set up a theocratic government there, his messages became more and more a product of reflection. At the same time they became prosaic and lengthy. Carlyle was no doubt impressed by such characteristics when he said of the Koran, "It is as toilsome reading as I ever undertook. A wearisome, confused jumble, crude, incondite. . . . Nothing but a sense of duty could carry any European through the Koran." After more careful study Carlyle added that in the Koran "there is a merit quite other than the literary one. If a book come from the heart, it will contrive to reach other hearts; all art and authorcraft are of small account to that."[10]

When or how the Koran came to be written is not known. That Muhammad himself did not write the Koran is confirmed in sura 7, verse 156: "Who shall follow the Apostle, the unlettered Prophet. . . ."[11] It is generally believed that at least some of the revelations were written down by disciples during Muhammad's lifetime, and that others were recorded from the disciples' memories shortly after his death, lest any of it be lost. Then within a few years thereafter the first compilation was made from "scraps of parchment and leather, tablets of stone, ribs of palm branches, camels' shoulder-blades and ribs, pieces of board and the breasts of men."[12] Subsequently Othman, the third Caliph, approved an authoritative text at Medina and distributed official copies. Some modifications of the text have occurred since then, mainly through glosses in copying.

Essentially, however, the text is accurate and well preserved. Even the recitation or intonation of the Koran is undertaken, to this day, in imitation of the style of its original delivery.[13]

The Traditions

Besides the Koran, and differing from it only in degree of authority, are the traditions of the prophet. The Arabic word for tradition is "sunna," which is the equivalent of the Latin "mos." Of course all peoples have mores, and that was the case with the pre-Muslims as well as with the Muslims. In Islam, however, the sunna took on new meaning, signifying the oral traditions about the prophet, and referring to the custom established for Islam by those traditions. Short statements or narratives establishing such traditions were called "hadīth," as were also the whole body of such narratives. They were accepted as the oral accompaniment of the Koran, and were themselves gradually reduced to writing. Their authority was the companions of the prophet, and the companions of the companions—any one who could claim some direct or indirect proof for what Muhammad was said to have taught or done.

The Koran needed supplementation, even during Muhammad's lifetime. That is why he sought new revelations from time to time, which proved to be inferior to the earlier revelations in expression and insight. The prophet had felt that Arabia needed a book just as much as the Jews and Christians did, and he supplied that need by producing the Koran. But no one book can ever satisfy all the needs of a people permanently. Experience changes and new problems arise which cannot be solved by appealing to old insights or authorities. Therefore stories about the prophet and what he said were recovered from the memories of those who had been close to him. When this source had been exhausted, then new stories were invented. Legends always grow about great men, and they were very prolific in Muhammad's case. "Legal maxims, Jewish and Christian materials, even aphorisms from Greek philosophy, were put into the mouth of the Prophet and there seemed no limits to the process of fabrication."[14] In time the Islamic community set up controls to test the reported hadīth, first, in order to aid the sound growth of Islamic law and second, to weed out the untrustworthy reports. It is claimed that al-Bukhārī (d. 870) studied some 200,000 hadīths and from them selected 2,762 as well-authenticated. Other scholars added to this collection as times changed and new unsolved problems arose. Furthermore a collection of hadīths which might satisfy one Islamic sect would not satisfy another. Therefore rival collections of the traditions were made, and their number increased. The growth of Islamic law was conditioned by the development of the traditions, since the Koran was obviously an inadequate basis for the law of a large community.

The importance of Islamic tradition should not be underestimated. It did not quite have the authority of the Koran. Yet some of the most essential elements of Islam are derived not from the Koran but from tradition. For example, nowhere in the Koran do we find the creed which is so often and so universally repeated, that "There is but one God, and Muhammad is the Apostle of God." The creed must be recited in Arabic: *lā ilāha illa 'llāh muhammadun rasūlu 'llāh*. Its substance but not its form may be found in sura 4, verse 135. Muhammad's message is only partly to be found in the Koran, and partly in the traditions.

God's Nature and Sovereignty

One of the deepest sources of the prophet's inspiration was his view of God. His concept of Allāh as a high God differed from that of Arabian tradition only negatively. Muhammad insisted that there is no God but Allāh, and that all animism and idolatry were wrong. Furthermore God is only one, not three as the Christians assert. He thought of the Christian trinity as consisting of the Father, the Son Jesus, and Mary his mother. God is the creator and ruler of all things. Everything takes place according to his will.

The doctrine of predestination is emphasized by Muhammad. Yet his view of predestination does not exclude human free will. The prophet is not consistent in this, for he often insists that sinners are made to do as they do because God so wills it. In one verse he says, "Wilt thou force men to become believers?" implying human freedom; in the next he states, "It is not for any person to believe save by the permission of God. . . ."[15] He holds man's will responsible while he insists that God is sovereign even over the will of man. His emphasis is on that sovereignty, as suggested in sura 18, verses 55-56:

> Verily, we . . . place veils upon their hearts lest they should understand, and dulness in their ears!
>
> And if thou shouldst call them to the guidance, they will not be guided then for ever.[16]

Allāh even vows, "I will surely fill hell with the jinns and with men all together."[17]

Is, then, Allāh a capricious God as Christians and others have described him? Is he, like "the typical sultan" or oriental despot, a being motivated by an exalted opinion of himself rather than by a sense of justice? Of two things we can be sure. First, God is "the Compassionate, the Merciful," as every sura in the Koran proclaims in its invocation. God deals with man not strictly according to his sin, but in accordance with the divine mercy. Second, the awfulness of the judgment, conceived throughout the Koran, is based upon the conviction that God will judge us according to our deserts. The judgment is to be feared not because God is unkind, for he is on the contrary merciful; it is to be feared rather because of our deeds and because God is just.

And yet God's sovereignty is the ruling concept of Muhammad. Ultimately his will is inscrutable, unfathomable. This truly leads us to the heart of "Islam"—a word which sums up the whole attitude of this religion. Submission to the will of God is the very heart and essence of Islam, as the name indicates. After all, it is God's doing. Who are we to question it? Let us be good Muslims: let us submit and obey the divine will, and God will be merciful. Let us adore his divine majesty and do the best we can, and on the day of judgment his great compassion will be manifested.

In the concept of God's unity Islam compares favorably with Judaism and with Christianity as many Christians understand it. In fact, Islam surpasses the earlier Jewish concept of God as national or racial. It is true that Muhammad thought of his revelation as a favor which the Arabians deserved, since the Jews and Christians already had their book. Yet the prophet of Islam considered his religion to be the culmination of Judaism and Christianity, and his God to be the sole God of all the earth. Being late-comers in the divine fold, the Arabian worshipers were predisposed to feel that God should not be exclusive nationally or racially.

Last and Greatest of the Prophets

The most provincial aspect of Islam consists of the doctrine that Muhammad is the last and greatest prophet of Allāh. His doctrine that there were other prophets, including Adam, Noah, Abraham, Moses, and even Jesus—virgin-born[18] and worker of miracles—was in a way an acknowledgment of his debt to Judaism and Christianity. At the same time it represented his bid for the support of Jews and Christians in his religious enterprise. In this, of course, he was bitterly disappointed.

Muhammad's claim to prophethood—rather than his insistence on the unity and spirituality of God—may have caused the rejection of his message. His fellow citizens at Mecca were not opposed to the idea of Allāh as supreme God, and might have accepted his doctrine of the evils of idolatry and animism. Many writers have repeated the suggestion that Muhammad's rejection had an economic basis, in that business would decline if idolatry ceased, since the pilgrimages to Mecca were motivated by its sacred idols and animistic well, and of course the pilgrims brought much trade to Mecca. There seems to have been more to it than that, however. For if Muhammad were recognized as a divinely sent prophet, that would constitute the basis for a new theocratic community at Mecca. It would disrupt the inherited religio-political custom as it functioned in his day. This was opposed by the Koreish clan which was in power in Mecca in Muhammad's day, and which would have to yield some of its power to Muhammad if his claim were recognized. There was also, of course, the matter of inherited beliefs.

If Muhammad was unwanted in Mecca, the opposite was true in Yathrib, later known as Medina—"the city of the prophet." This city was about two hundred miles to the north, and was experiencing division and conflict. Pilgrims to Mecca from Yathrib heard the doctrines of Muhammad and were impressed by them—and by the personality of the prophet. They came to believe that he could do much for their city. So they invited him to come and try. He accepted on condition that he be permitted to bring along his followers from Mecca. This was agreed, and the move began. The plan was kept secret largely on account of Meccan opposition. The Meccans feared what a successful organizer might accomplish in Medina. They sought not to kill him, as the legend states, but more likely to prevent his escape. So Muhammad sent his followers to Yathrib a few at a time. When they had all gone, then Muhammad, Abu Bekr and Ali, his son-in-law, escaped and fled in the opposite direction. This was the famous "hijra" or "hegira," the flight of Muhammad in 622 A.D. from which the new Muslim era is dated. When pursuers were unable to find them, then they left their providential cave, circled Mecca, and proceeded northward to Medina. There he united the two clans of Arabs and sought the support also of the three Jewish clans. But the Jews rejected his religious claims and ridiculed his ignorance of Jewish traditions. He made concessions such as ruling that in prayer one should turn one's face toward Jerusalem. When this failed to appease, he counter-ruled that believers should face Mecca in prayer.[19]

When Muhammad became convinced that his religion could not be reconciled with the prejudices of the Jews, he despaired of Jewish support and at the same time experienced a revival of sympathy for Mecca. After all, the Meccan mosque was Allāh's holy temple. But his reversion to Mecca was not at all a complete surrender of his former convictions. The three goddesses whom he had formerly rejected he continued to reject. Stone worship and jinn worship he continued to ban. But in turning his eyes once more to Mecca he rationalized the kaaba and its meteorite. These became symbols of God's relation with man and of his special interest in the Arabians to whom he had sent this token of his favor. And the spirit-well nearby he reinterpreted as a sign of God's historic intention by bringing Ishmael and Hagar to it, at which time the well again began to flow. These are good illustrations of how one who has been enlightened may with integrity continue in an old tradition by reinterpreting rather than breaking completely with the past. Man needs symbols even after he is enlightened.

Appeal to Abraham

Another development also took place. That was the prophet's appeal to Abraham as the true Hanif, or monotheist. In this way Muhammad defended himself against the Jews by appealing to one whom they all accepted but who was not himself a Jew. He was the traditional ancestor of Israelites and of Ishmaelites, who were believed to be the ancestors of the Arabs. Muhammad charged the Jews with having corrupted the pure monotheism of Abraham. Christians had improved the Jewish religion generally, but in turn had corrupted it by deifying Jesus. This was sacrilegious, since God has no son nor ever had one. God is too transcendent to beget a human son.

Eden Paradise

The transcendence which Muhammad asserted in his doctrine of God he abandoned in his teachings about paradise, heaven, and hell. One is led to believe that paradise or heaven is a place on earth, and hell is deep within the earth. Wherever it is, it is very much like the world we are used to, except that paradise is free from all imperfection and limitation while hell is full of pain and punishment. The worst punishment imaginable for one living in hot Arabia was to have to drink boiling water, but that was exactly what was done in hell, in addition to having his limbs crushed with iron clubs and being clothed with garments of fire. In heaven:

> Verily, for the pious is a blissful place,—gardens and vineyards, and girls with swelling breasts of the same age as themselves, and a brimming cup; they shall hear therein no folly and no lie;—a reward from thy Lord, a sufficient gift![20]

According to tradition the prophet taught that the virgins of paradise were formerly, on earth, "devout wives, and those who with grey hair and watery eyes died in old age. After death Allah remakes them into virgins."[21] Women and children shared the joys of paradise with the men.

Belief in angels was picturesque. Gabriel, the chief angel, of course played an important part in the formation of the Koran, according to tradition.[22] Muhammad rejected local animism only to bring angels and jinn back into his theology as messengers of God or as devils.

Islamic Prayer

Prayer, in Islam, is practiced as an act of worship rather than as petition. There was a place for petition and talking with God, but for the most part Islamic prayer was understood as repeating the scriptures, and ritualistic bowing, kneeling, prostration, and touching the ground with the forehead. Originally only two periods of prayer daily were required, at sunrise and at sunset. The ceremonies and the five required periods of prayer daily arose through the growth of custom, perhaps as early as Muhammad's own lifetime, but do not appear in the Koran.[23] Congregational assembly is called for only on the Islamic sabbath, at noon on Friday. At other times one may simply pray wherever one is. When in a mosque for prayer, an imām, or leader in prayer, stands in front of the worshipers and times the ritual. The only rest required on the sabbath is during the noontime congregational prayer. The call to prayer by the muezzin dates back to the times of Muhammad, although minarets belong to a later time.

Alms, fasting, and the pilgrimage complete the formal requirements of Islam. Almsgiving developed into an institution, out of what was at first regarded as merely a freewill offering. Later Islamic law required one-fortieth of one's income to be given as alms. This was not conceived as a tax, nevertheless was obligatory and collectable. Fasting was required during the month of Ramadān, in commemoration of the first revelation which was given to Muhammad. The fasting was required, however, only during the hours of daylight, although no feasting was approved even during the hours of darkness. From the times of the prophet in Medina, pilgrimage has been required to the sacred mosque at Mecca. This rule has always been modified in accordance with a realistic appraisal of an individual's ability, financial and otherwise, to make the pilgrimage.

Five Pillars of the Faith

Islam's five "pillars of the faith," as developed by tradition, include recitation of the creed; prayer five times daily; almsgiving; fasting during the month of Ramadān; and the pilgrimage to Mecca. These elements of Islam have indeed been pillars of the faith, giving to the religion of Muhammad a certain cohesion, purposiveness, common practice, and basis for reflection which has helped it to succeed phenomenally.

Moral Standards

Besides formal religious requirements, Islam provides a number of ethical norms. The Koran prohibits the drinking of wine, the eating of pork, and the practice of gambling or usury. It regulates divorce and marriage relationships, and provides for proper treatment of slaves. Honesty and truthfulness are strongly urged, and their opposites are severely condemned.

Islam's concept of the position of women has been an object of attack by Christian writers. There are two sides to this issue. In a desert environment where survival was difficult and women outnumbered the male survivors it had become customary to permit the killing of infant girls. This practice Muhammad condemned but sanctioned the customary polygamy, limiting the number of wives to four, plus jurisdiction over slaves. It was a kind of compromise with nature and as such merits our understanding. Judged by the standards of his culture we may say that Muhammad took care to guard the interests of infants, slaves and women. Divorce he permitted while at the same time pleading for justice and kindness on the part of the master sex. The wearing of a veil was not original with Islam but was taken over later from Persian and Syrian Christians. With the advance of democracy over the world today, Muslim lands are making progress in the emancipation of women.

Islamic tradition interprets piety according to the spirit in which an act is done.

It is almsgiving if you make adjustment between a couple; and if you help a man in the matter of his riding-animal and mount him upon her or lift his baggage for him upon her. A good word is almsgiving; and in every step you walk towards prayer there is an act of almsgiving; and it is almsgiving when you ward danger off the road.[24]

The Koran has resources of genuine piety far beyond the formalities of ritualism and rules. Muhammad perceived, for example:

Righteousness is not that ye turn your faces towards the east or the west, but righteousness is, one who believes in God, and the last day, and the angels, and the Book, and the prophets, and who gives wealth for His love to kindred, and orphans, and the poor, and the son of the road, and beggars, and those in captivity; and who is steadfast in prayer, and gives alms; and those who are sure of their covenant when they make a covenant; and the patient in poverty, and distress, and in time of violence. . . .[25]

From the Koran itself we derive a form of the golden rule:

Wrong not, and ye shall not be wronged.[26]

And from the traditions we derive the rule in a more complete form:

No one of you is a believer until he loves for his brother what he loves for himself.[27]

XXXIX. EXPANSION OF ISLAM

IMPORTANT CHANGES took place when Muhammad and his followers emigrated from Mecca to Medina. For one thing, the prophet became a judge and ruler over the affairs of all his followers who became united in a common loyalty to him. As we saw in the last chapter, Muhammad, disappointed in his hopes to win the Jewish clans, thereupon ceased to favor Jewish traditions and turned once again toward Mecca and its Arabian traditions. This required some compromises, but Muhammad was a diplomat as well as a prophet, and he managed to make the compromises. When the Jews rejected him, he could still call on Abraham, whom he brought into relationship with the Meccan mosque. He held to his conviction that he had received a monotheistic revelation. As a believer in a transcendent God he was perhaps no more inconsistent than his Christian or Jewish contemporaries in admitting the existence of angels and demons and in picturing a paradise and hell in vivid terms. His inclusion of the fetish meteorite was the single exception of its kind, and it was reinterpreted as a symbol of God's relationship with non-Jews and non-Christians, that is, with Arabs.

War in the Desert

Practical problems necessitated an amazing innovation. When the Jews failed to measure up to expectations and contribute to the support of the emigres something had to be done. The prophet and his band could not be allowed to starve. Ali, the prophet's son-in-law, made his living by becoming a brickmaker's helper, receiving as wages one date for each bucket of water which he carried. He shared his wages with the prophet. Even if such stories are legendary they dramatize a situation which must have seemed hopeless. They help to explain why Muhammad turned to banditry.

In the course of his eight years at Medina Muhammad sponsored three successful raids on caravans as they passed from Mecca to Syria. An earlier raid was unsuccessful and unmarked by bloodshed. The first successful raid occurred during the second year at Medina. It was marked by bloodshed; even worse, for Meccan Arabs, it was undertaken during a holy month when no fighting was supposed to be done. Pious Muslims have tried to make the record read differently, but scholarship has established the fact that Muhammad did sponsor the attack on the caravan, and that when widespread disapproval followed he repudiated his part in it.[1] Without defending him, some commentators have excused him. Muhammad himself ultimately received a revelation which relieved the situation:

> They will ask thee of the sacred month,—of fighting therein. Say: Fighting therein is a great sin; but turning folks off God's way, and misbelief in Him and in the Sacred Mosque, and turning His people out therefrom, is a greater in God's sight. . . . They will not cease from fighting you until they turn you from your religion, if they can. . . .[2]

About six weeks later Muhammad learned that a large caravan from Syria was returning home to Mecca, and that a thousand camels bore the merchandise. By superior tactics Muhammad's 305 men and 70 camels defeated Mecca's 950 men, 700 camels, and 100 horses. Muhammad was like a general in the field on this occasion, though he did not do any actual fighting—at the age of 54! He had, however, instructed his men on the tactics of fighting in closed ranks. He interpreted the victory as a sign of the miraculous intervention of Allāh in much the same manner as in the Red Sea incident of old. With God's help his men had killed 49 Meccans and captured an equal number. Generous treatment of the captives may have influenced future developments.[3] Muhammad's revelation later gave Allāh the glory for this second victory over the Koreish of Mecca:

> Ye did not slay them, but it was God who slew them; nor didst thou shoot when thou didst shoot, but God did shoot.[4]

Encouraged by this sign of divine approval, he instructed his men:

> Fight them then that there be no sedition, and that the religion may be wholly God's.[5]

Success encouraged the prophet to extend his control. First he consolidated his leadership in Medina by removing a whole Jewish clan. This occurred after a single act of violence on the part of one Jew had led to clan retaliation. On removing the clan to Syria Muhammad secured the distribution of its property among his followers. Other Jews who had ridiculed Muhammad in poetry or otherwise were executed or assassinated.

The next encounter between Muslims and Meccans took place about a year later, with both sides well organized. This time the Meccans won but failed to follow up their victory, which though indecisive, led to instability at Medina. The Jews there continued to hope for the end of Muhammad's rule. The prophet then secured the expulsion of another Jewish clan and the distribution of its property among his followers.

During the fifth year at Medina Muhammad inspired the divorce of his adopted son in order that he might marry his son's wife. This was contrary to Arab custom, but the prophet received a special revelation in the matter and managed to weather the storm. In all, the prophet married nine wives after the death of Khadijah, justifying his behavior by special revelations since he had limited the number of wives which other Muslims might have to four.

It was during the same year that the Meccans made a final attempt to crush Muhammad. The prophet learned of their plan to attack Medina. On the advice of a Persian he had certain vulnerable parts of the city surrounded by a moat and a wall. The Meccans finally gave up the siege and went home.

Sometime later Muhammad got rid of the third Jewish tribe in Medina. Fearing treachery during a siege he resolved on drastic measures. Indirectly he secured a verdict which called for the execution of all the men and the enslavement of their women and children. This was one of the most culpable acts of his whole career.

Journey to Mecca

In the year 6 Muhammad resolved to take his followers with him on a personal pilgrimage to the shrine at Mecca. Hearing of their approach the Meccans came out to learn what the prophet's intentions were and to prevent him from entering the city. It would have been contrary to Arabian custom for the Muslims to attack the holy city. Muhammad at one stage proposed such a course, but was strongly opposed by Abu Bekr. After lengthy negotiations with the Koreish Muhammad made a truce, agreeing to make a pilgrimage the following year in return for a promise that the Koreish would leave the city while the Muslims were there. In this way the Meccans saved their city from a dangerous precedent in case the Muslims should have attacked. At the same time Muhammad saved his reputation of piety by not using force against the holy city.

It was Muhammad who profited most by the truce. For his attitude gained the approval of Bedouin tribes who had already been inclined to follow his leadership. Many of them joined him freely at this time. There is also evidence that Muhammad's following was increasing even in Mecca. There were enough leaders there who believed in peace, added to those who were convinced of the benign and pious sincerity of Muhammad, to give the prophet a great moral victory. This occurred when in the year 8 (630 A.D.) he led an army of 10,000 men from Medina to Mecca. He entered the city virtually unopposed.

In the holy city Muhammad entered the shrine in triumph. His first act was to destroy the idols within and without the Kaaba. Towards the Koreish he acted with amazing forbearance, pardoning all former enemies whom he believed he could win to his side.

Mecca was thenceforth under Muslim control, although Medina continued to be the headquarters of the prophet. Before his death in 632 A.D. he had brought about the surrender of some petty Christian sheikhs, who bought their cultural independence by paying extra taxes. From the very beginning Islam had a policy of allowing subject people to reject Islam provided they pay a special poll tax. Many Arab tribes voluntarily joined Islam, religiously and politically, not waiting to be visited by an army. Others accepted Islam under military pressure. At the time of Muhammad's death practically all Arabia had submitted to Islam and, with the exception of Christians, were instructed in the faith.

Evaluating the Prophet

Opinion has long been divided regarding the character of Muhammad. Some, like Dante, would consign him to the lowest level of

Inferno, while others like Carlyle think of him as sincere, magnanimous and inspired. The truth must lie somewhere between the extremes. I do not doubt the initial sincerity of Muhammad, nor a certain statesmanship which enabled him to draw people to him. No doubt he did resort to calculations which were opportunistic at times, but his calculations were not purely cold and hypocritical. It is most likely that he never abandoned his original conviction that idolatry and animism were wrong, and that monotheism was the proper religious philosophy. He must have believed in himself and the fundamental inspiration of his message. It is a generally accepted fact that mystical experiences among all peoples are expressed in terms of the concepts of the culture to which the mystic belongs. Muhammad's revelations therefore could have no more objectivity than the breadth of his own experience. It is understandable that he should have erred regarding the Jewish traditions, and that his rulings regarding the role of women and the various forms of belief should have been influenced by his Arabian milieu. His fear of the day of judgment and his confidence in the mercy of Allah dominated all else in his experience, and made of him a great man and the founder of a great religion. It is significant that while Islamic dogma views Muhammad as sinless, the prophet himself, as revealed in the Koran, never so thought.[6] It is a mark of his sincerity that he knew his own weakness and would not be the hypocrite, claiming to be a sinless prophet when he knew himself to be subject to motives of vengeance and fear. On one occasion he took more than his share of booty, and quickly regretted his sin.[7] That he could inspire so many of his contemporaries and subsequent millions to an attitude of reverent piety is a real witness to his greatness.

Muhammad's Successors

Muhammad's sudden death in 632 left the enlarging Muslim community without a head and without a plan of succession. The prophet's closest companions thought that the succession should be determined by the current leaders of the community. Others felt that the succession should be kept in the prophet's own family. That would have made Ali, husband of Muhammad's daughter Fatima, his successor. Still others thought that the successor should be selected by Muhammad's native tribe, the Koreish, or the smaller clan, the Omayyads. The first four caliphs ("successors") were chosen by the prophet's companions.

Abu Bekr was the first caliph, who lived to lead Islam only a year. During that year he suppressed some revolts by Arabian tribes and sent three armies into Syria. Arabia and Syria were being unified for further conquest. During that year also the assembling of the Koran began.

The second caliph was Omar (634-644). To him Damascus fell in 635, and Jewish and Christian inhabitants of Damascus and Syria were easily pacified by the generous terms offered them. Palestine and Egypt followed next.

Othman, an Omayyad and a close companion of Muhammad, became the third caliph when Omar was stabbed by a Christian captive. He remained in office from 644 to 656, when he was assassinated by Muslims. Ali then became caliph but spent his four years fighting to maintain his position, and then was assassinated like his two predecessors. Moawiya in 660 established the Omayyad dynasty and moved the permanent Muslim capital to Damascus. In the meantime Islam had subdued Asia Minor and Persia.

Under the Omayyad dynasty Islam spread over north Africa and across into Spain. It was succeeded in 750 by the Abbaside caliphate which moved its capital from Damascus to Baghdad. About 1000 A.D. Islam reached India and in the course of time this conquest came to have far reaching consequences religiously and politically, there and farther east.

It might seem that the prospects of cultural achievement were poor, in the light of Muhammad's relative ignorance and misinformation. Two things are to be said in answer to this. First, there was a native intelligence and insight on the part of Muhammad which made his personality magnetic to large numbers of people. He succeeded in organizing a way of life which appealed to the common people of Arabia in his day, and to others like them through the years since. Second, as Islam spread, the initial momentum which was started by Arabs was taken over by people of other cultures. It was inevitable that changes would occur in the interpretation of Islam. The abstractions of Greek philosophy and science were cultivated by Muslim scholars. When in the crusades of the twelfth century the Christian armies sought to displace the 'uncouth" Muslims from the Holy Land they found, to their surprise, that the Muslims were more highly cultured than they. The Christian crusaders took back with them to Europe new and valuable ideas

Mosque's traditional dome and minaret remind the Muslim of the piety expected of him.

which led to a cultural ferment there. Architecture, literature, science and philosophy profited in Europe by Christian contact with Islam, both in the Near East and in Spain.

Muslim Sects

Theological differences plagued Islam for centuries. It was inevitable that human beings with different cultural backgrounds should think differently about the interpretation of Islam. One group which dared to think independently has been called the Mutazalites. They are sometimes described as rationalists, although this name scarcely distinguishes them. It was pinned on them by their opponents in the oriental schools of thought, who insisted that God was essentially arbitrary, absolute in power and infinite in love and mercy. The Mutazalites asserted, on the contrary, the justice of God. They argued that God could not act in any way except the way of justice. Furthermore, said the Mutazalites, God is not made of flesh and blood, he has no ears, mouth, eyes, nor arbitrary will. The Mutazalites may be characterized as Hellenists[8] who tried to reinterpret Islam for non-Arabs whose traditions were more sophisticated. They mediated, at the end of the first century of Islam, between the extreme positions of the Kharijites (party of "works") and the Murjites (party of "faith without works"). During the next century they opposed the extreme dualism of the Gnostics and Manicheans. Early in the third century the Mutazalites were active in translating into Arabic some Greek works on logic and philosophy, laying the basis for their reputation as rationalists. Yet aside from its opposition to the doctrine of predestination, the Mutazalite school even then was puritanical in its adherence to Islamic custom. The Mutazalites are also remembered for their opposition to the dogma that the Koran is eternal and uncreated. For them it had a history.

The right wing of the Mutazalite school used the Greek dialectic to develop a kind of scholastic orthodoxy. The best known representative of this line of thought was Ashari (d. 935). He defended the sunna and is therefore classed as a sunnite or traditionalist, in opposition to the Mutazalite views against which he reacted. Ashari approached the problem of reconciling tradition with religion by means of a pantheistic doctrine of Allāh. However his pantheism seems to have been an intellectual construction rather than a mystical experience.

Following in the scholastic path, though hardly classified as orthodox, were the contributions of Avicenna and Averroës in Muslim Spain, in the eleventh and twelfth centuries. These men made important contributions to medical science and to philosophy—contributions which were to have far reaching effects in the Christian west.[9] St. Thomas Aquinas was indirectly but significantly influenced by Averroës.

Most of the schools (sects) of Islam have lived in peace with each other. Four of the schools reaching back to early times are the Hanifite, the Malakite, the Shafiite, and the Hanbalite. The Hanifite school (its founder, Abu Hanifa, died 767 A.D. in Iraq) stressed analogy as the principle by which the teachings of the Koran might be applied to new situations in new cultures. The Malakite school stressed "consensus" as the principle by which the Koran and the Hadīths might be applied to new and difficult situations. This meant the consensus of Islamic scholars and jurists—the Ulamā. The Shafiites urged the primacy of Hadīths over the Koran, since they represented Islam in process of growth. The Hanbalites insisted on the doctrine that the Koran is eternal and uncreated, and is absolutely binding in faith and conduct. The Hadīths served to interpret and uphold the Koran, as they insisted.

There was one sect which has never been reconciled to the others, and which cannot be classified as primarily a school of thought as the others can. That is the Shiite sect, which from the beginning has insisted that the successors to Muhammad should be his legitimate descendants. This view, of course, makes the Shiites fundamentally a political sect. Morocco is till Shiite in political doctrine, but otherwise generally orthodox or sunnite. The Shiites have broken up into sub-sects according to the precise manner in which they trace the line of descent from Muhammad. There has been a tendency for the Shiites to attribute to the Imām an esoteric knowledge which was handed down to Ali and his descendants. They conceive the Imām as sinless and infallible. The Imami (Shiite) sect is strongest today in Persia, with some strength in India, Iraq, and Syria.

Sufism

More significant than the Shiites, and perhaps influenced by them in certain ways, are the Sufis. Sufism is a school of thought which has had profound influence in Islam, not always recognized. Nor is the influence of Christianity recognized in Sufism. The fact seems to be that Sufism arose from the religious experience of the people of the Near East at a time when Christian piety was strong, infiltrating, as it were, into Islam. Hallaj (d. 922) applied the concepts of Gnosticism and the Gospel of John to the character of Muhammad. Said he:

> All the Lights of the Prophets proceeded from his Light; he was before all, his name the first in the Book of Fate; he was known before all things and all being, and will endure after the end of all. By his guidance have all eyes attained to sight. . . . All knowledge is a drop from his ocean, all wisdom a handful from his stream, all times an hour from his life.[10]

The Sufis seem to have originated from an ascetic movement common to Christianity and Islam. As such the religious experience which they cultivated was not intellectual but emotional. Problems of orthodoxy did not trouble the Sufis. Consequently they rather easily allowed their experiences to carry them beyond the borders of orthodoxy. When Hallaj identified himself with Allāh—as Jesus is represented in the Fourth Gospel as having identified himself and, through him, his followers with God—the orthodox were horrified. He became a martyr to the cause of mysticism.

The scholar who did most for the way of Sufism was Ghazzali (d. 1111). He was educated as an orthodox Asharite but turned to skepticism and, unsatisfied still, he became a Sufi. Just as Ashari had taken the rational methods developed by the Mutazalites and turned them to the uses of scholastic orthodoxy, so Ghazzali made a new synthesis of scholastic orthodoxy and Sufism. The result was a moderate sort of mysticism in which the experience of religion was supremely important while doctrines were of value only as they contributed to religious experience. What Ghazzali taught Islam was that it is not necessary to be unorthodox in order to have the essential experience of religion. Mystics have tended toward heterodoxy because they have been satisfied with any beliefs which have produced the mystical experiences. Sufism has done for Islam what the evangelical movement did both for Hinduism and for Christianity. The Islamic world of scholarship has lamented the mystical tendency to disregard intellectual standards. Since Ghazzali's day there has arisen in Islam some basis for this criticism by the scholars. It is true, however, that a religion in order to be vital must concentrate on experience rather than on doctrine. Happy is the religion in which the two complement each other, as Ghazzali believed they could.

Sufi orders were established in most Muslim lands and have followed a variety of patterns. At first the asceticism which has always characterized Sufism did not include celibacy, but in time came to embrace it also, as Christian asceticism did. Sufi doctrines, being intrinsically unimportant, took startling forms at times. In India and Moorish Africa animism, the old enemy of Muhammad, became very popular and remained so for a long time. Muhammad Iqbal of India complained about this feature of Indian Islam. Iqbal was himself a Sufi mystic and greatly desired to reform and revitalize Islam.

Recent Movements

In recent times the community of orthodox Islamic scholars—the Ulamā—has sought to overcome the doctrinal laxity of popular Sufism. This they attempted by organizing a system of education which has gone far toward reviving a popular understanding of Islamic traditions. The efforts of the Ulamā have been supported, through the pride of tradition, by local daily and periodical journals in Muslim lands.

One remarkable movement in modern Islam has been the Wahabis. With its roots far back in the Hanbali school of thought, the Wahabis in the eighteenth century sought through violent action to call attention to the facts that Islam came from Arabia and that since its origin long ago it has lost the unique "Arab idea." The Wahabis captured Mecca in 1806 and "purified" it of foreign influences. The Ottoman Empire suppressed the rebels in 1818. But its influence spread. Sufism was recognized as a foreign (non-Arabian) development and opposed as such. The Ulamā tried to steer a middle course between the fundamentalism and fanaticism of the Wahabis and the heterodoxy of the Sufis. The scholars would do well to combine the religious insight of the Sufis with the resolution of the Wahabis to restore Islam to its original monotheistic purity—its Arab idea.

Divergent currents of thought are evident in modern Islam. One is westernism, insisting that Islam has much to learn from western science and enlightenment. This might be expressed as secularism, as in Republican Turkey, or on the other hand it may take the form of modernism. There is also a typical movement known as Salafīya, which stresses the value of Islamic tradition but claims the right of private interpretation in theology and other areas of thought. Modernism, Salafism and Wahabism are all opposed to the saint-worship of Sufism, and to its general tendency to conceive of the prophet as sinless and authoritative.

Typical of recent currents of thought in Islam is the work of Ali Saiyid Ameer, Shiite jurist, who in 1891 first published *The Spirit of Islam.* In his effort to restore the pride of Islam he presented a biography of Muhammad which described him not as sinless or superhuman, as Sufism likes to do, but simply as a great man. The Koran, he said, is the work of Muhammad, not the inerrant word of God; nevertheless, it is a great contribution to mankind. Ali also relates the spirit of Muhammad to modern problems, commends prayer, fasting, almsgiving, and the pilgrimage, and suggests modifications of primitive Islamic customs such as slavery, polygamy and divorce. He also reminds his readers of the magnificent cultures of Baghdad and Cordova in their eras. Since Islam stimulated the Renaissance of Christian Europe, it is only fair now that it should receive again the scientific enlightenment which is its proper heritage.

This point of view was seconded by Muhammad Iqbal (1876-1938), who combined Sufism with modernism and demanded political independence for Pakistan.

I have suggested only a few of the divergent factors, personalities, and tendencies of Islamic thought and practice. It is evident from this brief survey that there is no unanimity among Muslims any more than there is among Christians. Muslim sects are not organized like Christian denominations; they are rather schools of thought. The Sufi orders or brotherhoods remind us of monastic orders in Roman Catholicism or Anglicanism. The Shiites are the most divisive among Islamic groups historically. Otherwise and in general it should be said that Muslim sects exist without organization.

In view of the divided and nationalistic nature of Islamic lands today there is small likelihood of a modern "jihad," or holy war about which we hear westerners speculate. It is true that the Koran urges such a war,[11] especially against Christians and Jews,[12] although the prophet's counsel is inconsistent on this point. Those who die fighting thus are promised direct passage to paradise.[13] Despite the Christian impression to the contrary, Islam has generally spread peacefully and without compulsion. "There is no compulsion in religion," were Muhammad's words in the Koran.[14] In any case, however, the jihad about which Muhammad spoke in the Koran belongs to primitive times when Islam was united and inspired by a living leader. Normally courteous diplomacy with Islamic lands should maintain good relations between us and all Muslim nations, whose present interests are as concrete as ours.

The future of Islam seems still to lie with the Ulamā, those scholars, teachers and jurists who know the facts of Islamic tradition and who ought to be abreast of modern enlightenment in general. Therefore it is their responsibility to guide the confused people of Islam into an experience of religion to which every human being has a right, while at the same time they try to reinterpret their traditions in such a way as to lead to intellectual and moral freedom and responsibility in harmony with modern enlightenment. The principle is no different from one which should be applied equally to Christianity or any other religion which possesses the potentialities of spiritual maturity. Let the Ulamā maintain the Islamic tradition that religion is not to be authoritarian. Let the teachers teach enlightenment. An enlightened Christian would rejoice to see such growth take place in another great religion of mankind.

Maturity of Islam

There are in Islam certain taboos, like those against eating pork or feasting during the month of Ramadan. And there are prescribed rites, like the pilgrimage to Mecca and the five daily prayers. These may be likened to magic, depending on the interpretation given them by the individual. Probably Muhammad himself was not entirely free from the influence of magical notions, and certainly many of his professed followers have been far less enlightened than he. Many have failed to understand the real message of the founder of Islam, as also of other great prophets.

Probably Muhammad himself was quite literal in his understanding of the myths of the Semitic and Christian traditions, as well as those which he himself told describing his own mystical experiences. In this respect we should regard him as less than mature, although it is not easy to judge him on this point. Relative to his immediate cultural background we should perhaps rate him rather highly. And as his followers become enlightened they tend to interpret his message in terms of its essential monotheism, its spirituality, and its missionary zeal for human brotherhood—universalistic factors.

When we think of the cultural inspiration which Christianity received from Islam in late medieval times, we are impressed by the ability of Islam to respond to the challenge of truth in science, philosophy, history, art, and human relations. We may witness the reforms that are taking place in Muslim lands today as enlightenment increases. It becomes clear that there is no fundamental antagonism between Islam and the commitment to all truth.

The criterion of commitment to the principles of psychological health calls for two comments. First, Islam has not cultivated the repressions of asceticism such as we have known in the history of Christianity. Second, on the other hand, Islam is a religion of submission, which may not be the healthiest attitude toward God and his universe. We do need, of course, to know the limitations of life and to accept them realistically. But perhaps a more wholesome attitude would be to think of God as eternally creative and inspiring, and to regard our relationship with him as that of co-workers in a great enterprise. This would be less negative; it would stress achievement.

As to the ethical and social influences of Islam, we must recognize the prophet's insights, his condemnation of infanticide in a primitive culture, his encouragement of the spirit of brotherliness and of temperance. There are many moral values in Islam. Yet in Muslim lands we have not yet seen great zeal for universal education, for organized social work, for hospitals and sanitary engineering. The emphasis in the Koran is theological, whereas in my opinion, in the New Testament the emphasis is upon moral perfection and social sensitivity. Muhammad's own moral imperfections and his resort to arms and to retaliation, even to a limited extent, are in contrast to certain other great religious prophets.

I have already commented on the Islamic cult. It has much beauty and can be made to have deep symbolic meaning. Consistently with the Islamic condemnation of idolatry, its symbolism should not be a magical end in itself, lest idolatry thus creep in unintentionally. As a matter of fact, Islam through the centuries has suffered from a puritanical fear of idolatry and has, in effect, deprived itself of intrinsically innocent art-forms, lest man should turn them to the uses of idolatry.

Muhammad was certainly a great mystic, aware of a presence which he conceived as an infinite personality with an almighty will. There may be a philosophical question which should be raised on this point, but that is something which must be postponed until the next chapter. At any rate, there is in Islamic tradition a sincere awareness of the existence of a universal power which may strengthen the individual or the group in times of need. This in itself is one sign of religious maturity. On the other side of the ledger, its puritanical fear of idolatry has deprived Islam of instrinsically innocent religious art-forms.

PART NINE

Philosophy

XL. PROSPECT

HAVING SURVEYED, compared, and evaluated the religions of mankind we are now faced with the necessity of doing some original and systematic thinking about religion as such. What are some of the persistent problems of religion, and what conclusions—if any—can safely be reached? Is there one and only one perfect and final religion for all men? Since most readers of this text will probably be Christians, ought we not to ask certain questions about the truth and possible interpretation of certain Christian ideas? Many of the important Christian ideas or doctrines belong also to other traditions than merely the Christian, and may lead us into a universal outlook.

First of all, let us again raise the question of the nature of religion, as we did in Chapter I. There we suggested that religion is commitment to a way of life, based on the conviction that such a way will contribute to the conservation and growth of life's dearest values. The maturity of a religion varies, we said, in inverse proportion to the magic involved in its practice, and the literalness of its interpretation of its myths. Religious maturity also varies in direct proportion to its commitment to ethical values, truth values, and mystical concepts, and likewise proportionally to its practical results in psychological health. A mature religion will also have developed meaningful symbols which are recognized as symbols rather than idols, and which influence persons in wholesome living.

May the scales of Maat prevail in all our thinking.

Some attention has recently been given to religious language, and at least one author[1] insists that language is religious not because of its subject matter alone, nor merely because of the attitude which is encouraged, apart from subject matter. Religious discourse is recognized as primarily concerned with the development of an attitude of special regard for the essential values of life.

It is not necessary at this point to explain in detail the exact nature of the values which religion strives to cultivate. Those values vary with the maturity of a religion. And the most mature religion—or phase of a given religion—is that which ministers most effectively to the psychological health of the individual, and to peaceful, helpful, and loving relations between the members or groups of a society.

Since religious language is language which tries to develop certain attitudes toward a certain subject matter, we need first to ask what such subject matter is, and then decide what the attitude should be.

One essential part of the subject matter of religion is the idea of God: his nature and his existence. Another element of religious subject matter is the idea of man: his nature and destiny. Now science, philosophy, and art are also concerned with some of the same subject matter, but not with the same attitude as religion. The philosophy of religion tries to distinguish these relative aspects of subject matter and attitude.

God

What is God like? God is the name generally applied to that supreme power in the universe which—or who—guarantees the survival of a world order and of those treasured values which depend on that world order. Some reject this concept of God, insisting that God is related only to spiritual experience, not to nature. Those who regard God as related solely to the realm of values should realize that values cannot exist in a vacuum. God is power as well as love and logos. So far as our experience goes, there can be no love in a universe where there are no physiological organisms capable of loving. Nor can there be a logos except in a universe wherein law can express the cosmic order or truth-relations, in which there are intelligent beings capable of knowing the truth.

Does God, then, exist? If religion assumes a supreme power, does that not mean that it assumes God's actual existence? Here a misunderstanding arises. Too often it is assumed that existence implies a physiological organism having individuality, the power to think as we think, and the power to feel and do. This is an unwarranted assumption. It is a part of the background of human mythology which may be retained poetically but rejected literally.

However, though God may not exist as a physical individual, there must be some organization or principle of power inherent in the structure of the universe, on which we may rely. Otherwise the values which we cherish as the supreme religious goal would have no basis in power.

Now our desire to secure values is not in itself a guarantee that they will be secured. We have no knowledge, either *a posteriori* or *a priori,* that values will survive, or that anything we can do will help them to survive. This is primarily a matter of faith. And this act of faith is the essential religious attitude—the commitment to a way of life based on the belief that that way of life is harmonious with the structure of the universe. Through one's commitment and heart-felt convictions one hopes to share in the cultivation and enjoyment of those values which are the object of religious concern.

Just what is meant by our insistence that "there must be some organization or principle of power inherent in the structure of the universe"? The existence of such principle is what we have in mind when we think of God as "existing." In other words, even if we think of God as spirit, that spirit must have some kind of relation to the physical world such that the spirit influences the cosmos creatively or directively. Aristotle's world of forms, as functions or purposes, was essentially a world of spirit which was believed to have a controlling power over the world of matter. The philosophy which Christianity shares with Mahayana Buddhism, that love is the heart of the cosmos, and that love is more real than the physical world, is a variant of the Aristotelian-Thomist philosophy of forms. The Christian logos doctrine implies that the physical world depends on the spiritual or mental world. This is no proof that the logos creates the cosmos, since proof is either a logical or an empirical construction. Yet there is no disproof of such a relationship either, and the belief in it seems to be a persistent intuition of the religious consciousness.

To illustrate the power of logos (spirit, wisdom, truth, love, value), we may point to the fact that wisdom and love actually do make a great difference in the physical world. The dreams of architects, composers, scientists, and prophets have changed physical reality tremendously. Through their knowledge of the internal relationships between numbers, mathematicians have ascertained that there are parallel relations between various elements of the universe and ultimately predicted the internal structure of the atom. Mind does seem to have a determinative, superior relation to matter, up to a certain point. To carry this doctrine beyond that certain point by insisting that, since matter depends on mind, therefore mind—mine or yours—may change the course of a river from flowing downhill, would be magic. But to say that logic is an orderly reality which determines the nature and relationships of matter as such, universally—this is not magic; it is a basic intuition which is sustained by much analysis.

Is God omnipotent? In saying that God, as logos, is power and as such is related to nature, we do not mean that God is omnipotent. There is an element of cosmic dualism in the Persian-Jewish-Christian tradition. This may be based on the honest and realistic observation of the presence of evil in man and nature. Much of the evil in man's character is due to his inherent biological structure. In seeking to satisfy his innocent biological needs, man gets into trouble with himself and with others. The conflict of biological needs within each individual, as well as between individuals and groups, is the real cause of much evil. This kind of evil cannot be avoided in any conceivable universe. That is, God could not avoid the accident of evil in our cosmos. Therefore God's power is limited. But this does not mean that God is not powerful. It only means that his power is bounded by logical and physical realities inherent in the nature of any cosmos conceivable by man. This is the meaning of the dualism of our own tradition. It is the best explanation of what Zoroaster meant.

Albert Schweitzer argues[2] that Christianity is an ethical mysticism while the mysticism of the Orient is logical. In this, he says, lies the superiority of Christianity over other religions. Logical mysticism teaches that God is related to the physical world, and that both man and nature may be absorbed into the divine nature. Ethical mysticism, on the other hand, insists that God is ethical will, and that only in the moral life do we come in contact with God. Wrote Schweitzer, "Christians have tried again and again to make of Christianity a doctrine in which the activity of the ethical God and the course of events in the natural world are brought into harmony with each other. Never has the attempt been successful."[3] Natural evil is therefore irrelevant to Christian faith, and salvation is a moral experience, not a supernatural intervention into the realm of nature. Only by uniting our moral wills with God do we realize the experience of salvation.

Schweitzer's emphasis on the moral character of Christianity is good, but his analysis is not completely logical. His analysis is not logical because morality must have some basis in power, and power is derived only from association with the world of nature. It seems more realistic therefore to say that love, truth, and goodness do have a vital connection with the physical world of human experience—in fact, they are the very heart of the universe; but they are not omnipotent. God as love, truth, and goodness, is both ethical and powerful, though limited in a dualistic universe. It is purely a matter of faith that all power will eventually be united with the goodness that is God.

Nevertheless the emphasis on the character of the divine nature should be ethical. Without ignoring the divine power, we should stress the divine love and goodness. We should be good not because we fear hell but because we are attracted by goodness itself. We should love all men not because we fear to hate but because we are in love with God as all love and all compassion. As we are drawn into complete union with this essence of the divine nature we come to realize that nothing else really matters, and that in him we have found the power that overcomes the world.

What is God's essence? Power is not of the essence of God; it is merely one of the necessary characteristics of the divine nature. The essence of God is love, goodness, truth and blessedness. God is the perfection of all positive values, and comes to be known to man as his experience conforms to the right. Man cannot live without learning from experience the compelling nature of truth and goodness. The good man freely lives the good life, impelled by the ideal of realizing the most harmonious fulfilment of his nature and his social and natural functions. The evil man is essentially an ignorant man who does not understand his own nature and needs. The evil man may seem to be successful, that is, powerful, but if he fails to realize his relationships with his family and society he is not truly happy or blessed. The natural world is not a moral world as such, and it is a real struggle for the good man to maintain his poise in a world where disease and disaster have no regard for merit. But the intrinsic moral life is an experience in which the right shines by its own light. It is this light of goodness, truth and love that, being freed from all imperfection, constitutes the divine nature itself.

Is God personal? This is not a new problem for the philosophy of religion, but it is being debated anew by theologians today. Personal idealists argue that reality is a community of persons in cosmic relation, with God as the supreme person having ethical will and creative power. On the other hand we find theologians like Professor Paul Tillich who insist that it is insufficient to describe God as personal. Rather, God is transpersonal. It is inconceivable that God, the creator of man and nature, should be lower in the scale of value than man who has personality. But it is also inconceivable that God should be merely personal, since that implies a consciousness inseparable from a physiological organism. It is inconceivable that God should think thoughts as we do, basing piecemeal judgments on the evidence at hand. We may believe that God is conscious. It is a part of religious faith that God is aware of human persons, and that he judges them justly and helps them in their need. God both knows and cares. This may be a myth in the sense that there is no simple cosmic personality who listens—without ears—to each man's prayer and does what is best for him.

If it is a myth, however, it seems to mean that God is not sub-personal but super-personal, or transpersonal, and that in a way that we cannot understand, the divine spiritual resources come to our aid in time of need.

Prayer and Cosmology

Modern cosmology leaves no room for magic or miracle in a literal sense. Many an atheist has become an atheist because he prayed for a miracle, such as the healing of his child or the safe journey of a loved one. When the prayer did not work like magic, that proved to the naive one that God did not really exist. He was mistaken in this conclusion. What it actually proved was that the naive one had not attained religious maturity, and was confusing religion with magic.

Is prayer magical? Prayer is a proper relation between man and God. Even the atheist prays in times of stress. It is simply human nature to turn to the creative spiritual resources of the universe in time of need. He who maintains constant contact with those resources through prayerful communion and meditation is more likely to survive life's emergencies with integrity than he who neglects such help.

There are different types of prayer. In expressing reverence toward God we are trying realistically to develop in ourselves a proper attitude toward nature and value. If this is God's world, and if there is an order of values, then through alerting our intuition we may truly and sincerely achieve a spiritual integrity which will make us more harmonious with God's world and more of an instrument of good will among men.

Should we pray for material things? A preacher once told how a young woman prayed for a pink skirt which she ardently desired. The end of the story is that she got the skirt, and that was supposed to prove the power of prayer. All that it really proved was that the preacher—and the young woman—confused prayer with magic. Said the Confucian, Hsun Tzu, "If men pray for rain and get rain, why is it? There is no reason. If they hadn't prayed it would have rained anyway."[4] Usually when some one prays for rain some one else is praying that it will not rain—like enemies in battle praying to the same god for victory.

Yet it is not altogether incongruous that we should pray for the satisfaction of our needs. We are more likely to find our spiritual than our material needs satisfied as a result of prayer. Yet even in praying for material things we may accomplish two things. First, we may learn against the stark background of God's pure will that our desires are unworthy or incoherent with the values to which we are already committed. Second, if our desires prove in prayer to be worthy and coherent, we may be equipped psychologically by prayer to cooperate in answering our own prayers.

We need not disdain the psychological value of prayer. There are many ways in which we may tap the spiritual and material resources of the universe. The psychological path is a perfectly good one. If by confession we relieve our hearts of heavy inhibition and release our own powers of positive achievement, is that not God responding to our prayer of confession? Prayers for health and guidance, prayers of intercession, prayers of gratitude and aspiration, all have potentialities for a mature religious life.

Man

What is man? Is he a worm or an angel? Certainly he is neither without qualification. It is grossly misleading to insist on the total depravity of man. For one thing, while theologians may define total depravity as imperfection in all phases of human nature, that is not what the phrase means to the average man. To say the least, therefore, it is a case of poor communication.

Man does possess a certain nobility, both physically and spiritually. Physically he has mastered most other forms of life and most of the elements of nature. The conquest of physical nature continues year by year. And spiritually man is morally autonomous, giving to himself the moral law by which he restrains his own actions. He is ideally governed by emotions of tenderness and self-sacrifice for those whom he loves, and by a feeling of right against those who injure him. Humanity produces many mean and mixed-up specimens, but it also produces many prophets and saints. The creative spirit of man is like the creative spirit of God. The best of men have motivations and temptations which reveal human imperfection. But it is also true that the worst of men are at times moved by the best sentiments. So man deserves neither universal condemnation nor universal praise.

Immortality

Does man, then, belong with the angels or with the beasts? Does he have an immortal soul which will live on into the future with the angels of God, or will his spirit expire with his breath, like the beasts?

There is no logical answer to this question. Since we do not know anything about angels, and since the nature of God himself is not that of an individual physical being, it is hard to classify man as to his destiny. Yet it is true that for a time men share in the creativity of the divine spirit. All men are potentially creative, morally autonomous and self-restrained in love and mercy. Having once shared in the image of God, one may assert that man always shares in that image, and in this sense is eternal in his present experience. Perhaps this sounds like double-talk.

What is immortality? The difficulty of deciding on man's immortal destiny may lie in part in the obscurity of the definition of immortality. There are at least six definitions. It may logically be argued, for example, that man does possess *biological* immortality. That is, by the process of reproduction he continues to live forever in his descendants—or as long as the human race survives. Or it may be argued that man possesses immortality of *fame*—or notoriety! This would be true only of a small proportion of men. Third, there is the immortality of *influence*. One's influence may even be small, yet like the pebble thrown into the ocean, that small influence may expand until it becomes imperceptible; nevertheless it is there. Or one may conceive of what has been called *Epicurean* immortality.[5] Having once experienced pleasure—or pain—that experience can never be erased from the soul of the universe. Then there is logical or *impersonal* immortality. Aristotle and Spinoza seemed to believe that one achieved immortality by completely identifying oneself with the truth which is eternal. This thought may console some, as the preceding thoughts may also. But most people who desire or believe in immortality regard all the above concepts as inadequate double-talk. The only kind of immortality that will satisfy them is the survival of *personal* consciousness.

The traditional doctrine of immortality presents some problems. One serious problem is, *how can personal consciousness survive the death of the body?* Consciousness fails even in sleep or in a fainting experience. Consciousness seems to be conditioned by an organism. What we think of as the higher type of consciousness is conditioned by an organism having a brain with a highly developed frontal cortex. In any of these cases, when the organism dies the consciousness ceases.

Experience within the compass of nature does not support the traditional belief in immortality. Yet the tradition of immortality is one of the oldest of mankind, extending back into prehistoric times when men accepted the tenets of animism and revered the souls of departed ancestors. Perhaps there is some logical value in the very fact that the belief in the soul's survival is a primitive intuition which even modern enlightened man can scarcely give up. The animistic belief is so basic that it may almost be regarded as an instinct, and for every instinct there is a natural fulfilment—so it was argued by Bishop Butler,[6] for example.

Perhaps since the doctrine of immortality has no logical coherence, the only way to represent its truth is by means of myth. As a myth, the age-long belief in human immortality may mean that man as an individual personality has intrinsic and infinite worth, and that he ought never to perish. Instead of perishing, if he has been bad his soul should be punished. If he has been good his soul should be rewarded. But this is really an evaluation of man's present existence rather than a judgment of his eternal fate. Yet since a myth is not intended to be logical, it may indeed be true that in some sense which our natures cannot visualize, man does have an immortal destiny. Without naivete one may by faith believe in such a myth. Any one who insists on a concrete description of the condition of souls in heaven or hell certainly is naive.

There is, of course, the view of the mystic. Substantially this view is that man's present existence, like all the rest of nature, is merely an aspect of God. Ceasing to exist as an individual organism is not to cease to exist in some other relationship to God. Within his infinite being nothing dies. All is transformed in the infinite being of God. Therefore man does have an infinite destiny, though the precise description of that destiny is forever hidden from the mind of man as he now exists.

Perhaps this mystical view is obscurantist. Perhaps it is double-talk. Perhaps the use of myth to express the immortal destiny of man's soul is likewise obscurantist double-talk. On the other hand philosophers have always dealt with questions of existence and value which could not be precisely answered. The alternatives are always plausible. That is what makes philosophy interesting.

Plato pretty well sums up the arguments for immortality in the *Crito* and *Phaedo,* with supplementary remarks elsewhere. In all his arguments he assumes that if there is immortality it has to do with a kind of substance which is indestructible. The definition of the soul as a spiritual substance is as suspect as any of the arguments which he bases on this concept of the soul. And ultimately there is no proof, just as there is no disproof.

Christian tradition is said to have added a kind of historical evidence to the other arguments; but we have already seen that the tradition of a historical resurrection is unfounded from the point of view of historical science. If the physical resurrection of Christ were even proved, that still would leave the question of the nature of the soul, since in that case it would have been a body, not the soul, that revived.

Kant and Josiah Royce added the moral argument for immortality. Kant first pointed out that all moral judgments assume freedom of the will in a moral universe, which in turn implies a future life in which to realize moral justice, since justice is not realized in this life. Royce added that the moral life implies infinite time in which to realize moral perfection, since there is no last act of achieving moral perfection.

All these arguments are interesting and deserve more attention than we can give them here. The consensus, however, is that none of the arguments proves immortality, which remains in the realm of faith—or at least of hope. Few men are free from the hope of immortality. Even in Oriental mysticism most devotees continue to hope for some kind of individual immortality, despite the philosophy of the Brahmins and the Taoist Sages. Even the authors of the Upanishads expected bliss unspeakable to be the experience of the soul reunited with God. How could the soul experience bliss if it ceased to have some kind of individuality? This is a paradox—but mysticism is full of paradoxes, and so is life.

Salvation

What is salvation? Is there a mature concept of this common experience of the religions of man? Certainly there is a variety of meanings. To the Hindu, salvation means being freed from the weary round of transmigration, the absorption of the individual soul in the soul of God. To the Confucian it means the restoration of the individual to the enjoyment of the confidence of the other members of one's family and ancestors. To the Christian it has traditionally meant the assurance of heavenly immortality.

Beneath the surface we may find a common essence of salvation in all religions. The Christian experience, whether of the emotional or intellectual type, means essentially that the individual has ceased working against God—and against himself—and is now at one, in spirit and intent, with the divine will in all human relations. The Hindu experience of salvation really means about the same thing. By coming into complete harmony with Brahman the Hindu also dedicates himself to a life of piety as he conceives the divine will. Confucian rationalism achieves somewhat the same results. Either mystical union with God or rational reconciliation with the soul or souls of the universe brings to the individual a sense of peace and integrity which may be described as blessedness. Such is the human experience of salvation in the great religions of mankind.

Theology

Is Jesus the divine son of God? Is there any mature value in the Christian doctrine of the incarnation, or similar teachings of other religions?

First, it must be admitted that many Christians confess the divine sonship of Jesus as if the words were a magical formula which guaranteed heavenly salvation to the believer. Probably few Christians in any age have critically analyzed the doctrine of Christ's divinity. They must feel that it would be an impiety even to ask what it means.

What can the divine sonship of Jesus mean? That Jesus was the son of God surely cannot mean that God was his physiological progenitor. This was the concept which Muhammad associated with the Christians when he insisted that "God has no son." Even Muhammad revered Jesus as the greatest prophet prior to himself.

If the incarnation does not mean that Jesus was the physiological son of God, then it must mean that he was his son spiritually. It is obvious, therefore, that the word *son* in this case must have a figurative meaning, since sonship as we use the term means the relationship of being a male offspring of a parent. While we are on the subject of sex, since most people will probably admit that God is not a physiological organism, then logically we should conclude that the distinction between male and female should not apply to God. Reference to God as *he* rather than *she* should be regarded as a custom of convenience which is philosophically unjustified. The motherhood of God may be as justifiable as the fatherhood of God. Similarly the sonship of Jesus must be regarded as a concept of the spiritual likeness between Jesus and God such that when we think of Christ's spirit we are reminded of God. Like Jesus, God is thought of as truthful, wise, just, merciful and compassionate—all positive values to the degree of perfection. Christ's followers sensed these values in him even during his lifetime. In the decades and still more in the centuries following his dramatic ministry and death, his disciples and their followers came to feel the same way in increasing degree.

The creed of Christ's divinity was an outgrowth of experience. All vital religion is based on some realistic experience. Creeds cannot create vital religion. Creeds are not revealed like bulletins dictated by the office boss. Therefore the ultimate interpretation of the doctrine of the incarnation should be in terms of the individual's commitment to a way of life which he regards as most certain to cultivate the values that he holds most dear. "If you keep my commandments, you will abide in my love, just as I have kept my Father's commandments and abide in his love" (John 15:10). The experience of spiritual likeness between Jesus and God is identical with our own mystical experience: "that they may all be one; even as thou, Father, art in me, and I in thee, that they also may be in us" (John 17:21). "He who abides in me, and I in him, he it is that bears much fruit" (John 15:5).

Other religions have had their "avatars" or divine incarnations, and have meant by this the same essential experience as Christianity has meant. When Hinduism made Buddha an avatar it meant that he had revealed God's perfection and his way of life to men. The Hindu avatar-myths, when interpreted literally, meant something different from this, no doubt. But when one stops to analyze it in terms of experience, this is what it had to mean.

Is Christianity the Final Religion?

Is Christianity, then, not superior to all other religions? Is it not the final religion of mankind, as Christians have long believed? If Christianity is not superior to all other religions, why send missionaries? In fact, is any good accomplished by going to church? Why be good at all?

A mature religion is one which turns away from credal magic and concentrates on experience. It really is not very worthwhile to export a magical brand of Christianity. If, however, we become fully mature, our religion will be greatly needed by the people of other traditions. The hope is that by this means Hindus, Buddhists and Confucians will learn of the way of life which many of us praise but few practice. Learning of the Christian perfection they will see God in it and will formulate new creeds from new experiences.

Other Christian writers on comparative religion and religious philosophy have felt impelled to emphasize the uniqueness of Christianity. The present writer has felt rather the need to point out the excellencies of all faiths. It really should not be necessary to teach a formal doctrine of the superiority and exclusiveness of Christianity. If Christian missionaries recognize the virtues of other religious traditions and cultivate the Christian way along with the others, it should not be hard for simple folks everywhere to recognize the real virtues of the Christian tradition. True, there are unlovely elements in other religions. We should not forget, either, the unlovely elements of Christian history and of contemporary Christian civilization.

This brings us back to the beginning: the credal basis in Christian experience. The best way to win the world for Christ is for us, his professed followers, to "abide in his love," to reveal to the rest of the world the real superiority of Christianity as it is lived in our personal lives, in our economic, class, and race relations, as well as in international and all human relations. This is Christ's challenge to us.

Chapter Notes

I. TOWARD A MATURE PHILOSOPHY OF RELIGION

1. Ferm, "Religion," *An Encyclopedia of Religion*, edited by Ferm.
2. Martineau, *A Study of Religion*, p. 1; Schleimacher, *History of Religion*, p. 11; Kant, *Religion within the Limits of Reason Alone*, p. 142; Brightman, *Philosophy of Religion*, p. 15; Leuba, *A Psychological Study of Religion*, Appendix, pp. 339-361.
3. Perry, *Realms of Value*, p. 463.
4. Cassirer, *Language and Myth*, pp. 1-6 *et passim.*
5. Tsanoff, *Religious Crossroads*, pp. 7-12.
6. Karsten, *Origins of Religion*, p. 35, cited hereafter as Karsten, *OR*.
7. *Ibid.*, pp. 35-36.

II. PREHISTORIC AND PRIMITIVE RELIGION

1. Weiss, *Nature and Man*, pp. 139-144.
2. Luquet, *The Art and Religion of Fossil Man* (cited hereafter as Luquet, *FM*), p. 154; cf. Chapter VI, "The Cult of the Dead"; see also Kroeber and Waterman, *Source Book in Anthropology*, pp. 60-62.
3. Luquet, *FM*, p. 172.
4. *Ibid.*, p. 159.
5. *Ibid.*, p. 191.
6. *Ibid.*, p. 184; he may also be wearing stag antlers; see also Chapter VII, "Religion and Magic."
7. *Ibid.*, p. 198.
8. Ackerman, "Dawn of Religions," in Ferm, ed., *Forgotten Religions*, pp. 1-24; cited hereafter as Ferm, *FR*.
9. Lowie, *An Introduction to Cultural Anthropology*, p. 303; cited hereafter as Lowie, *CA*.
10. Ackerman, "Dawn of Religions," in Ferm, *FR*, p. 4.
11. Lowie, *CA*, pp. 298-300.
12. Karsten, *OR*, p. 152.
13. Lowie, *CA*, p. 258.
14. *Ibid.*, pp. 299-300.
15. Karsten, *OR*, p. 129.
16. *Ibid.*, p. 35.
17. *Ibid.*, p. 133.

III. RELIGION IN ANCIENT EGYPT

1. See Albright, *From the Stone Age to Christianity*, pp. 98-100.
2. Hayes, *The Scepter of Egypt*, pp. 8-10.
3. Noss, *Man's Religions*, p. 47 (cited hereafter as Noss, *MR*); Hayes, *Scepter*, pp. 11-12.
4. Albright, *Stone Age*, pp. 96-98; Hayes *Scepter*, pp. 8, 34-36.
5. Murray, *The Splendour That Was Egypt*, p. 8; cf. Hayes, *Scepter*, p. 22, n. 5.
6. Hayes, *Scepter*, p. 21.
7. *Ibid.*, pp. 34-36; Murray, *Splendour*, p. 330; Albright, *Stone Age*, p. 441. Frankfort, *Kingship and the Gods* (cited hereafter as *KG*), p. xxiv, suggests 3100 B.C., "based on the work of Sidney Smith, Thorkild Jacobsen, and Richard A. Parker." I shall follow the chronology of Hayes wherever possible.
8. Winlock, "The Origins of the Ancient Egyptian Calendar," *Proc. Am. Phil. Soc.*, LXXXIII (September 10, 1940), 444-464. See Hayes, *Scepter*, p. 40.
9. Finegan, *Light from the Ancient Past*, p. 76.
10. Peet, *A Comparative Study of the Literatures of Egypt, Palestine, and Mesopotamia*, pp. 101-103.
11. *Ibid.*, p. 118.
12. Finegan, *Light*, p. 85.
13. *Ibid.*, pp. 105-108; Albright, *Stone Age*, p. 195.
14. Breasted, *The Dawn of Conscience*, pp. 372, 375.
15. Murray, *Splendour*, pp. 72, 102-103.
16. Breasted, *The Dawn of Conscience*, pp. xi-xii, 129.
17. Finegan, *Light*, p. 116.
18. Mercer, "The Religion of Ancient Egypt," in Ferm, *FR*, p. 40; cf. Hayes, *Scepter*, p. 75.
19. For a systematic effort to interpret prehistoric Egyptian art, see Raphael, *Prehistoric Pottery and Civilization in Egypt*, esp. p. 14.
20. Albright, *Stone Age*, p. 131.
21. Mercer, "Religion of Ancient Egypt," in Ferm, *FR*, p. 30; see also Murray, *Splendour*, pp. 172-173, and Noss, *MR*, pp. 46-47.
22. Herodotus III, 27-28, trans. by Cary.
23. Murray, *Splendour*, p. 162.
24. Prehistoric art is full of magical significance; cf, Raphael, *Prehistoric Pottery*, pp. 93-94.
25. Frankfort, *KG*, Chap. V; cf. Hayes, *Scepter*, Pt. I, p. 79.
26. Frankfort, *KG*, p. 5.
27. Some very early Pyramid texts foreshadow this doctrine by suggesting that Ptah is the one ultimate god, in whom other gods, kings, and all creation have their being. See Frankfort, *KG*, pp. 28-29.
28. Murray, *Splendour*, pp. 54, 298; cf. Mercer, "Religion of Ancient Egypt," in Ferm, *FR*, p. 31.
29. Breasted, *The Dawn of Conscience*, pp. 281-286.
30. *Ibid.*, p. 118.
31. *Ibid.*, p. 125.
32. *Ibid.*, pp. 125-126.

33. Browne, *The World's Great Scriptures*, pp. 51-53, quoted in Budge, tr., "The Papyrus of Ani," in *The Book of the Dead.*
34. Breasted, *The Dawn of Conscience*, pp. 143-145.

IV. RELIGION IN THE ANCIENT NEAR EAST

1. Finegan, *Light*, pp. 13-15; also Speiser, "Ancient Mesopotamia: A Light That Did Not Fail," *National Geographic Magazine*, XCIX (January, 1951), 46.
2. Albright, *Stone Age*, pp. 90-91.
3. The dates are in harmony with Finegan, *Light*, *passim*, and Albright, *Stone Age*, p. 364.
4. Finegan, *Light*, p. 17.
5. Albright, *Stone Age*, p. 97.
6. Finegan, *Light*, p. 17.
7. *Ibid.* A reconstruction of this temple is pictured in *National Geographic Magazine*, XCIX (January, 1951), 60.
8. Kramer, "Sumerian Religion," in Ferm, *FR*, p. 52.
9. *Ibid.*
10. Albright, *Stone Age*, p. 9.
11. Finegan, *Light*, p. 38.
12. *Ibid.*
13. Tr. by A. Jeremias, in Hastings, ed., *Encyclopedia of Religion and Ethics*, V, 445-446; cited hereafter as *ERE*.
14. Albright, *Stone Age*, p. 146.
15. Finegan, *Light*, p. 28; cf. Gaster, *Oldest Stories in the World*, p. 37. Speiser has a more literal translation of this in Mendelsohn, ed., *Religions of the Ancient Near East*, p. 92.
16. Heidel, *Gilgamesh Epic*, pp. 50-52.
17. Kramer, *Sumerian Mythology*, pp. 88-96.
18. Finegan, *Light*, p. 28; cf. Mendelsohn, *Religions*, p. 92; Gaster, *Oldest Stories*, p. 37; *Ancient Near Eastern Texts*, p. 90.
19. Langdon, *Semitic Mythology*, p. 220.
20. *Ancient Near Eastern Texts*, p. 95; cf. Mendelsohn, *Religions*, p. 104; Gaster, *Oldest Stories*, pp. 39-40.
21. *Ancient Near Eastern Texts*, p. 67; cf. Mendelsohn *Religions*, pp. 33-35.
22. Gaster, *Oldest Stories*, p. 66.
23. Finegan, *Light*, pp. 49-50.
24. *Ibid.*, pp. 48-49.
25. Albright, *Stone Age*, p. 176.
26. Gaster, *Oldest Stories*, chap. 13.
27. Obermann, *Ugaritic Mythology*, pp. 83-87, 90-92.

V. THE DEVELOPMENT OF GREEK RELIGION

1. Cf. Dow, "Minoan Writing," *AJA*, LVIII (1954), 77.
2. Cf. Myres, *Who Were the Greeks?*
3. Cornford, "Eleusinian Mysteries," *Cambridge Ancient History*, III, 529-531; cited hereafter as *CAH*.
4. Wace, *Mycenae*, pp. 21-22 and *CAH*, II, 451-452.

5. Pendlebury, "Egypt and the Aegean," in *Studies Presented to David M. Robinson*, I, 184-197.
6. Blegen, Caskey, Rawson, *University of Cincinnati Excavations in the Troad*, 1932-1938 (in progress; Vols. I, II, and III have appeared).
7. Aeschylus, *Eumenides*, lines 1-14.
8. Mylonas, "Religion in Prehistoric Greece," in Ferm, *FR*, p. 148.
9. *Ibid.*, p. 150.
10. *Ibid.*, p. 153.
11. *Ibid.*, p. 154.
12. *Ibid.*
13. Murray, *Five Stages of Greek Religion*, pp. 34-35.
14. *Ibid.*, p. 37.
15. *Odyssey*, V, 49-54, tr. by Mackail.
16. *Ibid.*, X, 277-279.
17. *Ibid.*, XXIV, 1-14.
18. Harrison, *Mythology*, pp. 6-7.
19. *Ibid.*, p. 27.
20. Murray, *Five Stages*, p. 75.
21. Harrison, *Mythology*, p. 65.
22. *Ibid.*, p. 94.
23. *Odyssey*, XI, 488-491, tr. by Butcher and Lang.
24. Mylonas, "Religion in Prehistoric Greece," in Ferm, *FR*, p. 182.
25. Harrison, *Mythology*, p. 137.
26. Mylonas, "Religion in Prehistoric Greece," in Ferm, *FR*, p. 175.
27. Euripides, *Bacchae*, lines 1017-1019, tr. by Murray. See Harvard Classics VIII, 396.
28. Euripides, *Bacchae*, lines 726-727, tr. by Murray. See Harvard Classics VIII, p. 380.
29. Mylonas, "Religion in Prehistoric Greece," in Ferm, *FR*, p. 180.
30. *Ibid.*, p. 185.
31. *Ibid.*, p. 187.
32. Angus, *Mystery Religions and Christianity*, p. 276.
33. Murray, *Five Stages*.
34. Sophocles, *Antigone*, lines 450-468, tr. by Whitelaw.
35. Fragments 35, 119, 36, 98-99 (Bywater), 57, 42, 67, 82-83 (Diels) tr. by Burnet.
36. Fragments 11, 14, 15, 16, 23, 24, 25, (Diels) tr. by Freeman, *Ancilla to the Pre-Socratic Philosophers*, pp. 22-23.
37. Tr. by Palmer, in Bakewell, *Source Book in Ancient Philosophy*, pp. 277-278.
38. Epictetus, *Discourses*, cvii, xxiv, tr. by Crossley.
39. Bakewell, *Source Book*, p. 325.

VI. UNIQUE QUALITIES OF ROMAN RELIGION

1. *CAH*, II, 563-565.
2. *Ibid.*, II, 570.
3. *Ibid.*, II, 574.
4. *Ibid.*, IV, 389.

5. *Ibid.*, IV, 415-421; Moore, *History of Religions*, I, 559; cited hereafter as *HR*.
6. Gjerstad, "The Agger of Servius Tullius," in *Studies Presented to David M. Robinson*, I, 412-422.
7. Cato, *de agri cultura*, p. 139, tr. by Bailey in *CAH*, VIII, 431.
8. Bailey in *CAH*, VIII, 429.
9. *Ibid.*
10. Altheim, *History of Roman Religion*, pp. 192-193.
11. Bailey, *Phases in the Religion of Ancient Rome*, p. 55.
12. *Ibid.*, p. 57.
13. *Ibid.*, pp. 50-51. Moore (*HR*, I, 543) says the Lares "preside over fields," but this interpretation of the function of the Lares seems inaccurate.
14. Bailey, *Phases*, pp. 59-60, 155.
15. *Ibid.*, p. 43.
16. Altheim, *Roman Religion*, p. 194.
17. Bailey, *Phases*, p. 70.
18. *Ibid.*, p. 102.
19. *Ibid.*, p. 154.
20. *Ibid.*, pp. 16-17.
21. *Ibid.*, p. 158.
22. *Ibid.*, p. 16.
23. *Ibid.*, p. 19.
24. Rose, *Primitive Culture in Italy*, p. 114.
25. Bailey, *Phases*, p. 28.
26. *Ibid.*, pp. 121-123.
27. Moore, *HR*, I, 554.
28. *Ibid.*, p. 556.
29. *Ibid.*
30. Bailey, *Phases*, p. 140.

VII. PRIMEVAL INDIA

1. Without citing the evidence, Finegan (*Archeology of World Religions*, p. 123; cited hereafter as *Arch.*) dates this civilization between 2500 and 1500 B.C.
2. Finegan, *Light*, p. 19.
3. Sen, *The Pageant of India's History*, pp. 23-24, 28.
4. *Ibid.*, p. 18.
5. *Ibid.*, p. 25; see also Finegan, *Arch.*, p. 124.
6. Goshal, *The People of India*, p. 14.
7. Sen, *Pageant*, pp. 26-27.
8. *Ibid.*, pp. 29-30.
9. Finegan, *Arch.*, p. 127 and fig. 49.
10. Sen, *Pageant*, pp. 30-31.

VIII. VEDIC RELIGION

1. Radhakrishnan, *Indian Philosophy*, I, 65; cited hereafter as *IP*.
2. Sen, *Pageant*, p. 55.
3. Radhakrishnan, *IP*, I, 67.

4. Sen, *Pageant*, p. 34.
5. Radhakrishnan, *IP*, I, 72-73.
6. *Ibid.*, p. 76, n. 1.
7. From *Hymns of the Rig Veda*, tr, by R. T. H. Griffith.
8. Rig Veda v.85.6-8, tr. by Griffith.
9. Radhakrishnan, *IP*, I, 79.
10. Rig Veda vii.60, tr. by Griffith.
11. Radhakrishnan, *IP*, I, 80.
12. *Ibid.*, p. 81.
13. Rig Veda ii. 12, tr. by Griffith.
14. Rig Veda i.1, tr. by Griffith.
15. Radhakrishnan, *IP*, I, 84, quoting Rig Veda viii, 48.
16. Radhakrishnan, *IP*, I, 84, quoting Rig Veda. *Sacred Books of the East*, Vedic Hymns, part i; hereafter cited as *SBE*.
17. Rig Veda x.129, tr. by Griffith.
18. See Dasgupta, *History of Indian Philosophy*, I, 16-17.
19. *Ibid.*, I, 118.
20. *JAOS*, III (1848), 307-308; see Radhakrishnan, *IP*, I, 120-121.
21. Radhakrishnan, *IP*, I, 122.

IX. POETS, PRIESTS, AND PHILOSOPHERS

1. Radhakrishnan, *IP*, I, 123.
2. Shatapatha Brahmana ii.2.2.6; ii.4.3.14. Tr. by Eggeling, in *Sacred Books of the East*, American edition, IX A, 309, 374; cited hereafter as *SBEA*.
3. Radhakrishnan, *IP*, I, 128.
4. Shatapatha Brahmana, xiii.7.1.1. See Radhakrishnan, *IP*, I, 131.
5. Shatapatha Brahmana, i.8.1-44, in *SBEA*, IX, 216-230.
6. Dasgupta, *History*, I, 14; Nikhilananda, *The Upanishads*, I, 4.
7. Nikhilananda, *The Upanishads*, I, 4-5; Radhakrishnan, *IP*, I, 132.
8. Brihadaranyaka i.1.1., tr. by Hume.
9. Sen, *Pageant*, p. 54.
10. Dasgupta, *History*, I, 33-35.
11. Chandogya Upanishad, iv.4.1-5, tr. by Hume.
12. Radhakrishnan, *IP*, I, 223; see Bridhadaranyaka Upanishad, iii.7.1; Chandogya Upanishad, v.3.
13. Dasgupta, *History*, I, 28; Radhakrishnan, *IP*, I, 141-142.
14. Vol. I, 1949; Vol. II, 1952.
15. Radhakrishnan, *IP*, I, 142.
16. Cf. Radhakrishnan, *The Principal Upanishads.*
17. Chandogya Upanishad III, 16-17, *passim*, tr. by Radhakrishnan.
18. Chandogya Upanishad vii.1.2-3, tr. by Müller.
19. Mundaka Upanishad i.1.4-5, tr. by Müller.

X. MAIN TEACHINGS OF THE UPANISHADS

1. Radhakrishnan, *IP*, I, 163-164, n. 1.
2. Maitri Upanishad iv.5-6, tr. by Müller.
3. Maitri Upanishad vi.17 tr. by Hume.
4. Chandogya Upanishad iii.14.1, tr. by Hume.

5. Radhakrishnan, *IP*, I, 146.
6. Chandogya Upanishad viii.3-12.
7. Chandogya Upanishad viii.12, tr. by Müller.
8. Radhakrishnan, *IP*, I, 157-158, quoting Mundaka Upanishad, i.1; Chandogya Upanishad, iii.12.7; cf. Nikhilananda, *The Upanishads,* I, 282.
9. Brihadaranyaka iv.4.25, tr. by Müller.
10. Chandogya vi., tr. by Müller.
11. From *The Upanishads,* II, 223-248, by Swami Nikhilananda. Translator's brackets are included but not his generous quotations from Shankara and Guadapada.
12. Katha Upanishad I.ii.23, tr. by Nikhilananda, I.
13. Katha Upanishad I.ii. 20, tr. by Nikhilananda, I.
14. Isha Upanishad 5, tr. by Nikhilananda, I.
15. Radhakrishnan, *IP*, I, 190-203, esp. p. 198.
16. Mundaka II.i.1, tr. by Nikhilananda, I.
17. Mundaka II.ii.10, tr. by Nikhilananda, I.
18. Mundaka III.ii.9, tr. by Nikhilananda, I.
19. Chandogya vi.12, tr. by Müller.
20. Brihadaranyaka Upanishad i.4.6-10, tr. by Hume.
21. Acts 17:28; I John 4;16.
22. Schilpp, *The Philosophy of Sarvepalli Radhakrishnan*, p. 806, n. 18.
23. Kaushitaki Brahmana, xxv.1.
24. Chandogya Upanishad, viii.14.1, tr. by Müller.
25. Chandogya Upanishad v.10.7, tr. by Müller.
26. Chandogya Upanishad v.10; Dasgupta, *History*, I, 54.
27. Radhakrishnan, *IP*, I, 254.
28. Isha Upanishad ii.
29. Chandogya Upanishad, viii.1.6, tr. by Müller.
30. Radhakrishnan, *IP*, I, 186.
31. Brihadaranyaka Upanishad i.5.23, tr. by Müller.
32. Maitri Upanishad vi.18, tr. by Müller; cf. Prashnna Upanishad v.1; Kena Upanishad iv.6.
33. Chandogya Upanishad, iii.14.1, tr. by Radhakrishnan.

XI. THE JAINIST PROTEST

1. Finegan, *Arch.*, pp. 182-186.
2. Radhakrishnan, *IP*, I, 288-289.
3. Hopkins, *The Religions of India*, p. 284.
4. Tr. by Hermann Jacobi in *SBEA*, X B.
5. *SBEA*, X B, 194.
6. *Ibid.*
7. *Ibid.*, p. 259.
8. *Ibid.*, p. 200.
9. *Ibid.*, pp. 82-86.
10. *Ibid.*, pp. 201-202.
11. Hopkins, *Religions*, p. 293.
12. *SBEA*, X B, 267-268.

13. Noss, *MR*, p. 154, gives the former figure; Sen, *Pageant*, p. 88, the latter.
14. Radhakrishnan, *IP*, I, Chap. VI.
15. Hopkins, *Religions*, p. 296 and n. 3.
16. *SBEA*, X B, 33.
17. Radhakrishnan, *IP*, I, 331.
18. Noss, *MR*, pp. 147-148.
19. Uttaradhyayana, Lect. 36, quoted by Finegan, *Arch.*, pp. 206-207.
20. *SBEA*, X B, 52.
21. Hopkins, *Religions*, pp. 293-295.
22. Radhakrishnan, *IP*, I, 329.
23. Hopkins, *Religions*, p. 297.
24. *Ibid.*, p. 291.
25. *Ibid.*, pp. 291-292.
26. *Ibid.*, p. 290.
27. Uttaradhyayana, *SBE*, XLV, 140.

XII. ORIGINAL BUDDHISM

1. See Pratt, *The Pilgrimage of Buddhism*, pp. vii-viii.
2. *Ibid.*, p. 3, note; also Radhakrishnan, *IP*, I, 343-346.
3. Finegan, *Arch.*, p. 236, holds to the former and Radhakrishnan, *IP*, I, 343, to the latter dates.
4. Sen, *Pageant*, pp. 84-85. Radhakrishnan, *IP*, I, 347, describes him as "heir to the Shakya kingdom."
5. Hopkins, *Religions*, pp. 302-305.
6. Majjhima Nikaya, in Chalmers, *Further Dialogues of the Buddha*, I, 56 (l. 80).
7. *Ibid.*, p. 176 (l. 246).
8. Radhakrishnan, *IP*, I, 350.
9. *SBEA*, VII B, 146-149.
10. Hopkins, *Religions*, p. 308.
11. Noss, *MR*, p. 163; Hopkins, *Religions*, p. 307, note.
12. *SBEA*, IV A, 112.
13. Sen, *Pageant*, pp. 100-103.
14. *SBEA*, VII B, 96-97, 102, 114.
15. Cf. Radhakrishnan, *IP*, I, 685-686.
16. Radhakrishnan, *IP*, I, 386.
17. Majjhima lxiii, tr. by Chalmers.
18. Radhakrishnan, *IP*, I, 375.
19. Pratt, *Pilgrimage*, p. 81.
20. Radhakrishnan, *IP*, I, 409.
21. Hopkins, *Religions*, p. 322.
22. Samyutta xxii.87, tr. by Mrs. Rhys Davids.
23. Majjhima lxxii, tr. by Chalmers.
24. Radhakrishnan, *IP*, I, 357.
25. Pratt, *Pilgrimage*, p. 15, quoting the Anguttara and the Majjhima, *passim*.
26. Samyutta xxii.87, tr. by Mrs. Rhys Davids.
27. Pratt, *Pilgrimage*, pp. 97-98.

28. Vasalasutta 21, *SBEA*, XII C, 23.
29. Radhakrishnan, *IP*, I, 693.

XIII. THE GROWTH OF BUDDHISM

1. Mahavagga x.
2. Smith, *The Edicts of Asoka*, pp. 18-19; see Finegan, *Arch.*, p. 261.
3. Pratt, *Pilgrimage*, p. 105.
4. Smith, *The Early History of India*, p. 197.
5. "Questions of King Milinda" ii.i.6.
6. Finegan, *Arch.*, p. 279.
7. Mahavamsa xix.
8. Pratt, *Pilgrimage*, pp. 119-120.
9. *Ibid.*, pp. 128-129.
10. *Ibid.*, p. 131.
11. *Ibid.*, p. 140.
12. Reischauer, "Buddhism," in Jurji, *Great Religions of the Modern World*, p. 121; cited hereafter as *GR*.
13. Pratt, *Pilgrimage*, p. 221.
14. *SBE*, XLIX, 98-99; see Conze, *Buddhist Texts*, pp. 198-202.
15. See Lafugie, "A Woman Paints the Tibetans," *National Geographic Magazine*, XCV (May, 1949), 659-692, for vivid paintings of monastic life and worship.
16. Reischauer, "Buddhism," in Jurji, *GR*, p. 126.
17. Pratt, *Pilgrimage*, pp. 524-537.
18. Ashvaghosha, *Awakening of Faith in the Mahayana*, tr. by Suzuki, p. 87.
19. Pratt, *Pilgrimage*, p. 266.

XIV. THE GROWTH OF HINDUISM

1. Sen, *Pageant*, p. 141.
2. Archer, "Hinduism," in Jurji, *GR*, p. 61.
3. Finegan, *Arch.*, p. 160.
4. Radhakrishnan, *IP*, I, 517.
5. *Ibid.*
6. *Ibid.*, p. 518.
7. Sen, *Pageant*, pp. 69-70.
8. *Ibid.*
9. Radhakrishnan, *IP*, I, 506.
10. *Ibid.*, pp. 523-524.
11. *Ibid.*, p. 519.
12. Gandhi, *Young India*, pp. 1078-1079; see Radhakrishnan, *The Bhagavadgita*, p. 9.
13. *Bhagavad-Gita*, tr. by Prabhavananda and Isherwood, Chap. XII, p. 130; cf. Radhakrishnan's translation, p. 294.
14. *Bhagavad-Gita*, tr. by Prabhavananda and Isherwood, p. 131.
15. *Ibid.*, p. 172.
16. *Ibid.*, p. 109.
17. *Ibid.*
18. *Ibid.*, pp. 109-110.

19. *Ibid.*, pp. 110-111.
20. Shvetashvatara Upanishad, iii.11, 14, 16; iv.3.
21. Rig Veda i, 136.3.
22. Finegan, *Arch.*, p. 163 and Plate 54.
23. *Ibid.*, p. 177 and figs. 66, 67, 68.
24. *Ibid.*, figs. 67, 66.
25. *Ibid.*, p. 177 and figs. 61, 69.
26. Archer, "Hinduism," in Jurji, *GR*, pp. 83-84.
27. Baronte, *Twilight in India*, p. 12.
28. Cf. Woodroffe, "Shakti and Maya, a study in the Shakta Tantra;" Avalon (= Woodroffe), "Shakti."
29. Avalon, "Shakti," pp. 29-30.
30. Archer, "Hinduism," in Jurji, *GR*, p. 83.
31. Soper, "The Modern Revival of Hinduism," *Motive*, XIII (May, 1953), 11.
32. Archer, "Hinduism," in Jurji, *GR*, pp. 48, 63-65.
33. *World Almanac*, 1954, pp. 355-356, 326; 1956, pp. 325-326, 355-356.
34. The worst features of Hinduism and its caste system are described by Baronte, *Twilight in India, passim.*
35. *World Almanac*, 1954, pp. 355-356; cf. Archer, "Hinduism," in Jurji, *GR*, p. 64; UNESCO, *Progress of Literacy in Various Countries*, p. 218; UNESCO, *World Survey of Education*, 1955, p .15.
36. Archer, "Hinduism," in Jurji, *GR*, pp. 48, 63-65.
37. Latourette, *History of the Expansion of Christianity*, VII, 294-295.
38. Noss, *MR*, p. 261.
39. For an excellent and sympathetic biography of Gandhi see Shean, *Lead Kindly Light.*

XV. THE HINDU SCHOOLS OF PHILOSOPHY

1. Radhakrishnan, *IP*, II, 36.
2. *Ibid.*, p. 43.
3. *Ibid.*, p. 46.
4. *Ibid.*, p. 65.
5. *Ibid.*, p. 75.
6. *Ibid.*, p. 86.
7. *Ibid.*, p. 93.
8. *Ibid.*, p. 96.
9. *Ibid.*, p. 103.
10. *Ibid.*
11. *Ibid.*, p. 107.
12. *Ibid.*, p. 125.
13. *Ibid.*, p. 127.
14. *Ibid.*, p. 129.
15. *Ibid.*, p. 131.
16. *Ibid.*, p. 136.
17. Bernard, *Hindu Philosophy*, p. 43.
18. *Ibid.*, p. 47.
19. Radhakrishnan, *IP*, II, 246.

20. *Ibid.*, pp. 254-255.
21. *Ibid.*, p. 283.
22. *Ibid.*, p. 289.
23. *Ibid.*, p. 309.
24. *Ibid.*, p. 338.
25. *Ibid.*, pp. 352-353.
26. *Ibid.*, p. 415.
27. *Ibid.*, p. 427.
28. *Ibid.*, p. 428.
29. *Ibid.*, p. 431.
30. *Ibid.*, p. 482.
31. *Ibid.*, p. 522.
32. *Ibid.*, p. 523.
33. *Ibid.*, p. 524.
34. Nikhilananda, *The Upanishads* I, 28 and 49.
35. Radhakrishnan, *IP*, II, 557.
36. *Ibid.*, pp. 600-601.
37. *Ibid.*, p. 618.
38. *Ibid.*, p. 705.
39. *Ibid.*, p. 711.

XVI. SIKHISM AND MODERN INDIA

1. Latourette, *Expansion*, VII, 307; Soper, "Modern Revival," *Motive*, XIII (May, 1953), 27.
2. Finegan, *Arch.*, p. 537.
3. Archer, *Sikhs in Relation to Hindus, Moslems, Christians, and Ahmadiyyas*, p. 50.
4. Finegan, *Arch.*, p. 545.
5. Archer, *Sikhs*, pp. 53-54; Finegan, *Arch.*, p. 547.
6. Archer, *Sikhs*, p. 70.
7. *Ibid.*
8. *Ibid.*, p. 75.
9. *Ibid.*, p. 120.
10. *Ibid.*, pp. 123-124.
11. *Ibid.*, p. 125.
12. *Ibid.*, p. 122.
13. *Ibid.*, p. 123.
14. *Ibid.*, p. 125.
15. *Ibid.*, p. 126.
16. *Ibid.*
17. *Ibid.*, p. 127.
18. *Ibid.*, pp. 170-171.

XVII. EARLY CHINESE RELIGION

1. Tsui Chi, *Short History of Chinese Civilization*, pp. 15-16.
2. *Ibid.*, p. 3.
3. Latourette, *The Chinese: Their History and Culture*, pp. 37-38.
4. Chou Yü, I, 10, quoted in Fung, *History of Chinese Philosophy*, I, 32, cf. Fung, *Short History of Chinese Philosophy*, p. 138. The latter

was composed, in English, more recently than the former, which has been translated into English by Derk Bodde.

5. Fung, *Chinese Philosophy,* I, 31.
6. Tsui, *Chinese Civilization,* p. 29.
7. *Ibid.,* p. 30.
8. Finegan, *Arch.,* p. 328.
9. Chan, *Religious Trends in Modern China,* pp. 257-258.
10. Creel, *Birth of China,* pp. 180-181.
11. *Ibid.,* pp. 181-182.
12. Creel, *Confucius, the Man and the Myth,* p. 118.
13. Shih Ching xi.6, tr. Legge in *The She King, or Book of Poetry.*

XVIII. CONFUCIAN HUMANISM

1. Fung, *Short History,* p. 1.
2. *Analects,* 9.6.3, tr. Waley.
3. Creel, *Confucius,* p. 291.
4. *Ibid.,* p. 37.
5. *Analects* 5.9.2, tr. Waley.
6. *Analects* 2.22, tr. Legge, in *Chinese Classics.*
7. *Analects* 4.14, tr. Waley.
8. *Analects* 14.29, tr. Waley.
9. *Analects* 3.26, tr. Waley.
10. *Analects* 17.11; cf. *Li Chi,* I, 400-401, in Legge, tr., *The Chinese Classics.*
11. *Analects* 8.2.1, tr. Waley.
12. *Analects* 15.17, tr. Waley.
13. *Analects* 6.16, tr. Waley.
14. *Analects* 14.31, tr. Waley.
15. *Analects* 17.9; 8.8, tr. Legge.
16. See *Analects* 3.9; 3.15; 3.17; 11.25.7; cf. Creel, *Confucius,* p. 115.
17. See *Analects* 14.43; 17.21.
18. *Analects* 11.11.
19. *Analects* 7.34, quoted in Creel, *Confucius,* p. 55.
20. *Analects* 12.5.3-4; cf. Creel, *Confucius,* pp. 121-122.
21. *Analects* 4.8, tr. Waley.
22. *Analects* 12.5.4, tr. Waley.
23. *Analects* 17.4, tr. Legge.
24. Creel, *Confucius,* p. 129.
25. *Analects* 7.15, tr. Legge.
26. *Analects* 4.14, n. 7 *supra.*
27. *Mencius* 2(1) 2.7, tr. Legge.
28. *Analects* 9.25, tr. Waley.
29. *Analects* 15.23, tr. Legge.
30. *Analects* 6.28, 2-3, tr. Legge.
31. *Analects* 17.3, tr. Waley.
32. *Analects* 17.2, tr. Legge.
33. Creel, *Confucius,* p. 134; cf. *Analects* 14.34.
34. *Analects* 4.10, tr. Legge.
35. *Analects* 19.21, tr. Waley; cf. 1.8; 7.3; 7.21; 9.23; 9.24; 15.19.

36. Creel, *Confucius,* pp. 165-166. The whole of Chapter X is most stimulating, and is entitled "The Reformer."

XIX. TAOIST MYSTICISM

1. Fung, *Short History,* p. 93.
2. Finegan, *Arch,* p. 387.
3. Lin Yutang, *Wisdom of Laotse,* pp. 8-9.
4. Fung, *Short History,* p. 104.
5. Lin, *Laotse,* p. 9, n. 5.
6. *Analects.* 14.39.
7. *Analects.* 14.41, tr. by Waley.
8. *Yang Chu's Garden of Pleasure,* tr. by Anton Forke; cf. Fung, *Short History,* pp. 61-63, 232.
9. Mencius 7a. 26. See Fung, *Chinese Philosophy,* II, 203.
10. Fung, *Short History,* p. 61.
11. *Ibid.,* chapter 6.
12. *Ibid.,* p. 63.
13. *Book of Tao,* tr. by Waley, *The Way and Its Powers;* cf. Lin, *Laotse,* p. 41, where the translation, though poetic is not so clear as that quoted here.
14. Ch. 25, trans. by Blakney. All translations of *Lao Tzu, Tao Te Ching* from here on by Blakney unless otherwise noted.
15. Fung, *Short History,* p. 96.
16. Giles, *Chuang Tzu, Mystic, Moralist, and Social Reformer,* chap. 11, pp. 130-131.
17. *Chuang Tzu,* Chapter 10, tr. by Waley, in *Three Ways of Thought in Ancient China,* p. 106.
18. *Ibid.,* p. 107.
19. Giles, *Musings of a Chinese Mystic,* p. 107.
20. Finegan, *Arch,* pp. 383-384.
21. Ch. 57, tr. Giles, in *Sayings of Lao Tzu,* p. 38.
22. Ch. 43.
23. Ch. 47.
24. *Tao Te Ching,* tr. by Ch'u Ta-Kao.
25. *SBE,* XXXIX (English Edition) *The Texts of Taoism,* p. 91, tr. by Legge; Noss, *MR,* p. 320.
26. Ch. 81.
27. Ch. 67, tr. Giles, *Sayings,* p. 35.
28. Ch. 8, tr. by Giles, *Sayings,* p. 24.
29. Cf. Giles, *Sayings,* p. 31.
30. Giles, *Chuang Tzu,* chapter 32, p. 428.
31. Giles, *Musings,* pp. 98-99.
32. Giles, *Sayings,* pp. 31-32.
33. Cf. Giles, *Chuang Tzu,* chs. 14 and 22, especially pp. 280, 283.
34. *Chuang Tzu,* chapter 18, tr. Waley, *Three Ways,* pp. 21-22.
35. *Chuang Tzu,* tr. Giles, *Musings,* p. 89.
36. Giles, *Chuang Tzu,* chapter 22, p. 285.
37. *Chuang Tzu,* chapter 2, tr. Waley, *Three Ways,* p. 54.

XX. EARLY CONFUCIAN APOSTLES AND RIVALS

1. Finegan, *Arch*, pp. 347-348.
2. *Ibid.*, p. 348.
3. Creel, *Chinese Thought: From Confucius to Mao Tse Tung*, p. 48; cited hereafter as *CT*.
4. Fung, *Short History*, p. 49.
5. Mei, tr., *The Ethical and Political Works of Mo Tzu*, p. 229, quoted in Creel, *Confucius*, p. 184.
6. Mei, *Mo Tzu*, p. 56, quoted in *ibid.*, p. 184.
7. Mei, *Mo Tzu*, pp. 62-63, in *ibid.*, p. 185.
8. Fung, *Short History*, pp. 50-52.
9. Mei, *Mo Tzu*, ch. 16; cf. *ibid.*, pp. 54-55.
10. Creel, *CT*, pp. 56-57.
11. Mei, *Mo Tzu*, ch. 16.
12. Mei, *Mo Tzu*, p. 139, in Finegan, *Arch*, p. 355.
13. Fung, *Short History*, p. 52.
14. Creel, *Confucius*, p. 115.
15. Creel, *CT*, p. 58; the last quotation is from Legge's translation of *Li Chi*, II. 127.
16. Cf. Fung, *Short History*, p. 68, and Creel, *CT*, p. 72.
17. *Mencius* III (2) 2.3, tr. Legge.
18. Creel, *CT*, pp. 82-83.
19. *Mencius* VI (1) 6, tr. Legge.
20. *Mencius* VII (1) 4.1; VII (1) 1.1; tr. by Legge.
21. *Mencius* I (1) 1, tr. Legge.
22. Creel, *CT*, pp. 89-91.
23. *Ibid.*, p. 119.
24. Dubs, tr., *Works of Hsuntze*, quoted in Creel, *CT*, p. 120.
25. Dubs, *Hsuntze*, in *ibid.*, pp. 120-121.
26. Dubs, *Hsuntze*, in *ibid.*, p. 125.
27. Duyvendak, trans., "Hsun-tzu on the Rectification of Names," quoted in *ibid.*, pp. 128-129.
28. *Ibid.*, p. 130.
29. *Ibid.*, p. 146.
30. Creel, *Confucius*, p. 216.
31. *Ibid.*

XXI. EMERGENCE OF NEO-CONFUCIANISM

1. Dubs, tr., *History of the Former Han Dynasty*, chap. 56; quoted in Fung, *Short History*, p. 205.
2. Creel, *Confucius*, p. 201.
3. Creel, *CT*, p. 177.
4. Fung, *Short History*, p. 138.
5. Hughes, *Chinese Philosophy in Classical Times*, p. 317.
6. Creel, *CT*, p. 184.
7. Hughes, *Classical Times*, pp. 335-336.
8. *Ibid.*, pp. 324-325.
9. Fung, *Short History*, pp. 210-211.

10. Creel, *CT*, pp. 192, 196-197.
11. *Ibid.*, p. 197.
12. Fung, *Short History*, pp. 235, 237-238.
13. Creel, *CT*, p. 195.
14. Fung, *Short History*, p. 307.
15. *Ibid.*, p. 298.
16. Gung-Hsing Wang, *The Chinese Mind*, pp. 136-137, quoted in Finegan, *Arch*, p. 379.
17. Chan, Wing-tsit, "The Story of Chinese Philosophy," in Moore, *Philosophy—East and West*, p. 64.
18. Fung, *Short History*, p. 316.
19. Shryock, *The Origin and Development of the State Cult of Confucius*, pp. 182, 184.

XXII. TAOISM, CONFUCIANISM, AND MODERN CHINA

1. *Chuang Tzu*, tr. by Giles, p. 5, quoted in Finegan, *Arch*, p. 395.
2. Finegan, *Arch*, p. 396; cf. Giles, *Taoist Teachings from the Book of Lieh Tzu*, pp. 50, 58-61, 90-92.
3. Fung, *Short History*, pp. 232-233.
4. Finegan, *Arch*, p. 397; Noss, *MR*, p. 330.
5. Hodous, "Taoism," in Jurji, *GR*, p. 32.
6. Chan, *Religious Trends*, pp. 151-152.
7. Noss, *MR*, pp. 329-331, presents a trustworthy account of Taoist history.
8. Wieger, *History of the Religious Beliefs and Philosophical Opinions in China*, pp. 395-401, *passim;* quoted in Noss, *MR*, p. 331.
9. Chan, *Trends*, p. 147.
10. Giles, *Confucianism and Its Rivals*, p. 221; cf. Finegan, *Arch*, p. 337.
11. Wieger, *Beliefs and Opinions*, p. 603; cf. Noss, *MR*, p. 333.
12. *Ibid.*
13. Finegan, *Arch*, p. 411; Giles, *Confucianism*, p. 221.
14. Finegan, *Arch*, p. 410, quoting Suzuki and Carus' translation of *T'ai-Shang Kan-Ying P'ien, Treatise of the Exalted One on Response and Retribution.*
15. Noss, *MR*, p. 334.
16. Finegan, *Arch*, p. 402; cf. Ling, *Journal of the North China Branch of the Royal Asiatic Society*, XLIX, 53-75, and Giles, *Chinese Biographical Dictionary*, s.v.
17. Chan, *Trends*, p. 145.
18. Noss, *MR*, p. 386.
19. Shryock, *State Cult*, p. 123.
20. Noss, *MR*, p. 386; cf. Shryock, *State Cult*, pp. 122-124.
21. Shryock, *State Cult*, pp. 97-99.
22. Finegan, *Arch*, p. 364; Hodous, "Confucianism," in Jurji, *GR*, p. 8. See Noss, *MR*, p. 394, and Shryock, *State Cult*, pp. 97-99.
23. Shryock, *State Cult*, p. 98.
24. *Ibid.*, pp. 99-100.
25. *Ibid.*, p. 120.

26. *Ibid.*, p. 138.
27. Finegan, *Arch*, p. 372.
28. Shryock, *State Cult*, pp. 189-190.
29. *Ibid.*, p. 188.
30. Creel, *CT*, p. 220.
31. Shryock, *State Cult*, p. 191.
32. *Ibid.*, p. 202.
33. *Ibid.*, p. 206.
34. Shryock, *State Cult*, pp. 169-171. The sacrifice is described in greater detail in the chapter cited here, pp. 165-176.
35. *Ibid.*, pp. 175-176. Shryock witnessed the sacrifice to Confucius conducted by officials of the Chinese Republic.
36. Mao Tse-tung, *China's New Democracy*, p. 61, quoted in Creel, *CT*, p. 255.
37. Creel, *CT*, pp. 256-257.

XXIII. SHINTO, THE JAPANESE RELIGION

1. Ballou, *Shinto*.
2. Oguchi, "The Religions of Japan," *Atlantic*, *CXCV* (January, 1955), 122.
3. Finegan, *Arch*, p. 424.
4. *Ibid.*, p. 421; see also Hara, *An Introduction to the History of Japan*, pp. 21-49.
5. Ballou, *Shinto*, pp. 7, 97.
6. Noss, *MR*, p. 401; Finegan, *Arch*, p. 430; *Kojiki*, Sect. XXX, in Ballou, *Shinto*, p. 98.
7. Ballou, *Shinto*, p. 7, citing Inazo Nitobe, *The Japanese Nation*, p. 52.
8. Aston, *A History of Japanese Literature*, pp. 6-9, 48.
9. Hara, *Introduction to the History of Japan* (*supra* n. 4), pp. 55-56; cf. Noss, *MR*, p. 406.
10. Aston, *Japanese Literature*, pp. 7, 9-13; Ballou, *Shinto*, pp. 116-118.
11. Aston, *Japanese Literature*, pp. 34-48; Ballou, *Shinto*, pp. 108-116.
12. Chan, *Religious Trends*, pp. 247-248, 257-258.
13. Holtom, "Shintoism," in Jurji, *GR*, p. 147.
14. Codrington, *The Melanesians, Studies in Their Anthropology*, p. 118.
15. Holtom, "Shintoism," p. 148, quoting from Toyokai Motoöri (ed.), *Motoöri Norinaga Zenshu* (Complete Works of Motoöri Norinaga) I, 150-152. See also Holtom, "The Meaning of Kami," *Monumenta Nipponica*, III, nos. 1 and 2, IV, no. 2, 1940-1941.
16. Holtom, "Shintoism," p. 149.
17. *Ibid.*, p. 151.
18. Finegan, *Arch*, p. 427.
19. *Kojiki*, Sect. III, tr. by Basil Hall Chamberlain, *Transactions of the Asiatic Society of Japan*, Suppl. to Vol. X, 1882.
20. *Kojiki*, Sect. IV.
21. *Kojiki*, Sect. V.
22. *Kojiki*, Sect. VI-X.

23. Ballou, *Shinto,* p. 20.
24. *Kojiki,* Sect. VI-X.
25. Anesaki, *History of Japanese Religion,* p. 27; cited hereafter as *JR.*
26. *Kojiki,* Sect. XII-XVI.
27. Finegan, *Arch,* p. 430; cf. Ballou, *Shinto,* p. 98; *Kojiki,* Sect. XXXIII.
28. Finegan, *Arch,* p. 433.
29. Ballou, *Shinto,* p. 20.
30. Holtom, *National Faith of Japan,* p. 113; cf. Noss, *MR,* p. 403.
31. Noss, *MR,* p. 403.
32. *Ibid.,* p. 405.
33. Kato, Genchi, *A Study of Shinto: The Religion of the Japanese Nation;* Holtom, "Shintoism," in Jurji, *GR,* p. 152.
34. Hara, *History of Japan,* p. 59.
35. Noss, *MR,* p. 405.
36. Anesaki, *JR,* pp. 52-53.
37. *Ibid.,* p. 53.
38. Ballou, *Shinto,* p. 91.
39. Finegan, *Arch,* p. 445.
40. Anesaki, *JR,* pp. 89, 99; cf. Finegan, *Arch,* pp. 444-445.
41. Anesaki, *JR,* p. 133; see also pp. 123-133, 137, 143.
42. *Ibid.,* p. 127; cf. Moore, *HR,* I, 120, 126.
43. Ballou, *Shinto,* p. 30.
44. Finegan, *Arch,* p. 451, gives the dates as 1185-1392 A.D., contrary to the usual report. Cf. Anesaki, *JR,* p. 167, and Okakura, *Awakening of Japan, passim.*
45. Japanese Constitution of 1889; Ballou, *Shinto,* p. 168.
46. Anesaki, *JR,* pp. 240-253.
47. *Ibid.,* p. 243.
48. *Ibid.,* p. 244, note; cf. Anesaki, *Religious Life of the Japanese People,* p. 97, and Noss, *MR,* p. 400, note.
49. Anesaki, *JR,* p. 247; Ballou, *Shinto,* p. 51, note.
50. Kuno, *Japanese Expansion on the Asiatic Continent.*
51. Ballou, *Shinto,* pp. 129-131.
52. Anesaki, *JR,* p. 250, note.
53. Okakura, *The Awakening of Japan,* p. 70; Ballou, *Shinto,* pp. 56-58.

XXIV. RELIGION AND NATIONALISM IN MODERN JAPAN

1. Anesaki, *Religious Life,* pp. 84-85; cf. Oguchi, "The Religions of Japan," *Atlantic,* CXCV (January, 1955), 122.
2. Anesaki, *Religious Life,* p. 73.
3. *Ibid.,* p. 74.
4. *Ibid.,* p. 57.
5. *Ibid.,* p. 58.
6. *Ibid.,* pp. 59-60.
7. *Ibid.,* p. 61.
8. Anesaki, *JR,* p. 214; cf. pp. 210-212.
9. Anesaki, *Religious Life,* p. 62.
10. *Ibid.,* p. 53.

11. Harper, Coates, and Ishizuka, *Honen, the Buddhist Saint.*
12. Anesaki, *Religious Life,* p. 54.
13. Anesaki, *JR,* pp. 279-280.
14. Noss, *MR,* pp. 422-423.
15. *Ibid.*
16. Anesaki, *JR,* p. 281; cf. pp. 280-283.
17. Anesaki, *JR,* pp. 237-238; Ballou, *Shinto,* p. 39.
18. Anesaki, *JR,* p. 307; Ballou, *Shinto,* pp. 45-46.
19. Ballou, *Shinto,* pp. 46-47.
20. Kamo-no-Mabuchi, "The Revival of Pure Shintau," tr. by Sir Ernest Satow, *Transactions of the Asiatic Society of Japan, Reprints,* Vol. II, 1927.
21. Young, *Rise of a Pagan State,* p. 181.
22. Anesaki, *Religious Life,* pp. 28-29.
23. *Ibid.,* pp. 26-35.
24. Ballou, *Shinto,* p. 76; Noss, *MR,* p. 421.
25. Ballou, *Shinto,* p. 206.
26. Holtom, "Shintoism," in Jurji, *GR,* p. 173.
27. Holtom, *Modern Japan and Shinto Nationalism,* pp. 4-5.
28. Ballou, *Shinto,* p. 65.
29. Noss, *MR,* pp. 411-412.
30. Anesaki, *Religious Life,* p. 16.
31. Holtom, "Shintoism," in Jurji, *GR,* pp. 170-171.
32. Anesaki, *Religious Life,* Plate 4 B.
33. Aston, *Japanese Literature,* p. 197.
34. *Ibid.,* pp. 199-214.

XXV. ZOROASTER, PROPHET OF IRAN

1. *Life,* XXX (May 21, 1951), 113-116.
2. Finegan, *Arch,* p. 75; Ferm, *Encyclopedia of Religion,* p. 49.
3. *Enc. Brit.,* XXIII (1950), 942, s.v. "Zend-Avesta."
4. *Ibid.*
5. Clemen, "Persian Religion," in Clemen, *Religions of the World,* p. 140.
6. *Ibid.,* p. 142.
7. *Ibid.*
8. *Ibid.*
9. *Ibid.,* p. 140.
10. Moore, *HR,* I, 359.
11. Jackson, *Zoroaster the Prophet of Ancient Iran,* p. 14 and Appendix I, pp. 147-149.
12. Jackson, *Zoroaster,* pp. 15-16, and Appendix II, p. 150; cf. Noss, *MR,* p. 437.
13. Finegan, *Arch,* pp. 77-85.
14. Trevor, *History of Ancient Civilization,* I, 112.
15. Jackson, *Zoroaster,* p. 27; cf. Ballou, *BW,* p. 650, citing Dinkard VII, chaps. I, II, III.
16. Jackson, *Zoroaster,* p. 31.
17. *Ibid.,* p. 32.

18. Yasna 46:11, in Jackson, *Zoroaster,* pp. 42-43.
19. Jackson, *Zoroaster,* p. 40.
20. *Ibid.,* p. 50.
21. *Ibid.,* p. 54.
22. *Ibid.,* pp. 95-96.

XXVI. DESTINY AND DECAY OF ZOROASTRIANISM

1. Yasna xliv.3-5,7, tr. by Moulton.
2. Yasna xxx.5, tr. by Moulton.
3. Yasna xxviii.1-2,7, tr. by Moulton.
4. Yasna xlv.2, from *The Hymns of Zoroaster,* tr. by Guthrie.
5. Yasna xxx.3-4,10, tr. by Moulton.
6. Yasna xxxi, based on Moulton but rearranged and paraphrased in Browne, *World's Great Scriptures,* pp. 364-365.
7. Moulton, *The Treasure of the Magi,* p. 37.
8. Finegan, Arch, p. 95; Kent, *Journal of Near Eastern Studies,* IV (1945), 41.
9. Jackson, *Zoroaster,* p. 60.
10. Farvardin Yast xxx.152, tr. by Darmesteter, *SBEA,* III B, 229.
11. Khorshed Yast vi.5, *SBEA,* III B, 86-87.
12. Farvardin Yast xxx.153-156, *SBEA,* III B, 229-230.
13. Dadistan-i Dinik xxi.3-9, tr. by West, *SBEA,* XI B, 48-49.
14. Dadistan-i Dinik xxvi.2-3; xxvii.2-3, *SBEA,* XI B, 57-58.
15. Bundahis xxx.7-10, tr. by West, *SBEA,* XI A, 123.
16. Müller, *SBE,* V, 248; Noss, *MR,* p. 456.
17. Noss, *MR,* pp. 452-453.
18. Yasna XII, tr. by Guthrie.
19. Zad-Sparam xxiv, tr. by West.
20. Vendidad, Fargard iii.1-6, tr. by Darmesteter, *SBEA,* III A, 22-24.
21. Vendidad, Fargard xiii.8-9, *SBEA,* III A, 157-158.
22. Vendidad, Fargard xv.20, *SBEA,* III A, 180.

XXVII. EARLY HEBREW TRADITION

1. Pfeiffer, *Introduction to the Old Testament,* pp. 159-167; cited hereafter as *Intro.*
2. Heidel, *The Gilgamesh Epic and Old Testament Parallels,* pp. 255-257; cf. Gen. 8:21. (All Biblical references are to the Revised Standard Version, 1946-1952).
3. Exod. 3:1-6, 13-15; notes e and f.
4. Bailey and Kent, *History of the Hebrew Commonwealth,* p. 3.
5. Hitti, *The Arabs,* p. 5.
6. *Ibid.,* p. 6.
7. Cf. Hastings, *ERE,* XI, 379-380; Barton, "Semites."
8. Della Vida, "America and the Arab Heritage," in Faris, ed., *Arab Heritage,* pp. 29, 34.
9. See Harmon, ed., *Interpreter's Bible,* I, 272-273; cited hereafter as *IB.*
10. Finegan, *Light,* p. 56.
11. Weber, *Ancient Judaism,* p. 3, *passim;* Finegan, *Light,* p. 57.

12. Cf. Albright, *Archaeology of Palestine,* pp. 236-237.
13. Wallis, *The Bible Is Human,* pp. 115-116.
14. *Ibid., passim.*

XXVIII. FROM EGYPT TO CANAAN

1. Gen. 46:27; Exod. 1:15; cf. 1:5-7; Deut. 26:5.
2. Gen. 48:21, 22; cf. Gen. 14:14.
3. Bailey and Kent, *Hebrew Commonwealth,* summarizing Albright in *ASOR, Bulletin* 58 (April, 1935).
4. *CAH,* II, 353-358, and p. 356, note 2.
5. Gen. 46:34; 47:1, 3, 4, 6; 15:13; Exod. 8:22; 9:23, 26.
6. Exod. 11:2; 12:13, 35, 36.
7. Exod. 14:21, 26; 15:1-21.
8. Gen. 19:1-19; 39:21; II Sam. 9:3; Hos. 6:6; Mic. 7:18; Psa. 33:18; 147:11.
9. Wallis, *Bible Is Human,* pp. 251-253.
10. Exod. 6:2, 3; cf. 3:13-15.
11. Jud. 1; 3:28; 4; 5; 7; 8; 11.
12. *IB,* I, 882; cf. Josh. 5:2ff.
13. Wallis, *Bible Is Human,* pp. 42-43.
14. *CAH,* II, 283-287 and 294-295.
15. Pfeiffer, *Intro.,* p. 320.

XXIX. RISE OF THE HEBREW MONARCHY

1. Wallis, *Bible Is Human,* p. 123.
2. Bailey and Kent, *Hebrew Commonwealth,* p. 98, noting the variant dates of Pfeiffer, Albright and Skinner.
3. *IB,* III, 44, on I Kings 3:16-27.
4. *IB,* III, 105-107, on I Kings 11:14-25.
5. Barrois, "Chronology, Metrology, Etc." in *IB,* I, 148. Barrois here follows Albright.

XXX. LEGACY OF ISRAEL

1. Sachar, *History of the Jews,* p. 148.
2. *Ibid.;* cf. Grayzel, *History of the Jews,* p. 208.
3. Cohen, *Everyman's Talmud,* Introduction, p. xxvi.
4. *Ibid.,* p. 3.

XXXI. THE JEWISH TORAH

1. Spinoza, *Tractatus Theologico-Politicus.* Preface.
2. See Bewer, *Literature of the Old Testament,* Chap. I.
3. Bentzen, *Introduction to the Old Testament,* I, 217; cited hereafter as *Intro.*
4. Pfeiffer, *Intro.,* p. 211.
5. Bentzen, *Intro.,* I, 222.

XXXII. THE PROPHETS

1. Bentzen, *Intro.*, II. 82.
2. Cf. Pfeiffer, *Intro.*, p. 296.
3. Bentzen, *Intro.*, II, 88.
4. *Ibid.*, pp. 93-94; cf. Pfeiffer, *Intro.*, p. 356.
5. Peiffer, *Intro.*, p. 600; cf. Bentzen, *Intro.*, II, 154.
6. Pfeiffer, *Intro.*, p. 596; Bentzen, *Intro.*, II, 149.
7. Bentzen, *Intro.*, II, 152.
8. Pfeiffer, *Intro.*, p. 492.
9. *Ibid.*, p. 470.
10. *Ibid.*, p. 459.
11. Bentzen, *Intro.*, II. 156.
12. Pfeiffer, *Intro.*, p. 604; cf. Bentzen, *Intro.*, II, 158.
13. Pfeiffer, *Intro.*, p. 586; Bentzen, *Intro.*, II, 144.
14. Pfeiffer, *Intro.*, p. 614; cf. Bentzen, *Intro.*, II, 162.
15. Pfeiffer, *Intro.*, pp. 575-576; cf. Bentzen *Intro.*, II, 136.
16. Bentzen, *Intro.*, II, 144.

XXXIII. "THE WRITINGS"

1. Pfeiffer, *Intro.*, p. 106.
2. *Ibid.*, pp. 811-812. Bentzen, *Intro.*, II, 215-216.
3. Bentzen, *Intro.*, II, 213-215; Pfeiffer, *Intro.*, pp. 808-811.
4. Ecclus. 49:11-13.
5. *IB*, III, 879.
6. Pfeiffer, *Intro.*, pp. 678-683; cf. Bentzen, *Intro.*, II, 178.
7. So believes Pfeiffer, *Intro.*, p. 637.
8. *Ibid.*, p. 632.
9. *Ibid.*, p. 630.
10. *Ibid.*, pp. 621-622.
11. Bentzen, *Intro.*, I, 20.
12. *Ibid.*, I, 21.
13. *Ibid.*, II, 236.

XXXIV. BEGINNING THE NEW TESTAMENT

1. Burrows, *The Dead Sea Scrolls*, pp. 347-415; Dupont-Sommer, *The Dead Sea Scrolls*, pp. 18-84; Sukenik, *The Dead Sea Scrolls of the Hebrew University*.
2. Cross, "The Scrolls from the Judaean Desert," *Archaeology*, IX (March, 1956), 41-53; Howlett, "Faith and History," *Atlantic Monthly*, CXCVII (April, 1956), 64-67; Burrows, *Scrolls*, p. 344; Wilson, *The Scrolls from the Dead Sea*, pp. 95-96; Dupont-Sommer, *The Jewish Sect of Qumran and the Essenes*, p. 151; Dupont-Sommer, *Scrolls*, pp. 85-100; Davies, *The Meaning of the Dead Sea Scrolls*. But see Graystone, *The Dead Sea Scrolls and the Originality of Christ*.
3. Barnett, *The New Testament, Its Making and Meaning*, p. 15; cited hereafter as *NT*.

4. Davies, *Meaning*, pp. 102-106.
5. Walker, *History of the Christian Church*, p. 49.
6. Latourette, *History of Christianity*, p. 85; Latourette, *History of the Expansion of Christianity*, I, 137-138.
7. Barnett, *NT*, pp. 23, 28, *passim.*
8. *Ibid.*, pp. 39-41.
9. *Ibid.*, p. 75.
10. *Ibid.*, pp. 79-81, 87.
11. *Ibid.*, pp. 87-89.

XXXV. THE GOSPELS AND ACTS

1. Grant, "Introduction to Mark," in *IB*, VII, 633.
2. *IB*, VII, 63-64.
3. Barnett, *NT*, p. 111, nn. 47 and 48; Gilmour, "Introduction to Luke," in *IB*, VIII, 16-18.
4. Barnett, *NT*, p. 118, n. 71; p. 119; cf. Taylor, *Formation of the Gospel Tradition.*
5. Barnett, *NT*, p. 95; Bacon, *Introduction to the New Testament*, p. 176.
6. Grant, *The Earliest Gospel*, p. 34.
7. *Ibid.*, p. 53.
8. Barnett, *NT*, p. 134.
9. Grant, "Introduction to Mark," in *IB*, VII, 637.
10. Translation from the Teubner text of *Annals*, XV, 44.
11. Grant, "Introduction to Mark," in *IB*, VII, 633.
12. Johnson, "Introduction to Matthew," in *IB*, VII, 240-241; Barnett, *NT*, pp. 150-152.
13. Eusebius, *Church History*, III, 39.16. See Schaff and Wace, *Nicene and Post-Nicene Fathers*, Series Two, Vol. I, p. 173; see Barnett, *NT*, p. 147.
14. *IB*, VII, 239-240; Barnett, *NT*, p. 148.
15. Barnett, *NT*, pp. 8, 152.
16. *Ibid.*, pp. 152-153; *IB*, VII, 231; Streeter, *Four Gospels*, pp. 500-523.
17. Wilson, *The Scrolls*, p. 89; Davies, *Meaning*, p. 104; Testament of the Twelve Patriarchs: Joseph I: 5-6.
18. Jerome, *Epistles* XX.4; Gilmour, "Introduction to Luke," in *IB*, VIII, 3.
19. Luke is favored by Barnett, and by Macgregor, "Introduction to Acts," in *IB*, IX, 6-9; a later author is favored by Gilmour, "Introduction to Luke," in *IB*, VIII, 9-10, and by Windisch, "The Case against the Traditions," *Beginnings of Christianity*, II, 298-348.
20. Streeter, *The Four Gospels*, pp. 531-539; Gilmour, "Introduction to Luke," in *IB*, VIII, 10.
21. Barnett, *NT*, p. 173.
22. *IB*, VIII, 7.
23. *Ibid.*, p. 15.

XXXVI. THE LATER NEW TESTAMENT

1. Goodspeed, *An Introduction to the New Testament,* p. 239; Barnett, *NT,* pp. 184-185; cf. Goodspeed, *The Meaning of Ephesians;* Barnett, *Paul Becomes a Literary Influence.*
2. Beare, "Introduction to Ephesians," in *IB,* X, 604.
3. Scott, *Literature of the New Testament,* p. 180; *The Epistles of Paul to the Collossians, to Philemon and to the Ephesians,* p. 121; cf. Beare, "Introduction to Ephesians," in *IB,* X, 599.
4. Barnett, *NT,* p. 195.
5. *Ibid.,* pp. 196-197; cf. Knox, *The Fourth Gospel and the Later Epistles,* p. 89.
6. Barnett, *NT,* pp. 206-210.
7. *Ibid.,* pp. 233-237.
8. Howard, "Introduction to John's Gospel," in *IB,* VIII, 450-451.
9. *Ibid.,* pp. 451-452; cf. Smart, *The Spiritual Gospel,* p. 24.
10. Barnett, *NT,* pp. 275-285.

XXXVII. THE CONTINUING CHRISTIAN TRADITION

1. Burrows, *Dead Sea Scrolls,* p. 294; Dupont-Sommer, *Dead Sea Scrolls,* p. 88; Dupont-Sommer, *Jewish Sect,* IX, 147-166; Davies, *Meaning,* p. 70.
2. Cross, "The Scrolls," *Archaeology,* IX (March, 1956), 44.
3. Schweitzer, *The Quest of the Historical Jesus,* pp. 357-358; Taylor, "The Life and Ministry of Jesus," in *IB,* VII, 125-126.
4. *IB,* VII, 129-130.
5. Latourette, *Expansion of Christianity,* I, 309-311; Spencer, *Beyond Damascus,* pp. 10-11.
6. Latourette, *Expansion of Christianity,* I, pp. 311-312.
7. Barnett, *NT,* p. 285, n. 55; Latourette, *History of Christianity,* p. 135.
8. Latourette, *History,* p. 167.

XXXVIII. THE RELIGION OF MUHAMMAD

1. Gibb, *Mohammedanism, An Historical Survey,* p. 22; cited hereafter as *Moh.;* cf. Jurji, *GR,* p. 214, where the earlier estimate was 275,000,000.
2. Andrae, *Mohammed: The Man and His Faith,* pp. 19-29; cited hereafter as *Moh.*
3. Ap. Syr. iii, p. 563 in Andrae, *Moh.,* pp. 120-121; cf. Sura 17, verses 31-36.
4. Andrae, *Moh.,* pp. 125-126.
5. Sura 28, verse 86, tr. Sale.
6. 75:16, tr. Palmer. The following passages from the Koran are tr. by Palmer in *SBEA,* VI, except in those cases indicated otherwise.
7. Andrae, *Moh.,* pp. 65-67.
8. 4:156.
9. Sura 1, tr. Rodwell.

10. Carlyle, *Heroes and Hero Worship,* pp. 86-89; cf. Gibb, *Moh.,* p. 36.
11. 7:156, tr. Rodwell.
12. Gibb, *Moh.,* p. 49.
13. *Ibid.,* pp. 50-51.
14. *Ibid.,* p. 75.
15. 10:99-100.
16. 18:55-56.
17. 32:13.
18. 19:20-22.
19. 2:139.
20. 78:31-36.
21. Tabari, Tafsir xxvii, p. 96, in Andrae, *Moh.,* p. 77.
22. Cf. 2:19-21.
23. Gibb, *Moh.,* pp. 62-63; cf. Andrae, *Moh.,* pp. 110-112.
24. "The Forty-Two Traditions of An-Nawawi," no. 26, tr. by Bishop.
25. 2:172.
26. 2:279, tr. Pickthall and Rodwell, who agree on this translation.
27. "The Forty-Two Traditions of An-Nawawi," no. 13, tr. Bishop.

XXXIX. EXPANSION OF ISLAM

1. Andrae, *Moh.,* pp. 196-199.
2. 2:213-214.
3. Andrae, *Moh.,* pp. 201-205.
4. 8:17.
5. 8:40.
6. Cf. 48:1; 3:141.
7. Andrae, *Moh.,* p. 228.
8. Gibb, *Moh.,* p. 111.
9. Hitti, *The Arabs,* pp. 157-158.
10. Quoted in Gibb, *Moh.,* p. 131.
11. 2:186.
12. 9:5, 29.
13. 3:163-164.
14. 2:257.

XL. PROSPECT

1. Kennick, "The Language of Religion," *Philosophical Review,* LXV (January, 1956), 56-71.
2. Schweitzer, *Christianity and the Religions of the World,* pp. 35-37, 73-80, 84.
3. Quoted from Mourant, *Readings in the Philosophy of Religion,* p 108.
4. Creel, *CT,* p. 130.
5. Santayana, *Reason in Religion,* chaps. XIII and XIV.
6. Butler, *The Analogy of Religion.*

Bibliography

Akhilananda, Swami. *Hindu Psychology*. New York: Harper and Brothers, 1946.

Albright, William Foxwell. *Archaeology of Palestine*. Richards Lectures at the University of Virginia, 1931. New York: Fleming H. Revell Co., 1932.

———. Bulletin 58, *ASOR*, April, 1935.

———. *From the Stone Age to Christianity*. Baltimore: Johns Hopkins Press, 1946.

Altheim, Franz. *History of Roman Religion*. London: Methuen and Co., 1938.

Ameer, 'Ali Maulavi Saiyid. *The Spirit of Islam*. Revised ed. London: Christophers, 1935.

Ancient Near Eastern Texts Relating to the Old Testament. James B. Pritchard, ed. Second Edition. Princeton: Princeton University Press, 1955.

Andrae, Tor. *Mohammed: The Man and His Faith*. Trans. by Theophil Menzel. New York: Charles Scribner's Sons, 1936.

Anesaki, M. *History of Japanese Religion*. London: Routledge and Kegan Paul, 1930.

———. *Religious Life of the Japanese People*. Series on Japanese Life and Culture, vol. II. Tokyo: Society for International Cultural Relations, 1938.

Angus, Samuel. *The Mystery Religions and Christianity*. London: John Murray, 1925.

———. *Religious Quests of the Graeco-Roman World*. London: John Murray, 1929.

Archer, John Clark. *Faiths Men Live By*. New York: Thomas Nelson and Sons, 1934.

———. *The Sikhs in Relation to Hindus, Moslems, Christians and Ahmadiyyas*. Princeton: Princeton University Press, 1946.

Arnold, Edwin. *The Light of Asia*. Chicago: Homewood, n.d.

Ashvaghosha, *Discourses on the Awakening of Faith in the Mahayana*. Trans. by Daisetz T. Suzuki. Chicago: Open Court Publishing Co., 1900.

Aston, W. G. *A History of Japanese Literature*. New York: Appleton, 1899.

Avalon (Woodroffe, Sir John G., q.v.).

Avey, Albert Edwin. *Historical Method in Bible Study*. New York: Charles Scribner's Sons, 1924.

Bacon, Benjamin W. *An Introduction to the New Testament*. New York: The Macmillan Company, 1924.

Bailey, Albert Edward and Charles Foster Kent. *History of the Hebrew Commonwealth*. Revised ed. New York: Charles Scribner's Sons, 1949.

Bailey, Cyril. *Phases in the Religion of Ancient Rome*. Berkeley: University of California Press, 1932.

Bakewell, C. M. *Source Book in Ancient Philosophy*. Revised ed. New York: Charles Scribner's Sons, 1939.

Ballou, R. O. *Shinto: The Unconquered Enemy*. New York: The Viking Press, 1945.

Bardothodol. *The Tibetan Book of the Dead*. Edited by W. Y. Evans-Wentz. New York: Oxford University Press, 1949.

Barnett, Albert E. *The New Testament: Its Making and Meaning*. New York: Abingdon-Cokesbury Press, 1946.

Baronte, Gervee [Mrs. Charles Breckenridge]. *Twilight in India*. New York: Philosophical Library, 1949.

Bentzen, Aage. *Introduction to the Old Testament*. 2nd ed. Copenhagen: Gad, 1952.

Bernard, Theos. *Hindu Philosophy*. New York: Philosophical Library, 1947.

Bettenson, Henry J., ed. *Documents of the Christian Church*. London: Oxford University Press, 1947.

Bewer, Julius A. *The Literature of the Old Testament in its Historical Development*. New York: Columbia University Press, 1922.

Bhagavad-Gita: The Song of God. Trans. by Swami Prabhavananda and Christopher Isherwood. Hollywood: Marcel Rodd, 1944.

Bhagavadgita. Trans. by S. Radhakrishnan. New York: Harper and Brothers, 1948.

Bible of the World. Edited by R. O. Ballou and F. Spiegelberg. New York: Viking Press, 1939.

Bible: *The Complete Bible*. Trans. by Smith and Goodspeed. Chicago: University of Chicago Press, 1939.

Bible: *Holy Bible*, Revised Standard Version. New York: Thomas Nelson and Sons, 1952.

Bishop, Eric F. F., tr. "The Forty-Two Traditions of An-Nawawi," *The Moslem World*, XXIX (April, 1939) 163-177. Published by the Hartford Seminary Foundation, Hartford, Connecticut.

Blakney, R. B. *The Way of Life: Lao Tzu*. A new translation of the *Tao Teh Ching*. A Mentor Book. New York: New American Library of World Literature, 1955.

Blegen, Carl W., John L. Caskey, and Marian Rawson. *University of Cincinnati Excavations in the Troad, 1932-1938*. Princeton: Princeton University Press, 1952.

Book of the Dead, trans. by E. A. Wallis Budge. Second edition. New York: E. P. Dutton and Co., 1923.

Breasted, James Henry. *The Dawn of Conscience*. New York: Charles Scribner's Sons, 1947.

Brightman, Edgar Sheffield. *A Philosophy of Religion*. New York: Prentice-Hall, 1945.

Brown, Brian. *The Wisdom of the Hindus*. New York: Brentano's, 1921.

Browne, Lewis. *The World's Great Scriptures*. New York: The Macmillan Company, 1946.

Bruce, Joseph Percy. *Chu Hsi and His Masters*. London: Arthur Probsthain, 1923.
Buddha. *Further Dialogues of the Buddha*. Vol. I. Trans. by Robert Chalmers, from the Majjhima Nikaya, for the Pali Text Society. London: Oxford University Press, 1926.
Burnet, John. *Greek Philosophy*. London: The Macmillan Company, 1914.
Burrows, Millar. *The Dead Sea Scrolls*. New York: Viking Press, 1955.
Burtt, E. A. *The Teachings of the Compassionate Buddha*. New York: New American Library of World Literature, 1955.
Butler, Joseph. *The Analogy of Religion*. New York: E. P. Dutton and Co., 1927.
Cadbury, Henry Joel. *Jesus: What Manner of Man?* New York: The Macmillan Company, 1947.
Cambridge Ancient History. J. B. Bury, S. A. Cook and F. E. Adcock, eds. Cambridge: Cambridge University Press, 1923-1939.
Carlyle, Thomas. *Heroes, Hero-Worship and the Heroic in History*. New York: The Macmillan Company, 1921.
Carus, Paul. *The Gospel of Buddha*. Chicago: Open Court Publishing Co., 1917.
———. *The Canon of Reason and Virtue, being Lao-tze's Tao Teh King*. Chicago: Open Court Publishing Co., 1927.
Case, Shirley Jackson. *Jesus: A New Biography*. Chicago: University of Chicago Press, 1927.
Cassirer, Ernst. *Language and Myth*. Trans. by Susanne K. Langer. New York: Harper and Brothers, 1946.
Chan, Wing-tsit. *Religious Trends in Modern China*. New York: Columbia University Press, 1953.
Chiera, Edward. *They Wrote on Clay*. Chicago: University of Chicago Press, 1938.
Chuang Tzu, Mystic, Moralist, and Social Reformer, tr. Herbert A. Giles. Second edition. Shanghai: Kelly and Walsh, 1926.
Chuang-Tzu. *Musings of a Chinese Mystic*. Trans. by Lionel Giles. Wisdom of the East series. London: John Murray, 1906.
Ch'u Ta-Kao, tr. *Tao Teh Ching*. London: The Buddhist Lodge, 1937.
Clemen, Carl C. *Religions of the World*. Trans. by A. K. Dallas. New York: Harcourt-Brace and Co., 1931.
Codrington, Robert H. *The Melanesians: Studies in Their Anthropology*. Oxford: Clarendon Press, 1891.
Coe, George Albert. *The Psychology of Religion*. Chicago: University of Chicago Press, 1916.
Cohen, A., ed. *Everybody's Talmud*. New York: E. P. Dutton and Co., 1932.
Confucius. *The Analects of Confucius*. Trans. by Arthur Waley. London: George Allen and Unwin, 1938. Reprinted 1945.
Conze, Edward, ed. *Buddhist Texts through the Ages*. New York: Philosophical Library, 1954.
Coomaraswamy, Ananda Kentish. *Hinduism and Buddhism*. New York: Philosophical Library, 1943.
Creel, Herrlee Glessner. *The Birth of China*. New York: Raynal and Hitchcock, 1937.

———. *Chinese Thought: From Confucius to Mao Tse-tung.* Chicago: University of Chicago Press, 1953.
———. *Confucius: The Man and the Myth.* New York: The John Day Company, 1949.
Cross, Frank M. "The Scrolls from the Judaean Desert," *Archaeology,* IX (March, 1956), 41-53.
Dasgupta, Surendranath. *Indian Mysticism.* Chicago: The Open Court Publishing Co., 1927.
———. *History of Indian Philosophy.* Cambridge: Cambridge University Press, 1932.
Davids, Mrs. Rhys, and F. L. Woodward. *Kindred Sayings* (Samyutta), 3 vols. London: Oxford University Press, 1917, 1922, 1925.
Davids, Mrs. Rhys. *A Manual of Buddhism.* New York: The Macmillan Company, 1932.
Davies, A. Powell. *The Meaning of the Dead Sea Scrolls.* New York: New American Library of World Literature, 1956.
Dhalla, Maneckji Nusservanji. *History of Zoroastrianism.* New York: Oxford University Press, 1938.
Dhammapada, The. Trans. by Irving Babbitt. New York: Oxford University Press, 1936.
Diels, H. *Fragmente der Vorsokratiker.* 5th ed. Berlin: Weidmann, 1934.
Dnyaneshwar, Maharaj. *Gita Explained.* Trans. by Manu Subedar. 3rd ed. Bombay: Kodak House, 1945.
Donaldson, Dwight M. *The Shi'ite Religion.* London: Luzac, 1933.
Dubs, Homer H., trans. *The Works of Hsuntze, Translated from the Chinese, with Notes.* Probsthain's Oriental Series. London: Probsthain, 1928.
———. *History of the Former Han Dynasty,* Vol. II. Baltimore: Waverly Press, 1944.
Ducasse, C. J. *A Philosophical Scrutiny of Religion.* New York: Ronald Press, 1953.
Dunham, James H. *The Religion of Philosophers.* Philadelphia: University of Pennsylvania Press, 1947.
Dupont-Sommer, Andre. *The Dead Sea Scrolls.* Oxford: Basil Blackwell and Mott, 1952.
———. *The Jewish Sect of Qumran and the Essenes.* New York: The Macmillan Company, 1954.
Duyvendak, J. J. L., trans. "Hsun-tzu on the Rectification of Names," *T'oung Pao,* XXIII, 221-254. Leyden: 1924.
Eddington, Arthur Stanley. *The Expanding Universe.* New York: The Macmillan Company, 1933.
———. *Nature of the Physical World.* Cambridge: Cambridge University Press, 1928.
Epictetus. *Discourse.* Trans. by Hasting Crowell. London: The Macmillan Company, 1903.
Erman, Adolph. *The Literature of the Ancient Egyptians.* Trans. by Aylward M. Blackman. London: Methuen and Co., 1927.
Evans, Arthur. *The Palace of Minos,* Vol. I. London: Macmillan & Co., 1921.
Faris, Nabih Amin, ed. *The Arab Heritage.* Princeton: Princeton University Press, 1944.

Feibleman, James. *The Theory of Human Culture*. New York: Duell, Sloan, and Pearce, 1946.

Ferm, Vergilius T. A., ed. *An Encyclopedia of Religion*. New York: Philosophical Library, 1945.

———. *Forgotten Religions*. New York: Philosophical Library, 1950.

———. *Religion in the Twentieth Century*. New York: Philosophical Library, 1948.

Ferre, Nels F. S. *Faith and Reason*. New York: Harper and Brothers, 1946.

Fifteen Greek Plays. Trans. by Gilbert Murray and others; introduction by Lane Cooper. New York: Oxford University Press, 1943.

Finegan, Jack. *The Archeology of World Religions*. Princeton: Princeton University Press, 1952.

———. *Light from the Ancient Past*. Princeton: Princeton University Press, 1946.

Foakes-Jackson, F. J. and Korsopp Lake, eds. *Beginnings of Christianity*. 2 vols. London: The Macmillan Company, 1920-1933.

Fosdick, Harry Emerson. *A Guide to Understanding the Bible*. New York: Harper and Brothers, 1938.

———. *The Modern Use of the Bible*. New York: The Macmillan Company, 1925.

Frankfort, Henri. *Ancient Egyptian Religion*. New York: Columbia University Press, 1948.

———. *Kingship and the Gods*. Chicago: University of Chicago Press, 1948.

Frazer. James G. *The Golden Bough*. 3rd ed. 12 vols. New York: The Macmillan Company, 1911-1915.

Freeman, Kathleen. *Ancilla to the Pre-Socratic Philosophers*. Cambridge: Harvard University Press, 1948.

Fromm, Erich. *Psychoanalysis and Religion*. New Haven: Yale University Press, 1950.

Fung Yu-lan. *History of Chinese Philosophy*. 2 vols. Trans. by Derk Bodde. Princeton: Princeton University Press, 1952-1953.

———. *A Short History of Chinese Philosophy,* ed. by Derk Bodde. New York: The Macmillan Company, 1948.

———. *The Spirit of Chinese Philosophy*. Trans. by E. R. Hughes. London: Routledge and Kegan Paul, 1944.

Gandhi, Mohandas K. *Young India*. New York: Viking Press, 1927.

Garnett, Arthur Campbell. *God in Us*. Chicago: Willett Clark and Co., 1945.

Gaster, Theodor Herzel. *The Oldest Stories in the World*. New York: Viking Press, 1952.

Gibb, H. A. R. *Mohammedanism: An Historical Survey*. London: Oxford University Press, 1953.

Giles, Herbert A. *Chinese Biographical Dictionary*. London: Quaritch, 1898.

———. *Confucianism and Its Rivals*. New York: Charles Scribner's Sons, 1915.

Giles, Lionel. *Sayings of Lao Tzu*. London: John Murray, 1905.

———. *Taoist Teachings from the Book of Lieh Tzu*. London: John Murray, 1912.

Goldin, Hyman Elias. *A Treasury of Jewish Holidays*. New York: Twayne Publishers, 1952.
Golub, Jacob S. *Israel in Canaan*. Cincinnati: Union of American Hebrew Congregations, 1930.
Goodspeed, Edgar J. *An Introduction to the New Testament*. Chicago: University of Chicago Press, 1937.
———. *The Meaning of Ephesians*. Chicago: University of Chicago Press, 1933.
———. *The Story of the Old Testament*. Chicago: University of Chicago Press, 1934.
Goshal, Juman. *The People of India*. New York: Sheridan House, 1944.
Grant, Frederick C. *The Earliest Gospel*. New York: Abingdon-Cokesbury Press, 1943.
Graystone, Geoffrey. *The Dead Sea Scrolls and the Originality of Christ*. New York: Sheed and Ward, 1956.
Grayzel, Solomon. *History of the Jews, from the Babylonian Exile to the End of World War II*. Philadelphia: Jewish Publication Society, 1947.
Grenier, Albert. *The Roman Spirit in Religion, Thought and Art*. London: Kegan Paul, 1926.
Griffith, Ralph T. H., tr. *Hymns of the Rig-Veda*. 2 vols. Benares: E. J. Lazarus and Company, 1896.
Guthrie, Kenneth S., trans. *The Hymns of Zoroaster*. Brooklyn: Comparative Literature, 1914.
Halidah, Adib. *Inside India*. London: George Allen and Unwin, 1937.
Hara, Katsuro. *Introduction to the History of Japan*. New York: G. P. Putnam's Sons, 1920.
Harper, Havelock Coates, and Ryugaku Ishizuka. *Honen, the Buddhist Saint*. Kyoto: Chionin, 1925.
Harrison, Jane Ellen, *Mythology*. Boston: Marshall Jones Co., 1924.
Hartog, Mabel Helene (Kisch). *India in Outline*. Cambridge: Cambridge University Press, 1945.
Hartshorne, Charles. *The Divine Relativity*. New Haven: Yale University Press, 1948.
Hastings, James, ed. *Encyclopedia of Religion and Ethics*. 13 vols. New York: Charles Scribner's Sons, 1924-1927.
Hawkridge, Emma. *Indian Gods and Kings*. New York: Houghton Mifflin Co., 1935.
Hayes, William Christopher. *The Scepter of Egypt*. New York: Harper and Brothers, 1953.
Heidel, Alexander. *The Gilgamesh Epic and Old Testament Parallels*. 2nd ed. Chicago: University of Chicago Press, 1949.
Herodotus, *A New and Literal Translation,* by Henry Cary. New York: Harper and Brothers, 1859.
Herzl, Theodor. *The Jewish State*. Trans. by Sylvie d'Avigdor. London: Central Office Zionist Organization, 1936.
Hitti, Philip K. *The Arabs: A Short History*. Princeton: Princeton University Press, 1944.
———. *History of the Arabs*. London: The Macmillan Company, 1937.
Hodous, Lewis. *Folkways in China*. London: Probsthain, 1929.
Holtom, Daniel. *Modern Japan and Shinto Nationalism*. Revised ed. Chicago: University of Chicago Press, 1947.

———. *The National Faith of Japan*. London: Kegan Paul, 1938.
Homer. *Iliad*. Trans. by William B. Smith and Walter Miller. New York: The Macmillan Company, 1944.
———. *Odyssey of Homer*. Trans. by S. H. Butcher and A. Lang. New York: The Macmillan Company, 1888.
———. Odyssey. Trans. by J. W. Mackail. Oxford: Clarendon Press, 1932.
———. *Odyssey*. Trans. by A. T. Murray. 2 vols. Cambridge: Harvard University Press, 1919.
———. *Odyssey*. Trans. by T. E. Shaw, New York: Oxford University Press, 1932.
Hooton, Earnest Albert. *Twilight of Man*. New York: G. P. Putnam and Sons, 1939.
Hopkins, Edward Washburn. *The Religions of India*. Boston: Ginn and Co., 1895.
Howlett, D. "Faith and History," *Atlantic Monthly*, CXCVII (April, 1956), 64-67.
Hoyle, Fred. *The Nature of the Universe*. New York: Harper and Brothers, 1951.
Hughes, Ernest Richard, trans. and ed., *Chinese Philosophy in Classical Times*. New York: E. P. Dutton and Co., 1942.
Humphries, Christine, ed. *The Mahatma Letters to A. P. Sinnett*. London: Unwin, 1923.
Inge, William Ralph. *God and the Astronomers*. London: Longmans, Green and Co., 1933.
Interpreter's Bible. George A. Buttrick, and others, eds. 12 vols. New York: Abingdon-Cokesbury Press, 1952-1957.
Iqbal, Muhammad. *The Reconstruction of Religious Thought in Islam*. London: Oxford University Press, 1934.
Izzeddin, Neyla. *The Arab World*. Chicago: Henry Regnery Co., 1953.
Jack, Homer A., ed. *The Wit and Wisdom of Gandhi*. Boston: Beacon Press, 1951.
Jackson, Abraham V. Williams. *Zoroaster the Prophet of Ancient Iran*. London: The Macmillan Company, 1899.
———. *Zoroastrian Studies*. New York: Columbia University Press, 1928.
Jeans, James Hopwood *Through Space and Time*. New York: The Macmillan Company, 1934.
Jeffery, Arthur. *The Qur'an as Scripture*. New York: Russel F. Moore Co., 1952.
Jones, W. T. *History of Western Philosophy*. 2 vols. New York: Harcourt-Brace and Co., 1952.
Jurji, Edward Jabra, ed. *The Great Religions of the Modern World*. Princeton: Princeton University Press, 1946.
Kamo-no-Mabuchi. "The Revival of Pure Shintau," trans. by Sir Ernest Satow, *Transactions of the Asiatic Society of Japan, Reprints,* Vol. II. London: Kegan Paul, Trench, Trubner and Co., 1927.
Kant, Immanuel. *Religion within the Limits of Reason Alone*. Trans. by T. M. Green and H. H. Hudson. Chicago: Open Court Publishing Co., 1934.
Karsten, Rafael. *The Origins of Religion*. London: Routledge and Kegan Paul, 1935.

Kato, Genchi. *A Study of Shinto: The Religion of the Japanese Nation.* Tokyo: Meiji Japan Society, 1926.
Kegley, Charles W. and Robert W. Bretall, eds. *The Theology of Paul Tillich.* New York: The Macmillan Company, 1952.
Kent, Roland G. "Darius Inscriptions." *Journal of Near Eastern Studies,* IV (1945), 41.
Klausner, Joseph. *From Jesus to Paul.* Trans. by W. F. Stinespring. New York: The Macmillan Company, 1943.
———. *Jesus of Nazareth.* New York: The Macmillan Company, 1925.
Knox, John. *The Fourth Gospel and the Later Epistles.* New York: Abingdon-Cokesbury Press, 1945.
Koran (Qur'an), *The.* Trans. by E. H. Palmer in *Sacred Books of the East,* Vol. VI. New York: Charles Scribner's Sons, 1900.
Koran: Meaning of the Glorious Koran. Trans. by Mohammed M. Pickthall. New York: New American Library of World Literature, 1953.
Koran, The. Trans. by J. M. Rodwell. Everyman's Library. New York: E. P. Dutton and Co., 1909.
Koran, The. Trans. by George Sale. 5th ed. Philadelphia: J. B. Lippincott and Co., 1859.
Kramer, Samuel Nathan. *Sumerian Mythology.* Philadelphia: American Philosophical Society, 1944.
Kroeber, Alfred L. and T. T. Waterman. *Source Book in Anthropology.* Berkeley: University of California Press, 1920.
Kuno, Yoshi S. *Japanese Expansion on the Asiatic Continent.* Berkeley: University of California Press, 1937.
Langdon, Stephen Herbert. *Semitic Mythology.* Boston: Marshall Jones Co., 1931.
Latourette, Kenneth Scott. *The Chinese: Their History and Culture,* New York: The Macmillan Company, 1926.
———. *History of Christianity.* New York: Harper and Brothers, 1953.
———. *A History of the Expansion of Christianity.* 7 vols. 6th ed. New York: Harper and Brothers, 1937-1945.
Legge, James. *Chinese Classics.* Boston: Houghton, Mifflin and Company, 1882.
Leuba, James H. *A Psychological Study of Religion.* New York: The Macmillan Company, 1912.
Lieh Tzu. *Taoist Teachings from the Book of Lieh Tzu.* Trans. by Lionel Giles. London: John Murray, 1912.
Lin Yutang. *The Wisdom of China and India.* New York: Random House, 1942.
———. *The Wisdom of Confucius.* New York: Random House, 1938.
———. *The Wisdom of Laotse.* New York: Modern Library Series. Random House, 1948.
Lorimer, Helen L. *Homer and the Monuments.* London: The Macmillan Company, 1950.
Lowie, Robert H. *An Introduction to Cultural Anthropology.* New York: Farrar and Rinehart, 1940.
———. *Primitive Religion.* London: Routledge, 1925.
Luquet, Georges Henri. *The Art and Religion of Fossil Man.* Trans. by J. T. Russell, Jr. New Haven: Yale University Press, 1930.
MacNair, Hartley F. *China.* Berkeley: University of California Press, 1951.

Mao Tse-tung. *China's "New Democracy."* Bombay: Peoples, 1944.
Martineau, James. *A Study of Religion, Its Sources and Contents.* Oxford: Clarendon Press, 1900.
McGiffert, Arthur Cushman. *A History of Christian Thought.* New York: Charles Scribner's Sons, 1932-1933.
McNeile, A. H. *Introduction to the Study of the New Testament.* 2nd ed. Revised by C. S. C. Williams. Oxford: Clarendon Press, 1953.
Mei Yi-Pao. *Mo Tzu: The Neglected Rival of Confucius.* London: Arthur Probsthain, 1934.
Mendelsohn, Isaac. *Religions of the Ancient Near East, Sumero-Akkadian Religious Texts and Ugaritic Epics.* New York: Liberal Arts Press, 1955.
Millikan, Robert A. *Evolution and Science in Religion.* London: Oxford University Press, 1927.
———. *Science and Life.* Boston: Pilgrim Press, 1924.
Moore, Charles A., ed. *Philosophy—East and West.* Princeton: Princeton University Press, 1944.
Moore, Frank G. *The Roman's World.* New York: Columbia University Press, 1936.
Moore, George F. *History of Religions.* 2 vols. New York: Charles Scribner's Sons, 1922-1937.
Moshan, Ali. *Oriental Literature; or, The Dabistan Translated from Persian.* Trans. by David O'Shea and Anthony Troyer. New York: Tudor Publishing Co., 1937.
Motoöri, Toyokai, ed. *Motoöri Norinaga Zenshu* (Complete Works of Motoöri Norinaga). Tokyo, 1901.
Mo Tzu. *The Ethical and Political Works of Motse.* Trans. by Mei Yi-Pao. London: Probsthain, 1930.
Moulton, James H. *Early Zoroastrianism.* London: George Allen and Unwin; Williams and Norgate, 1913.
———. *The Treasure of the Magi.* London: Oxford University Press, 1917.
Mourant, John A. *Readings in the Philosophy of Religion.* New York: Crowell, 1954.
Müller, Max. *Sacred Books of the East.* 50 vols. Oxford: Clarendon Press, 1879-1897.
Muhtar-Katircioglu, Mahmud. *Wisdom of the Qur'an.* London: Oxford University Press, 1937.
Murray, Gilbert. *Five Stages of Greek Religion.* New York: Columbia University Press, 1930.
Murray, Margaret Alice. *The Splendour That Was Egypt.* London: Sidgwick and Jackson, 1949.
Mylonas, George and Doris Raymond, eds. *Studies Presented to David M. Robinson.* 2 vols. St. Louis: Washington University, 1951-1953.
Myres, J. L. *Who Were the Greeks?* Berkeley: University of California Press, 1930.
Nies, James B. and Clarence E. Keiser. *Historical, Religious, and Economic Texts and Antiquities.* 2 vols. New Haven: Yale University Press, 1920.
Nikhilananda, Swami. *Essence of Hinduism.* Boston: Beacon Press, 1948.
———, ed. and trans. *The Upanishads.* 2 vols. New York: Harper and Brothers, 1949, 1952.

———. *Vivekananda: The Yogas and Other Works*. New York: Ramakrishna-Vivekananda Center, 1953.
Nilsson, Martin P. *Greek Piety*. Trans. by H. J. Rose. Oxford: Clarendon Press, 1949.
———. *Greek Popular Religion*. New York: Columbia University Press, 1940.
———. *History of Greek Religion*. Trans. by F. J. Pielden. Oxford: Clarendon Press, 1925.
———. *The Mycenaean Origin of Greek Mythology*. Berkeley: University of California Press, 1932.
Noss, John B. *Man's Religions*. Revised Edition. New York: The Macmillan Company, 1956.
Obermann, Julian. *Ugaritic Mythology*. New Haven: Yale University Press, 1948.
Oesterley, W. O. E. and Theodore H. Robinson. *Hebrew Religion, Its Origin and Development*. 2nd ed. New York: The Macmillan Company, 1937.
Okakura, Kakuzo. *The Awakening of Japan*. New York: Century Co., 1904.
———. *Ideals of the East, with Special Reference to the Art of Japan*. London: John Murray, 1920.
Old, Walter Gorn. *The Simple Way: Laotze*. Philadelphia: David McKay Company, 1913.
Olmstead, A. T. E. *Jesus in the Light of History*. New York: Charles Scribner's Sons, 1942.
Oshima, Masanori. *Japan from Within*. Tokyo: Hokuseido, 1940.
Oxford Book of Greek Verse in Translation, The. Ed. by T. F. Higham and C. M. Bowra. Oxford: Clarendon Press, 1938.
Patterson, Charles. *The Philosophy of the Old Testament*. New York: Ronald Press, 1953.
Peet, T. Eric. *A Comparative Study of the Literatures of Egypt, Palestine, and Mesopotamia*. London: Oxford University Press, 1931.
Perkins, Ann L. *Comparative Archaeology of Early Mesopotamia*. Chicago: University of Chicago Press, 1949.
Perry, Ralph Barton. *Realms of Value*. Cambridge: Harvard University Press, 1954.
Persson, Axel W. *The Religion of Greece in Prehistoric Times*. Berkeley: University of California Press, 1942.
Pfeiffer, Robert H. *Introduction to the Old Testament*. 2nd ed. New York: Harper and Brothers, 1941.
Pratt, James Bissett. *India and Its Faiths*. New York: Houghton Mifflin Company, 1915.
———. *The Pilgrimage of Buddhism*. New York: The Macmillan Company, 1928.
———. *The Religious Consciousness*. New York: The Macmillan Company, 1946.
Prentice, William Kelly. *The Ancient Greeks*. Princeton: Princeton University Press, 1940.
Radhakrishnan, Sarvepalli. *The Dhammapada*. London: Oxford University Press, 1950.
———. *Eastern Religions and Western Thought*. London: Oxford University Press, 1940.

———. *Indian Philosophy*. 2nd ed. 2 vols. London: George Allen and Unwin; New York: The Macmillan Company, 1948.

———, ed. and trans. *The Principal Upanishads*. New York: Harper and Brothers, 1953.

———. *Religion and Society*. London: George Allen and Unwin, 1947.

Ramakrishna. *The Sayings of Ramakrishna*. Abhedananda. New York: The Vedanta Society, 1903.

Raphael, Max. *Prehistoric Pottery and Civilization in Egypt*. Bollingen Series 8. New York: Pantheon Books, 1947.

Raven, Charles. *Natural Religion and Christian Theology*. Gifford Lectures, 1951. Cambridge: Cambridge University Press, 1953.

Rose, Herbert J. *Primitive Culture in Italy*. London: Methuen, 1926.

Rowley, Harold Henry. *From Joseph to Joshua: Biblical Traditions in the Light of Archaeology*. London: Oxford University Press, 1950.

Russell, Bertrand. *Religion and Science*. New York: Henry Holt and Co., 1935.

Sachar, Abram Leon. *History of the Jews*. 2nd ed., revised to 1940. New York: Alfred A. Knopf, 1943.

Sacred Books of the East. Edited by Max Müller. American Edition. 12 vols. New York: Charles Sribner's Sons, 1897-1901.

Santayana, George. *Reason in Religion* (series in The Life of Reason). New York: Charles Scribner's Sons, 1905.

Schaeffer, Henry. *Social Legislation of the Primitive Semites*. New Haven: Yale University Press, 1915.

Schaff, Philip, and Henry Wace, eds. *Select Library of Nicene and Post-Nicene Fathers of the Christian Church*. Two series, 14 vols. each. New York: Charles Scribner's Sons, 1892-1900.

Schilpp, Paul A., ed. *The Philosophy of Sarvepalli Radhakrishnan*. New York: Tudor Publishing Co., 1952.

Schleiermacher, Friedrich E. D. *On Religion: Speeches to Its Cultured Despisers*. Trans. by John Oman. London: Kegan Paul, 1893.

Schmidt, Wilhelm. *Origin and Growth of Religion*. Trans. by H. J. Rose. London: Methuen, 1931.

Scholem, Gershon Gerhard. *Major Trends in Jewish Mysticism*. Jerusalem: Schocken House, 1941.

Schuchert, Charles and Carl Dunbar. *Outlines of Historical Geology*. 3rd ed. New York: John Wiley and Sons, 1937.

Schweitzer, Albert. *Christianity and the Religions of the World*. Trans. by Johanna Powers. New York: The Macmillan Company, 1923.

———. *The Quest of the Historical Jesus*. New York: The Macmillan Company, 1948.

Scott, Ernest Finley. *The Epistles of Paul to the Colossians, to Philemon, and to the Ephesians*. London: Hodder and Stoughton, 1930.

———. *The Literature of the New Testament*. New York: Columbia University Press, 1932.

Sellars, Roy Wood. *Religion Coming of Age*. New York: The Macmillan Company, 1928.

Sen, Gertrude Emerson. *The Pageant of India's History*. New York: Longmans, Green and Co., 1948.

Shean, Vincent. *Lead Kindly Light*. New York: Union House, 1949.

Shryock, John K. *The Origin and Development of the State Cult of Confucius*. New York: The Century Co., 1932.

Siqueira, T. N. *The Education of India.* London: Oxford University Press, 1952.

Smart, W. A. *The Spiritual Gospel.* New York: Abingdon-Cokesbury Press, 1946.

Smith, Vincent Arthur. *The Early History of India.* 4th ed. Oxford: Clarendon Press, 1924.

———. *The Edicts of Asoka.* Edited in English with an Introduction and Commentary. Broad Campden: Essex House Press, 1909.

Sorokin, Pitirim A. *Social Philosophies of an Age of Crisis.* Boston: Beacon Press, 1950.

Spence, Lewis. *Myths and Legends of Ancient Egypt.* London: George G. Harrap and Co., 1915.

Spencer, F. A. *Beyond Damascus: A Biography of Paul the Tarsian.* New York: Harper and Brothers, 1934.

Spinoza, Benedict. *Tractatus Theologico-Politicus.* London: Trubner, 1862.

Stace, Walter T. *Religion and the Modern Mind.* Philadelphia: J. B. Lippincott Co., 1952.

Steinilber-Oberlin, Emile. *The Buddhist Sects of Japan.* Trans. by Marc Loge. London: George Allen and Unwin, 1938.

Streeter, B. H. *The Four Gospels.* London: The Macmillan Company, 1930.

Sukenik, E. L. *The Dead Sea Scrolls of the Hebrew University.* Jerusalem: Magness, 1955.

Sullivan, John W. N. *The Limitations of Science.* New York: Viking Press, 1933.

Suzuki, Daisetz Teitaro. *Essays in Zen Buddhism.* 2nd Series. Boston: Beacon Press, 1952.

———. *An Introduction to Zen Buddhism.* New York: Philosophical Library, 1949.

——— and Paul Carus, trans. *Treatise of the Exalted One on Response and Retribution.* Chicago: Open Court Publishing Co., 1906.

Swift, Emerson H. *Roman Sources of Christian Art.* New York: Columbia University Press, 1951.

Taylor, Vincent. *The Formation of the Gospel Tradition.* London: The Macmillan Company, 1935.

Toynbee, Arnold J. *Civilization on Trial.* New York: Oxford University Press, 1948.

Trever, Albert A. *History of Ancient Civilization.* New York: Harcourt Brace and Co., 1936.

Tsanoff, Radoslav A. *Religious Crossroads.* New York: E. P. Dutton and Co., 1942.

Tsui Chi. *A Short History of Chinese Civilization.* New York: G. P. Putnam's Sons, 1943.

UNESCO. *Progress of Literacy in Various Countries.* Paris, 1953.

———. *World Survey of Education.* Paris, 1955.

Upanishads: The Thirteen Principal Upanishads. Trans. by Robert E. Hume. 2nd ed. London: Oxford University Press, 1931.

Valmiki, *The Ramayana and the Mahabharata.* Trans. by Romesh Dutt. New York: E. P. Dutton and Co., 1929.

Wace, A. J. B. *Mycenae.* Princeton: Princeton University Press, 1949.

Waley, Arthur. *Three Ways of Thought in Ancient China*. London: George Allen and Unwin; New York: The Macmillan Company, 1939.
———. *The Way and Its Power*. New York: Houghton Mifflin Co., 1935.
Walker, Williston. *A History of the Christian Church*. New York: Charles Scribner's Sons, 1918.
Wallis, Louis. *The Bible Is Human: A Study in Secular History*. New York: Columbia University Press, 1942.
Wang, Gung-Hsing. *The Chinese Mind*. New York: The John Day Company, 1946.
Weber, Max. *Ancient Judaism*. Trans. by Gerth and Martindale. Glencoe: Free Press, 1952.
Wei, Francis C. M. *The Spirit of Chinese Culture*. New York: Charles Scribner's Sons, 1947.
Weiss, Paul. *Nature and Man*. New York: Henry Holt and Co., 1947.
Wheeler, Post. *Sacred Scriptures of Japan*. New York: Henry Schuman, 1952.
Wheelwright, Philip. *The Burning Fountain*. Bloomington: Indiana University Press, 1954.
Whitehead, Alfred North. *Religion in the Making*. New York: The Macmillan Company, 1926.
———. *Science and the Modern World*. New York: The Macmillan Company, 1925.
Wieger, Leon. *History of Religious Beliefs and Philosophical Opinions in China*. Trans. by E. C. Werner. Hsien-hsien: Hsien-hsien Press, 1927.
Wilson, Edmund. *The Scrolls from the Dead Sea*. New York: Oxford University Press, 1955.
Wilson, John Albert. *The Burden of Egypt*. Chicago: University of Chicago Press, 1951.
Winlock, H. E. *The Rise and Fall of the Middle Kingdom in Thebes*. New York: The Macmillan Company, 1947.
Woodroffe, Sir John G. *Shakti; or, The World as Power*. London: Women's Printing Society, 1920.
———. *Shakti and Maya: A Study in the Shakti Tantra*. Bombay: Oxford University Press, 1917.
Wright, William Kelley. *A Student's Philosophy of Religion*. New York: The Macmillan Company, 1935.
Yang Chu. *Yang Chu's Garden of Pleasure*. Trans. by Anton Forke. London: John Murray, 1912.
Young, Arthur Morgan. *Rise of a Pagan State*. New York: William Morrow, 1939.
Zimmer, Heinrich, *Philosophies of India*. Edited by Joseph Campbell. New York: Pantheon Books, 1951.

Glossary

Agni—Vedic fire god.
Ahura Mazda—Zoroastrian one god.
Allah—Islamic one god.
Ananda—supreme bliss in Hindu mysticism. Name of Buddha's beloved disciple.
Angra Mainyu—Zoroastrian devil.
Animism—belief that souls dwell within the objects of nature, making those objects conscious and purposeful.
Arahant—Buddhist saint.
Arhat—same as arahant.
Atman—soul, or self, used of the individual and universal self, or Brahman.
Aum (Om)—mystic Hindu symbol of diety and of reverence.
Avatar—incarnation of a deity in Hindu and Buddhist tradition.
Avesta (Zendavesta)—Zoroastrian Bible.
Bhakti—love and devotion.
Bodhisattva—A Buddha-in-the-making, or one who postpones Buddhahood in order to help others.
Brahmā—the Hindu creator-god, first of the trinity with Vishnu and Shiva.
Brahman—Hindu absolute reality, worthy of mystic aspiration.
Brahmana—the priestly part of the Vedas, detailing the ritual for the Brahmins.
Brahmin—Hindu priestly caste.
Buddha—the "enlightened," referring principally to Gautama Siddhartha.
Ch'i—Taoist soul of the universe.
Chit—consciousness (Hinduism).
Chuang Tzu—historic founder of philosophical Taoism.
Confucius (Kung Fu Tzu)—founder of Confucianism.
Devas—mythical Hindu gods or Zoroastrian demons.
Dharma (Dhamma)—the law in Hindu or Buddhist tradition. Virtue. (Other meanings).
Dhammapada—Buddhist sacred scriptures.
Dyaus—Hindu sky god, like Greek Zeus.
Dynamism—belief that nature is pervaded by an impersonal force, the presence of which accounts for unusual behavior, success, or power.
Fravashi—a departed soul or one's genius (Zoroastrianism).
Gathas—ancient Zoroastrian psalms.
Gita—Hindu psalm or song.

Guru—Hindu teacher or spiritual guide.
Islam—the religion founded by Muhammad, meaning "submission" (to Allah).
Jen (pronounced ren)—Chinese word for human-heartedness or sympathy.
Jinn—Arabian mythical spirits, good and bad.
Kaaba—black cubical enclosure at Mecca housing the revered meteorite.
Kami—Japanese equivalent of mana.
Karma—the law of action and its reward or punishment.
Krishna—an avatar of Vishnu, prominent in the Bhagavad Gita.
Kshatriya—ruler or soldier caste in India.
Kuan Yin—Chinese goddess of mercy.
Lao Tzu—legendary founder of philosophical Taoism.
Maitreya—the messianic Buddha still to come.
Mana—Polynesian word for dynamistic force.
Mantra—the hymn section of the Vedas. A prayer or a magical formula.
Maya—illusion, describing the relative world.
Mencius (Meng Tzu)—great interpreter of Confucius in ancient times.
Mithra—Persian sun god, reverenced in mystery cult of Mithraism.
Mitra—Hindu god like Mithra.
Moksha—release from individuality and transmigration.
Monotheism—belief in the existence of one god only, generally conceived as spiritual.
Muslim—one who submits to Allah's will.
Myth—imaginative tale, the truth of which may be apprehended by intuition only.
Nirvana—blissful state of being in which desire is absent and phenomena are known to be unreal.
Pantheism—theory that god is the only absolutely real being, while all individual things are dependent on it—or him—for their relative being.
Polytheism—belief in the existence of many gods.
Puranas—ancient legends, part of popular Hindu scriptures.
Raja—ruler in India.
Ramadan—holy Islamic month of abstinence.
Ramayana—Hindu epic.
Rishi—Hindu seer.
Sannyasin—Hindu ascetic seeking holiness.
Sat—Sanskrit for reality.
Shakti—goddess of female energy and motherhood in Hinduism.
Shakyamuni—Buddha, "sage of the Shakyas."
Shiva—one of the Hindu trinity, a negative deity, who destroys in order that Brahma may create.
Shudra—lowest of four main castes of Hinduism.
Soma—intoxicating juice of a plant in India and (Haoma) Iran.
Stupa—a burial mound or vault, popular in Buddhism.
Sufi—mystic sects of Islam.
Sunna—Islamic traditional sects.
Tao—the Way, the object of Chinese mystic contemplation.
Tao Te Ching (King)—classic book of Taoism.
Theism—theory that god is personal, having a kind of consciousness.

TOTEMISM—a primitive cultural concept believed to unite the tribe through common descent from an animal or other species.
UPANISHADS—scriptures of Hindu mysticism.
VAISHYAS—third caste of Hinduism; artisans, farmers, middle class.
VEDAS—Hindu sacred scriptures, consisting primarily of mantras (hymns), brahmanas, and upanishads.
VEDANTA—Vedic school stressing monism or pantheism.
VISHNU—popular member of Hindu trinity, the Preserver.
YAMA—the Adam of Hindu lore, who became god of the dead.
YANG—Chinese male principle, creative, aggressive.
YIMA—Iranism counterpart of Yama.
YIN—Chinese female principle, quiescent, sustaining.
YOGA—Hindu school stressing mental power through discipline.

Index